details the development of such recent issues as busing, bilingual education, feminism, and affirmative action.

Even-handed and compelling, *The Troubled Crusade* puts clearly into perspective the controversial issues that have plagued American education for thirty-five years: the struggle for equal educational opportunity; the debate over the quality of American education; the repeated challenges to academic freedom. This is more than a book about schools: it is a fascinating history of the social, political, and economic forces that have made American education what it is today.

PHOTO: INGER MCCABE

DIANE RAVITCH is on the faculty of Teacher's College, Columbia University and is the author of among other works, *The Great School Wars* (Basic, 1974) and *The Revisionists Revised* (Basic, 1978). She is also a frequent contributor to both scholarly and popular publications.

The Troubled Crusade

THE TROUBLED CRUSADE

American Education, 1945–1980

DIANE RAVITCH

Basic Books, Inc., Publishers *New York*

10563

Library of Congress Cataloging in Publication Data

Ravitch, Diane.
  The troubled crusade.

  Bibliographic References.
  Includes index.
  1. Education—United States—History—20th century.
I. Title.
LA209.2.R33   1983   370'.973   83-70750
ISBN 0-465-08756-6

For Richard

CONTENTS

ACKNOWLEDGMENTS   *ix*

INTRODUCTION   *xi*

CHAPTER 1:
Postwar Initiatives   *3*

CHAPTER 2:
The Rise and Fall of Progressive Education   *43*

CHAPTER 3:
Loyalty Investigations   *81*

CHAPTER 4:
Race and Education: The *Brown* Decision   *114*

CHAPTER 5:
Race and Education: Social Science and Law   *145*

CHAPTER 6:
From Berkeley to Kent State   *182*

CHAPTER 7:
Reformers, Radicals, and Romantics   *228*

CHAPTER 8:
The New Politics of Education   *267*

Contents

EPILOGUE:
From 1945 to 1980   321

NOTES   331

A NOTE ON SOURCES   357

INDEX   372

ACKNOWLEDGMENTS

In the course of writing a book that covers so much ground and requires several years of research and writing, many debts are inevitably incurred. I have been extremely fortunate in having the support and friendship of many people, who pointed me to new sources of information, read chapters, told me about articles or books, directed me to knowledgeable participants, shared their views about issues and events, and encouraged me in the dark days when it seemed that I might never finish.

I am particularly grateful to the John Simon Guggenheim Memorial Foundation, whose research fellowship in 1977–78 permitted me to devote a year to reading, sorting out the issues, and planning my research and writing. The generous support of the Spencer Foundation enabled me to complete the writing of the book and to obtain valuable research assistance. I was also the beneficiary of the superb resources and helpful staff of the Teachers College Library, the Harry S. Truman Library in Independence, Missouri, and the Dwight D. Eisenhower Library in Abilene, Kansas.

For their thoughtfulness, resourcefulness, and thoroughness as research assistants, I thank Katy Bordonaro, Susan Mason, and Barbara Martinsons. Virginia Brereton helped me gather information about religious issues, and Tim Counihan tracked down elusive references in the final days before publication.

The many good colleagues who answered questions, asked questions, pointed me to important data, tried to help me understand some of the issues I was wrestling with, but bear no responsibility for the final product, include Martin Trow, John Bunzel, Abigail Thernstrom, Gary Sykes, Patricia Graham, Leslie Lenkowsky, Marguerite Barnett, Harold Noah, and Derrick A. Bell, Jr. I particularly want to thank Rita Kramer, who not only read each chapter as it emerged, but raised my spirits when they sagged. It was my good fortune to have Jane Isay as my editor; her good editorial judgment and her steady moral support were invaluable. I am especially grateful to Julia Strand, the copy editor of this book, for her carefulness,

Acknowledgments

her insight, and her admirable respect for the integrity of the language. Words can scarcely express my debt to Lawrence A. Cremin, who has been a teacher, mentor, colleague, and friend, since the day I first walked into his office in 1969 and told him that I intended to write a book about education in New York City.

It is customary for authors to thank the other members of their family for putting up with the inconvenience of living with a person possessed by words and ideas. Where my family is concerned, customary thanks do not suffice. My husband, while burdened with his own fairly awesome responsibilities, willingly pitched in with certain household chores to give me more writing time; over the years, his integrity, common sense, and pragmatic idealism have been a constant source of inspiration. My younger son, Michael, taught me to use a word-processor, jumped to my assistance when I messed up, sympathized with me when I mistakenly wiped out pages of copy, and often made good editorial suggestions. My older son Joseph—fortunately for him—was away at college during the most intense writing periods, and so was not impressed into my cottage industry.

It is with love and admiration that I dedicate this book to my husband, Richard.

DIANE RAVITCH

INTRODUCTION

In 1786, Thomas Jefferson, at that time the American minister to the French government, wrote his friend and adviser George Wythe in Williamsburg, Virginia. He was delighted that the Virginia legislature had finally agreed to enact the statute for religious freedom that he had proposed some seven years earlier. However, he wrote Wythe, the most important bill before the state legislature, which had still not passed, was that "for the diffusion of knowledge among the people. No other sure foundation can be devised for the preservation of freedom, and happiness." For Jefferson, any doubt of this was removed by what he had seen of the common people of France, who were surrounded by "blessings from nature" and yet miserable because they remained in the grip of "ignorance, superstition, poverty and oppression of body and mind in every form." Jefferson exhorted his friend, "Preach, my dear Sir, a crusade against ignorance; establish and improve the law for educating the common people. Let our countrymen know that the people alone can protect us against these evils, and that the tax which will be paid for this purpose is not more than the thousandth part of what will be paid to kings, priests and nobles who will rise up among us if we leave the people in ignorance."[1]

This book is a report on the state of the crusade against ignorance during a particularly tumultuous time in American history. Many other crusades stormed through the nation's educational institutions during these thirty-five years, sometimes complementing the crusade against ignorance, at other times subordinating it to some other worthy or unworthy cause. More than at any other time in American history, the crusade against ignorance was understood to mean a crusade for equal educational opportunity. At every level of formal education, from nursery school to graduate school, equal opportunity became the overriding goal of postwar educational reformers. Sometimes those who led the battles seemed to forget why it was important to keep students in school longer; to forget that the fight for higher enrollments was part of a crusade against ignorance, and that institutions would be judged by what their students had learned as well as by how many were enrolled.

Probably no other idea has seemed more typically American than the belief that schooling could cure society's ills. Whether in the early nineteenth century or the late twentieth century, Americans have argued for more schooling on the grounds that it would preserve democracy, eliminate poverty, lower the crime rate, enrich the common culture, reduce unemployment, ease the assimilation of immigrants to the nation, overcome differences between ethnic groups, advance scientific and technological progress, prevent traffic accidents, raise health standards, refine moral character, and guide young people into useful occupations. While it has become fashionable in recent years to assert that schools and universities do little more than preserve the status quo and parcel out credentials, this hard-edged cynicism has less truth in it than the "myth" it is intended to debunk. Throughout history, Americans have expected much of their educational institutions; sometimes schools have been expected to take on responsibilities for which they were entirely unsuited. When they have failed, it was usually because their leaders and their public alike had forgotten their real limitations as well as their real strengths.

Defined as they so often were as instruments of national purpose, educational institutions became focal points for large areas of consensus (there is much, after all, on which Americans agree), but they also served as magnets for dissension, attracting all those who wanted to change the social order, preserve threatened traditions, challenge historic wrongs, or make sure that the next generation was not tainted by the errors of their predecessors. Ideology, social turmoil, racial and ethnic tensions, national and international events brought reformers to the schools and universities, eager to know what they were teaching; what books they were using; what kinds of ideas were espoused; who was being permitted to teach; what kinds of students were admitted, promoted, going to college, and winning degrees.

In 1945, American education had the strengths and weaknesses of a highly decentralized, pyramidal system. Everyone could go to school, but the difference in quality between the best schools and the worst schools was enormous. There were first-rate school districts and outstanding preparatory schools which sent large numbers of their graduates to great institutions of higher education. But there were also poor schools with narrow offerings, located in poor areas, where few students prepared for college. Good schools and good teachers were not equally available to all children; access to higher education was not open on an equal basis to all talented youths. One's educational chances were limited by the accident of birth and by the color of one's skin.

As the nation emerged from the Second World War, its idealism and aspirations raised high, the inequitable features of American education seemed more unacceptable than at any time in the past, though the problem of unequal opportunity was no worse than before. At the very least, the American crusade against ignorance required that the opportunity for education be made available to all young people, without regard to race, creed, national origin, sex, or family background. The obstacles to change were formidable. Idealism and aspiration alone were not enough to shake loose the shackles of the past; not enough, perhaps, to win the day, but enough to stir the nation's conscience and to keep alive the campaign for equal educational opportunity until the right political and social circumstances made success possible.

The Troubled Crusade

CHAPTER 1

Postwar Initiatives

I N EARLY 1945, with the war in Europe coming to an end, the Senate Committee on Education and Labor opened hearings on a proposal for federal aid to education. The most insistent claimants for federal help were poor districts, which had a difficult time adequately financing their public schools from local property taxes. In addition to the usual statements of support and opposition from interest groups, several teachers told the senators about conditions in their schools. Miss Wilma Upchurch, a teacher from rural Nebraska, stated that her school had 487 pupils and twelve teachers, only seven of whom had college degrees. Because of low salaries, teacher turnover had been 50 percent the year before, and one out of every five teachers in the state had a temporary emergency teaching certificate, usually because of lack of qualifications. Her district, a poor one, taxed itself to the limit and yet was able to spend only forty to forty-seven dollars per pupil annually. "I am sure I could get a job in another state, or maybe I could work at the bomber plant," Miss Upchurch testified, "but I would rather stay in the teaching profession. Somebody has got to teach those children, and I would like to do it."[1]

Mrs. Florence Christmas, a black teacher from Copiah County, Mississippi, described her school of 190 children and three teachers. As principal, she taught all subjects in four grades (fifth through eighth) and received $60 per month for six months. The other two teachers were paid, respectively, $292 and $288 for the six-month term. Mrs. Christmas said:

Our school is called Antioch and is located on the same ground as the Antioch Baptist Church. Some of our people in the community are small truck farmers. They have a great love for education. They built their own schoolhouse. It has grown from one room to a three-teacher type school. The money for the building was raised by the teachers, children, and patrons. We gave programs, entertainments, secured pledges from the parents and friends, and gave money from our salaries to help with the building. We have been able to put on one coat of paint, inside and out.

Parents and teachers were still trying to raise $12.57, Mrs. Christmas said, to "finish paying for the paint," and their next project was to get enough benches "so that all the children may have seats, especially those in the primary room."[2]

Of six thousand Negro teachers in Mississippi, said Mrs. Christmas, five thousand received less than $600 per year. During the months when school was not in session, she held a factory job, making containers for vegetables, where she earned almost as much in a week as in a month of teaching. When he heard this, Senator William Fulbright of Arkansas asked her, "Why do you do teaching?"

Mrs. Christmas responded, "Teaching is my profession. I would rather teach."

It was matter-of-factly noted in the record that in Copiah County, where Mrs. Christmas taught, the average salary for white teachers was $889.53, compared to an annual average for black teachers of $332.58; the length of the school term was eight months for whites and six months for blacks; of 91 white teachers in the county, 44 had no college degree, while of 126 black teachers, 122 had no college degree. The daily attendance rate for white children was 48 percent; for black children, it was 60 percent. At the Antioch school, the black parents dug down into their pockets to keep the school open for a seventh month.

Educational conditions throughout the South, particularly in rural areas, were equally depressed. Dr. E. B. Norton, the chief state school officer of Alabama, noted that "the only difference between our state and some of the others is that our emergency is not temporary, ours seems to be a permanent emergency." Some eleven thousand of Alabama's twenty thousand teachers had left their jobs in the three years after Pearl Harbor; many of their replacements had no college training. Low pay was one reason: the annual salary for white teachers was $976, and for black teachers only $600. Furthermore, more than half the school buildings in the state were heated with open stoves, and more than half lacked electricity.[3]

Other states, though not so desperately poor as those in the South, echoed similar complaints about teacher shortages caused by low salaries and competition from defense industries. The Colorado Education Association held that "the schools of Colorado are facing the gravest crisis in all their existence. The salaries are so woefully low that we are losing hundreds of our best teachers to industry and to other States. . . . one out of every three teachers in Colorado is a temporary teacher." A spokesman from Utah declared that 25 percent of the state's teachers did not have proper certification, and in Iowa some eight hundred rural schools were altogether without a teacher.[4]

There were no supplicants at the hearings from city schools, which were generally well staffed and well financed; suburbanization had not yet become a major trend, and city schools provided the standard for teachers' salaries, class size, and facilities, against which rural schools seemed needy and inadequate.

The issue of federal aid to education had been raised periodically in the Congress since the 1870s and had consistently failed to pass, no matter how compelling the demonstration of educational calamity. Invariably, federal aid became a national question when some crisis riveted national attention on the schools. It was debated for several years after World War I, when the army discovered that large numbers of its draftees were illiterate; it became an issue during the Great Depression, when plummeting revenues forced school districts to close schools, fire teachers, cut salaries, and eliminate programs. The education lobby, led by the National Education Association (NEA), the nation's largest group of teachers and supervisors, kept up the battle for federal aid during and after the war. Each era produced its own rationale for federal aid, and the major theme of the 1945 hearings—which teachers like Miss Upchurch and Mrs. Christmas dramatized—was the lack of equal opportunity in American education. The plea of the education interest groups was not just that American education was in a state of dire need, but that the incontrovertible fact of sharp inequalities from district to district and from state to state was manifestly unfair.

With the war coming to an end, the NEA and its allies—such as organized labor, the National Association for the Advancement of Colored People (NAACP), and the National Congress of Parents and Teachers—believed that the time was right to launch a new campaign for federal support of the nation's schools. As they well knew, the obstacles were formidable. Bills for federal aid had traditionally foundered for three reasons: race, religion, and fear of federal control. No matter how bleak the plight of the schools, every effort to formulate legislation had been stymied by conflicts over whether to fund the South's racially segregated schools; whether to fund nonpublic (largely Catholic) schools; and how to prevent federal subsidization from becoming federal domination of local schools.

Every time the issue was raised, different coalitions formed, depending on how these questions were framed in potential legislation. Southerners, whose need for federal aid was greatest, supported it as long as it did not threaten their system of racial segregation. Blacks, organized labor, and liberal congressmen would support federal aid proposals only if they guaranteed equal funding without regard to race. The public school lobby, headed by the NEA, would not support a bill that offered any form of aid to nonpublic schools. But any bill that aided only public schools was opposed by Catholics and by congressmen from districts with large Catholic constituencies. The distribution formula was also a problem: a bill that granted money only to the poorest states risked losing the votes of representatives from states that would get nothing, while a bill that distributed money to every state was either too expensive or spread the aid too thinly to help the poorest states. A sizable number of conservative congressmen, mostly Republicans, opposed any federal aid to education, for fear that it would destroy local control of public schooling.

Yet there was reason to hope that the end of World War II might be the right time to break through these traditional grounds for deadlock. During the war years, Americans had talked a great deal about defending the ideals of democracy and the American way of life, and the education lobby sensed that the time had come to base its appeal on the promise of democratic ideology. But beyond ideology was compelling need. The teacher shortage was a national problem, as were low salaries. There was also a critical need for new classrooms and schools, not only because replacement and repair had been deferred by the Depression and the war, but because as early as 1946 and 1947, it was clear that the fast-rising birthrate would produce a "baby boom" that would overwhelm existing classroom capacity. No less important than sheer physical need was awareness, at least among educational leaders, that the nation was entering an age of technological and scientific advance that required rising levels of education in order to maintain economic growth. And, perhaps more sharply than at any time in the past, there was concern that both of these trends—the growth of population and the rising levels of education—would exacerbate divisions within the society along lines of race and class and intensify inequality unless educational opportunities were equalized across the nation.

Only crisis would stir the Congress to action, and in the years immediately following the war, America's schools were in deep enough trouble to gain a hearing. Benjamin Fine, the education editor of the *New York Times*, wrote in 1947, "America's public school system is confronted with the most serious crisis in its history." After a six-month tour across the coun-

try, Fine reported that three hundred and fifty thousand teachers had left
the public schools since 1940 for war service or better jobs; that one of
every seven teachers held an emergency ("substandard") certificate; that
seventy thousand teaching jobs were unfilled; that six thousand schools
would close because of the teacher shortage; that sixty thousand of the
nation's teachers had only a high school education or less; that the average
teacher's salary was $37 per week, which was lower than the pay of the
average truck driver, garbage collector, or bartender; that 20 percent of all
teachers—one hundred and seventy-five thousand—were new to the job
each year, a turnover double the prewar rate; that fewer students were
entering teaching, and that men were deserting the teaching profession;
that twelve major teachers' strikes had taken place in the six months
following September, 1946; that teacher morale was at a new low; that
"appalling" inequities existed throughout the nation, from the best classrooms (where as much as $6,000 was spent per classroom unit) to the
poorest (where as little as $100 was spent per classroom unit); that the
United States was spending less of its national income on schools than
either Great Britain or the Soviet Union; and that school buildings were
in a "deplorable state all over the nation."[5]

The sense of crisis extended well beyond the physical and financial
needs of American education to larger questions of social policy that were
unresolved as the postwar period began. In higher education, educators
debated the problem of access, of who should be educated and for how
many years, and at whose expense. Should higher education be available
only to those who could afford to pay for it and to those talented enough
and lucky enough to win a scholarship? Should a greater proportion of
young people receive a postsecondary education, and if so, who should pay
for it? Should public funds be given only to public institutions or should
private colleges and universities also receive federal assistance? In elementary and secondary education, equally vexing problems pervaded the on-
going debates: What was to be done to improve the poor conditions in
certain districts and states? How could already poor districts afford to pay
higher teacher salaries or to build new schools? Since only the federal
government had the taxing and spending power to redistribute funds from
wealthy regions to poor regions, how could the traditional stalemate in
Congress be broken to pass a federal aid bill? Should federal aid go only
to schools that did not permit racial segregation or should it go to all
schools based only on need? Should public money go only to public
schools or should it go also to nonpublic schools? Was it possible to
establish federal "standards" that would not turn into federal domination
of local schools? And then there were questions of pedagogy. The rapid

growth of the high school enrollment in the 1930s had been followed by the introduction of new courses and new curricula on behalf of young people who presumably would not benefit from the traditional academic curriculum; the projected growth of postsecondary education, it was believed, would pose similar problems in higher education. This prospect divided educators between those who welcomed the new challenge to higher education to serve a mass enrollment and those who feared that large numbers would require a debasement of the curriculum and a lowering of standards. Until there was consensus on these issues, there would not be any federal funding of the schools or of higher education.

The new political and social conditions in the nation after the war did not provide an auspicious atmosphere for resolving ideological disagreements or launching policy innovations. The war was followed by a national mood of jubilation, then uncertainty and insecurity. There were good reasons for worry. To begin with, many people feared a resumption of the Depression, which was still relatively fresh in memory. Many who had benefited by the social reforms of the New Deal wondered whether the country would take a sharp turn to the right, as it had after World War I. The earlier world war had been followed by a period of retreat from international involvement, reaction against domestic reforms, the collapse of the League of Nations, the rise of xenophobia, and the excesses of the "Red Scare." Beyond these fundamental concerns about the relationship of the past to the present, there was the awesome new fact of the atomic bomb, the very existence of which presented a compelling argument for international cooperation and for the substitution of reason for coercion in politics. In the atomic age, there was fresh urgency to H. G. Wells's observation that "human history becomes more and more a race between education and catastrophe."

The mood of the electorate did turn more conservative after the war than it had been during the Roosevelt era. The Republicans gained control of Congress in 1946 for the first time in sixteen years. But even more significant was what did not happen: the New Deal social reforms were not repealed, and the United States did not withdraw from its international responsibilities. For the first time in the nation's history, domestic welfare programs and foreign assistance had broad bipartisan support. Yet the new consensus on issues like social security and the United Nations coexisted with a rising tide of social conflict. A nation that had been disciplined by the exigencies of war and unified by the leadership of a powerful president, both through the Depression and the world war, now found itself in a time of unruliness, labor unrest, shortages of goods, fear of renewed international tensions, and anxiety about domestic subversion. And something more was amiss: the helmsman, loved by many, hated by some, was gone, replaced by a man who was an unknown factor. The new president, one Harry S. Truman, was a man without a mandate or even a clear identity. The Republican victory in 1946 indicated that a substantial portion of the public did not wish to see an expansion of the reformism of the New Deal, and the absence of a sympathetic Congress limited any initiatives by Truman.

Besides the obvious political changes, there were subtle social and economic changes that contributed to an uneasy sense of dislocation. Rapid advances in technology and communication, the growth of suburbs, the breakdown of regional traditions, the pursuit of material security, the increase in juvenile delinquency, and the strains on the family—such trends, rarely the stuff of headlines, fed mistrust and anxiety. The very forces that made American society dynamic—technological change, modernization, urbanization, social fluidity, and innovation—contributed to the erosion of cohesive community life.

Perhaps it was only the same yearning for a golden past that every generation seems to feel, yet there was an almost tangible sense that traditional American values were under assault. In this time of tension and flux, many looked to the schools and colleges to protect the heritage of the past and instill traditional values in the rising generation. Others, less concerned with the past, wanted to plan the future and believed that the nation's educational system was key to realizing equal opportunity and economic plenty. Both kinds of critics of education were disappointed by the institutions on which their aspirations rested.

America's schools, it seemed, were fated to be judged by standards that were ever beyond reach, for behind the highly publicized crisis in the schools was a remarkable transformation in the availability of education. The buildings may have been inadequate and the teachers scarce and poorly paid, but more than anywhere else in the world, the children of the United States were going to school. With each passing decade, American youth went to school for a longer portion of the year and for a longer period of their lives. From 1870 to 1940, while the population tripled, school enrollment rates soared. Students in secondary schools increased by a multiple of almost 90, from eighty thousand in 1870 to 7 million in 1940, while college enrollment leapt from sixty thousand to 1.5 million (with another one million part-time students in postsecondary adult education programs).[6]

The rise in educational participation was due both to economic and social factors. In 1900, most male workers were either farmers or laborers.

As the century advanced, fewer men worked in these occupations, while more men held white-collar occupations and skilled blue-collar jobs, becoming a majority by midcentury. Technological change created a need for an educated people, and educated people stimulated technological change. Of no less importance was the national commitment to schooling as a means of self-improvement. Even before the tightening-up of compulsory education laws in the 1930s, most children attended school. Schooling was held in high regard even though teaching and intellectuality were not. It helped the individual "get ahead"; it stimulated economic progress by producing an industrious and resourceful work force; it promoted social harmony by teaching children about the history and culture of the nation; it contributed to the nation's well-being by teaching children how the government works and why they should participate as citizens. The value of schooling was an idea on which almost everyone agreed, even though they might differ about what should be taught or who should have the power to pick teachers or textbooks. Indeed, it was the substantial agreement on the power of schooling to affect the future that made educational controversies so emotionally charged.

Educational participation rose steadily during the twentieth century. Not until the 1930s did the idea of universal high school attendance gain currency, after the compulsory schooling age was raised to remove teenage workers from a depressed job market. The high schools had traditionally served as college preparatory institutions, and they adjusted to the new, diverse population with some difficulty. With most children between the ages of five and seventeen in school, new questions were raised. Why did some of them leave school before graduation? What could be done to the high schools' curriculum to extend their "holding power" and keep everyone enrolled until graduation time? During the 1930s—and in some cases, even earlier—high schools began to add new courses for children who were "not bookish": vocational courses, such as bookkeeping and typing, home economics and automobile mechanics; courses on contemporary issues and on the social problems of the teenager. Soon, some high schools offered different kinds of high school diplomas; in addition to the college-preparatory diploma, there was a vocational course, a business course, and a general course.

Because of this new situation in the high schools, educators had two kinds of concerns in the mid-1940s. First, there were school superintendents and leaders in professional groups like the NEA who wondered whether the high schools had diversified their curriculum enough to hold the interest and attendance of all children. They believed that the expansion of the high school enrollment had given the schools a special mission in a democratic society. Rather than serving only the college-bound, the schools had to become an agency of social adjustment for all American youth, guiding them into adulthood and preparing them to enter occupations suited to their needs as well as to society's. In this new mission, the schools had to meet young people's needs, not only for education in the traditional sense but also for vocation, health, recreation, citizenship, and social competence.

At the same time, there were college and university spokesmen who worried that the extreme diversification of the curriculum in the high school and the growth of specialization in higher education had gotten out of hand. They understood that the rapid multiplication of the number and kinds of courses in high school had been a direct result of the expansion of the high school enrollment and was an effort to provide something of educational value for young people of widely different ability, background, and interests. In response to these developments, they advocated "general education," and in the late 1940s calls for general education were heard throughout secondary and higher education.

Perhaps the most characteristic statement of the case for general education was made in 1945 in "The Redbook," written by Harvard University's Committee on the Objectives of a General Education in a Free Society. The expansion of the high school enrollment and of the secondary curriculum created two dangers, the committee said: "the alienation of students from each other in mind and outlook because their courses of study for the various diplomas are so distinct, and the disjointedness of any given student's work because instead of being conceived as a whole it falls into scattered parts." As an antidote, they recommended that secondary school youth spend about half their time in a common core of studies, ranging in level of difficulty and in method but sharing the same educational ideals. While others had their own versions of a "core" curriculum, the Harvard committee had correctly identified the central problems of education in a democratic society: How should education be provided for a high school population that was widely varied in talent and need? Should all study the same materials? Should students pursue only the courses that interested them most? Was there some way to strike a balance?[7]

One question that the Harvard committee never raised was whether school was the appropriate place for all of a community's youth. It was never raised because, presumably, it had been settled. In days gone by, restless youngsters had left school to go West, to go to sea, or to find a job in the community. Those options were rapidly disappearing, though many teenagers no doubt would continue to be restless or to find the institution-

11

alized life of school too limited, no matter how diversified the curriculum. It was not the kind of question that was likely to be raised in the late 1940s, for the more pressing issue to most educators was how to keep more students in high school until graduation and to increase the proportion of the population that was able to attend college. In the middle 1940s educators were concerned that for every 1,000 children who entered fifth grade in 1932, only 455 graduated from high school and only 160 entered college. While these figures represented substantial increases over previous years, the feeling was growing that too much talent was wasted and that the benefits of education must be more broadly, if not universally, dispersed throughout the population.[8]

After the Second World War, when a college education was seen as a ticket to a good job or entry into the professions, the question of access to higher education became a major public issue. It was no secret that admission to college or university was not based solely on ability. Though more youngsters were in school than ever before, it was nonetheless true that some never had a chance to go to college because the elementary and secondary schools they attended were too inadequate to give them a decent preparation. Some were excluded because of their race or religion. Others were prevented from attending college because their families could not afford the cost or the loss of their children's earnings. Nothing had so dramatic an effect on the way the public thought about the issue of opportunity for higher education than a remarkable—and relatively spontaneous—experiment in mass higher education known as the GI Bill.

The GI Bill of Rights, formally known as the Servicemen's Readjustment Act of 1944, offered the sixteen million men and women who served in the armed forces a federal subsidy to continue their schooling or training. Though the GI Bill ultimately provided a telling argument for expansion of educational opportunity, its sponsors had concerns other than education or opportunity. One group of proponents, the veterans' organizations, lobbied hard to get the best possible package of benefits for their constituents, the returning servicemen, and the final bill included job placement services, unemployment benefits, mortgage guarantees, and educational benefits. Another sponsor, the federal officials in charge of postwar planning, were chiefly interested in preventing joblessness and economic distress. To the veterans, the educational subsidy was one more "goody" in the total package; to the planners, it was a promising way to reduce the number of job-seekers in the period after demobilization.[9]

Signed into law on June 22, 1944, the GI Bill subsidized tuition, books, and fees, as well as providing a monthly subsistence allowance for veterans. The Veterans Administration determined whether veterans were eligible, the veterans selected the school they wanted to attend, and the school decided whether it wanted to admit them. One of the chief reasons for the success of the education program was that it maintained the freedom of servicemen to select their schools, and the freedom of the schools to control their admission policies and their curricula without federal intervention.

When the bill was passed, most educators welcomed the prospect of subsidized students as a way of making up for the underenrollments of the wartime years. But not everyone found the prospect pleasing. James B. Conant, president of Harvard University, worried that the bill would cause a lowering of academic standards; he preferred to see a bill that financed the education of "a carefully selected number of returned veterans." Even more outspoken was Robert M. Hutchins, chancellor of the University of Chicago. In December, 1944, Hutchins wrote an article for the popular magazine *Collier's* called "The Threat to American Education." While he approved of severing the relationship between "the education of a citizen and the income of his parents," he feared that the GI Bill would encourage vocational education in colleges and universities, which would prostitute themselves to get federal dollars. "Educational institutions," he wrote, ". . . cannot resist money. The GI Bill of Rights gives them a chance to get more money than they ever dreamed of and to do it in the name of patriotism. They will not want to keep out unqualified veterans; they will not want to expel those who fail. . . . Colleges and universities will find themselves converted into educational hobo jungles." Candidates for higher education should be chosen through national examinations, he believed, and colleges should be required to provide half the veterans' tuition, to be sure that only serious students were admitted. Hutchins thought it was outrageous to use education "as a substitute for a dole or for a national program of public works."[10]

Hutchins's critique had no effect in Congress or among educators. Few shared his singular devotion to the idea of liberal education untainted by vocationalism or utilitarianism, and no one was in a mood to be stingy with the veterans. By the fall of 1945, with some 88,000 veterans enrolled in college under the GI Bill, Congress liberalized the education benefits in order to make more GIs eligible and to increase the monthly subsistence payments.

Government officials and educators consistently underestimated the number of veterans who would use their education benefits. In the fall of 1946, to the surprise of those who had confidently predicted that veterans would shun higher education after their years on the battlefield, 1,013,000 veterans enrolled, nearly doubling the nation's college student population. Campus life was transformed by their presence. Quonset huts sprouted to house the students and, in some cases, their spouses. Many colleges doubled their usual enrollment to make room for the veterans. Certain sophomoric traditions such as freshman "beanies," student mud-fights, and freshman paddling, disappeared with the arrival of the older students. In many colleges, classes began early in the morning and concluded late at night. Inexperienced teachers, some of them graduate students, were pressed into duty to teach the bumper crop of undergraduates. Classes were jammed, facilities were strained beyond capacity, but somehow everyone took the situation in stride.[11]

What was even more surprising than the deluge of veterans on campus, however, was their academic performance. Far from undermining academic standards, as Hutchins and Conant had feared, the veterans consistently outperformed other students. Among educators, the veterans quickly established a reputation as the hardest working, best motivated generation ever to pass through the nation's colleges. Harvard's president, James B. Conant, withdrew his earlier criticism and concluded that the veterans at Harvard were "the most mature and promising students Harvard has ever had." *Fortune* described the class of 1949 as "the best class the country has ever produced . . . the most mature . . . the most responsible . . . the most self-disciplined group the colleges have ever had."[12]

The GI Bill was the most ambitious venture in mass higher education that had ever been attempted by any society. During the seven years in which the benefits were available, 7.8 million veterans used them to attend universities, colleges, high schools, trade schools, and training programs. Of that number, 2,232,000 attended institutions of higher education. No other society had ever subsidized so large and nonselective a portion of its population in institutions of higher education. For the first time, the link between income and educational opportunity was broken: every GI, without regard to background, was entitled to the same educational subsidy. The number of veterans who would probably not have gone to college or university without the subsidy has been estimated at between 20 to 25 percent, or between 450,000 and 550,000 people. These men and women (2.9 percent of the veterans in college were women) undoubtedly contributed to the dramatic expansion of American science and technology in the decades after the war. The veterans' presence on campus broke the genteel cocoon in which much of higher education had been wrapped, in some cases only temporarily, in others, permanently. This meant, for example, the introduction of married students' quarters, new flexibility of scheduling and calendar, and the discovery that age was an irrelevant criterion for higher education. The GIs' "uncritical acceptance" of "larger classes, larger colleges, and increased use of graduate students as teachers" may have been, in the view of one scholar, "a major legacy of the G.I. Bill." In 1948, only ten universities had an enrollment bigger than 20,000; by 1967, there were fifty-five. One historian called the GI Bill "the most important educational and social transformation in American history."[13]

Whatever else it was, the GI Bill was a successful investment in human resources. For educators and for the public, its great lesson was that college should not be reserved for the children of the well-to-do. The doors were opened for all who wished to come, and those who came helped themselves and added to society's stock of skilled and productive citizens. On the tenth anniversary of its passage, *Newsweek* summarized its benefits, but noted dourly that not everyone who went to college at government expense gained from the experience: "Their appearance at college came largely from a growing—and debatable—American conviction that everyone, regardless of ability, ought somehow to go to college." Though it originated in a compromise between officials who wanted to stave off unemployment and veterans' groups that wanted a good package of benefits, the GI Bill's most lasting effect was probably its encouragement of the conviction that "everyone, regardless of ability, ought somehow to go to college."[14]

The problems of overcrowding caused by the GI Bill presented a rare opportunity for educators who had a vision of a vastly expanded system of higher education. As professional educators saw it, the great struggle of the nineteenth century had been the fight to establish the principle of free universal public schooling; the great struggle of the first half of the twentieth century had been to make secondary schooling universal; and the goal for the present was to make higher education a right, not just a privilege, for all Americans. In the summer of 1946, the American Council on Education, an association of some six hundred colleges and universities, called together a conference to discuss the crisis on American campuses, which was associated with the doubling of enrollments, the rapid erection of housing and classrooms, and the recruitment of inexperienced faculty members. The leadership of the American Council on Education had been deeply involved in drafting the education section of the GI Bill, and they were eager to use the present crisis to encourage even greater expansion of higher education. In response to the council's requests, President Truman appointed the President's Commission on Higher Education in July 1946.

The Commission issued a series of reports between December, 1947, and February, 1948, collectively entitled *Higher Education for American Democracy*. It was a many-sided answer to the question, "How can higher education make society more democratic?" The thesis of the report was that, with the advance of science, technology, and industrialization, more and more students would seek higher education to prepare them for effective participation in contemporary society. Institutions of higher education should welcome this expansion, remove all barriers to its progress, and change in whatever ways were necessary to meet the diverse needs of students. A vastly expanded network of postsecondary institutions, the commission believed, would promote international understanding, the solution of social problems, general education for individual development, vocational education for occupational development, and a fuller realization of democratic living. Specifically, the commission maintained that the number of students in higher education should double to 4.6 million by 1960. According to its estimates, "at least 49 percent of our population has the mental ability to complete 14 years of schooling" and "at least 32 percent of our population has the mental ability to complete an advanced liberal or specialized professional education." The kind and amount of education people receive, the commission insisted, should depend solely on their abilities, "not on the family or community into which they happened to be born, or, worse still, on the color of skin or the religion of their parents." It vigorously condemned racial segregation, which was legal in seventeen states and the District of Columbia, and the denial of educational opportunity to black youth in states where segregation was not legal. The commission denounced the "quota system" or *numerus clausus* in higher education, which was an unacknowledged but widely practiced method of restricting the admission of blacks and Jews.[15]

The ultimate educational goal of the American people, the commission urged, should be "an educational system in which at no level—high school, college, graduate school or professional school—will a qualified individual in any part of the country encounter an insuperable economic barrier to the attainment of the kind of education suited to his aptitudes and interests." The commission recommended, first, that each state create administrative machinery for statewide planning of new institutions of higher education; second, that state planners prepare for a rapid expansion of two-year community colleges (not junior colleges), which would "fit into the community life as the high school has done"; third, that the federal government establish a program of scholarships, based primarily on need, for at least 20 percent of all undergraduates, and a program of graduate fellowships, based on ability; fourth, that the federal government provide financial aid for public institutions; and fifth, that segregation legislation be repealed and that new laws be passed banning discrimination in admissions.[16]

The public debate about the commission's report revealed a good deal about how educators and others viewed the prospect of a vastly enlarged mission for higher education in American society. The *New York Times* predicted that the report "may well become a landmark in the history of higher education in this country." *Life* magazine, one of the most popular mass magazines, declared in an unusual full-page editorial that access to college should be "a civic birthright," like high school: "Almost any experience of two years of full-time post-high-school study would be more humanizing than instantly to freeze, as so many young people must, into a rigid life pattern." Their clinching argument was an appeal to the American belief that education was good in and of itself: "Education alone cannot heal the world's wounds. But it can help. A basic principle of American democracy is the more education, the better."[17]

Many supporters and critics of the report wondered whether Americans put too much emphasis on the college degree for its own sake. Several mentioned a popular movie, *The Senator Was Indiscreet,* in which "Senator Melvin Gassaway Ashton" promised in his presidential campaign to have the federal government send every man, woman, and child in the nation to Harvard. Others quoted a remark of Barrett Wendell, a Harvard professor who years before had proposed facetiously that every American be endowed at birth with a college degree, so that only those who were truly interested in the pursuit of learning would go to college.

Critics of the report expressed a variety of concerns: first, that an increase of college enrollment to 4.6 million would dangerously lower academic standards, thereby destroying the educational environment that produces leaders; second, that this expansion would force institutions of higher education to adopt a vocational orientation; third, that the proposed federal role would establish political control over public institutions and drive private institutions out of existence; and, fourth, that there might be a dangerous oversupply of degree-bearers for whom there were not enough jobs. In short, the critics raised serious questions about whether democratization of higher education was feasible or desirable, and about whether it would change the nature, purpose, and control of public and private institutions.[18]

The Very Reverend Robert I. Gannon, president of Fordham University, warned that the commission's program "threatens to suffocate us with tides of mediocrity." He complained that "the fraud in the present campaign for educational inflation consists in spreading our national culture perilously thin and calling it 'democracy of education.' " In a more temperate vein, the liberal Catholic journal *Commonweal* objected, "To make higher education available to every American of genuine college caliber regardless of his purse it seems hardly necessary to gather everybody in, regardless. Or is the idea growing that higher education is primarily a useful social—rather than an intellectual—experience, which should be open to all?"[19]

Many college presidents attacked the report as a threat to academic standards or to the future of private colleges, but the most searing critique came from the University of Chicago's iconoclastic Robert M. Hutchins, who held that the report was like the educational system itself:

> It is big and booming. It is confused, confusing, and contradictory. It has something for everybody. It is generous, ignoble, bold, timid, naive, and optimistic. It is filled with the spirit of universal brotherhood and the sense of American superiority. It has great faith in money. It has great faith in courses. It is antihumanistic and anti-intellectual. It is confident that vices can be turned into virtues by making them larger. Its heart is in the right place: its head does not work very well. . . . The cry is "more": more money, more buildings, more professors, more students, more everything.

Hutchins was particularly exercised by what he called the "omnibus fallacy" of education, the idea that "there is nothing which education cannot do and it can do everything equally well." He saw no reason to "increase the number of students, to prolong the period of their incarceration in schools, to spend twice the money, but spend it in the same way, when the system is headed in no direction, or in the wrong direction, or in all directions at once."[20]

After the dust of the debate settled, what impact did the report of the President's Commission on Higher Education have? In an immediate sense, very little: the president and the Congress, embroiled in other problems, ignored its recommendations—no hearings were called, no legislation was offered. But in other, less tangible ways, its effects were widespread. First, it gave great impetus to the burgeoning community college movement, and especially, to the drive to convert junior colleges, which had been regarded as either adjuncts to universities or extensions of high schools, to community colleges designed to meet the educational needs of the local community, with comprehensive offerings and little or no tuition. Second, members of the commission spread out in the states, colleges, and communities as bearers of the report's message, and they were a considerable network; among their number were future college presidents, planners of state systems of community colleges, state commissioners of education, and even a future U.S. commissioner of education (Earl McGrath, who served in Truman's administration from 1949 to 1953). Third, while little was done to implement the proposals of the commission at a national level, its recommendation that enrollment double to 4.6 million students by 1960 was uncannily close to actual enrollment figures. Even without the proposed federal assistance to students and public institutions, the commission's proposal had proved an accurate prediction by 1963. Last, the commission's stern denunciation of segregation and discrimination helped to chip away at the legitimacy of such policies; in the eyes of leading educators, there could be no defense of discrimination. In future discussions of education and social policy, the issue of racial inequality could no longer be ignored.

Although racism was deeply embedded in American life and law, the experience of the war heightened the contradiction between the reality of racism and the ideals of American democracy. The painfulness of the contrast was presented most acutely to blacks, particularly the one million blacks who served in the armed forces. They had encountered racism in their daily lives before the war, but as members of the armed services, they found themselves in the odd position of being discriminated against by the American government, a government that daily proclaimed that the goal of the war was to defend the principles of democracy and to defeat malignant exponents of racial superiority. Northern blacks stationed in the South were subjected to the humiliating laws and practices of the segregated states; southern blacks who traveled North realized that the rigid racial separatism of their home communities was not immutable; and those who were sent overseas encountered cultures where racial prejudice was unknown. Among many who served in the military or who had, for the first time, a good job in a war industry, the war years were the beginning of a new consciousness, a new willingness to insist that the society make real the promises of its democratic creed.

The war and the democratic rhetoric it inspired contributed to delegitimating prejudice. Recognizing that the United States could not fight racism abroad while practicing it at home, a growing number of whites began to criticize openly the nation's racial caste system. Wendell L. Willkie, the unsuccessful Republican presidential candidate in 1940, wrote in 1944 that the war "has made us conscious of the contradiction between our treatment of our Negro minority and the ideals for which we are fighting." The perpetuation of racism, he declared, would harm America's standing in the world, for so long as "we continue to practice an ugly discrimination at home against our minorities . . . we cannot expect small nations and men of other races and colors to credit the good faith of our professed purposes." *Fortune* magazine sharply criticized both employers and labor unions for their continuing exclusion of blacks from employment. Racial discrimination, wrote the editors in 1942, impaired the war effort, damaged America's relations with other nations, and corroded the national conscience. "No serious review of the nation's status could ever overlook the contradiction between America's dream and the Negro reality," they stated. "In the consciousness of all peoples in the world this war is being fought for and against the idea of racial superiority. America's Constitution, like Christianity, is based on the principle that every man is born with the inalienable right to equality of opportunity. Whether or not this assumption is 'realistic'—we must either stick to it or change sides." The erosion of prejudice was also advanced by social scientists, whose research on the irrationality of group prejudice undermined the ideology of white supremacy. Of particular importance as a powerful indictment of racism was Gunnar Myrdal's *An American Dilemma,* published in 1944, which surveyed racial relations and summarized the findings of modern social science.[21]

Nonetheless, the outlook for political change on racial matters was not promising at the end of the war. Reactionaries and racists held key seats in Congress, and the Democratic party—which had won the allegiance of blacks during the Depression—was dependent on the electoral votes of the "solid South." Even President Roosevelt, beloved as a friend of the underdog, avoided making specific commitments on behalf of the civil rights of blacks, to appease his powerful southern allies. So bland was the Democratic party's 1944 platform on the issue of civil rights that the NAACP said sarcastically, "To call the section on the Negro a plank is a misnomer. It is best characterized as a splinter."[22]

No one knew what to expect on civil rights issues from Harry S. Truman. When he unexpectedly assumed the presidency on April 12, 1945, Truman had been vice-president for only eighty-two days; before then he had been known as the senator from Missouri who had investigated war profiteers. Lacking the artfulness of his predecessor, Truman was not able simultaneously to command the loyalty of blacks and white southern politicians. Though the political ramifications did not become clear until the 1948 election, Truman cast his lot on December 5, 1946, when he appointed a President's Committee on Civil Rights to study the status of civil rights and civil liberties and to recommend new legislation. It was no accident that the committee of fifteen consisted entirely of moderates and liberals and included two Catholics, two Jews, two labor leaders, two blacks, two liberal southerners, and—perhaps to enhance its credibility—the president of General Electric as its chairman. In his memoirs, Truman wrote that he set up the committee "because of the repeated anti-minority incidents immediately after the war in which homes were invaded, property was destroyed, and a number of innocent lives were taken."[23]

As a former senator, Truman knew that the chance of getting civil rights legislation through the Congress, with its southern committee chairmen, was nil. When the leadership of the Committee on Civil Rights asked him whether he wanted them only to make recommendations or to engage in "mass education as to our findings," the president told them that "the one thing he was interested in was in going to the public." In addition to documenting the extent of the problems, he told them "that the most practical and far-reaching aspect of our work would be whatever plans we devised for mass education of the public." The job of the committee, the president said, was to put before the American public an agenda for change, a list of particulars, and to begin the process of public education that must precede political and social change.[24]

In late 1947, the Committee for Civil Rights delivered its report to the president. It was a concise documentation of civil rights violations, accompanied by specific proposals for governmental action. For the first time, a presidential commission declared that the problem of civil rights was not a Negro problem or a Jewish problem, but a national problem, a problem of bringing America's practice into congruence with its ideals. In prose that was simple and direct, the committee detailed the severity of discrimination in the United States:

- Six blacks had been lynched by mobs in 1946. Twenty-two people had been rescued from lynch mobs. All but one of the would-be victims were Negroes. Due to the attitudes of local police and juries, members of lynch mobs were rarely prosecuted, rarely arrested, rarely convicted.
- Police brutality was flagrant in the South. The police in some communities subjected prisoners to beatings, third-degree tactics, pistol whippings, and illegal searches.
- In some communities, prisoners could not get a fair trial, either because members of minority groups were systematically excluded from jury service or because the accused could not afford to hire legal counsel.
- The right to vote was restricted unconstitutionally in many states in order to prevent or minimize black participation. Some southern states, for example, had imposed a poll tax or had required prospective voters to interpret the state constitution to the satisfaction of local officials. Such devices kept the electorate small and unrepresentative; in the 1944 election, 18.3 percent of potential voters in the eight poll-tax states had voted, compared to 68.7 percent in the other forty states.
- Discrimination in the armed forces persisted despite proclamations to the contrary. Negroes were barred from enlistment in any branch of the Marine Corps except as stewards; 80 percent of Negro sailors were cooks or stewards;

the army maintained a limit of 10 percent in all its sectors for Negroes. Only a tiny proportion of officers in any of the services were Negroes.

- Blacks were the victims of unfair employment practices and of wage discrimination. Whites and blacks with the same education were paid differently for the same work.

- Blacks were routinely excluded from hotels, restaurants, and other places of public accommodation.

- Health care facilities discriminated against Negroes. Many hospitals did not admit Negro patients or permit Negro doctors on their staff. Negro students were barred from most medical schools. "Medical schools graduate approximately 5,000 students a year, but only about 145 of these are Negro. And of these 145, 130 are from two Negro schools."

- School segregation, enforced by law in seventeen states and the District of Columbia, was manifestly unfair. "Whatever test is used—expenditure per pupil, teachers' salaries, the number of pupils per teacher, transportation of students, adequacy of school buildings and educational equipment, length of school term, extent of curriculum—Negro students are invariably at a disadvantage."[25]

The committee unanimously recommended the elimination of segregation and discrimination based on race, color, creed, or national origin from all aspects of American life. It proposed a federal antilynching law; abolition of the poll tax; strengthening of the civil rights section of the Justice Department; federal protection of the right to vote; new legislation to end all discrimination in the armed forces; a ban on segregation and discrimination in employment, housing, health facilities, interstate transportation, and places of public accommodation.

Only two issues split the committee, and both were educational issues. While everyone agreed that segregation was wrong, the committee argued at length whether to recommend a ban on federal aid to racially segregated schools. Even as the committee was deliberating, the Congress was considering a program of federal aid to elementary and secondary schools that had a good chance of passing. The members of the committee realized that their recommendations might affect the fate of the bill before Congress. The committee had to choose whether to recommend that federal aid be equitably divided between black and white schools in the South or to recommend that no federal aid go to any segregated school. The choice was not that simple: only three years before, in 1944, a federal aid bill had been killed when conservative Republican Senator William Langer attached an amendment to deny federal aid to segregated schools; as he expected, the bill's southern supporters voted against it and defeated the bill. Because of the dire financial needs of southern schools, and especially black southern schools, the NAACP in 1947 was supporting federal aid so long as it was fairly apportioned between white and black schools.

The southern members of the committee argued that the South would reject federal aid rather than permit the federal government to dictate its way of life. Some nonsouthern members opposed federal sanctions because they believed that prejudice stemmed from inferior education and that no step should be endorsed that might retard the improvement of southern schools. To cut off funds from communities that were blighted by ignorance, worried one member, was to remove "the very means of redemption." Morris Ernst, a liberal lawyer from New York, led the fight for federal sanctions against segregated schools; he held that the committee would look foolish if it endorsed "segregation plus a lot more money." Others agreed, including Sadie Alexander, a black lawyer from Philadelphia, who objected to permitting the South "to set a pattern for the entire United States." The most telling argument came from Rabbi Roland B. Gittelsohn of New York:

> I am deeply disturbed by this notion that by putting more money and better teachers into a segregated school system in the South you will thereby take an appreciable step toward the eventual elimination of segregation. You won't. Children don't learn from books, but from the life they are living, and the basic truth of a Southern educational system lies not in what you teach but in the fact that the white child knows that the colored child isn't good enough to go to school with him, and I don't care how much money you put into it, so long as you tell a white child, merely by implication, that the Negro child can't sit next to him in school, you are licked.

Channing Tobias, a black social worker, pointed out that a recommendation for sanctions against segregated schools might well cause the defeat of the federal aid bill, but he believed that the time had come "to say what is really in our hearts on this question of segregation and be willing to take what comes." And those who worried that the Congress would never pass federal sanctions were rebuked by James Carey, an official of the Congress of Industrial Organizations. Carey insisted that it was not the job of the committee to decide what was acceptable to the Congress, but to declare what was right: "If we could get a report and give it widespread publicity where people can see it, that this is the opinion of the people, of a cross section of the American society, it is the policy of the Federal Government, it goes way beyond what we expect to get even during the present Administration. . . . This represents our aspirations, and this is what we should seek." With an apologetic dissent from its two southern members, the committee endorsed the principle that no federal aid should be given to racially segregated schools.[26]

The second issue that split the committee was whether, in admissions to educational institutions, there should be an absolute ban on discrimination based on race, color, creed, or national origin. No one favored racial or religious discrimination, but John Dickey, president of Dartmouth College, contended that educational institutions should have the right to take race, religion, and social background into account in order to have a diverse student body; he was especially interested in keeping a balance among students from different religious backgrounds at Dartmouth. Members who were associated with denominational schools worried that an absolute ban might destroy the character of their institutions. However, the black and Jewish members of the committee resolutely defended an absolute ban for all but denominational schools, since it would be impossible to determine whether an institution had discriminated for reasons of diversity or for reasons of bigotry. The final report recommended laws "prohibiting discrimination in the admission and treatment of students based on race, color, creed, or national origin," exempting denominational schools. The report noted: "There is a substantial division within the committee on this recommendation. A majority favors it."[27]

Even before the committee issued its report, President Truman dramatically asserted his own civil rights views in an address to the NAACP on June 29, 1947. He was the first president ever to accept an invitation to speak to the NAACP. The night before he spoke, he wrote his sister: "I've got to make a speech to the Society for the Advancement of Colored People tomorrow and I wish I didn't have to make it. Mrs. R. and Walter White, Wayne Morse, Senator from Oregon, & your brother are the speakers. . . . Mamma won't like what I have to say because I wind up quoting Old Abe. But I believe what I say and I am hopeful we may implement it." Whatever his inner qualms, Truman delivered a forthright pledge to make the federal government the defender of the "rights and equalities of all Americans. And when I say all Americans—I mean all Americans." He stated that "every citizen in a truly democratic society" should have "the right to a decent home, the right to an education, the right to adequate medical care, the right to a worthwhile job, the right to an equal share in the making of public decisions through the ballot, and the right to a fair trial in a fair court." Truman won praise from the NAACP, the black press, and metropolitan newspapers in the North, but he was roundly criticized by the press in the South and the West, especially for his statement that everyone has the "right" to a home, a job, education, and medical care. These, said his critics, are to be earned, not guaranteed by government.[28]

Truman made civil rights the centerpiece of his 1948 state of the union address to Congress. "Our first goal," he held, "is to secure fully the essential human rights of our citizens." He condemned the fact "that some of our citizens are still denied equal opportunity for education, for jobs and for economic advancement, and for the expression of their views at the polls. Most serious of all, some are denied equal protection under the laws. Whether discrimination is based on race, or creed, or color, or land of origin, it is utterly contrary to American ideals of democracy." Less than a month later, on February 2, 1948, Truman sent the Congress a special message on civil rights, incorporating the recommendations of his Committee on Civil Rights.[29]

The president's advocacy of civil rights infuriated southern politicians. Senator James O. Eastland of Mississippi predicted that the South would withhold its votes in the presidential election and throw the election to the House of Representatives, where "a southern man would emerge as president." Others threatened to filibuster against the president's proposals. Southerners showed their contempt for Truman by walking out of the Democratic convention in 1948 and endorsing Governor Strom Thurmond of South Carolina as the "Dixiecrat" candidate for president. At the same time, the left wing of the Democratic party, irked by Truman's firm stand against Soviet expansionism in Europe, abandoned him to support Henry Wallace, the former vice-president, as the candidate of the Progressive party. Though Truman eked out a victory in 1948 against Republican Thomas Dewey, no one might reasonably have predicted that alienating both the right and the left wing of the party was a prescient political strategy.[30]

Each year, in his State of the Union message, Truman proposed a civil rights program, and each year the southern-dominated Congress quietly killed it. But there were things he could do without the Congress. On July 26, 1948, he issued an executive order ending racial segregation in the armed forces and banning discrimination in federal employment. The Federal Housing Administration was directed to drop its ban on insuring homes in racially mixed neighborhoods. And Truman's Justice Department established a significant precedent by filing an amicus brief in the Supreme Court supporting the NAACP's attack on racially restrictive covenants in housing.[31]

Through the work of the Committee on Civil Rights and by his own willingness to take a stand, President Truman set in motion a process of public education. In the struggle to resolve "the American dilemma," the contradiction between ideals and practices, the first requirement was to make the public aware of the dilemma. This was the tack of the Committee on Civil Rights. The value of its work—and of the president's doomed proposals—was to give legitimacy and encouragement to the growing movement for civil rights. Segregationists claimed that the nascent civil rights movement was led by agitators and Communists; the president of the United States said that its goals embodied the highest aspirations of the Constitution. In the decades ahead, events moved so quickly and public opinion shifted so decisively that the views of Truman and his Committee on Civil Rights came to sound commonplace, when in fact they had been uncommonly courageous.

When the war ended, the NEA had many reasons to feel hopeful about the prospects for federal aid to education. For one thing, there was wide recognition that many of the nation's elementary and secondary schools were in dire straits; the teacher shortage was a national problem, and many districts had exhausted their taxing powers. For another, President Truman was the first chief executive to support it. And then, the race issue, which had killed federal aid in 1944, was neutralized since the NAACP was willing to go along with the principle of fair apportionment of federal funds to white and black schools. But most important, Senator Robert Taft of Ohio, ranking Republican on the Senate Education and Labor Committee and one of the leaders of the conservative wing of the Republican party, switched sides. Taft's recruitment to the cause of federal aid to education was a significant coup for the education lobby. He had been instrumental in defeating federal aid during the war, and his change of heart surprised friend and foe alike. Though he was an outspoken critic of the New Deal and of big government, Taft became persuaded—after private meetings with NEA spokesmen—that federal aid to education was necessary. Several years later, when he was asked why he was so "conservative" in some areas and yet so "liberal" in support of federal aid to education, Taft explained that children "were entitled, not as a matter of privilege but as a matter of right, to a decent roof, decent meals, decent medical care and a decent place in which to go to school. The rest, as they grow older, was up to them." And, he added, "Education is socialistic anyway, and has been for a hundred and fifty years."[32]

With Taft enlisted, the leaders of the NEA renewed their campaign for federal aid. They knew they could count on the backing of a broad spectrum of civic, professional, religious, and social welfare organizations. The NAACP was prepared to support federal aid so long as it guaranteed an "equitable" distribution of funds between white and black schools in the South. Southern congressmen, whose schools were the poorest in the nation, could be counted on so long as prospective legislation offered no threat to racial segregation or to the states' control and distribution of their own school funds. Southerners had another reason to press for federal aid: beginning in 1938, federal courts began to require equalization of the salaries of black and white teachers and of facilities in segregated districts. The implications of the trend were clear, and southerners realized that equalization had to move faster in order to ward off new challenges to their separate-and-still-unequal school systems.

The only serious problem for the education lobby was the religious issue. The NEA was a public school organization, and it traditionally opposed the granting of any federal funds to nonpublic schools; in this position it was supported by some important allies, particularly by Protestant and Jewish groups that rejected any compromise of the principle of separation of church and state. But this posture was deeply offensive to Catholics, who opposed the passage of any federal assistance program that excluded children in nonpublic schools. To exclude their children, Catholics argued, would discriminate against them solely on religious grounds, would penalize them for exercising their religious freedom, and would deny Catholics benefits for which they were taxed. Until the mid-1930s, Catholics had resolutely opposed any federal aid to education; they feared that it would inevitably lead to federal control of education, to centralized efforts to homogenize the schools, and to the destruction of Catholic schools. However, by the mid-1940s, Catholic schools had participated beneficially in the New Deal's National Youth Administration, the federal school lunch program, and the GI Bill. These experiences made them willing to support federal aid to education if it included a fair share for Catholic schools. To the extent that benefits were available to public school children, argued Catholic spokesmen, they should be equally available to children in nonpublic schools.

The major opposition to federal aid legislation came from business and industrial groups, led by the U. S. Chamber of Commerce. The chamber insisted that the financing and control of education should remain at the state and local level. In part the chamber was concerned about economy, but principally it objected to federal involvement in education. The most zealous opponents of federal aid were ultraconservative groups like the Daughters of the American Revolution (DAR), which believed that federal aid would destroy local initiative and traditional values by empowering a centralized bureaucracy. While the DAR never faltered in its stand, the Chamber of Commerce went through a brief period of irresolution after the war because of the national teacher shortage. Also fearful of federal control, the National Association of Manufacturers consistently opposed federal aid, but other groups wavered: the American Legion and the American Farm Bureau Federation supported federal aid until the early 1950s, when they switched to the opposition.

Since at least the early 1940s, federal aid to education had the potential to command a majority of Congress. Those who opposed federal aid on principle were a minority, but those who supported it on principle were persistently divided among themselves. The religious issue, and to a lesser extent the racial issue, kept supporters of federal aid at odds with each other. By the time the war ended, the devastating effects of the teacher shortage and the glaring inequalities among schools were documented in thousands of pages of testimony. Every new congressional hearing brought forth many of the same witnesses and, frequently, the same recitation of facts. The cause seemed to have reached a stalemate, and even President Truman's support was not enough to move it forward. Though Truman was committed to federal aid, it was but one of many issues before him; he never authorized the preparation of an administration bill nor threw his support to any bill in particular nor made any effort to produce a compromise among the interested groups. It was only when Taft took over the leadership of the fight for federal aid in the Senate that new life was breathed into the campaign.

With Taft in charge, the federal aid to education movement became bipartisan, and even more important, gained skilled leadership and a legislative strategy. Taft's considerable skills went into the drafting of a new bill. To attract the votes of the "have" states, Taft provided a flat grant of five dollars per child in all states (but divided only among children in public schools); to defuse the religious issue, Taft permitted each state to decide whether to distribute federal funds to nonpublic schools; to resolve the racial issue, Taft included a provision for equitable distribution of funds as well as an amendment barring federal interference in segregation. In the compromises that were hammered out, no interest group emerged victorious, which made it possible for all of them to join behind the Taft bill, though grudgingly. The NEA approved the bill even though it included the possibility of limited public aid to nonpublic schools. The NAACP endorsed the bill, while complaining that southern states could not be trusted to distribute federal funds fairly. Catholics were unhappy about the very limited concessions to their interests, but they did not oppose the bill. Introduced in 1946, the Taft bill emerged from committee in 1947 and was finally passed by the Senate on April 1, 1948, by a vote of 58 to 22. It was the first time in sixty years that the Senate had approved general federal aid to education.[33]

Unfortunately, there was no advocate of federal aid in the House of Representatives with the stature of Robert Taft. Aside from his talents as a legislator, Taft had the advantage of being a Republican leader in a Republican-controlled Senate. In the House, neither Republicans nor Democrats were committed to passing a bill, and the presidential campaign of 1948 created a new reason to defer action. The Republican candidate, Thomas Dewey, ignored the issue, and President Truman excoriated the "Do-Nothing" Eightieth Congress for failing to pass it. Consequently, the Republican majority in the House was in no mood to press for legislation that might appear to give the president a political victory.

Federal aid legislation was blocked not only by partisan politics but by the eruption of religious conflict. Taft's compromise—to let each state decide whether to grant public funds to nonpublic schools—had satisfied the Senate but it was a tenuous compromise. A Supreme Court decision in 1947 made it increasingly difficult to find a middle ground between those who favored public funds for nonpublic schools and those who absolutely opposed it.

The township of Ewing, New Jersey, reimbursed parents for the cost of school bus transportation, regardless of whether their children went to public or Catholic schools. A taxpayer had sued, claiming that it was unconstitutional to use public funds on behalf of church schools. In early 1947, the Supreme Court ruled 5 to 4 that the town's policy was constitutional. Speaking for the majority, Justice Hugo Black held that the state subsidy for school bus transportation was comparable to providing

> such general government services as ordinary police and fire protection, connections for sewage disposal, public highways and sidewalks. Of course, cutting off church schools from these services . . . would make it far more difficult for the schools to operate. But such is obviously not the purpose of the First Amendment. That Amendment requires the state to be a neutral in its relations with groups of religious believers and nonbelievers; it does not require the state to be their adversary. State power is no more to be used so as to handicap religions than it is to favor them.

In an apparent effort to quell the fears of those who might see the decision as a dangerous precedent, Black stated, "The First Amendment has erected a wall between church and state. That wall must be kept high and impregnable. We could not approve the slightest breach. New Jersey has not breached it here."[34]

The four dissenting justices maintained that the purpose of the First Amendment had been "to create a complete and permanent separation of the spheres of religious activity and civil authority by comprehensively forbidding every form of public aid or support for religion." They held that "Payment of transportation is no more, nor is it any the less essential to education, whether religious or secular, than payment for tuitions, for teachers' salaries, for buildings, equipment and necessary materials." There was no legal discrimination against Catholic children by denying them transportation funds, they held, because all children had the same right to attend public school.

Known as the *Everson* decision, the Court's narrow ruling provoked cries of outrage from Protestant groups, which saw it as the first step toward full public support for parochial schools. In an editorial entitled "Now Will Protestants Awake?" the liberal Protestant *Christian Century* charged that Catholics were "using these apparently insignificant matters as the thin edge of the wedge which would ultimately crack open the Constitution and give the Church the privileged position in the United States which it professedly seeks." What was at stake, the editorialist warned, was nothing less than "the ultimate character of American culture and the destiny of Protestantism in this country." A Southern Baptist spokesman warned that "this ominous decision casts a shadow" that might in time "darken the torch of religious liberty in our beloved land." Other national Protestant leaders characterized the decision as a serious threat to the public schools and to religious liberty, called on their followers to resist new Catholic demands for public funds, and urged President Truman to recall his envoy to the Vatican. Their responses echoed nineteenth-century fears of a Catholic "plot" to dominate America.[35]

Catholics interpreted the *Everson* decision to mean that their schools were ineligible to receive public funds for teachers or buildings, and they abandoned their demand for full and equal participation in any future federal aid. They did, however, insist on their right to public subsidies for auxiliary services such as transportation, nonreligious textbooks, and health services. The "child benefit" theory was that if the state provided textbooks or health services or some other benefit to children in public schools, it should provide the same benefit to all children, regardless of the school they attended, because the benefit went to the child, not the school, and served a public purpose. Although Catholics adjusted their goals to the limits set by the Supreme Court, they believed that the wall-of-separation argument was a cover for anti-Catholic pleading, since there were numerous examples of productive relationships between the federal government and nonpublic institutions, such as the GI Bill, the federal school lunch program, and federal aid to hospitals, in which federal funds were dispersed without discrimination between public and nonpublic recipients. The "child benefit" theory was the basis of not only the *Everson* decision, but also the *Cochran* decision of 1930, when the Supreme Court had approved a Louisiana law permitting the state to furnish nonreligious textbooks to children in parochial schools. By 1946, five states (Louisiana, Mississippi, New Mexico, Oregon, and West Virginia) provided free textbooks to all children.[36]

In a different climate, the *Everson* decision might have provided the basis for a compromise between the NEA and Catholics, which would have removed the major barrier to federal aid legislation. But the effect of the decision was to sharpen the polarization between Catholics and public school partisans. Catholics became convinced that there was no reason to accept legislation that gave them less than the Supreme Court approved. On the other side, the decision inflamed anti-Catholic opinion and unleashed a torrent of attacks on Catholic motives.

To prevent any further Catholic inroads on public funds, a new organization was established in January 1948: Protestants and Other Americans United for Separation of Church and State (POAU). Its founders included prominent Protestant leaders, such as Dr. Louie D. Newton, president of the Southern Baptist Convention, the Reverend G. Bromley Oxnam, Bishop of the Methodist church for the New York area, and Dr. John A. Mackay, president of the Princeton Theological Seminary. POAU became a vehement opponent of any form of public aid to nonpublic schools; it treated the Catholics' demand for auxiliary services as a step toward "total support" of parochial schools and warned that the Roman Catholic church had made "ominous progress in its strategy of winning for itself a position of special privilege in relation to the state."[37]

The temperature of the religious conflict was raised even higher as a result of several articles in the *Nation* by Paul Blanshard attacking the Catholic church. Blanshard acknowledged candidly "the tremendous revival" of anti-Catholic feeling in the United States, especially among liberals, which he attributed not to bigotry but to "a growing educational aggressiveness on the part of the [Catholic] hierarchy." Anti-Catholicism was spreading, he asserted, because of "the extension of bus transportation at public expense to pupils of parochial schools in nineteen states and the fight of various Catholic lobbies in Washington against any federal aid to education in which parochial schools do not share." In other words, Catholics were responsible for provoking bigotry by claiming the benefits approved by the Supreme Court in the *Everson* decision.[38]

The central thesis of his articles, which ran in the fall of 1947 and the spring of 1948 (and which were then expanded into a book, *American Freedom and Catholic Power*), was that Catholic policies and Catholic power threatened American freedom. He criticized the church for its policies in medicine, morals, science, and education; its hierarchical organization; its undemocratic character; its sympathy for fascism; its censorship of books and movies; and its efforts to impose on non-Catholics its views on divorce, birth control, and abortion. Though he tried to disassociate himself from traditional anti-Catholic nativism, he nonetheless criticized Catholic rituals and religious practices, such as clerical garb, celibacy, and the medievalism of Catholic ceremonies. He called Catholic schools "a system of segregated schools under costumed religious teachers" which cultivated "separatism and intolerance." He claimed that priests were encouraging their followers to procreate in order to gain numerical supremacy in America, and he warned that if Catholics became a majority, "the most striking and immediate result . . . would be the transfer of control of education, religion, and family relationships to the Catholic hierarchy." To rouse public opinion against any federal aid for nonpublic schools, Blanshard forecast that the "struggle between American democracy and the Catholic hierarchy depends upon the survival and expansion of the public school."[39]

Blanshard's anti-Catholic polemic created a sensation. School officials in New York City and Newark, New Jersey, canceled their subscriptions to the *Nation,* which led to charges that the Catholic church was crushing freedom of the press. The New York City superintendent of schools, a Lutheran, contended that the schools should neither promote nor attack religion and that the New York schools had not violated the *Nation*'s rights by not subscribing to it. A committee of more than a hundred prominent New Yorkers signed "An Appeal to Reason and Conscience in Defense of the Right of Freedom of Inquiry in the United States" to protest the removal of the *Nation* from school libraries, but the state commissioner of education defended the right of the local school board to "determine the periodicals to which it wished to subscribe." Meanwhile, the *Nation* printed an extra 50,000 copies of the Blanshard series to meet public demand, and Blanshard's book was a national best-seller for six months. Though some newspapers would not advertise it and some stores would not sell it, it eventually went through twenty-six printings and sold 240,000 hardcover copies.[40]

In March, 1948, in the midst of the controversy over the Blanshard articles, the Supreme Court announced the *McCollum* decision, which offered yet another definition of the height of the wall separating church and state. In an 8-to-1 decision, the Court found that an Illinois law permitting released-time for religious instruction in public schools during regular school hours was unconstitutional. Justice Hugo Black declared for the majority (which included the Court's only Catholic member) that a public school system could not be used "to aid any or all religious faiths or sects in the dissemination of their doctrines and ideals."[41]

It was in this rancorous atmosphere that the Congress once again took up the question of federal aid to education. After the 1948 election, the chances for federal aid seemed better than ever. Truman had won the presidential election, and the Democratic party had gained control of both houses of Congress. In his 1949 State of the Union message, the president urged Congress to pass federal aid to education, though once again he avoided endorsing any particular bill. The Senate acted promptly to draw up legislation that was similar to the previous year's Taft bill, which had passed the Senate and stalled in the House.

Catholics tried to convince the Senate to incorporate the child-benefit theory of the *Everson* decision in its legislation. Baltimore's Archbishop Francis P. Keogh, chairman of the Department of Education of the National Catholic Welfare Conference, testified: "All we want for our children are just the necessary services where they are now difficult to get— a textbook, a bus ride, some medical and dental aid. We don't want anyone to build our schools. We don't want a penny for the salaries of our teachers." The Senate responded by passing a separate health services bill, which provided $35 million for medical and dental examinations for all children, as a companion measure to the general federal aid bill. Taft insisted that the federal aid bill should neither compel nor forbid the use of public funds for nonpublic schools; his view was that the issue should be fought out in the states, so that the states could maintain control of their schools without federal interference. The federal aid bill passed the Senate on May 5, 1949, by 58 to 15, with bipartisan support.[42]

Now the focus shifted to the House Committee on Education and Labor, which was known as an ideological battleground. Because it handled labor issues, the committee attracted the extremes of both parties, the most conservative Republicans and the most liberal Democrats. It was a committee in which it was easy to provoke dissension but difficult to build consensus. On May 9, 1949, the chairman of the committee, John Lesinski, a prolabor Democrat and Catholic from Detroit, assigned federal aid legislation to a subcommittee headed by Graham A. Barden, the second ranking Democrat on the committee, a conservative former schoolteacher from North Carolina, and a supporter of federal aid for public schools.

Although the Senate bill had been carefully drafted to satisfy a diverse coalition, Congressman Barden decided that it was unacceptable. The bill had strong language forbidding any federal agency from interfering in local schools, but Barden insisted that it was not strong enough: "I have taken part in the authorization of appropriations and the passing of laws and thought I knew what I was doing, and then spent the rest of my time crawling on my knees to some administrator, please, won't he please, do what we had in mind when we passed it. . . . Now, that is why we are afraid to let them get their hooks, so to speak, in our school system." He explained that "there are some features in the Senate bill so objectionable to me that I could not find myself going over to it. I am not going to accept it; that's all." One feature that was particularly objectionable to Barden was the Taft bill's laissez-faire attitude toward public funding of nonpublic schools. When a spokesman from the National Catholic Welfare Conference appeared before his committee, Barden told him, "I am just as far in one direction as you can possibly be in the other. So we could not get together." During three weeks of hearings, Barden scuttled the Senate bill and pushed his own bill to the fore. The Barden bill differed from the Senate bill in three important respects: it limited federal funding solely to public schools, it expressly barred federal expenditures for transportation and health services, and it removed the language that required southern states to make a "just and equitable" distribution of funds between white and black schools. On July 7, 1949, the Barden subcommittee reported the Barden bill to the full committee.[43]

The emergence of the Barden bill as the center of attention shattered the fragile consensus that Taft had carefully constructed between the partisans of public and nonpublic schools. The public school coalition got everything it wanted, and the Catholics were cut out altogether. Instead of holding out for the Senate bill, which had a good chance of passing because of its minimal concessions to Catholic interests, the NEA quickly embraced the Barden bill and urged its members to support it. The Barden bill was acclaimed by leading educators, by POAU, and by numerous organizations representing Protestants, Jews, veterans, and civic groups; the education editor of the *New York Times* testified before Barden's subcommittee that the bill was "the best thing . . . that has ever come out in the halls of Congress in 30 years in an effort to bring about a Federal measure."[44]

Predictably, Catholics were outraged. They had reluctantly abandoned their claim to participate fully in any federal aid program, and now the Barden bill denied them even auxiliary services. An official of the National Catholic Welfare Conference called it "the worst and most objectionable federal aid to education bill ever approved by any congressional committee." Barden was sharply attacked by Francis Cardinal Spellman, the archbishop of New York, on June 19, 1949, at a meeting of fifteen thousand Catholics. Spellman received first-page treatment when he denounced Barden as a "new apostle of bigotry," called his supporters "disciples of discrimination," and accused them of venting "venom upon children" in "a sin shocking as it is incomprehensible." Advocates of the

Barden bill, said Spellman, were "conducting a craven crusade of religious prejudice against Catholic children" by advancing an "irrational, un-American, discriminatory thesis that the public school is the only truly American school." The archbishop declared, "We must oppose any bill that fails to guarantee at least non-religious textbooks, bus rides and health services for all the children of all Americans." On the following Sunday, the Barden bill was attacked in Catholic churches throughout the country, and Catholics were urged to write their congressmen. The Catholic press inveighed against the Barden bill, and congressional offices received an "avalanche of letters and telegrams from angry Catholic voters."[45]

John Lesinski, the chairman of the House Committee on Education and Labor, was not happy with the Barden bill. On June 27, he declared that the bill was "anti-Catholic and anti-Negro. It is my opinion that he drew it up purposely because he did not want any aid to education and wanted to kill it." Lesinski was supported by John W. McCormack, majority leader of the House, who called the Barden bill "grossly unfair" to Catholics and Negroes. Barden insisted that the real issue was his prohibition against public funds for nonpublic schools, because his bill provided equal spending for all pupils, without regard to their race, and he implied that his critics were acting on behalf of the Catholic hierarchy. Lesinski refused to convene a meeting of the full committee to consider the Barden bill and vowed that "as long as I have the breath to prevent it, the Barden bill will never come out."[46]

Any chance of moderating the rising level of religious animosity was dashed by a public controversy between Cardinal Spellman and Mrs. Franklin Delano Roosevelt in the summer of 1949. The Spellman-Roosevelt exchange was one of those public events that serves as a symbolic vehicle for large political issues, in this instance dramatizing the depth of hostility and misunderstanding between Catholics and liberals. In his June attack on Congressman Barden, Cardinal Spellman had already expressed his bitter opposition to the Barden bill and its supporters, especially to those liberals who posed "as angels of light and liberty" while crusading against the rights of Catholic children. Mrs. Roosevelt, a revered figure among American liberals, had not hesitated to disagree with Catholic leaders in the past. According to Joseph P. Lash, her biographer,

> the leaders of the Catholic church responsible for its political interests had long been unhappy about Mrs. Roosevelt. Her friendliness toward Loyalist Spain in the thirties, her support, even though discreet, of birth control, her sponsorship of the American Youth Congress and other organizations in which the Communists had been heavily represented had vexed the clergy to

the point of public expression of its displeasure even while she was First Lady. She, on her side, had become increasingly concerned over the growth in temporal power of an institution that she felt was aggressively conservative in social and political matters . . . .

In 1948, she had incurred the displeasure of Catholic leaders when she joined the protest against the banning of the *Nation* from the New York City schools. Mrs. Roosevelt believed that Cardinal Spellman and his associates were particularly angry because she had been instrumental in maintaining the diplomatic isolation of Franco Spain at the United Nations.[47]

On June 23, 1949, four days after Cardinal Spellman's denunciation of the Barden bill, Mrs. Roosevelt disagreed with the cardinal in her column in the *New York World Telegram*. She wrote:

> The controversy brought about by the request made by Francis Cardinal Spellman that Catholic schools should share in Federal aid funds forces upon the citizens of the country the kind of decision that is going to be very difficult to make.
>
> Those of us who believe in the right of any human being to belong to whatever church he sees fit, and to worship God in his own way, cannot be accused of prejudice when we do not want to see public education connected with religious control of the schools, which are paid for by taxpayers' money.

Private schools, she believed, should receive "no tax funds of any kind." After receiving several letters accusing her of anti-Catholic bias, Mrs. Roosevelt reiterated her views in another column on July 8. Many of her correspondents apparently assumed that she was endorsing the Barden bill, which coincided with her own position, for in a third column, published on July 15, Mrs. Roosevelt noted, "I have not read the [Barden] bill carefully, and I have been rather careful not to say if I am for or against any particular bill or bills."[48]

On July 21, Cardinal Spellman sent to the press and to Mrs. Roosevelt a vitriolic attack on the views of the former first lady. The cardinal accused Mrs. Roosevelt of allying herself with Congressman Barden and of condemning Spellman "for defending Catholic children against those who would deny them their constitutional rights of equality with other American children." Spellman declared, "You could have acted only from misinformation, ignorance or prejudice, not from knowledge and understanding!" He too, he said, opposed religious control of tax-supported schools. But, he insisted, "If the Federal Government provides a bottle of milk to each child in a public school it should provide milk for all school children. I believe that if Federal funds are used to transport children to public schools they should be used to transport parochial school children. I believe if through the use of Federal funds the children who attend public schools are immunized from contagious diseases that all children should be protected from these diseases." He accused Mrs. Roosevelt of flagrant anti-Catholic bias. "Why," he asked, "do you repeatedly plead causes that are anti-Catholic?" He warned Mrs. Roosevelt that

> even though you may again use your column to attack me and again accuse me of starting a controversy, I shall not again publicly acknowledge you.
>
> For, whatever you may say in the future, your record of anti-Catholicism stands for all to see—a record which you yourself wrote on the pages of history which cannot be recalled—documents of discrimination unworthy of an American mother![49]

Mrs. Roosevelt responded to the cardinal, denying any religious bigotry and restating her opposition to public funding of nonpublic schools. In closing her letter, she said, "I assure you that I have no sense of being 'an unworthy American mother.' The final judgment, my dear Cardinal Spellman, of the worthiness of all human beings is in the hands of God."[50]

The exchange of letters was front-page news across the nation. Four thousand letters were sent to Mrs. Roosevelt and 90 percent of them were favorable. Mrs. Roosevelt was defended by editorials in large metropolitan newspapers, by Protestant and Jewish leaders, and by organizations such as the American Civil Liberties Union; she was defended also by some Catholics who agreed with her views and by some who were embarrassed by the vituperative language used by the cardinal. Although Mrs. Roosevelt was told by a Washington journalist that she had been "attacked by Catholic priests in pulpits here last Sunday, so it is Church policy," Cardinal Spellman attracted few supporters. In the court of public opinion, Mrs. Roosevelt was a clear winner, largely because Cardinal Spellman blundered in turning legitimate Catholic grievances into a personal attack on Mrs. Roosevelt.[51]

The substantive issues were muddied by the controversy, for Mrs. Roosevelt was uninformed about the status of the federal aid legislation at the time she wrote her columns. She did not seem to realize that the Supreme Court had already approved the use of state funds for bus transportation and nonreligious textbooks, nor that there was a conflict within the Congress between the Senate bill and the Barden bill. In her columns, she erroneously implied that the Catholic church sought full public funding for its schools. In letters that Mrs. Roosevelt wrote during the summer of 1949, she expressed doubts about the true motives of Cardinal Spellman. She would not be surprised to learn, she wrote to a friend, "that the

Cardinal had had word from the Vatican and that the letter was partly written there. . . . The whole episode with Cardinal Spellman, as far as I am concerned, is only part of a much larger situation. I think they felt the time had come to form a Catholic party in this country and hoped it could be accomplished. It was a disappointment to them that it did not turn out quite the way they hoped." Like the POAU, Mrs. Roosevelt treated the Catholic appeal for auxiliary services as part of a long-range, foot-in-the-door strategy to win not only full public support of their schools, but political power on a national scale.[52]

The public acrimony was brought to a close, at least rhetorically, when worried leaders of the New York Democratic party brought about a reconciliation. In early August, the cardinal called her and asked for her comments on a new statement of his views; a representative of the cardinal traveled to her home and together they worked on the text of the cardinal's statement and Mrs. Roosevelt's response. The cardinal restated his position that nonpublic schools should receive auxiliary services and said clearly that Catholics did not expect "general public support" or public funds for buildings or teachers. While he said nothing new, his tone was conciliatory, and Mrs. Roosevelt wrote that his statement was "clarifying and fair." A few weeks later, Cardinal Spellman paid a social call. In the days after her public reconciliation with Cardinal Spellman, Mrs. Roosevelt confided her continuing distrust of Catholic intentions in a letter to Agnes Meyer, a journalist, partisan of public school aid, and wife of the *Washington Post* publisher. Mrs. Roosevelt said, "I am more convinced than ever that they will never help us to get federal aid for education unless they think they are going to get it too for parochial schools." And she remained convinced that "auxiliary services" would never satisfy Catholic demands. According to Joseph P. Lash, she predicted "that the church would work to get as many states and as many Supreme Court decisions as possible upholding the constitutionality of state funds for parochial schools, 'and in the long run they are sure if it is constitutional for states, it may be declared constitutional for federal funds to be used not only for auxiliary services but for all services equally. Once that is done they control the schools, or at least a great part of them.' "[53]

While Mrs. Roosevelt, because of her great personal dignity, scored a clear triumph in the encounter, Cardinal Spellman forcefully made the point that the Barden bill was unacceptable to the Catholic church. The point was not wasted on John Lesinski, the chairman of the House Committee on Education and Labor, who refused to convene the committee during the month of July. Under pressure from other committee members, Lesinski finally called a committee meeting on August 2, which promptly turned into a debacle. The committee refused to vote on the Barden bill and voted down every other measure that was proposed. Federal aid to education was dead for 1949.

Federal aid proponents, having tried so hard for so many years, were not about to quit. With the opening of the 1950 session, hopes rose once again that the deadlock might be broken. Once again, President Truman called for passage of federal aid to education. Lesinski announced that the committee would begin in February to work out their differences and compose an acceptable measure. Catholics, who had previously asked for an allocation of 10 percent of the total federal funds for auxiliary services, moderated their position and stated that 2 percent would be acceptable to them. Another compromise acceptable to the Catholic leaders was offered by Representative John F. Kennedy of Massachusetts; he suggested passing the Senate bill with an amendment permitting federal subsidy of bus transportation for nonpublic school children, which was consistent with the Supreme Court's *Everson* decision. After meeting in closed session for a month, the committee voted not to report any bill until the president assured them that there would be no federal control of schools; their concern was prompted because the Federal Children's Bureau had published a pamphlet, "Your Child from Six to Twelve," in which one passage appeared to speak "slightingly" of home ownership and another passage dealt with sex education. Within a day, Truman responded with a vigorous assertion of opposition to federal control of schools: "When I say I am opposed to Federal control of schools, I mean I am opposed to control by any officer or department of the Federal Government, whether it be the United States Office of Education, the Federal Security Agency [predecessor to the Department of Health, Education, and Welfare] or any other bureau or official." With no further reason to delay, the committee prepared to vote. But on the very same day, Graham Barden publicly attacked Cardinal Spellman at a New York meeting of a group opposed to aid for parochial schools. Though the Spellman-Roosevelt controversy had been amicably settled eight months earlier, Barden used the occasion to brand Spellman "a cruel authoritarian" for having "attacked a great, noble American lady and mother." Barden recounted the abuse that had been heaped on him the previous year by Spellman and other Catholics and intoned, "Let there be no question as to who injected the religious issue into the Federal school aid problem." Given the timing of his remarks, there could be little doubt that Barden was using the occasion to rekindle the religious animosity that had killed federal aid in 1949. Barden shared the rostrum with Mrs. Roosevelt, who avoided any reference to personalities or to her confrontation with the cardinal. But Mrs. Roosevelt stated her firm opposition to both the Senate bill, which permitted states to spend federal funds in accordance with their own state laws, and the Kennedy amendment, that would permit the use of federal funds for school bus transportation.[54]

On the following day, March 7, the House Committee on Education and Labor voted down the Kennedy amendment, 16 to 9; it was defeated by an alliance of Republicans and the public school bloc. On March 14, 1950, the unamended Senate bill was brought to a vote and defeated 13 to 12 by a coalition of seven conservative Republicans and six Democrats; the six Democrats included two who opposed any aid whatsoever. And that was the end of federal aid to education in 1950. Seventeen of the twenty-five members of the House Committee on Education and Labor favored the principle of federal aid, but it proved to be impossible to compromise the differences among them, particularly the religious differences.

In May 1950, John Lesinski died and was replaced as chairman of the House Committee on Education and Labor by Graham Barden. Predictably, Barden was objectionable to Catholics, organized labor, and blacks. Where federal aid to education was concerned, only the NEA was pleased, and his ascension to the leadership slot made the NEA less willing to consider any compromise on the issue of aid to nonpublic schools. Though Barden was the hero of the NEA and of many liberals and Protestants during the controversy over his bill in 1949, his record as committee chairman suggests that he was an inconstant champion. One study, published in 1962, notes that in his eight years as chairman, "Barden led the Committee in such a way as to create rather than resolve internal conflicts. Most of the time, he worked tirelessly to defeat federal aid legislation; and on the single occasion, in 1949, when he accepted a federal aid bill he did so on such restrictive and uncompromising grounds that he triggered the most acrimonious of all Committee conflicts."[55]

During his tenure as committee chairman, Barden used "a skillful combination of formal prerogative, informal maneuver and personal talent" to block federal aid bills. According to his biographer, Barden believed that what he kept from happening was even more important than what he caused to happen; he liked to say that he "never knew the Republic to be endangered by a bill that was not passed." He decided after the contretemps over federal aid in 1949 "that the question of Federal aid to public schools *is not as important to the future welfare and happiness of this nation as separation of church and state*—and if it has reached the point that that is the choice, then my choice is already made." Like northern liberals and the public school lobby, Barden wanted federal aid, but not if it meant a penny for nonpublic school children. His hard-line tactics, which were supported by the leadership of the education lobby, undoubtedly prevented the passage of federal aid in 1949, at a moment when its prospects were good.[56]

A ground for compromise was always available, based on Supreme Court decisions. The Court had already ruled that nonreligious textbooks and bus transportation could be provided by the states to children in nonpublic schools, if they were already provided to children in public schools; very likely, this "child benefit" theory would have permitted government to provide all children with essential health and welfare services. Spokesmen for the Catholic church, after the *Everson* decision, continually reiterated their willingness to accept only auxiliary services, forsaking any claim to teachers' salaries and construction funds. But there was among the leadership of Protestants, liberals, and professional educators a deep distrust of the Catholic church that was stronger than their desire for federal aid to education. When Catholic educators talked about the right of parochial school children to immunizations, their critics reacted in terms of Franco, the Vatican, and the threat of a clerical state. If the Catholic leadership sometimes did a poor job of separating its spiritual activities from its political interests, so also did its critics fail to distinguish between their political grievances against the Catholic church and the legitimate claims of Catholic children.

It became an accepted axiom of the American political scene in the years between 1950 and 1965 that it was impossible to pass general federal aid to education. Truman's successor, the immensely popular Dwight D. Eisenhower, tried repeatedly to get the Congress to pass federal aid for school construction to ease the strains caused by the baby boom. But the moment had passed, and it was no longer possible to fashion a consensus. Not only was the religious issue an apparently immovable obstacle, but after the Supreme Court declared school segregation unconstitutional in 1954, the racial issue became another irreconcilable dispute. Blacks and liberals insisted that federal funds must not be allocated to racially segregated schools, and southern congressmen opposed any legislation that would meddle with their racially separate school systems.

When the campaign for general federal aid to education foundered in 1950, Congress fashioned a substitute measure that served as a sort of consolation prize for some of the rejected claimants. As prospects for the larger program faded, Congress approved a program of aid to "federally impacted areas," which updated a program enacted in 1940 to help districts whose schools were temporarily overcrowded by children of federal defense workers. The districts that became eligible in 1950 for this categorical assistance were concentrated in the South, where many defense installations were located. It was supposed to offset the expenses of districts burdened by an influx of military personnel and their families, who used local schools without paying real estate taxes. Over the years, Congress redefined eligibility for impact aid to include ever larger numbers of districts across the nation, and the program survived into the 1980s as a covert version of federal aid, entirely untouched by the political controversies that blocked the passage of general federal aid to education.

By midcentury, many of the apparently settled questions in American education were open for debate. None was resolved, but the important fact was that the status quo was no longer secure. Major educational issues, previously considered the proper province of local school districts or of individual institutions of higher education, had begun to move into the arena of national politics, to be discussed by national commissions, congressional committees, federal courts, and the political parties. The change was an abrupt departure from the past, too abrupt perhaps to permit political consensus and decision making. Whatever the future might bring, the clear implication of the postwar years was that American education had become the object of a variety of campaigns and crusades to change it, to save it, to improve it, to use it for social and economic purposes. The collapse of the battle for federal aid was only one facet of the changing politics of education: the efforts of so many different interests to control or redirect educational institutions raised the stakes, increased the number of participants, and changed the nature of the issues. The question in educational controversies became not, what kind of curriculum or teaching is best? but more often than not, what kind of society will such an arrangement promote? As the tendency grew to think about educational issues as social problems, the issues themselves became national in scope, and educational institutions were often thrust into the center of major social conflicts, serving as a hostage or a prize for partisans in ideological and political disputes.

CHAPTER 2

The Rise and Fall of Progressive Education

ESPITE the objective problems of American schools in the immediate postwar years—the teacher shortage, the low salaries, the need for buildings, and the uncertainty of future funding—American educators took pride in the fact that they shared a common philosophy about the role and the purpose of the schools. They knew what they needed—more money—and they knew why—to educate all American youth. By the 1940s, the ideals and tenets of progressive education had become the dominant American pedagogy. If one were to judge by the publications of the U.S. Office of Education, the various state departments of education, city school boards, and professional education associations, as well as by the textbooks that were required reading in schools of education, progressive education was the conventional wisdom, the lingua franca of American educators. Whether progressive practices were equally commonplace is another issue, but there can be little doubt that the language and ideas of progressive education permeated public education.

The triumph of progressive education consisted largely in the fact that by the mid-1940s it was no longer referred to as progressive education but as "modern education," the "new education," or simply, "good educational practice." The education profession's view of itself, its history, and its aspirations had been shaped during the 1920s and 1930s by progressive ideology. The teacher-in-training learned of the epochal struggle between the old-fashioned, subject-centered, rigid, authoritarian, traditional school and the modern, child-centered, flexible, democratic, progressive school. The regional accrediting agencies and state evaluators judged schools by progressive criteria: Were the classrooms teacher-dominated or was there joint pupil-teacher planning? Were pupils too involved in acquiring facts or were they actively solving problems? Was there undue stress on the distant past or were "learning situations" based on the present and future? Was the school relying too heavily on books or was it moving beyond the walls of the school to find learning experiences? Was the high school curriculum for all youth or only for those with academic ability?[1]

While there was never a clear-cut definition of progressive education —other than to say that it was an attitude, a belief in experimentation, a commitment to the education of all children and to democracy in the school—what progressive education was not was abundantly clear by this time. Among the features of traditional schooling that progressive educators rejected were: the belief that the primary purpose of the school was to improve intellectual functioning; emphasis on the cultural heritage and on learning derived from books; the teaching of the traditional subjects (like history, English, science, and mathematics) as such; the teaching of content dictated by the internal logic of the material; adherence to a daily schedule with specific subject matter allotted specific periods of time; evaluation of the school program by tests of the mastery of subject matter; competition among students for grades and other extrinsic rewards; traditional policies of promotion and failure; reliance on textbooks; the use of rote memorization or drill as a teaching method; the domination of the classroom by the teacher, either as a source of planning or as a disciplinarian; corporal punishment.

While educators differed in their conception of its necessary features, "modern" education generally emphasized: active learning (experiences and projects) rather than passive learning (reading); cooperative planning of classroom activities by teachers and pupils; cooperation among pupils on group projects instead of competition for grades; the recognition of individual differences in students' abilities and interests; justifying the curriculum by its utility to the student or by the way it met identifiable needs and interests of students; the goal of "effective living" rather than acquisition of knowledge; the value of relating the program of the school to the life of the community around it; the merging of traditional subjects into core curricula or functional problem areas related to family life, community problems, or student interests; the use of books, facts, or traditional learning only when needed as part of students' activities and experiences. In the pedagogical literature, the new education was consistently described as democracy in action, because it substituted teacher-pupil cooperation for teacher authoritarianism, stressed socialization to the group instead of individualism, and championed an educational program that was for all children in the here-and-now rather than for the minority that was college-bound.

Both its admirers and detractors acknowledged that progressive ideas had transformed the American public school during the first half of the twentieth century. Progressive concepts proved to be particularly appropriate in easing the transition to mass secondary education. At the opening of the century, about half a million students (about 10 percent of the age-group) attended high schools, where the curriculum was strongly academic, though only a minority graduated or went on to college; by midcentury, high school enrollment was over five million (65 percent of the age-group), and the secondary curriculum was remarkably diverse. Progressive education offered a rationale to include vocational and other nonacademic studies, thus enabling the high schools to retain an ever larger proportion of youth and to fulfill what the education profession believed was its special role in a democratic society.

Armed with the conviction that their philosophy was a democratic faith and that history was on their side, educational leaders were taken by surprise when attacks on their ideas and programs mounted in intensity in the late 1940s. The critics, said the educators, were reactionaries who objected to the cost of good schools, enemies of public education, apostles of hatred linked to the anti-Communist crusade of Senator Joseph McCarthy, know-nothings who wanted to return American schools to the dark ages and the three Rs. Schools hired public relations specialists and engaged in community relations to rebut the critics, but the debate continued. It was not understood, initially, that what Dean Hollis Caswell of Teachers College called "the great reappraisal" of American public education was aimed not at a particular progressive administrator or program but at a generation of educational thought.[2]

In his classic history of the progressive education movement, *The Transformation of the School,* Lawrence A. Cremin describes progressive education as "the educational phase of American Progressivism writ large." As such, Cremin says, the movement was "always closely related to broader currents of social and political progressivism"; it "had its origin during the quarter-century before World War I in an effort to cast the school as a fundamental lever of social and political regeneration." While he notes that it is impossible to write "any capsule definition of progressive education . . . for throughout its history [it] meant different things to different people," nonetheless he identifies progressivism in education with the following purposes:

> First, it meant broadening the program and function of the school to include direct concern for health, vocation, and the quality of family and community life. Second, it meant applying in the classroom the pedagogical principles derived from new scientific research in psychology and the social sciences. Third, it meant tailoring instruction more and more to the different kinds and classes of children who were being brought within the purview of the school. . . . Finally, Progressivism implied the radical faith that culture could be democratized without being vulgarized, the faith that everyone could share not only in the benefits of the new sciences but in the pursuit of the arts as well.

As the educational arm of the larger progressive reform movement, progressive education was "a many-sided effort to use the schools to improve the lives of individuals." As Cremin demonstrates, progressive education in its formative years was enriched by the thought and work of a wide variety of pioneers in social work, psychology, politics, philosophy, and education; its forebears included Jacob Riis, Lincoln Steffens, Jane Addams, John Dewey, William James, and scores of others who participated in the larger progressive reform movement.[3]

But something happened to the larger progressive movement, as well as to progressive education, in the aftermath of World War I. The larger movement, which had played a robust part in American life since the 1890s, did not survive the war. The progressive education movement, however, took on a new life even as the larger movement subsided. As it separated from the social and political reform movement of which it had been a vital part, the progressive education movement was itself transformed. In its new phase, the progressive education movement became institutionalized and professionalized, and its major themes accordingly changed. Shorn of its roots in politics and society, pedagogical progressivism came to be identified with the child-centered school; with a pretentious scientism; with social efficiency and social utility rather than social reform; and with a vigorous suspicion of "bookish" learning. That the tendency of these trends veered away from the original meaning of the progressive education movement was not at once apparent, since the prewar movement and the postwar movement shared, at least rhetorically, a reverence for John Dewey and a spirit of antiformalism. It was a long while before it was recognized, even by Dewey himself, that the form of progressive education seized upon by the emerging profession was a bastard version, and in important ways, a betrayal, of the new education he had called for.

Dewey was a prolific author whose prose style was dense and difficult. His inaccessibility as a writer did not prevent him from attracting followers and disciples, however, for he understood better than anyone else of his generation that education was changing decisively, both in its pedagogy and in its social function. By philosophical conviction and by his own experience as director of an experimental school, Dewey rejected the rigid, lockstep practices that typified public schools in the nineteenth and early twentieth centuries; the uniformity of curriculum, the stress on passivity, and the teachers' excessive reliance on rote memorization and drill tended to suppress the child's powers of interest and engagement. In his philosophy of education, the school took on many of the socializing functions that had once been performed by the family, the workplace, and the community. He believed that the school might become a fundamental lever of social progress by virtue of its capacity to improve the quality of life for individuals and for the community. In Dewey's conception, children should learn through experiences and activities that were carefully selected as starting points from which the teacher would direct them to higher levels of cultural, social, and intellectual meaning. Teachers in a progressive school had to be extraordinarily talented and well educated; they needed both a perceptive understanding of children and a wide knowledge of the disciplines in order to recognize when the child was ready to move through an experience to a new understanding, be it in history or science or mathematics or the arts. Because Dewey's ideas were complex, they were more easily misunderstood than understood, and his disciples proved better at discrediting traditional methods and curricula than at constructing a pedagogically superior replacement.

The publication of the *Cardinal Principles of Secondary Education* in 1918 launched pedagogical progressivism into the mainstream of the organized education profession. This report, which represented the best thinking of the leaders of the profession, launched "a pedagogical revolution" and ushered in "a whole new age in American secondary education" by redefining the role of the high school. In terms of both its authors and its educational philosophy, the *Cardinal Principles* contrasted sharply with a document issued twenty-five years earlier by the NEA's "Committee of Ten," which recommended that all secondary students, regardless of whether they intended to go to college, should be liberally educated and should study English, foreign languages, mathematics, history, and science. The Committee of Ten included five college presidents (its chairman was Charles Eliot, president of Harvard University) and the U. S. Commissioner of Education, William T. Harris. The *Cardinal Principles* pamphlet, which was circulated by the U.S. Bureau of Education and sold in the tens of thousands, was written by the NEA's Commission on the Reorganization of Secondary Education (CRSE). In contrast to the academically oriented Committee of Ten, the CRSE was chaired by Clarence D. Kingsley, State Supervisor of High Schools in Massachusetts, and consisted of professors of education, secondary principals, educational bureaucrats, and a college president who had been a professor of education.[4]

The cardinal principles of secondary education, by which educational offerings were to be judged, were: "1. Health. 2. Command of fundamental processes. 3. Worthy home-membership. 4. Vocation. 5. Citizenship. 6. Worthy use of leisure. 7. Ethical character." The objectives of secondary education should be determined, said the report, "by the needs of the society to be served, the character of the individuals to be educated, and the knowledge of educational theory and practice available." So little did the commission think of traditional, school-bound knowledge that the original draft of the report failed to include "command of the fundamental processes," its only reference to intellectual development, as a main objective of secondary education. The final document stressed that schools should derive their goals from the life activities of adults in society. That this was a tricky business was revealed, for instance, by the commission's statement that college-preparatory studies were "particularly incongruous with the actual needs and future responsibilities of girls," which led them to urge that homemaking be considered of equal value to any other school work. The social efficiency element of the *Cardinal Principles*, which inverted Dewey's notion of the-school-as-a-lever-of-social-reform into the-school-as-a-mechanism-to-adjust-the-individual-to-society, became the cornerstone of the new progressivism.[5]

The appeal to science and scientific method that characterized prewar progressivism was converted in the 1920s and 1930s into a polemical tool to be wielded on behalf of innovative methods and was often used to justify widescale use of testing in order to divide students into ability groups for administrative purposes. Progressives insisted that their reforms had been validated by science, not recognizing the tentative nature of scientific investigation, nor the difference between science and social science. One progressive leader, advising parents to heed the advice of experts, pointed to "conclusive proof" that reading must not be taught by attention to the alphabet, phonics, or any other kind of word-analysis, and that it was harmful for parents to read to children, since this "makes it easier to get information through the ear than through the eye." William

Heard Kilpatrick of Teachers College, in his lectures and books, spoke of "laws of learning" established by educational science, which supported his advocacy of projects and activities in place of subject matter as the method of education. In fact, few of the supposedly "scientific" findings of the period had any validity. William C. Bagley of Teachers College, a steadfast critic of progressive extremism, pointed out in 1934 that, "The study of the learning process by the experimental method has been on the whole disappointing. The 'laws' which seem at a given time to be well established have an irritating habit of collapsing as evidence accumulates."[6]

Probably the most egregious misuse of inconsistent experimental data was the misrepresentation of the mental discipline issue. Experiments at the turn of the century cast doubt on whether study of a given subject improves general mental functioning. Though there were scores of studies and their findings were ambivalent, advocates of progressive education repeatedly asserted that the "theory" of mental discipline had been decisively discredited and that all learning is specific (that is, the study of mathematics teaches mathematics, not precision and concentration). Since teachers of studies like Latin and advanced mathematics had defended their subjects on the ground that they taught students to think more clearly and logically, the experiments that purported to show that mental discipline could not be transferred contributed to the demise of requirements in these subjects. Other academic subjects were also challenged to defend their worth on utilitarian grounds, since "mental discipline" was supposedly refuted by scientific evidence. But the claims for the "scientific" investigations were inflated, and the issue was never conclusively settled. Ultimately, the question of whether the study of a given subject, like science or language or mathematics, makes one more logical or better organized may not even be subject to proof. Walter Kolesnik, who examined the issue exhaustively, concluded that "experimental psychology, in the last analysis, has shed but little light on the problem, and . . . may be incapable of shedding very much more." Richard Hofstadter has charged that the progressive educators' "misuse of experimental evidence . . . constitutes a major scandal in the history of educational thought." Nonetheless, the progressives' conviction that mental discipline had been utterly discredited was an essential element in attacking the teaching of traditional subjects and in asserting the importance of teaching specific how-to courses.[7]

To these educational currents was added the impact of a new branch of educational "science" called "curriculum making." The arrival of the curriculum expert was heralded by the appearance of Franklin Bobbitt's *The Curriculum* in 1918, the first book in the field. Bobbitt, a professor of education at the University of Chicago, rejected the traditional notion that the school program consisted of the sum of the subjects taught. Human life, wrote Bobbitt, "consists in the performance of specific activities. Education that prepares for life is one that prepares definitely and adequately for these specific activities." The curriculum is best determined by studying the activities of men and discovering what forms of knowledge men need to know: "These will be the objectives of the curriculum. They will be numerous, definite, and particularized." In *How To Make a Curriculum* (1924), Bobbitt identified 821 objectives for the curriculum maker; he made clear that the starting point in the shaping of a curriculum was an analysis of life activities, such as language activities, health activities, leisure activities, parental activities, vocational activities, and the like. The field of curriculum development, as it emerged, was firmly linked to this sort of social utilitarianism, which set the task of the school as the adjustment of the individual to the society.[8]

Another element of the new progressive education was a cluster of romantic views of the child, typified by Harold Rugg and Ann Shumaker's book *The Child-Centered School,* published in 1925. The hallmarks of the new school were freedom, activity, and creative self-expression. The old school was described as "the listening regime," a place of "fears, restraints, and long, weary hours of suppression," whose philosophy was based on outmoded allegiance to discipline and subject matter. The new school was devoted to "self-expression and maximum child growth," a place where children were eager to go to school because "they dance; they sing . . . ; they model in clay and sand; they draw and paint, read and write, make up stories and dramatize them; they work in the garden; they churn, and weave, and cook"; its philosophy was "the concept of Self." Reflecting the influence of the avant-garde thinking of the 1920s, particularly the fascination with artistic self-expression and Freudianism, Rugg and Shumaker wrote that "education in the Century of the Child aims at nothing less than the production of individuality through the integration of experience. The whole child is to be educated. Hence the materials of education are as broad and interrelated as life itself. For experience is not only an intellectual matter; it is physical, rhythmic, emotional."[9]

The most influential proponent of the new education was William Heard Kilpatrick, a popular professor at Teachers College who is said to have taught thirty-five thousand students in his long career. Kilpatrick advocated "the project method" as the best way to educate children through their own experiences, rather than through what he derisively called "subject matter fixed-in-advance." He held that a good teacher brings in subject matter only when needed as part of a student's experiences, that learning activities may be judged by their contribution to future growth (one of his graduate classes voted Greek, Latin, and mathematics the subjects offering the "least likely possibilities for educational growth," while selecting dancing, dramatics, and doll playing as holding the greatest possibilities), and that good education is "life itself, living now—the opposite of education as a mere preparation for future living." Not only did Kilpatrick combine in his work the romanticism of the child-centered school, the full-blown scientism of the authoritative pedagogue, and the anti-intellectualism of the social utilitarians, but he contributed to progressivism many of the phrases that became part of the arcane language of the education profession.[10]

The utilitarian message of the *Cardinal Principles,* the emphasis on experience and projects as the best method of learning, the emergence of the new field of curriculum development, the discovery and celebration of the child-centered school, the appeal to educational science to discredit the practices of traditional schools—these ingredients, despite some internal inconsistencies, suggested to progressive educators in the nation's professional education associations and schools of education the outlines of the philosophy and practice that should characterize a good school. Indeed, there was much in the progressive program that promised to improve education: the attention to the importance of motivating children through their interests and through use of contemporary issues, the concern for child health, the criticism of exclusive reliance on memorization and the textbook, and the efforts to diversify the school's offerings. But the positive contributions of progressive education were often at war with, and sometimes even submerged by, their own implicit distortions: the extremes of permissiveness in the child-centered movement, the hostility toward books and subject matter that grew out of the emphasis on "doing," the excessive vocationalism that emerged from social utility, and the notion that the school was uniquely qualified to meet all needs without establishing priorities among them.

Given the decentralized character of American elementary and secondary education, the dissemination of progressive philosophy and programs appeared to be a formidable task. Popularization of the new ideas proceeded through the activities of the Progressive Education Association (formed in 1919 to advance the cause), the NEA (which had sponsored the *Cardinal Principles* report), and schools of education (where progressive ideas had begun to take on the trappings of a religious faith, with a sainted leader, zealous disciples, and sacred writings).

Before long the ferment and excitement that stirred the educational leaders reached the schools themselves. One medium of influence was the school survey, which was first used in 1910. Typically, a city school system invited an expert from a school of education to prepare a study of its performance and needs. In addition to examining the schools' physical and financial condition, the surveyor would evaluate the system's curriculum according to whether it incorporated the latest pedagogical thinking. Besides giving school officials ammunition with which to seek additional funds from local government, the survey served as a means of spreading the curriculum ideas shared by progressive educators. Many schools of education established special programs to conduct surveys; Teachers College alone surveyed nearly one hundred school districts.

The survey could make recommendations, but it could not implement them. For that purpose, the most important vehicle for translating the new ideas into practice was the curriculum revision movement. Beginning in the 1920s, school systems started to study and revise their curricula to make them "modern" and "dynamic," and to adjust the content to "functional values" and "child needs." Among the first cities to launch curriculum revision were Denver, St. Louis, and Houston. By the late 1920s, the Houston superintendent reported that "Almost every school system of any size or importance in the country is now revising its curriculum or planning to do so." In 1931, Herbert Bruner, the director of the Curriculum Laboratory at Teachers College, reported that more than thirty thousand revised courses had been prepared in the previous six years alone, and the number of students in the curriculum division of the university had jumped during the same period from 6 to 762. By the mid-1930s, 70 percent of cities with a population greater than 25,000 had set up curriculum-development programs, as had nearly half the communities with a population of 5,000 to 25,000. At least thirty-seven states initiated statewide curriculum revision programs. A 1937 survey of "curriculum thinking" found a remarkable similarity of belief among teachers in cities with curriculum development programs, converging around progressive principles.[11]

Typically, a curriculum revision program was started by an administrator who had gone to a graduate school of education, where he encountered the overwhelming consensus around the new educational trends and learned that his own school's program, no matter how successful it might seem, was outmoded. He would return to his school to tell the teachers that they were going to work cooperatively to revise the curriculum to meet the diverse needs of the growing school population and to take account of the latest findings of educational science. First, the teachers were organized into study groups, where they were directed to read current pedagogical works, such as Kilpatrick's *Foundations of Method*, Ellsworth Collings's *An Experiment with a Project Curriculum* (a demonstration of Kilpatrick's methods, written by one of his students), and Rugg and Shumaker's *The Child-Centered School.* Outside consultants were brought in from schools of education to direct the teachers' study, perhaps even to set up an extension course on trends in education. After the teachers had informed themselves, the administrator might then ask them to do a survey of the community and to think about whether the curriculum of the school was meeting the needs of the community. Study and survey complete, the teachers' committees would then set out to reorganize the curriculum, under the guidance of the school-of-education expert, whose contribution was invariably described as "an impartial point of view."[12]

Not surprisingly, the results of these deliberations, instead of reflecting variations from one group of teachers to the next, and from one community to the next, demonstrated a remarkable sameness. Whether the community was rural, suburban, or urban, whether the local economy was based on farming, mining, or trade, whether the children came from wealth or poverty, the curriculum revisions echoed the language of the progressive textbooks. Schools that revised their curriculum reported agreement that since the world is dynamic, the curriculum must be dynamic; that education consists of a continuous reconstruction of experience; that education must embrace the total life experience of the child; that the goal of education must be to achieve effective living for all; that curriculum objectives had to be stated in terms of useful activities; that the focus of instruction had to shift from subject matter to the experience of the child; that college-preparatory studies were narrow and aristocratic, and that the curriculum had to embrace the interests of all children, not just the college-bound; that textbooks had to be supplemented or replaced by newspapers, magazines, excursions, projects, audiovisual aids, and activities; that promotion and failure were anachronistic concepts when applied to the continuous growth of the child; that marks and other extrinsic rewards were undemocratic and inappropriate sources of motivation.

When curriculum revision first got underway, superintendents and principals tried working with representative committees of teachers but found that the teachers who did not participate in the study group failed to share the group consensus. So, it became a matter of principle that all teachers must participate in curriculum revision. In every such program, the leaders said over and over again that the process of building a new curriculum must be a democratic process, that all decisions arrived at were democratic group decisions, and that in the nature of a democracy, all members of the group must abide by decisions of the group. Progressive educators acknowledged that they used techniques of group dynamics to engineer consent for their philosophy and programs. There is no indication that any progressive leader questioned the ethical implications of manipulating teachers, parents, and students. Hollis Caswell, dean of Teachers College and a leader in curriculum revision programs, suggested that teacher resistance to curriculum reform was best dealt with by "the setting of group goals": "A variety of studies, many in industry, have shown that when a group sets a goal the individuals who compose the group will exert greater effort to achieve the goal than when it is entirely an individual matter. In other words, an individual tends to work harder and with greater enthusiasm when he is cooperating with other people in an undertaking and when he knows that for him to fail will affect unfavorably those with whom he is working." It was a curious notion of the democratic process, since the goals of curriculum revision were never truly open for discussion; despite the rhetoric about participation and cooperation, the outcome of curriculum revision was fixed-in-advance by the experts.[13]

As part of the process of curriculum revision, there were usually efforts to achieve a consensus around a guiding philosophy, a shared set of goals and values, from which progressive practices would flow. Much was made of the importance of having a common viewpoint. Reports written by participants, often the supervising principal or superintendent, reveal that there were often teachers who refused to join the consensus, who resisted all efforts to change their philosophy or point of view. Teachers who impeded the "democratic" group process were fired; in one school, the principal fired half the faculty and replaced them with teachers who had been trained in progressive methods. In Philadelphia, the system's curriculum guide stated that the curriculum would be developed in accordance with "the democratic way of working together. That way is one in which the total personnel works together cooperatively and intelligently in the formulation and realization of common ends." However, said the guide, if teachers refused to behave "intelligently and cooperatively," then "protective measures" would be taken "in the interest of the common welfare." Since curriculum revision was always set in motion by school officials, who had the power to remove uncooperative teachers, those in charge never knew whether they had succeeded in winning the teachers over or in merely silencing the opposition to change.[14]

Because the schools of education were so strongly identified with progressive education, professionalization served as the medium for the promotion of progressive philosophy and practices. Whether in Kingsport, Tennessee, or Battle Creek, Michigan, the curriculum revision program aimed to transform the teacher through workshops, conferences, summer courses, visits to progressive schools, and enrollment in degree courses. The professional literature acknowledged that the goal of curriculum revision was not so much to change the curriculum as it was to change the attitudes, values, and perceptions of the teacher, so that the teacher would behave differently in the classroom. To be sure, even within schools of education there were articulate critics of the pretensions and tendencies of progressive education, like William C. Bagley and I. L. Kandel of Teachers College, but their attacks were brushed aside in the flush of success, and they were not among the phalanx of energetic professors who brought the news about curriculum development to America's school systems.[15]

Aside from altering the rhetoric of school documents, what effects did the curriculum revision movement have? The overall impression that emerges from a sampling of diverse districts is a pronounced shift in the stated goals of schooling, away from concern with intellectual development and mastery of subject matter to concern for social and emotional development and to the adoption of "functional" objectives related to areas such as vocation, health, and family life. Generally, the revised curriculum was not an effort to balance intellectual, social, and emotional needs, but a conscious attempt to denigrate the traditional notion of "knowledge for its own sake" as useless and possibly worthless. Many districts reported efforts to blur lines between subjects by creating something like a "core curriculum" course. The usual core course merged English and social studies, though some merged other subjects as well. The core course, with a title like "Basic Living" or "Common Learnings," concentrated on "personal and social development," and dealt with such problems as: how to earn a living, how to get along with other people, how to be a good consumer, how to behave on a date, and how to stay healthy.

There is little evidence that social reform entered the public schools as a consequence of the curriculum revision movement. Ten southern states engaged in statewide curriculum revision and dutifully recorded their desire to advance democratic living through the school, but not one of the state commissions noticed a conflict between democratic ideals and the practice of racial segregation. Nor did any of the city school systems which revised their curriculum offer any criticism of the social order. They saw their task to be one of fitting the children to the needs of the social order, in the social efficiency spirit of the *Cardinal Principles*. The leader of the program in Hackensack, New Jersey, observing that "many trades and occupations would not employ colored persons," concluded that "since 20 percent of the population of the school was of this race, the school was compelled to face realistically this issue and to provide an educational program in harmony with the needs of this race." This was "realism" unencumbered by any vision of the school as a source of social reform.[16]

An important, measurable, and intended outcome of curriculum revision was a decrease in the number of students enrolled in college preparatory courses. Since social utility was the guiding star of curriculum revision, the college preparatory subjects served no "function" for the large majority who were not going to college. The school official who started curriculum revision in Hackensack, New Jersey, reported with satisfaction that enrollment in the college preparatory course had been cut from 30 percent to 15 percent of the high school. Similarly, the school district of Battle Creek, Michigan, invited experts from the University of Chicago to survey its educational needs, hired a director of curriculum, revised its curriculum, and ended up with a new course focused on young people's personal problems called "Basic Living," and a reduction by one-half of those enrolled in the college preparatory curriculum. In Alameda County, California, curriculum revision resulted in a "functional" curriculum, which meant, for example, that a course in "World Problems," which "had degenerated into chronological history," was shunted aside "to make room for something 'more important,' " namely, safety and driver education. In Westwood, California, the revised curriculum offered everyone a "Basic Course," devoted to the functions of social living, and reserved courses like physics and chemistry for the college-bound.[17]

Many schools understood the spirit of curriculum revision as a mandate to expand vocational education, always at the expense of academic studies. One rural southern community, prodded by the regional accrediting agency to revise its traditional curriculum, stressed the practical arts: boys learned how to be farmers, printers, barbers, electricians, carpenters, and so forth, and girls learned bookkeeping, beauty culture, stenography, and home economics. In another school, which "moved from a narrow academic college preparatory program to one that is largely vocational," the principal lamented the fact that 30 percent of his students insisted on enrolling in academic courses, even though only 10 percent would actually go to college. In the new program, the only common courses were English, social studies, physical and health education. According to the principal, who "converted" the teachers to the new philosophy, "the backbone of the whole business is the vocational training. The pupils must leave us ready and willing to work, able to pay their own way and to earn their living. The day has passed when it suffices for the applicant for work to say, 'I have a high school diploma.' Any graduate can say that. We want ours to be able to say in addition, 'I can cook your meals.' 'I can type your letters.' 'I can repair your automobile.' 'I can paint your house.' 'I can tend your garden.' " The motto of the school was: "Call us when you need workers."[18]

The biggest obstacle faced by the leaders of the curriculum revision movement was the resistance of teachers and parents. When a school decided to abolish grades and report cards, to institute automatic promotion, or to divert students away from the college preparatory curriculum, parents complained. Some parents failed to understand why the school's new enlarged social role required it to inquire into intimate details of the family's life. One school district in Granite, Utah, took responsibility for knowing "what every single child in the community between 6 and 18 is doing with his life in school, before school, and after school, and even during summer vacation," and sent a school nurse to "score" every home for evidence of thrift, neatness, cleanliness, income, health, harmony or discord, presence of reading matter, and make, type, and year of automobile.[19]

Of course, teachers who became "trouble makers" by criticizing the new approach were ousted, but even those who tried their best to cooperate were constantly in danger of backsliding. In Ann Arbor, Michigan, a progressive administration eliminated all textbooks, and let it be known that "teachers were free to do what they wanted in the classroom, but they were not free to use a textbook." Spelling, for example, was taught through games and projects, but eventually it became necessary to bring back a spelling book; when asked to evaluate the new texts, "each school was so happy to get a spelling book again that each school thought the one it was using was the best."[20]

And then there was the persistent problem of what happened in the classroom after the new program was presumably implemented. Texas conducted a statewide curriculum revision in the mid-1930s. Like most other states, it devoted the first year to study; the second year to producing new courses; the third year to testing the new courses; and the fourth year to installing them in the schools. According to plan, the elementary school curriculum was to disregard subject matter and to be organized around five core areas: language arts; social relations; home and vocational arts; creative and recreative arts; nature, mathematics, and science. In 1943, the Texas State Department of Education asked teachers to submit descriptions of "A Typical Child's Day in My Class or School." More than a thousand entries were analyzed. Instead of finding the schools organized around the five core areas, the evaluators discovered that the typical elementary school day was organized into separate subjects taught by daily assignments. Long after the principles of progressivism had won general acceptance by professional leaders of city, state, and nation, educational authorities continued to complain that teachers were failing to "vitalize" or "humanize" or "socialize" the classroom and were clinging to outmoded academic traditions.[21]

Even as progressive education was on the ascendancy, the popular press began to reveal undercurrents of dissatisfaction. Mortimer Adler, an associate of Robert Hutchins at the University of Chicago, charged that progressives were trying to turn the school into "a grandiose 'Institute for Individual and Community Development' . . . which would be all things to all men, regulating everything from the pre-natal care of the child to his vocational preparation, and solving the social problems of the community on the side." He worried that the progressive ideal would corrupt the community by providing a "feeble palliative" which encouraged it to evade its problems and would corrupt the schools by diverting their energies "from the primary task of the basic intellectual disciplines." Others complained about poor discipline in progressive schools; about poor mastery of the fundamentals; about the abandonment of Western culture for practical studies; about the failure to teach respect for hard, sustained effort; about the absence of any common standards or values in the schools; about the tendency to adopt the latest fads from child study experts; about the use of children as guinea pigs; about children who were so well "socialized" that they lacked the ability to play alone; about the sacrifice of individuality to group-conformity; about the experts' contemptuous attitudes toward parents; about parents' dependency on expert opinion; about the introduction of psychological ratings and personality inventories in place of report cards and grades; about the education profession's impenetrable patois, which was unintelligible to laymen.[22]

Not all the critics could be dismissed out of hand as uninformed reactionaries. William C. Bagley, Kilpatrick's leading adversary, warned of the dangers of the narrowly utilitarian version of progressive education that had become the dominant pedagogy; he complained in 1934 that substituting "activities" for "systematic and sequential learning would defeat the most important ends of education in a democracy," in particular, the goal of insuring "as high a level of common culture as possible." An official of the U.S. Office of Education noted in 1937 that the secondary curriculum was evolving away from formal classroom work to "successful adjustment and learning to live," and that "the problem is one of developing techniques and procedures for introducing these important adjustments into the educational program of the schools without succumbing to a system of soft pedagogy which makes no demands on anybody anywhere."[23]

The most devastating criticism of the new progressive education came from an unexpected source: John Dewey. In 1938, in *Experience and Education,* Dewey rebuked those whose extremist zeal was corrupting progressive principles. He chided latter-day progressives for believing that organized subject matter should be jettisoned, for proceeding "as if any form of direction and guidance by adults were an invasion of individual freedom," and for mistakenly thinking that education should concentrate on the present and future to the exclusion of the past. Dewey warned that "it is not too much to say that an educational philosophy which professes to be based on the idea of freedom may become as dogmatic as ever was the traditional education which is reacted against." To those who had insistently confused progressive education with the removal of external controls, Dewey cautioned that "the only freedom that is of enduring importance is freedom of intelligence," which is the result of *"intelligent* activity," not of activity which is based on whim and impulse.[24]

Others might have been disheartened by criticism from the patriarch of the movement, as well as the complaints of parents and the backsliding of teachers, but progressive educators were not easily dismayed. The movement's success was undeniable: *Time* magazine ran a cover story in 1938 which declared that "No U.S. school has completely escaped its influence." Earlier the same year, when a group of professional educators, calling themselves "Essentialists," launched an attack on progressive education, Kilpatrick said scornfully, "The Essentialists represent the same sort of reactionary trend that always springs up when a doctrine is gaining headway in the country. The astonishing thing is not the fact of the reaction but that it is so small and on the whole comes from such inconspicuous people." Not only were progressive educators fortified by a sense of certainty, but they were able to explain whatever difficulties they encountered by invoking the concept of "cultural lag." According to Paul Mort, a professor of education at Teachers College, "Typically in the American school system fifty years elapse between the recognition of an unmet need and the first adaptation intended to take care of this need. Another fifty years are typically required to spread the new adaptations throughout all the schools of a state." With this kind of faith in the future, the most obdurate critics could be ignored.[25]

Even as the volume of criticism began to rise, largely from people who were dismissed as uninformed laymen or angry medievalists wedded to dead subjects, the consensus around progressive ideas became stronger. The best evidence of this appeared in a series of publications issued in the last years of the 1930s by such prominent organizations as the NEA's Educational Policies Commission, the National Association of Secondary-School Principals, and the American Council on Education. With one exception, these reports reinforced the social utility role of education. The exception, *The Unique Function of Education in American Democracy,* was written primarily by the historian Charles Beard and appeared in 1937. Beard's statement was striking because of its unambiguous commitment to the transmission of knowledge as the major goal of the school. He wrote that "The primary business of education, in effecting the promises of American democracy, is to guard, cherish, advance, and make available in the life of coming generations the funded and growing wisdom, knowledge, and aspirations of the race. This involves the dissemination of knowledge, the liberation of minds, the development of skills, the promotion of free inquiries, the encouragement of the creative or inventive spirit, and the establishment of wholesome attitudes toward order and change—all useful in the good life for each person. . . . " He added, perhaps with awareness of the aggressively utilitarian spirit that informed the curriculum revision movement, that "Education would cease to be education if it ruled out of consideration Plato's Republic, the Bible, or the writings of all such thinkers as Thomas Aquinas, John Ruskin, or Ralph Waldo Emerson." Beard was a progressive in the old sense of the word, but subsequent publications proved that he was clearly out of step with the new spirit of progressive education, perhaps because as a historian, he was a "subject matter specialist."[26]

In the same year, Harl R. Douglass's *Secondary Education for Youth in Modern America,* a report to the American Youth Commission of the American Council on Education, summarized the dominant themes of social utility and curricular differentiation that Beard had ignored. A professor of secondary education at the University of Minnesota, Douglass asserted that "the aim of education is to affect beneficially the activities of life for which youth is educated." By its nature, the public school exists to further certain social objectives, and it was developed "for the purpose of controlling human behavior." The objectives of education, he wrote, were preparation for citizenship; for home and family life; for vocational life; for physical health; for effective personality; for effective use of leisure time; and for development of information, interests, and skills. Like many other progressive educators, Douglass noted that high school enrollment had doubled every ten years since 1890, that the student population now included many of low intelligence, and that this required the high schools to diversify their offerings to "meet the needs of children of mediocre or inferior ability who lack interest in abstract and academic materials." With this new population, "It cannot be expected that the great mass of the populace will spend its leisure time with the classics, the arts, or higher mathematics. Leisure education must then be attuned to the primitive instincts for physical and practical activity, the more familiar pursuits of the masses—the home and its furnishings, nature, sports, games, the radio, and social activities." Furthermore, the curriculum "need not include subjects, or aspects of them, merely because they have made significant contributions to civilization. It is impractical to confuse, as is so commonly done, such values with the utility of subject matter for the education of the masses of young people today, however essential it may be that a small number of experts be well trained in these matters."[27]

The mainstream was promptly swelled by a new document from the Educational Policies Commission, *The Purposes of Education in American Democracy,* written primarily by William G. Carr, an NEA official. Carr asserted that education must be chiefly concerned with the objectives of "self-realization," "human relationships," "economic efficiency," and "civic responsibility." Too much emphasis, he held, was placed on the teaching of grammar and the classics in English: "Whatever may be the merits of such exercises as a preparation for a career as an author, the great majority of American boys and girls will profit more by a wide-ranging program of reading for enjoyment and fact-gathering." Relying on utility as the criterion for educational worth, Carr urged a reduction of the number studying advanced mathematics, advanced science, and foreign languages, and an emphasis instead on everyday applications of mathematics and science.[28]

The following year, 1939, the National Association of Secondary-School Principals published B. L. Dodds's *That All May Learn,* which utterly jettisoned the humane tradition of liberal education that Beard had championed. Dodds, a professor of education at Purdue University, held that it was absurd for the high school to adhere to an academic curriculum unsuited to "the new fifty percent," the students of low intelligence who stayed in high school as a result of the steady rise in the compulsory school age and the lack of jobs for youth. She claimed to be concerned about the "educationally neglected," but in fact was equally contemptuous of those at both extremes of ability. The "educationally neglected," she said, were not "abnormal"; on the contrary, "the academic person who can happily devote a lifetime to the pursuit of work dealing largely in abstract symbols of experience as reported through writing could with far more justification be considered abnormal." The trouble with the academic curriculum, said Dodds, was that it had "fostered and definitely encouraged" unrealistic ambitions and made too many "unselected" youth aspire to enter managerial and professional jobs for which they were not fitted. Too much time, effort, and money was wasted trying to teach the conventional subjects to the "educationally neglected," Dodds complained. In her view, not many adults need specialized knowledge in mathematics and science, and only those who can profit by it should get it. Nor do they need a high level of reading comprehension, only enough to use as an "essential tool" for newspaper and magazine fare. There is no reason to teach them the classics, and they do not need much in the way of writing skills for "the small amount of writing they will have to do." Their courses in social science should be devoted to the present, since "students of limited imagination" find no reality in the study of "heroes long dead" or other nations. Their curriculum, she recommended, should be based on their needs and interests and should be as lifelike as possible; what they want to know is how to dress attractively, how to make friends with the opposite sex, and how to get a job.[29]

The reports from the professional associations continued to pour forth, reiterating the need for a fundamental reconstruction of the secondary school program based on the needs of youth and recognition that the high school was no longer a college-preparatory institution. Seldom was there recognition of the responsibility of the school to transmit knowledge or to stimulate appreciation for the great achievements of mankind or to improve the intellectual development of all youth, even those who were not college bound. Instead the "needs of youth" became a catechetical slogan, invoked as evidence of the proper progressive orientation. In 1942, one progressive educator took the slogan a step further; he noted that although educators agreed on the paramount importance of the "needs of youth," there was little agreement on just what those needs were and how they should affect the curriculum. To correct this deficiency, he queried 2,069 youths and found that their actual needs were: how to find a job, how to make friends, how to behave on a date, how to protect one's health, how to get the most for one's money, and how to make life worthwhile. Few of them wanted to know about the causes of the war then raging in Europe or to learn a foreign language, and less than 10 percent cared about "the contributions of European culture to American culture"; boys wanted to study science, girls did not. The author concluded that his findings suggested the necessity of "considerable shift in the character and content of the prevailing secondary curriculum," including differentiation of the curriculum for girls and boys.[30]

The major report of the Educational Policies Commission, which summed up all that had gone before (except, of course, for Beard's idiosyncratic contribution), was *Education for All American Youth*, published in 1944. Again, the updated *Cardinal Principles* was set forth as the ideal education. Again, a distinguished panel of progressive educators described the ideal curriculum, restructured to meet "the imperative needs of youth," defined in terms of preparation for citizenship, vocation, consumption, family living, economic understanding, and so forth. While there was reference to stimulating intellectual curiosity, it was also proposed that in the school of the future, "There is no aristocracy of 'subjects'. . . . Mathematics and mechanics, art and agriculture, history and homemaking are all peers." Again, there was almost nothing that needed to be done that could not be done by the schools.[31]

Across the country, schools experimented with new curricula and new methods, to stay abreast of the best progressive thinking. In one junior high school in Tulsa, all traditional subject matter was merged into a single core period, taught by one teacher; students spent the rest of the day in shop, playground, or laboratory; the core period, which included English, science, mathematics, and history, was called "social relations." In an Oakland, California, high school, students could take courses in "Leisure Activities" or "Personal Management" for credit. The high school in Altoona, Pennsylvania, reorganized its curriculum in terms of needs, so that science instruction concentrated on housing, fuel, and clothing; social studies on group and personal adjustment; English on free reading; mathematics on practical applications; and home economics on consumer practices. In Holton, Kansas, the English department prepared a core curriculum that was based on the study of students' homes; groups were formed to study metals, landscaping, woods and finishes, and masonry. The Goldsboro, North Carolina, high school stressed practical applications: in physics, shop work replaced laboratory and textbook study; trigonometry was studied through its use in surveying; and one group of girls received credit for equipping the girls' restroom (picking materials, taking measurements, making estimates, selecting colors, and so forth).[32]

Innovative programs were reported in numerous other school systems. Their common features were: centering the curriculum around basic areas of human activity, instead of traditional subject matter; incorporating subject matter only insofar as it was useful in everyday situations; stressing functional values, such as behavior, attitudes, skills, and know-how, rather than "bookish" or abstract knowledge; reorienting studies to the immediate needs and interests of students; using community resources; introducing nontraditional materials (for example, audiovisual equipment or magazines) and nontraditional activities (for example, panel discussions, dramatizations, and work projects) in addition to or instead of direct instruction and textbooks.

In the face of the growing consensus, there was little criticism of the mainstream pedagogy within the profession. I. L. Kandel, professor at Teachers College and editor of *School and Society*, was a notable exception. In *The Cult of Uncertainty*, published in 1943, Kandel blasted progressive education as not only vapid and superficial but an approach so set against tradition, authority, and the past that it must inexorably produce "rootlessness." Despite the complaints of dissidents like Kandel, the consensus among progressives remained unshaken. A summary of typical progressive thinking was contained in Paul R. Mort and William S. Vincent's *A Look at Our Schools: A Book for the Thinking Citizen* in 1946, which attempted to show why the "modern school" was better than the old-fashioned school. The purpose of the public school, they said, was "to mold a people and to contribute to individual effectiveness and happiness." The way to judge an educational system is to ask "To what desirable patterns of group behavior does it contribute?" That this put educators, rather than individuals or elected representatives, in control of defining the future of society did not seem to trouble the authors. The special strength of the "modern school" was that it recognized that whatever is taught must have real use. Therefore, only those who intend to be scholars study "bookish" subjects: "With any child the secret for success is being fitted. The materials which go into houses are not those which go into clothing or those which make locomotives. But houses, clothing, locomotives are all needed. It is vain and wasteful to take a girl who would make a fine homemaker and try to fit her into the patterns of training which make a lawyer, or to take a boy who would be successful in business and try to fit his training to that which produces doctors." This sort of statement, a commonplace when it was written, revealed some of the inherent flaws in the conventional wisdom: first, that it reflected prevailing practices uncritically; second, that it presumed to know the occupational destinies of its pupils; and third, that it disparaged intellectual values.[33]

This grand consensus among professional educators did not go for nought. When World War II ended, events brought this school of thought to its logical conclusion and opened what became a great debate about American education. Its beginnings were inauspicious enough. On June 1, 1945, a group of vocational educators met in Washington, D.C., at the invitation of the U.S. Office of Education's Division of Vocational Education to discuss the problems of young people whose needs were not being met by either vocational or college preparatory programs. No one seemed to have any good ideas, and then the chairman of the meeting asked Charles A. Prosser, a veteran vocational educator, to summarize the conference. Prosser, in words that were soon described as "historic," offered the following resolution:

> It is the belief of this conference that, with the aid of this report in final form, the vocational school of a community will be able better to prepare 20 percent of the youth of secondary school age for entrance upon desirable skilled occupations; and that the high school will continue to prepare another 20 percent for entrance to college. We do not believe that the remaining 60

percent of our youth of secondary school age will receive the life adjustment training they need and to which they are entitled as American citizens— unless and until the administrators of public education with the assistance of the vocational education leaders formulate a similar program for this group.

We therefore request the U.S. Commissioner of Education and the Assist- ant Commissioner for Vocational Education to call at some early date a con- ference or a series of regional conferences between an equal number of repre- sentatives of general and of vocational education—to consider this problem and to take such initial steps as may be found advisable for its solution.[34]

The "Prosser Resolution," as it was immediately labeled, was adopted unanimously by an enthusiastic conference and forwarded to the commis- sioner of education. In 1946, regional conferences were convened in New York City, Chicago, Cheyenne, Sacramento, and Birmingham to consider "the meaning and implications of the resolution" and ways to implement it. The regional conferences agreed that there was urgent need for "life adjustment education" for "a major fraction" of high school youths and that a national conference should be convened to develop a plan of action. The Prosser Resolution was reworded to eliminate any reference to a specific percentage of youth with unmet needs, and a national conference was convened in Chicago in May, 1947. While there was still some uncer- tainty about just what the historic resolution meant, the educators at the conference understood that it represented a call to implement the profes- sion's persistent demands for "functional" education. The conference de- scribed educationally neglected youths as coming from low-income homes with low cultural environments; as retarded in school; as making low scores on intelligence tests and achievement tests; as less emotionally mature than other students, with lower grades and less interest in school work. What these students needed was "life adjustment education," which consisted of guidance and education in citizenship, home and family life, use of leisure, health, tools of learning, work experience, and occupational adjustment. Participants in the conference agreed further that "life adjust- ment education" must not be restricted to the educationally neglected, for indeed it was the very education best suited to meet the imperative needs of *all* American youth.

Prosser, who had addressed each of the regional conferences, told the national conference: "Never in all the history of education has there been such a meeting as this one. . . . Never was there such a meeting where people were so sincere in their belief that this was the golden opportunity to do something that would give to all American youth their educational heritage so long denied. What you have planned is worth fighting for—

it is worth dying for. . . . I am proud to have lived long enough to see my fellow schoolmen design a plan which will aid in achieving for every youth an education truly adjusted to life." Prosser, who had begun his career as a lobbyist for vocational education in 1912, had spelled out his educational values in a 1939 lecture, in which he insisted that every subject taught in high school must be judged by its utility for everyday living. He claimed that "business arithmetic is superior to plane or solid geometry; learning ways of keeping physically fit, to the study of French; learning the technique of selecting an occupation, to the study of algebra; simple science of everyday life, to geology; simple business English, to Elizabethan classics." If school subjects were judged by utility, he believed, all mathematics and foreign languages would be dropped as required studies. He saw no point in "a system of education-for-more-education," other than to select out students for higher education and to keep certain faculty employed. "The biggest, most difficult, and most important job in the world," he held, "is the job of living." This was the rationale and the vision that progressive educators hailed as "life adjustment education."[35]

The U.S. Office of Education threw its full support behind the campaign for life adjustment education. In 1947, John W. Studebaker, commissioner of education, appointed a National Commission on Life Adjustment Education for Youth, which included representatives from such major groups as the NEA, the American Association of School Administrators, the American Vocational Association, the National Association of High School Supervisors and Directors of Secondary Education, the National Association of Secondary-School Principals, the National Council of State School Officers, and the National Catholic Welfare Conference. This commission sponsored conferences and numerous publications, issued by the Government Printing Office, and spurred the creation of state commissions on life adjustment education. A second national commission was appointed in 1950, which continued the promotion of this concept, until the commission's term ended in 1954.

What was life adjustment education? In the eyes of its promoters, it was the direct descendant of every major progressive initiative, from the *Cardinal Principles of Secondary Education* right down to the NEA's *Education for All American Youth*. Its arrival was warmly greeted as the opportunity to implement thirty years of progressive proclamations, but it was nonetheless difficult for its sponsors to explain without becoming remarkably prolix. The official definition was that life adjustment education "better equips all American youth to live democratically with satisfaction to themselves and profit to society as home members, workers, and citizens." What *that* meant required fourteen additional statements (for example, "It is appropriate for all American youth and offers them learning experiences appropriate to their capacities. . . . It recognizes that many events of importance happened a long time ago, but holds that the real significance of these events is in their bearing upon life of today.") But even with all of this elaboration, its meaning was still unclear, though it surely meant a stress on "functional" objectives, like vocation and health, and a rejection of traditional academic studies.[36]

Precisely how much impact the life adjustment movement had on American schools is difficult to measure, particularly since life adjustment was indistinguishable in everything but name from many other, already established versions of progressive education, such as core curriculum courses, activity programs, and "common learnings" courses. At one national life adjustment conference, reports on current practice were offered by teachers from Ann Arbor, Michigan; Forest Hills, New York; Spencer, New York; Washington, D.C.; Springfield, Missouri; Philadelphia; New Britain, Connecticut; Midland, Michigan; Rockville, Maryland; Ashland, Virginia; and Pittsburgh. In addition, federal education officials cited the following as districts where life adjustment programs had been started: Amarillo, Texas; Bloomfield, New Jersey; Coffeyville, Kansas; Denver, Colorado; Hornell, New York; Peoria, Illinois; Saint Paul, Minnesota; Springfield, Missouri; Tulsa, Oklahoma; and Wilmington, Delaware.[37]

In 1949, the U.S. Office of Education surveyed the nation's schools and found that 20 percent of the junior high schools with more than 500 pupils had a core curriculum, as did 11.3 percent of the high schools of similar size. Most core courses were in seven states: California, Maryland, Michigan, Minnesota, Missouri, New York, and Pennsylvania. Fourteen of the fifteen junior and senior high schools in Denver, Colorado, offered a core course (which included English, social studies, guidance, health, "democratic living, personal and social growth, intergroup education, human relationships," and "general living units"), as did most of the secondary schools in Wichita, Kansas; Springfield, Missouri; Albuquerque, New Mexico; Eugene, Oregon; Long Beach and Pasadena, California; Minneapolis, Minnesota; Grand Rapids and Detroit, Michigan. The schools of Garrett County, Maryland, organized the curriculum for grades seven through twelve entirely around adolescent "needs," with no reference to subject matter; the curriculum for grade twelve, for example, consisted of "family living; role of education; making a living; health and safety; consumer problems; and technology of living." The schools of Harford County, Maryland, had no curriculum selected in advance, since teachers "are free to select from or reject them in light of the needs of pupils as they discover them." These districts were cited by the U.S. Office of Education as examples of advanced educational practice which were meeting "the imperative needs of every youth."[38]

By whatever name it was called, modern education by the late 1940s was clearly identified with "functional" teaching, which used everyday situations as the medium of instruction, with the purpose of changing students' attitudes and behavior to conform to social norms. The ideal was the well-adjusted student, who was prepared to live effectively as a worker, a home member, and a citizen. High school students in Atlanta, Georgia, took a social studies course that integrated art, music, mathematics, science, and other subjects into a unit on "Housing and Home Building," which aimed to teach such functional values as how to build a healthful home and how to beautify the home and grounds. In Peekskill, New York, the shift to a core curriculum was understood by parents and teachers to mean that the school was emphasizing behavioral change rather than subject matter acquisition. In Springfield, Missouri, teachers were trained by a school of education team to engage in child study techniques in order to make teachers aware of their role in "the development of desirable social attitudes and values in children." In Denver, Colorado, high school students participated in a unit on "What is expected of a boy on a date?" which covered such problems as "Do girls want to 'pet'?" and "Should you go in with a girl after a date (to raid the ice box)?" In Des Moines, Iowa, students were taught "correct social usage" and appreciation of "the satisfactions to be derived from being an approved member of the group" as part of a course in "Developing an Effective Personality." Junior high school students in Tulsa, Oklahoma, learned what kind of clothing was appropriate, what shade of nail polish to wear, and how to improve one's appearance. The object of courses like these was to teach children what kind of behavior was socially acceptable and how to adjust to group expectations.[39]

One likely casualty of the strain of progressivism that stretched from the *Cardinal Principles* to life adjustment education was foreign language enrollments in high school. According to Edward Krug, the high point in foreign language enrollment was 1910, when 83.3 percent of the nation's high school students studied a foreign language. By 1915, the proportion had slipped to 77 percent. The widespread abandonment of German instruction during World War I and the subsequent attack on foreign language requirements by progressive educators accelerated the decline to "catastrophic" proportions; by 1955, only 20.6 percent of high school students studied any foreign language. "Moreover," notes Krug, "46 percent of the public high schools in the middle 1950's offered no foreign language study whatsoever, either ancient or modern, while 54.6 percent offered no modern foreign language."[40]

While it is impossible to know with certainty the extent to which the purposeful de-emphasis of "mere knowledge" actually affected what was taught and learned in the nation's classrooms, and while it seems likely that many teachers ignored the strictures from the centers of pedagogical theory, a trend is suggested by changes in some major tests. The examination given by the College Entrance Examination Board, once firmly rooted in a common liberal arts curriculum, was replaced in 1947 by the Scholastic Aptitude Test (SAT), a standardized, multiple-choice test of verbal and mathematical skills, which was virtually curriculum-free; the switch had the effect of opening prestigious colleges to students whose schools did not follow the curricular practices of .the elite preparatory schools, but it also relieved schools of the necessity of requiring a liberal arts curriculum. The individually graded "college-boards," which stressed essay questions, gave way to the machine-scored SAT because of the increase in college applicants. A clearer reflection of curricular change is found in the New York State Regents' examinations, given annually to all high school seniors in the state. In 1927, tests were offered for those who had studied either two, three, or four years of a foreign language; those who had studied four years of English were asked to write an essay on a subject like "science in modern life," "heroes and hero worship," or "personal tastes and critical standards"; on the history examination, students were tested on the social, economic, and political history of Greece, Rome, Europe, and the United States. Ten years later, the same examination tended more toward multiple-choice questions and contemporary essays (for example, "the sit-down strike as an instrument of labor" or "achievements of outstanding Negroes"), but its substance was not dramatically dissimilar from that of 1927. By 1948, however, there were no longer any fourth-year language examinations; knowledge of all history other than American had shrunk into a minor portion of a multiple-choice examination called "American History and World Backgrounds"; and the fourth-year English test, while emphasizing multiple-choice questions, asked for an essay on such life-adjusted topics as "three problems facing seniors," "drawbacks to being an honor student," or "advice to parents."[41]

Criticism of progressive education had been continuous since 1930, both from respected scholars like Robert M. Hutchins, William C. Bagley, and I. L. Kandel and from writers in the popular media. Hutchins and his supporters were ignored, or when taken note of, scorned as Thomists, neoclassicists, elitists, and the like. Secure in their convictions, allied in their activities with federal, state, and city education agencies, nothing prepared the progressive educators for the deluge of attacks that began in 1949 and reached a peak in 1953. Both critics and defenders of the status quo referred to this period as "the great debate," and most felt that it would decisively influence the future of American education.

Critics of progressive education, whose charges previously had fallen on deaf ears because they could point only to isolated examples of foolishness, now found in life adjustment education a bloated target: it had the blessing of the U.S. Office of Education and almost every major education group; it was practiced in public school systems across the country; it contained an abundance of slogans, jargon, and vacuous anti-intellectualism; it carried the utilitarianism and group conformism of latter-day progressivism to its ultimate trivialization. This vast outpouring of criticism, coming as it did at the same time as the teacher shortage, the schools' appeal for federal aid, and the onset of the "baby boom," made it clear that the schools were in a crisis too fundamental to ignore.

The critics of the public schools were a diverse lot. Some were extremists who believed that progressive education was part of a Communist plot and who demanded the elimination of subversive teachers and controversial books. A few critics, like Bernard Iddings Bell, were concerned that the secularism of the public school prevented it from promoting any values other than relativism. Some, like Hutchins, criticized the schools on essentially philosophical grounds. Others, like Mortimer Smith, Albert Lynd, Arthur Bestor, and Paul Woodring, criticized the schools primarily for their curricular inadequacies. Since the target, progressive education, was the same, there was a certain amount of overlap among the critics, but the differences among them were as significant as the similarities. Smith, Lynd, Bestor, and Woodring shared many of Hutchins's concerns about the fundamental inadequacies of progressivism, but none of them agreed with Bell's complaint about the divorce between education and religion or with the coercive superpatriotism of the extremist groups. Yet defenders of public education responded to the critics by labeling them collectively as "enemies of the public schools."

The extremist organizations tapped a current of right-wing paranoia that roiled the country in the postwar decade. At least half a dozen organizations exploited fears that a vast and sinister conspiracy had subverted American education and had turned it against not only traditional education but traditional American ideals. These groups published books, pamphlets, and magazines, asserting, among other things, that public schools were failing to teach the fundamentals, failing to discipline children, wasting money on fads and frills, and espousing progressive education, which promoted collectivism, godlessness, and juvenile delinquency. Their materials—which contained half-truths, scurrilous distortions, and outrageous charges—surfaced in many of the communities where progressive programs came under attack; in some of those communities, like Houston, Texas, and Pasadena, California, local groups subscribed to the conspiracy theory and believed that they were engaged in a patriotic crusade to cleanse the schools of subversive influences. However, even in Pasadena, the antiprogressive forces had educational grievances based on their perception that the progressive superintendent was more interested in shaping their children's attitudes and values than in developing their minds.[42]

Nor were all the other attacks on progressive education at the local level inspired by militant anti-Communism. In Minneapolis, the school system's "common learnings" program became the focus of a community rebellion. "Common learnings" was a core program that met for a minimum of two hours each day, merging English and social studies, "during which youth study their personal and social problems so as to meet their common needs for present and future citizenship." It rejected traditional practices, such as the reading of classic literature, and adopted instead instruction in problems "meaningful to youth," with the goal of "the building of right attitudes," such as "understanding human behavior" or "developing into a good citizen." Initiated in 1945, "common learnings" was adopted systemwide by 1949/50. In 1950, a group called the Parents Council asked the board of education to make the program optional and to offer courses in subject matter for those who requested them. Though school officials claimed that children were learning more than ever, they failed to persuade the Parents Council, whose leaders were university professors. Some eight hundred people attended a mass meeting called by the Parents Council, where the poet and novelist Robert Penn Warren spoke caustically about "the minimum standards" of the "common learnings" program and the "patronizing attitude" of progressive educators, who exhibited "condescending democracy on the one hand and smug authoritarianism on the other hand." Bowing to pressure, the board of education agreed to make the program optional. Progressive educators analyzed this situation as typical of the efforts of a "militant minority" to disrupt a modern educational program; unable to understand how well-informed people could fail to agree with them, they lumped the critics of programs like "common learnings" together with other "enemies of the public schools."[43]

While communities debated and sometimes battled, the publication of several critical books made it respectable to question progressive education.

First to appear was Mortimer Smith's *And Madly Teach* (1949). Smith, a former school board member in Connecticut, complained that progressive education had become "the official philosophy of American public education," that teachers, administrators, and schools of education "have a truly amazing uniformity of opinion regarding the aims, the content, and the methods of education," and that this philosophy was both anti-intellectual and undemocratic. When the public schools expanded to include all children, said Smith, educators turned to progressivism to rationalize their failure to educate all: "Here was a doctrine that released the teacher from his responsibility for handing on the traditional knowledge of the race, a doctrine that firmly implied that one need not adhere to any standards of knowledge but simply cater to individual interests. . . . With the acceptance of this doctrine American public school education took the easy way to meet its problems. . . . " The easy way was to embrace utilitarian how-to courses, while abandoning the effort to "reach every student, bookish and nonbookish, with the world's wisdom." The elimination of intellectual and moral standards, wrote Smith, meant that "no subject is intrinsically of any more value than any other subject . . . training in mechanical skills is put on a par with the development of mind and imagination . . . hairdressing and embalming are just as important, if not a little more so, than history and philosophy." Smith complained that the schools' effort to educate "the whole child" was not only ridiculous, "covering everything except a course in how to come in out of the rain," but was dangerous, because it enlarged the power of the social group and the state at the expense of the individual and his family. The emphasis on adjusting the individual to society, he warned, eroded individual freedom and fed the tendency in modern society to bureaucratic control by experts accountable to no one. Smith insisted that it was progressives who were authoritarian, since they compel the individual to adjust to the social values of the group, and it was progressives who were undemocratic, since they betrayed a "profound distrust of the ability of all youth to 'take' education."[44]

For the next five years, the "crisis in education" filled the pages of the nation's magazines with arguments for and against contemporary practices. *Time* magazine described life adjustment education as "the latest gimmick among U.S. educators" and defined it contemptuously as "a school of thought which seemed to believe that the teacher's job was not so much to teach history or algebra, as to prepare students to live happily ever after." In the *Scientific Monthly,* the president of the University of Illinois chapter of Phi Beta Kappa ridiculed education professors; they had, he said, belittled "the pursuit of knowledge of literature, of languages, of philosophy, of the arts, of the sciences," and converted teachers into "wet nurses, instructors in sex education, medical advisors, consultants to the lovelorn, umpires in the battle of the vertical versus the horizontal stroke in tooth-brushing, and professors of motor-vehicle operation."[45]

Public educators were taken aback by the sudden deluge of critical commentaries, ridicule, and invective directed at them: in education journals alone, the number of articles attacking or defending current practice rose from seven in 1948 to forty-nine in 1952, and articles in *Life,* the *Readers Digest,* the *Atlantic Monthly,* the *Saturday Review of Literature, McCall's* and scores of other national publications doubled or trebled the volume of critiques. While it had been customary in the 1930s and early 1940s to ignore or belittle the critics of progressive education, this was no longer possible.[46]

The response of progressive educators revealed their inability to be self-critical or to examine their own assumptions in the pragmatic spirit to which they paid homage. At best, the defenders of current practice argued that the programs under attack had been validated by evidence garnered from the social sciences and were designed to recognize the diversity of abilities among students; to go back to the mythical "good old days," when the curriculum was appropriate for the few, not the many, would be unscientific and undemocratic. Far more typically, however, defenders of the new education were simply defensive. The schools, they insisted, were better than ever. Studies were cited to demonstrate that school children were learning the fundamentals better than did their predecessors. This answered the extremists who condemned the schools for ignoring the Three Rs, but it sidestepped the serious charge that "how-to" courses and socio-personal adjustment had been substituted for history, science, mathematics, foreign languages, and literature. Some of the defenders insisted that progressive education could not be responsible for the failings of the schools because it had never been implemented, which raised the question of how progressive practices made the schools better than ever if they had not been used.

Another reaction was to assail the critics as reactionaries, bigots, zealots, and enemies of public education, who were part of a massive, well-organized, well-financed national organization that was scheming to destroy public education. The editor of *Progressive Education* noted that there were three elements in the usual organized attack on the schools: first, local malcontents and critics; second, a local self-constituted organization; and third, national organizations that supply "ammunition and strategy" to local groups. What kind of people joined in the attacks? Certainly not honest critics, for honest critics keep themselves well informed, "are willing to work with the schools, and generally favor the same lines of progress as the educators." In short, an "honest critic" was not a critic at all, while anyone who did not agree with the schools' program was by definition a malcontent and a dishonest critic.[47]

A writer in the *Saturday Review of Literature* defined the critics as: "(a) the 'chronic tax conservationists' who resist every addition to the public expense; (b) the 'congenital reactionaries' who are suspicious of everything that 'isn't like it used to be when I was in school'; (c) numerous tribes of 'witch hunters,' especially those to whom every political or social change since 1900 is 'red'; (d) numerous 'religious tongs' which whet their axes on many forms of prejudice." James B. Conant, the president of Harvard University, told a convention of school administrators that critics should reveal whether they were attacking the public schools in order to help private schools get tax money; at the same meeting, a Harvard educator pronounced that those who joined in trying to discredit the schools were "among the emotionally least stable members of the community." The Defense Commission of the NEA characterized the critics somewhat differently, as: "confirmed subversives who want to destroy free public education in order to undermine our democratic way of life; disgruntled teachers who have not kept abreast of the latest educational methods and attempt to justify their own shortcomings; unreasonable parents who try to blame all of their children's shortcomings on the schools; racketeers who capitalize on the nation's legitimate concern over the education of our children and milk unsuspecting citizens for their own gain." Another author succinctly defined the "enemy" as: "real-estate conservatives, super-patriots, dogma peddlers, and race haters." There was no doubt that such disreputable types of school critics existed, but there could also be no doubt that the counterattackers preferred to focus on the extremists and crackpots rather than confront the fact that there were also well-informed individuals who honestly disagreed with the schools' practices.[48]

Despite the vigorous efforts by educators to discredit their enemies, the year 1953 was a banner year for slashing critiques of progressive education. The publication of books by authors who were in no way connected either with reactionary fringe groups or with religious organizations made it apparent that progressivism was in deep trouble.

In *The Conflict in Education in a Democratic Society*, Robert M. Hutchins asserted that modern pragmatic education was philosophically bankrupt. Progressive education, he said, consisted of four principles; first was "the doctrine of adjustment," which "leads to a curriculum of miscellaneous dead facts"—that is, information rather than knowledge—and to vocational training. Such a doctrine, he cautioned, was inadequate because it prizes conformity and devalues independent thought: "Our mission here on earth is to change our environment, not to adjust ourselves to it." Second was "the doctrine of immediate needs," which promotes the disintegration of the school's program since there are so many needs, and which fails to equip the young with "that intellectual power which will enable them to meet new situations and solve new problems as they arise." Third was "the doctrine of social reform," which he rejected because public schools would not advocate anything that was not already accepted by society; the way that schools reform society, he insisted, was by making men more intelligent, not by becoming propaganda machines for current political fashions. Fourth was "the doctrine of no doctrine at all," which he attributed to educators who refuse to ask the aims and purposes of education and who pride themselves on having no curriculum: "Perhaps the greatest idea that America has given the world is the idea of education for all. The world is entitled to know whether this idea means that everybody can be educated, or only that everybody must go to school."[49]

In *Quackery in the Public Schools,* Albert Lynd, a businessman and school board member, ridiculed the "educationist" monopoly of the public schools. Lynd charged that the pedagogues had wrested control of the schools from the people and had arrogated to themselves sole competence to decide not only the technical questions of method but also the social aims of education. Educationists, he complained, had contrived "one of the neatest bureaucratic machines ever created by any professional group in any country anywhere," since no one was permitted to teach in a public school without studying under an educationist and future salary increases were tied to further "vassalage to these superprofessionals." Instead of studying history, literature, science, and the arts, Lynd charged, children were learning "trivia" such as "How can my home be made democratic?" and "How can I make my room more attractive?" Despite his tendency to exaggerate for the sake of dramatic effect, Lynd raised important issues: To whom do public schools belong? Who has the right to select the social aims of education? The community or the educators? These were questions that progressive educators had not considered for more than thirty years.[50]

The challenge to the new education was joined by Arthur Bestor, whose credentials were impressive: Bestor was a well regarded historian at the University of Illinois who had taught at Teachers College and had himself attended the Lincoln School, the best-known progressive school in the nation. His articles and books, most notably *Educational Wastelands* (1953), have been called "the most serious, searching, and influential criticisms of progressive education to appear during the fifties." Not all critics of contemporary education, said Bestor, were reactionaries or classicists; they included liberals as well as scientists, mathematicians, and others

"directly connected with the problems of a modern technological world."
The educationists were profoundly wrong, wrote Bestor, because they
denied that the purpose of schools is to teach "the power to think." This
is not the only responsibility of schools and colleges, but if *they* do not
emphasize "rigorous intellectual training, there will be none." The very
essence of democracy is that all citizens are entitled to receive the liberal
education that was once reserved for the privileged few; because they
rejected this basic premise, because they believed that many or most high
school students lack the capacity to benefit from intellectual training, the
pedagogues had betrayed the ideal of democratic education. The degrada-
tion of education was caused not by "progressive education," which at
Lincoln School was used to improve the teaching of subject matter, but by
"regressive education," which was hostile to intellect, derisive of subject
matter, and isolated from the world of science and scholarship. Bestor
scorned the substitution of "life needs" for the basic disciplines: "It is a
curiously ostrichlike way of meeting life needs to de-emphasize foreign
languages during a period of world war and postwar global tension, and
to de-emphasize mathematics at precisely the time when the nation's
security has come to depend on Einstein's equation. . . . " Liberal education,
he claimed, produces self-reliance, but instruction in the problems of daily
life assumes that the student cannot deal with a matter unless he has taken
a course in it. "The West was not settled by men and women who had
taken courses in 'How to be a pioneer,' " he asserted; " . . . I for one do
not believe that the American people have lost all common sense and
native wit so that now they have to be taught in school to blow their noses
and button their pants." He believed that the notion that the school must
meet every need was "a preposterous delusion that in the end can wreck
the educational system without in any sense contributing to the salvation
of society." Bestor called for reforms to break the power of the "interlocking directorate" that controlled schools of education, state and federal
agencies of education, and public school administration, in particular by
requiring prospective teachers to take more academic training and by placing teacher training institutions under the stewardship of those in the arts
and sciences.[51]

In *Let's Talk Sense About Our Schools,* Paul Woodring, a professor at the
Western Washington College of Education, brought to the discussion a
perspective free of hostility and sarcasm yet fundamentally critical of
progressive education. The more that educators failed to meet the complaints of the critics honestly, he wrote, the more the criticism grew. Much
of the present discontent stemmed from the view that professional educators had "preempted the responsibility for policy making to such an extent

that interested citizens, even members of elected boards of education, feel that they no longer have an adequate part in the establishment of basic educational policies." Furthermore, he believed that most Americans would not accept the pragmatic philosophy of modern education if they understood it. The dilemma, as he saw it, was inherent in the rapid expansion of universal education: the school of the past did not know what to do with the slow learner, other than to flunk him, and the new school used social promotion to advance him with his age group but without teaching him how to read. In neither case was the problem solved. Woodring thought that it was time for the education profession to admit that it did not have answers to all the problems, to tolerate differences of opinion within the ranks, and to "get away from the prevailing notion that anyone who raises questions about basic principles is antisocial, unprofessional, or reactionary." The time had come, he held, to abandon attacks on the critics and to acknowledge that "American education in 1953 is evolving not *toward* progressive education, but *past* it."[52]

Woodring admitted that neither he nor any other educator had the answer to what I. L. Kandel had earlier called "the democratic dilemma." Does universal education imply differentiation of courses and curricula, according to students' ability? The progressive educators said yes and called it democratic to set up curricula which took account of students' diverse interests and aptitudes; the critics said no and said that it would be democratic to teach all children the same basic materials, even if at varying rates. What was to be done about the students who were bored in school by the traditional subjects as they were traditionally taught? The progressives' answer to the question was to identify whatever students were interested in, no matter how limited or limiting, and to turn it into a course or a unit; the critics failed to confront the question at all.

Despite the tidal wave of criticism, progressives continued to advocate the same programs that were now the subject of intense attack. Even as the onslaught gained full force, progressive pedagogical textbooks confidently described the steady advance of progressive reforms in school systems throughout the nation, and curriculum bulletins reflecting the progressive point of view continued to issue forth regularly from state and city education agencies. Yet the progressives' frustration at the slow pace of change occasionally showed. Harold Alberty, a prominent progressive at Ohio State University, acknowledged in his teacher-training textbook, *Reorganizing the High-School Curriculum,* that the creative curriculum reorganizer faced an uphill struggle against the opposition of teachers, parents, and students. Alberty noted glumly that "the time-honored, well-established academic fields representing accepted logical organizations of knowledge are still a very powerful influence in the curriculum and consume a large part of the student's time." He bemoaned the fact that the majority of teachers had neither interest in nor understanding of the need for change; in Bloomington, Illinois, for example, when high school teachers were asked for ideas to improve the school, only 5 percent suggested improving the curriculum. Furthermore, high school students "show a surprising lack of desire to pursue new curriculums and methods of work. . . . One needs only to ask college freshmen to express their opinions of their high schools to discover that most of them have been completely satisfied with their program." Worse, "Laymen's opinion polls all seem to indicate that the public is fairly well satisfied with the schools and the products which they are turning out." And, even though colleges no longer required Latin, many parents still wanted their children to study it because of an antiquated respect for "the time-honored tradition of culture and scholarship." Even in the face of all this apathy and resistance, Alberty heedlessly insisted that curriculum planning must be based on adolescent needs, including such problems as: being underweight, being overweight, poor teeth, poor complexion, foot trouble or "ill-fitting shoes."[53]

At the height of the controversy, the progressive education movement —what was left of it—crumbled. In 1955, the Progressive Education Association went out of business, and two years later the magazine *Progressive Education* quietly folded; it was not the critics that ended their lives but the fact that neither the organization nor the magazine had much of a following. If either had represented a vital, significant perspective, the controversy would have brought them new members and subscribers. In 1919, as Patricia A. Graham has observed, "progressive education meant all that was good in education; thirty-five years later nearly all the ills in American education were blamed on it," and the phrase itself "shifted from a term of praise to one of opprobrium." Educators who once prided themselves on their identification with progressivism as a symbol of modern thought now shunned the label.[54]

Who or what killed progressive education? It died for several reasons, but largely of old age. With all their talk of being forward-looking and future-oriented, in reality the spokesmen for the movement had become keepers of the sacred texts, defending ideas and practices of the past, ignorant of the emerging issues in American life and education. For all the talk of linking school to society, progressives failed to assert leadership on the already explosive racial issue and remained blind to the social implications of their separation of children into academic, general, and vocational curricula. As society and global conditions changed, they did not: the need for international understanding might have been reason to stress the teaching of foreign languages; the mobility and rootlessness of postwar society might have been reason to stress the teaching of history; the persistence of international tension might have been reason to stress the teaching of the history and literature of other cultures; the rapidity of technological change might have been reason to emphasize science and mathematics; the widespread concern about the plight of the individual in mass society might have been reason to elevate the teaching of literature; instead, they continued to talk on about the needs of youth in a way that reflected their insulation from events and their habitual, unthinking dependency on their own tradition and authority. Well before 1955, progressivism had become synonymous with professionalism, to the detriment of both; the ideas that once bound together individuals from a variety of diverse fields became increasingly remote from reality as they became ossified in the textbooks of the schools of education. The call for democracy, originally intended to invigorate the school and to improve society, by midcentury had come to mean the use of techniques of group dynamics to encourage consensus decision making and to convince others to accept predetermined outcomes. As the movement pursued utilitarianism in headlong fashion, the "radical faith" of the early progressives that "culture could be democratized without being vulgarized" was forgotten, and in some well-known progressive programs it seemed that culture could be democratized *only* by being vulgarized.[55]

The "great debate" about American education continued to rage until the fall of 1957, when the Russians orbited Sputnik, the first space satellite. Post-Sputnik shockwaves led to demands for federal funds for mathematics and science, greater emphasis on language instruction, and higher academic standards. In one sense, the Russians settled the great debate, but in another sense, it was already moot when Sputnik orbited. Progressive education had long before lost the ability to be self-critical or to adapt to new conditions. The variant of progressive education that had become established within the profession by the activities of the NEA, other professional groups, the schools of education, and the public education agencies had strayed far from the humane, pragmatic, open-minded approach advocated by John Dewey; it had deteriorated into a cult whose principles were taught as dogma and whose critics were treated as dangerous heretics. Life-adjustment education, which offered so fertile a field for satirists of contemporary education, was not an accidental excrescence but rather the logical outgrowth of tendencies that were already fullblown by 1940.

Neither the Russians nor the critics killed progressive education. It died because it was, ironically, no longer relevant to the times; it did not meet the pragmatic test of "working" in public schools except as curricular innovations for below-average students, which was far from its stated intentions. In a nation suddenly conscious of the need for skills and intelligence, progressive education seemed out of joint with the needs of the present and the future. When at last it disappeared in the mid-1950s, there was scarcely a trace of what it originally meant to be, though surely the influence of its pioneers was present wherever projects, activities, and pupil experiences had been intelligently integrated into subject-matter teaching, wherever concern for health and vocation had gained a permanent place in the school program, and wherever awareness of individual differences among children had replaced lockstep instruction and rote memorization.

CHAPTER 3

Loyalty Investigations

IN THE YEARS following the war, the only thing of which Americans could be certain was change. How could life go back to "normal," when for the previous sixteen years the country had known only crisis? In the field of education, national leaders sensed that the fluidity of the postwar situation provided the right atmosphere in which to press for egalitarian advancements in race relations, higher education, and the financing of public education. To men and women who wanted to improve the status quo, the aura of change seemed a welcome opportunity in which to advocate new solutions.

But while the climate of flux inspired some with reformist zeal, it filled others with a sense of insecurity and fear. At the same time that leading citizens on national commissions were calling for new initiatives at the federal level, a querulous mood was emerging at the state and local level. The new mood was one of hostility toward change and suspicion of those who advocated change. In one state legislature after another, concern was expressed about threats to domestic security and about the danger of subversive persons in important places. During the decade after the war, as Soviet-American relations soured, the issue of loyalty and internal security became a major preoccupation of American politics. Both state and federal legislators conducted investigations, wrote new laws, and used the harsh glare of publicity to expose persons believed to be subversive. These years came to be known by such epithets as "the nightmare decade," "the age of suspicion," and "the McCarthy era," though the investigations were underway well before Senator Joseph McCarthy of Wisconsin attached his name to the governmental search for disloyal citizens in 1950.

Because of their important role in shaping the minds and values of the younger generation, educational institutions invariably attracted the attention of those who were concerned about disloyalty and subversion, particularly at the state and local level, where most schools and institutions of higher education were financed and controlled. Publicly supported schools and universities became "a leading target . . . if not the primary target, of state legislative investigations into un-American activities." Most states adopted laws aimed at protecting the educational process from subversion, such as loyalty oaths for teachers, bans against the employment of members of certain organizations as teachers, and prohibitions against the teaching or advocacy of "un-American" or subversive doctrines (such as advocating the violent overthrow of the state or federal government). Vocal critics of the loyalty oaths and investigations charged that the schools and institutions of higher education were in no danger from subversives, but were in great peril as a result of the accusations directed at them by legislators and free-lance vigilantes; in communities where support for controversial causes or where radical activism was considered "un-American" or "subversive," the political climate inhibited freedom of thought and freedom of speech among those who were likeliest to exercise it.[1]

While many of the themes of the overall controversy were deeply rooted in American history—the fear of conspiracy and sedition, the xenophobia and nativism, and the populistic anti-intellectualism and anti-elitism—the immediate crisis grew out of the ideological struggles of the Depression era. Typically, the controversies about subversion in education in the late 1940s and early 1950s were marked by certain characteristics: intense politicization; a deep split within the American left over the relationship of Communism to liberalism; an insistence by the American right that the left was a seamless, unpatriotic whole; a shrill tone of recrimination, with antagonists trying to discredit and destroy each other; charges of disloyalty by some and claims of "Red-baiting" by others. The style and substance of these events originated in the 1930s, when the lines were drawn between partisans of different ideologies; their struggle for cultural dominance subsided during the war, and then flared anew in the postwar period, magnified and made ominous by world and national events.

The economic collapse that began in 1929 wrought profound change in the cultural and political milieu. The Depression's dire consequences were everywhere apparent: the number of unemployed rapidly grew; breadlines, apple-sellers, and Hoovervilles sprang up in the cities; banks failed; mortgages on farms and businesses were foreclosed. The spreading sense of crisis undermined traditional values and spurred critical reexamination of the nation's basic social, political, and economic arrangements. The economic calamity created new audiences for extremists and demagogues of all stripes, as well as a hunger for solutions and action. Most Americans shunned extremism and reacted either with hope in Franklin D. Roosevelt's New Deal programs or with apathetic resignation.

But others reached out for radical answers, and a "purposeful minority" found them in the Communist party. Some of "the most intelligent, selfless, and idealistic" of their generation were attracted to the party, according to Irving Howe and Lewis Coser, because of "their sense that American society seemed utterly adrift, that no large moral purpose animated the world of business and of work, that the idea of social crackup had become the common possession of millions of people who did not think of themselves as radicals." On college campuses, the Communist party made significant inroads among students, especially in New York City, where there was a critical mass of radical activists. Throughout the 1930s, Communists organized a succession of student organizations, like the National Student League, and exerted a dominating influence in many others. James Wechsler, a student at Columbia University in the early 1930s, described his own turn to communism at that time as a response to the widespread sense of breakdown in American life; the choice he perceived was between a liberalism that was tired, hesitant, and confused, and a Marxism that was confident and certain. He recalled the vivid contrast between the liberal Walter Lippman's *A Preface To Morals*, with its message that the old gods were dead and the new ones hard to find, as against the Marxist John Strachey's bold assertion in *The Coming Struggle for Power* that Americans could end poverty by eliminating private ownership.[2]

The lure of the Russian revolution was enhanced by the contrast between what Americans knew first-hand of their own situation and what they had heard about the achievements of the new Soviet society. They knew that American farmers and workers were in desperate straits; they heard that the measures taken by Stalin had transformed Russian agriculture and industry and created full employment. Aside from its pragmatic claims, the revolution offered the trappings of a secular religion: sacred texts, discipline, martyrs, holy leaders, and a vision of utopia. Since the revolutionary faith was so compelling, its admirers were willing to overlook the arbitrary means employed as a transitory manifestation of "the dictatorship of the proletariat." What especially impressed intellectuals was that the new state was constructed on ideas and theories, which meant that intellectuals, no less than workers, were essential to the success of the revolution, in contrast to their evident marginality in the United States.

Yet despite the favorable circumstances, the American Communist party experienced constant turnover in membership. Because of its interminable factionalism and its obedient adherence to Moscow-directed doctrines, the party was unable to take advantage of capitalism's enfeeblement. From 1928 to 1935, party dogma required hostility toward Socialists and liberals (both were scornfully called "social fascists" by Communist party members) and the ouster from the Communist party of Trotskyites and other left-wing deviationists. The party's hard-line policy, typified by its virulent attacks on Roosevelt and the New Deal and by its physical disruptions of Socialist party meetings, isolated it from potential allies on the left. Some of the staunchest left-wing anti-Communists were shaped by this period. Those who became Communists because they were rebels found themselves in an organization that was obsessed with purging dissenters, and many dropped out.

In 1935, party doctrine abruptly changed. In response to the growing fascist threat in Europe, the Communist International promulgated a new policy of collective security and called for a united front among the Communist party, trade unions, Socialists, liberals, and other antifascists. To conform to the new line, the American party elevated a new leader, Earl Browder of Kansas, who proclaimed that "Communism is the Americanism of the twentieth century" and that its heroes were not only Marx and Lenin but also Jefferson and Lincoln. The new line inaugurated a brief but significant era known as the "Popular Front," in which Communists joined with non-Communists in a galaxy of paper organizations to protest the rise of fascism, to oppose war, to rally support for the Spanish Republic, and to champion similar causes. During the years of the Popular Front, from 1935 to 1939, the party reached its zenith in influence. The numerous Popular Front organizations attracted thousands of sympathetic members and exploited a widespread yearning for fraternity and a desire to take a stand against fascism abroad and injustice at home. The Popular Front organizations gathered long lists of names for their "manifestoes, open letters, petitions, declarations, statements, pronouncements, protests and other illusions of opinion ground-swells in the land."[3]

In the glow of the Popular Front mood, any criticism of the Soviet Union or the American Communist party was apt to raise a hue and cry of "Red-baiting." Attitudes toward Stalinism and the Communist party sharply divided intellectuals of the left during the Popular Front, especially as news trickled in about Stalin's "show trials" of Bolshevik leaders and about mass arrests and executions of prominent writers, scholars, poets, artists, educators, and engineers. Some intellectuals lost faith, while others refused to question anything done by the Soviet Union. The Popular Front mentality proved resistant to challenge, unshaken even after the distinguished educator John Dewey, then in his late seventies, led a commission to investigate Stalin's charges against Leon Trotsky and found them baseless. It was not until the signing of a nonaggression pact between the Soviet Union and Nazi Germany in September 1939 that the Popular Front collapsed. Overnight, the Soviet Union and its American surrogates lost credibility as the leaders of the fight against Nazism. When the American party dutifully reversed course and defended the friendship pact with yesterday's villain, all but the most unregenerate Stalinists abandoned the party and its Popular Front organizations.

The radical climate of the 1930s found expression among professional educators, not through the activities of the Communist party but through the thinking and writing of a relatively small group of men centered around Teachers College, Columbia University. The most outspoken was George S. Counts, who was known both for his trenchant critiques of class bias in American education and for his studies of education in the Soviet Union. Counts attained a measure of renown and notoriety in 1932 with the publication of *Dare the School Build a New Social Order?* Counts challenged progressive educators to cease focusing on the individualistic, child-centered school and to consider instead how to use the school to build a better social order. Progressive education, he complained, was too much involved with "the liberal-minded upper middle class who send their children to the Progressive schools." He warned that

> If Progressive Education is to be genuinely progressive, it must emancipate itself from the influence of this class, face squarely and courageously every social issue, come to grips with life in all of its stark reality, establish an organic relationship with the community, develop a realistic and challenging vision of human destiny, and become less frightened than it is today at the bogies of *imposition* and *indoctrination*. [4]

Teachers, urged Counts, "should deliberately reach for power and then make the most of their conquest." They should avoid neutrality and use their power to project a vision of what America might become. And what were the outlines of this future society? It was not to be capitalistic, for capitalism was based on selfishness, which was morally reprehensible, and was, besides, a demonstrated failure. The future order should be planned, coordinated, socialized, humane, and collectivist; it should be built on the democratic and revolutionary traditions of America's past. But, he held, democracy "should not be identified with political forms and functions—with the federal constitution, the popular election of officials, or the practice of suffrage." No, democracy "has little to do with our political institutions: It is a sentiment with respect to the moral equality of men; it is an aspiration towards a society in which this sentiment will find complete fulfillment." In building the new social order, it was the end itself that mattered, not the means necessary to get there.[5]

In 1934, Counts and like-minded colleagues at Teachers College launched a new publication, the *Social Frontier,* as a forum for those who believed that education should lead the way in "the reconstruction of American society." Counts was its editor; its directors included such well-known progressive educators as John Dewey, William Heard Kilpatrick, John Childs, and Harold Rugg. The group associated with the magazine came to be called "Frontier Thinkers" or "Social Reconstructionists." Its first editorial summed up "the dominating reality" of the present age: "For the American people the age of individualism in economy is closing and an age of collectivism is opening." The monthly lobbied vigorously for socialism and collectivism and against capitalism and individualism, particularly in its early years. In the April, 1935, issue, for example, the editors confidently declared that "a collectivist social order has the promise of genuine freedom, an abundant, rich, colorful, socially significant life for the many where they now can find comfort only in an empty legalistic formula." In contrast, "there can be no freedom of thought and expression . . . [in] an economy based on private property in the means of production and private profits. . . . History has pronounced this verdict." In the same credulous vein, the editors opined that "Russia is moving toward greater democracy and away from dogmatism in art and in education while in most democratic countries the trend toward authoritarianism is in the ascendant." The editors' curious notion of cultural freedom was expressed in their question: "Dare the President harness the press, the radio, the cinema, the public educational system to the star of a new, economically secure and culturally free, social order?"[6]

During the course of the 1930s, the *Social Frontier* eventually provided remarkable documentation of the gradual disillusionment of the most politically conscious group of American educators. Its early issues were marked by militant radicalism and the belief that education "has an important, even strategic, role to play in the reconstruction of American society." In the fall of 1935, the magazine urged teachers to join in the class struggle, since "there is no hope for the significant practice of education in a social order based on private property and profit." Theodore Brameld, a Marxist philosopher of education at New York University, chided other progressives for their reluctance to endorse Marxian principles of class conflict and the dictatorship of the proletariat. In February, 1936, the editors defended the "class conflict" theory of society and asserted that society consisted of two classes, the owners and the workers, only one of which was conscious of its interests: "In view of the absence of a class mentality among the workers, it would be reasonable to assume that it is the problem of education to induce such a mentality rather than to take an existing mentality and base a course of action upon it."[7]

However, reconstructionists disagreed among themselves about the appropriateness of the Marxist analysis for American society. In 1936, Harold Rugg opposed the "class conflict" approach. He argued that American society did not consist of two warring classes, and that government proceeded through "the interplay of many small special interest-groups," based on such factors as religion, race, profession, and neighborhood. "Thus, we are compelled to view the American people today, not as a nice dichotomy of clear-cut antagonistic classes but as a kaleidoscope of many shifting groups, some of which from time to time are mutually exclusive and antagonistic, but most of which overlap in membership and interest and are both partly conflicting and partly co-operative." Similarly, William Heard Kilpatrick lambasted Brameld in an article titled "High Marxism Defined and Rejected." Kilpatrick flatly rejected "the class struggle," "the workers' dictatorship," "indoctrination by teachers," "teacher class consciousness," "class war morality," and other tenets of what he called "High Marxism." High Marxism should be repudiated, he maintained, because it "rejects democracy, rejects education as a process of social change and rejects . . . the ethical regard for the personality of others." The same spring of 1936, John Dewey questioned the usefulness of the class concept for educators and suggested that it conflicted with democratic traditions and methods (Dewey, of course, was already anathema to Communists for his role in exonerating Trotsky).[8]

The political complexion of the magazine was substantially altered when George Counts, the foremost radical firebrand, "underwent a change in attitude" after learning that educators he knew had been killed in the Soviet purges. In 1937, Counts left the editorship of the *Social Frontier* to assume the leadership of the anti-Communist group within the college teachers' union. In 1939, the final deradicalization of the major "Frontier Thinkers" became public: Counts wrote about a struggle within the Teachers College faculty union between liberals and a Communist faction. The Communists, Counts said, "seemed far less concerned with the improvement of the conditions of labor than with exacerbating and making capital out of the passions aroused." Not only did the Communist faction operate anonymously, but it tried to attribute its program and methods to liberal faculty members: "We realized then that sooner or later we would have to issue a declaration of independence from its influence." The publication of the Communist faction was "always malicious, provocative, and irresponsible. On every occasion it baited and misrepresented the administration. It sought to impose on the College the 'orthodox' pattern of the class struggle." Finally, the liberals on the faculty formally condemned the Communist party unit at Teachers College, to demonstrate that they would not "serve as a front for irresponsible and anonymous actions of any faction employing the methods of conspiracy." Counts blamed the Communists for creating reactionary attitudes by their tactics of vilification and provocation:

> They profess to be defending democracy against reaction and preach the united front of all popular forces. Yet they proceed to violate the most elementary democratic virtues of fairness and integrity, and by their methods bring inevitable discord into the ranks of the popular cause. They meet fundamental criticism with the cry of 'red baiting'. . . . One lesson contemporary history teaches with unmistakable clarity—ends and means cannot be separated—undemocratic means destroy democratic ends.

Counts had traveled a long way since 1932.[9]

By May, 1939, the *Social Frontier* had turned against the Communists, even though the Popular Front was still in full swing. The editors wrote:

> Ever since we began to whack away at Stalinist influences within the Teachers Union, the American League for Peace and Democracy, the American Student Union, and other organizations which the Communist Party considers worthy of its attention, *The Social Frontier* has been subjected to an organized barrage of attacks that are clearly intended to wear down our editorial morale. . . . The reasons why we are no good differ diametrically, but they all point to the common conclusion that The S.F went to the dogs the day it decided that the Communist Party had been too deferentially treated in its columns. A political gang that *pretends* to be concerned about the principles of a progressive education that is officially banned in Russia and feigns a devotion to democracy while defending a regime that would kill unmercifully the writer of this editorial for the crime of composing it expects us to remain silent about it. What colossal gall![10]

Although the *Social Frontier* is considered the quintessential progressive journal of the 1930s, its circulation never exceeded 6,000. Despite the fact that the leaders of reconstructionism became disenchanted with Marxism and Communism, the magazine never outlived its reputation as a radical publication. It ceased publication in 1943. "In the end," noted Lawrence A. Cremin, "the journal left one more image of progressive education in the public mind, the caricature of the radical pedagogue using the school to subvert the American way of life. . . . " In reality, the radical pedagogues of the early and middle thirties were deradicalized by events, by the purges in the Soviet Union, and by the undemocratic tactics of the Communist factions within the labor movement, especially within the teachers' unions.[11]

Nowhere was the struggle for control of organized teachers more dramatic than in New York City, where there was the greatest concentration of Socialists and Communists. Of the more than sixty organizations vying for the loyalty of New York City's thirty thousand teachers in the 1930s, only the Teachers Union was affiliated with organized labor. Founded in 1916 by Socialists and chartered as Local 5 of the American Federation of Teachers (AFT), American Federation of Labor (AFL), the Teachers Union was an outspoken defender of academic freedom and teachers' rights, as well as a scarred battleground of left-wing factionalism. In the early 1930s, the Teachers Union was split by a bitter power struggle between its Socialist leadership and a Communist-led opposition group. In 1935, when the opposition outmaneuvered the union leaders, the leaders walked out and formed a new organization called the Teachers Guild, which was staunchly anti-Communist. But the Teachers Union continued to hold the AFT-AFL charter. One of its new leaders was Bella Dodd, who served as its legislative representative and chief strategist from 1935 until 1944, when she publicly became a Communist party functionary.

During the remainder of the 1930s, various left-wing factions competed to control not only Local 5 but the parent AFT as well. In 1939, George Counts led the battle to oust the leadership of the New York City college teachers union; he ran for president of the local and was soundly beaten. He then became a candidate for president of the national AFT. News of the Nazi-Soviet pact arrived on the day that the vote was taken in national convention, and Counts narrowly won. By 1941, the Counts-led AFT had expelled the Communist-dominated locals.[12]

While the left fought out its internecine battles, a tide of militant anti-Communism was slowly rising in the country, fed by publications like Elizabeth Dilling's *Red Network: A 'Who's Who' and Handbook of Radicalism for Patriots* (1934), which identified four hundred and sixty organizations and thirteen hundred individuals as having "knowingly or unknowingly . . . contributed in some measure to one or more phases of the Red movement in the United States." Since Dilling's list included not only Communists, but also anti-Communists of the left, Socialists, liberals, pacifists, and people active in civil rights, civil liberties, and trade unions, it was not surprising to find the leaders of progressive education —men like John Dewey, William Heard Kilpatrick, Harold Rugg, Sidney Hook, and George Counts—listed as part of "the Red network." Since New Deal liberals were firmly in control of the national government, Dilling's charges could easily be ignored as the rantings of a paranoid reactionary.[13]

But Dilling's concern about a vast Communist-Socialist-pacifist-anarchist plot to subvert the nation's institutions, however absurd, revealed an undercurrent of feeling that existed outside the worlds of the cosmopolitan elites in Washington and New York. While some parts of the culture were turning left in the thirties, others—with a longstanding hatred of radicalism, Communism, Socialism, and every other -ism of the left— were doing a slow burn. One indication of this growing reaction was the spread of state loyalty oaths for teachers. Several states had enacted them during the antiradical period in the 1920s, and about a dozen additional states adopted them in the 1930s. In 1935, Congress attached a "little Red rider" to the District of Columbia school appropriation bill, stipulating that no pay could go to anyone teaching or advocating Communism (it was repealed in 1937). In 1938, the House of Representatives approved funding for its new Committee on Un-American Activities, created to investigate subversive activities by fascists and Communists. And in 1940, the New York State Legislature authorized a committee (called the Rapp-Coudert committee) to investigate the finances of the schools and colleges in New York City, as well as allegations of subversive activities. The Rapp-Coudert probe eventually led to the ouster from the city's municipal colleges of about three dozen faculty members who had been identified as members of the Communist party.[14]

The first successful ambush by the Red-hunting vigilantes was directed at a series of social studies textbooks developed by Harold Rugg. The Rugg books were adopted by thousands of schools in the 1930s and used by millions of children; they combined history, geography, sociology, economics, and political science, were attractively illustrated and well written, and were livelier than many older texts. In 1940, the Rugg textbooks became the target of national attacks; one called "Treason in the Textbooks" appeared in the *American Legion* magazine, and the other "Our 'Reconstructed' Educational System" was published in *Nation's Business*. Rugg and other "Frontier Thinkers" were described as "radical and communistic" educators who wanted to use the schools to introduce a collectivistic social order. The authors quoted statements made by George Counts in 1932 to demonstrate his radicalism, unaware that Counts by

1940 was the leader of the successful effort to end Communist domination of the AFT.[15]

By substituting "social studies" for the separate study of history and other disciplines, said the critics, Rugg was able to insert his propagandistic interpretations, which derogated the traditional version of American history and promoted socialism. The critics quoted liberally from Rugg's textbooks, as well as from the *Social Frontier* and Rugg's 1933 book, *The Great Technology,* in which he explained the role that educators should play in devising a new, scientifically planned social order. In a sense, the critics were right: in the early 1930s, Rugg and his colleagues at the *Social Frontier* did project a vision of educators as expert social engineers, preparing the way to a collectivist social order by building a new consensus among the people; they did believe that educators should exert leadership in the reconstruction of the social order along noncapitalist lines. This was not the role that the critics, or most Americans for that matter, expected of teachers and textbook writers, who were supposed to extol patriotic values and the American past, not attack them and put in their place a new ideology.

But the critics were wrong in labeling Rugg a communist. It was not just that the entire group had turned against Stalinism well before the Hitler-Stalin pact, but that even in 1933, Rugg's proposals were set forward as a middle way between a failed capitalism and a brutal Communism. And more important, the textbooks themselves were critical of American society but not propagandistic; this is why the case against Rugg had to be made, not on the basis of the textbooks, but by referring to Rugg's polemical writings. Nonetheless, as a result of the attacks by the American Legion and the Hearst press, school districts across the country withdrew the Rugg books from use.[16]

When the United States entered the war, these bitter controversies were temporarily set aside. Since the Soviet Union was an ally, the anti-Communist mood receded—or was temporarily suspended—and those who had been enemies in the battles of the 1930s joined together to defeat fascism. Yet the events of the 1930s, however limited in importance they may have seemed to nonparticipants, were precipitating factors in the legislative investigations of subversion after the war and provided the raw material for the postwar age of suspicion.

At the conclusion of the Second World War, there was widespread hope for a new era of peace and international cooperation, symbolized by the new United Nations. In the spirit of the times, the United States offered to transfer its monopoly of atomic energy to international control; the Soviet Union's rejection of the proposal was one of a series of events that revealed the deterioration of the Soviet-American wartime alliance. Concern about the intentions of the Soviet Union deepened when it failed to permit free elections in Eastern Europe, as promised at Yalta, and when the Canadian government exposed a Soviet espionage ring in 1946. In 1947 the Truman administration dispatched military and economic aid to Greece and Turkey to repel Communist guerrillas, and in 1948 the United States launched the Marshall Plan, a multi-billion dollar program of aid to rebuild the devastated economies of Western Europe (the Soviet Union declined to participate). That same year, a Communist coup in Czechoslovakia and a Soviet attempt to blockade Berlin dashed any remaining illusions about the new international situation. All too suddenly, Americans discovered that wartime amity was dead, and new terms—like "cold war," "iron curtain," and "containment"—entered the national vocabulary.[17]

As postwar optimism soured, Americans began to fear a new war and to worry about the threat of Communist subversion. To allay public concern, President Truman instituted a loyalty program for government employees in 1947. But public fear of Communist subversion continued to build, stoked by the sensational spy trials and congressional hearings of the late 1940s and early 1950s. At a time of great insecurity, when the headlines were dominated by charges of espionage and betrayal, Senator Joseph McCarthy of Wisconsin aggressively used his position in Congress to command the national leadership of a campaign to identify and root out subversives in important institutions. His name became a symbol of governmental efforts to oust allegedly subversive persons; in the educational field, the Congressional investigations were carried forward by the Senate Internal Security Subcommittee and the House Committee on Un-American Activities, where McCarthy was not a member.

Right-wing extremists who had hawked conspiracy theories since the 1930s found new audiences for their allegations of Communist infiltration into government, the mass media, unions, schools, and other vital institutions. There was a climate of credibility for these charges because they offered a coherent explanation for perplexing and ominous events: the resumption of tension between the United States and the Soviet Union; the absorption of Eastern Europe into the Soviet orbit; the Communist conquest of mainland China; the explosion of a Soviet atomic bomb; and the outbreak of war in Korea in 1950. In the questions raised in the trials and investigations of the period, the common thread was a sense of betrayal: Who gave the Russians our atomic secrets? Who lost China? Why had the United States trusted the Russians at Yalta? Which writers, government officials, teachers, and public figures were to blame for deceiving the American people about the true nature of the Communist threat?

Fear of Communism was not a new phenomenon in the United States; it had been fairly continuous since the Russian revolution. In the aftermath of World War I, fear of radicalism spread like an epidemic across the country; in a single year, 1919, twenty-six states enacted laws banning the display of red flags, and the United States attorney general, A. Mitchel Palmer, deported a boatload of alien radicals to Russia. During the 1930s, there continued to be a deep reservoir of popular antipathy toward the Soviet Union and American Communists, manifested at the state level by legislative investigations and by the passage of loyalty oaths. But during the Popular Front period and then again during the war, anti-Communist sentiment was submerged. By war's end, however, the Congress was dominated by a conservative coalition of Republicans and southern Demo-crats, and in 1946 the Republican party won control of Congress and of many state legislatures and governorships. Still, despite the eagerness of many Republicans to discredit the party that had been in power for four-teen years and that still held the presidency, there was no massive outbreak of anti-Communist activity until 1948, when Soviet actions abroad and espionage trials at home created a sense of national peril.[18]

In the decade after the war, fear of Communist subversion in the schools provoked a flurry of state legislative activity. By 1950, thirty-three states had adopted legislation permitting the ouster of disloyal teachers. In twenty-six states, teachers were required to sign a loyalty oath. Most such oaths consisted of a pledge to support the state and federal constitutions and to discharge faithfully the duties of a teacher. In fourteen states, embellishments were added: some states required teachers to promote patriotism; or to promise that the teacher was not a member of the Com-munist party or any other organization that advocated the forcible over-throw of the government; or to pledge not to teach or advocate the forcible overthrow of the government.[19]

But legislative proscriptions did not always satisfy the search for security. Following the pattern established by the House Committee on Un-American Activities (HCUA), several state legislatures opened investi-gations designed to expose teachers who were present or past members of the Communist party or who had been involved in Popular Front organiza-tions. The HCUA, in addition to supplying a model for its state counter-parts, offered them documentary records and expert witnesses. HCUA's research director, Benjamin Mandel, was one of the first Communist mem-bers of the New York Teachers Union. The expert witnesses—such as Benjamin Gitlow, Louis Budenz, Bella Dodd, and J. B. Matthews—had been prominent Communists or fellow travelers. Gitlow had been one of the founders of the American Communist party, a two-time Communist party candidate for vice-president, and the subject of a landmark Supreme Court decision in 1925 affirming his conviction on a charge of criminal anarchy. Budenz had been a member of the party's Central Committee and a managing editor of the *Daily Worker*. Bella Dodd had been legislative representative of the New York Teachers Union in the late 1930s and early 1940s, then became an official of the Communist party and the party's candidate for New York State attorney general. The ex-Communists brought to the crusade against subversives the same single-minded dedication that had once characterized their commitment to radical causes. Because of their knowledgeability and credentials, they brought credibility, substance, and coordination to the congressional investigations of the late 1940s and early 1950s.

No defector from the radical 1930s proved more valuable than J. B. Matthews, a one-time Methodist missionary who spent his life in the service of causes. Matthews had joined or led dozens of radical organizations until 1935; in 1938 he was hired by HCUA and devoted himself thereafter to the anti-Communist cause. Matthews, who prided himself on having been America's foremost fellow traveler, brought systematization to the search for Communists and their sympathizers. Having been on scores of radical letterheads himself, Matthews compiled extensive files of Communist-front organizations and lists of the thousands of individuals who had been members or who had signed petitions sponsored by fellow-traveling organizations. His lists were not perfect, however; some people were misidentified, some names had originally been used without permission, some had joined an organization or signed a petition in support of a particular issue, without regard to its sponsors. Murray Kempton described Matthews as "the legatee of the thirties, the custodian of their archives, the patcher and pumper of all their deflated balloons." Matthews, he said, was dependent on preserving the files of the thirties because his life "would be without meaning if he could not believe that it had all been terribly important, not as the tragedy of the few but the guilt of the many."[20]

One of the first states to set up an investigation of subversion after the war was Washington, where in 1946 Republicans took control of the legislature away from Democrats who had been active in Popular Front politics. After the election, a fact-finding committee on "un-American activities" was created, under the chairmanship of freshman Republican Albert F. Canwell. One of its targets was the University of Washington. Hearings were conducted in the spring of 1948, and testimony was taken both from local ex-Communists and from HCUA expert witnesses. As a result of the hearings, the University of Washington fired three tenured professors (against the recommendation of a faculty tenure committee). Two admitted current membership in the Communist party, and a third was judged to have been "evasive" in withholding information from the university about his political affiliations; in addition, three former party members were directed to sign affidavits declaring that they had left the party, and they were placed on probation for two years.[21]

The events at the University of Washington reverberated on other campuses, where it was noted with alarm that tenured professors had been fired, and in other state legislatures, where it was noted with interest that the Canwell committee had unearthed past and present Communists on the faculty of the state university. The major issue of the controversy was whether Communists should be permitted to teach, and the educational world began to take sides. The AFT, which had expelled its Communist-dominated locals in 1940, voted in the fall of 1948 against allowing Communists to teach. In its 1949 convention, the NEA endorsed the same stand by a vote of 2,995 to 5. Although most university presidents thought that Communists were unfit to teach, the American Association of University Professors held that the teacher should be judged by his individual acts and his professional competence and not by his political affiliations (efforts to indoctrinate students would be grounds for dismissal). The American Civil Liberties Union opposed the automatic exclusion of Communists from teaching, even though in 1940 it had voted to exclude from its own govern ing committee any person "who is a member of any political organization which supports totalitarian dictatorship in any country, or who by his public declarations indicates his support of such a principle."[22]

The controversy at the University of Washington prompted a lively debate in the *New York Times* between Sidney Hook, chairman of the philosophy department at New York University, and Alexander Meiklejohn, former president of Amherst College. The area of agreement between them was broad. Both believed that faculty members should be absolutely free to think and teach whatever they believed to be true, and both maintained that the faculty (not legislators) should be the ultimate judge of professional competence. Like Meiklejohn, Hook believed that the university was a privileged haven for unfettered thought. Hook wrote:

> If in the honest exercise of his academic freedom an individual reaches views which bring down about his head charges of "Communist," "Fascist," or what not, the academic community is duty bound to protect him irrespective of the truth of the charges. And since these words are often epithets of disparage-

ment rather than of precise description, there is all the more reason why the university must stand firm. It places its faith in the loyalty of its teachers to the ethics and logic of scientific inquiry. The heresies of yesterday are often the orthodoxies of today. It is better to err on the side of toleration than of proscription.[23]

Where Hook and Meiklejohn parted company was on their understanding of the meaning of membership in the Communist party. Hook argued that the Communist party was not a political party like any other. Citing Communist party documents, Hook asserted that the party was a secretive, highly disciplined organization, that it existed to advance the interests of the totalitarian regime in the Soviet Union, and that it had no passive or ignorant members. In his view, those who belonged to the party willingly surrendered their intellectual freedom, abandoned the search for truth, and violated the basic tenets of academic freedom. There is a party line, said Hook, "for every area of thought from art to zoology. No person who is known to hold a view incompatible with the party line is accepted as a member." Communist teachers, he pointed out, "taught in 1934 that Roosevelt was a fascist; in 1936, during the Popular Front, a progressive; in 1940, during the Nazi-Stalin pact, a warmonger and an imperialist; in 1941, after Hitler invaded the Soviet Union, a leader of the oppressed people of the world." What mattered, he held, was not whether the Communist teacher was right or wrong: "What is relevant is that their conclusions are not reached by a free inquiry into the evidence. To stay in the Communist Party, they must believe and teach what the party line decrees." To the argument that teachers should be judged by their acts, Hook replied that joining the party and submitting to its discipline was an act, not merely an opinion.

Disagreeing with Hook, Meiklejohn held that the significant feature of the University of Washington affair was that "if, in his search for the truth, [a teacher] finds the policies of the American Communist Party to be wise, and acts on that belief, he will be dismissed from the university." By its very nature, he argued, academic freedom exists to protect the expression of the teacher's views, no matter how unpopular or unconventional they may be, and to guarantee that the teacher's opinions may not be proper grounds for dismissal. While Meiklejohn agreed that Communist party members accepted a party line, which shifted over time, and party discipline, which was "unusually rigid and severe," nonetheless party members willingly accepted the party line and discipline because the party's views coincided with their own. Because joining the party represented a free expression of the teacher's beliefs, Meiklejohn believed that

Communists could not be ousted from the teaching profession without abridging their intellectual and academic freedom.[24]

Furthermore, Meiklejohn maintained that it was impossible to teach the value of intellectual freedom while denying it to those whose views were offensive:

> Whatever else our students may do or fail to do, they must learn what freedom is. They must learn to believe in it, to love it, and most important of all, to trust it. . . . With respect to the world-wide controversy now raging between the advocates of the freedom of belief and the advocates of suppression of belief, what is our American doctrine? Simply stated, that doctrine expresses our confidence that whenever, in the field of ideas, the advocates of freedom and the advocates of suppression meet in fair and unabridged discussion, freedom will win. If that were not true, if the intellectual program of democracy could not hold its own in fair debate, then that program itself would require of us its own abandonment. That chance we believers in self-government have determined to take.

The essential problem for Hook, as for many others on the left who had battled Communists during the 1930s and who had continued to fight Communist attempts to dominate labor unions and liberal organizations after the war, was the nature of the Communist party. Right after the war, for example, a bruising power struggle between Communists and liberal non-Communists had paralyzed and finally destroyed the American Veterans Committee, the only liberal veterans' organization. Convinced that American Communists sought power in order to further the foreign policy goals of the Soviet Union and that its rule-or-ruin tactics were crippling the liberal movement instead of advancing it, leading liberals established the Americans for Democratic Action to stake out a position that was opposed to totalitarianism of left and right. The question that split the left was, what was the proper relationship of liberals to Communists? Were they natural allies, at different points on the left side of the political spectrum? Or were liberals, devoted as they were to human liberty and to the democratic process, bound to oppose the totalitarianism of the left as vigorously as they opposed the totalitarianism of the right? Those who refused to criticize the Communists insisted that the left would be weakened unless it maintained a united front; liberals who were anti-Stalinist insisted that liberalism would be morally bankrupt and politically discredited unless it opposed both Communism and facism. Norman Thomas, the leading American Socialist, concluded that "the right of the Communist to teach should be denied because he has given away his freedom in the quest for truth. . . . He who today persists in Communist allegiance is either too foolish or too disloyal to democratic ideals to be allowed to teach in our schools." During the war, one-time radicals George Counts and John Childs predicted that the American Communist party would be a barrier to postwar reconciliation between the United States and the Soviet Union because it was "not a political party in the ordinary sense" but an arm of the Communist International which had engaged in disreputable, undemocratic tactics to subvert liberal organizations to the interests of the Soviet Union. Others, however, shared the view expressed by Herbert Davis, president of Smith College: "I do not fear the influence of any extreme opinions in the academic world," he said, "as much as I fear the attempt to stifle them and limit freedom of debate."[25]

While liberals debated how to deal with the issue of Communist teachers and how to protect free institutions without destroying freedom, those who controlled the legislatures of state and nation saw no such fine distinctions; to them, the problem was simply how to rid the schools and universities of Communists and fellow travelers. Amidst daily headlines chronicling accusations, arrests, trials, investigations, and hearings related to Communism and espionage, public officials and educational administrators sought to devise measures to demonstrate to an uneasy public that the nation's schools and universities were free from Communist influence.

In March 1949, soon after the dismissals at the University of Washington, the University of California's Board of Regents approved a loyalty oath for all faculty members in order to head off a legislative investigation of the state university system. In 1940 the regents had declared that "membership in the Communist Party is incompatible with membership in the faculty of a State University," and since 1942 all faculty members had been required to affirm their loyalty to the federal and state constitutions. The 1949 addition to the oath required a pledge "that I am not a member of the Communist party, or under any oath, or a party to any agreement, or under any commitment that is in conflict with my obligations under this oath."[26]

The oath controversy created a turmoil within the faculty which lasted for more than two years. The faculty supported the regents' policy of excluding Communists, but it opposed the firing of faculty members who refused to sign the oath, regardless of tenure or of traditional due process guarantees. One faculty statement said:

> The faculty is not trying to defend Communism or Communists. It abhors all totalitarian beliefs and has said so repeatedly. It has not challenged the right of the Regents to fire Communists. But virtually to a man, the faculty protests the Regents' right to wreck the University by firing men for no other reason

than non-signing of a particular oath, created by the Regents, without the Regents ever bothering to investigate whether these men are in fact Communists or otherwise disloyal.[27]

Despite the opposition of the faculty, the regents dismissed thirty-one professors who refused to sign the oath. Twenty of them sued for reinstatement and invalidation of the oath. By the time the state courts ruled in their favor in 1952, the legislature had adopted a new anti-Communist oath required of all state employees, including university faculty. Reinstatement of the nonsigners was, as one account notes, "a hollow victory," for they were required to sign an oath "more offensive than the one they had fought earlier."[28]

Unlike the University of California and the University of Washington, both publicly supported state universities, the independent University of Chicago confronted and bested a hostile state investigation. The state senate's Seditious Activities Commission, known as the Broyles commission (for its chairman, Paul Broyles), opened an investigation of the University of Chicago and Roosevelt College in April, 1949, in reaction to a raucous student demonstration against proposed anti-Communist legislation. Before the hearings began, the University of Chicago received an unequivocal statement of support from its board of trustees, which included Chicago's leading businessmen. The chancellor of the university, Robert M. Hutchins, opened the hearings with a point-blank declaration that he could not testify "concerning subversive activities at the University of Chicago because there are none." Hutchins unreservedly defended "absolute and complete academic freedom" and denied that any member of his faculty was a Communist. He disparaged charges that some of his faculty belonged to Communist-front organizations, because "the University of Chicago does not believe in the un-American doctrine of guilt by association. The fact that some Communists belong to, believe in, or even dominate some of the organizations to which some of our professors belong does not show that those professors are engaged in subversive activities. All that such facts would show would be that these professors believed in some of the objects of the organizations."[29]

Nor did Hutchins know of any student who engaged in subversive activities. There were, he said, eleven members of the Communist Club, who might be sympathetic to Communism, but he failed to see "how the sympathetic feelings of ten or a dozen students at the University of Chicago can be a danger to the state." The students who protested the Broyles commission's proposals may have been impolite, said Hutchins, but "Rudeness and Redness are not the same." Indeed, Hutchins argued that the protesting students were "entirely right to disapprove of this pending legislation," since the proposals, in his opinion, were not only unnecessary and unconstitutional, but un-American, because they "aim at thought control." Hutchins was sure that there were enough laws on the books to punish those engaged in subversive acts without enacting laws to restrict free thought. Since the university fully supported the rights of professors to say whatever they wished and to join any organization they chose, the recitation of faculty members' Communist-front affiliations could not lead to reprisals, as it had at the University of Washington. Not willing to give up, State Senator Broyles proposed that tax exemption be withdrawn from the University of Chicago and Roosevelt College because of the continued presence of "undesirables." Not only did his proposals fail in the legislature, but his commission was discontinued. Far from gaining general support and intimidating would-be critics, Broyles was opposed by three of Chicago's four newspapers, by clergymen and labor unions, civic associations and the city bar association.[30]

The University of Chicago demonstrated that it was possible to rebuff political interference into the internal affairs of the university, but it was an example that many institutions were unwilling or unable to follow. The American Association of University Professors (AAUP) and the American Civil Liberties Union (ACLU) received a steady flow of complaints from faculty members who were discharged for their left-wing political activities, such as campaigning for Henry Wallace in 1948 (Wallace, a former vice-president, headed the left-wing Progressive party ticket) or signing an amnesty petition for the Communist party leaders convicted of violating the Smith Act (a 1940 law making it illegal to teach or advocate the violent overthrow of the United States government). Some institutions, seeking to placate critics or to ward off hostile investigations, imposed their own loyalty oaths, banned controversial speakers, and took other steps to avoid trouble.

Nonetheless, the pressure on educational institutions intensified in 1952 and 1953 when the Senate Internal Security Subcommittee (SISS) and the HCUA opened investigations of subversion in education, with SISS concentrating on New York City's public schools and municipal colleges and the House committee concentrating on Harvard and the Massachusetts Institute of Technology (MIT). Former party members who testified disagreed about whether Communists should be permitted to teach. Granville Hicks believed that "every member of the Communist Party is an actual or potential agent of the Soviet Union," but he contended that "you cannot protect all college students a hundred per cent. Some of them take to drink, and some of them take to Communism, and lots of other things happen to them, and there's nothing that anybody on God's earth can do that will look out for all college students. I think you have to say that is a risk you run." At the hearings of the two committees, nearly one hundred teachers invoked the Fifth Amendment and refused to testify when they were questioned about their relationship to the Communist party. The witnesses who "took the Fifth" did not protect themselves from opprobrium, since the press and inquiring congressmen presumed they had something to hide. Pleading the Fifth, however, prevented witnesses from being compelled by congressmen to "name names" of others involved in the Communist party.[31]

New York City's Board of Higher Education dealt swiftly with its recalcitrant professors by invoking a section of the city charter that permitted automatic dismissal of those who refused to testify in official inquiries. Other institutions fumbled toward a response to the presence of a "Fifth Amendment professor" on their faculty. Some, like New York University, Rutgers, and the University of Kansas City, dismissed them; others, like Harvard, MIT, and Cornell, suspended them without pay until state and federal charges against them were dropped.[32]

The academic world remained deeply divided, not only about how to deal with those who avoided answering questions about themselves or their associates, but about whether a Communist had the right to teach. Those on the political left split along lines that had developed during the 1930s, between those who were anti-Stalinist liberals and those who were convinced that attacks on Communists and fellow travelers endangered civil liberties. The first group, typified by men like Arthur Schlesinger, Jr., Roger Baldwin, Norman Thomas, George Counts, and Sidney Hook, insisted that it was not only possible but absolutely necessary for defenders of democratic principles to be both anti-Communist and anti-McCarthy. Others, however, like Alan Barth, Henry Steele Commager, Robert M. Hutchins, and Harold Taylor argued that all ideas and political associations should be protected, no matter how odious they might be. Each group claimed that the other was playing into the hands of the right-wing inquisitors.[33]

As the congressional investigations wore on, the AAUP continued to insist that neither refusal to testify nor membership in the Communist party was a sufficient ground for dismissal. "A teacher who misuses his classroom or other relationships with his students for propaganda purposes or for the advocacy of legally defined subversive action, or who in his extra-mural relationships is guilty of a legally defined subversive act," said the AAUP, violated professional standards or the law; but any disciplinary action must be based on evidence and must respect the principles of procedural due process.[34]

The view of most college presidents was expressed in a statement by the Association of American Universities in 1953. Thirty-seven major college presidents held that there must be no curb on academic freedom, but that membership in the Communist party, because of its principles and methods, "extinguishes the right to a university position." The principles of the party that the association found inimical to the search for knowledge were, first, the "fomenting of world-wide revolution"; second, the "use of falsehood and deceit as normal means of persuasion"; and third, "thought control—the dictation of doctrines which must be accepted and taught by all Party members." Regarding the question of those who took the Fifth Amendment, the association declared that the professor "owes his colleagues in the university complete candor and perfect integrity, precluding any kind of clandestine or conspiratorial activities. He owes equal candor to the public. If he is called upon to answer for his convictions, it is his duty as a citizen to speak out." Consequently, invoking the Fifth Amendment "places upon a professor a heavy burden of proof of his fitness to hold a teaching position and lays upon his university an obligation to re-examine his qualifications for membership in its society."[35]

The primary target of the SISS investigation of "Subversive Influence in the Educational Process" was the New York City public schools. In 1949, the New York State Legislature passed the Feinberg Law, which required school officials to certify the loyalty of every teacher. While the law proved cumbersome and inefficient, its passage spurred a systematic effort to remove Communist teachers. The anti-Communist drive centered on the New York Teachers Union, which had been kicked out of the AFT in 1940 and had been the object of a state subversive investigation in 1940/41. After its ouster from the AFT, the Teachers Union joined the United Public Workers, which was affiliated with the Congress of Industrial Organizations (CIO). In 1950, the CIO expelled the United Public Workers on grounds that it was Communist-dominated. Between 1950 and 1959, New York school officials used information supplied by informers and defectors to single out teachers for questioning about the Communist party; nearly two hundred resigned while under investigation, and another two hundred were dismissed for refusing to answer questions or for perjury in denying party membership.

The New York City Board of Education's vigorous antisubversive program was sanctioned by the United States Supreme Court's approval of the Feinberg Law in 1952. Speaking for the 6 to 3 majority, Justice Sherman Minton wrote that a teacher works in a sensitive area in a schoolroom. There he shapes the attitude of young minds toward the society in which they live. In this, the state has a vital concern. . . . That the school authorities have the right and the duty to screen the officials, teachers, and employees as to their fitness to maintain the integrity of the schools as a part of ordered society, cannot be doubted. One's associates, past and present, as well as one's conduct, may properly be considered in determining fitness and loyalty. From time immemorial, one's reputation has been determined in part by the company he keeps.

The school system's efforts to identify and oust Communist teachers received additional momentum as a consequence of the SISS hearings in 1952 and 1953, where the star witness was Bella Dodd, who told the Senate committee about her role as a link between the New York Teachers Union and the Communist party.[36]

There was never much likelihood that the congressional hearings would lead to legislation, the usual purpose of legislative investigations, since Congress had no control over the employment practices of schools, colleges, and universities. Their purpose has been described as "prescriptive publicity," that is, public exposure intended to instruct, to deter, to punish, and to destroy. It was expected that public identification of teachers who were Communists or unrepentant former Communists would cause them to be fired, and indeed this was usually true for those who refused to testify. In a political climate deeply affected by the war against Communist troops in Korea and by Senator Joseph McCarthy's inflammatory accusations of Communist infiltrations into vital areas of American society, there was little public sympathy for teachers who were fired for refusing to talk about their ties to the Communist party.[37]

In removing teachers believed to be Communist, educational institutions were responding both to immediate pressure from state and federal legislators and to a broad public consensus. A public opinion survey conducted for the Fund for the Republic in 1954 found that about 90 percent of a national sample believed that an admitted Communist teacher should be fired. Even among college professors, who were considerably more tolerant of unorthodoxy than the public, there was considerable opposition to Communist teachers. A poll of social science teachers, taken in 1955, revealed that 35 percent would permit a Communist to teach, 45 percent would not, and 20 percent were undecided. Nonetheless, many in the academic community believed that Communist teachers were less of a threat than misguided efforts to impose political conformity on teachers. One major study cited reports from college professors about colleagues who had been fired or passed over for promotion because of their political views, about pressure from administrators or the local community to stop using certain books or engaging in controversial political activities, about teachers accused of being Communists because of their views on race relations or other issues, about an atmosphere in which a significant minority worried that their opinions might imperil their job security.[38]

There was a significant gap between the perceptions of those within the academic world and those outside it. To those who were directly affected, who were questioned by the FBI or pressured to cooperate with the FBI or called before a congressional committee or fearful of expressing their views, there was an atmosphere of hysteria, a "witch hunt," a "Red scare," which endangered academic freedom and civil liberties. But according to the Fund for the Republic poll, the public did not perceive such a climate nor did it share the sense that basic liberties were in peril. And there was the rub, for only those who dealt in the realm of ideas and opinions recognized the danger of permitting government to monitor and regulate the acceptability of ideas and opinions.

The widely publicized congressional investigations confirmed the fears and suspicions of those who were unsettled by the rapid dislocations in American society since the 1930s. In a society where mobility and change and technological innovation were becoming the rule rather than the exception, where people puzzled about the apparent breakdown in traditional morality, the rise of juvenile delinquency, and the loss of something indefinable—whether it was called character or community spirit or respect for authority or religious faith—some people were quick to believe that Communists were responsible. The fact that the Communist party often operated in a clandestine fashion lent an air of plausibility to even the most implausible speculations. Whatever was new and undesirable could be attributed to Communist influence, and nowhere was this more true than in the schools. In communities where there had never been an equivalent of the New York Teachers Union, where no organized group of Communists had ever played an active part in the schools, the postwar "Red scare" added a sinister dimension to what otherwise might have been garden-variety controversies over curriculum, personnel, and policy.

The charge of "Communist" or "subversive," thrown into educational debates, was not only difficult to refute but tended to damage, and sometimes destroy, the reputation of its target. Educational changes, usually associated with progressive education, were frequently denounced in anti-Communist rhetoric. Did the schools eliminate grades and de-emphasize competition? If so, it was because the Communists wanted to weaken the moral fiber of America's children and undermine our ability to compete with the Soviet Union. Did textbooks debunk American heroes, stress the defects of American society, or fail to excoriate Soviet totalitarianism? If so, it was because the writers had been unduly influenced by leftist authors in the academic world. Did schools promote the United Nations too enthusiastically? If so, it was because of dark designs to undermine our national sovereignty and to advance the schemes of world federalists and Communist internationalists. Did young people seem to be of weak character, prone to juvenile delinquency, and lacking in patriotism? If so, it was because the schools had absorbed the "godless pragmatism" of John Dewey.

The oft-repeated assertion that progressive education (which was, by that time, the ascendant pedagogy in public education) was subversive became an idée fixe among a large number of groups and individuals, who undertook to save the schools from subversion by routing progressive educators, progressive policies, and "left-wing" textbooks from the schools. The claim, as one book was titled, that *Progressive Education is REDucation* rested largely on a spurious understanding of the radical period of the Frontier Thinkers. Those who believed that progressive education was radical and hostile to American institutions found copious documentation for their claims in the progressive works of the early 1930s. There was, for example, the oft-quoted statement by the American Historical Association's Commission on the Social Studies in 1934 that "The age of individualism and laissez faire in economy and government is closing and a new age of collectivism is emerging." And there were numerous damning quotes from George Counts's famous 1932 publication *Dare the School Build a New Social Order?*, calling on teachers to seize power, and from Harold Rugg's *The Great Technology* (1933), which sounded like a blueprint for a collectivist state.[39]

It was true that progressive educators had flirted with Marxism, had toyed with the notion of indoctrinating children, had advocated the reconstruction of society along collectivist lines, and had expressed in unambiguous terms their belief that schools should be used to prepare the way for a new, noncapitalist society. But it was also true—and this the aghast critics of 1950 did not know or would not believe—that by the end of the 1930s, all of the leading Frontier Thinkers had repudiated Marxism, Communism, indoctrination, and the other radicalisms of a radical age. Dewey was anathema to the Communist party for his role in exonerating Trotsky and for his persistent anti-Stalinist socialism; Rugg was one of the first Frontier Thinkers to disavow the Marxist class analysis of American society; Counts had led the anti-Communist forces in the AFT, and, additionally, had written a scathing indictment of Soviet totalitarianism in 1949 (*The Country of the Blind: The Soviet System of Mind Control*); and William Heard Kilpatrick had ridiculed the tenets of "High Marxism" at the height of the radical era. Yet regardless of what they had done or said in the intervening years, the early statements of the Frontier Thinkers were used repeatedly to pillory progressive education, with which they were closely associated. Thus, not only were the antiprogressives locked in debate without opponents on the other side, they did not understand that the radicalism of the Frontier Thinkers was a minor strand in the development of the progressive pedagogy. Nonetheless, the conviction that these men and these works had captured American education became unshakeable to those who believed in the progressive conspiracy.

The thesis was stated clearly in an article by John T. Flynn in the *Reader's Digest* in 1951. Flynn charged baldly that "a group of educators—not numerous but influential—has set out to introduce into the social-science courses of our high schools a seductive form of propaganda for collectivism—chiefly of that type which we call socialism." Their propaganda, he held, rested on three claims: "First, that our American system of private enterprise is a failure. Second, that our republic of limited powers is a mistake. Third, that our way of life must give way to a collectivist society in which the central State will own and operate, or plan and finance and control, the economic system." He cited what was by now the customary evidence, a string of quotes from the early writings of Counts and Rugg. The belief that a sinister, un-American plot had been unmasked and demonstrated to all who had eyes to see became undisputed doctrine among anti-Communist zealots. The theme that American education was being subverted by Communists and Socialists was publicized through the activities of such groups as Milo McDonald's American Education Association, Colonel Augustin Rudd's Guardians of American Education, Lucille Cardin Crain's *Educational Reviewer,* and Allen Zoll's National Council for American Education. Their attacks on suspect textbooks and progressive education were reinforced by the support of the politically potent American Legion and by the localized activities of militant groups like the Sons and Daughters of the American Revolution and the Minute Women. The best known of these organizations was Zoll's group, which supplied speakers (on subjects like "How Red is the Little Red Schoolhouse?") and pamphlets ("They Want Your Child" and "Progressive Education Increases Delinquency") to disgruntled community groups. In addition, Zoll published a periodical, the *Educational Guardian,* and disseminated critiques of "un-American" textbooks, as well as something called the

"Red-ucator Series," which listed the Communist-front affiliations of professors at leading colleges and universities.[40]

Egged on by the charges and insinuations of extremist propagandists, pressure groups in a number of communities demanded censorship of textbooks and library books and the ouster of "controversial" educators. Just how poisonous this politicization of public education could be was demonstrated in Houston, Texas, where control of the elected school board alternated between hostile factions, one made up of moderate liberals, the other of radical-right conservatives. The liberals (who did not necessarily favor either progressive education or racial integration) supported the federal school lunch program and professional control of the curriculum. The rightists, led by members of the extremist Minute Women, opposed federal aid, racial integration, the United Nations, "creeping socialism," and progressive education.

In 1940, the conservative school board banned Harold Rugg's social science textbooks. After the war, Frank Magruder's widely used textbook *American Government* was withdrawn (over the objections of the city's civics teachers) after it was attacked in the first issue of Crain's right-wing *Educational Reviewer*. The problem with the text, which had been approved for use in all forty-eight states, was that it contained a statement that "the postal system, power projects, and progressive taxes are bits of Socialism; and public free education and old age assistance are examples of Communism." Under radical-right control, books about Russia were removed from school libraries, a United Nations essay contest was withdrawn, and "controversial" teachers and administrators were ousted. Fearful of being denounced by vigilante groups or offending whichever bloc was in control, Houston's teachers learned to avoid doing or saying anything that might provoke criticism or attention. While there was never evidence of a single Communist in the school system, manipulation of the Communist issue put teachers, textbooks, and the curriculum at the mercy of radical-right pressure groups.[41]

The most celebrated school controversy occurred in Pasadena, California. In the spring of 1948, the Pasadena Board of Education hired Willard Goslin, the progressive superintendent of schools in Minneapolis, to be Pasadena's superintendent. Having established the "common learnings" program in the Minneapolis schools, Goslin was regarded as an outstanding administrator; the Minneapolis program did not become the subject of controversy until after Goslin had left for Pasadena. Goslin believed that he had an opportunity to build a model district, since Pasadena had had a progressive superintendent for the previous twenty years. What he did not anticipate was that a substantial segment within the community not only disliked progressive education but thought it was part of a far-flung Communist conspiracy to undermine the character of American youth.

Goslin did nothing that was not standard operating procedure for a progressive school administrator. Nonetheless, it was too much for a newly formed community group, the School Development Council, which complained bitterly that progressive education was ruining the schools; that the schools under Goslin were ignoring the fundamentals, eliminating grades, minimizing competition, and using textbooks that were "subversive in character." The council was appalled when Goslin invited the famous progressive educator, William Heard Kilpatrick of Teachers College, to lecture Pasadena teachers in a summer workshop and aghast when Goslin introduced curriculum materials about minority groups and planned to rezone racially isolated neighborhoods. Conservative parents heard Goslin's description of the school as a community center and himself as a community leader, and they envisaged a power-grab, undercutting parental authority and elected officials. They suspected school officials of using "group dynamics" techniques to steer parent opinion and to manipulate the outcome of meetings. The more they objected, and the more their objections were ignored, the more certain they became that the professionals were trying to put something over on the people.[42]

Two years after Goslin arrived, the voters of Pasadena turned out in record numbers to reject by a 2-to-1 margin a school tax increase; the election was generally considered a referendum on Goslin and progressive education. Six months after the election, the school board asked Goslin to resign. The uproar that followed Goslin's resignation brought national attention to Pasadena. A journalist wrote a book about the affair, called *This Happened in Pasadena,* which was widely reviewed as an object lesson about what happens when reactionary forces gang up on an enlightened superintendent. Progressives and liberals believed that the School Development Council of Pasadena was acting under instructions, or at least under the influence, of Allen Zoll, and the Pasadena story seemed to prove the dangers of outside agitators and smear techniques.[43]

From the other side, the Dilworth Committee of the California legislature, already well known for its interest in "un-American activities," conducted an investigation and demonstrated that California had no need of outside agitators. The committee pointed out that Kilpatrick belonged to several "Communist-front" organizations; that the authors of many books used in the Pasadena schools were members of "Communist-front" organizations; and that the school system's "controversial" methods of teaching (especially the elimination of grades and competition) were similar to those favored in Communist countries. The committee concluded that there was "no clear cut evidence of known subversives actually within the school system itself," but it did think that the school administration could do a better job of listening to parent and community opinion.[44]

In the end, progressives remained convinced that there was a well-financed, frightening plot to purge a reputable administrator and to destroy modern education, while the leaders of the School Development Council were equally convinced that there was a long-range, frightening plot by left-wing educators to take over the schools and build a collectivist social order. The progressives could not understand why anyone other than an ignoramus or a fascist would attack a program that represented the best professional thinking, and the local vigilantes could not understand how the traditional relationship between parents and educators had been reversed or why the progressive educators seemed to sneer at the three Rs. What happened in Pasadena revealed an extraordinary lack of understanding between professional educators and a significant number of the lay public; such controversies became entangled in the language of McCarthyism without being explained—on either side—by the ready charges of fascism and communism.

This kind of victory for the radical right, however, was far from typical, and it was invariably temporary. Goslin's opponents in Pasadena never gained control of the school board. In other communities, like Scarsdale and Port Washington, in New York, the demands of would-be censors were rejected. After Houston's ban of the Magruder book, the Texas State Board of Education renewed its adoption of the book for a six-year period as the only state-approved text, which meant that the Houston school district had to buy a different text out of its own funds. The propagandists of the radical right never achieved respectability; they were treated contemptously in national publications like *McCall's* and the *Saturday Review* and were attacked as fascistic bigots by national organizations like the National Education Association and the Anti-Defamation League of B'nai B'rith. Just as the publicists of the left fringe had found fertile territory for their ideas and theories in the Depression era, the alarmists of the right fringe discovered a receptive audience in the climate of the early 1950s. And in both periods, events changed the political atmosphere and effectively dissipated the constituency for the claims of the extremists.[45]

Dwight D. Eisenhower was elected president of the United States in 1952, when Senator Joseph McCarthy of Wisconsin—by now the national leader of the congressional search for subversives—was at the height of his demagogic powers. While Eisenhower purposely avoided confrontation with McCarthy, it was only a matter of time until the Republican administration realized that McCarthy's ruthless and reckless tactics had to be curbed, and until the Republicans in the Senate acknowledged that he had become an embarrassment to the party, the Senate, and the nation. In December 1954, the Senate voted to censure McCarthy, and almost overnight he was discredited as a national figure. The rapidity of his decline was due not just to the Senate's decisive rebuke, but to the disappearance of most of the sources of his influence. The end of the Korean war removed that emotional issue, and the election of a moderate, conservative Republican administration eroded the credibility of McCarthy's assertion that the administration was "soft on Communism." With Eisenhower as president, McCarthy could no longer feed upon and sustain an atmosphere of suspicion. The efforts to oust teachers suspected of Communist ties continued for a time in some school districts, but by the end of the 1950s the heresy hunters had been reduced to the obscure margins of American politics.

Even as the political system tried haltingly to resolve the competing claims of security and civil liberties, the U.S. Supreme Court began to strike down, one after another, the antisubversive laws that had given the states the power to inquire into the beliefs and associations of teachers. In 1952, the Supreme Court declared unconstitutional an Oklahoma loyalty oath that required teachers to swear that they had not belonged to a subversive organization during the past five years; the oath "offends due process," said the Court, because the teacher may have joined the "proscribed organization unaware of its activities and purposes."[46]

In other key decisions, the high court reversed the dismissal of a professor who had been fired after pleading the Fifth Amendment before a congressional committee, on grounds that he had been denied due process (1956); declared unconstitutional the section of New York City's charter that permitted the city to terminate employees who invoked the Fifth Amendment, also on grounds of violation of due process (1956); voided all state sedition laws, because they had been superseded by the federal Smith Act (1956); overturned New Hampshire's contempt citation against a Marxist professor who had refused to disclose the contents of a lecture, because it was "an invasion of the petitioner's liberties in areas of academic freedom and political expression" (1957); reversed an Arkansas statute that compelled teachers to file annually a list of organizations to which they had belonged or contributed during the past five years, because the statute interfered with the teachers' freedom of association (1960); invalidated a Florida statute requiring teachers to sign an oath that they had never aided the Communist party, because it was unconstitutionally vague and inhibited the exercise of freedoms protected by the Constitution (1961); declared unconstitutional a loyalty oath imposed by Arizona which subjected state employees to prosecution for knowingly belonging to the Communist party, because the oath "threatens the cherished freedom of association protected by the First Amendment" (1966); threw out New York State's Feinberg Law (overruling its own 1952 decision), because it was unconstitutionally vague (1967); and approved simple state loyalty oaths that were similar to those sworn to by other public officials (1967, 1971, 1972). Ironically, the decade of sustained efforts to place political restrictions on teachers led ultimately to the elimination of all state-imposed limitations on academic freedom and to the establishment of strong procedural safeguards for free expression.[47]

In the view of Robert Iversen, "the most important single consequence of American Communist activity in the field of education has been the massive retaliation it provoked." Other writers contend that the massive retaliation was the result of cold war hysteria, unrelated to any real threat presented by Communist teachers. There can be little doubt that those who defended the right of Communists to teach were in a small minority. At a time when Stalin was still dictator of the Soviet Union and when reports of his regime's brutality were fresh, there was no more sympathy for the right of a Communist to teach than there was for the right of a Nazi to teach. The price paid for finding present and former members of the Communist party was high: institutions were polarized, careers were destroyed, and communities were factionalized.[48]

The distinguished jurist Learned Hand warned education officials in New York State in 1952 that what was most in jeopardy was the cement, the mutual confidence, that holds the society together:

> Risk for risk, for myself I had rather take my chance that some traitors will escape detection than spread abroad a spirit of general suspicion and distrust. . . . I believe that that community is already in process of dissolution where each man begins to eye his neighbor as a possible enemy, where non-conformity with the accepted creed, political as well as religious, is a mark of disaffection; where denunciation, without specification or backing, takes the place of evidence; where orthodoxy chokes freedom of dissent; where faith in the eventual supremacy of reason has become so timid that we dare not enter our convictions in the open lists, to win or lose.[49]

The McCarthy era is appropriately remembered for its excesses, for the efforts by government to police ideas. But it should not be forgotten that these efforts ultimately failed and that freedom of dissent was never choked off. Fortunately, the state and federal governments had no direct power to impose their edicts, other than through the power of publicity. McCarthyism in its various manifestations was unequivocally denounced by journalists and scholars like Walter Gellhorn, Robert M. Hutchins, Arthur Schlesinger, Jr., Alan Barth, Edward Shils, Elmer Davis, Lawrence Chamberlain, Vern Countryman, Edward L. Barrett, Jr., Henry Steele Commager, James Wechsler, Murray Kempton, Telford Taylor, Carey McWilliams, Nathan Glazer, David Riesman, Daniel Bell, Richard Hofstadter, Robert MacIver, and Seymour Martin Lipset. At no time were the voices of McCarthyism's critics stilled.

As a result of the era, there was undoubtedly a dampening of student and faculty interest in social and political issues; Iversen believed that "Communist control of some student activities proved to be the kiss of death for politics on the campus." He wrongly predicted that "the political hyperactivity of the students of the Depression will probably never return." Because of their disinterest in protests and mass activities, the college students of the late 1950s were dubbed "the silent generation." It was not that they were intimidated, but that they came to political consciousness in an age that was weary of ideology, skeptical of utopias, and alert to ambivalence. Extremism, they learned early, was bad form; the right was discredited by the abuses of McCarthyism, and the left was discredited by its apologetics for Soviet totalitarianism, especially after the Soviet invasion of Hungary in 1956.[50]

Why had schools loomed so large as a target for antisubversive legislation and radical-right political activists? It was not because schools were especially rife with subversive activity; true, there were Communist teachers, but their numbers were never large, and their influence was negligible. Colleges and universities were vulnerable because they were, or were supposed to be, centers of unfettered, critical thinking, which naturally made them offensive to those who wanted to rein in unfettered, critical thinking. Schools were vulnerable because, in a time of frustration, there they were in every community, a public institution that was "get-at-able," an agency in which the power to educate might be construed as the power to indoctrinate. The knowledge that the Communist party often operated in secret, coupled with the fact that state and federal prosecutions were driving members of the Communist party underground, tended to arouse fear that the Communists could be anywhere, a fear that headline-seeking congressional investigators amplified. And there was, finally, the persistent uncertainty about whether schools were supposed to reflect the values of parents and society or to project a new set of values—different from those students brought with them. Those who saw the schools as the leading edge of social change believed that they could shape the values of children in ways that were broader, more humane, and more liberated than those of their parents; those who expected the school to respect parental and community values were appalled by the arrogance of educational theorists who presumed to impose their values on other people's children.

But in the end, it was not the schools that attracted the attackers, it was the attackers who sought out the schools. To weed out controversial books and teachers and speakers was an effort to control the present and to direct the future; it was a way of doing something to stave off the Communist menace that was advancing in other parts of the world; it was a way of saying no to the progressive forces that had dominated Washington and the education profession for a generation. For a time there was a powerful national consensus that supported the right of government to inquire into the individual's ideas, opinions, and associations—past and present. All that stood between government and the individual educator was, first, an unwritten set of principles called academic freedom, which was an unreliable shield since it depended on conscience rather than power; and second, a pluralistic political structure that restricted Congress's ability to impose its will on private and public educational institutions. When the rage for conformity ended, it was like a fever that broke, taking with it the other symptoms of illness as well. Like McCarthy, all of the others who had briefly held center stage disappeared, along with their crusade to purify American education of its political and ideological errors.

CHAPTER 4

Race and Education: The *Brown* Decision

W HILE some issues in American education waxed and waned, like interest in methods of instruction, and other issues flared and dissipated, like the fear of subversion, the problem of racial inequality in education grew in significance with each passing year. With the success of the legal attack on school segregation in 1954, the process of dismantling the segregated structures and of transforming racial attitudes was set in motion, a process that moved slowly, fitfully, sometimes violently, and continued for decades. For a long time the clear and unambiguous goal of the civil rights movement was to make America a color-blind society, to remove the race line from American law and life, to establish once and for all that each person is equal as a citizen and an individual, regardless of race, religion, or national origin. Yet after formal segregation and legalized discrimination were abolished, massive problems remained, a legacy of years of racial inequality. In time, the pursuit of color-blindness came to be characterized not as a noble goal, but as racism in a new form. Efforts to right the wrongs of history thrust the racial issue into the midst of such decisions as how schools are funded, how teachers are trained and hired, how school officials are promoted, how educational progress is assessed, and how students are assigned to school. A wrong so many generations in the making was not to be undone easily or quickly.

White southerners liked to say that there were not enough troops anywhere in the world to make the South give up its segregated way of life. The southern way of life may have been incomprehensible to critical outsiders, but it was solidly entrenched in the folkways, mores, customs, and manners of the South. The southern way of life was at one and the same time enormously simple and enormously complicated: simple in that it was firmly grounded in the notion of the superiority of the white race and the subservience of the Negro race, and complicated in that it was practiced through elaborate, usually unwritten rules of behavior and etiquette. State and local laws segregated the races in schools, hospitals, transportation, hotels, theaters, and in most other public and private facilities, and absolutely banned marriage between whites and nonwhites; unwritten but well-understood race etiquette prescribed the deference that black people were expected to show to white people, such as entering a white person's home only through the back door or stepping off the curb to let a white person pass. White southerners believed that theirs was a biracial culture, that whites and blacks were each evolving in their own way, and that this was best for both races. But the relationship was decidedly asymmetrical, for whites controlled all the instruments of public power and almost all of the instruments of private power as well. Not necessarily through state law, but certainly through state action, Negroes were disenfranchised and thereby left politically powerless; they were systematically excluded from jury duty; they lived in neighborhoods that were last to get paved roads, lights, sewers, and other public amenities; they went to schools with shorter terms and poorer facilities than those attended by whites; they were vulnerable to the whims of lawless whites, who could enlist the support of white police, white juries, and white prosecutors.

The essence of racism was the belief that differences in skin color represented real and substantial differences among people; that "whites" and "Negroes" were essentially different kinds of people; and that people who were "Negro" or "white" should be dealt with by the state as group members rather than as individuals. To give legal meaning to racism, southern state laws contained various definitions of "Negro," such as Arkansas's declaration that a Negro is "any person who has in his or her veins any Negro blood whatever," or Alabama's explanation that "the word 'mulatto' or the term 'person of color' means a person of mixed blood descended on the part of the father or mother from Negro ancestors, without reference to or limit of time or number of generations removed." Black people were at the bottom of a system that was designed to keep them there, and the likelihood of upending this system must have seemed as unlikely as a summer snowstorm in Mississippi.[1]

Yet two unusually keen observers sensed during the Second World War that something new was percolating inside the system and that the old order was rumbling and creaking. Howard Odum, a southern sociologist, captured a sense of the regional mood by collecting rumors that had become widespread among southern whites during 1942. A crisis was building, Odum observed, and evidence of it was to be found in the tensions, violence, conflict, riots, and fears that infected relations between the races, North and South. He described "an almost universal assumption on the part of the rest of the Nation that 'something must be done about' the South's treatment of the Negro," and an almost universal southern determination to resist any interference in its traditional folkways. Among the "flood of rumors and stories" that spread across the South, four were typical: the rumor that the Negroes would "take over" when the war was over, often expressed in conjunction with the fear that black soldiers would return with dangerous aspirations and knowledge of weaponry; the rumor that Negro men intended to "take over" the white women while the white southerners were away at war; the rumor that blacks were stockpiling weapons, such as icepicks, to seize power at a propitious moment; the rumor that Negro domestics, inspired by the egalitarian ways of Mrs. Roosevelt, had joined "Eleanor Clubs," had become "uppity" and demanding, and had adopted as their motto the pledge that white women would be back in the kitchen by Christmas 1942 or 1943.[2]

Behind the rumors, said Odum, was a changing situation: the availability of jobs in defense industries and at military bases in the South had created a scarcity of black labor, even of domestic help; the atmosphere engendered by the war itself, with the constant reiteration of brotherhood and democracy, must have heightened the southerner's guilty defensiveness and uneasiness, making him quicker to find fault with black people, thereby justifying whatever was done to blacks to keep them in their place. And beneath the fears of a Negro uprising, the rumors of black men "taking over" and of black women who were suddenly verbally rebellious, was the tacit admission that whites sensed a loss of control, a loosening of the tight reins that had traditionally held black people in check. Blacks were restless, Odum observed, and whites were uneasy; but the potential for trouble lay in the fact that while blacks were changing in their attitudes and expectations, whites were apparently becoming more defensive, more determined to hold onto things as they were without giving ground.

Gunnar Myrdal, in his classic *An American Dilemma,* also saw changes in the making that were of enormous significance to the status of the Negro. The labor shortages induced by the war economy gave black workers an opportunity to get a foothold in industries where they had previously been excluded; President Roosevelt's fair employment practices order, issued in 1941, not only banned discrimination in defense industries and created an agency to investigate complaints of discrimination, but represented *"the most definite break in the tradition of federal unconcernedness about racial discrimination"* in the economy. Nor could one minimize the effect of war propaganda in revitalizing American ideals, for Myrdal felt certain that the blacks' greatest opportunity for justice lay in exposing the gulf between what he called the American creed—which extols freedom, opportunity, justice, equality, and liberty—and the commonplace practices of racial prejudice and segregation. Myrdal believed that the long trends of history were moving inexorably toward eliminating racial discrimination, which was nothing less than "the survivals in modern American society of the slavery institution."[3]

Several trends persuaded Myrdal that the "dilemma"—the conflict between America's ideals and its practices—was moving toward a favorable resolution. Since the tradition of government noninterference in the economy had been broken during the New Deal, and on an even larger scale during the war, he predicted that government planning would continue when the war was over and that this would benefit the Negro: "As time goes on," he foresaw, "it will become more and more apparent that either the Negro will have to be cared for as a more or less permanent relief client or positive measures must be taken for his integration into the regular economy." Myrdal saw, too, as few Americans did, that "the whole unique political system" of the South, based on its disenfranchisement of the Negro, was "increasingly shaky" and was dependent "mainly on illegal measures." Racism as a political ideology had been stripped of any intellectual legitimacy by advances in social science. As industrialization and urbanization combined to integrate the South into the national culture, its racial ideology would not survive. Still, like Odum, Myrdal had to admit that white southerners "do not see the handwriting on the wall. They do not study the impending changes; they live again in the pathetic illusion that the matter is settled. They do not care to have any constructive policies to meet the trends." The white South had its collective head in the sand, but the social forces bringing change would continue to move nonetheless.[4]

For the southern system of rigid racial segregation to persist, several conditions were necessary: whites had to continue to control the political process; blacks had to continue to believe that the system would never change and that to challenge it was not only futile but dangerous; and blacks had to be isolated as much as possible from those who were opposed to the status quo. The laws and practices of the southern states were intended to protect this situation, to keep blacks from participating in the political process and to suppress the voices and agencies that advocated racial equality.

But the South could not wall out the social and economic forces that were moving through the nation at midcentury. As industrialization came to the south and the need for farm labor declined, blacks left the rural areas, where they were easily controlled and where their access to information was limited, and moved to the cities in search of jobs. In the cities, there were better schools than those they left behind, as well as black newspapers and sometimes even liberal white newspapers (as in Little Rock, Louisville, and Atlanta). Readers of the black press learned of the growing tempo of protest activities by organizations like the National Association for the Advancement of Colored People (NAACP) and the National Urban League. After the war, the number of whites who agitated against racial discrimination increased, and—as Myrdal had predicted— racism had become an embarrassment that no representative national organization would endorse and that some, like the President's Commission on Higher Education and the President's Committee on Civil Rights, vigorously denounced.

Ironically, the South's own efforts to maintain its peculiar system of biracialism planted the most vigorous seeds of the system's destruction, for the segregated Negro schools of the South, however unequal they were, did eventually produce high school graduates, then college graduates, then a small and discontented group of professionals. As the number of educated Negroes expanded, as black aspirations grew, the limits imposed by the segregated system became increasingly intolerable. The very schools meant to contain Negroes produced not only a demand for graduate education (which was rarely available in segregated states) but trained the black leaders who conducted the fight against the segregated system. To maintain the fiction of "separate equality," the South had to provide literacy, and literacy proved to be subversive of segregation, for it provided access to new information and ideas which could not be controlled by the segregationists. The technological expansion of the national media meant that ideas hostile to racism would regularly enter the South via magazines, radio, television, movies, and books; the rising level of black literacy meant that blacks could not be isolated from the national culture. It was also significant that white educational levels were rising, for in all parts of the country, rising education was associated with declining prejudice and with awareness of the discrediting of racist ideology.

But even with all of the positive social and economic forces at work, there remained an enigma: How was segregation to be broken if the white South held all the levers of power and was adamantly opposed to yielding? How would the institutions of American society change? What would break the political impasse? Certainly, Congress would not initiate any departure from the past, in view of the power and seniority of southern congressmen, most of whom were elected by virtually all-white constituencies. State legislatures in the South, which determined voting qualifications, were dominated not only by whites but by rural whites who were entirely unsympathetic to any effort to democratize the political process. Not even the president could get the Congress to move on civil rights proposals, as Truman's unsuccessful efforts in the late 1940s showed.

There was an avenue, however, through which the advocates of equal rights for blacks could press their cause: the judiciary. It was altogether fitting that this was so, for it was the Supreme Court that had permitted the erosion of the rights of blacks during the last three decades of the nineteenth century. Beginning in 1873, the Supreme Court had invalidated the civil rights legislation of the Reconstruction-era Congresses and reinterpreted the post–Civil War amendments to the Constitution in ways that denied that their purpose was to guarantee the full citizenship of blacks. As a result of Supreme Court decisions, the southern states were able to ignore the egalitarian intent of the Reconstruction era amendments; white supremacy was restored in the former slave states, blacks were removed from the voting rolls, and Jim Crow laws were passed to maintain strict segregation of the races. The culmination of this process was the Supreme Court's *Plessy* v. *Ferguson* decision in 1896, which upheld the constitutionality of a Louisiana law segregating rail passengers by race. Eight of the Court's nine justices reasoned that so long as the facilities available to the two races were equal, there was nothing wrong with racial separation. If colored persons believed that "enforced separation of the two races stamps the colored race with a badge of inferiority," the majority held, "it is not by reason of anything found in the act, but solely because the colored race chooses to put that construction upon it."[5]

Only Justice John Marshall Harlan dissented from the *Plessy* decision, and his dissent was for many decades a rallying-cry for the civil rights movement. Harlan denied that the states had the power to regulate their citizens solely on the basis of race: "In respect of civil rights, common to all citizens, the Constitution of the United States does not, I think, permit any public authority to know the race of those entitled to be protected in the enjoyment of such rights." The Reconstruction amendments to the Constitution, he held, "removed the race line from our governmental systems." In what was destined to be the most famous passage of his dissent, Harlan protested that the regulation of citizens solely on the basis of their race was repugnant to the Constitution:

> in view of the Constitution, in the eye of the law, there is in this country no superior dominant, ruling class of citizens. There is no caste here. Our Constitution is color-blind, and neither knows nor tolerates classes among citizens. In respect of civil rights, all citizens are equal before the law. The humblest is the peer of the most powerful. The law regards man as man, and takes no account of his surroundings or of his color when his civil rights as guaranteed by the supreme law of the land are involved.

The principle of "separate but equal," validated by the Supreme Court in the *Plessy* decision, stood as the law of the land for more than half a century. Thus it was the Supreme Court that sanctioned the principle of racial segregation in the law and daily life of the southern states, as well as in many areas beyond the South.

The legal strategists of the interracial NAACP steadily chipped away at the edifice of segregation during the 1930s and 1940s, winning cases that involved such issues as the exclusion of Negroes from juries, the equalization of the salaries of white and black teachers, the denial of Negroes' right to vote, the use of racially restrictive covenants in housing, and segregation in interstate bus travel. Yet no one of these decisions served as a sweeping and irresistible commandment to end segregation, because the *Plessy* principle of "separate but equal" remained in force. States that wanted to keep blacks from voting proved ingenious in substituting new schemes for those that were invalidated by the courts. It was not a single law that had to be overthrown; it was a way of life, and governmental compulsion of racial segregation was its bedrock.

In the early 1930s, the NAACP developed a coordinated legal campaign against school segregation. Instead of taking up miscellaneous cases as they emerged, the association began to follow a carefully planned effort to create a body of legal precedent, steadily undermining the validity of the "separate but equal" principle in education. The principle itself provided its enemies with ammunition to assail it, for the states that maintained segregated schools were supposed to offer equal provisions for both races, in conformity with the *Plessy* holding. But despite the asserted commitment to separate equality, the dual school systems in the southern states were grossly unequal; while the extent of disparity varied from state to state, and from year to year, the educational opportunities available to white students were markedly superior to those available to black students. In schools for whites, more public funds were spent, school terms were longer, teachers were better paid and usually better prepared, and more was expended on physical facilities than in schools for blacks. In South Carolina, one of the states where racial inequality was greatest, the number of white and black students was nearly equal in 1945, but the state spent nearly three times as much for each white pupil as for each black pupil; the value of white school property was six times the value of black school property; and the state spent 1/100 as much transporting black pupils to school as it did transporting white pupils. Unfair as this division of public funds was, it represented a decided advance over the comparative statistics for 1930, when South Carolina spent eight times as much for whites as for blacks. Still more egregious was the division of funds in Mississippi, where in 1945 the state spent 4½ times as much for each white student as for each black student, also an advance, since the adverse ratio in 1929 had been 9 to 1. Even federal funds allocated to the states for vocational education and teacher training were apportioned inequitably between white and black schools: blacks, who were 21.4 percent of the pupil population in states with segregated systems, received only 9.8 percent of federal dollars in the mid-1930s. To the fundamental inequity in distribution of public resources were added the casual insults implicit in a racist system, for example, black schools were supplied with the used textbooks discarded by white schools.[6]

In higher education, opportunities for black students were limited; white students had five times as many colleges to choose from, and white colleges offered a richer curriculum and were more likely to be accredited than black colleges. The availability of graduate and professional education was severely restricted for black students: no Negro institution offered work leading to the Ph.D.; only two Negro institutions (Howard University and Meharry in Nashville) offered medical training; graduate training in engineering and architecture was not available in any southern Negro institution; while white students could study dentistry, law, pharmacy, and library science in a large number of public and private universities, professional programs for Negro students existed in only one or two institutions in the entire South.[7]

The legal campaign to abolish segregation began with suits seeking the admission of qualified black students to public graduate and professional schools. The decision to concentrate at this educational level had several strategic advantages. First of all, the inequality was clear-cut and undeniable, since most southern states offered graduate and professional programs for white students but none at all for Negroes. The number of students involved was small, thus presumably presenting less of a threat initially to segregationists than a frontal attack on elementary and secondary schools. The students were mature and college-educated, which dramatized the arbitrariness of excluding them on racial grounds from a state-supported institution of higher education. The *Plessy* doctrine's guarantee of equal treatment opened the way for the NAACP's line of argument.

In the first major trial of this strategy, the NAACP represented Lloyd Lionel Gaines, a black resident of St. Louis who sought admission to the University of Missouri Law School. Gaines, a graduate of Lincoln University, a public black college in Missouri, was rejected by the all-white state law school and advised either to apply to Lincoln, in which case the state would create a new law school for blacks, or to an out-of-state law school, for which the state of Missouri would provide tuition assistance. Gaines's NAACP attorneys argued that the state was obligated under the "separate but equal" rubric to provide him with educational opportunities equal to those provided for whites. Missouri's promise to build a new law school or to provide an out-of-state scholarship was not equal treatment, as called for under the *Plessy* doctrine. In 1938, in a 6-to-2 decision, the Supreme Court agreed. It concluded that the validity of segregation laws "rests wholly upon the equality of the privileges which the laws give to the separated groups within the State." But Missouri had created a privilege for white law students that was denied to Negroes. "The white resident is afforded legal education within the State; the Negro resident having the same qualifications is refused it there and must go outside of the State to obtain it." The plaintiff was entitled to admission to the state law school; although Gaines never enrolled and failed to test his victory, what was significant was the legal precedent established.[8]

The attack was renewed after the war, when Ada Lois Sipuel, a graduate of Oklahoma's State College for Negroes, was rejected by the all-white University of Oklahoma Law School and told to wait until the state had built a law school for Negroes. In arguing Sipuel's right to admission, the NAACP forcefully insisted that "Classifications and distinctions based on race or color have no moral or legal validity in our society." The Supreme Court, while not yet ready to agree with the NAACP that segregation was inherently inconsistent with equality, declared in 1948 that Oklahoma, to conform with the equal protection clause of the Fourteenth Amendment, must provide Sipuel with a legal education "as soon as it does for applicants of any other group." The state lost no time in setting up a makeshift law school for Negro students, and the Supreme Court refused to consider whether Oklahoma's response failed to meet the constitutional standard of equality.[9]

Two years later, the Supreme Court ruled on two additional challenges to segregation in professional and graduate education. Heman M. Sweatt, a black letter-carrier, applied for admission to the all-white University of Texas Law School and was, of course, rejected. The state hastily established a new black law school to show that it had complied with the "separate but equal" mandate; the new law school opened with a part-time faculty of three, three classrooms, and one student: Heman M. Sweatt. The question put to the Supreme Court, which it had ducked in the Sipuel case, was whether such an arrangement amounted to equal treatment, when blacks were not allowed to enter the state's major, recognized law school and were eligible only to attend a new, quickly contrived law school. At the same time, the case of George W. McLaurin reached the Supreme Court. McLaurin, a sixty-eight-year-old educator, applied for entry as a doctoral student in the University of Oklahoma graduate school of education. A federal court ordered his admission, but after his enrollment, he was segregated from other students within the university, whether in the classroom, library, or cafeteria.[10]

With these cases, the issue was sharply drawn. The state of Texas pledged to build a Negro law school for Sweatt that would be the equal of the one available to whites at the University of Texas, but the two law schools clearly would not be "equal" in any meaningful sense. McLaurin had access to all the same facilities and books as whites in his program, but he was cordoned off and treated differently from white students. The action of the state, in both instances, was based solely on the race of the student. The NAACP zeroed in on the indefensibility of racial classifications in a democratic society. In both the Sweatt and McLaurin cases, the NAACP insisted that classification by race was unreasonable and irrational. Not only did the NAACP gain the support for the first time of the Justice Department, which filed an amicus brief in the two cases, but its position also was resoundingly endorsed in an amicus brief by the Committee of Law Teachers Against Segregation. Drafted by Yale professor Thomas Emerson and signed by 187 law professors, the brief stated the case against racial classifications unambiguously:

> Laws which give equal protection are those which make no *discrimination* because of race in the sense that they make no *distinction* because of race. As soon as laws make a right or responsibility dependent solely on race, they

violate the 14th amendment. Reasonable classifications may be made, but one basis of classification is completely precluded; for the Equal Protection Clause makes racial classifications unreasonable per se.[11]

The Supreme Court avoided deciding whether segregation and the policy of classifying citizens by race was unconstitutional, but ruled unanimously in favor of both Sweatt and McLaurin. The University of Oklahoma was ordered to remove all state-imposed restrictions for they handicapped George McLaurin "in his pursuit of effective graduate education," making it difficult for him to study, to engage in interchange with his fellow students, and to learn his profession. On the same day in 1950, the Supreme Court ordered the University of Texas Law School to admit Heman Sweatt, because the state did not offer "substantial equality" to white and Negro law students. Aside from the measurable differences between the university law school and the law school created for Sweatt and other black students, the University of Texas Law School "possesses to a far greater degree those qualities which are incapable of objective measurement but which make for greatness in a law school." These intangibles include "reputation of the faculty, experience of the administration, position and influence of the alumni, standing in the community, traditions and prestige. It is difficult to believe that one who had a free choice between these law schools would consider the question close." The *Sweatt* and *McLaurin* decisions signaled clearly that the Supreme Court intended to take the "equal" half of the "separate but equal" formula seriously, so seriously that it was doubtful whether any segregated institution of higher education could pass its muster.

Buttressed by the unanimous *Sweatt* and *McLaurin* decisions, the NAACP mounted a direct challenge to state-enforced segregation in elementary and secondary schooling. In 1952 and 1953, the Supreme Court heard challenges to segregation laws in Kansas, South Carolina, Delaware, Virginia, and the District of Columbia, a group of cases known collectively as *Brown* v. *Board of Education* (the title of the case from Topeka, Kansas). The verdicts against segregation in graduate education did not cause white southern leaders to reexamine their course or to prepare for the possibility of a decision against school segregation. As Myrdal and Odum had observed earlier, the white South seemed determined to prevent change by ignoring it. White southerners did not believe that the Supreme Court would overturn laws that affected the daily lives of nearly half the nation. Their lawyers insisted that the *Plessy* decision had settled the matter of segregation for all time and that the Supreme Court would not abrogate the states' traditional power to control their educational affairs. Spokesmen for the white South pointed proudly to the strides made in recent years toward upgrading black school systems, which suggested, if not a bad conscience, at least a recognition that the courts might not continue to tolerate separate and unequal schools.

The NAACP attack on school segregation, then compulsory in seventeen states and permitted in four others, was based on one overriding principle: that the use of racial classifications was forbidden by the Fourteenth Amendment. The NAACP brief eloquently recited the history of the egalitarian tradition in the United States, which was defined as dedication to the belief that the Constitution is (as Justice Harlan had written in 1896) color-blind, that every citizen is equal before the law regardless of race, color, creed, or national origin. Basic to the egalitarian tradition was the concept that each person should be dealt with as an individual, not as a group member. Speaking for the plaintiffs, Robert L. Carter told the Supreme Court: "We have one fundamental contention which we will seek to develop in the course of this argument, and that contention is that no state has any authority under the equal protection clause of the Fourteenth Amendment to use race as a factor in affording educational opportunities among its citizens." Similarly, Thurgood Marshall argued "that there were no recognizable differences from a racial standpoint between children," and that it was unreasonable for states to classify people on the basis of their race or ancestry.[12]

When the lawyers for the South stressed the long line of decisions upholding the *Plessy* rule of "separate but equal," the lawyers for the NAACP countered by stressing the numerous decisions in which the Supreme Court had invalidated racial classifications in areas such as jury service, property occupancy, voting, employment, and graduate education. The chief argument against *Plessy* was that "the Fourteenth Amendment precludes a state from imposing distinctions or classifications based upon race and color alone." The state, said the civil rights lawyers, may "confer benefits or impose disabilities upon selected groups of citizens," but the selection of such groups must be reasonable and related to real differences; clearly, distinctions based solely on race and color were "patently the epitome of that arbitrariness and capriciousness constitutionally impermissible under our system of government. A racial criterion is a constitutional irrelevance. . . . " There was no ambiguity in the NAACP view that the Fourteenth Amendment absolutely prohibits any state action based on race and color and "compels the states to be color blind in exercising their power and authority."[13]

125

Lawyers for the plaintiffs enlisted the support of social scientists to support their charge that state-imposed racial segregation damaged the social and psychological development of black children. While the constitutional appeal of the lawyers rested unequivocally on the color-blind principle, the social science testimony on behalf of the Negro plaintiffs contained a double-edged argument whose inner contradiction was not then apparent. Some social scientists testified that racial differences were meaningless, that white and Negro children learn in the same manner, and that there was no rational or scientific justification for classifying children by race; nor was it even clear that conventional definitions of race were reasonable, since so much intermixture had already taken place. They argued further that harm was done to children when they were denied access to some public schools solely because of their race and sent to a school that was open only to others of the same race. This was the thrust of a statement endorsed by thirty-two prominent social scientists, who defined segregation as "that restriction of opportunities for different types of associations between the members of one racial, religious, national or geographic origin, or linguistic group and those of other groups, which results from or is supported by the action of any official body or agency representing some branch of government. We are not here concerned with such segregation as arises from the free movements of individuals which are neither enforced nor supported by official bodies. . . . " But other social scientists testified that the harm to minority children was caused by the absence of interracial contact, by lack of exposure to majority group children. The first strand of social science testimony supported the color-blind principle, while the second pointed to the necessity of interracial schooling. In the difference between these two conflicting interpretations of desegregation lay the ingredients of future controversy, for the first implied that the abolition of segregation could be achieved by forbidding all state-imposed racial classifications, while the second contended that segregation must be replaced by integration, the mixing in classrooms of children of differing races, which might *require* racial classification.[14]

Perhaps because the potential conflict between these understandings was not apparent, the lawyers spoke in terms of making government color-blind but assumed that integration would follow the barring of racial classification by the state. The lawyers were not concerned about the proportion of blacks and whites in the same school, so long as the states ceased coercing black children to go to segregated schools. When Justice Felix Frankfurter asked Thurgood Marshall, the chief counsel for the NAACP's Legal Defense Fund, "to spell out in concrete what would happen" if the Court ruled in his favor, Marshall said:

I think, sir, that the decree would be entered which would enjoin the school officials from, one, enforcing the statute; two, from segregating on the basis of race or color. Then I think whatever district lines they draw, if it can be shown that those lines are drawn on the basis of race or color, then I think they would violate the injunction. If the lines are drawn on a natural basis, without regard to race or color, then I think that nobody would have any complaint.

Similarly, when Spottswood W. Robinson, III, counsel for the Virginia plaintiffs, was asked to describe the remedy he envisioned, he responded, "what you do is, you simply make all the facilities in the county available to all the pupils, without restriction or assignment to particular schools on the basis of race." It was Marshall who made the most conclusive statement about the constitutional issue before the Court. He firmly insisted that the Fourteenth Amendment deprived the state "of any power to make any racial classification in any governmental field." Racial distinctions in the law, he said, were "invidious," "odious," "suspect," and "irrational," because there were no real differences between people whose skin color was not the same.[15]

The Supreme Court ruled unanimously for the Negro plaintiffs on May 17, 1954, declaring state-imposed racial segregation in the public schools unconstitutional. Education had become so important in modern society, wrote Chief Justice Earl Warren, that "it is doubtful that any child may reasonably be expected to succeed in life if he is denied the opportunity of an education. Such an opportunity, where the state has undertaken to provide it, is a right which must be made available to all on equal terms." Even when physical facilities and other tangible factors are equal, said the Court, segregation in public schools solely on the basis of race deprives the minority group children of equal educational opportunity. The Court concluded that "in the field of public education the doctrine of 'separate but equal' has no place. Separate educational facilities are inherently unequal."[16]

The decision, ever after known as "the *Brown* decision," was a historic affirmation of the egalitarian ideals of American society. Though the verdict was entirely consonant with the line of decisions that followed the *Gaines* case in 1938, it was nonetheless startling in its implications. Never before had the Supreme Court reached so deeply into the lives, laws, and mores of so many people; nearly half the states of the nation were living according to laws that the Court had ruled unconstitutional. Approximately 40 percent of the public school pupils in the nation were enrolled in segregated systems. While the ruling was hailed throughout the North, described as inevitable by liberal southern newspapers, and received contemptuously by Deep South politicians, no one knew for sure what it would mean or how it would be implemented. Since the Court issued no decree, but invited the lawyers on both sides to return to discuss how the decision should be implemented, it was not clear how or when compliance would occur.

A year before the decision was announced, the Court asked the competing lawyers to present their views on the nature of a decree abolishing segregation. One of the questions posed by the Court suggested the range of remedies under consideration: "Assuming . . . that segregation in public schools violates the Fourteenth Amendment," asked the Court, "(a) would a decree necessarily follow that, within the limits set by normal geographic school districting, Negro children should forthwith be admitted to schools of their choice, or (b) may this Court, in the exercise of its equity powers, permit an effective gradual adjustment to be brought about from existing segregated systems to a system not based on color distinctions?" Both in their brief and in later arguments, the civil rights lawyers appealed for a decree to admit the plaintiffs "forthwith to public schools without distinction as to race or color"; they argued that the rights acknowledged by the decision should be "personal and present," applying to the plaintiffs as individuals. Lawyers for the South argued that time, flexibility, and patience were needed to permit the districts to adjust to the new situation.[17]

On May 31, 1955, the Court issued what was known as *Brown II*, which was generally interpreted as a victory for the South, since it left the implementation of desegregation to local school authorities, subject to the supervision of federal district judges. The lower courts were directed to require local school boards to make "a prompt and reasonable start toward full compliance" and to enter whatever decrees were necessary "to admit to public schools on a racially nondiscriminatory basis with all deliberate speed the parties to these cases."[18]

Despite the Court's effort to placate the South by deferring the right of the black plaintiffs to be admitted at once to desegregated schools, the *Brown* decision was nonetheless vehemently denounced by southern leaders as an unprecedented, tyrannical exercise of judicial power; demagogic accusations of Communist subversion, as well as fruitless demands to impeach Chief Justice Earl Warren and several of his colleagues, filled the air. In the heat of the moment, there was a tendency to regard the decision either as a monumental usurpation of states' rights or as a moral command of breath-taking eloquence. But there were also, in muted tones, friendly critics who voiced principled concerns while welcoming the decision. Their questions and doubts survived long after the shouts of the demagogues had died away and presaged problems that would remain to plague the effectuation of the decision.

First, there was concern about the failure of the Court to issue a firm decree implementing desegregation. By permitting school boards to move with "all deliberate speed," instead of directing them to acknowledge the "personal and present" right of the plaintiffs to a nonsegregated education, as the lawyers for the NAACP had urged, the Court placed in the hands of those who operated segregated schools the decision about when to phase out their unconstitutional practices and guaranteed that the process of desegregation would drag on for many years. In the higher education cases, the Court had ordered the universities forthwith to admit the plaintiffs or to cease discriminating against them once admitted. The introduction of the "all deliberate speed" formula denied the plaintiffs the immediate relief from discrimination to which they were entitled. In effect, the Court dealt with the plaintiffs as representatives of a group—Negroes—rather than as individuals whose rights had been denied. The Court seemed to agree with the southern lawyers that the South would not tolerate immediate desegregation. However, even the NAACP lawyers, at the time, doubted that the Court could have compelled the South's cooperation. Robert L. Carter and Thurgood Marshall observed that the Court's failure to impose a time limit for compliance probably would make little difference, for they expected that some border states would comply regardless of the Court's formula and a few others would follow after some pressure was applied, while the bitter-end stalwarts of the Deep South—like Georgia, Alabama, and Mississippi—would desegregate only "after a long and bitter fight, the brunt of which will have to be borne by Negroes." And this would have been the case, they believed, "no matter what kind of decision the Court had handed down." Perhaps the Court feared that a direct decree would be ignored or provoke violent resistance; surely, the high court in the 1950s was not so accustomed to imposing unpopular decisions as it later became. Yet it remains challenging to speculate what would have happened if the Court had required the defendant school districts to admit Negro children "to schools of their choice," instead of deciding to "permit an effective gradual adjustment . . . to a system not based on color distinctions."[19]

Second, the decision was criticized for its reliance on sociological and psychological evidence. Edmond Cahn of New York University School of Law worried that the prominent role of sociological evidence in the outcome of the case was dangerous because he "would not have the Constitutional rights of Negroes—or of other Americans—rest on any such flimsy foundation as some of the scientific demonstrations in these records."

Cahn pointed specifically to Kenneth B. Clark's famous doll study, in which black children were offered a choice between white and colored dolls; the results, Cahn complained, seemed predetermined: "For example, if Negro children say a *brown* doll is like themselves, he infers that segregation has made them conscious of race; yet if they say a *white* doll is like themselves, he infers that segregation has forced them to evade reality."[20]

In a related vein, Herbert Wechsler of the Columbia University School of Law expressed concern that the reasoning of the decision was not based on a neutral principle of constitutional law. The Court did not say, as the NAACP had urged, that the Fourteenth Amendment forbids government to classify its citizens by race, which would have provided a neutral constitutional principle. What then did the decision rest on? If segregated education was inherently unequal because of the importance of education today, as the Court said, what principle could be extended to ban racial segregation in public bath houses and beaches? If segregated education is unconstitutional because social scientists say that it causes psychological harm to children, what happens if new sociological evidence emerges in the future to support a different finding? And, after school systems cease assigning children by race, what are they constitutionally required to do in the future, in the absence of a clearly defined principle? Opinions like those of Cahn and Wechsler were in turn criticized, but their doubts were not refuted; the flaws in the Court's analysis which they identified grew more problematic over the years, as sociologists became more divergent in their views and as the problems of implementing desegregation became more complex.[21]

Third, the vagueness of the decree and of the underlying constitutional principle created uncertainty about what the *Brown* decision required, which encouraged resistance and noncompliance. The failure of the Court to specify what was permitted and what was forbidden generated confusion among federal district judges, led to conflicting opinions in the lower courts, and contributed to delay in implementation of desegregation. Although the Court never retreated from the principle that "separate educational facilities are inherently unequal," fourteen years passed after the *Brown* decision before the Supreme Court set forth minimal requirements for compliance. And the Court did little to clear up uncertainty over the following years about whether what was forbidden was state-imposed racial segregation or racial isolation, regardless of its cause.[22]

Aside from angry editorials and political rhetoric, the South reacted to the *Brown* decision with something like calm incredulity. The calm did not signify acceptance so much as skepticism that segregation, the cornerstone of the southern way of life, could be overturned, even by a Supreme Court decision. The example of *Plessy* proved the point, for the requirement of equal treatment of both races had been ignored with impunity. In those states where white supremacy had been imbedded in law and practice for as long as anyone could remember, there was reason to doubt that the *Brown* decision would change anything. Derogation of the decision was commonplace among public officials in the Deep South; physical defiance —that is, demonstrations and mob action—did not erupt until there were efforts to enforce it. Every instance of implementation in the early years after 1954 had paradoxical qualities: it both intensified white racist rage by demonstrating that the decision could not be ignored and, at the same time, established the inevitability of desegregation.

As Carter and Marshall had predicted, negative reactions to the decision were strongest in the states of the Deep South, where the percentage of Negro population was greater, where fears of black domination were more intense, and where Negrophobia prevailed. In border states like Missouri, Tennessee, Delaware, Kentucky, and Maryland, politicians and the press responded constructively to the Court's decision and urged acceptance of the *Brown* decision. Many border state communities, with few black students, desegregated their schools without incident. Several major cities, with substantial black enrollment, also began desegregation. Among those that promptly desegregated were Baltimore, Wilmington, San Antonio, the District of Columbia, St. Louis, and Louisville. These cities adopted plans to eliminate their dual schools by redistricting and assigning children on a nonracial basis to the nearest school or by permitting students to transfer to the school of their choice.

The successful desegregation of Louisville attracted national attention, and Omer Carmichael, the southern-born superintendent who planned it, was invited to the White House to confer with President Eisenhower. As soon as the *Brown* decision was announced, he explained, the educational and political leaders of the city and state stressed their readiness to comply, and he devoted a year to building community support for desegregation. The program began in September, 1956, and it applied to the entire system, from kindergarten through adult education. Though the school system was redistricted without regard to race, and students were assigned to their local schools, the novel feature of the plan was its permissive transfer policy: students could transfer at their parents' request to any school with space available. Carmichael believed that this feature minimized the opposition of those who were adamantly opposed to desegregation and made it unlikely that any school could remain segregated. When assignments went out, 45 percent of the Negroes assigned to formerly white schools asked to be returned to the formerly Negro schools, while 85 percent of the whites assigned to formerly Negro schools requested transfers. Nonetheless, when school opened, 73.6 percent of all students were in racially mixed schools (a school was considered racially mixed if it contained even a single student of the other race). The *New York Times* covered the opening day of school in Louisville and predicted: "When the history of this proud Southern city is written, this day will undoubtedly go down as an historic landmark. Historians will note that a social revolution took place that may advance the cause of integration by a generation."[23]

Though for several years civil rights leaders pointed to cities like Louisville, Wilmington, and Washington as proof that desegregation could be carried out quickly and peacefully when good will and leadership prevailed, each of the big cities that promptly desegregated eventually became resegregated by population movements. In time, their public school enrollments became predominantly black, and Louisville, Wilmington, and Washington were all found guilty of maintaining racially segregated schools, long after the applause for their early desegregation had been forgotten. The problem was not only that whites had fled to the suburbs and/or to private schools, but that the definition of desegregation had changed over time. In the immediate aftermath of the *Brown* decision, a district could successfully desegregate by requiring all students to attend their neighborhood school; by removing all racial restrictions, as San Antonio did, and permitting students to go wherever they and their parents chose; by permitting students to transfer at will, as Louisville did. Such policies were, at the time, laudable because they abolished the old dual system where blacks and whites were automatically assigned to school on the basis of their race. First-generation responses of liberal southern cities aspired to achieve a color-blind policy (for example, the neighborhood school or the free-choice policy); under segregation, blacks were often bused past the neighborhood school (as Linda Brown, the child of the NAACP's lead plaintiff in the *Brown* decision, had been) and were always denied the right to choose which school to attend. Time and events, however, cast a bad light on the very desegregation policies that in 1959 could be described by civil rights lawyer Jack Greenberg as "thorough and striking" examples of social change.[24]

For many white southerners, any accommodation to the *Brown* decision was heresy, and in Deep South states like Alabama, Mississippi, South Carolina, Louisiana, and Georgia an expression of willingness to accept the decision was a courageous act for a politician, a school official, a newspaper editor, or a religious leader. Negrophobia was a powerful force, long supported by law and custom, and few were able to stand against it, not merely because of fear of ostracism but because of fear for one's physical safety. With rare exceptions, elected leaders did little to promote compliance with the decision; on the contrary, they used their positions of leadership to encourage their constituents to believe that resistance was a viable course of action. Southern political leaders shaped a policy of "massive resistance," on the premise that a solid front of opposition by southern states would frustrate, defer, and eventually defeat efforts to impose desegregation. In March, 1956, southern congressmen issued a "Southern Manifesto," which decried the *Brown* decision as "a clear abuse of judicial power" and declared their intention "to resist enforced integration by any lawful means." The manifesto was signed by 19 of the South's 22 senators (only the senators from Tennessee refused to sign, and Senate Majority Leader Lyndon B. Johnson was not asked to sign), and by 82 of its 106 congressmen (including the entire delegations of Alabama, Arkansas, Georgia, Louisiana, Mississippi, South Carolina, and Virginia).[25]

To stave off the anticipated incursions by the NAACP and the federal judiciary, the legislatures in the eleven southern states passed scores of new laws to protect segregation. The measures passed included such provisions as: the denial of state funds to schools attended by pupils of different races; threats to close the public schools in the event they were integrated; delegation of control of the public schools to the governor or the state legislature, in hopes of frustrating federal court orders; the abolition of compulsory schooling; tuition grants for those who did not wish to attend integrated schools; criminal penalties for teaching in or attending an integrated school. The Georgia legislature called for the impeachment of six Supreme Court justices; the Alabama legislature provided for firing teachers who advocated desegregation; the Mississippi legislature banned speeches at state institutions by advocates of antistate action; the South Carolina legislature barred members of the NAACP from public employment. Three types of laws were adopted by most southern states: first, laws intended to impede the NAACP's legal activities; second, laws embracing the doctrine of "interposition," which was an assertion of the power of the state to nullify federal authority within its borders; and third, pupil assignment laws, which set up complicated administrative machinery to regulate assignments and transfers. The pupil assignment laws established elaborate criteria for pupils who wished to transfer and were administered by local boards; some states used them to control the flow of Negro applicants to white schools and to create "token" desegregation, while others used them to prevent any Negro admissions to white schools on seemingly nonracial grounds, such as the student's psychological or academic profile or the possibility of community disorder.[26]

In the fall of 1956, two districts became testing grounds for desegregation—with markedly different results. In Mansfield, Texas, when crowds of angry whites assembled to block the court-ordered desegregation of the local high school, Governor Alan Shivers sent two Texas Rangers to restore peace and urged the local board to remove the dozen Negro students whose presence incited disorder. The same fall, Tennessee Governor Frank Clement dispatched tanks and hundreds of state troopers to the town of Clinton, where a mob of unruly whites was trying to prevent local school authorities from admitting a dozen Negroes to its high school. As a result of the governors' intervention, the federal court order was carried out in Clinton but was defied in Mansfield. President Eisenhower made no effort to uphold the federal court in Texas. It remained unclear how desegregation could be implemented when it was opposed by local and state officials, and whether federal court orders could be ignored by those who disagreed with them.[27]

If southern governors had the power to nullify court orders, as Governor Shivers of Texas had, there was no chance that the *Brown* decision could penetrate the bastions of massive resistance. And neither Congress, where southern representatives held powerful positions, nor President Eisenhower showed any inclination to interfere in the institutional conflict between the federal judiciary and the southern states. Eisenhower, a revered military leader who was elected to the presidency in 1952, firmly believed in the limited powers of the federal government in relation to state and local government. Though he was repeatedly pressed to endorse the *Brown* decision, Eisenhower refused. On May 19, 1954, a reporter asked the president whether he had any advice for the South, and Eisenhower would go no further than to say, "The Supreme Court has spoken, and I am sworn to uphold the Constitutional process in this country. And I am trying—I will obey it." Time and again, the president reiterated his deep commitment to gradualism; as he saw it, the district courts and local authorities would eventually work things out for the best, allowing adequate time to overcome the prejudices that had been built up over generations. Eisenhower was convinced that racial progress was being made, and that "extremism"—whether in resisting desegregation or in demanding it —was not helpful and might provoke violence, which would retard further progress. He often said that it was difficult "through law, and through force, to change a man's heart," and that readjustment of racial relations in the South would come about only through good will, common sense, and understanding.[28]

A year before the *Brown* decision was announced, Eisenhower had lunch with South Carolina Governor James Byrnes, who warned him that his support for the forthcoming ruling would "forever defeat any possibility of developing a real Republican or 'Opposition' Party in the South." Eisenhower recorded, in his personal diary, his response to Byrnes:

> I told him that while I was not going to give in advance my attitude toward a Supreme Court opinion that I had not even seen and so could not know in what terms it would be couched, that my convictions would not be formed by political expediency. He is well aware of my belief that improvement in race relations is one of those things that will be healthy and sound only if it starts locally. I do not believe that prejudices, even palpably unjustified prejudices, will succumb to compulsion. Consequently, I believe that Federal law imposed upon our states in such a way as to bring about a conflict of the police powers of the states and of the nation, would set back the cause of progress in race relations for a long, long time.[29]

When his attorney general developed a proposal for new civil rights legislation in the spring of 1956, Eisenhower gave it his approval but urged continued sensitivity to the feelings of white southerners; the president reminded his cabinet that "People have a right to disagree with the Supreme Court decision—since the Supreme Court has disagreed with its own decision of 60 years standing—but, of course, the new decision should now be carried out." While he wanted to avoid antagonizing the white South by his public rhetoric, Eisenhower agreed that new civil rights legislation was necessary to protect basic rights and to relieve the political isolation of the federal judiciary. Although the bill that passed was stripped of much of its force by compromises demanded by southern senators, it created a Civil Rights Commission and a civil rights division within the Justice Department, and it permitted the Justice Department to sue on behalf of Negroes denied the right to vote. It was noteworthy, furthermore, as the first civil rights legislation since Reconstruction and the first significant assumption of federal responsibility for the protection of civil rights.[30]

From the point of view of those advocating massive resistance, Eisenhower was an ideal president, for he gave little or no encouragement to the moral claims of the civil rights groups, and he was extremely unlikely ever to use federal power to override local authorities. Indeed, he sought to reassure anxious white southerners on July 17, 1957, that "I can't imagine any set of circumstances that would ever induce me to send Federal troops ... into any area to enforce the orders of a Federal Court, because I believe that common sense of America will never require it." Inevitably, however, the defiance of the South forced Eisenhower to choose between his belief in gradualism and his oath to uphold the Constitution. For Eisenhower, the choice was clear.[31]

The confrontation that began the end of the strategy of massive resistance took place in Little Rock, Arkansas, which was ironic since Arkansas was not one of the die-hard states, having already admitted Negro students in a handful of school districts and to all state-supported colleges. Yet what happened in Little Rock forced a major change in the role of the federal government and removed any uncertainty about the future enforcement of court orders.

In response to legal action, the Little Rock school board announced a plan to desegregate its schools over a period of several years, beginning with the admission of nine Negro students to Central High School in September, 1957. When Negroes challenged the plan as too gradual, it was upheld by the federal district court; when it was challenged by whites who predicted violence, the federal judge enjoined any interference in carrying out desegregation. On September 2, the day before school was to open, Governor Orval Faubus sent the Arkansas National Guard to Central High School to prevent the admission of the Negro students, ostensibly to "maintain or restore order," even though no disorder had occurred. Federal Judge Ronald Davies ordered the school board to proceed with the plan, and on September 4, the Negro pupils attempted to enter and were turned away by the national guardsmen, acting on the governor's instructions. The by-now well-publicized events attracted crowds of cheering, jeering whites and the attention of the world press.[32]

At this point, Governor Faubus was acting in opposition not only to the federal court, but to the Little Rock school board and the mayor of Little Rock, who complained that the governor had created tensions "where none existed." Under threat of an injunction to cease interfering with the federal court's orders, Faubus flew to a meeting with President Eisenhower and pledged "to accept the decisions of the court." When the injunction was issued, the governor withdrew the Guard from Central High.[33]

Faubus's maneuvering turned Little Rock into a symbolic battleground, which drew segregationists to the Central High campus to demonstrate their contempt for integration, for Negroes, for the federal court, and for the "Yankee" press. When school opened on September 23, Central High was beseiged by a disorderly mob of nearly one thousand, who screamed threats, attacked newsmen, battled the police, and demanded the ouster of the Negro pupils. Joined by several dozen students who left their classes, the mob could not be controlled by local police. As the situation deteriorated, the superintendent of schools sent the Negro students home in police cars. At 6:23 P.M., President Eisenhower issued a proclamation, commanding all those obstructing justice in Little Rock to "cease and desist" immediately. Calling the situation "disgraceful," the president warned that federal court orders "cannot be flouted with impunity by any individual or mob of extremists." The next day the president federalized the Arkansas National Guard and sent troops of the 101st Airborne Division into Little Rock to "insure the carrying out of the decisions of the Federal courts." It was up to local authorities and the courts to formulate desegregation plans, the president said, but the final order of the federal court "must be obeyed by state authorities and all citizens as the law of the land." The paratroopers moved quickly, decisively, and "with visibly overwhelming force," to carry out the court order and disperse the mob.[34]

By the end of November, 1957, the regular army troops were withdrawn from Little Rock; the federalized guard detachment remained until school ended in May, 1958. The story was not done, however, for in the middle of the school year the school board sought a two-and-one-half year delay in the desegregation plan, due to the tensions within the school and the disruption of the educational program. The Supreme Court refused to permit such a delay. In its *Cooper* v. *Aaron* decision (1958), the Court declared that "Law and order are not here to be preserved by depriving the Negro children of their constitutional rights." The right not to be discriminated against on account of race and color "can neither be nullified openly and directly by state legislators or state executive or judicial officers, nor nullified indirectly by them through evasive schemes for segregation whether attempted 'ingeniously or ingenuously.'" To emphasize the unanimity of their decision, the justices took the unusual step of affixing all nine of their names to the opinion. Fresh from an overwhelming victory in the Democratic primary, Governor Faubus responded to the decision by closing Little Rock's four high schools for the 1958/59 school year. Almost a year later, a federal court declared the Arkansas school-closing laws unconstitutional, in light of the Supreme Court's ruling in *Cooper* v. *Aaron* that the threat of violence cannot justify state action to deprive a citizen of his constitutional rights.[35]

Other states, emboldened by Faubus's flamboyant tactics, tried to follow his example by closing their public schools or otherwise evading their responsibility to end segregation. But while the drama in Little Rock temporarily added fuel to the segregationists' fires, its more enduring importance was its effect on the presidency and on the Supreme Court.

Though Eisenhower tried to remain aloof from the slow working-out of the issue, the governor's defiance compelled him to abandon his detachment and to defend the integrity of the federal judiciary with military force. The Supreme Court, in its Little Rock decision, made clear to the public and to judges in lower courts that it would not tolerate schemes that catered to segregationist opinion. After *Cooper* v. *Aaron*, federal judges were on notice that they could not permit nullification of the right of children "not to be discriminated against on grounds of race or color." From this time, there could no longer be any doubt that the cluttered statutory barricades erected by southern state legislatures must eventually fall. After Little Rock, neither inventive legislatures nor violent resistance could prevent court-ordered desegregation. Each major showdown varied in its particulars, but whether it was the angry, jeering white protesters in New Orleans in 1960, the riots at the University of Georgia in 1961, the bloodshed and loss of life at the University of Mississippi in 1962, or Governor George Wallace's stage-managed "stand-in-the-schoolhouse-door" at the University of Alabama in 1963, the segregationists lost.

Still, despite the steady string of victories in the courts, there remained the considerable question of how much difference the *Brown* decision would actually make. Segregation persisted throughout the South, not only in schools but as a way of life, and those who challenged it in protest activities continued to be at great personal risk. Most of the states that had operated dual school systems were desegregating as slowly as possible. By 1962, substantial progress had been achieved in the border states of Oklahoma, Missouri, Kentucky, West Virginia, Maryland, and Delaware, where 25 to 60 percent of black students attended biracial schools. But in eight southern states (Texas, Georgia, Virginia, North Carolina, Arkansas, Louisiana, Tennessee, and Florida), where about 2 percent or less of black students were in biracial schools, strategies of "tokenism" had been used to admit only a few blacks to white schools. And in Mississippi, Alabama, and South Carolina, not a single black attended school with a white. Most states continued to segregate their public school teachers, even when students were desegregated; and in Missouri, Oklahoma, Texas, and West Virginia, "a sizeable number of Negro teachers lost their jobs in the change to biracial schools."[36]

The process of social change, however, had begun, and there was no turning back. The movement for racial equality advanced on a broken front, faster in some areas than others, but its forward direction became inexorable when it acquired a mass base among southern blacks. The transformation of the equal rights struggle into a popular movement began in Montgomery, Alabama, in December, 1955, when Rosa Parks, a Negro seamstress who had recently completed a leadership training course at the

interracial Highlander Folk School in Tennessee, was arrested for refusing
to yield her seat on a crowded public bus to a white man. In response, the
Negro community of Montgomery boycotted the city's buses until, one
year later, the Supreme Court declared bus segregation unconstitutional.
No less valuable than the legal victory was the experience itself, for it
demonstrated the power of nonviolent, organized protest and produced a
charismatic black leader, the Reverend Martin Luther King, Jr., who immediately emerged as an eloquent spokesman for the cause of equality.
King understood that the gains won in the courts could be secured only
if a newly self-conscious black community was prepared to exercise them.
"Legislation and court orders tend only to declare rights," King wrote,
"they can never thoroughly deliver them. . . . Life is breathed into a judicial
decision by the persistent exercise of legal rights until they become usual
and ordinary in human experience."[37]

The mass base of the civil rights movement expanded rapidly in the
early 1960s. In February, 1960, four black college freshmen staged the first
"sit-in" at a segregated lunch counter in Greensboro, North Carolina.
Their example inspired similar demonstrations across the South, in restaurants, hotels, movie theaters, beaches, churches, and amusement parks. In
1961, black and white "freedom riders" traveled south on interstate buses
to protest segregation in southern bus terminals; the brutal treatment they
received in Alabama and Mississippi led to a federal ban against segregation in all trains, buses, and terminals. By 1962, civil rights workers from
several organizations—including the NAACP, Martin Luther King's
Southern Christian Leadership Conference, the Student Nonviolent Coordinating Committee (created in 1960 by student protest groups), and the
Congress of Racial Equality—were organizing voter registration drives and
conducting protest demonstrations across the South.

The racial protests of the early 1960s dramatized the inhumanity and
absurdity of racial discrimination. The national communications media,
and particularly television, changed the way these confrontations were
perceived by a national audience. In ways that Myrdal had presciently
understood, raw and undisguised racism was revealed as a direct challenge
to the American creed. It seemed outrageous to the distant television
viewer to see white men striking blacks, who were not resisting the blows,
in order to prevent the blacks from ordering a cup of coffee or from sitting
where they wished in a bus terminal. Part of the lesson was transmitted
through the power of the demonstrators' nonviolent tactics, which exposed the brutality of those attacking them. But a larger part was that the
demonstrators effectively communicated the simple justice of their plea to
be treated precisely as others whose skin color was different. Rarely have

a cause, a method, and a medium combined so effectively to educate the public.

As the civil rights movement spread across the South, as laws promoting massive resistance were one-by-one struck down by the courts, defenders of the southern position became increasingly isolated. With the election of John F. Kennedy in 1960, the executive branch was in the control of men sympathetic to the civil rights struggle. During his campaign, Kennedy chided Eisenhower for his passivity on civil rights issues; but when he was elected by a razor-thin margin, he too tried to avoid offending the powerful southern bloc in Congress. Yet by temperament, Kennedy was an activist president, intent on showing that words and deeds could make America a better society. The Kennedy administration sent federal marshals to protect freedom riders, pressed the Interstate Commerce Commission to end segregation in travel facilities, entered school desegregation suits on behalf of Negro plaintiffs, and actively negotiated with the governors of Alabama and Mississippi for the desegregation of their state universities.

Kennedy's attempt to maintain both his relations with southern congressmen and his support for civil rights was ended by the events in Birmingham, Alabama, in the spring of 1963. In order to focus national awareness on racial injustice, the Reverend Martin Luther King led the local black community in protest activities that were fought at every turn by local authorities, armed with cattle prods, police dogs, and firehoses. Federal efforts to negotiate a settlement between the leaders of both races were derailed by disorders, rioting, and bombings; eventually the president sent federal troops to restore order. The films and photographs of snarling police dogs attacking young men and women portrayed, as no words could, the brutality of the city's status quo. "A new climate of national opinion was created on the streets of Birmingham," wrote legal scholar Alexander Bickel. Shortly after the Birmingham demonstrations ended, Kennedy again had to intervene in Alabama when Governor George Wallace threatened to prevent the court-ordered enrollment of black students at the University of Alabama. After much posturing, the governor made his statement, the president federalized the Alabama National Guard, and the students were admitted.[38]

On June 11, 1963, two hours after Governor Wallace deferred to federal authority, President Kennedy went on national television to seek public support for a major new civil rights bill, the most significant such proposal since the Reconstruction era. Kennedy spoke simply, eloquently, and passionately of the "moral crisis" that confronted the nation:

140

If an American, because his skin is dark, cannot eat lunch in a restaurant open to the public; if he cannot send his children to the best public school available; if he cannot vote for the public officials who represent him; if, in short, he cannot enjoy the full and free life which all of us want, then who among us would be content to have the color of his skin changed and stand in his place? . . . not every child has an equal talent or an equal ability or equal motivation. But they should have the equal right to develop their talent and their ability and their motivation to make something of themselves. We have a right to expect that the Negro community will be responsible, will uphold the law. But they have a right to expect the law will be fair, that the Constitution will be color blind, as Justice Harlan said at the turn of the century.

Not only Birmingham, but scores of communities were experiencing rising tensions, sporadic rioting and violence because of their denial of black grievances. The time for "patience and delay" was past, the president declared; "the fires of frustration and discord are burning in every city, North and South." Kennedy pledged to ask the Congress to commit itself "to the proposition that race has no place in American life or law." A week later, the president proposed an omnibus civil rights bill that included significant federal protection against racial discrimination in voting, access to public accommodations, federally funded programs, education, and employment.[39]

The civil rights movement had forced white Americans to take notice, and in doing so, provoked violent reactions from white racists. The day after the president's address, Medger Evers, a field secretary for the NAACP in Mississippi, was murdered; three months later, a black church in Birmingham was bombed and four children were killed. And the movement, outraged by the rising tide of violence but exhilarated by the prospect of decisive federal action, set in motion a historic demonstration against inequality and injustice. Civil rights leaders organized a massive "March on Washington" in August, 1963, which attracted a quarter of a million persons to support a concerted rights-and-jobs program and which showed that the cause of nondiscrimination had been joined by a broad coalition of religious groups and labor unions.

After Kennedy's assassination in November, 1963, his successor Lyndon B. Johnson immediately pressed for adoption of Kennedy's civil rights legislation. In his first address to Congress, Johnson said, "We have talked long enough in this country about equal rights. We have talked for one hundred years or more. It is time now to write the next chapter—and to write it in the books of law." A southerner and a masterful politician, Johnson adroitly steered the civil rights bill through Congress and signed it into law on July 2, 1964. The Civil Rights Act of 1964 was a complex document of some eighteen thousand words, covering a wide range of activities. Title I extended federal safeguards of the right to vote (in 1965, the Voting Rights Act further strengthened the federal guarantees); Title II prohibited discrimination on account of race, religion, or national origin in places of public accommodation, such as hotels, restaurants, and theaters; Title III authorized the attorney general of the United States to sue to desegregate public facilities, such as parks and municipal auditoriums; Title IV directed the commissioner of education to prepare a survey on the availability of equal educational opportunity and to render technical assistance to localities trying to desegregate their schools; Title V extended the life of the Civil Rights Commission, a fact-finding body created in 1957; Title VI banned discrimination "on the ground of race, color, or national origin" in any federally assisted program; Title VII prohibited discrimination in employment on grounds of an individual's color, religion, sex, or national origin (Title VII was the only section that included "sex," a result of what was intended to be a derisive amendment by a southern congressman). The changed status of the civil rights movement in American life was indicated by the presence at the bill-signing of key black leaders, including Martin Luther King, Jr., and Roy Wilkins, the leader of the NAACP. Johnson explained that "The purpose of this law is simple. It does not restrict the freedom of any American so long as he respects the rights of others. It does not give special treatment to any citizen. It does say the only limit to a man's hope for happiness and for the future of his children shall be his own ability."[40]

Though it was not apparent at the time, the passage of the Civil Rights Act marked a turning point in the evolution of the civil rights movement as well as in the larger issue of the role of race and group consciousness in American life. Before the passage of the act, the major civil rights groups were interracial in character and dedicated to the elimination of racial distinctions from the law; the language of the act reflected, as President Kennedy had hoped, the proposition that "race has no place in American life or law." At hearings on the bill, witnesses frequently affirmed their commitment to the color-blind principles contained in Justice Harlan's dissent from the *Plessy* decision. It was in this spirit, for example, that Roy Wilkins told the House Judiciary Committee that the NAACP opposed racial quotas in employment: "We believe the quota system is unfair whether it is used for Negroes or against Negroes."[41]

But beneath the surface were troublesome hints of tensions unresolved by the seeming consensus against group discrimination. The desire to get the bill passed encouraged supporters to paper over potential conflicts between the rhetorical ideal of color-blindness and any consideration of future race-conscious policies. One issue that forced the question emerged because of several references in the Kennedy bill to "problems of racial imbalance" in the public schools. Southern congressmen feared that the purpose of the phrase was to empower the courts and the federal bureaucracy to promote integration without regard to neighborhood schools, and northern congressmen wondered if it might serve as a statutory basis to reassign children in northern districts. They peppered administration spokesmen with questions about the meaning of the phrase. Defending the bill, neither Attorney General Robert Kennedy nor Secretary of Health, Education, and Welfare Anthony J. Celebrezze seemed to understand what "racial imbalance" was, and neither would defend its obvious implications. When pressed by Senator Sam Ervin of North Carolina to say whether the Kennedy administration had a policy "to encourage transporting children away from their neighborhood schools to schools in other communities for the purpose of getting what some educators may conceive to be racially balanced schools in the other communities," Robert Kennedy responded, "No; we have no policy on that, Senator," and explained that "we will only be of help [in solving problems of racial imbalance] where there is a request from the local authorities for assistance." Under Ervin's persistent questioning about the meaning of racial balance, Kennedy insisted that the purpose of the language was to guarantee each child the right to attend his neighborhood school.[12]

Nor could Celebrezze explain what the references to racial imbalance meant; he said, "If you start drawing the line of demarcation that you should have 80 percent white and 20 percent Negroes, or 20 percent white and 80 percent Negroes, then you are promoting as much segregation as we are trying to get rid of. What I am saying is that these students ought to be able to go to classes without taking into consideration whether they are white or black." At the insistence of congressional critics, the Civil Rights Act of 1964 contained specific language defining desegregation as "the assignment of students to public schools and within such schools without regard to their race, color, religion, or national origin, but 'desegregation' shall not mean the assignment of students to public schools in order to overcome racial imbalance."[43]

At the time it seemed conclusively settled that the Civil Rights Act of 1964 had at last removed from government the power to classify people by race or group identity and had at last empowered the federal government to protect its citizens against arbitrary discrimination in the exercise of their rights. This consensus reflected the political coalition that had gathered under black leadership to protest all forms of discrimination associated with one's group identity. The idea that a person should be judged solely on the basis of his own ability was squarely grounded in what Myrdal had called the American Creed. As the leaders of the fight to end discrimination against all groups, black spokesmen moved to the center of the national stage and worked closely with the Johnson administration in forging the innovative social legislation of 1964/65: not only the Civil Rights Act, but also the Economic Opportunity Act (1964), the Voting Rights Act (1965), and the Elementary and Secondary Education Act (1965).

But the apparent triumph of color-blindness was ephemeral. Even as the coalition of liberals, labor unions, and civil rights groups achieved its greatest legislative victories, riots and civil disorders swept through urban black communities, and voices espousing black separatism and belittling nonviolent tactics grew louder. The expectations raised during the previous decade had unleashed the anger and frustration that had been pent up for generations. Race-consciousness in American life had been too powerful and too poisonous to be willed away in a day, or even in a decade.

CHAPTER 5

Race and Education: Social Science and Law

T HE COLOR-BLINDNESS that was mandated by passage of the Civil Rights Act of 1964 did not last long, if it ever existed at all. Race-consciousness was already too deeply ingrained in the American psyche to be obliterated by statute. Although liberals tried gamely during the years after the *Brown* decision to eliminate questions about racial identity from application forms for school and work, the push for racial equality had come to rely on racial information as a way of gauging, first, the pace of desegregation and, later, the effect of various measures on black advancement. And, of course, it immediately became apparent that the aspirations loosed by the black social upheaval would not be satisfied by a guarantee that race would no longer matter. Since an important element of the strategy of the civil rights movement had been to mobilize blacks as blacks, and to make whites aware of (and responsible for) the historic injustices perpetrated against blacks, it was naïve to believe that race-consciousness would suddenly disappear.

Indeed, soon after the passage of the act, changes began to occur that altered racial relations and affected subsequent public policy. Though it was not immediately apparent, the nature of the civil rights movement changed. As an interracial movement led by blacks, its goal had been a public policy in which the state treated persons as individuals, without regard to race, color, creed, or national origin. After this goal was written into law, the movement itself was transformed by the political climate into a black movement, dedicated to advancing the interests of blacks as a minority group. The nationalist strain that had always existed among blacks and within black organizations came to the fore, calling attention to the need of blacks for group recognition, for assertion of their own history and culture, for a legitimate and respected place among American ethnic groups. Indicative of this shift was that two of the leading civil rights organizations, the Congress of Racial Equality (CORE) and the Student Nonviolent Coordinating Committee (SNCC) abandoned their past interracialism and became exponents of black nationalism. As blacks began to act assertively in terms of their group interests, entering politics as other ethnic groups did, the notion of color-blindness seemed an affront, a requirement that they alone of all minorities must be invisible.

There were other reasons why the original understanding that animated the Civil Rights Act quickly seemed irrelevant. Color-blindness was not a remedy for the widespread poverty among blacks, nor for their exclusion from major sectors of the economy; disillusionment was expressed by the commonplace complaint that it did no good to gain entry to a restaurant if you did not have the price of a meal. Even while Congress was legislating what was supposed to be the elimination of the role of race in American law, black activists were demanding preferential treatment in hiring as reparation for historic racism. And, if further reminder were needed of the continuing role of race, it came from the South, where few black students attended school with whites.

As the urban slums grew denser and as fear of violent racial disorders mounted, it became increasingly clear that the legal victory over Jim Crow left untouched the deeper problems of American blacks, which could be documented in their high unemployment rates, their concentration in low-skill jobs that were most vulnerable to automation, their lack of education, and their concentration in crowded, rundown schools and housing. Regardless of the laws, blacks as a group were economically marginal and socially excluded from full participation in American life. Since the nation in the early 1960s was in a time of unusual prosperity, and since the Democratic administrations in office since 1960 were sympathetic to social reform, there was a growing constituency for action against poverty. Government policy makers, foundations, and university circles were abuzz with ideas to mount a campaign against the causes and effects of poverty. The discovery—or rediscovery—of poverty as a national problem was spurred by Michael Harrington's *The Other America: Poverty in the United States,* published in 1962. Harrington movingly described the grinding despair of nearly fifty million people whom he charged were without adequate housing, education, and medical care, left behind by the nation's economic progress and excluded from the benefits of the welfare state. His call for "a passion to end poverty" could not have come at a more opportune moment, not because America was hopeful but because it was worried.[1]

There was a broad perception in the early 1960s that the United States was in the grip of an "urban crisis," and that the viability of the nation's cities was in serious doubt. The perception of the "urban crisis," discussed intensively in the popular press and in policy-making circles, stemmed specifically from the changing racial composition of the cities. In the years from 1940 to 1966, as agriculture was mechanized, nearly four million blacks migrated from the South to other regions of the country, and most settled in urban areas. The black population in almost every major American city grew markedly during the 1950s and early 1960s. Between 1950 and 1966, the black population in the central cities nearly doubled, from 6.5 million to 12.1 million, growing from 43 to 56 percent of the nation's blacks. During the same period of time, the number of whites living in the central cities remained the same, but by 1966 had dropped from 34 to only 27 percent of all whites. With the black urban population rising sharply, residential segregation also rose. The newly arrived blacks settled in the poorest neighborhoods of each city; in the older cities of the Northeast, they moved into the same slum tenements previously occupied by the earlier waves of poor European immigrants. The rural migrants arrived with poor education and few skills at a time when the number of jobs for unskilled and semiskilled workers was rapidly diminishing.[2]

Like other immigrants, they came to the cities in search of greater opportunities, and some found them. Others, however, found urban poverty more debilitating than the rural poverty they had fled. The institutions they dealt with were impersonal and bureaucratic. Large sectors of the job market were closed to them because they lacked the right skills, education, dress, manner, or speech. And even in cities where the laws strictly forbade it, racial discrimination was pervasive. Blacks were concentrated in low-wage jobs as domestics, porters, and waiters; few had the education to become professionals, and even those with credentials discovered that there were stores, businesses, corporations, restaurants, hotels, and neighborhoods where people with dark skin were not welcome.

In 1963, and for several years after, urban racial disorders provided a counterpoint to the passive resistance tactics of the civil rights groups in the South. The articulate leader of the Black Muslims, Malcolm X, gained national attention as he aggressively asserted his contempt for white society, as well as for black integrationists who were seeking admission to the white man's world. Malcolm's bitter denunciations of whites found an appreciative public in the black slums of America, particularly in those nonsouthern cities where civil rights demonstrations raised expectations and group solidarity without affecting any of the objective conditions of life. The great legislative victories of the civil rights movement seemed to make poor urban blacks keenly aware that the drive for equal opportunity would not transform their condition and fearful that the egalitarian rhetoric of the moment was an empty hoax.

The "urban crisis" atmosphere had political implications for it galvanized the impulse to take action against poverty and to respond to black grievances and made possible a breakthrough on the long-stalled issue of federal aid to education. In 1961, Kennedy had tried to get a bill through Congress and failed because of the usual conflicts over race and religion. Seasoned observers concluded that the issue was hopeless for many years to come. After Lyndon Johnson's landslide victory of 1964, he was determined to pass a federal aid to education bill. His party held a commanding majority of both houses of Congress, 68 to 32 in the Senate, and 295 to 140 in the House of Representatives. With this kind of legislative support, no group was powerful enough to block a bill. Previous bills, phrased in terms of helping the schools or raising teachers' salaries or meeting the nation's needs, had foundered. Johnson's bill was cast as an antipoverty measure, and its largest benefits were aimed at improving the schooling of poor children. This focus on poverty made available a formula to compromise the differences between advocates of public and nonpublic schools, for while only public agencies would receive funds, poor children in nonpublic schools would be eligible to share services and facilities. The new formula was, in fact, an updated version of the child-benefit theory that the Catholic Church had embraced twenty years earlier and that opponents of nonpublic schools had vigorously resisted. Yet when the proposal was couched in terms of aiding poor children, the enmities of the past were set aside; both sides recognized that their past feuding had blocked federal aid, and neither had the votes to stop a bill going through.[3]

Not only was the religious issue resolved, the race issue was for the first time not a significant problem, as a result of the Civil Rights Act of 1964, which already prohibited discrimination in any federally-funded program. So, having finally broken the race-religion deadlock, the president's bill proceeded with remarkable celerity through the Congress. On April 9, 1965, only eighty-seven days after it had been introduced, the Elementary and Secondary Education Act (ESEA) passed the Congress. For nearly one hundred years, attempts to pass federal aid to education had failed; approval was made possible at last because of a broad consensus on the necessity of improving the educational opportunities of poor children. The political appeal of the program was assured by the antipoverty formula, which allocated federal funds on the basis of the number of poor children; this solution not only sidestepped the traditional debate about whether federal money should be appropriated on a per capita basis or for teachers' salaries or buildings, but also guaranteed that federal dollars would go to the overwhelming majority of the nation's school districts.[4]

The social reformism that produced the ESEA in 1965 had already stimulated intense concern among social scientists and educators about the education of poor children. During the decade after the *Brown* decision, the wide disparity between the achievement levels of white and black children was a major problem in desegregating school districts. Administrators in the newly desegregated schools of Washington, D.C., met the problem by assigning students to one of four different tracks on the basis of their ability; "tracking" was described as an appropriate response to the disparate learning needs of the children, but it was also reassurance to white parents that desegregation would not lower standards. Problems in the cities where the black population had grown since World War II came not from the mixing of black and white children, but from the growing number of predominantly black schools in poor neighborhoods. Slum neighborhoods had high rates of crime, youth gangs, alcoholism, drug addiction, illiteracy, disease, and unemployment. The schools of the slums were characterized by low achievement, poor discipline, truancy, and high teacher turnover. Disproportionate numbers of students dropped out before graduating with little education, few skills, and poor prospects for future employment. Teacher turnover figures revealed the reluctance of teachers to remain in schools where the conditions, inside and outside the school, ranged from discouraging to frightening.

Urban schools themselves were disadvantaged. James B. Conant wrote in 1961 that the per capita expenditure in wealthy suburban schools was more than twice as much as in big city high schools. The suburban high school "is likely to be a spacious modern school staffed by as many as 70 professionals per 1,000 pupils; in the slum one finds a crowded, often dilapidated and unattractive school staffed by 40 or fewer professionals per 1,000 youths." In the suburban school, 80 percent or more went on to college; in the slum school, as many as half dropped out before graduating. Nor could the social conditions in the surrounding slum be walled out of the life of the students: one junior high school principal told Conant that female students reported that their biggest problem was "getting from the

149

street into their apartment without being molested in the hallway of the tenement." Conant expressed a widely shared foreboding:

> . . . when one considers the total situation that has been developing in the Negro city slums since World War II, one has reason to worry about the future. The building up of a mass of unemployed and frustrated Negro youth in congested areas of a city is a social phenomenon that may be compared to the piling up of inflammable material in an empty building in a city block. Potentialities for trouble—indeed possibilities of disaster—are surely there.[5]

Research on the problems of educating the poor and minorities had an unusual urgency about it, since it was widely perceived that the schools and cities were in an unparalleled crisis. In questioning whether the cities could survive, it was repeatedly asserted that the public schools were failing to assimilate the tide of black migrants as they had previously assimilated millions of illiterate European immigrants. Behind this assumption, however, was a lack of historical perspective about the difficulties encountered by immigrants in urban schools. Few social scientists seemed to know that immigrant children had experienced high rates of "educational retardation" in the early twentieth century; that relatively few immigrant children had finished high school; and that midcentury schools were being judged by a far higher standard of success than early twentieth century schools ever attained. There was little recognition of the striking parallel between the hostility encountered by the "new immigration" in the late nineteenth and early twentieth centuries—which contemporaries thought to be so unassimilable, so backward, and so ill-fitted to American life that by the 1920s immigration was virtually cut off—and the fearful reaction to the postwar black migration.[6]

But a crisis there was, as the number of predominantly black schools continued to grow, and as educators admitted that the children in these schools fell further behind in academic skills with each year they stayed in school. In efforts to reverse the rapid decline of urban education, educators initiated programs of "compensatory education," and social scientists studied the relationship between race, social class, and learning. From the middle 1950s to the end of the 1960s, a vast literature was produced which sought to account for the low achievement of poor and minority children in urban schools. Books, articles, symposia, seminars, and conferences proliferated around the theme of how to educate the "culturally deprived," the "culturally disadvantaged," the "underprivileged," and the "lower-class child." Often, though not always, the terms were used as euphemisms for the black child.

A major impulse behind research on "cultural deprivation" was to discredit the common belief that black and low-income children did poorly in school because of genetic inferiority. The widespread use of IQ tests had given currency to the misconception that such tests actually measured innate intelligence, rather than an indeterminate mix of inherited and environmentally determined capacities. So long as the hereditarian interpretation held sway, there was little reason to believe that educational intervention could change what nature had ordained. The rapid expansion of interest in cultural deprivation reflected growing interest among social researchers in the environmental determinants of learning. The central finding of the cultural deprivation research was that children's ability to learn in school was impaired by the effects of poverty and racial prejudice. Some researchers, following the *Brown* decision's finding that segregation causes lasting psychological harm to minority children, attributed the poor academic performance of black children to racial segregation. But while the *Brown* decision referred only to segregation imposed by government, many post-*Brown* researchers argued that catastrophic damage was inflicted on the ego, the self-esteem, and the motivation of the child who lived in a black community such as Harlem.[7]

Most social research focused on the deleterious effects of poverty on the child's home environment, and a striking number of studies concurred about the way that poverty affected the learning process. Compared to the middle-class home, the poor home had few books, toys, games, or objects to stimulate the child's visual and auditory senses. Compared to middle-class parents, who had more leisure time and education, poor parents had less time to read to, talk to, and interact with their children in ways that promoted their acquisition of language skills and encouraged their curiosity. Compared to the middle-class child, the poor child could not be certain that his basic needs for food and rest and medical care would be met, which led to a fatalistic and passive attitude. Compared to the poor child, the middle-class child was rewarded for paying attention and for learning-to-learn, was taught to defer gratification of his immediate wants in return for future goals, and learned to look to adults for information and approval.[8]

Not only did poor children start school less ready to learn than did their middle-income peers, but they were further impaired by the inability of the school to adapt its methods and materials to the academic needs of its pupils. Progressive methods, wherever they had been accepted, had de-emphasized phonetics and the careful sequencing of instruction in language and reading, which were ususlly what children with underdeveloped verbal skills needed. Trained to teach children who were already motivated and prepared to begin reading, teachers in impoverished

151

neighborhoods were unequipped for the children in their classes; not knowing how to teach them, they struggled to maintain order. The psychologist Martin Deutsch, describing a school that was 99 percent Negro, found "an atmosphere of disorganization, an emphasis on disciplining, minimal academic teaching, and much emphasis on 'creative expression.' " The students were disruptive and challenging, and the mostly Negro teachers were cynical. ("Their aim was mainly to keep order, and their expectation was not in terms of the children actually learning.") The reading books, with their stories of pink-cheeked children in single-family homes, were foreign to the children, as was a writing assignment on "The Trip I Took" (65 percent of the children had never been more than twenty-five blocks from home). Most of the children came from crowded apartments and broken homes. Half said there was neither a pen nor a pencil in their homes, and many came to school without breakfast. The children had a short "auditory attention span," which meant that they were not accustomed to listening carefully or for long. When compared to poor white students, the black children fell farther behind as time went by. One reason was that in the black classes, 50 to 80 percent of classroom time was spent on discipline and other nonacademic matters, compared with no more than 30 percent of the time in the white classrooms.[9]

In June, 1964, thirty-one prominent social scientists met at the University of Chicago, with the support of the U.S. Office of Education, to review what was known about cultural deprivation and education and to recommend specific solutions. The participants were aware that the federal government was planning to invest massive funds in an anti-poverty program. The document that resulted from the group's meeting, written by Benjamin Bloom, Allison Davis, and Robert Hess, contained an unambiguous view of what "cultural deprivation" meant and how to reverse it. The authors used the term "culturally disadvantaged or culturally deprived because we believe the roots of their problem may in large part be traced to their experiences in homes which do not transmit the cultural patterns necessary for the types of learning characteristic of the schools and the larger society." It was recommended:

First, that the school and the community should provide each child breakfast and lunch, appropriate medical care, and necessary clothing, if his parents were not able to.

Second, that nursery schools and kindergartens be provided for culturally deprived children "with the conditions for their intellectual development and the learning-to-learn stimulation which is found in the most favorable home environment."

Third, each child should have an individual prescription for learning during the first three years of elementary school, which would enable the child to "master the fundamental skills in language, reading, and arithmetic as well as develop a general skill in learning itself." The object, the authors stressed, "is to start with the child where he is and to proceed by a carefully developed and sequential program to bring him up to a level where he can learn as well as other children and eventually under the same conditions as other children."[10]

The report revealed both the strengths and the weaknesses of the compensatory education field and of American education as well. It analyzed a mass of complex social data concisely and accurately; it set goals that were democratic, egalitarian, and properly focused on educational values. But it revealed a paucity of knowledge about how to accomplish what was proposed. There was no question about how to feed hungry children or set up medical clinics in schools. But when recommending nursery schools and elementary schools that would bring culturally deprived children to their full intellectual development, the authors had to call for the creation of a "national commission of teachers and other specialists . . . to develop the curricular guidelines, materials, and methods" for these special programs. The authors admitted that very little was known about how to educate en masse the children of the poor. American schools had excelled in identifying talented youth for advancement, but they had never actually accepted full responsibility for making all children literate. In earlier years, immigrant children who were unsuccessful in school had dropped out and gone to work; they were able to enter an economy that needed unskilled or semiskilled labor. As more youths stayed in school longer in the 1930s, in response to the enforcement of compulsory education laws and a tight job market, progressive educators had introduced flexible standards, social promotion, and nonacademic programs to keep them in school and busy. American educators, despite their professed ideals, had never made a sustained effort to break the correlation between social class and educational achievement. Was it possible to educate all children? Was it possible to overcome whatever cultural handicaps children brought with them to school? To say that it was possible was an act of faith—an admirable act of faith, to be sure, but one for which evidence was still scant.

In the jargon of the day, compensatory education was the answer to cultural deprivation. Like so much other pedagogical jargon of the era, the term compensatory education was a misnomer with an unnecessarily pejorative tone. What it meant, when properly defined and implemented, was intensive, individualized instruction in an encouraging, supportive environment—in other words, good education.

In response to the political climate and to their own embarrassment about the failure rates of minority children, more than one hundred communities created compensatory programs between 1960 and 1965. The first, and possibly the best known, compensatory program was the Demonstration Guidance Project at Junior High School 43 and George Washington High School in New York City. It began in 1957, continued until 1962, and served as the model for the citywide Higher Horizons program. The 365 children in the program, 80 percent black or Puerto Rican, were selected for their academic potential. These students were placed in the academic course, where they received intensive instruction in language and mathematics and individualized counseling; they were screened for medical problems; they went to museums, concerts, plays, and colleges; they were helped to find part-time jobs. When the five-year program ended, 108 of the project pupils graduated with academic diplomas, compared to 43 in the preproject classes; the drop-out rate (22 percent) was well below the citywide average; and several of the students ranked in the top ten of their graduating class of 800 to 900.[11]

If the early pattern of the cultural deprivation research pointed toward the radical idea that schools had the responsibility to educate all children with the goal of full participation in the common culture, there was occasional evidence that the goal itself was in doubt. And as time went by, the doubts grew into a broad schism about the means and the purposes of educating the culturally deprived.

A subtle shift in direction was reflected in Frank Riessman's *The Culturally Deprived Child,* probably the most widely read of the books on the subject. Where the University of Chicago group had defined cultural deprivation in terms of children's need for certain abilities and learning styles, Riessman argued that the "culturally deprived," while lacking the values and culture of the middle class, had their own culture with its own strengths. His thesis was that if educators understood the culture of "the deprived," they could achieve "much greater academic success." Riessman articulated and popularized the claim that the so-called middle-class values of the school stood in the way of the "deprived child's" ability to learn, and that lower-class culture might actually be superior to anything the schools could teach. The book's introduction by Goodwin Watson of Teachers College made this point clearly:

> Under-cultured children have much to learn from education, but educators could well take some lessons from some of these youngsters. Their language may not be grammatical, but it is often more vivid and expressive than is the turgid prose of textbooks. These children face some of the "facts of life" more

realistically than many of their teachers do. Even their pugnacity might be worth attention by some long-suffering, overworked, underpaid teachers. When it comes to making friends and standing by their pals, some children from underprivileged neighborhoods far outshine their priggish teachers.

Perhaps, speculated Watson, they prefer television and movies because of their "authentic awareness that print is actually a devious and impoverished medium in comparison with the presence of speaking, acting persons." Here was a romantic vision of the nonverbal child, already wiser and cannier than those who were supposed to teach him to read in an "impoverished medium" and to speak in the language of the larger culture.[12]

Riessman assailed the school both for failing to bring the child into the academic mainstream and at the same time for failing to accept the nonverbal learning styles that kept "the deprived child" out of the mainstream. "It would be easy to say, as many have said, that we must give these children what middle-class parents give their children—we must stimulate them in the use of language through reading, discussion and the like. However, it is probable that this would not work nor would it make the best use of the deprived child's particular mode of functioning." Such children, he believed, should be taught through techniques that "stress the visual, the physical, the active. . . . We must be careful not to try to make these children over into replicas of middle-class children." It was somehow presumed that poor children could win the rewards of schooling—academic success and college entry—without mastering the verbal skills that make such rewards possible and meaningful.[13]

Since no one could say for certain just what would lead to better educational achievement by poor children, one researcher's theory was as good as another's. Thus, while one group of social scientists believed that the school could teach the children the skills they lacked, others insisted that the children's difficulty in learning was caused by the nature of the school, not just by inappropriate materials and methods but by its middle-class values. The view began to emerge that the middle-class bias of the school alienated poor children, and this in turn precipitated a search for reforms that would make the style of the school consonant with the special cultural needs of disadvantaged children. Riessman said that disadvantaged children needed to be taught by methods that acknowledged their nonverbal modes of communication and their preference for physical activity, like role-playing and teaching machines. He also urged teachers to learn the argot of "deprived" children and helpfully supplied a glossary of slang emphasizing terms for sexual activity and drugs, so that teachers could understand the language of the "deprived".[14]

Others attacked the unreality of the reading books, with their pictures of white children in neat suburban houses. What the Negro student needed, one researcher insisted, was to encounter a realistic portrayal of his own slum life; it was squeamish adults who removed "the crumbling plaster, foul smells, brazen rats, crunchy cockroaches, sidewalks littered with paper and broken glass" from the children's reading books. Although there was no evidence that poor children would read better if their reading books showed drug pushers and decaying tenements, there was also no evidence that they would not. In any event, in contrast to those who had advanced the idea that poor children needed to learn those things that would make them part of the common culture, other researchers asserted that since the "lower-class culture" of the children was at odds with the "middle-class culture" of the school, the school must change.[15]

Much of the language used by researchers in the field revealed conceptual confusion. By using the terms "lower-class culture" and "middle-class culture" so freely, it was implied that such cultures actually existed, that in the real world there was a "culture" that characterized poor people as a group and middle-income people as a group. On both counts, this thinking was not only wrong but encouraged invidious stereotyping. It simply was not true that all poor people, or even most poor people, shared a common culture. They were alike (though not always) in terms of their common economic needs, which were a function of being poor, but the significant differences among poor people were blurred by the blanket terminology attached to them by social scientists. Those who by income could be labeled a member of the same social class were of different races, different religions, different national origins; they differed in terms of their parents' education and occupation and in their own occupational experience, as well as in their length of residence in a given neighborhood. Even among a given racial group, like blacks, cultural differences were broad for all of the same reasons, including birthplace, religion, family history, and individual experience. In the search for understanding, little was gained by lumping poor children together under the common term the "culturally deprived"; the label obscured the particular situation of individual students and encouraged the belief that there must be a special curriculum, special books, and special methods geared to the presumed needs of the "culturally deprived."

Even while the focus on cultural deprivation was in full cry, some social scientists doubted its validity. Sloan Wayland of Teachers College pointed out that an earlier generation of social researchers had also found strikingly high levels of juvenile delinquency, crime, and economic dependency among poor European immigrants, and he wondered about the contemporary suggestion "that this is something new and is a unique product of the large city." He observed that "the historic task of formal education has been an attack on cultural deprivation. In the sense in which cultural deprivation is used, all but a very small fraction of mankind has been in this category." Hylan Lewis, who conducted a long-term field study among low-income families in the District of Columbia, questioned whether a culture of poverty existed. He observed great diversity in the behavior and values of poor people, and only one common trait: a lack of money. Poor people, he argued, did not live as they did because of their values or preferences, but because they did not have the income or security to live as they would choose.[16]

The way in which "middle-class culture" and "middle-class values" were casually used in the cultural deprivation literature was equally egregious. As with the poor, the stereotype of "middle-class culture" assumed a coherent culture where none existed. "Middle class" was a term describing people of middle and upper income, who shared some values as Americans but who differed in their race, religion, ethnicity, occupation, and social origin. It was a crude social analysis that confused income, culture, social class, and race. For a time, the term "middle class" was used to define the aptitudes and attitudes that the culturally deprived lacked, and it was certainly true that the poor needed the verbal skills and work habits that the productive sector of the economy required. But as the idea of a "culture of poverty" gained credence and interpreters, an ersatz form of egalitarianism was employed to attack the "imposition" of "middle-class values" on the poor, as though the schools were bound by tenets of cultural pluralism to respect the "culture of poverty." To suggest that verbal skills are "middle-class," and to complain that the emphasis on the teaching of verbal skills is unfair to those who lack them, is to propose that the school cease to function as a school. Historically, the public schools have performed a vital socializing role, teaching children of diverse origins the skills, knowledge, and values necessary for participation in the mainstream of American society. It was an unfortunate irony that the scholarly and popular criticism of the socializing role of the school occurred at the very time that large numbers of poor children, recent immigrants from the South and Puerto Rico, most needed to learn the skills, knowledge, and values of the larger society.

A different critique of the cultural deprivation field was leveled by Kenneth Clark, the psychologist whose work had influenced the *Brown* decision. He attacked what he called the "cult of cultural deprivation" on grounds that the environmental explanation of failure had become as deterministic as the genetic explanation ever was, and so allowed prejudiced teachers to say that "these children" cannot learn because of their slum backgrounds. The crux of academic failure, he contended, was the low expectations of teachers: "these children, by and large, do not learn because they are not being taught effectively and they are not being taught because those who are charged with the responsibility of teaching them do not believe that they can learn, do not expect that they can learn, and do not act toward them in ways which help them to learn." This perspective was soon adopted by advocates of black community control, who asserted that black children failed because of the racism and low expectations of their teachers.[17]

Although social scientists and educators were not in agreement about whether there was a culture of poverty or how best to educate poor children, there was nonetheless broad support for the use of federal funds to support equal educational opportunity. As the Johnson administration was shaping its preschool Head Start program and its Title I compensatory program, several different approaches contended for the attention of policy makers. First there was the "deficit model," which held that schools should teach poor children certain skills and attitudes that they lacked in order to close the achievement gap between poor and middle-income children. What poor children needed, according to this analysis, was intensive academic preparation to improve their achievement levels. Second, there was the contrasting claim that poor children would do better in school if the school would respect their culture and values, rather than trying to impose middle-class culture and values on them. Partisans of this view believed that poor children fell behind because of alienation from the school, which could be overcome by the use of special techniques and materials appropriate to the culture of disadvantaged children. Third, there was the view, not inconsistent with either of the others, that the school ought to become a social service center for the entire community and that teachers and administrators should become involved in the political, social, and economic problems of the local community. The vigorous advocacy of differing theories obscured the fact that educators did not know how best to educate poor children or even whether it was possible to eliminate the achievement differences between poor and middle-income children.

The preschool Head Start program grew directly out of the optimism and environmentalism of the so-called deficit model. Initially, it was expected that educational intervention at a "critical period" would quickly and permanently enable poor children to enter school as ready to learn as were middle-income children. The original plan was intellectually oriented and aimed specifically to develop the "attitudes and aptitudes" associated with "middle-class culture." As Head Start began, President Johnson predicted that participation in the summer session would not only "rescue" the children from poverty but would "put them on an even footing with their classmates as they enter school."[18]

The expectation that Head Start would stress intellectual growth and transition to "middle-class" values was not realized, however, for a variety of reasons. First, due to its explosive growth, Head Start began with an insufficiency of trained teachers and without agreement on methods and goals; while its planners had recommended a pilot program for about twenty-five hundred children, the Johnson administration's desire to launch a visible, national antipoverty effort led to the enrollment of five hundred thousand children the first summer of Head Start. Second, whatever its originators may have intended, the priorities of each Head Start center were determined by "maximum feasible participation" of local residents, which meant that the educational goals of the program had to compete with other immediate concerns, like adult education and employment. Third, experts in early-childhood education were more attuned to a multifaceted, child-development approach than to the single-minded goal of intellectual growth; consequently, the typical Head Start project was "child-centered" and focused on "the development of the whole child with emphasis on social and emotional growth."[19]

The curriculum of the "traditional" center emphasized free play and permissive adult-child relations rather than structured learning. In typical Head Start centers, cognitive goals were no more important, and often less important, than social, medical, and psychological services, nutrition, adult career development, and parent involvement. Two years after Head Start began, according to one observer, many projects began to replace trained teachers with paraprofessionals; since professional educators "had not been able to define or defend a consistent educational approach," there seemed no reason to retain professional teachers instead of neighborhood residents who needed work. When national evaluations repeatedly showed that the academic effects of Head Start were limited and transitory, there was widespread disappointment; but the findings were unfair in that they judged Head Start by its original goals, without recognizing that the typical Head Start center put little emphasis on cognitive growth.[20]

The Title I program of the Elementary and Secondary Education Act (ESEA) of 1965, whose purpose was to meet the "special educational needs of educationally deprived children," was beset by some of the same operational and conceptual problems. Approximately five-sixths of all ESEA funds were allocated to Title I, with the expectation that federal funds would be used for compensatory programs to improve the achievement of poor children. One reason for the program's popularity was that almost every district in the country received Title I funding. Concerned that districts would use the money to subsidize ineffectual programs, Senator Robert F. Kennedy of New York insisted that the law require districts receiving Title I funds to submit, at least once annually, objective evaluations of the educational effectiveness of their programs. Furthermore, districts were specifically expected to share information about "promising educational practices."[21]

The programs designed by local educational agencies included not only improvement of academic achievement but also the provision of socialization skills, cultural enrichment, social work, parental involvement, libraries, speech and hearing therapy, nutrition, clothing, and medical services. The goals were diffuse, and school officials in 1965 did not have an educational strategy in hand to apply to the well-documented problems of the disadvantaged. As one observer put it, "Title I . . . asked schoolmen to launch an activity in what was essentially an uncharted area and to implement successful programs for the very group of children the schools historically had seemed least able to help." Few school districts submitted the achievement data required by law to the Office of Education; as a result, the first national survey "was not reported until 1970; the 1969 survey analysis was never released; the 1970 results consist of 1,200 tables which were never interpreted; and the 1971 data were never analyzed." When national evaluations could find scant evidence that Title I had closed the achievement gap between poor and middle-income children, it was seldom noted that the goal itself was shared more consistently by evaluators than by those in charge of the programs.[22]

Even though theories about cultural deprivation achieved their greatest recognition in the original conceptualization of the Head Start and Title I programs, other aspects of the Great Society soon impaired the credibility of such theorizing. First, the "community action programs" of the Economic Opportunity Act, which operated with "maximum feasible participation" of the poor, sought to mobilize poor residents and to create community solidarity and pride; with spokesmen for the poor involved in policy discussions, it became not only tasteless but politically awkward to talk about "cultural deprivation" and "cultural deficits." Social scientists employed by or sympathetic to community-action programs wrote instead of the cultural strengths of the poor, and representatives of the local groups insisted that what the poor needed was not cultural enrichment but power to run their own schools in order to oust incompetent teachers.

A second reason for the abandonment of the cultural deprivation model can be found in the cannonade directed against the Moynihan report on the Negro family. An assistant secretary of labor and an architect of the "war on poverty," Daniel Patrick Moynihan prepared an analysis of the social and economic plight of American Negroes, titled *The Negro Family: The Case for National Action.* The report argued for new federal policies directed at the root causes of family instability: unemployment, poverty, discrimination, poor housing and health care. President Johnson's speech at Howard University on June 4, 1965, drew heavily from the then-secret Moynihan report, calling for a new definition of equality. The president said:

> You do not take a person who, for years, has been hobbled by chains and liberate him, bring him up to the starting line of a race and then say, 'You are free to compete with all the others,' and still justly believe that you have been completely fair. . . . It is not enough just to open the gates of opportunity. All our citizens must have the ability to walk through those gates. . . . This is the next and the more profound stage of the battle for civil rights. We seek not just freedom but opportunity. We seek not just legal equity but human ability, not just equality as a right and a theory but equality as a fact and equality as a result. . . . To this end equal opportunity is essential, but not enough, not enough.

The speech was warmly applauded by black leaders. When, in the summer of 1965, the report itself began to leak to the press, it was sharply denounced, and critics claimed that Moynihan blamed the problems of blacks on their family structure instead of on racism and injustice (though it was difficult to see how anyone who had actually read the report, which recommended a major federal commitment to eliminate the economic sources of black poverty, could come to this conclusion). The attacks were so laden with unfair charges of racism, and the controversy became so acrimonious, that the report was buried. After the opprobrium heaped on the Moynihan report, it became clear to social researchers that certain issues involving race and culture were taboo, or at the very least to be approached with extreme caution.[23]

The hostile reaction to the report reflected extensive discord about the assumptions undergirding government social policy. Policy makers, following the lead of the social scientists, had gotten into problem areas where the connections between cause and effect were murky at best. In the past, the object of a housing program was to provide shelter; school aid was a matter of raising teachers' salaries or building new facilities or reducing class size; other programs, by and large, had equally explicit and measurable goals. Now, legislators and policy makers tried to stay abreast of the evolving debates among social scientists about the importance of self-esteem, of socialization skills, of community organization, and other goals that seemed unassailable yet intangible.

While social researchers and policy makers struggled to relate the emerging social programs to contending social theories, black neighborhoods in the cities began to erupt in rioting and violence. In the summer of 1965, only days after President Johnson signed the Voting Rights Act into law, a riot broke out in the Watts section of Los Angeles, leaving thirty-four dead, nine hundred injured, and more than four thousand arrested. The following summer, there were forty-three riots in other black communities. As tensions in society rose, so too did the feeling that something had to be done to stop the rising tide of disorder; in addition to black unrest, there was growing opposition to the escalation of the war in Vietnam, especially on the campuses. The first antiwar "teach-in" took place on March 24, 1965, at the University of Michigan at Ann Arbor.[24]

The broad national consensus that the president had mobilized to pass the Civil Rights Act, the poverty program, the ESEA, and the Voting Rights Act became increasingly fragile. Whites and blacks in the Johnson coalition began to defect, for different reasons. The established civil rights organizations seemed out of touch with the blacks who were rioting in the cities. The new black voices were angry and bitter, encouraged in their anger by federally-funded antipoverty agencies, which adopted confrontation tactics as a means of community organizing. The militant groups preferred to fight the system rather than to work within it. By choosing confrontation instead of cooperation, the militants challenged the very authorities who funded their activities and who had the power to expand or to curtail the government's social programs, while strengthening the hand of political forces who had always doubted the wisdom of such federal expenditures.

Whites, too, began to splinter away from the liberal consensus. Some moved decisively to the left of the president in anger over the Vietnam war and the failure to achieve racial equality. Other whites, however, reacted with hostility to the riots, demonstrations, and disorders; the phenomenon called "white backlash" had produced large votes for the presidential candidacy of Alabama Governor George Wallace in blue-collar districts in 1964. Even among liberal supporters of the civil rights movement there was growing resentment in reaction to the riots and to black expressions of antiwhite feeling and of separatist sympathies.

Something had to be done; the government had to respond in visible fashion to the spreading racial unrest. The most tangible symbol of black grievances was the slow pace of school desegregation. In May, 1964, ten years after the *Brown* decision, less than 2 percent of the black students in the eleven states of the South attended school with whites. Throughout the decade, the federal government had stood aloof from school desegregation, since the power to do anything other than enforce federal court orders was lacking. The entire burden of interpreting and carrying out the decision had fallen on the courts, with little uniformity from one district to the next. However, the impotence of the federal government ended with the passage of the Civil Rights Act, for its Title VI forbade discrimination in any federally-funded program, and it authorized a cutoff of federal funds from any program in which there was illegal discrimination. Title VI said that "No person . . . shall, on the ground of race, color, or national origin, be excluded from participation in, be denied the benefits of, or be subjected to discrimination under any program or activity receiving Federal financial assistance."[25]

There was initially some question as to how much coercive power the federal government would gain with the enactment of Title VI. When it was first proposed in 1963 by the Kennedy administration, southern congressmen complained that it would be used to impose "racial balancing" in the South. After men like Senator Sam Ervin of North Carolina charged that Title VI "would confer the power of a dictator upon the President," the final version of the Civil Rights Act carefully specified that " 'desegregation' shall not mean the assignment of students to public schools in order to overcome racial imbalance." And then, the possibility of a fund cutoff was not a powerful threat in 1964, since there was no general federal aid to education. However, when the Elementary and Secondary Education Act of 1965 passed, the weapon established by Title VI was suddenly loaded.[26]

The Office of Education in the Department of Health, Education, and Welfare (HEW) was in charge of disbursing federal funds and of devising a way to assure that districts were in compliance with Title VI. Federal education officials, eager to press desegregation as far as possible without igniting a rebellion among southern congressmen, issued guidelines in April, 1965, that described how a district could qualify for its federal funds. First, those districts that had eliminated all traces of segregation in pupil and faculty assignment and in all school activities could file an "assurance of compliance." Second, those that were desegregating under court order could file a copy of the court order, along with a report on the racial distribution of students and faculty in their schools and on the progress of their desegregation activities. And third, other districts could file a voluntary plan that would fully desegregate their schools by the fall of 1967, either by permitting students to choose their own schools or by adopting compact geographical attendance zones. Although the HEW guidelines were onerous only to those districts that had adamantly refused to acknowledge the existence of the *Brown* decision, they nonetheless evoked both howls of outrage from the South and complaints from civil rights groups about their permissive character.[27]

In the first year of implementing Title VI, the proportion of black children attending school with whites rose from 2 percent to 6 percent, and 1,563 districts started to desegregate, more in a single year than in the preceding decade. Deep South districts overwhelmingly submitted free-choice plans, permitting students to choose their schools, presumably to maintain segregation-by-choice or to establish token desegregation; the U. S. Civil Rights Commission identified 102 free-choice districts where not a single black student was in school with whites. Southern districts thought that the adoption of a free-choice plan fully satisfied the requirements of the Civil Rights Act, but the Office of Education considered free-choice only a means to the end of complete integration.[28]

Despite the progress of the first year, the Office of Education felt that the pace of integration was far too slow. New guidelines were issued in March, 1966, which virtually prohibited free-choice plans. Believing that the first year's guidelines represented a definitive interpretation of the law's requirements, the South was astonished to learn that the Office of Education had upped the ante. The new HEW guidelines set out percentages, or "performance criteria," that each district was required to meet. If 8 to 9 percent of a district's black pupils were integrated, then double that number would have to be integrated by 1966/67; if only 4 to 5 percent had been integrated, then triple that number was required. Where free-choice plans had produced no integration, a "very substantial start" was necessary. Every district was expected to make "significant progress" toward faculty integration.[29]

As federal officials tightened the enforcement vise through the fund cutoff threat in Title VI, southerners in Congress denounced the revised guidelines as arbitrary and dictatorial. They charged that HEW had initiated a policy of racial balancing, which was specifically prohibited in the Civil Rights Act. Commissioner of Education Harold Howe, II, who was entirely unsympathetic to their complaints, held that the percentages were devised "to give school officials some guidance as to a reasonable degree of progress." Resentment against the guidelines was loudly expressed in Congress, where—by the summer of 1966—the political climate had shifted sharply in response to the continuing riots and black militancy. HEW's efforts to withhold federal aid funds from Chicago pending an investigation of charges of segregation drew heated attacks from Illinois politicians and other northerners who had supported federal enforcement

activities in the South. The second session of the Eighty-ninth Congress
—the Congress that had been brought into office in Lyndon Johnson's
landslide and had enacted federal aid to education, Medicare, Model Cities, and the Voting Rights Act—refused to pass a new civil rights act. The
problem was that Congress and HEW had conflicting interpretations of the
goals of the Civil Rights Act of 1964. The same Congress had mustered
large majorities to remove racial barriers and to endorse nondiscrimination
in education; but HEW was enforcing in the South precisely those policies
of racial balance that southern congressmen thought had been proscribed
in the Civil Rights Act. In reaction to HEW's activism, the "most liberal
House since the depression" passed an antibusing amendment in 1966.
Every year for the next fifteen years, the House reflected the unpopularity
of what was called "racial balancing" by adopting legislation forbidding
HEW or the Justice Department to require the reassignment of students
away from their neighborhood schools in order to overcome racial
imbalance.[30]

But the fate of the HEW guidelines, which translated the mandate of
the Civil Rights Act from color-blindness to color-consciousness, was
decided by the courts, not by Congress. In the decade following *Brown,*
southern federal judges strove to determine precisely what the *Brown* decision required and what it forbade. Different interpretations emerged in
different jurisdictions, since the Supreme Court never provided a clear
definition of "segregation," "desegregation," and "integration" and had
made no major school decision since 1954 other than that on Little Rock.
To fill the vacuum left by the high court's ambiguity, many southern
judges and school boards relied on the "Briggs dictum," an interpretation
of *Brown* set forward in 1955 by a three-judge federal district court in South
Carolina. It ruled that the Supreme Court

> has not decided that the federal courts are to take over or regulate the public
> schools of the states. It has not decided that the states must mix persons of
> different races in the schools or must require them to attend schools or must
> deprive them of the right of choosing the schools they attend. What it has
> decided, and all that it has decided, is that a state may not deny to any person
> on account of race the right to attend any school that it maintains. . . . The
> Constitution, in other words, does not require integration. It merely forbids
> discrimination. It does not forbid such segregation as occurs as the result of
> voluntary action. It merely forbids the use of governmental power to enforce
> segregation.[31]

To those who wanted the courts and the federal government not only
to ban school segregation but to require integration, the Briggs dictum was

a formidable obstacle. Since it validated free choice, it stood in the path of the HEW guidelines, which required proof of actual racial mixing. The conflict between the two principles was resolved in the federal courts between 1965 and 1967 in the momentous *Singleton* and *Jefferson* decisions. Written by Judge John Minor Wisdom of the Fifth Circuit Court of Appeals, the decisions were a dramatic turning point in the evolution of desegregation in the South. As one legal scholar noted, these two decisions "presage the era of massive integration. Their importance cannot be overemphasized." Not only did they impose a uniform standard throughout the South, based on the HEW guidelines, but "they created *new* policy by reinterpreting settled desegregation law."[32]

Judge Wisdom upheld the legitimacy of the controversial HEW guidelines, which he said were "intended by Congress and the executive to be part of a coordinated national program." Furthermore, he held that public school officials had an affirmative duty "to provide an integrated school system," and that the Briggs dictum "should be laid to rest." Southern lawyers had understood "desegregation" to mean that Negro children had the right to go to any public school of their choosing. But Judge Wisdom contended that this interpretation left segregation largely undisturbed. The Constitution, he held, required the public schools "to integrate students, faculties, facilities, and activities." To the southerners' claim that the Civil Rights Act specifically prohibited "the assignment of students to public schools in order to overcome racial imbalance," Judge Wisdom found that this prohibition was meant to apply only to nonracially motivated—de facto—segregation (the segregation that arises as a result of demography) and not to prevent the disestablishment of de jure segregated school systems (those created by law and governmental actions). He approved HEW's use of racial percentages to prod the districts into providing a unitary, integrated system. *"The only school desegregation plan that meets Constitutional standards,"* wrote Judge Wisdom, *"is one that works."*[33]

The *Singleton* and *Jefferson* decisions, which involved districts in Alabama, Louisiana, and Mississippi that had resolutely refused to begin desegregation until HEW gained power over the federal purse-strings, immediately changed the legal meaning of desegregation. Before these decisions, the command of the *Brown* decision could reasonably be understood, in Alexander Bickel's term, as a "stop" order, commanding government officials to cease separating children on the basis of race; the *Singleton* and *Jefferson* decisions converted *Brown* into a "go" order, compelling school districts to take affirmative steps to mix children of different races. Judge Wisdom left no doubt that nothing less than actual integration would be tolerated; that henceforward the courts and HEW would work together to achieve the same result; that the evasive strategies of the past were finished; and that the delaying game of "deliberate speed" was unacceptable.[34]

Although the decisions were a great triumph for the civil rights forces, the victory was tempered by Judge Wisdom's necessary distinction between de facto and de jure segregation. In order to show that the Civil Rights Act's prohibition of racial balancing did not apply to de jure segregated systems and did not therefore invalidate the HEW guidelines, Judge Wisdom held that Congress intended this prohibition to apply only to de facto school systems. While this conclusion disappointed those who believed that racial isolation, regardless of the cause, violated the Constitution, it did establish the power of the courts and the federal government to compel southern districts to integrate their public schools. The partnership between HEW and the federal courts proved to be remarkably effective in eliminating school segregation in the South. In 1964, only about 2 percent of the region's black students attended schools with whites; by 1968, the proportion had grown to 32 percent, and by 1972, 91 percent of southern black students were in schools with whites.[35]

The steady progress that was made in desegregating the schools of the South did nothing to ease the tension that was building in the urban black ghettos. Each summer brought new disorders, new explosions of frustration and impatience. Martin Luther King, Jr., had repeatedly warned that black patience would wear thin, and now blacks were turning away from him as a symbol of the old, willing-to-compromise leadership. In 1966, the young leadership of the Student Nonviolent Coordinating Committee (SNCC) became increasingly radical and separatist in its outlook; some staff members declared that whites should get out of SNCC. On a march through Mississippi, Stokely Carmichael attracted national publicity by using the slogan "black power" as a rallying cry. King warned that the inflammatory slogan "would confuse our allies, isolate the Negro community and give many prejudiced whites, who might otherwise be ashamed of their anti-Negro feeling, a ready excuse for self-justification." But Carmichael was not interested in holding together a coalition of black and white supporters, as the older leaders were. On a rational level, he was reaching out to build an independent black political base, akin to the power that other ethnic groups had wielded. But on an emotional level, he was invoking racial consciousness and racial pride to purge the feelings of inadequacy and dependency instilled by past racism. Whites reacted to this new phase of militancy with anger, in which case they joined the backlash, or with guilt, in which case they agreed that something must be done, and soon, to placate the seething black masses.[36]

The sense of racial crisis that had given impetus to Lyndon Johnson's Great Society persisted, but the consensus necessary for political action had collapsed. In 1966, the push and pull of ideas and events were centrifugal. There were so many possibilities, and yet so many of them moved in contrary directions. The A. Philip Randolph Institute proposed a ten-year plan to spend $180 billion on public programs; called the "Freedom Budget," it aimed to eradicate poverty and slums by a program of full employment, an adequate minimum wage, decent housing and health care for all, and a guaranteed income for those who could not work. It was, in short, a domestic Marshall Plan. In another time, it might have captured the imagination of liberals, but in 1966, the liberal imagination was distracted. It was distracted by the escalation of the war in Vietnam, which was consuming ever larger quantities of human and physical resources; it was distracted by the riots and racial tensions in the cities; and it was distracted by the appearance in several major cities of black demands for community control.[37]

But even without political consensus, social scientists and educators continued to search for answers to the problem of educating poor blacks in the cities. One likely course of action was suggested by a massive report published in the summer of 1966. The report, called *Equality of Educational Opportunity*, had been commissioned by the Civil Rights Act of 1964 as a survey "concerning the lack of availability of equal educational opportunities for individuals by reason of race, color, religion, or national origin in public educational institutions at all levels in the United States." A large research team led by James S. Coleman of Johns Hopkins University and Ernest Q. Campbell of Vanderbilt University surveyed some four thousand public schools in the fall of 1965. The research team decided not only to examine such resource factors as facilities, materials, curricula, and laboratories, but also to scrutinize outcomes—that is, achievement scores. Thus, in defining their assignment, the researchers shifted the issue under investigation from equal opportunity to equal results. Coleman later argued that "the major virtue of the study" lay in the fact that by not accepting the traditional measures of school quality, it shifted policy attention to the question of how school resources affect pupil achievement. The major findings of the survey (popularly known as the Coleman Report) startled educational policymakers.[38]

The Coleman Report found that:

- Most American children attended schools where almost all of their fellow pupils were of the same race.
- Schools attended by white students had some advantages in physical re-

sources over those attended by blacks, but the differences were far less than anticipated, or, as one analyst pointed out, "American schools were virtually separate and equal" at the time of the survey.[39]

- The academic achievement of children from minority groups was one to two years behind that of whites at first grade; by twelfth grade, minority children were as much as three to five years behind their white peers.
- Achievement seemed to be related to the student's family background rather than to the quality of the school.
- Next to the student's own family background, the other factors related to achievement were social composition of the school and the student's sense of control of the environment.

The Coleman Report was debated, dissected, and reanalyzed, for while it drew conclusions, it made no recommendations. Others, however, were quick to see policy implications. The most important point to filter through the public prints was that "schools don't make a difference." If student achievement is determined largely by family background and scarcely at all by teachers, books, and facilities, the reasoning went, then improving the school is unlikely to have much effect on student achievement. This finding raised serious doubts about the likely value of compensatory education for poor children, which was just beginning to burgeon in response to the passage of federal aid to education only the year before.

But while school improvement received little support from the report, there was a strong suggestion that social class integration might effectively improve the achievement of lower-class students. And, since most Negro students were poor, racial integration was the best route to improve their test scores. Indeed, the report indicated that, "in the long run, integration should be expected to have a positive effect on Negro achievement." The report compared four groups of black students: those in classes with a white majority; those in classes that were half black, half white; those in classes with a black majority; and those in classes with no whites. Those in the first group generally got the highest scores, although the differences from group to group were small.[40]

The idea that the Coleman Report demonstrated that racial integration would improve black achievement was quickly disseminated. It was furthermore believed that the report conclusively showed that successful integration required a white majority. Actually, the evidence was not strong on either point. The tables of average test scores for Negro pupils did not show that black student achievement rose in proportion to the presence of white classmates. While black students in majority white classes generally had the highest scores, black students in all-black classes scored as high or higher than those in half-and-half or majority-black

169

classes. Oddly, in the Midwest, students in all-black classes outperformed even those blacks in majority white classes. Furthermore, there was no way of knowing that the proportion of whites or blacks had affected achievement levels. After all, the black students in integrated schools presumably lived in integrated neighborhoods, since there was no court-ordered desegregation in 1965 (no southern districts were included in the table of Negro test scores). So, the higher achievement of black students in largely white schools may have been related to the family background factors that enabled them to live in an integrated neighborhood in 1965, rather than to the independent effect of the number of whites in their school. A correlation was established, but not a cause.[41]

Nonetheless, the Coleman Report seemed to offer powerful ammunition to those who had become convinced that racial integration, and not quality of resources or instruction, was the key to improving black achievement. It appeared to provide solid documentation for the view that compensatory programs would have no effect, and that the North, West, and East would have to take the same strong medicine that HEW and the courts were giving the South. Furthermore, it appeared just when federal courts in the South declared that the *Brown* decision was not simply a guarantee of the right to choose one's school without regard to race but a requirement to disperse students of both races. As Alexander Bickel later remarked, "The enforcement of a requirement of racial dispersal of school populations in one region of the country but not in other regions is morally, politically, and, ultimately, therefore, legally, an untenable position on any permanent basis."[42]

It was hardly surprising that the *Brown* decision was increasingly defined not as a command to eliminate racial discrimination but a command to eliminate racial isolation. Even in 1954, many people had interpreted the *Brown* decision precisely that way. The president of the New York City Board of Education told a Harlem audience that the all-black schools their children attended caused "a psychological scarring." The board publicly pledged to end de facto segregation because "racially homogeneous schools damage the personality of minority group children," "decrease their motivation," and "impair their ability to learn." In 1963, the New York State commissioner of education held that any school in which more than 50 percent of the students were black was racially imbalanced and therefore incapable of providing equal educational opportunity. A similar policy statement was adopted by the Massachusetts Advisory Committee on Racial Imbalance and Education in 1965, recommending the elimination of all racially imbalanced schools (this recommendation was enacted into law by the state legislature). New Jersey's commissioner of education in

1963 held that: "in the minds of Negro pupils and parents a stigma is attached to attending a school whose enrollment is completely or exclusively Negro, and that this sense of stigma and resulting feeling of inferiority have an undesirable effect upon attitudes related to successful learning." Or, put another way, racist attitudes toward black institutions made it impossible for whites or blacks to believe that a school attended largely by black students could be equal to one attended largely by whites.[43]

Northern courts struggled with the problem of de facto segregation in the early 1960s, without guidance from the Supreme Court. A federal district court in 1961 found that the neighborhood school policy of New Rochelle, New York, was unconstitutional because it caused a predominantly black neighborhood to have an elementary school that was 94 percent black. The decision was upheld on appeal, and the Supreme Court denied a request to review the decision. The school in the black neighborhood was closed, and its students were distributed among other schools. Though New Rochelle was called the "Little Rock of the North," other northern courts ruled differently. In 1963, when a suit was brought against the neighborhood school system of Gary, Indiana, on the grounds that black students were segregated unconstitutionally, a federal district judge held that racial balance in the public schools was not mandated by the *Brown* decision or the Constitution. The decision was upheld on appeal. The Supreme Court refused to resolve the conflict between the lower court rulings on New Rochelle and Gary.[44]

But regardless of the irresolution in the courts, there was a growing consensus among social scientists that racial isolation, whatever its cause, was directly responsible for the low educational achievement of blacks. The most forceful and typical expression of the growing consensus was the U.S. Commission on Civil Rights' report, *Racial Isolation in the Public Schools,* issued in February, 1967. The report was written in response to a request from President Johnson, who in late 1965 had asked the commission to conduct a fact-finding study of racial isolation, presumably to lay the groundwork for federal action against de facto segregation. Numerous well-known educators and social scientists, including James Coleman and Kenneth Clark, served on the commission's advisory committee or as staff or consultants.[45]

Relying on the Coleman Report as "a basic fund of nationwide data on student achievement and attitudes," the report found that racial isolation was "intense" and "increasing"; that racial, social, and economic separation between city and suburb was growing; that geographical zoning in cities contributed to racial isolation due to residential racial concentration; that a student's academic achievement was strongly affected by his family background and by the social class of his classmates; that Negro students were more likely than whites to attend schools with mostly disadvantaged students, to have less qualified teachers, and to attend schools of lesser quality; and that Negro students in majority-white schools generally achieved more than did Negro students in majority-Negro schools.[46]

Racial Isolation went well beyond the Coleman Report in its conclusions about the educational benefits of placing disadvantaged Negro students in majority-white schools. Where the Coleman Report speculated about the potential benefits of social class and racial integration, the Commission on Civil Rights' report stated positively that: "Negro students in majority-white schools with poorer teachers generally achieve better than similar Negro students in majority-Negro schools with better teachers"; "Disadvantaged Negro students in school with a majority of equally disadvantaged white students achieve better than Negro students in school with equally disadvantaged Negro students"; disadvantaged Negro students in school with other disadvantaged Negro students were more than two grade levels behind equally disadvantaged Negroes in school with a majority of advantaged whites; the longer Negroes attend desegregated schools, the better their achievement and attitudes.[47]

The report's judgments about the value of compensatory education in Negro schools were devastatingly negative, although few of the programs providing intensive academic support and cultural enrichment to poor black students had been in existence for more than two or three years. It held that "Negro children attending desegregated schools that do not have compensatory education programs perform better than Negro children in racially isolated schools with such programs." In a review of prominent compensatory programs around the country, the report found little or no achievement gain for Negro students. In contrast, it held that Negroes who were bused to majority-white schools significantly raised their achievement levels. The commission held that compensatory education programs had been of "limited effectiveness" because the problems they attempted to solve stemmed in large measure "from racial and social class isolation in schools which themselves are isolated by race and social class."[48]

The commission recommended that Congress establish a "uniform standard providing for the elimination of racial isolation in the schools." A "reasonable" national standard, said the report, would permit no school to be more than 50 percent Negro. Schools that were more than 50 percent Negro "tend to be regarded and treated by the community as segregated and inferior schools."[49]

Racial Isolation posited two alternate remedies for black educational problems: on one hand were compensatory educational programs, which "rest upon the assumption that the major cause of academic disadvantage is the poverty of the average Negro child and the environment in which he is raised"; on the other was the dispersion of black students into majority-white schools, which was based on the assumption that any predominantly black school was stigmatized and perceived to be inferior by whites and blacks and therefore incapable of providing equal educational opportunity. Although the evidence to accept or reject either alternative was fragmentary, the commission came down strongly on the side of dispersion, in the belief that blacks would benefit even if their classmates were equally impoverished whites, so long as blacks remained in a minority. The lure of the dispersion remedy was strong; it promised that the achievement gap could be closed—not by intensive instruction or costly compensatory programs but by the extraordinarily simple (if extraordinarily difficult) act of placing black students in white-majority schools. Unable to imagine the possibility of a good school that had more blacks than whites, the commission's report was uniquely a document of its time, which could not extricate itself from the very racism that it so passionately denounced.[50]

Racial Isolation became the bible of the integration movement at the very time that some black intellectuals and community activists lost faith in the ideal of assimilation. As many urban school systems became predominantly nonwhite and the likelihood of integration (as the commission defined it, with a white majority) dimmed, it appeared that the ideology of the integration movement actually heightened the stigma attached to schools attended by minority pupils. The constant reiteration that schools in minority neighborhoods were inferior, no matter what their resources or programs, and the adoption of integration programs that drew away the most talented minority youth to schools in white neighborhoods had the effect, in the view of some black community leaders, of dampening "student motivation, parental interest, teacher investment and community practices." If all people are equal, regardless of their ethnicity, they wondered, why is it that a predominantly white school is a good school, but a predominantly black and Hispanic school is inherently inferior?[51]

Such questions, reflecting the rise of black militancy and racial separatism, precipitated the community control movement that began in the summer of 1966 at Intermediate School 201 in Harlem. IS 201 was a new school in the center of New York City's most famous black ghetto; it had splendid facilities and a hand-picked staff. Community organizers in the local antipoverty program saw the opening of the new school as a valuable opportunity to mobilize the community, initially to seek integration, ultimately to demand community control of the school. IS 201 was in tumult throughout the 1966/67 school year, and the leaders of its protests made common cause with activists from other neighborhoods to demand community control of their schools. After months of boycotts, picketing, and demonstrations, the New York City Board of Education agreed in the summer of 1967 to create three demonstration districts in minority communities, including IS 201, run by local governing boards. In short order, the local boards became increasingly radical in their demands for total control and in their attacks on the "white power structure" and the predominantly Jewish teachers' union. In May, 1968, the governing board of the Ocean Hill–Brownsville district in Brooklyn ousted a group of teachers without due process, and the United Federation of Teachers shut down the entire school system for two months in the fall. The following spring, the state legislature adopted a moderate school decentralization plan, which scuttled the three demonstration districts, dissipated any prospect for local control by autonomous boards, and placated the powerful teachers' union.[52]

The community control movement failed politically because it was perceived as a vehicle for black nationalism and racial separatism, thus threatening the fundamental notion of public schooling; because its leaders flagrantly assailed the very interests whose cooperation was needed; and because the inflammatory rhetoric it used to mobilize the local community alienated potential supporters outside the local community. Nonetheless, the movement gained a wide hearing for its critique of conventional educational and social ideas. It rejected the assimilationist goals of the integration movement and asserted the value of ethnic awareness. It disparaged the melting pot ideal of the common school in favor of the school as a reflection of the concerns and interests of the local community. Where integrationists had focused on absorbing blacks into the mainstream culture, advocates of community control appealed to racial pride and asserted the integrity of the black cultural heritage. But in their struggle for group recognition and solidarity, the activists at IS 201 and Ocean Hill–Brownsville blundered badly by resorting to antiwhite and anti-Semitic rhetoric. In a city (and nation) of many minorities, they violated the code of intergroup comity that permits a pluralistic society to function. Yet ironically, after the fiery political rhetoric faded from memory, the community control movement left as its legacy the conviction that blacks must not be seen as an inferior caste, to be pitied and dispersed, but as an ethnic group asserting its demands and interests like others in a pluralistic society.

Though scorned by militant blacks as hopelessly out of step with the black revolution and eclipsed in the popular media by those on the barricades, the NAACP continued to press for school integration in the courts.

In 1968, even as intellectuals like Kenneth Clark threw their support behind the struggle for black community control in New York, the Supreme Court issued its first major desegregation decision since Little Rock a decade earlier. In *Green* v. *New Kent County*, the Court struck down freedom-of-choice plans that did not produce measurable desegregation. New Kent County, Virginia, had two schools, one white and one black, and no residential segregation; under its free-choice plan, 15 percent of the blacks attended the formerly white school, but no whites chose to go to the black school. The Court required the local school board to develop a plan that "promises realistically to work now," one that would produce "a system without a 'white' school and a 'Negro' school, but just schools." The *Green* decision was a landmark; the Court for the first time since its 1955 decree, which decreed so little, specified that actual racial mixture was required to eliminate de jure segregation. The timing was significant. A free-choice policy in 1955 would probably have sufficed; by 1968, the federal courts had come to view free-choice as synonymous with evasion of the duty to comply with *Brown*. [53]

As the Supreme Court moved to require integration rather than merely the absence of discrimination, hostility to court-ordered racial balancing grew. The assignment of children to school in order to promote racial integration was never popular. Though social scientists proclaimed the educational benefits of racial integration and urged government to reassign pupil populations on the basis of race ("busing"), public opposition to such proposals remained unwaveringly high. The House of Representatives regularly approved antibusing amendments, which were defeated in the Senate, ironically, by the same parliamentary tactics that segregationists had once used to frustrate majority opinion. Political scientist Gary Orfield observed that "Committed civil rights supporters with positions of seniority have used conference committees, control of committee agendas, filibusters, muddled legislative language, and a variety of other strategems to frustrate antibusing majorities. Time after time the tactics the South used to preserve segregation have been used to defend desegregation requirements." Richard Nixon, elected president in 1968, vigorously denounced "wholesale compulsory busing," and his Justice Department opposed the racial balancing imposed by the federal district court in Charlotte-Mecklenburg, North Carolina. [54]

Despite Nixon's opposition, the Supreme Court unanimously upheld the reassignment of students by race in *Swann* v. *Charlotte-Mecklenburg* in 1971. Written by Chief Justice Warren Burger, a Nixon appointee, the *Swann* decision overturned a neighborhood school policy that produced many racially isolated schools. Following the *Green* principle that schools had to produce a remedy that "works now," the Court directed school authorities to "make every effort to achieve the greatest possible degree of actual desegregation." Local officials were told to do whatever was necessary—including the use of racial quotas, the gerrymandering of districts, busing, and the creation of noncontiguous attendance zones—in order to redistribute white and black pupil populations into the same schools. The remedy, in other words, for segregation was racial dispersion. Although the Court held that not every school in every community would be expected to reflect the racial composition of the school system as a whole, it was clear that school authorities had the burden of justifying the existence of any one-race schools.[55]

By 1972, the kind of racial segregation that had existed before the *Brown* decision had nearly been eliminated. In 1954, few black students attended schools with whites in the South. By 1972, as a result of the concerted efforts of the courts and HEW, 91.3 percent of all southern black students attended school with whites, compared to 76.4 percent in the border states, and 89.1 percent in the North and West. However, this standard was no longer relevant, since the effect of the Coleman Report and *Racial Isolation* had been to emphasize the necessity of placing blacks in majority-white schools. The switch to this new standard, which redefined "segregation" as racial imbalance or a predominantly black school, produced a far different picture: in the South in 1972, 46.3 percent of blacks were in majority-white schools, compared to 31.8 percent in border states, and 28.3 percent in the North and West.[56]

While the courts did not explicitly embrace the principle that blacks must be assigned to majority-white schools, the *Swann* decision endorsed the use of racial redistribution as a remedy for previous unconstitutional segregation. There was no reason why the logic of *Swann* should be limited to southern school systems, and the *Keyes* decision in 1973 established that it would not be. In that decision, the principles developed in a southern context were applied to a nonsouthern district that had never operated legally segregated schools. The Denver school board was found to have pursued certain policies, such as zoning, site selection, staff assignment, and assignment to neighborhood schools, that had the effect of segregating 38 percent of the black school population in identifiably black schools. Having determined that segregation existed "in a substantial portion of the district," the Court declared that Denver was unconstitutionally operating a dual system of de jure segregated schools. Denver's claims that racial concentration resulted from its neighborhood school policy and that the illegal actions had occurred before 1954 were rejected.[57]

After *Keyes,* it seemed likely, or at least possible, that federal courts would finally extinguish the line between de facto and de jure segregation and order racial balance in school systems throughout the nation. As Denver's experience showed, sufficient evidence could be assembled to prove that almost any de facto segregated school system was actually an unconstitutional de jure segregated school system. While school officials claimed that racial concentrations reflected residential patterns, over which the schools had no control, civil rights lawyers contended that school policies and other state actions were responsible for creating and maintaining segregated schools. Even before the Denver decision, a number of northern districts had been found guilty of de jure segregation and ordered to redistribute their white, black, Hispanic, Asian, and American Indian students into the same schools. Diligent research revealed documentation of policies, sometimes contained in school board minutes, intended to maintain racial segregation, through such devices as gerrymandering, discriminatory zoning, manipulation of feeder patterns from elementary to junior high schools, assignment of minority faculty to minority schools, and failure to relieve overcrowding in schools attended by one race while space was available in schools attended by the other race.[58]

Since the existence of a one-race school was not a constitutional violation, it was necessary to establish that school officials had intended to segregate pupils. But whether racial isolation resulted entirely from adventitious factors or from the constitutionally forbidden acts of school officials was not usually easy to determine. A permissive transfer policy was one such ambiguous piece of evidence. School officials claimed that they adopted it to minimize white flight, but civil rights lawyers argued that white students used such policies to escape schools that were growing blacker; conversely, a nonpermissive transfer policy could be characterized as evidence of intent to lock blacks into their neighborhood schools. A school board's decision to build a school in a minority community could be construed as a tacit effort to contain blacks; conversely, refusal to build in a minority community caused black students to attend antiquated and inferior schools. Furthermore, racial discrimination in the sale or rental of housing, which had been commonplace in every part of the country, as well as in federal mortgage policies, was easily obtainable evidence of state participation in the creation of racially homogeneous neighborhoods, though it did not show that the school board was responsible for residential segregation.

After the Denver decision, the civil rights movement was in an unusually strong position to attack racial isolation in the North, but demographic shifts had created a new problem. Since the Second World War, central cities had experienced a steady exodus of whites and an immigration of minorities. The whites who remained in the cities tended to have fewer children than did the minorities, and consequently, the proportion of minority students in urban schools was growing rapidly. By the early 1970s, white students had become a minority in such major cities as New York, Chicago, Philadelphia, Detroit, Cleveland, and Washington, D.C. Even if plaintiffs won a court order to redistribute students by race in such cities, it was no longer possible to integrate minority students into a majority-white school. The challenge, then, was not only to the neighborhood school, so long a fixture in American schools, but to the district lines that prevented the redistribution of students between city and suburb.

The city of Detroit was the ground on which the issue was drawn. Detroit had one of the most liberal school systems in the nation. Its superintendent and school board president had been honored by the NAACP for their commitment to school integration; its deputy superintendent, who was responsible for school boundary lines and pupil assignments, was a former director of the Detroit NAACP; it had a higher proportion of black administrators (37.8 percent) and black teachers (42.1 percent) than any other city in the nation; it pioneered in the creation of multi-ethnic instructional materials. Yet there was substantial residential segregation in Detroit, and the school board's efforts failed to eliminate de facto segregation. In 1971, a federal district judge declared in *Milliken* v. *Bradley* that the Detroit schools were racially segregated, due to the actions and inaction of its school board. Noting that Detroit's schools were already 63.8 percent black, and that they would be 80 percent black by 1980, the judge ordered the creation of a metropolitan school district, integrating the Detroit school district with fifty-three predominantly white suburban districts.[59]

The suburban districts appealed the order, and the issue presented to the Supreme Court was whether the federal courts could merge adjacent school districts in order to produce a majority-white enrollment. If upheld, the decision would open the way for similar challenges in other major cities with nonwhite majorities; if rejected, cities like Detroit would be left to figure out how to desegregate with few white pupils. The Court's widely anticipated ruling, delivered in 1974, reversed the lower courts. In a 5-to-4 decision, the Court held that the metropolitan remedy could not be imposed because, in the absence of constitutional violations by the fifty-three suburban districts, there was no reason to abrogate local control. Local autonomy, said the majority, "has long been thought essential both to the maintenance of community concern and support for public schools and to quality of the educational process." The schools of Detroit were ordered to eliminate segregation within the existing district lines, though the Court, as usual, did not define what was required to do so.[60]

The integration movement, while deeply disappointed by the Detroit decision, faced a different kind of threat. Throughout the decades of the 1940s, 1950s, and 1960s, the movement had enjoyed near-unanimous support from social scientists, and the legal battle moved forward with solid support from the field of social research. However, in 1972, dissension among social scientists surfaced, and for the first time, the assumptions of integration policy were directly challenged. David J. Armor of Harvard University, a desegregation researcher who had been one of the consultants to the Commission on Civil Rights' *Racial Isolation* report, reviewed several recent studies and concluded that racial balance had not led to higher achievement or self-esteem among black students and had not improved race relations. Pro-integration researchers criticized Armor's findings and countered with other studies whose results showed positive gains from integration, but the rift in the social science community continued to grow.[61]

In 1975, the integration forces were shaken by the public defection of James S. Coleman, the nationally prominent sociologist whose 1966 report was regularly cited in courtrooms as evidence on behalf of racial redistribution. Coleman had grown increasingly concerned about the "inappropriate" use of the report to argue for racial balancing. In April, 1975, he released a study that concluded that court-imposed school desegregation was contributing to the flight of whites from big cities and was thus a self-defeating policy. To the extent that individuals retained the power to move and defeat the policy, he held, "the courts are probably the worst instrument of social policy." Pro-integration social scientists responded by attacking Coleman's methodology and even his competence and by insisting that there was no correlation between desegregation and white flight.[62]

In time, when tempers cooled, Coleman's critics generally accepted his original assertion that school desegregation contributed to white flight from big-city schools, though not his policy implications. Where Coleman preferred voluntary inducements to desegregate, integrationist scholars advocated the creation of metropolitan districts so that whites could not flee to suburban schools to avoid desegregation. The controversy drew attention to the fact that white students had become a minority in most of the nation's large urban school districts, which negated the possibility of racially balancing those districts with a white majority in every school.[63]

The "white flight" issue was not the only one on which scholarly consensus dissolved. Studies began to appear from districts where racial balancing had been in effect for several years, and their findings were inconsistent about the expected benefits of desegregation on black achievement and attitudes. Nancy St. John, a scholar who had studied the effects of segregation and desegregation since 1962, analyzed more than one hundred studies to determine the effects of school desegregation on children, and specifically how it had affected academic growth, motivation, and interracial attitudes and behavior. Desegregation rarely lowered the achievement of whites or blacks, she noted, but there was no clear evidence that changes in the racial composition of the school closed or reduced the achievement gap between the races. Nor could she find support in the research findings for the belief that desegregation raised black self-esteem. Further, the research indicated that desegregation sometimes produced interracial friendships and sometimes produced racial conflict and stereotyping. "An outcome so variable," she observed, "must be affected by circumstances other than the mere fact of desegregation."[64]

While the social scientists debated methodological and ideological issues, racial balancing orders were applied in several major cities, among them Denver, San Francisco, and Boston. In Boston, the order to redistribute whites, blacks, and other minorities throughout the system was met with boycotts, protests, and violence by whites. During the two years in which the federal court's plan was implemented, one-third of the district's white pupils left the public schools, never to return. The district appealed unsuccessfully to the Supreme Court, which had long before determined in the Little Rock decision that community turmoil could not prevent the execution of a federal court order.[65]

What happened in the mid-1970s was that court orders based in part on social science findings proceeded even as social scientists lost their earlier certainty about the effects of desegregation on black achievement and attitudes. The collapse of consensus stemmed from several sources. Time and experience had revealed that putting black students in majority-white classrooms would not automatically improve their achievement or raise their self-esteem. While some social scientists continued to insist that the right conditions of desegregation would have the predicted benefits, others were unpersuaded. David K. Cohen, who had directed the "race and education" section of *Racial Isolation*, observed in 1977 that the increased sophistication of social research had led not to convergence but to greater complexity and greater mystification. Recognizing that social scientists no longer agreed or offered clear answers on the issues of race and education, Cohen reflected that social research should be understood as "a dialogue —rather than a problem-solving exercise."[66]

Dissension on issues of race and education was not limited to social scientists. Black critics of dispersionist policies became vocal as evidence accumulated about the uncertainty of educational benefits. Derrick A. Bell, Jr., a former civil rights lawyer, argued that the object of future litigation must be to ensure the educational gains that black parents want, which might not necessarily include the racial dispersion remedy. His ideas reflected a growing sentiment among blacks who approved of "busing" insofar as it represented a symbolic black victory, but preferred substantial improvement of their neighborhood school, with enhanced possibilities of effective parent-teacher-community relationships, to participation in a systemwide busing plan. To be sure, such views had little effect on the aggressive integrationist leadership of the NAACP and the Legal Defense Fund. But dissident black voices in such communities as Atlanta and Dallas persuaded federal district judges not to impose systemwide racial balancing. In Dallas, the Black Coalition to Maximize Education, which represented a broad array of parents, professionals, and ministers, intervened in school desegregation litigation to oppose expanded busing and to seek instead remedies "designed to improve educational quality and to eliminate the disparity in academic achievement" between minorities and whites.[67]

That blacks had begun to disagree openly with those who spoke on their behalf, that blacks did not feel that an institution was stigmatized by their participation in it, that black clients had found their own voice were indications not of a dissolution of the movement for black equality but of the success of the social revolution initiated by the *Brown* decision. In the quarter-century after *Brown,* race relations had changed dramatically. With the protection of court decisions and civil rights laws, blacks entered every walk of life, moved into formerly lily-white occupations, went to college in growing numbers, took an active part in political life, and destroyed forever the subservient, inferior role imposed by white racism in the past. A generation after *Brown,* there continued to be many predominantly black schools, located largely in the urban North and West, sustained by school district lines and demographic patterns, not by law. Whether these conditions represented a betrayal of the promise of the *Brown* decision or were in essence no different from the urban schools in which other ethnic groups had predominated was for another generation, unaffected by the ideas and passions of those who had led the struggle through its early years, to determine.

CHAPTER 6

From Berkeley to Kent State

AS THE 1960s BEGAN, the trouble spots in American education were plain to see. The persistence of racial segregation in the South guaranteed continued unrest; the migration of poor blacks and Hispanics to northern and western cities presented urban schools with new problems of race and poverty; the Soviet Union's successful launching of its Sputnik spacecraft stimulated anxiety about the state of the nation's schools; the repeated calls for federal aid to education continued to be ignored, even as the baby boom generation filled the nation's classrooms. The one sector of American education that seemed to be in sound health, responsive to the needs of its students and its society, was higher education.

Riding the crest of exuberant growth, thinking of themselves as leaders of vital and socially dynamic institutions, college and university officials had no reason to anticipate the era of crisis that lay before them. Going to college was the culmination of the American dream, the gateway to economic success and social status. As higher education grew bigger and opened its doors wider, there were no dark clouds on the horizon, not even the problem of financing, which seemed manageable in a thriving economy. In a time of unbounded optimism, no one could have predicted that many of America's campuses would come under siege in the late 1960s;

that they would become scapegoats for an unpopular war and for black grievances; that their openness and tolerance would make them convenient targets for youthful revolutionaries who ironically tried to destroy the one institution in American society that provided a sanctuary for their views. As young radicals expressed their rage by setting bombs in university offices, burning buildings that housed ROTC and defense-oriented research, forcibly occupying university facilities, shouting down speakers whose views they disliked, and disrupting the classes of professors who criticized them, higher education's commitment to reason and free thought was directly threatened. Only a decade after the McCarthyite assaults on education, academic freedom—the right to teach and the right to learn— was again under attack, not by the external forces of reaction but by student ideologues and their campus sympathizers.

After World War II, higher education entered into a period of remarkable growth. The expanding demand for higher education was compounded of expectations and economic reality. Not only did parents expect their children to have at least as much schooling as they had, but increased college enrollments accurately reflected the shift in the occupational structure to professional, technical, clerical, and managerial work. As ever larger numbers of students finished high school, the numbers entering college grew. This was no new phenomenon: in the years between 1870 and 1970, college enrollments doubled every fourteen or fifteen years.[1]

Yet nothing in past experience was comparable to the dramatic growth in higher education in the postwar decades. In 1946, the nation's colleges and universities enrolled more than two million students, including veterans, and employed about one hundred and sixty-five thousand faculty. By 1970, higher enrollment rates combined with the maturing of the postwar baby-boom generation to produce eight million students in higher education, taught by a faculty of more than five hundred thousand. In part to prepare new teachers and other professionals, but also because of unprecedented funding for research, the number of graduate students increased from one hundred and twenty thousand in 1946 to nine hundred thousand in 1970.[2]

The transformation of higher education was spurred on by the heavy commitment of state funds for public institutions. In the late 1940s, there were more students in private institutions of higher education than in public. In the mid-1950s, public enrollments began to outdistance private enrollments, and by 1970, approximately three-quarters of the eight million students in higher education were in public institutions. This vast opening up of higher education changed the nature of college-going in

America. No longer was it a privilege reserved for the brightest or the most affluent in the high school graduating class. In 1946, one of eight college-age youths was enrolled in higher education; by 1970, one of three was a college or university student. This had the paradoxical effect of making a college degree less of a rarity, less of a badge of status, but more of a necessity for entry to white-collar occupations. It also meant that an ever larger proportion of American youth would enjoy—or endure—extra years of dependency before entering the world of work.[3]

In the internal life of the university, the transformation had other effects. During the great growth spurt, many state universities and a few private universities reached enrollments well in excess of twenty thousand students. Outstanding professors, sought after by many universities, were able to negotiate arrangements permitting them to concentrate on their research and writing and to teach advanced courses in their speciality, leaving little time for undergraduates or for general education. As the size of the institution grew, the number of administrators grew also, and complex bureaucratic structures emerged to administer admissions, fund raising, financial aid, physical plant, relations with the legislature, faculty relations, and governmental programs. Expansion of enrollment also meant larger classes and a lessening of contact between faculty and students. As the university grew bigger and more diverse, its sense of purpose became more various. And at the same time that the campus's sense of community diminished, changing cultural patterns eroded the authority of administrators to regulate student social life.

In postwar America, the university had become a prime generator of knowledge, analysis, and data, performing vital functions in a society where knowledge was necessary in devising foreign and domestic policy, in securing scientific and technological advancement, and in analyzing basic economic and social trends. Faculty members in certain fields found their services in demand as consultants to government, foundations, and private industry. The university was no longer, as Clark Kerr put it, "a village with its priests." In keeping pace with the dynamic social and economic changes in the United States, in meeting demands for new and useful knowledge, the university had become a "multiversity . . . a city of infinite variety." Yes, Kerr agreed, the multiversity had less sense of community and less sense of purpose than the old university, but it was also less confining, more various in providing ways to excel and to participate in the life of the larger society. Writing in 1963, Kerr saw the university as "a prime instrument of national purpose" because it was essential to the "knowledge industry" on which government and business had come to rely: "Knowledge has certainly never in history been so central to the conduct of an entire society," he wrote. "What the railroads did for the second half of the last century and the automobile for the first half of this century may be done for the second half of this century by the knowledge industry: that is, to serve as the focal point for national growth. And the university is at the center of the knowledge process."[4]

As president of the University of California, Kerr had unusual insight into the forces that were reshaping the university and readying it for higher levels of service to government and industry. He did not fail to notice that the undergraduates had been neglected in the advancing rationalization of the multiversity. "Recent changes . . . have done them little good—lower teaching loads for the faculty, larger classes, the use of substitute teachers for the regular faculty, the choice of faculty members based on research accomplishments rather than instructional capacity, the fragmentation of knowledge into endless subdivisions." Undergraduates, he observed, "are coming to look upon themselves . . . as a 'class'; some may even feel like a 'lumpen proletariat.' "[5]

If there was in Kerr's *The Uses of the University* the tone of the liberal technocrat, the man who brings dispassionate reason to bear on knotty problems, it was a note characteristic of the brief Kennedy era. The Democrats who came to national power in the 1960 election saw themselves as hard-headed pragmatists—uninterested in ideology, willing to experiment with practical solutions, unafraid to exercise power. In their dispassionate, rationalistic approach to governmental problems, the Kennedy Democrats embodied sociologist Daniel Bell's claim that ideology had become irrelevant. In *The End of Ideology*, Bell described the disillusionment with apocalyptic thinking that reduced the appeal of ideological politics. After the experiences of the previous thirty years, after the outrages and perfidy committed by ideologues of the right and left, Bell believed that the old ideologies had lost their power to persuade people with their simplistic slogans. Any new utopia, he argued, would have "to specify *where* one wants to go, *how* to get there, the costs of the enterprise, and some realization of, and justification for the determination of *who* is to pay." Bell's vision was of a rational society, in which thinking people make choices with full awareness of the consequences and costs. Just as Kerr was aware of the restlessness of the undergraduates in the multiversity, so Bell recognized the stirrings of a new radicalism among young people who resisted the rational, technologically advanced society that was evolving. Bell noted that this "new left" was engaged in a desperate search for a "cause," which was all the more difficult because the ground was seemingly not fertile for radicalism.[6]

Yet, while objective conditions seemed unpropitious to radicalism as the 1960s opened, there clearly was something stirring, some seismic shifting within the culture. From the perspective of intellectuals and liberals, the 1950s had been "a captivity in Babylon" or "a dull, sad time." It was, wrote historian William L. O'Neill, "the age of television (ten thousand sets in 1947, forty million ten years later), tract houses, garish automobiles, long skirts, and bad movies." Democrats, liberals, and others of the left perceived the Eisenhower era as intellectually sterile, politically stagnant, and culturally bland, led by men who were self-righteous, business-minded, provincial, materialistic, conservative, and Philistine; Eisenhower was derided by the educated elite, partly for the way he mangled the English language in his press conferences, but also because he was the personification of middle-brow, bourgeois values.[7]

There was, to be sure, a good deal of caricature and exaggeration in this portrait, for—as O'Neill also points out—the arts flourished in the fifties, inflation was low, peace was maintained, and real economic gains were made by most ordinary citizens. But, once McCarthyism was decisively repudiated, pockets of cultural and political dissidence appeared. In the cultural sphere, bohemians calling themselves "Beats" rebelled against the cool, restrained, ironic style of the literary mainstream and celebrated spontaneity, sensuality, and experience. In the political sphere, a nascent radicalism formed to oppose nuclear testing, the Cold War, and militarism, and to support Third World revolutions, especially that of Fidel Castro in Cuba. The new radicals found inspiration in the works of C. Wright Mills and Paul Goodman.[8]

Mills's *The Power Elite,* published in 1956, provided a cogent explanation for those young people who were alienated by the mediocrity, the placidity, the seeming immobility of "the system." Ordinary men, Mills held, were powerless in modern American society, driven by forces beyond their control. Centralized decision-making power was actually concentrated in the hands of small cliques in government, the economy, and the military, which together formed an interlocking directorate, a "power elite." These men hold vast power over others, not because they are wise or meritorious but because they are "selected and formed by the means of power, the sources of wealth, the mechanics of celebrity," which prevail "within the American system of organized irresponsibility."[9]

Mills's concept of a power elite struck a responsive chord among those who were concerned about the size of the military establishment, the concentration of economic power in great corporations, the growing bureaucratization of public and private institutions, and the indifference of the national government to these concerns. To those who felt estranged by the drift of American politics, and especially to left-leaning youth who sought some way to understand their sense of ineffectualness, Mills's interpretation was a useful explanation. It suggested to those out of power that they might in fact be part of the great mass of hoodwinked citizenry, rather than a lonely minority, even while it failed to indicate how the many could break the strong and seamless bonds forged by the few.

Paul Goodman added to this nascent radical perspective his own idiosyncratic anarchism, which focused on the relation of the individual to society. As a social critic and gadfly, Goodman worried about everything that diminished the individual's opportunity to have a life of value, meaning, personal freedom, beauty, and utility. In *Growing Up Absurd,* published in 1960, Goodman complained that young men had a difficult time growing up because there was so little opportunity for what he called "man's work." The "semimonopolies" that run business, unions, and government, he held, worry about profit and jobs "without regard for utility, quality, rational productivity, personal freedom, independent enterprise, human scale, manly vocation, or genuine culture." As a consequence, men are prepared to assume jobs that are meaningless, to make useless gadgets or to fit into a faceless bureaucracy. In a society where so much activity was organized and systematized without regard to preserving human values, he wrote, the problem for young men was "how to be useful and make something of oneself." Unlike Mills, whose power elite appeared impregnable, Goodman believed that "if ten thousand people in all walks of life will stand up on their two feet and talk out and insist, we shall get back our country."[10]

As 1960 opened, there were abundant signs that college students were prepared to "talk out and insist." In January, the student affiliates of the social-democratic League for Industrial Democracy renamed themselves Students for a Democratic Society (SDS) and pledged themselves to begin the task of building a "new left" among American students. In February, four black college students ordered coffee at an all-white lunch counter in Greensboro, North Carolina, inspiring civil rights demonstrations by students across the nation over the next few years. In May, several hundred people, including many Berkeley students, participated in a raucous demonstration against the House Committee on Un-American Activities (HCUA) in San Francisco. In reaction against the American-sponsored invasion of Cuba in the spring of 1961, students joined "Fair Play for Cuba" committees on a number of campuses, and in early 1962, several thousand students demonstrated for peace at the White House.

Mindful of the new mood among students, C. Wright Mills saw them as the cutting edge of a revived radicalism. In his "Letter to the New Left," published in England in the fall of 1960 and reprinted in the United States in early 1961, he attacked Bell's end-of-ideology notion as "a slogan of complacency" proffered by "NATO intellectuals" to discourage commitment to socialism. Mills argued that radicals could no longer count on the working class to serve as the historic agency of social change. Who then could serve as the "immediate, radical agency of change"? Who is it, Mills asked, "that is getting fed up? Who is it that is getting disgusted with what Marx called 'all the old crap'? Who is it that is thinking and acting in radical ways? All over the world—in the bloc, outside the bloc and in between—the answer is the same: it is the young intelligentsia."[11]

The student activists who joined SDS in the early 1960s responded positively to the idea that students might become the "radical agency of change." SDS leader Tom Hayden had read Mills's works at the University of Michigan, and Mills's influence was reflected in the organization's manifesto, the Port Huron Statement. In that document, SDS set forward its wide-ranging critique of American society—of racial injustice, the danger of nuclear war, the failure to develop peaceful nuclear energy, the Cold War, reflexive anti-Communism, the maldistribution of wealth, the meaningless of work, the political apathy of students, the exhaustion of liberal and socialist thinking, the isolation of the individual ("from power and community and ability to aspire"). It was a call for a radically changed social order, for a "participatory democracy" in which individuals would take part in making the decisions that affect their own lives. Its animating spirit was an existential humanism, in which the political process would become the means of creating community, ending the isolation of the individual, and finding meaning in one's personal life. Many people who did not necessarily share SDS's radicalism nonetheless identified with the aspiration that individuals might break free of convention to take control of their destiny.

The route to radical change, declared the Port Huron Statement, lay not in the traditional political process nor even through mobilizing workers, but rather in the universities, which were seen as the "potential base and agency in a movement of social change." The university offered radical organizers several important advantages: they were distributed throughout the country; they offered a critical mass of the young intelligentsia who would make a new left; and radicals in the university had the time to pursue the political life and benefited from the protection that a university provided for controversial views.[12]

The process of turning students into political activists was grounded not in rhetoric, however, but in the experiences of the civil rights movement. In 1964, the Student Nonviolent Coordinating Committee (SNCC) enlisted one thousand white volunteers in the Mississippi Summer Project to teach in freedom schools, to register black voters, and to challenge segregation. SNCC leaders hoped to force a crisis of such dimensions in Mississippi that the federal government would be compelled to step in; the fact that the northern whites were children of affluent families also guaranteed publicity in the event of violence. In short order, the event that would provoke national outrage occurred: on June 21, 1964, a black Mississippian and two white New Yorkers disappeared; their bodies were found six weeks later. As expected, the Mississippi Summer Project helped to galvanize public support for the Civil Rights Act, but it also had a lasting effect on the minds and hearts of the white students who participated.[13]

White students were deeply affected by their involvement in civil rights work. First, they developed a sense of moral outrage as they became aware of the harsh injustice and oppressiveness of southern racism, as well as the discrimination routinely practiced in nonsouthern communities; knowing the abuse and physical violence that SNCC staffers exposed themselves to each day, white students were eager to show that they too were willing to take risks for social change. Second, civil rights activities demonstrated the efficacy of the tactics of confrontation and mass protest: a confrontation between a large number of demonstrators and authorities presents the authorities with a choice of doing nothing or using force. If the authorities use force, it solidifies the protesters and creates sympathy for the demonstration; the mass protest not only generates publicity but lessens the likelihood of punishment, since it is difficult to assign responsibility when several hundred people are arrested. Third, their racial association with the oppressors, involuntary though it was, filled white students with a sense of guilt which strained relations between white and black students and contributed to white attitudes that were sometimes condescending, sometimes patronizing, and sometimes deferential toward blacks. Additionally, as Tom Hayden later recalled, "what was so transforming" about civil rights activities was that those who took part did so "in a way that risked their life." It offered a means "to act existentially or to act as if you mattered." Hayden thought that characters like Holden Caulfield in *Catcher in the Rye* or James Dean in *Rebel Without a Cause* typified the feeling "of being in some kind of plight where you didn't know the name of it and you didn't know how to get out of it and there wasn't anything to do about it." Whether it was called alienation or boredom, would-be political activists found in direct action an opportunity to live what they believed and to give meaning to their comfortable but unchallenging lives.[14]

In the campus protests of the 1960s, white students utilized the moral outrage and tactics that they had learned from the civil rights movement.

But where oppressed blacks could successfully use demonstrations to win public support for civil rights legislation, the white students' frequent assertions that their struggle was the same, that they were just as oppressed as poor southern blacks, were received by the public with incredulity and hostility. Since cries of oppression arose most frequently from students at elite institutions like Berkeley, Columbia, and Harvard, the public most often was simply baffled.

By the early 1960s, the Bay Area surrounding San Francisco had a well-developed reputation for political activism, and much of the leadership and many of the troops were drawn from the University of California at Berkeley. Student activism sprouted in the late 1950s, when a coalition of liberal and radical student groups (known as Slate) gained control of student government. Slate attracted students concerned about such issues as the arms race, capital punishment, racial integration in local public schools, the hiring of minorities by local businesses, racial discrimination by fraternities, and the shortage of student housing. After the sit-in movement began in early 1960, student political involvement rose. In May, 1960, hundreds of Berkeley students were arrested for noisily protesting HCUA hearings in San Francisco. During the early 1960s, a few hundred students—and a growing number of nonstudents who lived near the campus—participated in civil rights marches and demonstrations, considering it a badge of honor to be arrested for their activities.*

As home base for numerous politically active organizations, Berkeley was in a delicate situation. To remain one of the nation's elite centers of scholarship, it had to protect zealously the academic tradition of free inquiry and free expression; but as a tax-supported institution dependent on the state legislature, it had to avoid political controversy. Given the past record of the legislature, there was an ever-present concern that conservatives might interfere in the university or cut its budget if it were seen as a hotbed of radicalism. This dilemma was seemingly resolved by the state Board of Regents' ban of political or religious proselytizing on campus. The university distinguished between on-campus political activity (which was restricted) and off-campus political activity (which was unlimited). The

*A matter of definition: in the discussion that follows, "liberals" worked to make changes within the political system, believing that a change in elected officials or laws could improve society; "radicals" believed that incremental reform, like a change in leaders or laws, was pointless because the system itself was hopelessly corrupt and had to be replaced; the most extreme radicals were "revolutionaries," who believed that armed violence was necessary to overthrow the system. "Activists," as used here, refers to students who were politically active, regardless of their political orientation. Although the New Left attracted many students on the left side of the political spectrum, it was primarily associated with student radicalism, such as that of SDS.

limitation of on-campus political activities was a source of continuing conflict over the years, since it required constant regulation and redefinition. As of early 1964, any partisan speaker could appear on campus, so long as a tenured faculty member chaired the meeting and seventy-two hours' notice was given the university. However, students had to restrict their fund raising and recruitment for off-campus causes (like civil rights, national and state elections, and so forth) to a strip of brick walkway outside the main gate of the university, which was considered an off-campus location. The solution seemed to work well enough, since spokesmen for every conceivable political view—from Communists to Nazis—spoke on campus. The extension of academic freedom had led the American Association of University Professors to confer its Alexander Meiklejohn award on Clark Kerr, the president of the University of California, in the spring of 1964.

In September, 1964, a series of events occurred that plunged the Berkeley campus into a crisis unprecedented in American higher education. Student activists returned to campus fired-up by the civil rights work of the previous summer. Of Berkeley's twenty-seven thousand students, about three hundred to five hundred were experienced political activists; several had spent the summer in Mississippi with SNCC. Furthermore, some had become overtly radical. Returning students received copies of the Slate publication that included a rambling, bitter indictment of the university and American society. Written by an ex-graduate student, "A Letter to Undergraduates" urged undergraduates to *"Organize and split this campus wide open!* . . . DO NOTHING LESS THAN BEGIN AN OPEN, FIERCE, AND THOROUGHGOING REBELLION ON THIS CAMPUS." The author demanded the immediate abolition of grades in undergraduate courses and of rules in student dormitories, as well as a permanent, independent student role in running the university.[15]

With the political consciousness of student activists at a keen edge, the Berkeley administration—headed by Chancellor Edward M. Strong—chose this moment to announce that students would no longer be permitted to use the heavily trafficked twenty-six–foot strip of walkway at the university entrance for their off-campus political activities. It seems that the walkway was actually owned by the university, not the city. Student organizations could no longer use this area—as they had for many years —to set up their tables for fund raising and recruitment, for supporting or opposing candidates or electoral propositions. The campus administration had decided during the summer of 1964 that it had to show consistency in its on-campus/off-campus policy: as president of the state university system, Clark Kerr had refused to dismiss students who had been arrested in off-campus civil rights demonstrations, and now the Berkeley authorities intended to enforce the ban against political proselytizing on university property.

The logic may have been sound, but the decision invited—indeed provoked—what followed. The eighteen student organizations affected, from conservative to radical, joined together to demand restoration of the rights withdrawn. During the fall of 1964, the leadership of the student protest (which called itself the Free Speech Movement) came to be dominated by leftist students who approached the situation as a classic civil rights contest, in which they were the oppressed and the university administration was the oppressor. Its leading spokesman was Mario Savio, a twenty-one-year-old junior in philosophy who had spent the summer in Mississippi as a SNCC volunteer; Savio saw the fight in Berkeley as the same fight, against the same enemy, as the civil rights struggle in Mississippi. The public drama appeared to be a match between a David—the embattled students—and a Goliath—the powerful and unresponsive officialdom of the University of California.[16]

In reality, the roles were quite different. While the students were knowledgeable about the dynamics of protest and about the use of symbols to discredit their opponents and to win allies, the administration was inept in presenting its own case, hobbled by the multiple levels of decision makers, uncertain about how to respond to challenges to its authority, and constrained by the necessity of acting according to the prescribed rules and procedures that govern a formal bureaucracy. At almost every point in the controversy, the students determined the agenda and kept the administration on the defensive. The Free Speech Movement (FSM), even in its choice of name, defined the central issue, and the administration was never able to convince anyone that the question was not one of free speech (which all protesters regularly exercised throughout the controversy) but—as the administration saw it—the necessity of keeping the university as a marketplace of ideas, not a staging ground for political action. The administration's clumsiness was in part generational; it failed to recognize that students in 1964 were more militant and less willing to accept paternalistic policies than were students a few years earlier. But its greatest difficulty was substantive: at a time when civil rights and civil liberties were being extended in every sphere, the administration was unable to persuade the majority of the faculty and students that its distinction between permissible activities and impermissible activities was justified.

In the first phase of the controversy, the affronted student organizations picketed, conducted an all-night vigil, and began a program of massive rule violations, which culminated in a dramatic act of civil disobedience: on October 1, 1964, when an ex-student was arrested while manning an "illegal" fund-raising table, the police car in which he was placed was surrounded by hundreds of students who sat down and immobilized it. The police car was held captive for thirty-two hours, and the demonstration did not end until Clark Kerr signed a pact with leaders of the FSM.

The FSM negotiated for several weeks with faculty members and administrators, and all sides agreed that advocacy of off-campus political action should be allowed on campus. However, they could not agree on the FSM's demand that the university permit on-campus planning of illegal off-campus activities, like stopping troop trains. The FSM broke away from the negotiations, reopened its campaign of massive rule violations, and ousted the moderate members of its steering committee who opposed the return to confrontation tactics. At this point in the drama, an ad hoc faculty committee—appointed as a result of the October 2 peace pact—all but nullified the penalties of eight FSM members who had been suspended at the beginning of the crisis for violating campus rules; the committee's leniency appeared to vindicate the FSM campaign against the administration.[17]

On November 20, the Board of Regents of the University of California voted to permit off-campus groups to do fund raising and recruiting of members on campus, but insisted that students would not be permitted to use campus facilities to plan illegal off-campus political action. Furthermore, the regents leveled symbolic punishments against the eight suspended students, changing the faculty's tap-on-the-wrist to a slap-on-the-wrist (the faculty committee had canceled the suspensions, but the regents upheld the suspensions, ending on November 20, the day of the regents' meeting). On the surface, the regents' decisions saved face for the administrators of the university while securing a great victory for the FSM by finally conceding precisely those rights that the Strong administration had resisted granting for two months. But the FSM leaders took the new policies as a devastating blow, a betrayal of their hopes. Their original objectives had changed: they no longer sought restoration of lost rights but abrogation of the university's power to regulate any of their political activities, legal or illegal. Since civil rights demonstrators were still subject to arrest for trespassing, the FSM believed that any stricture on illegal action was aimed at curbing civil rights protests. Besides, some of the leaders now endorsed the strategy of refusing to be reasonable and of forcing new crises. Jack Weinberg, the arrested man at the center of the captured police car incident, urged the FSM to treat the "enemy" as "monolithic" and to "resist the temptation to be reasonable." The object, he explained, was not the short-term goals but the building of widespread support for "the movement." The way to win was by "escalating the situation," which attracts more and more supporters. "We can always cap escalation with a student-faculty strike. . . . At the right moment, we can call for a general strike. We can say we just thought of it. Many people are with us in spirit, but against our methods. It is very tense in an escalating situation. They would join the strike to relieve the tension." The FSM called a rally, then tried a sit-in at Sproul Hall (the administration building), but failed to ignite the mass response they hoped for.[18]

But just as prospects seemed extremely bleak for the FSM, the campus administration—snatching defeat from the jaws of victory—committed an extraordinary blunder. During Thanksgiving recess, it notified four FSM leaders, including Mario Savio, that they were being charged with violations committed during the capture of the police car on October 1 and 2. Here was the issue that the FSM needed to revive its flagging fortunes. The FSM quickly established its "battle plan." It would demand cancellation of the charges against its leaders; when the administration refused, it would lead a sit-in at Sproul Hall on December 2. Demonstrators "would remain in the building overnight, hoping to be arrested. They were sure that a large number of arrests would lead to a general student strike." If the administration ignored the sit-in, they would call for a strike anyway, relying on the sympathy that had built up.[19]

Throughout the fall, FSM spokesmen had criticized the university as a soulless "knowledge factory," using Clark Kerr's *The Uses of the University* as a text to prove that the university was an adjunct of industry and government and that students were no more than raw material for the mass-production process. In the FSM rally preceding the sit-in, Mario Savio reiterated this theme in an eloquent speech that both expounded a critique of bureaucratic, impersonal, mass higher education and appealed to a spirit of existential revolt: "There is a time when the operation of the machine becomes so odious, makes you so sick at heart, that you can't take part; you can't even passively take part, and you've got to put your bodies upon the gears and upon the wheels, upon the levers, upon all the apparatus, and you've got to make it stop. And you've got to indicate to the people who run it, to the people who own it, that unless you're free, the machines will be prevented from working at all."[20]

An estimated 1,500 persons joined the Sproul Hall sit-in. In the middle of the night, Chancellor Strong sent police to clear the building, and 773 people were arrested. The shock of having police on the campus had the effect that the FSM anticipated: it created a strong reaction by faculty members and students against the administration and spread support for a strike against the university. According to one survey, about half the student body sympathized in some way with the strike, while the other half either opposed it or ignored it.[21]

The campus was thrown into turmoil. More than eight hundred professors met and called on the administration to drop all charges against students, to turn over to the faculty final control over discipline related to political action, and to nullify the regents' ban on illegal off-campus actions. Students picketed, carrying signs such as "I am a student. Do not fold, spindle, or mutilate." Chancellor Strong was admitted to a hospital, the victim of a gall bladder attack. President Kerr negotiated with the departmental chairmen and announced a campuswide meeting for December 7 to reveal a solution to the crisis. Facing sixteen thousand students, faculty, and staff, Kerr announced that the university would remain open; that the university would not discipline the students arrested in the sit-in beyond what the civil courts decreed; and that charges against the four FSM leaders would be dropped. As Kerr finished to a standing ovation, Mario Savio mounted the stage and approached the microphone; before he could speak, two university policemen dragged him away. By this action, which shocked onlookers, Savio provoked a response that turned Kerr's compromise proposal into a fiasco.

The next day, the faculty formally met and overwhelmingly adopted a series of resolutions that pleased the FSM. It urged, first, cancellation of all disciplinary proceedings in the controversy; second, "that the time, place, and manner of conducting political activity on the campus shall be subject to reasonable regulations to prevent interference with the normal functions of the University," but that the content of speech should be unrestricted; and that future disciplinary measures regarding political activity should be placed in the hands of the faculty. An amendment proposing that speech should be unregulated "on this campus provided that it is directed to no immediate act of force or violence" was defeated. FSM demonstrators, massed outside the meeting and listening to its deliberations over a public address system, applauded the results.[22]

When the faculty elected an Emergency Executive Committee a few days later, it became clear that the FSM had rejoiced too soon: of the six chosen, only one was identified with the pro-FSM faculty group, while the other five were experienced faculty leaders. This composition explains the temperate reaction of the Emergency Executive Committee to the regents' rejection on December 18 of important elements of the faculty's proposal. The regents "directed the administration to preserve law and order on the campuses of the University of California"; reiterated that authority for student discipline remains with the administration of the university (not the faculty); agreed to review their policies controlling political action on campus; asserted that they would impose no greater restriction on speech than the First and Fourteenth Amendments to the Constitution; and reaffirmed that students could engage in lawful off-campus political action, subject to regulation by university authorities. Their somewhat ambiguous statement was hailed by the Emergency Executive Committee and condemned by the FSM. There would be no new confrontations, however, for the faculty wanted nothing more than an end to turmoil, and the FSM had already won too much to make its cries of administrative repression credible.[23]

Two weeks later, Chancellor Strong was replaced by an acting chancellor who was considered sympathetic to student concerns. The change in leadership and the liberalization of campus rules was followed by a brief era of good feeling. University committees set about finding educational answers to Berkeley students' malaise, overlooking the results of a survey conducted during the fall of 1964, which showed that 82 percent of Berkeley students were "satisfied or very satisfied" with "courses, examinations, professors, etc.," while fully 92 percent agreed that "although some people don't think so, the president of this university and the chancellor (of this campus) are really trying very hard to provide top-quality educational experience for students here."[24]

There would be no lasting peace, however, on the Berkeley campus. The FSM was succeeded by the "Filthy Speech Movement," and for the next several years a loose alliance of radical students, hippies, and "street people" kept alive the spirit of protest. Throughout the balance of the 1960s, student demonstrations became a near-daily ritual, occurring every afternoon at the same place on campus, with adequate time for the television cameras to film the action for the evening news. The most dramatic confrontation occurred in May, 1969, around the issue of "People's Park," a recreational area created by community activists on university property. When the university tried to reclaim the three-acre tract, students and street people engaged in pitched battles with the police, who responded with shotguns and tear-gas; the disorders were forcibly ended by the National Guard, who sprayed the campus with tear-gas from a helicopter and patrolled with fixed bayonets.

The Berkeley story was of far more than local interest. The ripple effect spread first across the state, then across the nation, to some as an inspiration, to others as a warning. In California, a statewide poll showed overwhelming disapproval of the uprising at the state's most prestigious campus. In 1966, the film star Ronald Reagan ran for governor and launched his political career by campaigning for law and order on the state's campuses. To the New Left student movement, still few in numbers, the Berkeley example contained useful lessons: about the use of confrontation tactics in polarizing the campus and winning supporters; about the possibility of mobilizing faculty to intervene on behalf of student demands; about the value of reducing complicated issues to idealistic slogans that can be easily symbolized on picket signs; about the way to reach a mass audience by providing colorful footage for cooperative television crews; about the means by which a relatively small number of unified protesters can compel the administration of a great university to deal with them as equals. At a time when other channels of change seemed to be unpromising to young radicals—when the black movement was turning separatist, and the Democratic administration was unabashedly committed to pragmatic, incremental reforms—the Berkeley experience revealed the vulnerability of the liberal university and liberal administrators to radical challenge.[25]

After Berkeley, one thing seemed sure: America had a new radicalism, a new left spawned on the campuses among middle-class youths. To a nation grown accustomed since the end of the Depression to hard-working, striving, conformist students, Berkeley came as a shock; other than a handful of scholars, few people recognized that American student activism had historically increased in times of social tension or that there was a contemporaneous rise of student protest movements in other countries. SDS, the New Left student organization, quickly realized that Berkeley suggested the possibility of politicizing and radicalizing American students by relating campus grievances to national issues. In order for radicalization to occur, students had to be convinced that change within the existing system was impossible, that the liberal-labor forces that controlled the national government were part of the power elite and that the Johnson administration's efforts to end poverty and protect civil rights were a sham. SDS spokesmen contended that "the movement" for radical social change would be constructed by poor people and students, not only without the help of the powerful liberal-labor coalition but in opposition to it.[26]

Veterans of left politics wondered whether this new, student-led radicalism was the real thing. Irving Howe worried that the new radicals appeared to be more concerned about "personal style," about "how to live individually within this society, rather than how to change it collectively." He pointed, for example, to the young radicals' insistence on shocking the middle class by their distinctive modes of speech, dress, and appearance; to their fascination with an inner revolution of drugs and sex rather than a public revolution requiring compromise and strategy; to their contempt for potential allies among liberals and the labor movement; to their preference for rage rather than specific plans and programs for change. Michael

Harrington puzzled over the new radicals' belief that students and the poor could make a revolution. He thought that no social change of importance would occur unless there was an alliance among these groups and the labor movement.[27]

Even without a program or a strategy or the approval of their radical elders, in the spring of 1965 the new radicals gained an immensely important new issue when President Johnson committed American troops to the war in Vietnam. In March, American involvement in the war was debated in the first "teach-in" at the University of Michigan. In April, SDS led some twenty-five thousand antiwar demonstrators in Washington, D.C. The opportunity to connect the national issue to student self-interest was provided in the spring of 1966, when the government decided to draft students in the lower levels of class standing. The Selective Service System asked colleges and universities to submit class rankings. At a number of campuses, students demonstrated against the draft and against the university's cooperation with the draft. The largest protest occurred at the University of Chicago, where about four hundred students conducted a sit-in in the administration building; the administration refused to call the police or to negotiate, and after five days, the demonstration was called off.

As antiwar sentiment rose on the campuses, SDS was in the forefront of the student protest movement; the number of its campus chapters grew from 29 in 1964 to 247 in 1967. At all times the radicalization of SDS proceeded faster than the mood among the young in general or on any given campus (not until 1968 did a majority of students oppose the war). In 1965, SDS dropped from its constitution the clauses excluding Communists and "totalitarians" from membership, as relics of the Cold War. A few months later, in response to SDS's open-door policy toward Communists, the May 2nd Movement of the Progressive Labor Party (PL), a tightly-disciplined Maoist group, dissolved itself and joined SDS. Unlike the free-wheeling, anti-authoritarian SDSers, PL believed in strict "cadre control." As a faction within SDS, PL always had a "line," always demanded doctrinal purity, and constantly drove SDS farther and farther left. (PL ceaselessly advocated a "worker-student alliance.")[28]

Campus protests against the war spread. The teach-in spread to hundreds of campuses, at first as a forum for debating the war, but—after government spokesmen were repeatedly heckled and disrupted—it soon became a vehicle for antiwar protest. Students demonstrated against the draft, against ROTC, and against the presence of recruiters from the military and from war-related industries like Dow Chemical. Protesters demanded that universities sever their ties to military research, the Central Intelligence Agency, defense industries, and corporate interests. Radical students and intellectuals sponsored "free universities," which consisted of courses emphasizing revolutionary consciousness and personal liberation.

As the surge of activism gathered momentum, the university itself became a target for protest. Even before the war, FSM at Berkeley had criticized the offerings of the modern university as irrelevant to the great socio-political issues of the day and subservient to the needs of industry. This analysis, combined with the new charge that the university was guilty of complicity in the war because of its relations with government and industry, provided fuel for student rage. The realization grew that the university could serve as a "surrogate" for a corrupt society. For SDS, the decision to carry the struggle to the university campus had a certain unassailable logic, since whites had been ousted from SNCC in 1966, and SDS's efforts to organize black slums and white working-class neighborhoods had failed. The newly developed idea of "student syndicalism" provided a rationale for the focus on the campuses. As an SDS leader explained, the university is an assembly line to produce those who will sustain the system of "corporate liberalism": "Its elite are trained in our colleges of business administration. Its defenders are trained in our law schools. Its apologists can be found in the political science departments. The colleges of social sciences produce its manipulators. For propagandists, it relies on the schools of journalism. It insures its own future growth in the colleges of education. If some of us don't quite fit in, we are brainwashed in the divisions of counseling." SDS ideologists argued further that students were the vanguard of a "new working class," composed of professionals and technicians. The return to the campus coincided with a heightening of SDS's revolutionary consciousness; by late 1967, SDS emissaries were meeting with revolutionaries from North Vietnam, Cuba, and other Communist countries.[29]

As the hardy band of radicals in SDS moved decisively to the extreme left, an even larger number of young people embraced cultural radicalism. The summer of 1967 marked the emergence of the "counterculture," which, like the "Beats" of the 1950s, rejected middle-class ideas about family, work, career, religion, and authority. As the name suggests, the counterculture defined itself as a culture of opposition. Where the mainstream culture valued hard work, deferred gratification, achievement, and material possessions, the counterculture celebrated sensual experience, immediate gratification, and unrestrained naturalism. Its representative type was the "hippie," and it had its own art, lingo, music, clothing, and personal style. Because of its numbers, it soon had its own press, celebrities, rock stars, and movies. Drugs were an important element in the counterculture, and consciousness-changing drugs quickly permeated the youth culture, as did such countercultural symbols as long hair (on men and women), granny glasses, beads, psychedelic art, "be-ins," "happenings," sitar music, and fascination with the occult and Eastern religions. With its emphasis on personal liberation, particularly regarding drugs and sex, the counterculture posed a challenge to any institution attempting to assert authority over young adults, even teenagers. With its contempt for rationality and its reverence for immediacy, the counterculture openly opposed the self-discipline, order, and respect for reason that educational institutions rely on. While the hippies and street people were generally apolitical, they occasionally joined with political radicals in jousts with campus authorities.[30]

By the spring of 1968, American society was pervaded by a national mood of foreboding, which on many campuses was so intense as to seem apocalyptic. The war dragged on inconclusively, and antiwar protests became angrier and more frequent; for the first time, campus buildings were bombed and burned by the student left. The black urban riots had grown progressively more violent in each of the preceding four summers, and SNCC stridently endorsed armed rebellion. The assassination of Martin Luther King, Jr., in April 1968 set off a new round of rioting in the cities.

At Columbia University, perched on the western edge of Harlem, King's assassination inflamed an already troubled atmosphere. Until then Columbia students had ignored repeated attempts by SDS to capture the attention of the campus. Formed in the fall of 1966, the SDS chapter at Columbia had searched for the right issue to create a Berkeley-style confrontation with the administration. At first, it campaigned against military recruiting on campus, but a student referendum overwhelmingly endorsed open recruiting. Ignoring the vote, SDS sat-in to block a Dow recruiter in February, 1968; again, no mass response. In March, 1968, Mark Rudd was elected chairman of SDS on his return from a three-week trip to Cuba; a week after his election, he showed his eagerness to take action by throwing a pie in the face of the New York City director of Selective Service. Still seeking the conflict with the administration that would ignite mass sympathy, Rudd led one hundred followers into the administration building, in defiance of a ban on indoor demonstrations, to demonstrate noisily against the university's connections with the Institute for Defense Analysis (IDA). This time the administration responded by summoning six leaders of the protest to the dean's office, where they were placed on disciplinary probation. The next day, April 23, SDS began its "spring offensive" against Columbia with a protest rally.[31]

At this point, SDS had two issues: its opposition to IDA and to any disciplining of "the IDA six." Since the university had already begun to disaffiliate from IDA, a government-funded military research organization in which three professors participated, the issue had not generated much interest. Nor did the plight of the "IDA six" have much appeal, since their punishments were not harsh. But something new was added, for the SDS rally was joined by the Students' Afro-American Society (SAS), to enlist white opposition to the construction of a new university gymnasium in Morningside Park, a craggy area that sloped down from the university to Harlem. The gym was racist, the SAS asserted, because the university was usurping public parkland that belonged to the people of Harlem.

The gym had a long and complicated history. In the late 1950s, the university negotiated an agreement with the City of New York to build the gymnasium, with a portion reserved for public use. After the agreement was approved by the State Legislature, the university spent several years raising money for the new gym. When a new city administration took office in 1966, the parks commissioner opposed the use of a city park for the university gym. With the rise of black separatism and demands for community control, the gym became a target of sparsely attended demonstrations. While a politically conscious minority saw Columbia as an elite white institution that was insensitive to the needs of the local community, most people in Harlem who were aware of the proposed gym thought that it was a good idea, since it would provide recreational facilities for neighborhood youths. Nonetheless, once the gym became a racial issue, no Harlem leader dared to support it.[32]

Now the SDS rally had three issues: stop the gym; disassociate from IDA; cancel any disciplinary action against the "IDA six." After a march to the gym site, about four hundred and fifty supporters of SDS and SAS proceeded to occupy Hamilton Hall, a building with administrative offices and classrooms, where a dean was taken hostage (he was released twenty-six hours later). During the first night of the occupation, the black students told the white students to leave and take over their own building. They did, by breaking into Low Library and occupying the offices of the university president, Grayson Kirk. The following night, two more university buildings were taken over by dissident graduate students, and soon afterward a fifth building was added. Altogether about one thousand people— a significant number on a campus of seventeen thousand students—occupied the five buildings during the next several days. The onset of the occupation gave rise to new demands, the most important of which was total amnesty for all involved.

Initially, the administration hesitated to call in the police because of threats that blacks from Harlem would invade the campus if the black students were removed from Hamilton Hall; militants from Harlem CORE, SNCC, and other groups joined the students in Hamilton Hall, and it was reported in the campus newspaper that some were armed. The whites occupying the other four buildings apparently had a wonderful time, sharing a common existential experience, united by a common enemy, and involved from moment-to-moment in the decisions that affected their lives. While the black students organized a tightly disciplined community, the white students put participatory democracy to work, opening every decision to group discussion. Radical luminaries, like Tom Hayden, visited the "liberated" zones, lending the events a festive air. Red flags flew from the tops of two buildings, while inside the buildings the walls were festooned with posters of Karl Marx, Malcolm X, and Che Guevara and with revolutionary slogans. Students rifled the files of the university president, hoping to retrieve damaging evidence of the university's corruption, but came up empty-handed.[33]

Most importantly, the confrontation between students and administration created new support for SDS demands. Before the demonstration, there was scant evidence of campus opposition to the gym, to IDA, or to the discipline of SDS leaders. But once the buildings were occupied and the threat of violence hung over the campus, significant groups of students and faculty began to side with SDS and to agree that the only way to resolve the crisis was to accede to SDS's demands. The student newspaper, which had strongly endorsed the gym in March, declared soon after the takeover that the gym was a "political and moral abortion," and the faculty called for suspension of construction. The effect of the crisis was to magnify every flawed relationship, to transform the accumulation of diverse individual grievances into a raging sense of injustice against the administration and trustees of the university. The prolonged crisis brought to the surface widespread resentment of an administration that made important decisions without soliciting the opinion of faculty or students. To be sure, for the previous thirty years Columbia had had a succession of presidents who were ceremonial figures, remote from faculty and students. Who the president and trustees were and what they did was of little interest to students or faculty until 1968. Because of the political climate, SDS's die-hard stand against the administration was perceived as a symbolic action against the war and racism; the specific issues became far less important than the symbolism of rebuking unjust authority and involving students and faculty in the running of the university.[34]

As it quickly became clear that the administration would not negotiate with the radicals, a large number of the faculty—which had no formal leadership—intervened in the dispute as a third force between the students and the administration, calling themselves the Ad Hoc Faculty Group (AHFG). Their actions implied a repudiation of the administration, especially President Grayson Kirk, a distant and patriarchal figure who commanded neither respect nor loyalty. The AHFG pressed the administration to take a more flexible approach to the students' demands and to avoid calling the police. In response to pressure from the AHFG, the administration postponed calling in police and suspended construction of the gym. The AHFG believed that it was making progress in negotiating with the radical students, but the students never accepted any of the faculty's proposals nor yielded on any of their demands. Since the administration was willing to negotiate anything other than amnesty, the issue of amnesty became the major sticking point. The radicals insisted on amnesty, because it would constitute an admission by the administration that the radicals were right and that the administration was an illegitimate authority.

The administration was caught in the midst of irreconcilable forces: on one side were the trustees, who supported an uncompromising position; on the other was the faculty, whose vocal members were pushing for flexibility. And then there were the intransigent students in the buildings, who wanted nothing less than unconditional surrender from the administration. Meanwhile, university presidents from around the country were calling Kirk and urging him to stand firm. Unable to be tough without alienating the faculty, unwilling to capitulate for fear of abandoning its integrity, the administration was trapped by the situation. It was, in the radicals' parlance, "up against the wall," faced with a choice of summoning the police or acquiescing to the radicals' demands. Since both the administration and the faculty opposed a general amnesty, the AHFG worked feverishly to find a middle ground. On the seventh day of the occupation, AHFG offered both sides a set of compromise proposals, which included a de facto, implied amnesty: the administration reluctantly, with reservations, accepted the compromise; the students rejected them outright and demanded full amnesty as a precondition for negotiations.[35]

Since the radicals showed no willingness to compromise, the administration called in the police to clear the buildings at 2:30 A.M. on April 30. More than 700 people (of whom 524 were Columbia students) were arrested for trespassing. The black students in Hamilton Hall filed out quietly into police vans. The white students resisted, passively and actively, and 148 people were injured, including students and policemen. The intrusion of police on campus had the same effect as at Berkeley: it created mass support for the radicals among students and faculty. On the morning after the police action, a student strike began, and for most students, the semester was finished. A student strike organization was created, dominated by SDS and organized around its demands.

The strike organization was an uneasy alliance between SDS, which wanted to radicalize the university, and liberal students, who sought a "restructured" university in which students participated in decision making. Two weeks after the strike began, the strike organization split. The moderate students left to work on restructuring, while SDS insisted that restructuring diverted energy from revolutionary activities. A week later, SDS leaders brought five hundred students into Hamilton Hall and refused to leave. That night, police were called onto campus again. Inspired by the radical student uprising taking place in Paris, Columbia's radicals built barricades, set fires, threw stones at the police, and battled through the night. Remarkably, no one was killed, but scores were injured in the melee.

In the summer of 1968, Kirk retired. The faculty executive committee, created after the first police action, took command of the effort to "restructure" the university and put the university community back together again. More than a dozen student-faculty committees worked to hammer out new forms of participation, which led to student involvement on disciplinary panels, liberalized rules of conduct, and a unicameral legislative body of faculty, administrators, and students. Andrew Cordier, the new president of the university, dropped criminal-trespass charges against the students who had been arrested and reinstated most of those who had been suspended after the April uprising. The involvement of nonradical students in the restructuring process effectively isolated SDS; its repeated attempts to provoke another confrontation during the fall of 1968 and spring of 1969 (including the seizure of two buildings in May, 1969) failed; having worked once, the confrontation tactic no longer had the power to shock and radicalize other students. The university severed its ties to IDA and canceled its plans to build in Morningside Park. The much-needed new gymnasium was built on the campus, mostly underground, without provision for community facilities; Morningside Park remained as it had been, a seldom-used, glass-strewn rocky outcropping dividing Columbia from Harlem. Rudd and several other Columbia SDS leaders became the nucleus of the terroristic "Weatherman" group; one died in 1970 while constructing antipersonnel bombs, and another was arrested in 1982 in connection with the robbery of a Brinks' truck and the murder of two policemen in Nyack, New York.

A new and ominous note was introduced at Columbia: during the second occupation of Hamilton Hall in May, 1968, someone broke into the office of a professor who had opposed the demonstrators, ransacked his papers, and burned his research for projected books on the history of Paris and the reign of Louis XIV. In June, Tom Hayden praised the militant tactics of the radicals at Columbia and predicted even greater disruption in the future, including "raids on the offices of professors doing weapons research." The object, he wrote, was not to reform the university but to transform it into a new institution "standing against the mainstream of American society." That fall, at Columbia and other campuses as well, radical students disrupted the classes of professors they wanted to silence or humiliate and shouted down speakers whose views they disagreed with. The movement that had begun with the demand for free speech at Berkeley had become an effort to politicize the university and coerce those who disagreed.[36]

In the short run, the rebellion at Columbia was a stunning victory for the radicals: the administration was humbled, thousands of students were mobilized behind SDS leadership, a small band of insurgents captured the attention of the national media. Before Columbia, major disruptions of campus life involving property destruction and personal violence were rare. In the year after the crisis at Columbia, violent protests occurred on about one hundred and fifty campuses, which was a small percentage of all institutions (6 percent) but included many of the nation's most selective public and private universities. The epidemic of violent protests was not caused by Columbia's example, but Columbia was available as a well-publicized model. In making demands, whether for student power or the expulsion of ROTC or black studies or open admissions, protesters threatened to shut down the university or to use "whatever means necessary" to win acceptance of their "nonnegotiable" demands. Forcible actions—by protesters, counterprotesters, and police—became commonplace, and terroristic acts—arson, bombings, and attempts to intimidate faculty or administration—though by no means commonplace, occurred on scores of campuses.[37]

The collapse of civility on so many campuses was facilitated by the ambivalence of the faculty toward student activism. Poll data has shown that college faculty members are predominantly liberal to left in their politics and that professors were more opposed to the war than were students; faculties, however, were usually divided politically by their fields or departments, with the most liberal professors in the social sciences and the humanities and the most conservative in such applied fields as agriculture, business, and engineering. In 1969, a national sample of professors was almost evenly divided as to whether they approved of "the emergence of radical activism" (42 percent did). Most professors disapproved of disruptive tactics (77 percent believed that "students who disrupt the functioning of a college should be expelled or suspended"), but approved the "aims" behind such protests. In practice, this meant that militant students could always find a sympathetic faculty majority for their stated "aims," and even a sympathetic minority when their tactics were objectionable. While some professors supported student demands and others supported the administration, most preferred to get on with their work and entered the political arena "only at moments of great crisis," in hopes of finding some reasonable settlement to return the campus to normal.[38]

Attempts to return to normal were complicated not just by the internal stresses that existed in every campus community, but by the strains and fissures in American social and political life. The assassination of John Kennedy's younger brother, presidential candidate Robert Kennedy of New York, and the unsuccessful antiwar candidacy of Senator Eugene McCarthy of Minnesota disheartened students who worked in electoral politics to oppose the war. The pitched battles between radical demonstrators and the Chicago police during the Democratic convention in the summer of 1968 further polarized opinion, outraging both those who saw the police as stormtroopers beating idealistic students and those who thought that the police responded correctly to provocation by lawless hippies and radicals. The rising tide of violence and the nightly reports on television of battles and body counts in Vietnam made appeals to civility unrealistic, if not absurd.

Against this background of social disintegration, radical students believed that the university should stand with them "against the mainstream of American society." Their efforts to make the university an ally in their fight against the status quo met stiff resistance from most administrators and faculty members. Those who objected to politicization insisted that, while students and professors could say whatever they wished, the university as an institution had to remain politically neutral. Radical students asserted that the university's cooperation with government and industry and the domination of university boards by businessmen were proof that the university's claim to neutrality was mythical. To dramatize their arguments and to force students and faculty to choose sides, radical students disrupted classes and university functions. Liberal administrators and liberal professors were often the chief targets of radical students. Indeed, the most aggressive attacks on the university occurred at institutions noted for their permissiveness toward student misbehavior.

With no end in sight to the disruptions, administrators devised new responses. In early 1969, three hundred students occupied the administration building at the University of Chicago to demand the rehiring of a radical sociology professor and an equal student voice in the hiring and firing of faculty members. The students may have picked the wrong issue, for the latter demand invaded the powers of the faculty instead of symbolizing an attack on war and racism. The administration moved out of its headquarters, set up shop elsewhere, and appointed a committee to investigate whether the disputed professor had been unfairly judged by her colleagues. The university's position was: no force, no negotiations, speedy discipline. Eighty-two students were suspended; the controversial professor was offered a one-year extension, which she declined. The demonstrators failed to win support from faculty or students, and after two weeks they abandoned their sit-in.[39]

One tactic that proved disastrous was capitulation. Recognizing that student radicals sought confrontations, many administrators avoided imposing discipline for rule violations; this invited those seeking confrontation to find ever more spectacular ways to lock horns with the administration. Thus, the result of sympathetic concession was to heighten the next challenge to the university's authority. San Francisco State College's acquiescent president joined antiwar marches, refused to discipline students who disrupted his inauguration, reduced penalties placed on students who had beaten up the college newspaper editor, and aided students who organized a strike against the college cafeteria. All to no avail. Each concession produced new demands, and at one point an SDS leader crowed, "We have the administration on their knees. Now we're going to push them over on their backs." Not only did his concessions not win a reprieve from radical activism, they inevitably incited the fury of legislators and trustees, who forced the resignation of the president for appeasing disruptive students.[40]

One university that observed the travails of others and concluded that it was, if not immune from similar problems, at least well prepared, was Harvard. In the fall of 1968, SDS began a campaign to drive ROTC off the campus. While refusing to expel ROTC, the faculty voted to strip its courses of academic credit and to remove ROTC professors from the faculty, moves that were certain to cause the Defense Department to withdraw ROTC from Harvard. When the administration said that it would try to work out some arrangement so that students on ROTC scholarships could continue to prepare for military service, SDS became convinced that Harvard's President Nathan Pusey was trying to circumvent the faculty's recommendation.

Harvard SDS, split between a New Left caucus and a Progressive Labor caucus, debated whether to begin its spring offensive by occupying a building. The chapter voted not to seize a building, but the PL faction decided to ignore the vote. On April 9, 1969, several dozen students burst into University Hall, the administrative center, and forcibly ejected several deans from the building, which was promptly renamed "Che Guevara

Hall." The students perused the files in the deans' offices, copying confidential correspondence and records.⁴¹

On the advice of Archibald Cox, who had conducted a fact-finding study of the Columbia disturbances, the administration had developed guidelines well in advance. First, only one person, the president, would speak for the university in order to avoid confusion. Second, the faculty would not be convened immediately, because Cox concluded that the intervention of the Columbia faculty made the crisis much more difficult to resolve. Third, if the decision were made to call the police, they would be summoned promptly; the delay at Columbia was thought to have contributed to conflicting demands, multiple negotiators, and an uncontrollable situation. At 5 A.M., some seventeen hours after the building was seized, local police entered University Hall, where they clubbed many demonstrators. Of the 184 persons arrested, 145 were Harvard students.⁴²

The campus was stunned. Students and faculty were shocked by the brutality of the police; the faculty was outraged that it had not been consulted. Moderate students called a strike, demanding restructuring of the university and cancellation of charges against the demonstrators. The faculty, in a rebuke to President Pusey, recommended the dropping of criminal charges and the creation of a faculty committee to suggest changes in governance and disciplinary policy. The University's Board of Overseers adopted a strong statement supporting Pusey:

> The fundamental issue is whether violence can be allowed to interfere with scholarly inquiry and teaching at a university. A small minority has tried to impose its will on an institution that belongs to all of us. The invasion of University Hall, the forceable eviction of the deans, and the theft and copying of confidential files constituted conduct intolerable in a free academic society. Were we to condone such conduct, no professor would be safe in his classroom, no scholar safe to pursue unpopular inquiry, no group of students safe to oppose the fashion of the moment, whether it be of the radical right or the radical left.

This was the voice of decent liberalism, but it made no impact on the aggrieved students in Harvard Yard, who wore red armbands and tee-shirts emblazoned with a clenched red fist.⁴³

By Friday, April 18, the week-long strike had lost much of its momentum. Classes were over three-quarters full, and one radical told a reporter, "All I want to do is return to a normal schedule, even if it means having a fascist university." Radicals disrupted three classes during the week, and student parodies of radical rhetoric began to appear on campus. ("SMASH THE BOY SCOUTS: This organization is a CIA front. . . . END UNIVER-

SAL EXPANSION: For a great many years now, the universe has been rapidly expanding, having in this enterprise the full co-operation of the Harvard Astronomy Department.") That day, assuaged by commitments from the faculty, the students voted to end their strike.[44]

But before the campus crisis passed, one issue remained: black studies. The faculty had agreed in February, 1969, to establish a program in black studies; as approved, a B.A. degree in Afro-American Studies would be granted in combination with an allied field, like history or economics. But black students insisted that it was insulting to Afro-American Studies to require that it be tied to an "allied field." They also demanded that students have a role equal to faculty in controlling the program. Eager to calm the campus and to remove any potential issue from students who were threatening to commit "acts of sabotage," the faculty agreed to the black students' demands. (Three years later, both changes were canceled on the recommendation of an independent evaluating committee, which concluded that the Department of Afro-American Studies had become an "academic stepchild" because of its isolation from other disciplines, and that student participation in hiring was "counterproductive" in attracting faculty members.)[45]

After the crisis passed, discipline was in the hands of an elected student-faculty committee. In the past, discipline had been inconsistent and inconsequential. The new student-faculty committee held hearings (which SDS tried to disrupt) and recommended stiff punishment for those who had used force or who had past disciplinary records. The leaders of the University Hall seizure were expelled from Harvard, and others were suspended. The contracts of an instructor and teaching fellows who participated were terminated. The ironic effect of the SDS spring offensive was to bring into being a student-faculty disciplinary system that had legitimacy and authority. As a result of SDS's tactics, Harvard emerged greatly strengthened in its ability to ward off future disruptions of the university.

At most universities, the confrontation tactic turned out to be inherently self-limiting, for it rarely worked twice in the same place, and it led to changes that isolated the radicals. The great mass of students was only briefly "radicalized." Most students sincerely wanted to demonstrate their opposition to the war, their support for racial equality, and their conviction that students had a right to participate in university decision making; but they also wanted to get on with their education. In each crisis, student demands for reform were usually satisfied by the "restructuring" of the university—that is, by including student representatives on policy-making committees. Once students participated in the governance and judicial functions, SDS's continued resort to disruptive tactics struck a blow against the *community*, not just the administration. In addition, many university administrators learned from experience, theirs or someone else's, either to avoid getting drawn into a forceful confrontation or to adhere to a firm policy of prompt but nonviolent police action when faced with a protest that disrupted the effective functioning of the university.

If administrators learned slowly and painfully how to respond to challenges from white radical students, they were typically embarrassed, uncertain, and frightened when confronted by black demands. Antiwar tensions culminated at the same time that the status of blacks in higher education was undergoing a dramatic transformation. Under the impact of the civil rights movement and a booming economy, black college enrollment tripled during the 1960s from 174,000 to 522,000, then doubled to more than one million by 1976. In the 1950s, 80 percent of black college students attended historically black institutions; by 1970, 75 percent of black college students were enrolled in predominantly white institutions. Though it was the integration movement that had opened the doors of formerly segregated universities in the South and spurred efforts to increase black enrollment in selective northern institutions, black students in the 1960s were stirred by the same strong tides of anger, separatism, and nationalism that animated riots and demonstrations in black urban communities.[46]

New to higher education and uneasy in an environment that was unaccustomed (and often insensitive) to nonwhites, black students began in the mid-1960s to seek a campus version of "black power." Conscious of the progress that universities had made in recruiting black students and removing racial barriers in dormitories and fraternities, administrators were taken aback by the anger of their new students. Black students organized to demand such things as programs in black studies, more black faculty and administrators, increased black enrollments, special admissions for unprepared students, and separate black dormitories. The university administrators' expectations that black students would pursue their aims through regular channels or would express them in the spirit of the unwritten academic rules of polite discourse were quickly dashed. Whether they had been active in civil rights demonstrations or not, the experience of the civil rights movement convinced many black students that the "white power structure" responded positively only when confronted by militant tactics.

Even on campuses where white radical demands were ignored, black demands struck a sensitive nerve of guilt among white administrators, faculty members, and students. The combination of white guilt and black rage created an emotionally combustible situation; to this was added the administration's fear that the local black community would wreak havoc on campus (at San Francisco State, the Black Student Union imported local high school students who "ransacked the cafeteria, raided the bookstore, broke several windows, started a bookstore fire, destroyed a number of news photographers' cameras, and engaged in several fistfights." A national survey later showed that of three major types of campus protest—involving minority issues, student life (for example, food or parietal rules), or antiwar protest—the administration was most likely to respond positively to black protests and least likely to respond to antiwar issues.[47]

The most audacious attempt by black students to seize political power occurred at San Francisco State College, a commuter college with a national reputation for permissiveness, student participation in decision making, and educational experimentation. In May, 1968, the college president resigned under pressure after appeasing the demands of white radicals and militant blacks. Black students promptly confronted the new president, Robert Smith, with demands for the immediate creation of a black studies department and for the reinstatement of George Murray, a black teacher and minister of education in the Black Panther party, who was suspended after making several inflammatory statements, such as calling for the assassination of the governor (Ronald Reagan), the college president, and others and urging black students to bring guns on campus. When Smith, a man devoted to reason and due process, insisted that the new department would begin operations in the fall of 1969, after its curriculum was approved through regular academic channels, the Black Student Union launched a series of hit-and-run attacks on the college to protest Smith's refusal to open the new department without delay. In early November, 1968, roving groups of black students disrupted classes, beat up white students, overturned filing cabinets, started small fires, and committed numerous other acts of petty vandalism; pitched battles broke out between students and police when the latter arrived on campus.[48]

Their disruptions turned into a full-fledged strike, supported by SDS, an organization called the "Third World Liberation Front," and a committed minority of faculty members. The Black Students Union (BSU) had ten "nonnegotiable" demands, the centerpiece of which was a fully autonomous black studies department. Black student rhetoric was revolutionary, abusive, and extreme. As one BSU leader said to a college convocation:

> Our major objective is the seizure of power. Power must come to the people and black power will come to black people. As things now stand, you must

present your program to the pigs in power and they must approve it. Until we have power, everything is bullshit. The dog believes we want to participate in his political games and that if we demand ten things all the niggers really want is five. Each day the demands are delayed we will escalate our tactics. If armed struggle is what is needed for us to control our lives and our education, then that is what we will use.[49]

Less than three weeks after the strike began, after endless hours of inconclusive faculty meetings and repeated skirmishes between students and police, President Smith resigned and was immediately replaced by S. I. Hayakawa, a faculty member who was known as a firm advocate of law and order on campus. Hayakawa was chosen by the officials of the state college system to act as a military governor of San Francisco State College, and he did not disappoint them. Hayakawa promptly declared an emergency on campus: he banned firearms, forbade the unauthorized use of amplification equipment or of the centrally located "speakers' platform," directed the faculty to meet their classes, and warned that anyone who interfered with the functioning of the college would be suspended. Hayakawa lacked the support of the faculty or the students, but he had the solid backing of the governor, the trustees, and the public.

During the two weeks remaining until Christmas vacation, the campus was the scene of daily battles between students and police, of arrests and bloodied heads, arson and broken windows. When student radicals brought a sound truck on campus, the president himself ripped out its wiring system and became an instant hero on national television. A minority of the faculty launched its own strike on January 6. Many continued to teach, and some classes were disrupted by striking students. Black militants repeatedly packed and disrupted the classes of one target, John H. Bunzel, the liberal chairman of the political science department who had criticized the politicization of the black studies department (in the fall of 1968, an unexploded bomb had been found at the door of Bunzel's office). In mid-February, the faculty ended their strike after receiving assurances of new grievance procedures; the students concluded their strike on March 20, 1969, on the basis of an agreement that denied some of their demands and maintained that others had already been satisfied.[50]

When it was all over, an air of unreality hung over the exhausted campus. The administration had conceded nothing that had not been agreed upon in early December. The black studies department had been established long before the strike ended, but no one seemed to care. After the strike, Hayakawa looked the other way while militant black students took control of the new department, forced out those black faculty members who opposed them, filled most of its staff positions themselves, and shaped a curriculum intended to train revolutionaries; after three semesters, however, all were fired, and a committee of black professors was appointed to reconstruct the department. One of the black student leaders served a year in jail for firebombing the administration building. A black student was maimed when a bomb malfunctioned. Twenty-five professors who encouraged the student strike were fired. An institution that had prided itself on its permissiveness, its experimental courses, the autonomy of its faculty, and the participation of its students emerged from the five-month strike with an authoritarian administration, a divided and demoralized faculty, and deep uncertainty about what had been gained and lost. And Hayakawa was subsequently elected by the people of California to the U.S. Senate in 1976.[51]

While events at San Francisco State were shaped by the fact that it is a public institution, ultimately responsible to elected officials, and by the close ties between its black students and the black communities in San Francisco and Oakland (and, crucially important at the time, such organizations as the revolutionary Black Panther party), the problem of black militancy on campus played out somewhat differently at Cornell, a private university in upstate New York, far from any sizable black community. Yet for all the differences in circumstance, the great private university proved to be as inept and confused in responding to militant black demands as was the public commuter college on the West Coast.

When James Perkins, formerly an executive of the socially conscious Carnegie Corporation, was named president of Cornell in 1963, one of his chief goals was to expand the university's black enrollment, then only twenty-five in a student body of fourteen thousand. In 1964, the university set up a special program to recruit black students and focused its efforts on the very poor and disadvantaged, whose test scores were substantially lower than those of other students. In 1966, black students formed the Afro-American Society (AAS), for blacks only, which stunned white liberals on the faculty, who had fought for years to ban racial exclusivity in dormitories and fraternities. By 1968, there were two hundred and fifty black students, and they began a campaign against racism by barricading the head of the economics department in his office for seven hours in protest against an allegedly racist remark by a visiting lecturer. AAS demanded, among other things, separate living quarters, separate classes, and black studies. In the spring of 1968, the administration told departments to recruit more black faculty, and a black women's residence was set up. That fall, an Afro-American studies program was approved, with a governing committee of nine white faculty members and administrators and eight black students and a $1 million pledge from the university's trustees. As their militancy grew, the black students demanded an autonomous black college, entirely separate within the university. President Perkins was eager to placate the black students, but he advised the AAS that he could not establish a separate black college without the consent of the trustees and the State Board of Regents.[52]

The black students had in Perkins a man who was genuinely dedicated to racial equality, but nothing within his power could assuage their anger. The students complained that Cornell was trying to make them white and that their courses were "irrelevant" to the needs of the black community. One student told a reporter: "We've always questioned why we were brought here. I think they want to get us into this 'mainstream' thing. They figure that after four years up here in this isolated world, you'll go back and fall into your $20,000-a-year job and never think twice." The students wanted to control the black studies program and insisted that only blacks could teach in it. Some prominent black scholars disagreed with their aims. Martin Kilson, a black political scientist at Harvard, opposed student control of black studies and insisted that teachers should be selected by professional qualifications, not by their race. "Students are still *students,*" he held, "and that means they are not intellectually disciplined or trained people. Students must be trained by people who are. Otherwise these black-studies programs will be just a kind of revivalist situation where the recitation of the experiences that each black kid has had will give him a sense of cathartic gain or of therapeutic value, but this will not be an intellectual process. It'll really be a kind of group therapy."[53]

To dramatize their demands, almost all of which had been met, and their anger, which seemed to grow with every new concession by the administration, black students conducted a series of disruptive demonstrations in December, 1968, including a melee in a dining hall when black students walked on eating tables during a meal. Although the university had avoided disciplining blacks for infractions of university rules, six black students who were accused of misconduct (taking furniture from a girls' dormitory for the new AAS center and harassing students and visitors with toy guns) were called before a student-faculty disciplinary committee created by the faculty in 1967 to protect political dissent but to limit disruptive misbehavior. The students refused to appear for hearings. They claimed that an arm of the university was not competent to judge their actions, which were directed against the university, and besides, a racist university had no right to discipline black students. Finally, on the evening of April 17, the conduct board decided to clear three of the black students and to issue a reprimand to three others, the mildest possible disciplinary action.

Within an hour of the decision, a cross was burned outside the black women's residence, and eleven false fire alarms were turned in during the night. The next morning, April 19, at 6 A.M., from fifty to one hundred black students seized Willard Straight Hall, the student union building, evicting thirty parents who were visiting for parents' weekend. A few hours later, some white fraternity men tried to enter through a window and were ejected by the blacks. Administrators began to negotiate with the black students, and on April 20 announced an agreement. The administration promised to recommend to the faculty the nullification of the judicial procedures against black students; to provide legal assistance for those who occupied Willard Straight; to grant full amnesty; to assume full responsibility for damages to the building; to provide twenty-four–hour protection for the black women's residence; and to investigate the cross-burning incident. As the occupation ended, black students, many with bandoliers across their chests, filed out of "the Straight" brandishing shotguns and rifles. The photographs of this scene received national attention as an example of outrageous student behavior.

The next day, April 21, the faculty met and overwhelmingly condemned the seizure of Willard Straight Hall and the introduction of weapons on campus. Taking the position that it was wrong to negotiate under coercion, the faculty refused to dismiss the reprimands imposed on the three black students and agreed to meet again four days later to review the complaints of AAS. Blacks and their allies, the SDS, were outraged by the faculty's refusal to endorse the pact. SDS called a mass meeting in the gymnasium to demand faculty reconsideration. The meeting turned into an occupation, and several thousand students determined to sit-in until the faculty acted. Meanwhile, an AAS leader identified four administrators and three faculty members as "racists" who would be dealt with and warned that the university had only "three hours to live." A group of about thirty sympathetic faculty members, calling themselves "Concerned Faculty," promised to seize a building if the faculty did not reverse its Monday vote. By Tuesday evening, as tension and fear mounted, the faculty leadership called a new meeting for Wednesday noon and recommended repeal of the disciplinary penalties.[54]

On Wednesday, the atmosphere of duress was intense. If the faculty did not nullify the reprimands, buildings would be seized by SDS, AAS, Concerned Faculty, and perhaps others as well. The faculty, faced with the prospect of a collapse of civil order on the campus, overwhelmingly reversed themselves and nullified the reprimands. President Perkins went immediately to the student meeting, where some eight thousand were gathered, to embrace the leaders of AAS and SDS and to declare that their overnight sit-in was "probably one of the most constructive, positive forces that have been set in motion in the history of Cornell." In the end, fear of violence was the only principle that mattered at Cornell, and Perkins did the best he could to put a good face on it.[55]

As at other institutions, the university quickly plunged into "restructuring," soon devising a "constituent assembly" of nearly four hundred elected students, faculty members, administrators, alumni, and others. A small but influential group of professors loudly assailed Perkins's failure to defend academic freedom against student ideologues. A university spokesman defended the pact with the black students by saying that "It was a choice between surrender or extinction." Complaining that the freedom to teach had been sorely compromised by the administration's deference to student power, several leading members of the faculty submitted their resignations, including the chairmen of the government department and the history department. Apparently embarrassed by the university's submission to coercion, the trustees announced that in the future "tactics of terror" would be met by "firm and appropriate response." At the end of May, Perkins resigned as president.[56]

After Perkins left, after the black studies department was in full operation, after the university was restructured, Cornell remained troubled. A year after the occupation of Willard Straight Hall, the black studies center was burned, destroying the center's records and research materials and numerous individual manuscripts. The willingness to condone violence, so antithetical to the values of a university community, was an evil genie on the Cornell campus, neither easily controlled nor easily recalled once set loose.

The public response to campus unrest in the spring of 1969 was one of massive disapproval. The House of Representatives considered legislation to remove federal funds from any college or university in which there were protests. President Richard Nixon urged colleges to crack down on illegal student protests, and his secretary of health, education, and welfare reminded university administrators that the 1968 Congress had passed laws requiring withdrawal of federal support from students convicted of criminal actions in connection with campus disorders. Since so many campuses seemed unwilling to police themselves, state legislatures passed laws governing campus conduct and threatened investigations. The governor of Kentucky, expressing a widespread public reaction, declared, "If you'll pardon me, I'm damned sick and tired of this kind of thing." The Harris Poll reported that most Americans were "shocked and dismayed" by student disorders and could not comprehend black demands for separatism;

those who had never been to college and still considered a college education a great privilege could not understand student protests against their own colleges. Harris found that 68 percent of the public felt that campus demonstrations were unjustified, and that 89 percent supported college officials who called police or the National Guard to quell disorders.[57]

After the hectic spring of 1969, in which thousands of students were arrested, suspended, or expelled for protest activities, a strange quiet descended on the nation's campuses. Campuses that had experienced serious disorders were engaged in the process of "restructuring," and student leaders became involved in committee work. As a step toward a volunteer military, President Nixon replaced the draft with a lottery system, affecting only nineteen-year-olds, which significantly reduced the number of draft-eligibles and relieved men of the necessity of staying in college or graduate school to avoid the draft. Many colleges headed off black uprisings by initiating black studies programs, opening black dormitories, and committing themselves to higher black enrollments.[58]

One other element was no longer present: SDS had virtually ceased to exist. While chapters survived on some campuses, the national organization met in the summer of 1969 and split into two hostile factions, both committed to an armed revolution, each denouncing the other as "anti-Communist." One group, led by Columbia's Mark Rudd, became the Weathermen, dedicated to terrorism and armed struggle. When the Weathermen walked out of the national convention, the other faction, led by the Maoist Progressive Labor party—declaring its intention to lead a revolutionary mass movement composed of radical workers and students—took over SDS's name and its publication, but what was left was a shell of the former organization. Never in touch with reality, the Weathermen summoned their followers to begin "the revolution" by participating in "Four Days of Rage" in Chicago that October; in response, a few hundred radicals descended on Chicago, where they ran through the streets smashing windows and fighting the police. On January 1, 1970, the Weatherman group "went underground," that is, into hiding, to avoid government surveillance of their revolutionary activities. Almost overnight, SDS—the spark that turned campus protests into confrontation, resistance, and rebellion—had self-destructed. By attacking potential allies on the left, like liberals and labor unions, SDS removed itself from working within the political system for change; by admitting to membership those committed to totalitarianism, it brought into its midst the tightly disciplined cadres from the Progressive Labor Party, which ultimately dominated and decimated the organization.[59]

Despite the collapse of SDS, the eagerness of many students to be actively involved in the central political issues of the day was undiminished. At Yale University, which had avoided the angry confrontations that had shaken many other elite institutions, the opportunity to take part in radical politics presented itself in the spring of 1970. A year earlier, New Haven police charged several members of the revolutionary Black Panther party with the kidnapping and murder of a party member; two of those arrested admitted participating in the murder, and one claimed that he had acted on orders from Bobby Seale, national chairman of the party, who was then arrested. In April, 1970, white radicals and black sympathizers on the Yale campus, charging that the Panthers were victims of a national campaign of repression, demanded that Seale and the others be freed; they called for a student strike and scheduled a massive protest rally for May 1. Although the aims of the strike were vague, Yale undergraduates endorsed it, and by April 23, 1970, the college was on strike.

Everyone at Yale knew that other institutions had been severely damaged, morally and physically, by clashes between demonstrators and police, and the strong desire of many students to take a stand was tempered by a growing fear that the university and many individuals might be harmed on May 1. President Kingman Brewster and the faculty decided that the best course of action was to put Yale on the side of the demonstrators. At a faculty meeting on April 23, Brewster gave rhetorical support to the organizers of the forthcoming demonstration by saying, "I am skeptical of the ability of black revolutionaries to achieve a fair trial anywhere in the United States." With Brewster's encouragement and with the knowledge that one thousand students were waiting outside their meeting, the Yale faculty voted to permit the suspension of classes and the use of regular class time to discuss current issues. Brewster's blunt statement provoked outrage by some editorialists and politicians but won him the support of Yale students; when he was denounced by Vice-President Spiro Agnew, the Yale faculty and board of trustees rallied behind him as well.[60]

Though not an official sponsor of the May Day rally, the university cooperated with its organizers and provided food, housing, and medical care for the expected demonstrators. Some fifteen thousand people came to New Haven on May 1, and only scattered incidents marked an otherwise nonviolent weekend. Brewster's tactic worked: by joining forces with the Panthers and attacking the courts, Yale did not become a target of the demonstrators' wrath. The success of the ploy muted the voices of those who doubted the wisdom of politicizing the university. After the May Day weekend, attention turned back to the war in Indochina, and Yale students lost interest in the Panther trial. As the passions of spring 1970 faded, scarcely anyone noticed that Yale had purchased its safety by trashing the judicial system. The following fall, one Panther who had already confessed to the murder was convicted and sentenced, and when Bobby Seale's trial opened, fewer than sixty people sought admission to the courtroom. In the spring of 1971, the jury announced that it could not reach a verdict; the judge declared a mistrial, then dismissed all the charges because prejudicial publicity had made it impossible to have a fair trial.[61]

The student protest movement, which seemed to be losing steam during the winter of 1969 and spring of 1970, was instantly revived on April 30, 1970, when President Nixon announced that American troops had invaded Cambodia. Protest demonstrations began on campuses all over the nation, and student leaders urged a national student strike. The presidents of the nation's most prestigious universities jointly implored President Nixon to consider "the incalculable dangers of an unprecedented alienation of America's youth" and called on him to end American participation in the war. The governor of Ohio dispatched National Guard troops to Kent, Ohio, where protesters from Kent State University had rioted in the town, burned the campus ROTC building, and prevented firemen from saving the building. When National Guardsmen tried to disperse a large crowd of students on May 4, they were pelted with stones and other objects and taunted with verbal abuse. This kind of student behavior was by now unexceptional, indeed typical; students had come to believe law officers would never use any force stronger than a billyclub, and policemen familiar with campus demonstrations had learned to ignore student provocations. The National Guardsmen, however, for reasons that never became clear, fired on the students, killing four.[62]

In angry response to the killings at Kent State and the widening of the war, the student strike movement gained momentum, often supported by faculty and administrators; about three hundred and fifty institutions went on strike for a day or longer, and many institutions closed for the balance of the school year. Governor Ronald Reagan of California shut down the state's college and university system for a week, and other states called on the state police and the National Guard to control student demonstrations. While most campus protests were peaceful, there were numerous incidents of firebombing and arson, directed especially at campus ROTC facilities. At one of the campus uprisings, at historically black Jackson State College in Jackson, Mississippi, two youths were killed when police fired on a crowd of students who were raining rocks and insults on them.[63]

The killings at Kent State and Jackson State dramatized the danger of the by-now customary practice of forcing the university to summon outside law-enforcement officers. The tragic events at Kent State and Jackson

State were the national equivalent of a police bust, acts of repression that would be expected to "radicalize" hundreds of thousands, even millions of students. But since SDS had splintered the year before, each faction having become so extreme in its revolutionary posturing as to lose touch with ordinary students, there was no longer any radical leadership to direct the outpouring of student anguish in May of 1970. The following fall, many colleges gave students time off to campaign for antiwar candidates, precisely the kind of liberal political activity that SDS radicals scorned.

Other events accelerated the decline of the once-exuberant student left. In March, 1970, three leaders of the Weatherman group died while making bombs in a luxurious Greenwich Village townhouse; one had been a Columbia SDS leader, the other two had been Ohio-Michigan regional SDS leaders and frequent visitors at Kent State. A graduate student was killed in August, 1970, when a bomb set by radicals leveled the Army Mathematics Research Center at the University of Wisconsin. The illusion that radical students were the vanguard of a worker-student alliance was shattered when hundreds of hard-hatted construction workers attacked student peace demonstrators in New York City in May and forced city officials to raise the flag that had been lowered in honor of the students killed at Kent State. It was not just the war that divided the workers and the demonstrators. The workers focused their rage on the long-haired, bearded, beaded, shoeless hippies because the cultural style that the students flaunted derided traditional values of authority, family, work, patriotism, and morality. Many workers, like policemen brought in to control student demonstrations, resented the student radicals for belittling a privilege that few workers or policemen enjoyed: a high-quality college education.[64]

Although there continued to be campus protests against the war and about racial issues, their number and intensity fell sharply. Even with "the movement" in decline, however, some centers of radical activism remained. At Stanford University, the war within continued. Since the mid-1960s an unusually strong core of radical students and professors had led sit-ins, boycotted classes, burned the ROTC building (more than once), and firebombed the president's office; antiwar protests were directed, first, against war-related research, and later—after Stanford severed its ties with the defense-oriented Stanford Research Institute—against the university itself. Despite the fact that the faculty and administration opposed the war, radical students periodically rampaged through the campus, breaking windows and destroying university property, selecting targets that would cost the university as much as possible. Toward the end of 1971, Stanford President Richard W. Lyman took the unusual step, upon the advice of an elected faculty board, of dismissing a tenured professor for inciting students to engage in illegal actions.[65]

The bitter-end revolutionaries clung to their dream of politicizing the university, but intelligent radicals knew that it was dangerous to tamper with the political neutrality of the university. Robert Paul Wolff, a radical philosopher, warned students that even if the neutrality of the university was a myth, it was a valuable myth:

> the politicization of the university invites . . . the ever-present threat of pressure, censorship and witch-hunting by conservative forces in society at large. The universities at present are sanctuaries for social critics who would find it very hard to gain a living elsewhere in society. Who but a university these days would hire Herbert Marcuse, Eugene Genovese, or Barrington Moore, Jr.? Where else are anarchists, socialists and followers of other unpopular persuasions accorded titles, honors, and the absolute security of academic tenure? . . . It is a bitter pill for the radicals to swallow, but the fact is that they benefit more than any other segment of the university community from the fiction of institutional neutrality.[66]

Well before the war in Vietnam actually ended, the era of disruptive campus protest faded, and student activists became involved in feminism, ecology, mysticism, and religious cults. But long before the chants of "On strike, shut it down," "Power to the people," and "Up against the wall, motherfucker" faded into memory, analysts sought to interpret the underlying causes of student unrest. The New Left served as "a political inkblot test for outside observers."[67]

For those who had long criticized the mediocrity of American life, the student left represented the cutting edge of cultural revival. For those who had been active in left-wing politics in the 1930s and 1940s, the students were redeeming their hopes for radical change. Yet others, with different memories, viewed student radicalism with foreboding. One-time Socialists, remembering their battles in the 1930s with Stalinists, and European emigrés, recalling the rise of Hitler youth groups, looked apprehensively on the mass demonstrations, with their chants and slogans, and saw the readiness of students to shout down their enemies as a threat to the freedom of the university.

Those who defended the protesters tried to explain their actions in terms of their stated grievances. In the wake of Berkeley, some looked to the anonymity of the multiversity as a cause for student unhappiness; the faculty was too distant from the students, classes were too large, undergraduates were neglected, the university had become a factory, and the conditions of learning had been overly bureaucratized. When the revolt shifted to Columbia, analysts pointed to the autocratic nature of the administration, the failure of communication among faculty, administration, and students, and the need to restructure the university and include students in decision making.

Some of those who were dubious about the sincerity of the radicals looked to their motivations to explain their actions. Zbigniew Brzezinski compared the student revolutionaries to Luddites, who felt themselves left out of the emerging "technetronic society," whose revolution lacked either program or content, and who were therefore "historically obsolete" counterrevolutionaries. Bruno Bettelheim compared the student rebels with Nazi youth, in their anti-intellectualism, fascination with violence, and moral absolutism; he asserted that they were immature, socially useless adolescents who had drawn "extreme isolates and paranoids . . . to the ranks of Extremism." Others saw student protest as a classic generational conflict in a context that was both historic and international.[68]

For student participants, the rewards of political activism were many. It was an opportunity to "put one's body on the line" against war and racism, although until Kent State the actual physical danger was minimal (when police were called to clear a building, students were forewarned and urged to leave). In numerous memoirs, students recalled the enormous sense of power that they felt by defying authorities in a large group, as well as the sense of exhilaration that came from sharing a uniquely exciting experience. Occupying a building was not only a political act; it was an escape from boredom, an opportunity to meet likeminded people in interesting circumstances, and a chance to be an actor on the stage of history. Radical politics offered, above all, a means of personal transformation, out of the ordinariness of everyday life, away from exams and careers, beyond alienation and impotence into a moment of rare, communal intensity. In a characteristic comment, one veteran wrote: "What enlivened the Free Speech Movement was the exhilaration of feeling that you were, for once, really acting, that you were dealing directly with the things that affect your life, and with each other. You were for once free of the whole sticky cobweb that kept you apart from each other and from the roots of your existence, and you knew you were alive and what your life was all about." Whatever else it was, the protest movement was a route to recognition and power; student leaders found themselves negotiating as equals with the highest university officials, interviewed on the evening news, and courted by television talk shows.[69]

The student protest movement could not be easily characterized because it was not a single, definable movement, and it changed over time. It could be likened to a series of concentric circles, whose numbers expanded or contracted in response to the political climate and specific issues on a given campus. Most students joined demonstrations against the war because they felt a deep sense of rage about the war and were frustrated by their inability to change national policy; they wanted the war to stop, and dramatic protests seemed to be the only way to communicate the strength of their views to the public. But while many students participated in demonstrations to oppose the war, to seek student involvement in policy making, or to protest the presence of police on campus, radical leaders viewed the demonstrations and confrontations as tactics to build the radical movement. Radical leaders used issues to force a confrontation and to polarize the campus. There was a saying at Berkeley that "the issue is not the issue." Or as Mark Rudd boasted, "Let me tell you. We manufactured the issues. The Institute for Defense Analysis is nothing at Columbia. Just three professors. And the gym issue is bull. It doesn't mean anything to anybody. I had never been to the gym site before the demonstration began. I didn't even know how to get there." Paul Goodman recognized regretfully that the new radicalism had moved from blissful anarchism to authoritarian Leninism during the 1960s; the cynical effort to "radicalize" the student masses, he wrote, was "exactly the social engineering that the young object to. . . . it is authoritarian to manipulate people for their own good and incidentally to expend them for the cause by somebody else's strategy."[70]

Although large numbers of students participated in demonstrations and signed petitions in the 1960s, those who considered themselves radicals were about 3 to 12 percent of college students, depending on the campus and the political climate at the time. On any given campus, the activist radicals who regularly participated in protests were rarely more than 3 percent. Even at the height of the protests, only 25 percent believed that ROTC should leave the campus, only 30 percent believed that professors should not be permitted to do military research, and only 22 percent believed that defense companies should not be permitted to recruit on campus. Still, on a large campus like Berkeley, 3 percent of twenty-seven thousand students, augmented by nonstudents, could stage an impressive sit-in.[71]

Numerous studies of the social origins of the radical activists converge to create a collective profile. Compared to nonradicals, the radicals were from upper middle-class, high-income, professional families; both mother and father were highly educated, with a liberal-to-radical political orientation (a significant number of radicals were "red-diaper babies," children of 1930s radicals). Rather than revolting against their parents, they were carrying forward their parents' ideals by revolting against society. An extraordinary number of radical activists were of Jewish descent—at least 60 percent of "the movement's" leadership—or from liberal Protestant families, though few reported any current religious affiliation. Radicals were drawn disproportionately from highly verbal, high-scoring students in the social sciences or humanities at elite universities. One sociologist, himself a founder of SDS, described the student movement as "a revolt of the advantaged." Those social scientists who identified with the idealism of radical students hailed them as a new breed, a product of affluence and the postindustrial society. Less admiring social scientists saw the radicals as manipulative, power-seeking, leftist children of leftist parents.[72]

Subsequent studies showed that the protest-prone institutions were those that had a critical mass of radical students. The most selective institutions had the greatest incidence of protests, especially disruptive protests. The occurrence of protest, one national survey found, "depended less on the specific policies and practices of that institution than on the characteristics of its student body and faculty. Indeed, liberalness or permissiveness in the administrative policies of an institution made protests more likely to occur."[73]

The process of polarization left its mark on university faculties. Where there was a major crisis, the faculty split into factions that were characterized by their sympathy or opposition to student demands. Everett Carll Ladd, Jr., and Seymour Martin Lipset have observed that most troubled campuses passed through a two-stage process. The first stage was typified by sympathy for student protest; typically, the administration mishandled the situation and was discredited, and the "left" faction in the faculty gained strength. But in the second stage, when campus disorders continued, support for disruptive behavior ebbed, and moderate or conservative factions in the faculty won elections and set about restoring order to the campus. On many of the most troubled campuses, lifelong friendships among faculty members were destroyed. The disorders, the broken friendships, and the disputes between radicals and liberals shattered the broad liberal consensus that had prevailed on most campuses. At one end of the spectrum, a small but conspicuous number of disillusioned liberals began to shape a critique of the liberal tradition that came to be known as neoconservatism; and before long, the other end of the political and ideological spectrum on campus was represented by a sizable number of Marxist scholars, many of whom had been introduced to radicalism during their student days in the 1960s.[74]

When it was all over, no college or university was destroyed, nor was American reliance on higher education shaken: enrollments continued to increase, and—while some public budgets were cut for a time, and alumni in certain troubled institutions showed their displeasure by withholding contributions—when the era of disruptions ended, financial support for public and private institutions grew. The major effect of the period of disruption was to hasten several nascent trends. Even before the upheavals, some large institutions had begun to withdraw from their traditional *in loco parentis* role, in response to the growing diversity of their student body; after "the troubles," the enlarged importance of the student voice caused many more institutions, large and small, to abandon their supervision of student social life. At many institutions, students became part of policy-making committees, usually with the exception of faculty committees controlling the appointment and promotion of faculty members. In efforts to provide greater choice for students and more individual decision making, course requirements were widely eliminated. Student unrest was sometimes but a pretext for dismantling requirements. In many institutions, there was genuine confusion or disagreement about what knowledge was of most worth; in the large universities, the retreat from requirements was a triumph of specialized research over the liberal arts curriculum, rather than a response to student pressure.

One national survey found that "the number of institutions requiring English, a foreign language, and mathematics as part of everyone's general education declined appreciably from 1967 to 1974—from 90 percent of the institutions surveyed to 72 percent for English, from 72 to 53 percent for foreign language, and from 33 to 20 percent for mathematics." Gerald Grant and David Riesman in *The Perpetual Dream* concluded that "the most widespread and significant impact of the educational upheaval of the sixties was to bring about a greater degree of autonomy for students. They were free to plan their courses of study in a way they had never done before. The most important change was the virtual or complete abolition of fixed requirements in many departments and of mandatory distribution requirements, whether of breadth or depth, including class attendance and the time, mode and kinds of credits needed to secure a baccalaureate degree." The abandonment of requirements meant "the collapse of general education," since students in many institutions could largely plan their own courses of study, no matter how specialized or esoteric they might be.[75]

In some institutions, the innovative courses pioneered at radical "free universities," which focused on radical consciousness and revolutionary ideology, were incorporated into the regular curriculum. Black studies was widely introduced, either as a program or a department, sometimes taught in the original, consciousness-raising, nationalist mode, sometimes evolving as an area study in tandem with traditional disciplines. Grading standards changed, with the introduction of pass-fail options and other replacements for traditional competition. While most elite institutions continued to be elite institutions, the convergence of educational and ethnic demands caused some formerly selective institutions—like the elite City College of New York—to adopt "open admissions" for all high school graduates. Even severe protest, however, did not necessarily lead to educational change; Columbia, for example, preserved its required "contemporary civilization" curriculum and did not introduce black studies (black students never sought it). And at some institutions, notably Berkeley and Columbia, after the student uprisings, faculty members actually had less classroom contact with students than before.[76]

By the end of the 1970s, institutions of higher education began to reexamine their curricula and to wonder whether they had gone too far in dissolving requirements for admission and graduation. Following the lead of the colleges, high schools had also lowered graduation requirements; there seemed no reason for high schools to require students to study a foreign language or science if colleges did not require them for admission. Despite some public grumbling about the collapse of general education in college and high school, many professors found a free-choice curriculum to their taste since it kept unwilling students out of their courses.

Without the war in Vietnam, it is possible that the student uprising at Berkeley would have been an isolated event. So many proximate causes converged in time and place that no one of them can be isolated as a single cause of student unrest or radicalism. Certainly the war was a critical factor —perhaps *the* critical factor—as was the rising tempo of black urban riots and black demands for separatism and political power. The military draft kept male students in college who did not want to be there and made them feel both guilty and angry about the choice they had made to avoid the draft. However, student unrest also occurred in the late 1960s in many other countries which were neither involved in Vietnam nor struggling with racial problems. And it coincided in time with the arrival of the baby-boom generation on campus in 1964, the first generation to grow up in an age of steadily expanding affluence, untouched by war or depression. Unlike their parents, their own lives were relatively unaffected by struggle; many had grown up in comfort, strived to get into elite universities, and found their lives devoid of challenge, with little to look forward to other than following in their parents' professional footsteps. Further, the size of the baby-boom generation and its increased rates of college attendance contributed not only to the growth of multiversities but to the growth of an autonomous, affluent youth culture with a relaxed attitude toward drugs and sex. The ready availability of drugs was an important element of the counterculture, and affluence expanded the number who could afford to drop out and swell the ranks of the counterculture. While the counterculture was only one component of the student protest movement, it had an important effect on the movement's nature and direction.

At a time of intense public debate, the universities served as a platform and a sanctuary for opponents of the war. It was one of the paradoxes of the era that radical students made the university their target, even though the university was the one institution most congenial to dissenting views. Radical protests often directly threatened academic freedom—the freedom to teach and the freedom to learn. Radical students, attracting sympathizers by their opposition to war and racism, arrogated for themselves the right to decide who was entitled to free speech on the campus and declared war on their enemies by disrupting their classes, destroying their research, bombing their offices, and burning their buildings. Eugene Genovese, the Marxist historian, described them as "pseudo-revolutionary middle-class totalitarians," whose efforts to politicize the universities invited far more powerful conservative forces to purge *their* enemies.[77]

Institutions, it turns out, are not easily destroyed, though at many colleges and universities the fragile consensus that sustains openness and freedom was severely damaged; reputations were impaired, collegial relationships were disrupted, some permanently. A college campus cannot survive either as an armed camp or as an arena for violence and thuggery. The freedom to think and speak without regard to popular opinion is to a large extent dependent on the strength of the institutions that protect critical thinking from political interference. When political interference comes from right-wing elected officials, university trustees, and pressure groups, then faculty members and administrators join to defend academic freedom. When the challenge comes from radical students, teachers, and pressure groups, as it did in the 1960s, the university is internally divided, which puts academic freedom at risk from those who most need its protection.

CHAPTER 7

Reformers, Radicals, and Romantics

U NLIKE HIGHER EDUCATION, where the mood was one of confidence and optimism as the 1960s began, America's elementary and secondary schools were struggling to readjust to the new demands of the post-Sputnik era. The Soviet launch of the world's first artificial satellite on October 4, 1957, promptly ended the debate that had raged for several years about the quality of American education. Those who had argued since the late 1940s that American schools were not rigorous enough and that life adjustment education had cheapened intellectual values felt vindicated, and, as one historian later wrote, "a shocked and humbled nation embarked on a bitter orgy of pedagogical soul-searching." National magazines discovered a new crisis in education, and critics like Admiral Hyman Rickover—known as the father of the nuclear submarine—vociferously blamed the schools for endangering the nation's security by falling behind the Russians in science, mathematics, and engineering. Regardless of what was said, there was Sputnik itself, orbiting the earth as a constant reminder that political supremacy was tied to technological prowess. For the first time since the end of World War II, people of all political backgrounds agreed that the national interest depended on improving the quality of America's schools.[1]

Out of the new mood arose a clamor for the federal government to do something, and do it quickly. President Eisenhower had staunchly opposed any general federal aid to schools, on the grounds that federal aid would inevitably lead to federal control. Yet, aware that the baby boom had strained the finances of many school districts, Eisenhower repeatedly tried to gain congressional approval for a federal school construction program. Even so limited a purpose as school construction was stymied by the same political factors—race, religion, and fear of federal control—that had blocked previous federal aid bills. After Sputnik, however, the broad popular demand for a federal response to meet the Russian challenge prompted Congress to pass the National Defense Education Act in 1958 (NDEA). This act provided fellowships, grants, and loans to encourage the study of science, mathematics, and foreign languages and funded school construction and equipment. The active federal aid lobby, defeated so many times in the past, was happy to latch onto national security as a vehicle to establish the legitimacy of the federal role in supporting education.[2]

Well before Sputnik, there were clear signs of discontent with the quality of American schools. Government officials repeatedly expressed concern about the shortage of graduates in scientific and technological fields. Additionally, the critics of progressivism complained about the neglect of the basic academic disciplines—English, history, science, mathematics, and foreign languages. The historian Arthur Bestor insisted that scholars had a responsibility for the way their disciplines were presented in the public schools. Nor was Bestor alone in his belief that what was taught in the schools was obsolescent, trivial, or insufficiently challenging. Many others, in the academic world and the government, criticized the quality of secondary school teaching, especially in the fields of science and mathematics. In 1952, mathematicians at the University of Illinois organized a project to develop new materials for high school teachers, with the intention of introducing adolescents to the way that mathematicians think. In the spring of 1956, under the leadership of physicist Jerrold Zacharias, a group of scientists at MIT formed the Physical Science Study Committee, which aimed to revise the content and methods of physics teaching in secondary schools, in part to correct what was taught but also to attract more students into careers in science.[3]

Sputnik came to be a symbol of the consequences of indifference to high standards. In popular parlance, Sputnik had happened not because of what the Russians had done but because of what American schools had failed to do. The prototypical response to Sputnik was the Rockefeller Brothers Fund's report *The Pursuit of Excellence,* which appeared in 1958. While the NEA's *Education for All American Youth,* published in 1944, epitomized the progressive educators' expansive vision of the school as a grand social service center meeting the needs of the individual and the community, *The Pursuit of Excellence* presented a contrasting vision of the proper relation between school and society. It advocated the development of human potential as a national goal and insisted that the nation could encourage both excellence and equality without compromising either. It spoke of challenges and greatness, of high performance, of moral and intellectual excellence. Like most reports, it made nothing happen, but it accurately reflected hopes for the renewal of American society through the infusion of higher educational aspirations.[4]

During the late 1950s, the much-discussed "crisis in the schools" attracted the attention of the major foundations, which had previously focused their resources on higher education. In late 1956, almost a year before the orbiting of Sputnik, the Carnegie Corporation agreed to support a series of studies of public education by James B. Conant, former president of Harvard University and ambassador to West Germany. When Conant's first report, *The American High School Today*, was published in 1959, beleaguered school officials seized upon it as a set of practical recommendations to translate the exhortations of *The Pursuit of Excellence* into reality. Conant urged the spread of the comprehensive high school, which he defined (in progressive terminology) as one "whose programs correspond to the educational needs of *all* the youth in the community." To be comprehensive, a high school had to fulfill three tasks: first, to provide "a good general education for *all* the pupils" (which meant that all students were required to take courses in English and American literature and composition, as well as in social studies); second, to offer the noncollege-bound majority good elective nonacademic courses (such as vocational, commercial, and work-study); and third, to provide the academically talented students with advanced courses in fields such as mathematics, science, and foreign languages. He urged the elimination of high schools too small to be "comprehensive," that is, with a senior class smaller than one hundred. Conant opposed tracking of students into separate curricula (for example, "college prep" versus vocational), but he endorsed ability grouping, so that fast and slow students would get the appropriate level of academic challenge. A skillful blend of dedication to both academic excellence and democratic values, Conant's high school study became a surprise bestseller. Though some professional educators complained that Conant's recommendations were too conservative, John Gardner, president of the Carnegie Corporation (and, coincidentally, author of *The Pursuit of Excellence*) noted approvingly that Conant "became overnight the most quoted authority on American education," and his celebrated report "was debated in PTA's, school boards, superintendents' offices, and educational conferences throughout the nation."[5]

During the same period, the Ford Foundation addressed the "crisis in the schools" with two major efforts: a "Comprehensive School Improvement Program" (CSIP), which funded leading communities to serve as model districts for educational reform, and a "Great Cities–Gray Areas Program," to help big-city school systems create compensatory and remedial programs for their increasing numbers of low-income pupils. Unlike the Conant report, which sought to strengthen traditional secondary education, Ford's CSIP encouraged the implementation of innovative practices in curriculum, staffing, technology, and facilities, such as team teaching, nonprofessional personnel, flexible scheduling, programmed instruction, federally sponsored science curricula, teacher-devised curricula, independent study, language laboratories, open-space classrooms, nongraded programs, and school-university cooperation. Both programs were bellwethers of a sort, one by stressing innovation as the key to school improvement, the other by confronting the issues of educating poor children.[6]

The great flurry of public interest that followed the orbiting of Sputnik was invaluable for those who wanted the schools to pay more attention to gifted students and to raise academic standards. The Conant report provided parents and citizens' groups with a handy check-list to use in gauging the quality of their high schools. The definition of the "crisis" riveted the attention of school officials on such matters as enrollments in science, mathematics, and foreign languages. Able students were encouraged to enroll in advanced courses and to work hard to get into elite colleges. Standardized achievement scores rose steadily, as did high school enrollments in advanced academic courses. For the first time in the twentieth century, foreign language enrollments grew: in 1955, only 20 percent of high school students were studying any foreign language, a figure that rose to 24 percent by 1965.[7]

At the National Science Foundation (NSF), the furor over Sputnik significantly increased the agency's role in secondary school curriculum reform. Established by Congress in 1950 to promote basic research and education in the sciences, NSF initially had little to do with precollege programs. Soon, however, it began to sponsor science fairs and summer institutes for high school teachers of mathematics and science. In 1956, responding to governmental concern about manpower shortages in scientific and technical fields, NSF funded the MIT Physical Science Study Committee's revision of the secondary school physics curriculum. In the wake of Sputnik, NSF expanded its high school curriculum revision projects to include the fields of mathematics, biology, chemistry, and social science. From these efforts eventually came a number of innovative curricula, including "the new math," "the new social studies," and substantial revisions in the natural sciences.

Convinced that the right combination of talent and funding would correct the flaws of the schools, the curriculum reformers took up their task with missionary zeal. The flurry of activity by university scholars and high school teachers offered promise of transforming American education: "Action sprung up at schools and colleges across the land. Hundreds of talented persons—scientists, science teachers, psychologists, film makers, writers, apparatus designers, artists, etc.—formed themselves into groups according to shared notions of what high school science might become. At first this meant high school mathematics and the natural sciences, but then it became extended to high school social sciences, and then to elementary and junior high science." Each new curriculum package was tested, retested, and revised. Thousands of teachers attended summer institutes and inservice programs to learn how to use the new materials and methods.[8]

The curriculum reformers shared a common outlook. They hoped to replace current methods—characterized by teacher-led "telling" and student recitation—with curriculum packages that used "discovery," "inquiry," and inductive reasoning as methods of learning; the rationale was that students would find the field more interesting and would retain longer what they learned if they "figured out," through carefully designed exercises or experiments, the basic principles of the field. They hoped to end the traditional reliance on a single textbook by creating attractive multimedia packages that included films, "hands-on" activities, and readings. They emphasized the importance of understanding a few central concepts in a discipline, rather than trying to "cover" an entire field, the way current courses in science or history did. Where present curricula stressed the informational, descriptive, and applied aspects of a subject (the discipline's "product"), the new curricula would teach the structure of the academic discipline; students would learn how a scientist or mathematician or social scientist thinks (the discipline's "processes"). Put another way, instead of learning "about" science, students would "do" science. The reformers agreed on the importance of cognitive growth, in keeping with the principle enunciated by one of the moving forces of the curriculum reform movement, Harvard psychologist Jerome Bruner, that "any subject can be taught effectively in some intellectually honest form to any child at any stage of development."[9]

As the new curricula were devised and revised in the early years of the 1960s, the climate for educational change was unusually receptive. The political and social context seemed charged by the energy, youth, and dynamism of the Kennedy administration, and the status quo in every area of endeavor was under reexamination. For the first time, the problem of educational change was jointly attacked by federal agencies, university scholars, major philanthropic foundations, big-city school systems, and almost everyone else in the field. On all educational fronts, innovation was the watchword, and some observers confidently spoke of "the revolution in the schools." In 1963, Francis Keppel, U. S. commissioner of education, observed that in the past decade, "more time, talent, and money than ever before in history have been invested in pushing outward the frontiers of educational knowledge, and in the next decade or two we may expect even more significant developments."[10]

With funds from foundations and government, school systems experimented with the new (supposedly "teacher-proof") curricula, new patterns of staffing and scheduling, new ways of training teachers, and new technology. Admirers of behaviorist B. F. Skinner claimed that the teaching machine and programmed instruction would revolutionize the classroom. Others, touting the virtues of television teaching, talking typewriters, computers, and multimedia equipment, envisioned the advent of "the automated classroom." The new technology, it was believed, had made the traditional, egg-crate school obsolete; in a school where students sometimes worked individually, sometimes joined in large groups for television instruction, and sometimes worked in team-taught situations, it would no longer make sense to have equal-sized classrooms with fixed walls. "The new schoolhouse" would have flexible furnishings, movable walls, and open spaces, and indeed such schoolhouses already existed in places such as San Mateo, California; Wayland, Massachusetts; Boulder City, Nevada; and Newton, Massachusetts.[11]

The expected pedagogical revolution in the schools was not to be, however. It was swept aside by the onrush of the racial revolution, which presented a forceful challenge to the political, social, and economic basis of American schools. Between 1963 and 1965, the nation's social fabric sustained a series of jolts: violence against blacks and civil rights workers in the South; the assassination of President Kennedy; the rediscovery of poverty; the beginning of American involvement in Vietnam. Meanwhile, the movement of blacks to northern cities brought the problems of racial segregation and slums to urban schools. Civil rights leaders in North and South brought their demands for integration, equality, and justice to the doors of the public schools; in the context of such transcending demands, the pedagogical revolution was no revolution at all.

Before long, the pursuit of excellence was overshadowed by concern about the needs of the disadvantaged. As the racial crisis and the urban crisis became the nation's most pressing problems, the Cold War competition with the Soviets moved to the back burner and lost its motivating power. Identifying the gifted and stimulating high achievement paled as a national goal in comparison to the urgency of redressing racial injustice. Government agencies and foundations redirected their agendas to search for mechanisms to meet the needs of disadvantaged minority children, and scores of compensatory programs were created throughout the country. Such efforts were multiplied by congressional passage of the Elementary and Secondary Education Act in 1965, with its focus on educating poor children.

The many remedial and compensatory programs initiated by local school systems, state education departments, and federal agencies were born in crisis, and there was neither time enough nor knowledge enough to satisfy the rising expectations of long-denied and angry minorities. Programs were tried, hastily evaluated, declared a failure. In some cities, civil rights groups conducted demonstrations to demand integration and to protest inferior schooling. In others, black community groups demanded control of the public schools by the black community. Critics charged that the curriculum, the professionals, the tests, the bureaucratic organization, and the methods of the conventional school were inherently biased against blacks.

Since none of these demands for change was ever fully satisfied, and, more importantly, since none—even if fully satisfied—had the power to produce in immediate and tangible form the desired goal of full racial equality, the schools bore the brunt of black anger. No matter how well or how badly the schools taught reading or writing or history, poor black children still lived in slums, black unemployment was still double the white rate, and black poverty remained high. Even what the schools could do well, if they were good schools, was not equal to the burden placed on them. And so, because they could not solve the problem of racial inequality and did not have within their power the means to redress demands for justice, the schools became the targets of intense criticism.

Amid the extreme social dissension of the late 1960s, the schools—because of their role in generating values and teaching ways of knowing —were directly affected by antiwar protests, the splintering of the liberal center, the rise of the counterculture, the growth of racial separatism, and demands for "relevant" curricula by everyone who wished to change society. When the decade of the 1960s opened, the problems of the schools seemed solvable, if only enough talent, commitment, and money could be mobilized; by the late 1960s, the waning of national self-esteem was evident in the schools. Where once there had been a clear sense of purpose about educational goals, now there was uncertainty. The educational pendulum began to swing back toward a revival of progressivism. When the new progressivism burst forth in the mid-1960s, it sought to combine a critique of schools and a critique of society. It grew out of a bitter reaction against the inadequacies of American public schools in educating minority children and a profound hostility to the typical public school's commitment to such values as competition and order. It blamed American society for the persistence of racism and inequality; it blamed the bureaucratic nature of the educational system for failing to respond to children as individuals; it blamed the teaching profession for serving its own interests instead of the interests of children.

The rise of the new progressivism mirrored the social and political trends of the time and grew in response to racial unrest, antiwar sentiment, and student activism. While the new progressivism was eventually well supported by government and foundations, and its influence affected many public and private schools, its chief product was a substantial body of educational protest literature. The forerunner of the new movement was A. S. Neill's *Summerhill,* which appeared in 1960, the very time when post-Sputnik pressures to raise academic standards were widespread, an unfortuitous moment for a book celebrating the virtues of permissiveness. One of the book's few reviews came from Margaret Mead, who called it "a ghost of the 1920's" and worried that it might "set off a wave of uncritical behavior among a new class of parents just emerging into a literate interest in pedagogy."[12]

Despite Mead's dismissal, *Summerhill*—an autobiographical, anecdotal account of Neill's libertarian boarding school in England—was destined to become a classic of educational radicalism. Directly challenging the discipline that characterized traditional schools, Neill held that the child "is innately wise and realistic. If left to himself without adult suggestion of any kind, he will develop as far as he is capable of developing." At Summerhill, children did not have to attend classes unless they wanted to, and Neill was quite willing to wait until they wanted to; one of his students, he proudly noted, lived at Summerhill for thirteen years without ever going to a single lesson. "Parents are slow in realizing how unimportant the learning side of school is," wrote Neill. "Children, like adults, learn what they want to learn. All prize-giving and marks and exams sidetrack proper personality development. . . . All that any child needs is the three R's; the rest should be tools and clay and sports and theater and paint and freedom." These echoes from an earlier strain of American progressivism had scant resonance in 1960, at a time when American educators were striving to meet the public's demands for excellence. But by 1969, in a changed atmosphere, *Summerhill* was selling at the rate of more than two hundred thousand copies a year.[13]

Summerhill was soon followed by a plethora of scathing critiques of the American school. In *Compulsory Mis-Education,* Paul Goodman (an admirer of Neill's) attacked compulsory education and argued that the prolongation of schooling for adolescents "is psychologically, politically, and professionally damaging." Adolescents are "herded into" schools, where they are "brainwashed," bribed, and pressured, subdued, policed, and regimented. In place of this destructive, standardized system, Goodman suggested several alternatives: attendance should be voluntary, as at Summerhill; some children should have no school at all; some classes should use the city's resources as a school; unlicensed adults in the community should be engaged as educators; big urban schools should be decentralized into small units of twenty to fifty children and housed in storefronts or clubhouses. He believed that schools should be "havens for those scholarly by disposition" and that the nonscholarly majority should get job training and learn about life outside the school, in real-life situations.[14]

In 1967, criticism of the schools—and in particular, urban schools in black neighborhoods—reached a crescendo with the publication of Jonathan Kozol's *Death at an Early Age* and Herbert Kohl's *36 Children.* The two young men, former classmates at Harvard, became elementary school teachers, Kozol in Boston, Kohl in New York City. Kozol, whose book won the National Book Award, recounted a year in a school where the teachers were racist, cruel, and contemptuous of the children. Kohl described a year of teaching in which he set aside the sterile prescribed curriculum and encouraged the children to express themselves through creative writing.[15]

In the dozens of critical books published about the schools during the late 1960s, several types emerged: the account of the public school principal struggling against an uncaring society and bureaucratic system to educate black children (Nat Hentoff, *Our Children Are Dying*); the memoirs of the articulate young teacher who triumphs over his principal, the other teachers, and the system by treating his pupils as human beings (James Herndon, *The Way It Spozed To Be* and *How to Survive in Your Native Land*); the experiences of the dedicated radical who defies the public schools and social convention by creating an experimental private school, which is impecunious but educationally exciting (George Dennison, *The Lives of Children;* Steve Bhaerman and Joel Denker, *No Particular Place to Go*); the reflections of the teacher who has realized that the curriculum and the methods of the school actually crush the joy of learning (John Holt, *Why Children Fail*); the polemic by the journalist who discovers that education must be an extension of the human potential movement, a means to achieve moments of ecstasy (George Leonard, *Education and Ecstasy*), or by the educator who declares that intellectual goals must make way for "affective education," directed to students' feelings and attitudes (Terry Borton, *Reach, Touch and Teach: Student Concerns and Process Education*).[16]

The indictment of the school was overwhelming. In the eyes of the critics, the school destroyed the souls of children, whether black or white, middle-class or poor. It coerced unwilling youths to sit through hours of stultifying classes, breaking their spirits before turning them out as either rebellious misfits or conforming cogs in the great industrial machine. It neglected the needs of individuals while slighting the history and culture of diverse minorities. It clung to a boring, irrelevant curriculum and to methods that obliterated whatever curiosity children brought with them. It drove away creative teachers and gave tenure to petty martinets. For those who agreed with the critics, there was no alternative other than to change the schools or to abandon them.

As the school became the focus of criticism for everyone who found fault with American society or the American character, a consensus developed among education policy makers in government and foundations. The schools, went the new consensus, needed to be changed radically. The long-heralded "revolution in the schools," prophesied only a few years earlier, had not come to pass; teaching machines, team teaching, nongraded classrooms, and even the curriculum reforms supported by the National Science Foundation had not brought about the dramatic improvement that was anticipated. The new curricula, like the "new math" and the "new science," were conceived when the nation demanded excellence and were designed to stimulate the interest of college-bound youth; only a half dozen years later, the new curricula were seen as solving yesterday's problem. In terms of the current crisis, they were no longer relevant. They offered little promise of erasing racial inequality and none at all of radically transforming the school and the society. Thus the new consensus was founded on belief in the failure of the schools, the uselessness of piecemeal reforms like curriculum change, and the necessity for sweeping change. Every new idea had a constituency, whether it was racial balancing of schools, parent participation, black community control, or anything else that promised to break the grip of traditional practice. The courts began to order busing, the Ford Foundation supported demonstrations of community control in minority neighborhoods in New York City, the federal government funded scores of experimental programs. The underlying assumptions in the various approaches were, first, that there was little in the schools worth preserving; second, that anything innovative was bound to be better than whatever it replaced; third, that the pathology of the schools was so grave that the only change worth attempting must be of a fundamental, institutional, systemic kind; and fourth, that the way to change society and to turn it against war and racism was to change (or abandon) the schools.

It was in this atmosphere that a variety of new movements for educational change developed, distinguished from one another largely by the extent to which they assumed that the public schools could be "saved" or were even worth saving. The "open education movement," which achieved national prominence in the late 1960s and early 1970s, aimed to reform public schools by changing the methods and goals of schooling. The "free school movement," which emerged during the same period, consisted of a loose network of private schools animated by Summerhillian principles, aware of each other, hostile to traditional methods, and committed to radical politics. The "alternative schools movement" was an effort to bring some of the principles of the free schools into the public schools, in order to reduce student discontent. The "deschooling movement," which was stimulated by Ivan Illich's book *Deschooling Society,* was not so much an educational movement as it was a literary sensation. Its practical effect was to lend support to the fast-growing assumption that out-of-school activities were equal in educational value, and perhaps actually superior to, in-school activities. None of these movements was isolated from the others; they shared certain assumptions about the failure of the existing public schools, the corruptness of American society, and the need to adopt radical changes in school and society.

These movements and ideologies gained their greatest success at the same time that belief in the egalitarian potential of compensatory education faltered. Quickly developed in response to the racial turmoil of the mid-1960s, the Great Society educational reforms were oversold; extravagant claims were made—in part to pass legislation and in part to gain political credit for the new programs—that federal intervention in education would eliminate the achievement gap between white and black children and that poor children who participated in preschool Head Start programs would enter regular school on a par with middle-class children. That neither the knowledge nor the experience existed to fulfill such promises did not become apparent until 1969, when two critiques dashed hopes that education alone could end inequality and end it quickly. One was the Westinghouse assessment of Head Start, which concluded that the initial gains made by poor children in preschool programs were washed out in subsequent years; the other was a controversial article by educational psychologist Arthur Jensen, who argued that the genetic limitations of blacks explained why "Compensatory education has been tried and it apparently has failed." While both Jensen and the Westinghouse study were vigorously rebutted, their effect nonetheless was to dampen the enthusiasm of those who believed that more money and more schooling would produce a leveling-up of society.[17]

Yet for most radical critics of American schools, especially those who agreed with writers like A. S. Neill and Paul Goodman, the outcome of compensatory education was never a live issue, for it promised only to place minority students into a soul-deadening mainstream. What mattered to the radical critics was that even in supposedly successful schools with high test scores and good college admission records, students were expected to produce "right" answers, to compete against each other, to conform, and to acquiesce to the demands of the school system, in preparation for similar demands from the larger social system. The problem with the schools, the critics believed, was not just their curricula or their textbooks or their methods—none of which the critics liked—but their repressive nature, their demands for conformity. These critics were indifferent to reforms that attempted to raise test scores because such reforms did nothing to change the essential character of American education or American society.

In this climate of scorn, disappointment, and despair about American schools, Joseph Featherstone's articles in the *New Republic* about the British infant schools caused a minor sensation. In three articles in August and September, 1967, Featherstone reported "a profound and sweeping revolution in English primary education, involving new ways of thinking about how young children learn, classroom organization, the curriculum, and the role of the teacher." His straightforward, graphic, and admiring account of classrooms where children were busily and happily learning presented a sharp contrast to the current reputation of American schools. Featherstone's articles publicized the findings of Britain's Plowden Commission, which ringingly endorsed the activity-centered infant school. Within a year after Featherstone's articles appeared, the magazine sold one hundred thousand offprints, and the British model (which Featherstone referred to offhandedly as "the free day," the "integrated curriculum," or the "integrated day") became the talk of American education.[18]

Featherstone described a typical day at the Westfield Infant School in Leicestershire County. Early in the day, even before the teachers arrive, the children (ages five to seven) are "reading, writing, painting, playing music, tending to pets." Children work (and play) individually or in small groups, rarely as an entire class. The classroom is noisy, because the children move about and talk freely. Children learning and playing flow back and forth among the classroom, hallway, and playground. There are no assigned places, rather there are well-equipped tables and activity areas for art, number work, sand and water play, quiet reading, a play corner with dolls and furniture. The routine of the day "is left completely up to the teacher, and the teacher, in turn, leaves options open to the children. . . . there is no real difference between one subject in the curriculum and another, or even between work and play." Not only is the children's writing profuse and fluent, but the older children teach the younger ones how to read. The teacher who oversees all of this purposeful activity "sometimes sits at her desk, and the children flock to her for consultations, but more often she moves about the room advising on projects, listening to children read, asking questions, giving words, talking, sometimes prodding." The essential ingredient in the success of the British infant school, Featherstone concluded, was the teacher's belief "that in a rich environment young children can learn a great deal by themselves and that most often their own choices reflect their needs."

The impetus for the new methods, Featherstone believed, came about in part because the children involved were very young, and the infant schools were separate institutions; infant school teachers were trained together with nursery school teachers, and their "subject matter," in effect, was the development of the individual child, how he learns and grows. The best practice, he held, reflected developmental psychologist Jean Piaget's influence, particularly his belief that "children learn to think in stages, and that in the early stages they learn mainly from the testimony of their senses, and not so much through words." Thus, the emphasis in the infant school on concrete experience and activity. Another important element in the shift to individual learning was the influence of the government inspectors, who in many English counties had functioned as educational advisory agents, disseminating new ideas and training new teachers in progressive practices.

Before the publication of Featherstone's articles, there was a handful of Americans trying to adapt the methods of the British infant school to American schools. As news of the "revolution" in the British primary schools got out, more and more educators saw the British model as a potential answer to the urgent need for a reliable-but-revolutionary innovation. The British model offered everything: learning activities were individualized and based on play and experience; teaching was informal and responded to children's needs and interests; the children were learning, and they enjoyed school. British practices struck a responsive chord in part because they encompassed the tenets of America's own educational progressivism: that children learn at different rates; that children want to learn; that the best way to motivate learning is through projects, experiences, and activities; that, for children, the distinction between "work" and "play" is false; that division of knowledge into subjects is artificial; and that such external stimuli as grades and tests cannot compare to the power of the child's own interest. For American educators who had been brought up on the progressive creed of Dewey, Kilpatrick, and Rugg, the British "integrated day" sounded a familiar melody which had been drowned out by the attacks of academic critics and the hysteria of the post-Sputnik era. Young teachers who abhorred the "authoritarianism" of the traditional school saw in the British concept the possibility of infusing the classroom with a humane and democratic spirit. Part of its instant mass appeal was the fact that it offered so much to so many different audiences.

At some point, the approach that Featherstone described was christened "open education," and its fortunes soared as faith in the promise of compensatory education plummeted. Little more than three years after his articles appeared, open education experienced a meteoric success. State education departments, federal agencies, teacher-training institutions, magazines, network commentators, foundations, and individual educators flocked to its banner. In cities and towns across the nation, school officials knocked down the walls between classrooms or designed their new buildings without walls. In 1970, when the New York State Department of Education held a one-day conference on open education, more than two thousand teachers attended. In 1968, only about thirty articles mentioning the British primary reforms were published in the United States, but by 1971, the number had grown to over three hundred. The near-evangelistic appeal of open education created a boom in transatlantic travel; by 1969, study teams from twenty American cities made the pilgrimage to England to learn first-hand about informal education.[19]

Because the principles of open education attracted support across a wide spectrum, efforts to disseminate it were diverse. In the highly compressed history of open education, one of the pioneer practitioners was Lillian Weber, a professor at the City College of New York. Weber spent eighteen months observing British infant schools in 1965/66; she began the Open Corridor Program in the fall of 1967 in a Harlem public school. Working with teachers who volunteered, she brought together four or five classrooms, linked by a common corridor, as a school-within-a-school; she showed teachers how to encourage interaction among different age levels and to replace whole-group instruction with individual and small group lessons. Weber sought "a minimum of changes, taking hints from the scale and intimacy in English schools." Word of her understated approach and good working relationships with teachers spread, and the program was requested by several other public schools. In 1969, Weber established an advisory service to help teachers implement open education methods. Within a few years, the advisory center was conducting summer institutes, publishing a journal, and receiving funding from the federal government and the Ford Foundation. Its major purpose was to provide support and reinforcement for teachers interested in open education.[20]

Significant efforts to teach open education were made by such colleges and universities as the Bank Street College of Education, Wheelock College, Newton College, the University of Connecticut, the University of Illinois, and the University of Colorado. By far the most effective university-based program for disseminating open education was developed at the University of North Dakota. A statewide study had found that 59 percent of all elementary school teachers lacked a college degree and that the state ranked fiftieth in the nation in the educational level of its elementary teachers. A member of the state study committee had read Featherstone's articles on the British primary school, and the committee agreed that upgrading the credentials of so many teachers offered the opportunity to train a new kind of teacher with a new outlook and new methods. To pursue that goal, the University of North Dakota created the New School of Behavioral Studies in Education in 1968. Headed by Vito Perrone, an advocate of open education, the New School set up a teacher-swap, sending graduate students to district schools as interns while the regular teachers attended the New School. Both teachers and interns were trained in the theory and practice of open education. Because of its experimentation with new methods of training teachers, the New School received substantial federal funding.[21]

Probably the most influential source of thinking and practice on the subject of open education emanated from an unusual network of individuals and institutions clustered about the Shady Hill School in Cambridge, Massachusetts, and the Education Development Center (EDC) in Newton, Massachusetts. Shady Hill was a private progressive school, founded in 1915, and EDC was a major, federally funded regional laboratory for the improvement of education. As ideas and individuals flowed from one institution to the other, a link was forged between the old progressivism and the new progressivism, and between the post-Sputnik curriculum reformers and the advocates of open education.

Teachers at Shady Hill included William Hull, who had become enthusiastic about the practices of British infant schools after a visit to Leicestershire County in 1961; Hull's teaching assistant, John Holt; and David Armington, who visited Leicestershire with Hull in 1962. Subsequently, Armington worked at EDC (as did his wife, a former headmistress of a British infant school), and Holt left teaching to devote full time to writing critically about American schools. In the early 1960s, Hull, Holt, and Armington met frequently to discuss education and children's thinking. Their discussions were joined for a time by Anthony Kallet, a Shady Hill teacher who visited Leicestershire schools in 1963 and stayed on for ten years, maintaining a lively correspondence with his friends at Shady Hill about informal practices in British schools. It was Hull who suggested to Joseph Featherstone in 1966 that he travel to Leicestershire, where he visited Kallet and observed infant schools.[22]

EDC grew out of an organization called Educational Services Incorporated (ESI), which had been created in 1958 as a vehicle for disseminating and testing the PSSC secondary school physics course, the first NSF-funded new curriculum. In the early 1960s, ESI received additional support from NSF to develop a new elementary science curriculum called the Elementary Science Study (ESS). Like other scientists engaged in curriculum reform, David Hawkins, the director of ESS, believed that children should learn science by doing science, not by being told about science. Hawkins was responsive to progressive methods, in part because his wife had been a teacher in a progressive school in California in the 1930s. Hawkins's writings became classics among supporters of open education.[23]

One of the schools selected to try out ESS materials was Shady Hill. By the mid-1960s, the connections between Shady Hill and ESS were many. William Hull circulated Anthony Kallet's letters from Leicestershire to ESS staff, keeping them informed about the new methods in Britain, and ESS produced mathematical materials designed by Hull. ESS staff, including Hawkins, exchanged visits with educators from Leicestershire. Years later, Hawkins recalled that his trip to England came at a time when he felt disillusioned about the minimal effect of the NSF-funded curricula in high school science. In England, he and his wife, Frances, saw schools where teachers "were really doing the kind of thing that Frances had been trying to do in the thirties. That had great influence on us. In particular, I don't think that we saw anything that we couldn't have seen in San Francisco in a few classrooms in the thirties, but here it was widely practiced with lots of perceptive professional support. And that was something that hadn't existed in San Francisco."[24]

The curriculum developed at ESS consisted of a series of units which used concrete materials—both everyday objects and special equipment—to demonstrate the process of scientific thinking rather than "right answers." The curricula prepared previously for high school science students were tightly organized, logically sequenced, and supposedly "teacher-proof." The ESS units were intended to be used by individual students, in no special order, and to encourage what British infant school proponents called "messing about." Ironically, while NSF curriculum development had begun in the strongly cognitive, antiprogressive spirit of the late 1950s, the curriculum developers at ESS followed the concepts of "inquiry" and "discovery" full circle back to the progressive tradition. And the more they expected to revolutionize the classroom by introducing their new curricula, the more frustrated they were by the structure and values of the typical classroom. When they saw how teachers converted their carefully conceived experiments into verbalized, abstract lessons in skills instead of letting students use them to explore freely, the ESS scientists despaired of their ability to transport the culture of science into the school as it existed.[25]

By the mid-1960s, the ESS staff had become convinced that the production of new curricula was too limited a goal. Their hothouse discussions with innovative educators, their trips abroad, their exchanges with British practitioners, their grounding in progressive educational philosophy (both British and American) made them impatient with what now seemed to be merely piecemeal reform. In an internal memorandum at ESS, Hull noted that some staff had come to realize that a new science curriculum would change little unless there was "a revolution in the underlying assumptions which would permit basic changes in classroom organization. . . . It is now clearer than ever that there cannot be good science, or good anything else, in classrooms without basic changes in attitudes and expectations."[26]

Believing that its mission should be to act as a catalyst for large-scale institutional change, ESS asked NSF in 1964 to fund a teacher-training project whose object would be to spread innovative practices and break the school's reliance on the textbook and rote learning. NSF, which was authorized by Congress to underwrite scientific research and development, not organizational reform, turned down the request. A similar proposal by ESS to the U.S. Office of Education was also turned down. When federal funds became available in 1965, ESS and its parent organization became part of EDC, a new federal regional laboratory. Headed by a British educator from Leicestershire, EDC took a leading role in promoting open education, by sponsoring workshops, providing an advisory service for teachers, and preparing instructional materials for open classrooms. EDC received a major contract to administer a Follow Through program for post–Head Start children, based on the principles of open education. EDC ran British Infant School Model projects in Laurel, Delaware; Chicago; Washington, D.C.; Paterson, New Jersey; Philadelphia; Rosebud, Texas; Lackawanna County, Pennsylvania; Johnston County, North Carolina; and Burlington, Vermont. The projects stressed informal methods, physical reorganization of the classroom, provisioning of the classroom with manipulative materials, and other features of the British model. Over time, however, the emphasis faded as the original directors departed, teachers came and went, and the federal government began to demand evaluations based on standardized tests.[27]

Clearly, the movement toward open education was fueled by enthusiastic advocates who believed that it could transform American education. Yet, while there was vigorous activity in many cities and towns across the nation, the number of teachers trained to run an open classroom or of school board members who had heard of the British model was relatively small. Some leaders of the movement, like Lillian Weber, thought that it was best to grow slowly and to build understanding from the ground up. But in the nature of things, at least in American education, a new and exciting trend is rarely allowed to go unheralded for long, and such was the case with open education. In 1970, open education received the kind of publicity that turned it into a Movement with a capital M.

In May, 1970, Beatrice and Ronald Gross introduced readers of the *Saturday Review* to open education. In their account, they went further than Featherstone on some crucial matters. Where Featherstone had specified that British infant schools were for children ages five to seven, the Grosses stated that the new practices were appropriate for children between the ages of five and twelve. Where Featherstone pointed out that Piaget's views about how children learn were theories, the Grosses asserted that Piaget "proved that it is a waste of time to tell a child things that the child cannot experience through his senses." Where Featherstone had cited Piaget's belief that learning moves in stages from concrete experiences to abstract thinking, the Grosses wrote, "Piaget is critical of classrooms where the teacher is the dominant figure, where books and the teacher's talking are basic instructional media, and where large group instruction is the rule, and oral or written tests are used to validate the whole process." When children in need of stimulation are subjected to such an environment, they held, their minds may be damaged or "actually atrophy." These embellishments and simplifications of complicated pedagogical issues were symptomatic: open education was being turned into a crusade, an object of faith for true believers, capable of "saving" American education.[28]

A few months later, Charles Silberman's best-selling *Crisis in the Classroom* projected open education into the public limelight as nothing previously had done. An accomplished journalist, Silberman had been invited by the Carnegie Corporation of New York to prepare a study of teacher education. But Silberman saw another story breaking and, with his keen intuition, captured the zeitgeist of the late 1960s. He sought out the people who were in the forefront of innovative pedagogical activity, and he found that their thinking converged on the British model. His book brought open education to a vast public, in part because he had the imprimatur of the prestigious Carnegie Corporation behind his recommendations, but more because he was able to write, as few in the education profession could, in a powerful, vivid, and graceful style.[29]

Others had lauded the British model because, compared to traditional didactic methods, it seemed to be more enjoyable for students and teachers, better suited to the learning styles of different children, and more attuned to the way children think: in short, a better way of learning and teaching. Silberman put the case for informal education in a far broader context. It was not just the schools that were in a state of crisis, he noted; American society as a whole was gripped by a sense of disaster and an "apocalyptic vision . . . a new consensus of anxiety seems to have taken hold of the nation." Much of this anxiety stemmed from the realization that many of the young did not accept the authority of the older generation, nor care much for its accumulated knowledge. Citing a recent poll of young people, Silberman warned that as many as 40 percent of college students sympathized with radicalism (a figure far higher than the findings of other polls), and that "dissent and alienation [were] moving rapidly into the high school and even the junior high." He pointed to the large rock festivals in the summer of 1969 as evidence of "the reservoir of alienation that may lie beneath the surface."[30]

Silberman argued that the national crisis "may well be a religious or spiritual crisis of a depth and magnitude that has no parallel since the Reformation." Yet in the face of this profound upheaval shaking American society, the nation's educating institutions—its schools and colleges, churches, newspapers, magazines, television stations, and networks—had all failed. None was adequate to the needs of the present or the future. What was to be done? The problem of the collapse of "meaning and purpose in our lives, in our society, and in our world" was to be addressed by a "transformation of the schools." Like that of many a reformer in the past, Silberman's diagnosis of the ills of society turned quickly into a treatise on the ills of the public schools and how to cure them.[31]

Silberman's opinion of the public schools concurred with the most extreme views of the radical critics of the late 1960s. American schools, he complained, were "grim, joyless places . . . oppressive and petty . . . intellectually sterile and esthetically barren," preoccupied above all with "order and control," demanding "docility and conformity." The curriculum was characterized by "banality and triviality": "Much of what is taught is not worth knowing as a child, let alone as an adult, and little will be remembered." The blame for this terrible, repressive institution lay not with the teachers, who were on the whole rather decent, well-meaning people; no, the "central problem" of American schools was "mindlessness," the fact that so few people in the schools took time "to think seriously or deeply about the purposes or consequences of education." "Mindlessness" accounted for

> the preoccupation with order and control, the slavish adherence to the timetable and lesson plan, the obsession with routine qua routine, the absence of noise and movement, the joylessness and repression, the universality of the formal lecture or teacher-dominated "discussion" in which the teacher instructs an entire class as a unit, the emphasis of the verbal and de-emphasis of the concrete, the inability of students to work on their own, the dichotomy between work and play. . . .[32]

The antidote to the crisis in the classroom was "the new English primary schools." Like so many others, Silberman had gone to England and come back a missionary for informal education. In a chapter of his book titled "It Can Happen Here," he detailed the activities of such American practitioners as Lillian Weber of New York and Vito Perrone of North Dakota. But, while other champions of informal education limited their proposed reforms to the early years, Silberman extended the same principles to the high school years, which were also afflicted by "mindlessness." Like the elementary school, the high school needed a complete revamping and an infusion of student freedom. In the high school programs he admiringly described, students had a large measure of freedom in deciding which courses to take, which courses would be offered, whether to receive grades or some other kind of evaluation, how to spend large blocks of unscheduled time, how to dress and groom themselves, and whether to leave the school building for lunch.[33]

Crisis in the Classroom had a dramatic effect on the fortunes of informal education. Silberman did what none of the previous advocates of the British model had attempted: he universalized open education. It was not just that Silberman brought the story of open education to a large popular audience. Silberman transformed the British model from a teaching method appropriate for young children into a philosophy directed to all educational institutions and all age groups; he elevated it from a pedagogical approach into an ideology about children, learning, and schooling that was intended to revive society and the quality of life in America. Though Silberman warned that informal education was not a panacea for all educational ills, it was difficult to read his enthusiastic promotion of the British model without seeing it as the answer to the alienation, anomie, and other social ills that Silberman so eloquently described. Similarly, while he warned that it would be wrong for Americans to make the mistake of swinging too far in the direction of child-centered schools, his strictures on the need for balance were outweighed by his fervent endorsement of child-centered methods and child-centered ideas.

Silberman both reported the growing groundswell of interest in open education and added to it. By the time his book appeared, open education had already found a committed following; it was perceived as a pedagogical innovation well suited to the age of student disaffection and protest because it stressed participation, freedom, and feelings, while downplaying tradition, authority, and structured teaching. The New York State commissioner of education, Ewald B. Nyquist, publicly endorsed open education, saying that it offered "unique opportunities for humanizing and individualizing learning, making it relevant, meaningful, and personally satisfying." He described it as "person-centered, idea-centered, experience-centered, problem-oriented, and interdisciplinary," in contrast to traditional education with its "information-gathering, fact-centered, course-centered, subject-centered, grade-getting, and bell-interrupted activity." Under Nyquist's leadership, the state education department sponsored teacher workshops in open education and convened statewide conferences of teachers and principals to promote its implementation. Beginning in the late 1960s, the Ford Foundation actively promoted open education by subsidizing publications, teacher training projects, and experiments in elementary schools, high schools, and universities. Open education in the elementary school meant that children exercised a large degree of choice in selecting activities and materials; in the high school, like the Parkway School in Philadelphia (a "school-without-walls"), it meant that students used the city and its institutions as their classrooms and were freed from the usual subject-matter requirements; at the university level, it meant a significant increase in off-campus learning, independent study, student-designed courses, and unstructured programs.[34]

Open education was an idea whose time had come, and there was no shortage of enthusiasm for it. The problem, which became more acute as enthusiasm grew, was defining it. After Silberman, books and articles about open education proliferated, and each one seemed to define the theory and practice of open education somewhat differently. Some advocates refused to define it, since to practice open education meant, they said, to be flexible, open to new ideas, ready to respond to children's interests, and free from predetermined lesson plans. But other advocates believed that it would be impossible to disseminate open educational practice without giving teachers some reliable examples of what to do and how to teach.

So, one focus of proponents of open education was simply to try to explain what it was, how to do it, and how to evaluate it.

Its advocates tended to define it in terms of what it was not, which accounted for much of its appeal to those seeking to disassociate themselves from the old, discredited ways of teaching: it was not traditional; it was not achieved by merely removing walls; it was not the same as team teaching, individualized instruction (which relied on preprogrammed materials), or nongraded classes. One researcher, after trying to explain why open education seemed so vague and formless, concluded that the best way to define it was to observe an open classroom.[35]

Others, however, did try to rationalize it and showed, despite disclaimers to the contrary, that open education was not "open" to every educational strategy, or at least not to methods associated with traditional practice. One advocate, Charles H. Rathbone, explained the open classroom in terms of *how* children learn (through their own experience) and *what* they learn (only what they themselves experience). To Rathbone, the fundamental concepts of open education were, first, that every child is "a self-activated maker of meaning, an active agent in his own learning process . . . a self-reliant, independent, self-actualizing individual"; and, second, that there is no "inherently indispensable body of knowledge that every single child should know." Knowledge, in his view, comes only from personal experience, and no two people have the same experience: "Thus, what two children carry in their heads as 'chair' or 'aunt' or 'black' will never be absolutely identical."[36]

Proponents of open education envisaged a new role for the teacher in the open classroom as a "facilitator" of the child's experiences rather than as a transmitter of knowledge. The role of the teacher in such a classroom, wrote Rathbone, was not to provide either answers or questions but to observe the child, to anticipate his needs, and to provide opportunities for the child to find his own questions and answers. "This means that in open education the teacher is mainly *assistant to* not *director of* the child's activity." Both Rathbone and John Holt endorsed the idea that the teacher was like a travel agent, helping the child go where the child wants to go.[37]

Another prolific proponent of open education was Roland S. Barth, who published several articles in 1969 and 1970 describing British informal practices as grounds for "a revolution" in American education. In his book *Open Education and the American School,* Barth compiled a list of twenty-nine assumptions shared by open educators about children and learning. For example, open educators assume that: "children are innately curious and will explore without adult intervention"; "if a child is fully involved in and having fun with an activity, learning is taking place"; "objective measures of performance may have a negative effect on learning"; "there is no minimum body of knowledge which is essential for everyone to know." From these assumptions, Barth concluded that

> open education has no curriculum. . . . In a real sense, children's own experiences are the subject matter—the content—of their learning. These experiences are good and bad, productive and nonproductive, pleasant and unpleasant. Open educators worry less about whether a child has had a particular experience than about the quality and meaning for him of the experiences he has had. It is for time and future experience to assess the significance of a student's experience, not for the adult to judge.[38]

However, Barth's own experience tempered his initial zeal. He participated in a disastrous effort to introduce open education in a small, almost all black, urban school. Supported as a demonstration by the school system, a university, and foundation funds, the project was riddled with problems: the staff was overloaded with specialists; the old and new teachers regarded each other with suspicion; the school had unstable leadership. Meanwhile, the open educators were astonished to discover that the children did not welcome the opportunity to explore freely and make their own decisions; instead, they became disruptive and "ganged up by tens and twenties outside the bathrooms and at the water fountains." Fearful of choices, they became "merciless in their demands for teacher-imposed order." Before long, the new teachers began clutching at traditional practices; "they set up reading groups and introduced basal texts, required seats, and homework." Especially disheartening to the experimental teachers was the negative attitude of parents, who complained about the permissiveness of the teachers and the noisiness of the classrooms. As one parent explained to a teacher, "You have had a certain kind of educational experience . . . teacher as source of knowledge and control, child as respectful and obedient responder, and you made it. If our children have the same kind of educational experience, *they too* will make it." By the end of the school year, all of the open educators had quit or were dismissed.[39]

Open classrooms ran into difficulty, but nonetheless the spirit of innovation spread rapidly. Nearly three years after the publication of his book, Charles Silberman wrote that "Hardly a day has gone by . . . and certainly not a week, in which I have not heard of another teacher, or group of teachers, or school, or school system that is moving (or thinking about moving) in the directions I proposed and described." Indeed, it was not only the open classroom, however it was defined, that was gaining in influence in the early 1970s; schools large and small, in big cities and small

towns, were adopting educational innovations advocated by school reformers. Typically, such innovations emphasized the students' role in selecting their own activities; the introduction of student-designed and stu-
dent-taught courses; the elimination of traditional high school graduation
requirements; the replacement of traditional subject-matter courses with
courses and mini-courses organized around student interests; expansion of
the number of courses and activities available to the student; flexible
scheduling; de-emphasis or elimination of letter grades; random or mixed-
ability grouping of children, instead of grouping by age or ability;
academic credit for off-campus programs, community involvement, and
nontraditional study.[40]

That there was a pragmatic basis to such changes was apparent. The
extraordinary stress in the society outside the schools had created nearly
intolerable strains within many schools in terms of student resistance to
traditional authority. As authority in the larger society eroded, authority
in the schools also came under attack; discipline problems increased, as did
truancy and vandalism. When the Gallup organization began its annual
opinion poll about public education in 1969, lack of discipline was identified as the leading problem of the schools. Many schools adopted innovative programs with the hope that a loosening of academic demands, a more
relaxed relationship with teachers, and a curriculum more relevant to contemporary social issues would pacify student discontent, improve student
behavior, and reduce truancy. Such changes were also attractive to many
of the younger teachers, who had been college students in the mid-1960s
and shared their generation's ambivalence about the exercise of adult
authority. However, the loosening of adult authority only exacerbated the
public's perception that lack of discipline was the most important problem
in the schools and contributed to the steady decline of public confidence
in the schools during the 1970s.[41]

School critics disagreed on whether the public school was salvageable.
Those who thought there was still hope embraced open education, while
those who thought the public schools were beyond salvation set out to
create the "free school movement," entirely outside the reach of the public
schools. Beginning in the mid-1960s, these parent-controlled, privately
financed "free schools" were developed by people who had participated in
the civil rights movement, the New Left, and the counterculture. There
was a fringe even beyond the "free school movement" which opposed the
institution of the school altogether as an oppressive social device that
unjustly monopolized the power to assign people to social roles, to discriminate against those who do not hold its credentials, and to make them
dependent on its degrees for future advancement. The idea of "deschool-

ing," put forth by the radical priest Ivan Illich, was widely discussed when it first appeared in 1970, but it had little practical effect other than to give momentary impetus to interest in lowering the compulsory schooling age. Since Illich attacked even the free school movement, because it shared the conventional assumption "that social man needs a school if he is to be born" while reinforcing "the dominant system of compulsory knowledge," he found few allies to support his proposal for disestablishing schools and permitting people to devise their own "learning webs."[42]

While "deschooling" proved to be a rhetorical phenomenon rather than an educational movement, the free school movement grew out of the dissident political and social activism of the 1960s. As Ann Swidler points out in her study *Organization Without Authority: Dilemmas of Social Control in Free Schools,* the free schools were "only the most visible of a whole collection of alternative organizations," such as free clinics and legal collectives and communes, created by countercultural groups. "What united these diverse organizations was their rejection of authority as a valid principle for regulating group life." The free schools shared an information network called the New Schools Exchange, which published a newsletter, a directory of innovative schools, books, and position papers. Far more than the open education movement, which adapted to the bureaucratic, institutional requirements of the public schools, the free schools were the inheritors of the libertarian Summerhillian spirit. What this meant in practice, in the words of free school advocate Allen Graubard, was "doing away with all of the public school apparatus of imposed disciplines and punishments, lock-step age gradings and time-period divisions, homework, frequent tests and grades and report cards, rigid graded curriculum, standardized classrooms, dominated and commanded by one teacher with 25 to 35 students under his or her power." According to Graubard, the number of free schools grew rapidly during the late 1960s and early 1970s, reaching perhaps five hundred by 1972. The average free school had an enrollment of about thirty-three students, which meant that less than twenty thousand children attended a free school during this period.[43]

Free schools were an expression of both political and cultural radicalism. One free school guidebook was dedicated to "the millions of children still in prison in the United States and to the handful of adults trying to spring them." The authors observed that "it is a revolutionary act to be involved in a free school. Saying 'no' to the heart of a culture—their schools—and establishing an alternative system for learning is an explicit rejection of a *set* of beliefs, and the web of premises, myths, rituals—the underlying faith—that goes with a set of beliefs." In free schools, Swidler writes, "Adults allow children to explore their environment, to discover what they themselves want to learn, to play, make noise, move around, or even do nothing. But what is really distinctive about these schools is not so much their pedagogy or educational philosophy as their purpose: they are designed as models of a new kind of society. They abolish authority relations between teachers and students—not simply to educate children better but to create a new sort of human being and a new model of cooperative social life."[44]

The quest for ideological solidarity drew adherents to the free schools, but ideological conflicts split and destroyed the parent-run free schools at a dizzying rate. One researcher estimated that the average life span of a free school was eighteen months. This high mortality rate was due not so much to the difficulty of financing a complex undertaking as to the nature of free school ideology, which was vulnerable to schisms: it promised divergent ends (freedom and learning) to parents seeking ideological purity and then, because it eschewed leadership and representative democracy as means of governance, lacked mechanisms for resolving conflicts. Sometimes a free school divided between those who were "traditional" libertarians and those who wanted to impose their political radicalism. Sometimes it split between parents who wanted a completely unstructured environment and those who wanted teachers to place some limits on children and to instruct them in reading and writing.[45]

Despite the fact that so few students attended free schools, the existence of the free school movement was treated by the mass media as a major phenomenon, threatening the very survival of the public schools. Public secondary schools felt some of the same demands for change and for student participation that animated the free schools, and many responded by creating alternative schools. Sometimes this was accomplished by splitting up a large high school into "mini-schools," or schools-within-schools, in order to overcome the anonymity of the bureaucratic institution and to bring about closer contact between teachers and students. Typically, however, alternative schools borrowed countercultural mechanisms to achieve traditional goals. They were usually organized as separate institutions for problem students who were likely to drop out of school, including students "who have emotional problems that cause difficulty in a conventional school, students who have high academic ability and who want to learn in a place where they can be creative," and low-achieving students with poorly developed skills. Compared to the traditional high school, the usual secondary alternative school was small in size, its rules were fewer, and students had greater freedom in such matters as selecting courses and teachers, leaving campus, and smoking cigarettes. Close relationships with teachers and counselors were substituted for the customary rules and regulations. Academic credit was available for classroom studies, but also for work-study, participation in community agencies, and independent study. Although traditional subject matter was sometimes offered, classroom studies tended to reflect student interests, such as arts, crafts, political activism, environmentalism, transcendental meditation, and the occult. Instead of letter-grades, students often received written evaluations or pass-fail or credit–no credit assessments.[46]

Still, while alternative schools traced their roots to the countercultural influence of the free school movement, they proved to have staying power because they served a variety of purposes. Some districts saw in the alternative school a rationale for creating a special school for gifted students; others satisfied the complaints of conservative parents by establishing "fundamental" alternative schools that stressed basic skills, dress codes, and patriotism; some called the traditional high school or elementary school an alternative; still others designed interest-centered alternative schools around fine arts, science, physical education, the humanities, or the performing arts. In some districts, like Ann Arbor, Michigan, the alternative high school was an attractively packaged vocational program that placed students in paid and unpaid jobs in the community. In Houston, Texas, district officials replaced their technical and vocational high schools with alternative schools, established an alternative high school to train personnel to meet the needs of the local health-care industry, and set up special alternative schools for those interested in the arts and for the gifted. Despite their origin in the counterculture, the alternative schools became domesticated: successful ones reduced the dropout rate, removed troublesome or unhappy students from traditional schools, and provided programs tailored for the special needs of different groups of students.[47]

The alternative school idea survived because, lacking a definition, it became whatever school boards and principals chose to make of it. The open education movement, however, did not survive *as a movement* because, lacking a definition, it became identified with the ideas and practices of its extremely child-centered advocates, those who zealously opposed whatever was traditional in the structure, content, or methods of the classroom. Their ideological tenets stressed the freedom of the child, the passivity of the teacher, equality between teacher and child, the virtues of play and unstructured activity, and distrust of extrinsic motivation. Open classroom teachers who expected their methods to work as the ideology said it would were in for a rude awakening. Nothing prepared them for criticism from parents and other teachers about the noisiness of their classrooms and the neglect of "basics." They were taken aback when children demanded that teachers take a more active role or asked to learn from a textbook; they did not know how to deal with discipline problems because they were not supposed to have any. Advocates of open education saw the teachers' problems not as a failing of the theory but as a result of the teachers' incomplete commitment to a new way of life.[48]

As early as 1971, some proponents of open education began to warn that it was turning into a fad. Joseph Featherstone reported that of the American informal classrooms he had visited, "the best are as good as anything I've seen in England; the worst are a shambles." Alarmed by the camp followers who belittled skills and discipline, Featherstone wrote, "I'm growing wary of slogans like open education. . . . Currently I'm seeking to enlist everybody in favor of open, informal schooling into a movement whose one slogan will be a demand for decent schools." Shortly after Roland Barth's book about open education appeared, Barth wrote an article titled, "Should We Forget about Open Education?" in which he complained that open education had become a new orthodoxy and the source of futile ideological battles among teachers. By 1974, Donald A. Myers, who had studied open classrooms in New York State, speculated on "Why Open Education Died." Myers asserted that it was not "a discrete concept but rather a collection of best existing practices." American observers, he complained, failed to see that good teachers in informal British classrooms provided more structure, not less; emphasized the three Rs; and provided a sensible balance between intrinsic and extrinsic motivation. "What is our attraction to play," he wondered, "especially when it is advocated as a vehicle through which students learn cognitive concepts and skills? Why is it difficult for so many American educators to acknowledge that writing a sentence, speaking clearly, playing the piano, or learning inferential statistics, is simply difficult work?"[49]

As disillusionment grew among proponents and laymen, the movement dissipated. The number of articles about open education in professional education journals peaked between 1972 and 1974 and then dwindled rapidly. By the latter date, demands that schools go "back to the basics" had begun to be expressed in school districts across the country. In many districts, the "back to basics" forces blamed programs like open education for lowering academic standards and undermining discipline. By 1975, when the College Entrance Examination Board announced that scores on its Scholastic Aptitude Test had fallen steadily for a decade, experimental programs were on the defensive. Though many open classrooms in elementary schools survived the "back to basics" movement and budget cuts, they did so usually as alternatives available for parents and teachers who chose them rather than as the wave of the future for all American education.[50]

Very likely, the cause of informal education was harmed rather than advanced by its propagandists, who blew it up out of all proportion to the reality of either British or American schools. Some teachers found it a valuable technique, which they used well; others did not. Some children responded well to informal methods; others needed a more structured environment. British teachers understood this far better than did their American admirers. Smitten by British informal methods, American writers portrayed their advance in British schools as though it were a revolutionary contest between the forces of light and the forces of darkness. The reality was different. A 1976 study in Britain concluded that about 17 percent of teachers used informal methods, another 25 percent used formal methods, and the majority used "what have been termed mixed styles, incorporating elements of both formal and informal practice." Contrary to American belief, "A high degree of permissiveness does not appear to be the norm. . . . Teacher control of physical movement and talk is generally high. . . . eight out of ten teachers require their pupils to know their multiplication tables by heart." Similarly, a national survey conducted in 1978 by the British Inspectorate concluded that while most teachers varied their teaching method according to the circumstances, about three-quarters of the primary teachers "employed a mainly didactic approach, while less than one in twenty relied mainly on an exploratory approach."[51]

British scholars have challenged the simplistic notion that teachers can be easily divided between progressives and traditionalists; most, it turns out, use a variety of teaching styles. Nor is it at all obvious that individualization necessarily promotes student-directed "discovery" learning. Brian Simon, codirector of a major research study of primary schools in England, observed that while there was a "fundamental change" in primary schools, it is "extremely doubtful" that "it ever amounted to anything which might be called a revolution." Simon reported that a large-scale observation study of over one hundred primary school classrooms showed that most work was individualized, but most teaching was "didactic in character": "The promotion of enquiry or discovery learning appeared almost nonexistent. . . . Collaborative group work or enquiry was also found to be seldom realized. . . . Further, as regards the content of education, a major emphasis on 'the basics' was also found. . . . Certainly there was little evidence there of any fundamental shift either in the content of education or in the procedures of teaching and learning, in the sense that didacticism still largely prevails."[52]

As the federal government's role in financing public education grew larger, it became a major promoter of innovative practices. To some extent, almost every federal program encouraged local education agencies to do something that they might not otherwise do: to devote increased resources to the special needs of poor children, to monitor and correct racial segregation, to provide career education, to make special provision for non–English-speaking children, to offer free medical services and free lunches to poor children, and so on. Beyond its commitment to equity in the provision of educational services for all children, the federal government actively intervened to prod school districts to move away from traditional methods of teaching and learning. By the early 1970s, about 10 percent of all federal funds for public schools was allocated specifically to promote educational innovations; in 1974, this amounted to about $350 million annually, spent through a wide variety of programs.[53]

Federal policy makers believed that a major cause of the schools' troubles was their rigidity and traditionalism, and that federal dollars should be used to free the schools from existing practices. The lure of federal funds prompted a number of school districts to try innovative practices; the largest single federal "change-agent" program, Title III of the Elementary and Secondary Education Act of 1965, allocated money to states and local districts for "innovative projects" (its annual budget by 1974 was $150 million). Local school districts used Title III funds to initiate open classrooms, team teaching, multi-age grouping, and alternative schools, as well as for inservice training to prepare the staff to implement innovative practices. Federal funds also spurred experiments in teacher education, through such ambitious programs as the Teacher Corps (established in 1965 to recruit idealistic young people into teaching careers) and the Trainers of Teacher Trainers program (which from 1969 to 1974 expended about $40 million on a multitude of innovative activities, such as North Dakota's New School for Behavioral Studies and model open classrooms in Harlem).[54]

In 1970, the Nixon administration launched one of the most ambitious federal efforts to reform the schools. Educational policy makers in the new administration decided that the time had come to "pause and reflect" on the disappointing results of previous reform efforts. They concluded that federal reform programs had thus far failed to produce lasting improvement because: they had fostered piecemeal change with little overall coherence; education reform had been inadequately related to social science research; too much direction had come from the federal and state bureaucracies and not enough initiative from the local school officials; and there had not been enough involvement by the local community. In the end, the Nixon policy makers' conclusions dovetailed with the consensus shared by reform-minded analysts in the foundations and universities. What was needed, they decided, was *comprehensive* change. Toward this end, President Nixon announced the Experimental Schools Program (ESP), which he described, in his March, 1970, message to Congress, as a strategy for building "a bridge between educational research and actual practice." At the same time, the president proposed the creation of the research-oriented National Institute of Education, which later administered ESP.[55]

In order to win funding, local districts had to propose programs of comprehensive change. Although "comprehensive" was never defined, applicants were told that the plan must involve students at all twelve grade levels; must include curriculum, staff development, community involvement, administration, and organization; and must be organized around "a central theme or educational concept that reflects change from what exists at present to what education ought to be in terms of the needs and aspirations of the learners." Because ESP was supposed to use research to identify effective practices, between 25 and 30 percent of program funds were earmarked for research and evaluation. ESP officials planned three different evaluations: an in-house study by the local project staff; a second evaluation by outside social scientists; and a third to synthesize the findings of all the others.[56]

Eventually eighteen districts, both urban and rural, won substantial federal funding. Their proposals reflected the reform ideas and language that were currently in the air. They promised to individualize, to humanize, to stress process instead of product, to retrain teachers to use diagnostic approaches, and to provide learning environments in which every child would experience success. The Minneapolis district won its grant by describing a subsystem of alternative elementary schools that was already either underway or in the planning stages: a traditional school, a "continuous progress" (nongraded) school, an open school, and a free school. The Franklin Pierce district in Pierce County, Washington, pledged to individualize the learning experience of each student by introducing a dozen new curricula and by breaking free of "lock-step" programs, "and the typical regimentation of rigid course offerings, and rigid class schedules." Berkeley, California, won a five-year grant for $7 million by proposing to establish twenty-four alternative schools around the central theme of decreasing institutional racism. Whatever was avant-garde found a place in one of Berkeley's alternative schools. In addition to such standard innovations as nongraded classrooms and peer teaching, Berkeley ESP stressed ethnicity. One program, Black House, was for blacks only; another, Casa de la Raza, was for Chicanos only. Both were subsequently closed by the U.S. Office for Civil Rights for operating as segregated schools. There was a counterculture elementary school and high school, and a multicultural school whose students and faculty were balanced equally among whites, blacks, Chicanos, and Asians.[57]

In terms of the ambitious goals that it set for itself, ESP failed. For the $55 million that was expended over a five-year period, the results were meager. Districts that already intended to innovate, like Minneapolis, continued to do so. Some districts used the funds to help get through a fiscal crisis or to buy needed equipment but showed little evidence of lasting, "comprehensive" change. Of Berkeley's twenty-four alternative schools, only one survived; additionally, the Berkeley ESP diverted attention from the district's previous commitment to total, voluntary desegregation, and layoffs of controversial ESP staff after the program ended plunged the district into bitter wrangling.

The ten rural sites that received ESP money had other kinds of problems, due in part to the unreceptivity of rural districts to rapid change. Teachers resented programs they felt were imposed on them, and internal conflicts undermined many of the projects. In South Umpqua, Oregon, considered one of the most successful projects, the end of the project was followed by a conservative backlash: "many of the ES programs have been discontinued, library books and curriculum materials are now scrutinized by a watchdog committee, a new board has been elected, the superintendent and associate superintendent have left, and the new administration has a mandate to get things back to normal." While some of this backlash was attributable to the times, a federal evaluator concluded that "the swing of the pendulum is greater in South Umpqua because of ES."[58]

In many districts, the in-house evaluation was useless as an evaluation because of the close association between its authors and local school officials. Several of the professional evaluations commissioned by the National Institute of Education were rejected by the agency as deficient; even the social scientists stumbled on the difficulty of assessing a concept as broad and vague as "comprehensive" change: what could not be defined could not be evaluated. The final, synthesizing evaluation of the entire program was never carried out.

The program failed not because of the backwardness or insincerity of local school officials but because it laid bare the contradictions and vacuousness inherent in much of the contemporary rhetoric of educational reform. Like the policy makers at foundations and universities and many popular critics, the staff at ESP assumed that previous reform efforts had failed because they were too piecemeal; ESP intended to demonstrate that comprehensive, holistic change of an entire district or subdistrict was possible and that extensive community involvement would strengthen the process of comprehensive change. These goals were not attained because they were inherently unattainable.

First of all, neither federal nor local officials knew what "comprehensive" change meant, and yet federal officials insisted that each proposal had to claim that it would be "comprehensive." Saying that a project would be comprehensive did not make it so. Many local officials rewrote their proposals at the direction of federal monitors and used whatever words would satisfy the demands of ESP officials. Yet, the more they wrote to please the federal officials, the less the proposals reflected local interests. "Comprehensive" was a buzz-word, a word that local officials learned to invoke at the right time if they wanted federal funds. In the same way, school officials somewhat ritualistically described what they were doing as "humanistic," "affective," "individualized," and so forth, as though it were possible to change the reality of an activity by renaming it in warm, reformist terminology.

Nor did the federal insistence on the importance of community involvement contribute to meeting reform objectives. Instead, the inclusion of community participation multiplied the number of interests and demands to be included in the project and further frustrated the possibility of coherent, comprehensive educational change. When federal officials pressed local officials both for comprehensive change and for community participation, they made unwarranted assumptions about the unity of interests among administrators, teachers, parents, and community members. Federal reformers did not realize, a district superintendent later complained, that "the community represents such a diverse population that its involvement only created different factions of interest who wanted different things to happen in school."[59]

Perhaps a more important problem was that federal officials never understood that their priorities were not the same as the priorities of local school officials. The federal officials, like their predecessors in Democratic administrations, came to the project believing that the federal government had a responsibility to reform local schools and that their research-based ideas about educational theory and practice were superior to those held by people working in the schools. They further imagined that they could direct change by winning a written commitment from the local superintendent, who, with adequate federal monitoring, would see to it that the reform process was securely implemented. An insightful study of ESP by Peter Cowden and David K. Cohen concluded that the federal officials' hopes for comprehensive change "never approached fulfillment. What change occurred . . . did so in fragmented ways, and was typically modest and piecemeal." Federal officials imagined that the right mechanisms or processes could bring about sweeping change in an entire school district. "But a school district is not a single, centrally directed, coherent system that can, upon a decision, change direction. It consists of many units and individuals with different needs, interests, and opinions. And the work of central administrators, principals, and teachers is only weakly inter-dependent—they by no means all pull together."[60]

Local officials applied for ESP funds with the expectation that they would enhance the prestige of their district or get more money to hire specialists, buy new materials, or plan a program for a special group like potential dropouts. They did not usually see their schools as negatively as federal officials did. Furthermore, while they might promise comprehensive change, they knew that a school system is not a tightly organized, hierarchical chain of command. They could ask (or tell) teachers to participate in inservice training programs, and they could buy new curricula, but they could not force teachers to do what they did not want to do. Ironically, what ESP may have demonstrated is the impossibility of "holistic" change, and the likelihood that piecemeal, incremental change may be appropriate to the highly decentralized nature of school systems, which are made up of semiautonomous schools and staffed by relatively autonomous teachers.

How, then, did "piecemeal change" get such a bad reputation? In large measure, the assumption that piecemeal change had been tried and failed stemmed from the troubled history of the curriculum revisions sponsored by the NSF in the aftermath of Sputnik. What was thought of at the time as the single greatest venture in recasting American education had not transformed the schools. Seen from the perspective of the early 1970s, the NSF-funded programs had assembled the nation's best scholars, who had revised the curricula to reflect the latest knowledge and the best methodology, yet still the schools remained essentially untouched. This led reformers to conclude that tinkering with the parts of the system was insufficient and that some kind of sweeping, comprehensive change was necessary to change the system itself.

But this version of what happened to the NSF curriculum revisions was not the whole story, and the actual NSF experience sheds light on the politics of school reform. Between 1956 and 1975, NSF funded fifty-three projects, forty-three in mathematics and the natural sciences and ten in the social sciences. By the end of this period, when NSF conducted a review of its curriculum development activities, it was clear that the new science curricula had been far more successful than the others. In the 1976/77 school year, almost 60 percent of all school districts were using one or more of the federally funded science programs in grades seven through twelve; 40 percent were using more than one, and even in the elementary grades about 30 percent of the districts reported using at least one of the NSF science curricula. In addition, the NSF science programs had substantial secondary effects in that they prompted substantial revisions in the content and methods of the most popular commercial textbooks. Since it was not necessarily the purpose of NSF to put commercial textbook publishers out of business, but rather to improve the content and approach of science teaching, it can be judged to have achieved a significant influence through its relatively small investment in reforming the science curricula.[61]

Mathematics and the social sciences presented very different problems. The revisions in mathematics, like those in science, were begun before Sputnik, gathered considerable NSF funding after Sputnik, and were intended to improve the mathematical preparation of the college-bound. "The new math," as the revisions were called, was not a single program but rather the product or approach that evolved from several mathemathics reform groups. Students and teachers knew it as a collection of new concepts like "sets," "numeration in bases other than 10," and "prime numbers." One mathematics scholar, Bruce R. Vogeli, defined it as the premise that "Mathematical learning is more effective and efficient if the fundamental unifying ideas of mathematics are stressed—if the internal structure of the discipline is emphasized." The major NSF program was developed by the School Mathematics Study Group (SMSG), which wrote a new secondary curriculum and then a new elementary curriculum between 1958 and 1962. By 1967, according to Vogeli, not only were SMSG texts widely used and widely emulated by commercial publishers, but "no series was marketable that was not identified as 'modern.'"[62]

The initial victory of the "new math" was illusory, however. It was severely criticized by mathematicians who complained that it was too abstract and that it neglected significant applications of mathematics; it encountered unanticipated resistance from teachers, particularly at the elementary level, who found it difficult to teach; and it was strongly disliked by parents, who resented the mystification of the third R and worried about their children's lack of computation skills. By the end of the 1960s, the combination of criticism and resistance routed "new math" from most elementary schools and fed the emergence of a "back to basics" movement. By the late 1970s, when NSF surveyed the status of precollege mathematics, its reviewers found that such topics as sets and nondecimal numeration systems were "practically non-existent in newer elementary-school curriculum materials." The proportion of school districts using NSF mathematics curricula dropped from 30 percent in the early 1970s to only 9 percent by 1976/77. And while mathematics professors predicted that hand-held computers eventually would restore a reformulated version of modern mathematics to the classroom, mathematics teachers expressed satisfaction with the return to the methods and concepts they were comfortable with; they told NSF observers "with near perfect regularity . . . that they applaud the return to traditional content, [traditional] instructional methods, and higher standards of student performance."[63]

The new social science courses underwritten by NSF encountered other obstacles. Like NSF-funded courses in science, the new social studies encouraged the use of discovery methods and student inquiry and introduced multimedia materials to supplement written texts. By 1976/77, when the NSF survey was completed, about 25 percent of school districts were using NSF social science materials. However, the surveyors found that most social studies teachers continued to use the textbook as the most important source of knowledge and to be most concerned that students learn the content, the subject matter of the field. For the most part, the social studies curriculum had changed little; it was still devoted largely to history and government, and it followed the textbook, with little reference to the social sciences. At first glance, it appeared that nothing had changed, but in fact the survey caught a snapshot of a field rapidly retreating from an era of curricular fragmentation, characterized by minicourses and electives devoted to social activism, ethnicity, valuing, and self-realization.[64]

Why did teachers continue to hold a transmission-of-knowledge view of education when it was held in so little regard by university professors? In the view of spokesmen for the National Council for the Social Studies, the curriculum reformers had misunderstood the needs of classroom teachers. Teachers, they said, are primarily concerned with managing their classroom and teaching students good citizenship. Their failure to use new materials and new methods came not from any obstructionist motive. "Instead, it is simply more appropriate to them to continue doing what they have done before—practices consistent with their own values and beliefs and those they perceive, probably accurately, to be those of their communities. The new materials just don't fit." Teachers who were familiar with the new curricula thought they were best for elite groups of students "who had attained the basics and perhaps more important, proper self-discipline." Used with other students, the new materials threatened the teachers' ability to control the classroom. "Some of the support by teachers for the 'back to basics' movement," the authors believed, "may even be interpreted as reaction to the demands of the curriculum reform attempts of the 1960s—the new topics and content organizations, and unusual teaching roles not only seemed difficult to carry out but flew in the face of the teachers' view of the needs of students and the school."[65]

Controversy over "Man: A Course of Study" (MACOS), an NSF-funded anthropology course used in the upper elementary grades, brought the entire NSF curriculum-development effort under congressional scrutiny in 1976. Like other new curricula, MACOS was innovative in its content, its methodology, and its pedagogy. Its units included the life cycle and behavior patterns of salmon, herring gulls, baboons, and Netsilik Eskimos. Its developers at ESI (the same organization that was also instrumental in the dissemination of British informal methods) expected that the course would encourage children to speculate on "What is human about human beings? How did they get that way? How can they be made more so?" The course "touched on such inflammatory subjects as evolution, infanticide, wife sharing, senilicide, and 'communal living,' " which made commercial publishers reluctant to sponsor it. As the course began to be broadly disseminated, it came under attack in widely scattered communities by conservative critics who objected to its subject matter and its cultural relativism. When an Arizona congressman challenged the appropriateness of federal subsidy for a curriculum that was so offensive to local communities, a House subcommittee held hearings, NSF conducted an internal review of MACOS, and the General Accounting Office investigated the financial relationship between NSF and MACOS' developers. MACOS survived the criticisms and challenges, but its notoriety "brought about a precipitous drop in sales from which the course . . . never recovered."[66]

The era of curriculum reform, which began with great expectations, ended quietly. There had been substantial gains, especially in the physical sciences, and there had been losses. Even the losses could be turned into gains, however, if they advanced understanding of the conditions that impede educational change. There was much to be learned from the NSF efforts to revise precollege curricula. Both the way the new materials were prepared and the methods they incorporated later created problems for the new curricula that could not have been foreseen in the years of heady optimism. When the curriculum reform movement began in the 1950s, school critics persistently complained that existing curricula were mediocre and lacked rigor, and that the educational system was controlled by an "interlocking directorate" of professional educators. These assumptions shaped certain of the movement's characteristics.

- First, despite repeated references to curriculum "revisions," the reformers aimed to replace the existing curriculum, not just to improve it. This guaranteed not only substantial institutional resistance, but also the necessity of massive teacher retraining.
- Second, the reformers sorely underestimated the reluctance of teachers to discard their knowledge, their methods, and their beliefs about teaching. They did not anticipate the number of teachers who had difficulty utilizing inquiry and discovery methods, who believed in the value of "covering the field," who relied on the textbook to organize their courses, and who were unable to manage a classroom of individualized learners.
- Third, many of the materials were prepared for college-bound students; average and below-average students had difficulty dealing with the conceptual approach of the new courses.
- Fourth, the new curricula were prepared by prominent university scholars and teachers from leading secondary schools, with little participation by professors of education and teachers from typical secondary schools. The lack of involvement of teacher educators undoubtedly slowed the absorption of the new materials by those who trained new teachers, and the paucity of representative teachers probably deprived the projects of persons familiar with the wide range of abilities represented in the average public school classroom.
- Fifth, the new curricula were funded by foundations and federal agencies, which freed them of the political constraints of state and local education agencies and the marketplace constraints on textbook publishers. This freedom was a mixed blessing, however, because the "constraints" of politics and the marketplace tend to determine whether a new curriculum will be adopted.[67]

Like ESP, with its hopes for "comprehensive" change, the curriculum reform movement exemplified the pitfalls of trying to impose sweeping change on an institution as multidimensional as the American school. Regardless of what the state superintendent or the school superintendent or the principal may recommend, classroom teachers have a considerable degree of control over what and how they teach; even when a new curriculum is put in their hands, the way they use it may alter it beyond recognition. Recognizing the diversity of interests and individuals in the nation's thousands of school districts and hundreds of thousands of schools does not argue against the value of curriculum reform. It does suggest, though, that any planned reform is filtered through the experiences, intentions, and purposes of those who implement it. In view of the number of actors involved, and the degree of their autonomy, lasting change in an institution as various as the school is invariably incremental and piecemeal.

Although for nearly twenty years alternating waves of reforms and crusades had swept through the schools, they seemed to be in some ways unchanged. But every effort to make the school better had left its mark.

The more limited and specific the goal, the more likely was the reform to endure. More children were in school for more years than at any time in the past. School buildings were better equipped and more commodious. More teachers had college degrees. Classes were smaller. There were more curricula to choose from, more methods in use, and a greater variety of materials. The schools may not have been saved, but they had survived nonetheless.

CHAPTER 8

The New Politics of Education

URING THE DECADE AFTER 1965, political pressures con-
verged on schools and universities in ways that undermined their authority
to direct their own affairs. New responsibilities were assigned to educational institutions, even as effective authority was dispersed widely among
students, faculty, unions, courts, state and federal regulatory agencies,
state legislatures, Congress, the judiciary, and special interest groups. Educational administrators found themselves in the midst of unfamiliar power
struggles. In colleges and universities, students demanded enlarged powers
over the curriculum and the structure of governance; the courts and federal
civil rights agencies required adherence to affirmative action programs to
increase the representation of minorities and women on the faculty; faculties organized into unions; Congress, the courts, federal agencies, and state
legislatures devised burdensome and costly new mandates. In elementary
and secondary schools, almost no area of administrative discretion was left
uncontested: students demanded new rights and freedoms; teachers' unions asserted a new militancy; political-action groups complained about
books in the classrooms and libraries, for reasons of sexism, racism, or
immorality; the courts ordered the busing of students in many communities, as well as reassignment of faculty, to achieve racial integration; Con-

gress, the courts, federal agencies, and state legislatures imposed special mandates across a wide range of issues, such as restricting or requiring certain tests, setting standards for promotion and graduation, and establishing new requirements governing the treatment of handicapped students and of students who were either female or members of a racial or linguistic minority. Considering the traditional reluctance of the courts to intervene in the internal affairs of educational institutions, of the federal bureaucracy to violate local control of schools, and of the Congress to bestow federal aid upon education, it is all the more remarkable how rapidly the courts, the federal bureaucracy, and the Congress shed their doubts and hesitation after 1965.

The enlarged federal presence in educational institutions was founded in substantial measure on Title VI of the Civil Rights Act of 1964, which empowered federal officials to withdraw funds from any program violating antidiscrimination laws and regulations. The rapid expansion of federal funding for education at all levels after 1965 meant that the threatened cutoff of federal funds was a potent weapon. With Title VI as the stick and federal funds as the carrot, the federal government became a significant factor in setting rules for the nation's schools, colleges, and universities. A school system whose budget relied on federal funds for about 10 percent of its revenues or a major university that received several millions for research programs and fellowships was not in a strong position to oppose federal directives.

By 1966, racial issues had become a central element in debates about educational policy. In order to receive badly needed federal funds, southern school districts had to assign children by race in order to meet federal standards for racial integration, and the success of their efforts was judged by numerical standards. This shift from color-blindness to color-consciousness, from the rights of the individual to the concept of group rights, reflected the rise of ethnocentrism in American politics. Stimulated by uprisings in urban ghettoes, ethnocentrism spread beyond small nationalist groups like the Black Panthers and the Black Muslims to black leaders in SNCC, CORE, antipoverty agencies, and academe. The civil disorders in poor black communities in the mid-1960s had their counterpart in the world of education, in a rebellion by minority scholars against the conventional wisdom that for years had explained the low educational performance of minority children as a function of their "cultural deficiencies" or "cultural disadvantage." Some black educators and community-control activists charged that black children had been deprived of their own rich cultural heritage in feckless efforts to make them think and act like whites.

To the standard analysis of the defects of ghetto education, they responded that black children needed to study their culture, to identify with black heroes, and to find classroom acceptance for the "black English" with which they were comfortable. As the number of black students on traditionally white campuses expanded rapidly in the late 1960s, similar demands were presented for black studies programs. Eager to cool racial tensions, colleges and universities established courses, programs, or departments to grant the bachelor's degree in this relatively new field.

In courtrooms and classrooms, it proved impossible to address critical social issues without recourse to race-conscious solutions. Whether the cry was for racial integration or racial separatism, a vocabulary drawn loosely (and often inaccurately) from the social sciences was called upon to rationalize either course of action. When federal officials or judges imposed a racial integration plan on a school district, they relied on a substantial body of social science literature as evidence that segregated schooling psychologically and emotionally harmed black children, producing feelings of inferiority that limited black aspirations and achievement. Proponents of black separatism drew on some of the same arguments but turned them to their own purposes. They claimed that generations of black children had been psychologically and emotionally harmed by white domination; that the only way to eradicate feelings of inferiority among black children was to educate them in an environment where blacks were in control, providing role models of strong and effective leadership; and that a period of racial separatism was necessary in order to build economically and politically powerful black institutions as well as healthy black psyches. Social science research offered some support for all of these theories, even those that were diametrically opposed to one another. The problem lay not in social science, which produces divergent and limited evidence, but in those who expected tentative and partial findings to sustain complex social policies.

What emerged from this welter of conflicting claims was a unique constellation of social forces, at one and the same time egalitarian and particularistic. Normally the two tendencies are at war, since one insists on equal and similar treatment for all, while the other demands different treatment for special groups. But in this unusual time both egalitarianism and particularism traced their roots to the *Brown* decision. Egalitarians could point to the *Brown* decision to confirm their claim that racially separate schools were unconstitutional; advocates of black solidarity could respond that the *Brown* decision confirmed the psychological harm done to black children by white subordination, a harm they intended to reverse by restoring self-esteem and racial pride, even if it meant ignoring the Supreme Court's admonition that "Separate educational facilities are inherently unequal."

Initially the leaders of the traditional civil rights organizations resisted the turn to ethnocentrism and clung to the traditional liberal concept of individual rights (not group rights) and color-blindness (not color-consciousness). But their position was untenable because the new militants won real victories—concessions from school boards to hire and promote more blacks, agreements from universities to increase recruitment of black students and black faculty members and to create black studies programs and departments. Compared to these tangible gains, the lofty goal of formal legal equality seemed abstract and empty indeed, utterly lacking in the economic gains and the emotional rewards that came from a victorious confrontation with the power structure. Ethnocentrism was further legitimized by foundation support for programs that championed ethnic particularism (such as the Ford Foundation's projects demonstrating community control of schools in New York City, which were administered by ethnic separatists).

The revival of ethnocentrism, however, involved costs. For years American liberals had sought to reduce group prejudice by preaching the virtues not only of tolerance among different peoples but of the insignificance of group differences. The goal was to see each person as a person, a fellow human being, not as a group representative. But in the late 1960s, the call to black power and black pride was soon followed by other assertions of group consciousness. Chicanos, American Indians, and other minorities imitated the black model with calls for brown power and red power. By 1970, not to be outdone, descendants of immigrants from southern and eastern Europe proclaimed the arousal of a white ethnic movement and celebrated Italian power, Slavic power, Polish power, and Irish power, among others. Champions of "the new ethnicity," as it was widely called, declared that "the melting pot" had failed and that White-Anglo-Saxon-Protestants had foisted assimilation on immigrants in order to strip them of their cultural heritage and their identity.

The surge of the new ethnocentrism coincided with the intensification of the Vietnam war and of the protest movement against it on the streets and campuses of America. Against this background of social dissension, social crisis, urban riots, and antiwar fervor, the American system came under harsh attack for its defects. In the late 1960s, one scholar observes,

the view that America was systematically oppressive and immoral was not the majority view, but it had been advanced so vehemently by numerous partisans and acquiesced in so tamely by authoritative figures that national confidence and self-respect were severely shaken. Both domestic and foreign policy were castigated, not merely as wrong, but as evil and obscene. . . . The American creed, according to this interpretation, had never been anything but a sham; the American dream had always been a nightmare.[1]

In this atmosphere of discord and distrust, those with grievances turned naturally to the courts and the federal government to enforce their rights against local school boards and university administrators. Programs, regulations, and court orders began to reflect the strong suspicion that those in control of American institutions were not to be trusted with any discretion where minorities, women, and other aggrieved groups were concerned. The idea that schools and universities provided equal opportunity for all American youth to improve themselves and succeed on the basis of individual ability without regard to their origins was scorned, as ethnic groups complained that the schools forced them to give up their language and culture, as women complained that institutions of higher education discriminated against them because of their gender, and as blacks complained that white racism was so pervasive that institutional neutrality was impossible.

This was the context within which the federal government promoted several programs that proved to be highly controversial, among them affirmative action and sex equity in higher education and bilingual education in the schools. Carried along on the general egalitarian tide were such issues as the rights of the handicapped. Advocates and opponents of each new program disputed its worth, sometimes bitterly, as though each presented a choice between destroying the institution or saving the students. Some initiatives were absorbed, others foundered; what changed, probably permanently, was the relationship of the federal government and the courts to educational institutions in the United States.

The legitimization of ethnicity as a basis for public policy and the assertion that minority children were educationally damaged by the denial of their native culture were powerful themes in congressional hearings in 1967 on bilingual education. The original bill was intended to provide federal funding for demonstration projects "to meet the special educational needs" of Hispanic children only. The principal sponsor of the legislation, Senator Ralph Yarborough of Texas, claimed that the proposed benefits should be limited to Hispanics because other non–English-speaking groups had come voluntarily to this country and left behind their language and culture, while Spanish speakers in the Southwest had been conquered and "had our culture superimposed on them." Throughout the hearings, conducted in Texas, California, and New York (where the number of Hispanic children and voters was greatest), testimony was presented mostly by Hispanic spokesmen and local politicians who wanted to demonstrate their commitment to the welfare of their Hispanic constituents. To prove the need for bilingual education, several witnesses (including the U.S. commissioner of education) decried the fact that adult Mexican Americans in the Southwest (those twenty-five years and older) had completed 7.1 years of schooling, compared to 12.1 years for "Anglos" and 9 years for nonwhites, a disparity attributed to the failures of the American school. No one pointed out that among the adult Mexican Americans twenty-five and older were many who had been born and educated (or not educated) *outside* the United States.[2]

All of the congressmen and witnesses agreed that the purpose of bilingual education was to enable the Hispanic child to learn English. Yarborough explained that he proposed bilingual education because "unless a child becomes very fluent in English he will rarely reach the top in American cultural life. He might as a baseball player, but he could not as a performer on radio; he could not in law; he could not in medicine; he could not in any of the professions or in business."[3]

Four assumptions, which were usually stated as facts rather than as assumptions, dominated the hearings: first, that Hispanic children did poorly in school because they had a "damaged self-concept"; second, that this negative self-appraisal occurred because the child's native tongue was not the language of instruction; third, that the appropriate remedy for this problem was bilingual instruction; and fourth, that children who were taught their native language (or their *parents'* native language) and their cultural heritage would acquire a positive self-concept, high self-esteem, better attitudes toward school, increased motivation, and improved educational achievement. One bilingual educator testified that "When these children know their native language well, it is going to be very much easier for them to establish a bridge to English and learn it more effectively." A Puerto Rican spokesman complained that "the psychic cost of the melting pot" was probably responsible for the extent of "mental and emotional illness" in the United States; he held that the necessity of learning a new language gives children "a negative self-image."[4]

In the midst of a steady stream of extravagant claims made on behalf of bilingual education, one educator sounded a warning note. Hershel T. Manuel, professor emeritus of educational psychology at the University of Texas, warned Yarborough that any new legislation should emphasize research and experimentation because educators did not have answers to the problems of teaching children whose home language is not English.

"The school has been right in its emphasis on English," Manuel held, "and this emphasis on English must continue, but it has not been right in its neglect of the child's home language." He cautioned, however, that "no one best program is possible. . . . We know a great deal about teaching languages, but we do not know enough about teaching two languages together. . . . We desperately need carefully controlled experiments with measured results and we should be careful that, in our enthusiasm, we do not simply proliferate unproved and unwise programs which can only lead to disillusionment and delay."[5]

When Congress passed the Bilingual Education Act of 1968 (subsequently referred to as Title VII of the Elementary and Secondary Education Act), the act covered not just Hispanic children but "children of limited English-speaking ability" (a necessary political compromise in order to garner support for the bill in Congress), and it was focused on low-income children. Significantly, the bill neither defined "bilingual education" nor stated the purpose of the act, other than to provide money for local districts "to develop and carry out new and imaginative elementary and secondary school programs" to meet the special needs of non–English-speaking children. The vagueness of the legislation was intentional. Yarborough candidly admitted that "Every time people ask me, 'What does bilingual education mean?' I reply that it means different things to different people." Supporters of bilingual education thought that they had won a victory for preservation of non-English cultures and languages, but congressional supporters thought of bilingual education as a remedial program to help children become literate in the English language and then join English-speaking classes. This issue was central to debates over bilingual education during the next fifteen years. Was the purpose of bilingual education to provide a *transition* to the regular English-language school program or was its purpose to *maintain* the language and culture of non-English-speaking children?[6]

The Bilingual Education Act did not require any district to offer bilingual programs; it provided money ($7.5 million the first year) for what were supposed to be demonstration programs initiated by local districts. This permissive approach did not last long, however. In 1970, the Office for Civil Rights (OCR) in the Health, Education, and Welfare Department decided that discrimination against children who were "deficient in English language skills" violated Title VI of the Civil Rights Act (which provided that "No person in the United States shall, on the ground of race, color, or national origin, be excluded from participation in, be denied the benefits of, or be subjected to discrimination under any program or activity receiving Federal financial assistance"). OCR informed every school district "with More than Five Percent National Origin-Minority Group Children" that

> Where inability to speak and understand the English language excludes national origin-minority group children from effective participation in the educational program offered by a school district, the district must take affirmative steps to rectify the language deficiency in order to open its instructional program to these students.

Any special program for these children "must be designed to meet such language skill needs as soon as possible and must not operate as an educational dead-end or permanent track." Essentially, OCR took the reasonable position that school districts had to provide special assistance for those children who could not participate in the regular educational program because of their limited English skills.[7]

These guidelines were upheld by the Supreme Court in 1974, when it ruled against the San Francisco school system for failing to provide English language instruction to eighteen hundred non–English-speaking Chinese students. In the *Lau* v. *Nichols* decision, the Supreme Court held that "there is no equality of treatment merely by providing students with the same facilities, textbooks, teachers, and curriculum; for students who do not understand English are effectively foreclosed from any meaningful education." The Supreme Court suggested no particular remedy: "Teaching English to the students of Chinese ancestry who do not speak the language is one choice. Giving instruction to the group in Chinese is another. There may be others." Like the OCR guidelines of 1970, the Court's *Lau* decision of 1974 directed the schools to create special language programs for non–English-speaking children to "rectify the language deficiency," while prudently avoiding any pedagogical dictates.[8]

Prudence was not, however, the hallmark of guidelines fashioned in the summer of 1975 by a task force that was appointed by the commissioner of education, Terrell Bell, and was composed of bilingual educators and representatives of language minority groups. Known as the "Lau remedies," the task force's report prescribed in exhaustive detail how school districts were to prepare and carry out bilingual programs for non–English-speaking students. The districts were directed to identify the student's primary language, not by his proficiency in English but by determining which language was most often spoken in the student's home, which language he had learned first, and which language he used most often; thus a student would be eligible for a bilingual program even if he were entirely fluent in English. Although the Supreme Court had not endorsed any pedagogical approach, the Lau task force declared that non–English-speaking students were to receive bilingual education that emphasized instruction in their native language and native culture. Districts were discouraged from offering "English as a Second Language" (ESL), which was intensive, supplemental English-only instruction. ESL, said the task force, was "not appropriate" for elementary school children and could not be used as the only program for high school children. The task force overlooked the fact that the failure of the San Francisco schools to provide ESL to all Chinese children in the system was the basis of the *Lau* decision.[9]

The task force recommendations reflected a new consensus among proponents of bilingual education. At congressional hearings in 1974 on a bill to extend Title VII, it was clear that bilingual educators had come to see the program as a way to preserve non-English languages and cultures, even though congressmen still thought of it as a bridge to help learn English. While a strong supporter like Congresswoman Shirley Chisholm of New York City insisted that bilingual education had to be "a real priority" because "those students who do not understand English are effectively foreclosed from any meaningful education," the director of New York City's bilingual program insisted that "at no time should we simply view this as a way of providing the transition from the native language to English." Others vigorously protested suggestions that the program should be limited in time, since their ideal was to maintain students in a bilingual curriculum through twelve years of schooling.[10]

The 1974 hearings also revealed the effects of the ethnic revival, as speakers berated the melting pot and celebrated cultural pluralism. An Italian spokesman complained that "bilingual funds should be spread out amongst other nationalities" but admitted that the high dropout rate of Italian-American youth "was not primarily a language situation." A member of the New York City Board of Education waxed enthusiastic: "I believe in this bill for the Haitian children who are coming to New York, for the Chinese children . . . for the Greek and for the Italian kids who are coming in, and I believe in this for the Hungarian children and the Latvian and the German grandchildren of people who have a right again to know something about where their ancestors came from and why."[11]

The Nixon administration viewed the bilingual/bicultural approach with skepticism. Frank Carlucci, the undersecretary of HEW, testified that "We simply do not have firm evidence to embrace any one model to the exclusion of others. . . ." Carlucci reminded the House committee that the goal of language programs was to teach the English language to children who knew little or no English. Additionally, he insisted that it was not the role of the federal government to support the cultural interests of the

275

nation's many ethnic groups: "The cultural pluralism of American society is one of its greatest assets. But I believe such pluralism should be a matter of local choice and not subsidized by the Federal Government."[12]

Since the Bilingual Education Act was up for renewal during the crisis-ridden days in the summer of 1974 as pressure was building for President Richard Nixon to resign because of the Watergate scandal, his administration's opposition to the legislation merely strengthened its support in the Democratic Congress. The new version of Title VII, sponsored principally by Senators Edward Kennedy of Massachusetts and Alan Cranston of California, incorporated a version of bilingual education that satisfied ethnic militants. It was heavily weighted toward maintenance programs; no longer a demonstration program, bilingual education was now treated as a proven method of instruction. The 1974 act explicitly recognized that many children of limited English-speaking ability "have a cultural heritage which differs from that of English-speaking persons," and "that a primary means by which a child learns is through the use of such child's language and cultural heritage," and "that, therefore, large numbers of children of limited English-speaking ability have educational needs which can be met by the use of bilingual educational methods and techniques." Furthermore, the legislation made all limited English-speakers eligible for such programs, not just those from low-income homes. The Bilingual Education Act of 1974 was a landmark of sorts, for it represented the first time since the enactment of federal aid that the Congress had dictated a specific pedagogical approach to local educational agencies.[13]

By 1977, the U.S. Office of Education reported that it had allocated $115 million for bilingual programs in more than five hundred local districts to teach more than three hundred thousand children in their native language. In addition to providing training for about twenty-five thousand teachers and aides, the federal government funded the preparation of teaching materials in sixty-eight languages, including not only those with sizable numbers of speakers, like Spanish, French, Korean, Chinese, Italian, Greek, Russian, and Japanese, but also in seven Eskimo languages (Gwich-'in, Inupiag, Siberian Yupik, Sugpiag, Upper Kuskokwim, Aluet, and Upper Tanana) and a score of American Indian languages (some of which had no written form).[14]

The 1977 congressional hearings on the renewal of federal funding for bilingual education introduced a few jarring notes into the usual pas de deux between the congressmen and ethnic lobbyists. For the first time, educators raised pointed questions about the direction and efficacy of the programs. Gary Orfield of the University of Illinois, a desegregation specialist, complained that federal grants often provide for expensive, highly segregated programs of no proven educational value to children. Worse, I believe there is sometimes a tendency to train children who do not need the program and may be hurt by it. Some programs pursue not successful integration in American society but deeper cultural and linguistic identity and separation. . . . Congress began support of bilingual programs without any significant proof that they would work. The history of research on bilingualism is full of ambiguous findings and careless methods. . . . There is nothing in the research to suggest that children can effectively learn English without continuous interaction with other children who are native English speakers.[15]

Even more unsettling was the report of a four-year study of Title VII commissioned by the U.S. Office of Education. Prepared by the American Institutes for Research (AIR), a well-known research organization, the study sampled 286 classrooms in all 38 Spanish/English projects that had been in operation for at least four years as of 1975. The object of the evaluation was to determine whether the program was helping limited English-speaking children to gain competency in English while progressing in their other school subjects through the use of their native language.[16]

One congressman stated that he lost part of a night's sleep when he saw the results of the AIR study. The first finding was that while three-quarters of the children in the Title VII classrooms were Hispanic, less than a third had limited proficiency in English. Further, about 85 percent of the project directors told the evaluators that Hispanic students remained in bilingual classes after they had become competent in English. Bilingual educators saw nothing wrong with these figures, since they believed that children should learn bilingually from kindergarten through twelfth grade. But some congressmen were astonished because they had seen bilingual education as a transitional effort to prepare Hispanic children to move into the regular English-language curriculum.[17]

AIR's report on student achievement and attitudes was equally disappointing. On tests of English, Hispanic students in Title VII classes did not do as well as Hispanic students who did not learn bilingually. On tests of mathematics (given in Spanish and English), Hispanic students in both Title VII and non–Title VII classes performed at about the same level. Relative to national norms, both groups were far behind (at the twentieth percentile in English and the thirtieth percentile in mathematics). Students in Title VII classes did not have a more positive attitude toward school; both groups were said to feel neither strongly positive nor strongly negative toward school. The only area in which Title VII students could be said to have improved was in their ability to read Spanish. In short, the study found that studying Spanish improved the student's command of Spanish but not necessarily of English or of other subjects.[18]

The AIR study was attacked not only by bilingual educators but also by a spokesman from the bilingual/bicultural division of the National Institute of Education, the major federal research agency. But congressmen, accustomed only to statements about the positive effects of bilingual education, were deeply disturbed, particularly by the finding that so many children in federally funded bilingual programs already knew English. When asked what he thought of the latest evaluation, John Molina, the director of the Office of Bilingual Education, responded, "You actually can't evaluate a bilingual education program. It is philosophy and management. You can evaluate courses. For example, evaluation should be limited to reading, mathematics, science and social science. I think we need a tremendous amount of research in order to determine what are the best methods and if children learn in languages other than English." His was a blunt admission that bilingual education proceeded from ideological grounds, and not as a result of research validating the best methods of teaching children of limited English-speaking ability.[19]

Although it seemed in one sense astonishing that federal education officials still lacked any research basis for the practices they had been funding for ten years (and that Congress had mandated), Molina's answer struck to the core of the problem. As one scholar put it, "The proposition that the preservation of native language and culture would produce healthy children and a healthy polity could not be tested. Only the educational impact of the programs could be measured." To those who believed that the purpose of bilingual education was to promote ethnic solidarity, test results were beside the point; in their terms, the very existence of bilingual/bicultural education was a success. To those who thought that its purpose was to speed the transition of limited English-speakers into the regular English curriculum, bilingual education lost some of its luster.[20]

In the amended version of Title VII which passed in 1978, Congress limited the number of English-speaking children in bilingual classes to 40 percent and made clear that they were there to help the other children learn English. Programs were required in the future to form parent advisory councils, to be sure that the projects were providing what parents wanted for their children. Local schools were also instructed to evaluate individually any child who remained in bilingual programs for more than two years, a move intended to stress congressional disapproval of programs devoted to cultural maintenance rather than to transition to English-speaking classes.[21]

Even with these restrictions, bilingual education continued to be highly controversial. When the Department of Education proposed new regulations in 1980 to mandate bilingual education, there was broad-based opposition; not only did such professional organizations as the Chief State School Officers, the National School Boards Association, the National Association of Elementary School Principals, the National Association of Secondary School Principals, and the American Federation of Teachers object to this direct assertion of federal control of pedagogy, but thousands of letters from individuals were sent to Washington, denouncing this threat to their ideal of the melting pot. These regulations, which would have had the force of law, were never put into effect by the Carter administration and were subsequently withdrawn by Terrell Bell, the Reagan administration's secretary of education (who, ironically, had supervised the preparation of the 1975 "Lau remedies," which first committed the federal government to bilingual/bicultural methods).[22]

Like so many other issues, bilingual education merged both political and educational concerns in ways that were difficult to separate. It was originally advocated as a way to reverse low educational achievement and high dropout rates and to increase self-esteem among Hispanic and other non–English-speaking minorities. Real as the problems were, there was no evidence to demonstrate that they were caused by the absence of bilingual education. To the extent that belief in bilingual education was ideological and political, it was not subject to evaluation; to the extent that it rested on claims that it would improve the achievement of non–English-speaking children, it had finally to be measured against impartial research. In a 1982 survey of research about bilingual education, Iris Rotberg of the National Institute of Education found that "bilingual programs are neither better nor worse than other instructional methods." She cited an international study which concluded that "at the world level, the field of research on bilingual education is characterized by disparate findings and inconclusive results. . . . a study can be found to support virtually every possible opinion." Rotberg noted, significantly, that most language programs "may be more alike than their labels imply. For instance, bilingual components are typically included in immersion programs, and almost every bilingual program uses some ESL techniques." She concluded that there is "no legal necessity or research basis for the federal government to advocate or require a specific educational approach."[23]

By 1980, thirteen states mandated bilingual education, and some federal judges had ordered its use by school districts or even entire states, so there was no question that it would continue to be a controversial issue so long as it was perceived as a bulwark of cultural separatism. As the ethnic revival faded, deflating some of the political rationale for bilingualism, the possibility remained that advocates of bilingualism might merge their interests with the larger public concern about the decline of foreign language instruction in American schools and universities.[24]

Bilingual education was controversial because of disagreement about its purposes, and congressional debates revealed the very different expectations of congressmen and ethnic lobbyists. Affirmative action, on the other hand, was controversial in part because both proponents and critics clearly understood its purpose and disagreed vigorously, but also because it became government policy in the absence of either congressional debate or legislation. Neither bilingual education nor affirmative action enjoyed popular support; public opinion polls consistently showed overwhelming majorities opposed to both. Affirmative action symbolized the shift in government policy from color-blindness to color-consciousness, from individual rights to group rights, and from a government policy forbidding specific acts of discrimination to a government policy relying on statistical disparities among groups as presumptive evidence of discrimination. Private and governmental efforts to increase the number of minority students and faculty in higher education opened a national debate on the nature of equal opportunity and the question of compensatory justice.[25]

Affirmative action emerged in the late 1960s as an effort to speed up black economic advancement in light of paradoxical trends. A prolonged period of both racial turmoil and racial progress followed the landmark civil rights legislation of 1964 and 1965. Conspicuously in public view were urban riots and the rise of quasi-military groups like the Black Panthers. At the same time, black educational attainment and college enrollment rose dramatically, and for the first time, a sizable minority of educated blacks achieved middle-class incomes. Even though the second half of the 1960s was a time of unparalleled social and economic progress for blacks, black leaders continued to warn sympathetic federal officials that the slow pace of racial change would cause further unrest and disorders.[26]

However, the language of the Civil Rights Act of 1964 posed an obstacle to any governmental efforts intended to help blacks or any other specific racial, ethnic, or religious group. Aimed at guaranteeing an end to discrimination based on one's group identity, the act represented a clear affirmation of the equality of all persons before the law. During hearings on the bill, a number of congressmen had expressed concern that the law might be used to impose racial balancing in schools or preferential hiring; to allay these fears, the act explicitly barred the use of race, religion, or national origin in school assignment or in hiring practices (also, sexual discrimination was banned in employment). Title IV of the act included a definition of desegregation as "the assignment of students to public schools and within such schools without regard to their race, color, religion, or national origin, but 'desegregation' shall not mean the assignment of students to public schools in order to overcome racial imbalance." Title VII, intended to end employment discrimination, included a statement that "nothing contained in this title shall be interpreted to require any employer . . . to grant preferential treatment to any individual or to any group because of the race, color, religion, sex, or national origin of such individual or group on account of an imbalance which may exist with respect to the total number or percentage of persons of any race, color, religion, sex, or national origin employed by any employer. . . . " Both of these guarantees were enforced by Title VI, which declared that no federal funds would go to any activity or program that practiced discrimination: "No person in the United States shall, on the grounds of race, color, or national origin, be excluded from participation in, be denied the benefits of, or be subjected to discrimination under any program or activity receiving Federal financial assistance."[27]

Yet, as smoke darkened the sky over several of the nation's cities in the aftermath of black uprisings, an ominous sense of apocalyse intensified the need to do something for blacks that was visible. Harold Howe, II, the U.S. commissioner of education, explained bluntly in 1966 that "a revolution is brewing under our feet," and that "it is largely up to the schools to determine whether the energies of that revolution can be converted into a new and vigorous source of American progress, or whether their explosion will rip this nation into two societies." It became the task of federal officials to find ways to remedy past segregation without running afoul of the statutory commands in the Civil Rights Act. In the area of school desegregation, the imposition of racial integration on southern schools seemed a fitting recompense, not only because the South had degraded blacks for so many generations but because these districts had for more than a decade willfully ignored or evaded the *Brown* decision. Federal judges, in order to square their orders assigning children to schools by race with the Civil Rights Act's command not to assign children by race, adhered to the principle that a violation must be followed by a remedy. Once a district had violated the law by intentionally segregating children, then the remedy of racial balancing was appropriately invoked. Because the South did not have clean hands, its complaints to the rest of the nation about the new federal role won little sympathy.[28]

In the area of employment, discrimination was banned not only by Title VII of the Civil Rights Act but also by several presidential executive orders. President Franklin Roosevelt had first barred discrimination in defense industries in 1941; additional executive orders were issued by presidents Truman, Eisenhower, and Kennedy, extending nondiscrimination to other government contractors and strengthening its enforcement. In 1965, President Lyndon Johnson issued Executive Order 11246, which was amended in 1967 to include "sex" among the categories where nondiscrimination was mandated. Johnson's executive orders provided that "The contractor will not discriminate against any employee or applicant for employment because of race, color, religion, sex, or national origin. The contractor will take affirmative action to ensure that applicants are employed, and that employees are treated during employment, without regard to their race, color, religion, sex, or national origin."

Enforcement of the executive order was the responsibility of the Department of Labor, which in May, 1968, a few weeks after the assassination of Martin Luther King, Jr., and the ensuing disorders in Washington, D.C., issued regulations explaining what "affirmative action" meant. The government contractor was expected to post a statement of nondiscrimination in conspicuous places, to advertise job openings widely, and to notify collective bargaining agents of the agreement not to discriminate. Contractors were required to prepare a "written affirmative action compliance program" that included an analysis of "utilization of minority group personnel" in all job categories and, "when there are deficiencies, the development of specific goals and time tables for the prompt achievement of full and equal employment opportunity." For the first time, government contractors were told to prepare an ethnic census of their work force, to report the number of employees who were from designated minority groups ("Negroes," "Orientals," "American Indians," and "Spanish Americans"). But the overall emphasis was on enlarging the pool of applicants by aggressive advertising and recruiting, on expanding "opportunity" rather than on statistical representation by race, nationality, and gender.[29]

The election of a Republican president, Richard Nixon, with little support from civil rights groups evoked fears that federal enforcement efforts might slacken. Surprisingly, under the Nixon administration, the idea of affirmative action was transformed into a vigorous federal program to compel government contractors to increase their employment of persons of minority background and of women. J. Stanley Pottinger, the Nixon administration's director of the OCR, oversaw the transition to an affirmative action policy that was, in the language of the 1970 guidelines, "result-oriented." Each new set of guidelines advanced and clarified the government's requirement that employers analyze the number of minority persons and women in each job category, determine where these groups were "underutilized," and specify "goals and timetables" to correct the deficient utilization of these groups in every job classification. In effect, the federal government endorsed the concept that "underrepresentation" of a particular group implied a pattern of discrimination, even when no individual acts of discrimination could be identified. Despite the distrust between the Nixon administration and advocacy groups for women and minorities, OCR worked amicably with these organizations to extend its enforcement powers. Pottinger claimed that the pre-Nixon executive orders had been "unnoticed" in relation to higher education until they were "discovered" in 1970 by women's organizations and minority groups, which then helped his office gain new staff and a larger mission. The relationship, often observed in regulatory agencies, was symbiotic: protests by the aggrieved constituency groups increased the power of the agency, and each new grant of power to the agency enhanced the position of both the agency and its constituency of minorities.[30]

By the time OCR began doing compliance reviews of institutions of higher education in the fall of 1971, the concept of nondiscrimination had been decisively redefined: it no longer meant that contractors should hire and treat employees *without regard* to their race, color, religion, sex, or national origin but that they should act *with regard* to those factors. Typically, universities complied with federal requirements by supplying a description of the number of blacks, Hispanics, Asians, American Indians, and women in each department and job category, as well as an analysis of the availability of each group in the job market and a projection of the university's program to increase the representation of each "underutilized" group. During the early 1970s, federal grants to twenty leading universities were held up until the universities filed affirmative action plans that satisfied OCR. Complaints against colleges and universities could be filed not only with OCR but also with the Equal Employment Opportunity Commission, the Department of Labor, and state antidiscrimination agencies, all of which were authorized to launch investigations and compliance reviews. In addition to pressure from the federal government to hire more women and minorities, many institutions of higher education responded positively to demands by their own black students to increase black enrollment and to hire more black professors and administrators.[31]

Unwilling to risk federal grants, universities usually complied, but individual professors unleashed a barrage of criticism against affirmative action. Their concerns were, first, that academic merit (intellectual ability, teaching experience, scholarship, recognition by one's peers) should be the only consideration in selecting faculty members; second, that the pressure to hire minorities and women would force universities to hire less qualified people; third, that white males would be the victims of "reverse discrimination"; fourth, that the issue gave federal investigators access to confidential faculty files, thus endangering the traditional process of peer review among colleagues; and fifth, that government intervention in the internal affairs of the university infringed on academic freedom.

The underlying fear of the critics was that the government was trying to force universities to accept the principle of proportional representation —by race, gender, and national origin—in place of merit. What they saw, surrounded by euphemisms and bureaucratic jargon, was governmental power imposing hiring quotas on the university. It seemed unreasonable to extend preferential treatment to, for example, recent immigrants from the West Indies or Latin America merely because of the color of their skin or their Hispanic surnames. In the domain of the mind, they insisted, no qualifications should matter other than the ability to think, to write, and to teach. An unusual number of the critics were Jewish, and many were immigrants or children of immigrants. Those who had been educated in Europe recalled the ethnic and religious restrictions on education and employment; those who had been educated in the United States knew that quotas limiting the enrollments and employment of Jews, Catholics, blacks, and other groups had only recently been eliminated by many major universities. The critics defined equal opportunity as a fair chance for all individuals to compete for rewards on the basis of ability. "Quotas" for minorities meant that the federal government was redefining equal opportunity to mean equal representation for all groups, regardless of individual merit. That this policy was advanced in the name of "nondiscrimination" made it all the more galling.[32]

Those who defended the affirmative action policy argued that members of racial minorities and women would never gain equal opportunity for employment in the university, dominated as it was by an "old boy" network of white males, without government pressure; nor could equal opportunity enable members of the designated groups to overcome the effects of past discrimination in education and employment. Spokesmen for OCR insisted that the invocation of "quotas" was a scare tactic, that the government meant only to urge universities to determine whether women and minorities were adequately represented on their faculties in relation to their availability, and if they were not, actively to recruit and hire them. Scores of articles were written on whether OCR's "goals and timetables" were unconscionable quotas or were merely useful indicators of desirable changes in hiring patterns. What was indisputable, however, was that the antibias regulatory agencies imposed an inappropriate industrial model of employment on the university. For example, after its first three plans were rejected as inadequate, Harvard University submitted a five-volume affirmative action plan to comply with OCR's requirements, but its approval was contingent on Harvard's agreeing (among other things) to "develop and submit detailed criteria for selection and promotion for each job category and for faculty by rank by department where they have not been previously submitted," to "validate all tests presently used in selection, upgrading, or promotion," and to prepare a "salary equity analysis," which compared all employees in terms of such criteria as their years at the institution, their education level, their number of publications, and so forth. While such requests may have been easily answered by large industrial companies, the same rationalization of job categories simply did not fit the faculty model, where scholarly distinction and research interests could not be tailored to fit a conventional job analysis; where decisions about hiring and promotion are made by the tenured faculty (not by a personnel officer); and where two professors might have the same number of publications and the same years on the faculty without having equal stature within their field.[33]

Although most criticism was directed at government intervention into university employment practices, the major court tests of affirmative action challenged the use of racial preferences in graduate-student admissions programs. Competition for admission to graduate professional schools had become especially intense as the children of the baby boom came of age in the late 1960s; most law schools and medical schools had far more applicants than places. In 1971, Marco DeFunis filed suit against the University of Washington Law School after he was rejected for the second time. Competing with sixteen hundred others for only three hundred places, DeFunis complained that he had been unconstitutionally discriminated against because the university had classified applicants by race and preferentially admitted members of certain racial groups (blacks, Chicanos, American Indians, and Filipinos) whose qualifications were less than his. A state court ordered the University of Washington to admit him. In 1974, when DeFunis's case reached the U. S. Supreme Court, he was already in his last term of law school. By 5 to 4, the Court decided that his case was moot, since he would graduate regardless of their holding.[34]

Though the Court avoided rendering a decision, another case quickly appeared to test the same issue. Allan Bakke, a white engineer, charged that he had been discriminated against by the University of California at Davis Medical School. A new medical school, open only since 1968, Davis had a dual system of admissions: a regular admissions program, in which all applicants competed for eighty-four places; and a special admissions program, in which only members of disadvantaged minorities competed for sixteen places. When Bakke was turned down for the second time in

1974, he decided to sue. Other medical schools had turned him down because he was thirty-three, too old, some thought, to begin a career in medicine. His academic credentials, however, were excellent, and his scores on the Medical College Admissions Test were well above the average of those admitted under the regular admissions program and substantially above those admitted under the special admissions program. Bakke claimed that the special program operated as an unconstitutional racial quota that discriminated against him on the basis of his race.[35]

The California Supreme Court, noted for its liberal orientation, declared the Davis admissions program to be unconstitutional by a vote of 6 to 1 and ordered the university to admit Allan Bakke. The Court described the Davis special program as

> a form of an education quota system, benevolent in concept perhaps, but a revival of quotas nevertheless. No college admission policy in history has been so thoroughly discredited in contemporary times as the use of racial percentages. Originated as a means of exclusion of racial and religious minorities from higher education, a quota becomes no less offensive when it serves to exclude a racial majority.[36]

The state court advised the university to use "flexible admission standards" and to adopt aggressive programs to select disadvantaged students of all races, but to maintain a context of racial neutrality.

The University of California appealed to the U. S. Supreme Court. Many civil rights organizations tried to persuade the university to drop its appeal and to persuade the Supreme Court not to take the case. They were fearful, first of all, because their interests were represented by the University of California, which they did not entirely trust; they recognized also that the case was not strong from their point of view: it had already lost in the California courts; the Davis program separated minorities for special treatment; and the school itself was too new to have a record of prior discrimination to justify the adoption of a racial remedy.[37]

Once it became clear that the *Bakke* case would be reviewed by the Supreme Court during 1977, the sides were quickly drawn. The University of California, to allay concern about its seriousness, engaged Archibald Cox, former solicitor general of the United States, to defend the Davis program. Allan Bakke was represented by Reynolds Colvin, a prominent San Francisco attorney who had never argued a case before the Supreme Court. Fifty-eight "friend-of-the-court" briefs were submitted in the *Bakke* case, more than for any previous decision, including even the *Brown* decision, and about three-quarters of them opposed Bakke. Among the many defenders of the University of California's special admissions procedure were many private universities, the Justice Department, the American Civil Liberties Union, the National Education Association, the Association of American Law Schools, the Association of American Medical Colleges, and civil rights groups. Bakke's position was defended mostly by Jewish organizations, white ethnic groups (of Italian, Polish, and Ukrainian descent), and conservatives.

From the time the Supreme Court agreed to hear the *Bakke* case, hardly a week passed without an article in a journal defending discrimination in favor of minorities or attacking racial quotas. In a widely noted article in the *Atlantic Monthly,* McGeorge Bundy, president of the Ford Foundation, warned that the *Bakke* case had "an importance not exceeded by any single case from the past," including the *Brown* decision. The decision in California, he believed, threatened "the constitutionality of all forms of affirmative action that are aimed explicitly at helping racial minorities." To classify students by race in order to give them special help was "not only rational but necessary for compelling purposes." Racial neutrality, Bundy argued, would not suffice: "The reason is simple, if also painful: the gaps in social, economic, educational, and cultural advantage between racial minorities and the white majority are still so wide that *there is no racially neutral process of choice that will produce more than a handful of minority students in our competitive colleges and professional schools.*"[38]

Supporters of the Davis program argued that universities had an obligation to provide special help for racial minorities in order to overcome the effects of past discrimination. It was in the interest of society, they held, to increase the number of nonwhite professionals, both to improve the availability of legal and medical services in their communities and to provide role models of achievement for young people. Universities made two additional claims on behalf of the Davis program. First, they asked the Court to respect the University of California's freedom to select its students, and second, they insisted on the value of diversity in their enrollments. Harvard University explained that its admissions officers purposefully sought diversity in accepting students to the college; for many years, they had selected students from different geographical regions, with different talents and different aspirations. In recent years, they also sought diversity of economic, racial, and ethnic background, recognizing that "a farm boy from Idaho can bring something to Harvard College that a Bostonian cannot offer. Similarly, a black student can usually bring something that a white person cannot offer." Harvard claimed that it pursued diversity without using minimums or target-quotas but by paying "some attention to distribution among many types and categories of students." Harvard did acknowledge that "diversity" was emphasized more in the selection of undergraduate students than at the graduate or professional levels of the university.[39]

An indication of how much had changed since the *Brown* case was provided by the brief of the NAACP Legal Defense Fund (LDF). In 1952, LDF lawyers insisted that "the Fourteenth Amendment precludes a state from imposing distinctions or classifications based upon race and color alone" and submitted a lengthy history of the Fourteenth Amendment to prove that the framers intended "to eliminate race distinctions from American law." In the *Bakke* case, the LDF argued that "the Fourteenth Amendment prohibits any racial classification which has the purpose or effect of stigmatizing as inferior any racial or ethnic group," and presented a history of the Fourteenth Amendment to demonstrate "that the framers intended it to legitimate and to allow implementation of race-specific remedial measures."[40]

By the spring of 1978, as the debate raged, media coverage of the impending decision was intense. On June 28, when the decision was announced, Justice Powell explained, "We speak today with a notable lack of unanimity. I will try to explain how we divided." There was much to explain. Six of the nine justices wrote opinions, and the upshot was that the University of California was ordered to admit Bakke to the Davis Medical School, was permitted to take race into account in its future admissions decisions, but was directed to abolish Davis's two-track system for students of different races. "Perhaps there has never been a case before the Supreme Court with opposing arguments of more equal legitimacy," wrote one analyst. "The Court's own task in *Bakke* was to avoid a conclusive outcome. It must not, in this most divisive of cases, hoist the arms of a victorious contestant." The decision, a 4-1-4 split, was "a Solomonic compromise," "a brokered judgment," "a well-modulated counterpoint." Or as the cover of *Time* magazine put it, "QUOTAS:NO/RACE:YES."[41]

One bloc of four justices (William Brennan, Byron White, Thurgood Marshall, and Harry Blackmun) contended that the Davis program was a valid, voluntary effort to overcome the effects of societal discrimination and to reduce the underrepresentation of minorities in the medical profession, even though Davis had never been guilty of discrimination. The Brennan group argued that neither the Congress nor the Court had ever adopted the proposition that the Constitution must be color-blind. There could be no doubt, they held, about the permissibility of "racial preferences for the purpose of assisting disadvantaged racial minorities." In additional opinions, Justice Marshall held that historic discrimination against the Negro justified the provision of "greater protection under the Fourteenth Amendment where it is necessary to remedy the effects of past discrimination," and Justice Blackmun declared, "In order to get beyond racism, we must first take account of race."[42]

Another bloc of four justices (John Paul Stevens, Warren Burger, Potter Stewart, William Rehnquist) believed that Davis had violated Title VI of the Civil Rights Act by excluding Bakke from participation in a federally funded program on the basis of his race. They contended that "the meaning of the Title VI ban on exclusion is crystal clear: Race cannot be the basis of excluding anyone from participation in a federally funded program." The proponents of Title VI, they believed, "assumed that the Constitution itself required a colorblind standard on the part of government." The Stevens group voted to uphold the judgment of the California Supreme Court, voiding the special program and admitting Bakke.

Justice Lewis Powell delivered an opinion that was signed by no one else, but which became the judgment of the Court because he cast the deciding vote on different sides of the issue. Powell agreed with the Brennan group that it was appropriate, under certain circumstances, to take race into account as a factor in the admissions process, and he agreed with the Stevens group that the Davis program was unconstitutional and that Bakke should be admitted to the medical school.

Powell found that the Davis program was unconstitutional because it used an "explicit racial classification." Applicants who were not black, Asian, or Chicano were "totally excluded from a specific percentage of the seats in an entering class." He did not accept the claim that blacks were entitled to greater protection by the Fourteenth Amendment or that white males as members of the majority were entitled to less protection: "The guarantee of equal protection cannot mean one thing when applied to one individual and something else when applied to a person of another color. If both are not accorded the same protection, then it is not equal." Because the nation was composed of so many different minority groups, most of which "can lay claim to a history of prior discrimination," Powell rejected the idea that the Court could adjudicate preferences among racial and ethnic minorities because there would be no principled basis by which to adjudicate their competing claims: "Courts would be asked to evaluate the extent of the prejudice and consequent harm suffered by various minority groups. Those whose societal injury is thought to exceed some arbitrary level of tolerability then would be entitled to preferential classifications at the expense of individuals belonging to other groups." The danger of preferential programs, he asserted, is that they "may only reinforce common stereotypes holding that certain groups are unable to achieve success without special protection based on a factor having no relationship to individual worth."

Powell approvingly quoted Alexander Bickel, a prolific legal scholar at Yale University who had died in 1974. Coauthor of a brief on behalf of Marco DeFunis, Bickel viewed with concern the growing demand by government and civil rights groups for racial remedies, even in the absence of a constitutional violation. "The lesson of the great decisions of the Supreme Court," wrote Bickel, "and the lesson of contemporary history have been the same for at least a generation: discrimination on the basis of race is illegal, immoral, unconstitutional, inherently wrong, and destructive of democratic society. Now this is to be unlearned and we are told that this is not a matter of fundamental principle but only a matter of whose ox is gored. Those for whom racial equality was demanded are to be more equal than others. Having found support in the Constitution for equality, they now claim support for inequality under the same Constitution."[43]

Under what circumstances was the University of California entitled to consider the race of an applicant? Powell rejected any program whose purpose was to obtain a specified percentage of a racial or ethnic group in the student body: "Preferring members of any one group for no reason other than race or ethnic origin is discrimination for its own sake. This the Constitution forbids." Nor had the University of California demonstrated that racial classifications were appropriate in order to redress the injuries of societal discrimination or to improve the health-care services in underserved communities. However, Powell *was* persuaded that it was constitutionally permissible to take race into account as a way of achieving a diverse student body. Powell specifically commended Harvard University's admissions program, which avoided numbers or quotas, viewed all candidates as part of the same pool, but considered diversity of race or ethnic background as one element in selecting an entering class.

Because so much media attention had portrayed the case as a clash between the interests of minorities and those of the white majority, Bakke's personal victory was initially interpreted by civil rights spokesmen as a devastating setback. An NAACP official called it "a very sad day in the United States"; a Chicano official complained that the high court had removed the special protection that minorities had previously enjoyed; a black congressman called it "a racist decision by the Nixon court"; and the black-owned *Amsterdam News* in New York City ran the simple headline: "Bakke—We Lost." Other minority spokesmen, however, realized that little had been lost: Vernon Jordan of the National Urban League saw the decision as a "green light to go forward with acceptable affirmative action programs."[44]

Those in charge of implementing government affirmative action programs interpreted the decision as support for their activities. Eleanor

Holmes Norton, chairman of the Equal Employment Opportunity Commission (EEOC), said, "My reading of the decision is that we are not compelled to do anything differently from the way we've done things in the past, and we are not going to." Five months after the *Bakke* decision, EEOC issued new guidelines for affirmative action in which the *Bakke* decision was invoked to rebut those who continued to insist that employment decisions should be made "without consideration of race, color, religion, sex, or national origin." The lesson of *Bakke*, EEOC declared, was that the Supreme Court had approved consideration of such factors. Similarly, the chairman of the U. S. Commission on Civil Rights, Arthur Flemming, hailed the Supreme Court's "unequivocal support . . . for the consideration of race and ethnicity in admissions programs." To allay any further doubts, President Jimmy Carter issued a memorandum to all heads of government agencies advising them that the *Bakke* decision "enables us to continue" affirmative action programs "without interruption."[45]

The Supreme Court, perhaps to keep the matter in flux, avoided a definitive resolution of the issue in subsequent decisions in the late 1970s, but federal regulatory agencies pushed forward in their efforts to make statistical parity of groups the measure of "equal opportunity." By 1981, the U.S. Commission on Civil Rights had begun to gather data on "Euro-ethnic groups," which were defined as "the various and unique ethnic, religious, and nationality groups of Eastern and Southern Europe." In the offing, the commission implied, might be statistical analyses and affirmative action not just for blacks, women, Hispanics, Alaskan Natives, Asian or Pacific Islanders, and American Indians but for a whole new galaxy of minorities.[46]

The changes resulting from a decade of affirmative action in higher education are not easily assessed, largely because the effects of one policy are not clearly separable from the effects of other, concurrent policies and social trends. The enrollment of blacks and women in higher education and their receipt of advanced degrees rose substantially during the decade, a trend that was well underway before the onset of governmental pressure. Although most critics and proponents of affirmative action seemed to believe that institutions would be judged by whether their workforce reflected the proportion of women (50 percent) and blacks (11 percent) in the population, the actual changes in employment patterns in higher education by the end of the 1970s were far from those figures. Women, who had held about 20 percent of faculty positions during the 1960s, increased their share of faculty positions to 26 percent. Black representation on college and university faculties rose from approximately 3 percent in 1960 to 4.4 percent in 1979, a statistic that mirrored the limited supply of blacks with graduate degrees. According to an estimate by Harvard economist Richard B. Freeman, in 1973 blacks held 1.4 percent of all Ph.D. degrees. In the years from 1974 to 1980, about one thousand blacks received doctorate degrees each year, representing between 3 to 4 percent of new doctorates but not enough new degree-holders to augment substantially the number of black professors on the nation's twenty-five hundred campuses.[47]

While federal civil rights agencies shared a strong consensus about their mission, public opinion polls showed an equally strong consensus in opposition. In late 1980, after the issue had been thoroughly aired, only 10 percent of the Gallup Poll's sample believed that race, sex, and national origin should determine decisions about employment or college entry. The idea of group rights, regulated by the government, apparently was a political concept that most Americans—even most blacks and women—disliked. After a decade of discussion, few were convinced that the way to overcome a past in which benefits and burdens depended on race, sex, and national origin was to make permanent a system in which benefits and burdens depended on race, sex, and national origin.[48]

Since the early nineteenth century, the issue of equal rights for women had emerged periodically, usually in tandem with other social reform movements. It was not surprising, then, that militant feminism reappeared in the mid-1960s as factionalism within other protest movements. Activist women in the New Left and civil rights organizations, taking seriously the demands for equality and participatory democracy of their organizations, rebelled against their usual consignment to housekeeping functions within supposedly egalitarian movements. By the late 1960s, there were two different thrusts to the "new feminist movement." The public was most aware of the "Women's Liberationists," who specialized in the development of ideology and in the promulgation of consciousness-raising activities, through the formation of discussion groups, publications, films, and demonstrations. Women's Liberationists were relatively few in number, but attracted wide attention because of their flamboyance and studied outrageousness. WITCH (the Women's International Terrorist Conspiracy from Hell), with only a handful of members, captured headlines and television time by performing "guerrilla" theater in public places; other groups, like Redstockings, the Feminists, and the New York Radical Women, reflecting their radical origins, devised manifestoes, organized brigades, conducted ideology workshops, and debated such issues as the relationship of feminism to capitalism, to lesbianism, and to social relations within the family.[49]

Though temporarily overshadowed by the antics of the Liberationists, the other side of the new feminism—women's rights organizations—paved the way for momentous political and legal changes in the status of women in American society, and in time, absorbed the Women's Liberationists altogether. The National Organization for Women (NOW) was organized in 1966 to "take action to bring women into full participation in the mainstream of American society," and to "press for enforcement of laws which prohibit discrimination on the basis of sex." With chapters across the country, NOW persuaded President Johnson to revise his executive order to ban sex discrimination in the government and by federal contractors, lobbied for additional legislation against sex discrimination, and led the political battle for an Equal Rights Amendment to the Constitution, which was passed by the House of Representatives in 1971 and the Senate in 1972 (the amendment subsequently failed to receive the approval of three-quarters of the states, and it expired in 1982).[50]

NOW's political activities were enhanced by the establishment in 1968 of the Women's Equity Action League (WEAL), which pursued legal attacks against discriminatory practices in education, industry, and other institutions, and worked for legislative changes to strengthen the prohibition of sex discrimination. Hundreds of other feminist organizations were created in the late 1960s and early 1970s, including caucuses within professional organizations, women's groups on campuses and in industry, community-based organizations, centers for women's studies, and political-action committees to support legislation and promote the election of female candidates. Feminist publications, films, and books proliferated, and some, like Kate Millett's *Sexual Politics* and Germaine Greer's *The Female Eunuch,* reached a large popular audience. In addition, the spread of feminism on campus stimulated the production of hundreds of research studies documenting the existence of sex discrimination in education and society. A study published in 1974 reported the existence of nearly one hundred and thirty new feminist periodicals, most started in 1970 or 1971, and offered a sampling of the hundreds of articles, as well as books, newsletters, and bibliographies on the new feminism.[51]

As the issue of sex discrimination developed, the target of feminist anger was, to a marked degree, educational institutions. At one level, this focus was due to the stress that feminists placed on the way that schools "socialized" female students to accept an inferior status. But at another level, there was a practical consideration that directed special attention to education: an extraordinary proportion of feminist leaders were well-educated, middle-class and upper middle-class whites. One survey found that nearly 90 percent of the women's rights members had at least a B.A., and a third held graduate degrees. This suggests that most of them, though not disadvantaged by any measure, knew from their own experience that the university was, at its highest reaches, a male domain. As educated women, they turned naturally to education as the best possible lever in their campaign to reconstruct the social order.[52]

Perhaps the most remarkable achievement of the new feminism was that it was transformed in the span of a few years from the angry rhetoric of a few radical feminists to a political force to be reckoned with by both major parties. In 1970, Congresswoman Edith Green of Oregon opened hearings on discrimination in education. At that time, the major federal restraint on sex discrimination was contained in the presidential executive order requiring affirmative action and nondiscrimination. Green introduced a bill to prohibit sex discrimination in all federal programs. She proposed to amend the Civil Rights Act of 1964, which did not ban sex discrimination except in employment; to amend Title VII (the employment section of the Civil Rights Act) to remove the exemption enjoyed by educational institutions; to remove the exemption of executive, administrative, and professional employees from the Equal Pay Act; and to empower the U.S. Commission on Civil Rights to investigate discrimination against women. These changes, major items on the feminist agenda, would make institutions of higher education subject to the federal civil rights agencies, which were armed with the power to cut off their federal funds.

The Green hearings were considered a major landmark by feminists because for the first time their case against American education was presented in a prestigious forum. Witnesses testified to the underrepresentation of women in the higher levels of academic employment and to the exclusion of women from professional opportunities because of narrow conceptions of what was appropriate for women and men. The representative of WEAL complained that

> Half of the brightest people in this country—half of the most talented people with the potential for the highest intellectual endeavor are women. These women will encounter discrimination after discrimination as they try to use their talents in the university world.
>
> They will be discriminated against when they first apply for admission. They will be discriminated against when they apply for financial and scholarship aid. They will be discriminated against when they apply for positions on the faculty. If they are hired, they will be promoted far more slowly than their male counterparts; and furthermore, if hired at all, women will most likely receive far less money than their male colleagues.[53]

Others complained, in testimony recalling the by-now standard sociological arguments invoked by all minorities seeking special protection, that because of domination of the culture by males (blacks would say "whites," Hispanics would say "Anglos"), women were made to feel inferior, to have a negative self-image and lowered expectations. One speaker saw no contradiction between her statement that women at newly coeducational Yale University were "outdoing men by every measure of academic achievement" and her claim that women were psychically damaged by a "male-oriented, male-administered institution within an androcentric culture." Another witness called on Congress to "cure the causes" of sexism and denounced "the sexually negative atmosphere in which women live and work," which was characterized by "psychological warfare . . . [and] daily propaganda with regard to [women's] intrinsic weaknesses and inferiority." One speaker based her claim for federal intervention on the need to curb overpopulation. Contraceptives, she held, would not be enough: "Unless women have, from the moment of birth, socialization for, expectations of, and preparation for a viable significant alternative to motherhood as their chief adult occupation, women will continue to want and reproduce too many children instead of producing ideas, art, literature, leadership, inventions, and healthier social relationships." She argued, further, that "the only job for which no women can or could be qualified is sperm donor. The only job or jobs for which no man is or can be qualified would be human incubator or wet nurse, period."[54]

The leitmotifs expressed at the Green hearings came to characterize the rhetoric and activity of the decade ahead: that women had low self-esteem because of discrimination by males; that the principle of proportional representation was a proper measure of discrimination; that the federal government had a responsibility to correct statistical imbalances in university employment; and that, while there was much discussion of the plight of low-income women, the most compelling arena for federal concern about sex discrimination must be higher education.

Although the bill containing Congresswoman Green's amendment failed to pass in the summer of 1970, a victim of campus turmoil, by 1972 the women's movement had achieved its major legislative goals. Title IX of the Higher Education Act of 1972 stated that "no person in the United States shall, on the basis of sex, be excluded from participation in, be denied the benefits of, or be subjected to discrimination under any education program or activity receiving Federal financial assistance. . . ." The only exemptions were for single-sex undergraduate institutions, religious institutions, and military academies. In the same session, Congress amended Title VII of the Civil Rights Act of 1964 (which banned employment discrimination) to remove the exemption enjoyed by educational institutions and revised the Equal Pay Act of 1963 to remove the exemption of executive and professional employees. Educational institutions did not object, perhaps because the liberality and fair-mindedness on which they prided themselves made it unreasonable to question the goal of equality for women. Certainly they did not realize that Title IX was far more sweeping in its implications than affirmative action or any other grant of federal power over educational institutions.[55]

A combination of demographic, economic, and social factors had drawn women out of the labor market after World War II. During the postwar period of prosperity and low unemployment, women married earlier, fertility rates rose, suburbs grew, and many women stayed home to raise the children of the baby boom, which continued into the early 1960s. At the same time, college enrollments and university faculties experienced dramatic growth; the coinciding of the expansion of higher education and the baby boom meant that a large number of young women were caring for young children while their male peers participated in the great increase of new students and new faculty members. Although the number of female Ph.D.s grew steadily each year, the actual proportion of female doctorates declined in relation to that of male Ph.D.s, which soared to meet the demand for college professors and industrial researchers. Thus, in 1945/46, women received 19.1 percent of the doctorates awarded, but the proportion of female doctorates declined each year until the late 1950s. In 1970, women received only 13.3 percent of the doctorates awarded that year and held only 11.6 percent of all the doctorates awarded since 1930. Since women held about 20 percent of all full-time faculty positions in 1970, they were actually *overrepresented* relative to the number of women with doctorates.[56]

However, female professors were concentrated in the lower ranks of the faculty, as instructors and assistant professors, and they were clustered in certain traditionally "female" fields, like education, social work, library science, and nursing, where there were large numbers of women with advanced degrees. To some extent, the slow advancement of female professors resulted from the work patterns of married women, who left the labor market while their children were infants or received their degrees later than men of the same age in order to start a family or, because of family responsibilities, worked part-time or published fewer articles. The disproportionate number of female faculty members in the so-called "female" fields was due in part to their discriminatory exclusion from fields like medicine, law, and business, but it was also attributable to the fact that these were fields where the demands on one's time could be blended with family responsibilities.

Just as demography, economics, and social attitudes had merged in the postwar era to emphasize the role of women as homemakers, so did comparably powerful trends intersect in the late 1960s to bring women into the labor force and to oppose artificial barriers to women's occupational achievement. As the baby boom ended and as families sought to improve their economic situations, women's labor-force participation grew rapidly, including substantial numbers of women with school-age children and even preschool children. After 1960, the birthrate dropped; family size fell; the number of women who were single, widowed, or divorced increased; and women were marrying at a later age. At the same time, women students were staying in school longer, and beginning in 1976, more women entered college than men. With substantial numbers of women in the labor force (50 percent of women by 1978) and in higher education, occupations where women had been excluded or limited in the past by nothing more than "tradition" came under severe challenge.[57]

While education was supposedly a woman's field, not many women made it to the top. In public schools, where the preponderance of teachers were women, there were few female superintendents or principals. In higher education, there were only a handful of female college presidents or administrators. In the prestigious research universities, there were many departments that were all-male, even though a substantial number of their graduate students were women. Although many states had already equalized the pay scales for men and women doing the same job in public institutions, many colleges and universities paid women less on the common assumption that the head of a family (male) needed more income.[58]

After Congress expanded the prohibition against sex discrimination to cover educational institutions and professional positions in 1972, many institutions were sued by female faculty members and compelled to award them back pay, salary adjustments, and promotions. A number of standard practices became illegal because of Title IX. Anti-nepotism rules, adopted to prevent the hiring of faculty spouses, were declared to be discriminatory against women. OCR informed schools and universities that they could no longer spend disproportionate amounts of money on boys' athletics, nor award more scholarships to male athletes; they were also told that they must not favor male students in allocating financial aid. Nor could residential institutions enforce different parietal rules for girls' dormitories and boys' dormitories. Vocational education programs were advised that they could no longer steer men and women to different occupational activities. Beginning in 1973, OCR directed campuses and school districts to report whether there were any classes "comprised of [sic] 80% or more of students of one sex," presumably to identify potentially discriminatory activities.[59]

The legal guarantees won in 1972 set off a round of litigation and formal complaints to federal agencies, but still did not get to the heart of the matter. What remained after the laws were rewritten and enforced was sexism, the attitudes of males toward females, and even of females toward themselves. This, the leaders of the movement decided, must also be an issue for the federal government. So in the fall of 1973, Senator Walter Mondale conducted hearings on the Women's Educational Equity Act, which he sponsored. The purpose of the act was to provide federal funds for the development of nonsexist curricula and to support education, training, and research activities related to women; any organization or group could apply for federal funds, even one that had been in existence for less than a year. Representatives from several feminist organizations explained that it was essential to "counter sexism in education." It was clear that what they and Senator Mondale had in mind was "a national consciousness-raising concerning women's status and roles." Witnesses described how girls were taught to accept sex-role stereotyping by their teachers and textbooks:

> From the time a young girl enters school she learns more than just reading, writing, and arithmetic. Her textbooks are far more likely to be written about boys and men; girls and women are rarely major characters. She will read about boys who do interesting, exciting things; they build rafts and tree-houses; they have challenging adventures and solve problems, and they rescue girls who are "so stupid" that they get into trouble. One typical book pictures a 14-year-old girl standing on a chair, screaming because there is a frog on the floor; her 8-year-old brother rescues her.

Not only did girls see themselves depicted as weak and passive, but readers showed mothers in aprons, staying home all day as housewives. The witness complained that the "lives and talents and aspirations" of half the population "are crippled by a society which sees them as second-class citizens." When a witness told Senator Mondale about discrimination against women with advanced degrees at the University of Minnesota, he responded, "I cannot help but be struck by the almost identical recitation of problems in the civil rights movement, it is almost the same, the textbooks, poverty, the whole thing."[60]

It was not just textbooks and attitudes that the women's movement wanted to change, not just the male-orientation of the English language, in which "mankind" represented men and women and in which the pronoun "he" stood for each person, but the position of women in American life. The speaker from NOW expressed her contempt for the kind of education that women received in American universities:

What the universities are offering is an education designed to turn out efficient little suburban housewives with a minor marketable skill so they can be secondary earners until the babies come, with enough liberal arts so they can enrich their children's lives and not disgrace themselves in front of husband's business associates, so they can read Book of the Month, listen to Walter Cronkite, and participate with other housewives in a little steam-cleaned, organized, community good works.[61]

Concern about sex-role stereotyping in textbooks was so great, the director of OCR informed Senator Mondale, that he convened a meeting in October, 1973, "with representatives of major textbook publishing firms to discuss the sex stereotyping issue. As of now we believe that in order to realize corrective action on a broad scale, OCR must seek the cooperation of textbook publishers." Apparently OCR never wondered whether this kind of pressure from the government might be an invasion of the publishers' First Amendment rights. On the contrary, OCR sent Senator Mondale copies of an exchange with the superintendent of schools of Kalamazoo, Michigan, informing him that a complaint had been filed alleging that the district had violated Title IX by adopting readers that contained sex stereotypes. While OCR had not yet decided whether the use of such textbooks was covered by Title IX, it asked the superintendent to explain why these books had been selected. The superintendent responded with a six-page, single-spaced letter, defending the district's textbook adoption procedures, presenting a new "count" of the number of female characters portrayed in the series, promising to drop "certain words and questions" from the teachers' guides, and assuring OCR of the inclusion of new material that had the approval of such publishers as the Feminist Press. In his eagerness to avoid a federal investigation, the superintendent never questioned whether OCR had the right to monitor the district's choice of textbooks.[62]

Although the Nixon administration was not enthusiastic about the Women's Educational Equity Act, its own Office of Education prepared a lengthy report stating that women were second-class citizens, subjected to "exploitation and exclusion" along with "ethnic minorities, the handicapped and the poor." With virtually no opposition, the act passed in 1974, creating a twenty-member National Advisory Council on Women's Educational Programs (although HEW already had a nineteen-member Advisory Committee on the Rights and Responsibilities of Women). From 1976 to 1982, nearly $55 million was appropriated to the Women's Educational Equity Program, which granted funds to state and local education agencies, colleges and universities, nonprofit organizations, and individuals, to produce nonsexist textbooks, curricula, instructional materials, and other feminist educational activities.[63]

Legislation at the federal level was complemented by vigorous activity at the local level. Feminist critics studied children's books and textbooks for evidence of sex bias, counting the number of times girls or boys appeared in illustrations or as the major character in a story, the kinds of occupations or activities in which the different sexes were shown, and whether girls and boys were portrayed with "feminine" and "masculine" personalities. Through publications and NOW locals, feminists circulated lists of "sex-stereotyped" books; across the nation, parent groups and feminist organizations demanded the removal of "sexist" textbooks and stories. In Seattle, the school system launched a major study of sex-role stereotyping in every grade, "from teacher attitudes to textbooks." Teacher-training seminars were held in Ann Arbor, Michigan, where role reversal was practiced: "Male teachers served the coffee." Education journals featured articles exploring sex bias in every aspect of the classroom—in the social studies curriculum, history books, Dick-and-Jane readers, math and science textbooks, toys, standardized tests, and of course, in the sex-stereotyped placement of boys in auto mechanics and girls in home economics.[64]

Assertions to the contrary, it was impossible to demonstrate that girls were, in fact, "damaged" by textbooks that quoted men more often than women or by readers that showed mothers as housewives. Since girls achieved at least as well as boys (and usually better), both in school and in college, there was no evidence that the depiction of women in schoolbooks had destroyed the self-esteem or motivation of female students. Girls and boys finished high school in roughly the same proportions in 1970; more males finished college and received advanced degrees. Clearly, the intervening variables were demographic factors like women's age at marriage and the fertility rate, not the language of readers. To the extent that women married young and bore children early in their marriage, they were less likely to attain advanced degrees, less likely to be in the labor force, and more likely to earn less than men who had worked continuously. Nor was labor force discrimination against women in any way comparable to the situation of blacks and Hispanics, for by 1970, 60.5 percent of all white-collar jobs were held by women. Like the claim that bilingual education improved children's self-esteem, the charge that sex-role stereotyping in the school "damaged" girls' psyches was inherently untestable. It was a value statement about how things should be, and, like any other ideological concept, it was not open to proof or disproof.[65]

Feminists won their most significant victory in their efforts to "desex" the English language. Common usage, they charged, expressed sex bias and reinforced male domination of the culture. Why were women addressed as "Mrs." or "Miss," which identified them by their marital status, while all men were "Mr."? Why shouldn't all women be referred to by the neutral address "Ms."? Why did so many occupations have the suffix "-man" attached, thereby excluding women who might otherwise aspire to be a policeman, fireman, postman, or salesman? Why was the leader of a meeting the chair*man*? How could women not feel diminished when they constantly read and heard descriptions of "man's history," "the story of mankind," and similar male-oriented references. And then there was the nettlesome problem of the male referent ("each person has his book"), a practice dictated by standard English grammar.

Under pressure from feminists, the federal government adopted sex-neutral terminology in the mid-1970s; the title "Ms." and words like "personpower" and "personhours" entered the federal vocabulary. Professional associations devised guidelines to cleanse their journals of sexist language, especially by eliminating the generic use of "man," as a suffix, a pronoun, or a term for humankind. The American Psychological Association, for example, advised contributors not to use phrases like "mankind," or "the average man," or a verb like "to man a project"; the National Council of Teachers of English suggested avoiding the use of terms like "man-made" or "the common man" or "old wives' tale." Between 1974 and 1977, sensitivity to disturbances in the marketplace prompted such major publishers as McGraw-Hill; Scott, Foresman; John Wiley; Holt, Rinehart, and Winston; Harper and Row; and Prentice-Hall to publish guidelines to nonsexist language for their authors and editors.[66]

The enactment in 1972 of Title IX, which banned sex discrimination in all educational activities and programs receiving federal funds, and the revision of Title VII of the Civil Rights Act to bar sex discrimination in educational institutions put the full force of federal law and the federal civil rights bureaucracy on the side of the women's cause. Women who were denied promotion or tenure turned to the federal government or the courts for assistance. Sometimes a complaint to OCR or EEOC was sufficient to trigger a major compliance review of an institution, which would create enough pressure to compel a settlement in order to avoid a costly law suit. The threat of litigation was itself a powerful weapon: Brown University settled out of court after it was sued by a female professor who was denied tenure; even without a court battle or an admission of guilt, the university paid more than $1 million in legal fees.[67]

The increase of litigation required educational institutions to develop new administrative positions in order to handle legal challenges and to negotiate with federal and state agencies. WEAL filed suit against the systems of public higher education in seven states. A professor at the University of Georgia who refused to divulge how he had voted on a promotion decision involving a female professor was sent to jail for three months by a federal judge who rejected the claim that academic freedom protected the confidentiality of the academic review process. According to the Project on the Status and Education of Women, an organization created to monitor the progress of women, a public high school in North Carolina and a religious school in Iowa were ordered to reinstate teachers who had been fired because they were pregnant and unmarried; a federal court in California ordered several public colleges to provide day-care centers, because their failure to do so excluded women from participation; female coaches sued Washington State University, complaining that male coaches received a free car; female athletes sued West Texas State University on the grounds that outside "booster clubs" were providing extra scholarships for male athletes; and female basketball players sued the University of Alaska, charging that the men's team got newer uniforms and a bigger budget than did the women's team. Although athletic programs did not receive federal funds, the regulations written for Title IX directed educational institutions to spend the same amount on sports for men and women (however, certain sports—like wrestling, football, and basketball—did not have to be available to both sexes). Even unsuccessful suits, such as those based on the claim that the university's requirement of a Ph.D. discriminated against women because more men had such degrees than women, involved costly legal proceedings.[68]

The enforcement of Title IX brought federal regulations onto every campus, public and private, in the nation. Affirmative action, which applied to institutions receiving federal contracts or grants, covered only nine hundred of nearly three thousand institutions of higher education. Title IX was interpreted by HEW officials to cover every educational institution that received even indirect forms of federal assistance, like federal student loans or veterans' benefits. A handful of institutions of higher education that had never received federal contracts refused to sign the Title IX compliance form; charging that refusal to comply was itself a violation of Title IX, HEW threatened to cut off all student aid to these campuses and successfully sued the recalcitrant institutions in the lower federal courts.[69]

The new presence of the federal government and courts on the campus stimulated debate about governmental intervention in faculty personnel decisions and threats to academic freedom. The tendency of the government to treat the university like any other government contractor alarmed those who shared a view stated in one of the Supreme Court's McCarthy-era decisions:

> It is the business of a university to provide that atmosphere which is most conducive to speculation, experiment and creation. It is an atmosphere in which there prevail 'the four essential freedoms' of a university—to determine for itself on academic grounds who may teach, what may be taught, how it shall be taught, and who may be admitted to study.[70]

Traditionally, universities were zealous of their independence from any government control, fearful that government might stifle free thought or use the resources of the university for partisan purposes. Decisions to hire, fire, promote, or grant tenure to faculty members were customarily made by the faculty, using a confidential peer review process. In their own fashion, universities were as autonomous from government regulation as churches, because both vigilantly resisted infringement of their autonomy.

The growth of government regulation, designed for beneficent purposes, gave government investigators powers over higher education that they had never exercised before. Confidential personnel records, rigorously protected from the eyes of the FBI and state investigators during the McCarthy years, were opened to investigators from EEOC and the Department of Labor who were looking for evidence of sex discrimination. In 1972, an EEOC official admitted to a meeting of leaders of higher education that her agency knew little about "how faculty decisions are made; what employment processes exist," but assured them "that the Commission will attempt to apply what it has learned in seven years of combatting job discrimination in the industrial sector." At the same meeting, a feminist leader complained that "academic freedom" and "institutional autonomy" were "smokescreens" thrown up by universities to protect the "old boy" method of recruiting. Her subject was "Affirmative Action on the Campus: Like It or Not, Uncle Sam Is Here to Stay."[71]

One person who did not like affirmative action was former Congresswoman Edith Green of Oregon, the original proponent of Title IX. She was "surprised and dismayed" to learn that the ban against sex discrimination had become the basis for "reverse discrimination" favoring women. In 1977, no longer a member of Congress, she said that when Title IX was written, "we sought to be exceedingly explicit so that the establishment of quotas would be prohibited." She considered the distinction between "quotas" and "goals" to be "a game of semantics." She could not understand "the reasoning that now leads well intentioned people, in simplistic zeal, to institute reverse quotas. Do they believe that one injustice deserves another? Is the basis of judgment to be 'merit' or some strict ethnic or sex formula?" Of course, Title IX was not the source of affirmative action, but Title IX was interpreted by the civil rights bureaucracy as congressional authorization to extend the federal regulatory reach to virtually every campus in the nation.[72]

The interpretation of Title IX took a new turn in the late 1970s, when "sexual harassment" became an important issue. A Yale student sued a professor who had allegedly given her a lower grade after she had resisted his sexual advances; a federal judge dismissed the case because the student could not prove that the improper offer had been made or that she had been adversely affected. Other suits quickly followed, as students sued their professors and as female professors claimed that they had been denied promotion or tenure for refusing to have sexual relations with male professors. A survey of five hundred women who had received their doctorates in psychology in the previous six years revealed that one out of four had engaged in sexual relations with a professor, compared with only five percent who had received their degrees twenty-one or more years ago. Patricia Harris, the secretary of HEW, declared that sexual harassment was "a component of sex discrimination"; the Department of Labor issued guidelines prohibiting sexual harassment in the workplace; and EEOC instructed all federal agencies to prepare plans and to develop training programs to prevent sexual harassment. EEOC defined sexual harassment as "explicit or implicit unwelcome verbal or physical conduct of a sexual nature." The president of the University of Miami warned that sexist remarks would not be tolerated, and the university's women's commission agreed to meet with a professor who made sexist jokes, in order to devise a "joke guideline" to impermissible humor. A survey at the University of Florida revealed that 31 percent of women graduate students and 26 percent of women undergraduates reported sexual advances by professors. Meanwhile, on several campuses, male faculty members launched countersuits, claiming they had been libeled; and charges of McCarthyism were leveled at student organizations that kept secret lists of professors who were suspected to be sexual harassers.[73]

After a decade of decisive action by the federal government against sex discrimination, the barriers that had blocked women's educational and occupational advance were breached. Women outnumbered men among undergraduates, received 28 percent of the doctorate degrees by 1978/79, and accounted for 25 percent of the enrollment in legal and medical schools. (In a few medical schools, like Michigan State University, women were a majority of the entering class.) By 1981, there had been substantial increases in the number of female engineers, lawyers, judges, doctors, pharmacists, scientists, and insurance adjusters. Women who were full-time faculty members in colleges and universities increased from about 20 percent in 1970/71 to 26.4 percent in 1980/81. During the same period the number of women who were full professors edged up from 8.6 percent to 10.2 percent, a reflection of the low rate of turnover among tenured faculty.[74]

Many of these changes could be attributed to the effects of the feminist movement, insofar as it had stimulated women's ambitions, encouraging them to enter nontraditional fields and to compete on equal terms with men. Its influence may also have contributed to the marked shift of such vital demographic barometers as low birth rates and the higher age of women at marriage. That the changes of the 1970s represented a readjustment of the social structure rather than a revolutionary dissolution of sex roles was indicated by the fact that a majority of women who received advanced degrees majored in such traditionally female fields as education, social sciences, literature, home economics, fine arts, and library science.[75]

For women, the changes of the 1970s were substantial, as measured by degrees and occupational diversification. Even more substantial, however, was the changed relationship of the federal government to higher education; through the issue of sex discrimination, federal agencies gained access to confidential personnel records, compelled universities to divulge tenure deliberations, and caused the creation of new bureaucratic structures within the university to supervise their orders. In one university, a federal investigator surreptitiously monitored classes for evidence of bias in professors' lectures. By 1980, federal regulatory authority reached into every institution of higher education in the nation, even those that had never accepted federal contracts. This substantial encroachment on institutional autonomy, so long considered a necessary component of academic freedom, would have been resisted tooth-and-nail in the 1950s; because government purposes in the 1970s were perceived to be beneficent, the new order was quickly effectuated.[76]

The activities of the civil rights movement in the field of education provided a valuable model for others who sought structural change. The civil rights movement argued persuasively that blacks had been victimized by American schools and that the prejudice of local school officials made federal and judicial intervention necessary. The case for intervention rested on the documentation of the educational and social disadvantages suffered by blacks and the reasonable charge that those responsible for such injuries could not be trusted to rectify them. Advocates of bilingual education and the feminist movement adapted their strategies to the civil rights model because it offered a way not only to bypass local and state education authorities but to compel these officials to accept rules over which they had little control. The success of the strategy depended on the ability of the interest groups to ally themselves with congressmen on relevant committees and to gain a permanent voice within the executive branch to advocate their concerns regardless of who was president (for racial minorities—and after 1972, for women—this voice was the Commission on Civil Rights, OCR, and EEOC; for women, the National Advisory Council on Women's Educational Programs; and for linguistic minorities, the Office of Bilingual Education). Once these relationships were established, interest groups were able to dominate hearings on issues that concerned them and to have considerable influence when new legislation was under consideration or when new regulations were drafted.

In one important instance, the model itself helped to create a constituency that had not previously coalesced. Recognizing the effectiveness of the methods of the civil rights movement, advocates for handicapped children began to coordinate their political activities. When Congress passed its first comprehensive federal aid program in 1965, most organizations for the handicapped were busy fighting for programs and funds at the state and local level, often with disunity among the different organizations representing children who were deaf, crippled, blind, mentally retarded, and otherwise handicapped. Handicapped children could rightly claim the status of a neglected minority. Depending on the kind and degree of handicap, some children had been entirely excluded from the benefits of public education or had been placed in special classes with little opportunity to learn with nonhandicapped children. The critical needs were, first, to get all handicapped children into publicly supported educational programs; second, to train enough teachers to staff such programs; and third, to pay for both.

After 1965, advocates for the handicapped concentrated their efforts at the federal level. They sought an expansion of federal funding, but more significantly, they wanted the federal government to require the states to provide a free and appropriate public education to all handicapped children, as a matter of right. The handicapped constituency was composed of numerous organizations representing specific disabilities, as well as groups like the National Association for Retarded Citizens, which had been formed in 1950 by families of handicapped children, and the Council for Exceptional Children, which was the voice of special education professionals. There was no accurate count of the number of handicapped children, but, depending on how the term was defined and whether it included learning disabilities as well as physical and mental impairments, congressional staff and witnesses estimated that between five and eight million children were handicapped.[77]

Advocates for the handicapped proceeded to wage a brilliant political campaign for federal protection. Their assets were considerable. They represented the interests of the handicapped with deep conviction, and seldom did anyone oppose their demands. In addition, it is probable that almost every congressman had a friend or relative who was handicapped. The educational needs of handicapped children were beyond challenge, as well as beyond the resources of most states and local school districts. The question was not whether the federal government would assist the handicapped, but how this assistance would be framed and at what cost.

In 1966, the Democratic Congress established a Bureau of Education for the Handicapped (BEH), which was placed within the Office of Education in HEW, and created a National Advisory Committee on Education and Training of the Handicapped. This was a critical victory, because both BEH and the National Advisory Committee functioned (and were intended to function) as advocacy agencies for the handicapped within the federal government. The lobbyists for the handicapped worked closely with the education committees in the House and the Senate, and each body eventually created a subcommittee on the handicapped to prepare legislation. In 1970, the Congress passed new legislation, increasing the amount of federal aid for education of the handicapped and expanding the definition of "handicapped" to include learning-disabled children, such as those with perceptual problems and dyslexia.[78]

It was not simply money but a federal mandate that was needed, so the battle shifted to the federal courts, where handicapped plaintiffs won two important decisions. In 1971, the state of Pennsylvania was sued on behalf of severely retarded children who were not receiving public schooling; the state accepted a consent decree by a federal court, which required the state to provide a free public education to all retarded children in the state between the ages of six and twenty-one and established extensive due process mechanisms to provide for hearings, appeals, and continual monitoring. In 1972, the federal court in the District of Columbia held that under the due process clause of the Fifth Amendment to the Constitution every school-age child in the district must be provided with "a free and suitable publicly-supported education regardless of the degree of a child's mental, physical or emotional disability or impairment."[79]

After these legal victories, the Congress passed the Rehabilitation Act of 1973, which included Section 504, the handicapped person's equivalent of Title VI of the Civil Rights Act of 1964. Section 504 requires that

> No otherwise qualified handicapped individual in the United States . . . shall, solely by reason of his handicap, be excluded from participation in, be denied the benefits of, or be subjected to discrimination under any program or activity receiving Federal financial assistance.

Under Section 504, every recipient of federal funds was required to provide full access to the handicapped, without discrimination, and enforcement became the responsibility of OCR. The potential cost of 504 evoked substantial opposition, the most serious that the handicapped movement had encountered. President Nixon vetoed the bill, but the Democratic Congress overrode his veto. Enforcement was delayed during the Nixon and Ford administrations because of HEW's failure to draft regulations (even Joseph Califano, the secretary of HEW in the Democratic Carter administration, hesitated until a vociferous protest in his office by handicapped demonstrators changed his mind).[80]

The passage of 504 over the president's veto demonstrated that the handicapped interest groups were part of what political scientists call "the iron triangle." They had forged close relationships, as one study of legislation for the handicapped shows, with the staff and members of the congressional education committees and with the federal agency officers responsible for administering programs for the handicapped. Congressional staff worked with the representatives of the handicapped to develop new legislation, BEH urged stronger enforcement and more funds, and spokesmen for the interest groups were well prepared whenever hearings were called or when new regulations were being drafted. So well-organized and articulate was the constituency for the handicapped that Congress passed its legislation by overwhelming, bipartisan majorities.[81]

The most significant victory for handicapped children was the passage in 1975 of Public Law 94–142, titled the "Education for All Handicapped Children Act." Although the interest groups knew that "lack of funds, personnel, and an adequate delivery system were all real problems," they determined that such constraints should not prevent passage of tough mechanisms to compel states and local districts to supply services to all handicapped children. The basic purpose of Public Law 94–142 was to assure that all handicapped children receive "a free appropriate public education which emphasizes special education and related services designed to meet their unique needs." The act has been described as "probably the most prescriptive education statute ever passed by Congress." It is written "in the sort of detail that is generally found in regulations, not in statutes." The law required that each handicapped child receive an "individualized education program," which was defined as a written statement for each handicapped child . . . which statement shall include (A) a statement of the present levels of education performance of such child, (B) a statement of annual goals, including short-term instructional objectives, (C) a statement of the specific educational services to be provided to such child, and the extent to which such child will be able to participate in regular educational programs, (D) the projected date for initiation and anticipated duration of such services, and (E) appropriate objective criteria and evaluation procedures and schedules for determining, on at least an annual basis, whether instructional objectives are being achieved.

The law also contained elaborate due process safeguards for parents, so that any questionable action by the school or teacher would be subject to a speedy appeals process and litigation. Congress declared its intention to pay for a portion of the "excess costs" of special education, beyond the cost of the regular school program; the portion was supposed to start at 5 percent of costs, then rise in time up to 40 percent.[82]

Education for the handicapped, a program that had been beyond criticism for nearly a decade, was soon plunged into controversy. The cost to local districts put a strain on budgets around the nation at a time of rising inflation. In addition to hiring new personnel trained in special education and creating affirmative action plans to hire handicapped workers, districts had to bear the expense of eliminating architectural barriers to the handicapped and of paying tuition for severely handicapped children in private schools. School officials had supported the federal commitment on the assumption that the Congress would be willing to fund what it mandated. However, the congressional mandate was never matched even at the levels of partial funding that had been promised. Because of the Carter administration's efforts to reduce the federal budget, funding levels for the program never exceeded 12.5 percent of the districts' costs. Inevitably, local school budgets increased to satisfy the law's costs, which were often met by reducing services to nonhandicapped children. One writer described it as resembling "a regulation by the city council that you take your next-door-neighbor to dinner twice a week and pay for it out of your own pocket."[83]

Cost was not the only problem. The law mandated that handicapped children were to be educated with children who were not handicapped, "to the maximum extent appropriate." This became known as the requirement to "mainstream" handicapped children in "the least restrictive environment." Some parents of handicapped children preferred special schools; special education teachers wondered if mainstreaming might lead to renewed neglect or might threaten their jobs; regular teachers worried about their ability to teach classes that included children with physical and emotional impairments; and parents of nonhandicapped children feared that their children's education would be neglected or diluted. In addition, school officials and teacher organizations complained about the time and paperwork required by preparation of the "individualized education plan" and objected that the plan might be considered a legally binding contract, providing grist for new litigation.[84]

Uncertainty about the scope of the federal laws was settled to some extent by two Supreme Court decisions. In 1979, the Court ruled unanimously that a North Carolina college was not required by Section 504 to accept a deaf woman into its nursing program; her handicap disqualified her because "the ability to understand speech without reliance on lip reading is necessary for patient safety." Section 504, the Court held, "imposes no requirement upon an educational institution to lower or to affect substantial modifications of standards to accommodate a handicapped person." In 1982, in the first major test of Public Law 94-142, the Supreme Court held in a 6-to-3 decision that a school district in New York was not required to provide a sign-language interpreter for a deaf fourth-grader. Since the child was performing above average in regular classrooms and receiving special services, the Court concluded that her education was "appropriate." The intent of Congress, said the majority, was "more to open the door of public education to handicapped children on appropriate terms than to guarantee any particular level of education once inside."[85]

These decisions allayed the fears of educational authorities that the new legal requirements would prove unworkable but did not by any means relieve the obligation of educational institutions to educate all handicapped students. Nor did it relieve anxiety that local school districts would be left by Congress with an expensive, bureaucratic mandate but without the federal funds to comply, a scenario for endless litigation and disappointed hopes.

By the spring of 1980, OCR reported that more than 4 million handicapped children—representing 98 percent of all students in need of special education—had been evaluated and placed in special education programs in accordance with Public Law 94-142, far fewer than originally anticipated by Congress. Nearly two-thirds of the handicapped enrollment in local school districts consisted of children with specific learning disabilities or speech impairments. Almost 70 percent of the handicapped students were enrolled in regular classes. The programs were still underfunded and still capable of provoking resentment by parents of nonhandicapped children in a time of declining educational resources. But, nonetheless, in a short period of time, advocates of handicapped children had skillfully entered the political arena to establish the right of all children, whatever their condition, to a free public education.[86]

Whoever the claimant, whether representing blacks, women, the handicapped, or non–English-speaking minority groups, the avenue of political remedy was the same: to bypass educational authorities by working directly with sympathetic congressional committees and by gaining judicial supervision. Each victory led to the imposition of mandates on school and university officials, requiring them to do promptly what they otherwise would have done slowly, reluctantly, or not at all. By their very nature, these outside interventions diminished the authority of educational administrators, not only leaving them with less discretion but also introducing new levels of bureaucracy and new staff to administer the federally mandated programs and to determine whether the multiple federal, state, and local requirements had been met.

By the end of the 1970s, the universities had adjusted to the new relationship with the federal government, largely because it had so little bearing on the life of the average professor. Demands for affirmative action for women, blacks, and members of other minority groups were, as it turned out, easily deflected or absorbed because the available pool of female and minority-group professors with appropriate professional qualifications was extremely low in those fields where underrepresentation was most typical.

However, the public schools did not adjust easily or quickly to the new programs of the 1970s. For one thing, unlike college professors, who could go on teaching as they always had, schoolteachers were directly affected by some aspect of the new situation—by the introduction of bilingual education; by the mainstreaming of mildly retarded children into their classrooms; by busing of school children or by reassignment of teachers for racial balance; by the removal of a textbook because it was offensive to some particular group; by the splitting of history into courses on ethnic groups or women; or by the ethnic revival, which some professional educators joined by declaring that all students have the "right to their own patterns and varieties of language—the dialects of their nurture or whatever dialects in which they find their own identity and style."[87]

Besieged as they were by the rapidity of change, the public schools sustained yet another blow when the College Board revealed in 1975 that scores on the Scholastic Aptitude Test (SAT), taken each year by more than a million high school seniors, had declined steadily since 1964. More than any other single factor, the public's concern about the score declines touched off loud calls for instruction in "the basics" of reading, writing, and arithmetic. Complaints about lax standards in the schools increased in

1977 when the College Board's own blue-ribbon panel reported that, though the causes of the score declines were many and complex, they certainly included the findings "(1) that less thoughtful and critical reading is now being demanded and done, and (2) that careful writing has apparently about gone out of style." In response to public complaints and demands to restore "the basics," thirty-eight state legislatures passed laws requiring public schools to administer minimum competency tests in the basic skills.[88]

At the end of a decade in which interest groups, the courts, and the federal government had said repeatedly through enactments, directives, and court orders that the schools, if left to themselves, could not be trusted to do the right thing, it was somehow fitting, though at the same time profoundly sad, that the state legislatures communicated to the schools that they could no longer be trusted to do the very thing that everyone assumed schools did first and best: the teaching of literacy.

After the mid-1960s, well-intended efforts to improve, reform, or regulate educational institutions increased by leaps and bounds, and almost every level of government as well as numerous private organizations joined the fray. After generations of stand-offishness, federal lawmakers rolled up their sleeves: between 1964 and 1976, the number of pages of federal legislation affecting education increased from 80 to 360, while the number of federal regulations increased from 92 in 1965 to nearly 1,000 in 1977. Some of these legislative interventions had unintended consequences. The Buckley Amendment, for example, sponsored by a Conservative party senator from New York, was intended to protect the rights of students by opening their educational records to them; in reality, it meant that letters of recommendation could no longer be confidential, which destroyed their candor and made them worthless to college admissions officials (thereby giving added weight to SAT scores).[89]

The federal courts, of course, became deeply involved in educational matters: the number of federal court decisions affecting education numbered only 112 between 1946 and 1956, rose to 729 from 1956 to 1966, and climbed to "in excess of 1,200 in the next four years." There seemed to be no educational issue outside the courts' purview. In 1975, the Supreme Court ruled that a student could not be suspended from a public school in Ohio for even a single day without a hearing; the dissenting minority complained that for the first time "the federal courts, rather than educational officials and state legislatures" had assumed "the authority to determine the rules applicable to routine classroom discipline of children and teenagers." In Ann Arbor, Michigan, a federal judge required the school system to train teachers in Black English. In California, a federal judge banned the use of intelligence tests to place minority children in classes for the mentally retarded and ordered the state to "eliminate disproportionate placement of black children" in such classes. In Pennsylvania, federal courts ruled that public schooling must be provided for seriously handicapped children all-year round, not just 180 days per year. A university was ordered to reinstate a medical student who had been expelled for poor academic performance because the university had never formally defined what "marginal quality" meant. No matter seemed too far-fetched to bring suit, even though some were unsuccessful, like the Princeton senior who sued the university for denying her a diploma as a penalty for plagiarism or the high school graduates who sued their school districts for educational malpractice when they realized that they were illiterate.[90]

Some issues, like school finance reform, involved state courts, federal courts, interest groups, and state legislatures. The purpose of the school finance reform movement was to equalize school expenditures within states. Most states financed local public schools by relying largely on local property taxes. Even though the states often contributed additional revenues to offset the advantages of wealthy districts, wealthy districts generally had more money to spend on public schools than did poor districts. The first major victory of the school reform movement was the case of *Serrano* v. *Priest* in 1971, when the California Supreme Court ruled that it was unconstitutional to base the quality of a child's education on "the wealth of his parents and neighbors." Similar suits, challenging the property-tax basis of public school finance, were filed in many states. However, in 1973, the U. S. Supreme Court ruled in a 5-to-4 decision that the Texas system, based on local property taxes, was not unconstitutional; the Court held that "only relative differences in spending levels" were involved, not "an absolute denial of educational opportunities." After this ruling, the battle shifted to state courts, where state constitutions provided the basis for challenges to unequal spending. In some states, like New Jersey and Connecticut, reliance on local property taxes was found to be in violation of the state constitution; in New York, however, the highest state court found that it was not necessary to equalize school spending among districts. Responding to demands for equity, twenty-eight states revised their system of financing public education in the decade after *Serrano* in order to reduce disparities among districts.[91]

Another complicating factor for those responsible for managing educational institutions resulted from the dramatic growth of teacher unionism. In 1960, the American Federation of Teachers (AFT) represented more than fifty thousand teachers, and its rival, the National Education Association (NEA), had over seven hundred thousand. The AFT offered affiliation with the organized labor movement, and NEA boasted of its "professionalism." By 1978, the NEA claimed a membership of 1.7 million, and the AFT over 500,000. Thousands of other noninstructional school personnel became members of the American Federation of State, County, and Municipal Employees. By 1980, more than 75 percent of the nation's teachers were union members. Much of this rapid growth was attributable to the intense rivalry between the NEA and the AFT, but it occurred at a time when school systems were becoming larger, more impersonal, and more bureaucratic; when teachers were underpaid and not keeping pace with others of similar educational levels; when teachers, on the whole, were younger, better educated, and more likely to be male (male teachers were likelier to join a union than were female teachers); when the cultural context encouraged political activism and collective action; when educational decision making was increasingly removed to the state or federal level, where teachers had no influence; and when criticism of public education was rising rapidly.[92]

Teacher unions became involved not just in conditions affecting pay and other benefits but in "the entire range of policies related to conditions under which teachers teach and children learn . . . class size, number of classes taught, curriculum, textbooks and supplies, and hiring standards—in fact, anything having to do with the operation of the school." As the unions' power grew, the administrators' discretion over the same matters correlatively shrank. How these changes affected the tone and quality of instruction was by no means clear. Since the rise of unionism coincided with a period in which the schools were severely criticized for poor teaching, indifference to students, bureaucratic rigidity, and low standards, critics of the schools tended to direct much of the blame at unions. One critic (a one-time champion of teachers' unions), Myron Lieberman, charged that it was in the nature of collective bargaining to demand "less work for more pay" and to resist administrative control over assignments and transfers, even when such changes might improve the overall functioning of the schools.[93]

But a study by Susan Moore Johnson concluded that the effects of collective bargaining had been far less extensive than was generally believed. While it was true that "principals' formal authority had been restricted and teachers' formal authority had been increased," nonetheless "school site administrators in even the strongest union districts could manage their schools well. Principals were neither figureheads deferring to union representatives nor functionaries complying slavishly with the contract. . . . Schools were remarkably autonomous in interpreting and administering the contract." Johnson found that even among schools within the same district there were wide variations in labor practices. She concluded that the schools had been "altered, but not transformed by collective bargaining."[94]

By the mid-1970s, there was nothing tenuous about the position of teacher unions, regardless of their critics. Opinion surveys of educators and the public regularly indicated that Albert Shanker, the AFT president, was considered one of the nation's leading educators, a tribute to his staying power and to the burnout rate of college presidents and school superintendents. Indeed, both the AFT and the NEA had become major powers, not only in their school districts but in state legislatures and in the nation, and the real question was whether any school district had either the political power or legal resources to deal with them as equals. Because of their size and the activism of their members, both unions were courted by candidates for national office. The NEA was acknowledged to be one of the key power bases of President Jimmy Carter, who repaid his debt by persuading Congress to establish a new Department of Education in 1979 (over the objections of the AFT).[95]

The only impediment to the advance of teacher unionism occurred in the Supreme Court, which ruled in 1980 against faculty members in private colleges and universities who were trying to organize a union. In a 5-to-4 decision, the Court held that faculty members at Yeshiva University were "managerial" employees who were "in effect, substantially and pervasively operating the enterprise." Faculty members, said the majority, "make recommendations to the dean or director in every case of faculty hiring, tenure, sabbaticals, termination and promotion," and they "effectively determine its curriculum, grading system, admission and matriculation standards, academic calendars and course schedules." At the time of the decision, unions represented about half of the nation's professors, mostly those in public institutions. Although expert observers disagreed on the implications of the Yeshiva decision, it seemed likely to encourage resistance to unionization by private institutions and to block the path to power pursued by unions in public elementary and secondary schools.[96]

As the number of competitors hoping to share decision-making power over elementary and secondary schools increased, the states—which had traditionally been responsible for public education—intensified their legislative involvement in educational policy making. In the early 1970s, state legislatures seeking ways to improve the efficiency of the much-criticized schools mandated a wide variety of "accountability" schemes. Accountability laws required the schools to adopt new management systems for planning, budgeting, evaluation, and goal-setting. The object, certainly, was to make schools function more rationally, but the likely outcome was to add another level of bureaucratic measures and managers to already overburdened school districts.[97]

As though the schools did not have enough to cope with just trying to keep track of new directives from courts, legislatures, and other governmental agencies, citizen groups complained vigorously about the cost, quality, and nature of public education. In a widely-heralded taxpayers' revolt, voters in California and Massachusetts enacted propositions that restricted property taxes, on which schools depend; the probable effect was to speed the state takeover of the financing of public education that reformers had been unable to win in the courts. Textbooks and library books came under fire by opponents of sexism, racism, evolution, pornography, and sexually explicit language. In reaction against open education and declining test scores, parent groups pressed state legislators for more attention to basic skills, which fueled the passage of minimum competency testing and came to be known as the "back to basics" movement. Rightwing groups, resentful ever since the Supreme Court's ban against prayer in the public schools in 1963, complained about the intrusion of "secular humanism" in courses like the federally funded "Man: A Course of Study" (MACOS) and about the neglect of the Biblical account of creation.

To an extraordinary degree, the consensus that had undergirded American education for most of its history seemed to be dissipating, and the emergence of rival claimants mirrored growing uncertainty about the purpose of education. The lesson of the federal categorical programs (such as bilingual education, compensatory education, and special education), federal directives, and court orders, it appeared, was that each interest group had to look out for itself, to get as much federal protection and as many public dollars as possible, regardless of the effect on the institution. Lost in the new order of things was any conception of the common interest, the idea that made common schooling possible. Outside intervention assumed that local officials were not to be trusted to do the right thing, and distrust is a corrosive sentiment, especially in an institution where parents entrust their children to the care of strangers. According to annual Gallup polls, public confidence in the public schools declined steadily during the 1970s; while educators thought that the schools' greatest need was innovation, the public each year believed that "lack of discipline" was the biggest problem facing the schools. Two-thirds of the Gallup sample thought that educational decisions should be made by the local board, not by federal or state authorities.[98]

By the late 1970s, concern about distortion of the educational process by outside intervention came not just from parent groups and conservative critics but from liberal scholars of education policy. Arthur E. Wise, one of the early advocates of school finance reform, wrote in 1979 that well-meaning intrusions by Congress, federal agencies, the courts, and state legislators into education were bringing about "the bureaucratization of the American classroom." Each new requirement, he pointed out, was followed by new rules, new procedures to govern everyday decision making, more centralization, and more standardization; administration by rules was replacing administration by persons, and each new round of rule making was followed by more litigation and adversarial procedures, not less.[99]

In a similar vein, J. Myron Atkin, dean of the school of education at Stanford University, reflected somberly in 1980 that the nature of state and federal involvement in education policy had changed dramatically in the previous two decades. Until the 1960s, he wrote, few could have imagined that "politicians and civil servants might determine how mathematics was to be taught, how twelve-year-olds were to be tested, or how instructional plans for individual children were to be developed." Atkin described the Education for All Handicapped Children Act as "one of the sharpest intrusions of the federal government into the details of teaching practice" because of its unprecedented specification of teacher behavior. Following the federal lead, state legislatures too had begun to tell teachers how to teach and what to teach. "Increasingly," he warned, "local school administrators and teachers are losing control over the curriculum as a result of government action. . . . In this process, the local administrator becomes less of an educational leader and more of a monitor of legislative intent."[100]

Besides loss of leadership, Atkin believed that recent trends had stimulated the flight of middle-class parents, black and white, from troubled public schools:

> As a result of legislative directive, handicapped children increasingly are placed in regular classrooms, without additional resources provided for the teacher, forcing the teacher to redirect attention from "average" youngsters to the new group. As another example, judges frequently send delinquent children back to classrooms from which they had been excluded because they were extraordinarily disruptive. The courts act to protect the civil rights of the excluded children. But when many of these youngsters go back to the classroom, they continue to disrupt the regular educational activities and command disproportionate amounts of teacher time. There is little doubt that many of the new schools established by middle-class parents are a response to such developments.

Atkin's most withering criticism, however, was reserved for the federal curriculum development projects sponsored by the National Science Foundation in the 1950s and 1960s. These well-funded projects created new specialized roles: "text writer, subject-matter expert, test developer, classroom manager, program evaluator, curriculum planner." Before there was a curriculum reform movement, "the teacher considered it part of his or her professional responsibility to assume each of these roles." Thus, the latent impact of the curriculum reform movement may have been to narrow the autonomy of the teacher, to turn the teacher from a professional to a technician, and to reduce those areas in which the teacher exercises "sensitive and sophisticated judgment." Each new effort to impose reform on the school, Atkin implied, had simply undermined the schools' autonomy and effectiveness.

University presidents, burdened by the cost and complexity of federal regulations, joined the chorus of critics. Because of the burst of new laws and regulations in the 1970s, universities had to add new administrative staff to process the paperwork and had to spend millions of dollars to comply with the Occupational Safety and Health Act, with environmental regulations, with Section 504 for the handicapped, with requirements for affirmative action, and with Title IX's directives on providing equal athletics for men and women. In 1980, a new federal regulation (Circular A-21 from the Office of Management and Budget) outraged research universities by requiring that faculty members who had any portion of their salaries paid by federal research funds must account for 100 percent of their "time and effort," to the satisfaction of government auditors. Federal rule makers assumed that research universities, like other contractors, were hierarchically organized corporations of managers and employees; they could not understand the faculty's somewhat anachronistic conception of collegiality or its resistance to hourly monitoring of its time.[101]

Whether a university was public or private, it was subject to federal regulations affecting admissions, personnel policy, wage and salary administration, housing, athletics, record keeping, financial aid, research, physical plant construction and management, among other things. Some worried that this relentless standardization and bureaucratization would inevitably erode diversity in higher education. The president of Duke University, Terry Sanford, charged that "the avalanche of recent government regulations . . . threatens to dominate campus management." The president of Yale University, A. Bartlett Giamatti, assailed the "mounting wave of regulation" and "requirements for massive amounts of paperwork" that impaired the relationship between the federal government and the universities. Willis D. Weatherford, president of Berea College, complaining that he spent one-fourth of his time coping with government regulations, foresaw "a deadening monotony creeping across colleges and universities in America—a uniformity induced by excess government regulation." Derek C. Bok, the president of Harvard University, argued that there should be a presumption against government involvement in academic matters:

> if the government freely substitutes its judgment and overrules universities on academic issues, the results, on the whole, will be harmful to the quality of higher education . . . because government officials will not know as much about academic issues as educators and faculty members; because government rules are likely to impress uniformity and rigidity on a field of activity that needs diversity, experimentation, and change; because teaching and research do better under conditions of freedom rather than external direction; and because efforts to determine the academic policies of 3,000 separate institutions are likely to be expensive and difficult to enforce.[102]

The unhappiness of the colleges and universities was not the whole story, however. What had also changed was the dependence of many large universities on federal research funds, which by 1980 were close to $6 billion annually. Just as school districts had come to count on federal funding, even when it provided only 10 percent of the district's total budget, so universities found that their research faculties, their laboratories, their graduate students, and their prestige depended to some degree on maintaining their funding from the federal government, no matter how nettlesome their relationship with federal agencies might become. And while their complaints were well grounded, the fact was that in the most important matters colleges and universities had preserved their integrity and their freedom of action. With rare exceptions, the institutions continued to decide for themselves, on academic terms, who would teach, what would be taught, how it would be taught, and who would be admitted to study. Federal regulation was costly, and it added a new layer of administrators within institutions, but it did not destroy what was best about American higher education.[103]

Nonetheless, vocal criticism of federal intervention into the affairs of higher education and local school districts became especially intense during the administration of President Jimmy Carter, not necessarily because Carter's policies were unusually burdensome but because during his administration the regulations governing the treatment of the handicapped and women (laws passed during the Nixon and Ford years) were promulgated. Under Carter, the federal education budget was substantially increased and a federal Department of Education was established. Ironically, the first secretary of the new department was a federal judge rather than an educator, and the implicit signal from Washington was that the network of regulations and mandates would be administered by an experienced hand. Carter was defeated in 1980 by a conservative Republican, Ronald Reagan, who pledged to dismantle the Department of Education and to reduce federal regulation of education, both tasks that were easier said than done.

By 1980, regardless of who was elected president, there was no turning back to the days when local school boards were near-autonomous and when higher education was as remote from the government as were churches. The changed situation was a new fact of life, like the discovery of nuclear energy. No matter how much one might deplore it, and no matter how many might deplore it, it did not go away. As John Dewey might have observed, the new relationship between education and the government was a problem, and as a problem, it was a challenge to critical intelligence. As such, it was to be studied, debated, criticized, and acted on. No one could doubt the value of efforts to rethink flawed assumptions, to reconsider unsatisfactory regulations, or to rewrite legislation that had adverse consequences. Much had been gained because of the active dedication of the federal government and the courts to the rights of all children. To the extent that the pursuit of good ends jeopardized equally valuable ends, like academic freedom, institutional autonomy, and diversity; to the extent that absorption by educators in bureaucratic procedures overshadowed the educational function of the schools; and to the extent that government programs gave new responsibilities to academic institutions while depriving them of the authority needed to carry out those responsibilities, there remained a compelling agenda for future educational reformers.

Epilogue:
From 1945 to 1980

WHEN HEARINGS on federal aid to education were held in 1945 and teachers came from around the nation to tell the Congress about the needs of their schools, the problems of American education seemed nearly insoluble. It was no accident that the teachers who testified came from rural districts, because it was there that the schools were in the direst financial straits. Urban districts were conspicuous by their absence from these hearings, because they were considered relatively privileged, well staffed, and well financed. Rural schools, however, suffered from low funding, poor facilities, obsolete teaching materials, and a critical teacher shortage.

Inequitable funding was only the most immediate problem, however. Whether urban or rural, privileged or poor, American schools reflected the racial bias that was common in the larger society. In many states, this bias was institutionalized in racially separate schools where black students received fewer months of schooling and had teachers who had less training and lower pay than their white peers. So deeply imbedded was the practice of racial segregation that there seemed little reason to believe, at war's end, that any political change might be seismic enough to destroy the power of state-enforced racial segregation. Furthermore, access to higher education

—though by no means narrow when compared to other nations—was available to fewer than one of every six college-age youths. For black youths, the opportunity for higher education was far less, since they suffered the double burden of an inadequate preparation and exclusion from many "white" colleges and universities. The schools were part of a vicious circle, because exclusion from educational opportunity guaranteed exclusion from economic opportunity.

In the thirty-five years after the Second World War, American education was transformed, though not always in ways that were predictable or intended. Through the course of the fight for federal aid to education and the struggle to abolish racial segregation, the politics of American education changed substantially. In 1949, when Senator Taft's proposal for federal aid came close to passing, everyone agreed—Republican and Democrat, Catholic, Protestant, and Jew, black and white, representatives of labor and business—that there should be no federal control of education. Taft's bill stipulated that "nothing contained in this Act shall be construed to authorize any department, agency, officer, or employee of the United States to exercise any direction, supervision, or control over, or to prescribe any requirements with respect to any school, or any State educational institution or agency" which received federal funds. In 1965, when Congress was concerned above all about racial injustice, the issue of federal control was seen as a "red herring" thrown up by recalcitrant southern congressmen. Regardless of declarations, once federal dollars were involved, there was no quarantining the activities of school districts from the watchful eye of the courts, the Congress, and the federal civil rights agencies.[1]

Over these thirty-five years, educational decision making expanded beyond the traditional state-local district connection. What a given school decided to do regarding its curriculum, its personnel policy, its disciplinary procedures, and its allocation of resources was no longer a local matter. Not every wrong would be righted, but a serious misstep invited the attention of federal officials, state officials, the national press, civil rights organizations, powerful teachers' unions, and professional associations. The rhetoric changed: in the new situation, it seemed archaic to speak about keeping the schools "out of politics." Of course, the schools had always been "in politics," in the sense that they had to compete with other public agencies for funds, they awarded contracts for services, they selected teachers and administrators, and they made their peace with the mores of the surrounding community.

But the new politics of the schools rotated about a state-federal axis rather than a local-state axis. The good superintendent or principal in 1945 maintained good relations with the mayor, the city council, and the school board. By 1980, the alert school administrator had to stay informed about the activities of Congress, the Department of Education, federal regulatory agencies, the courts, and the state legislature in order to see whether some new program had been developed that might provide new funds or whether some current activity had been proscribed or curtailed. School politics became more like American politics in general, in which different interest groups lobbied for funds, sought special relationships with congressional committees, and fought off rival claimants.

Relations between the lay public and the teaching profession also changed in significant ways. In the 1940s, few teachers belonged to a union; strikes were uncommon; administrators were powerful within their school building or their district in hiring, promoting, and assigning teachers. Though their pay was low, teachers had more education than did the parents of their students and commanded the respect that went with the authority they wielded. Teaching attracted a number of gifted women, for whom other career opportunities were limited. In some communities, there were substantial restrictions placed on teachers' behavior; as models for the community's youth, teachers were expected not to smoke or drink or otherwise set a bad example.

The growth of higher education, and especially of community colleges, drew away from the high schools those teachers who preferred the higher status and higher pay associated with being a professor and the chance to teach without discipline problems. The growth of new opportunities for women in law, medicine, and business drew away many of the bright female college graduates who would have previously entered elementary and secondary teaching. The increased educational attainment of the population as a whole meant that teachers were no longer more educated than were parents and could not automatically count on the respect of parents; nor, after the rise of the youth culture in the 1960s, with its antiauthority attitudes, could teachers count on the respect of their adolescent students. These were part of the background conditions within which teacher unionism spread, giving teacher organizations more political power than any of the school boards they negotiated with and making teachers nearly invulnerable to the discontents of the lay public which previously had both admired and disciplined them.

So customary was it to criticize the public schools, whether in the 1940s, the 1950s, the 1960s, or the 1970s, that it was easy to forget the ways in which the schools had been amazingly successful. Americans had long ago decided, without too much discussion of the matter, that education would be the best vehicle through which to change society. The attack against racial segregation, characteristically, was fought out in the schools, and the dismantling of the racial caste system began in the schools and spread to other areas of American life. More than any other institution in American society, the schools became the means through which the goal of equity was pursued. The battle took place around the schools because they provided the setting in which children learned to get along with others beyond their immediate families and in which children and young people developed (or failed to develop) the skills, knowledge, and intelligence to realize their aspirations.

The goal of access to higher education was realized far beyond the most optimistic predictions of President Truman's Commission on Higher Education. The commission's hope that the states might establish extensive community college systems was fully realized by 1980. Its wish that 4.6 million students might attend college by 1960 was derided by many in higher education as both impossible because of the limited number of able students and undesirable because of the certainty that it would degrade the standards of higher education. But fantastic as its prediction sounded in 1947, by 1980 more than 12 million students were enrolled in institutions of higher education. And so fully engaged were colleges and universities in the life of the American people, that fully 38 percent of all their students in 1980 were over the age of twenty-five, returning to improve their minds, their skills, their credentials, or their hobbies. After 1972, college-going was substantially subsidized by a massive federal program of grants and loans, which amounted to more than $5 billion annually by 1980.[2]

Higher levels of participation in the colleges and universities reflected the rising level of educational attainment for the population as a whole. At the end of the war, about 40 of every 100 young people remained in high school long enough to graduate, and about 16 then entered college. By 1980, 75 of every 100 youths graduated from high school, and about 45 then entered college. The gap in educational attainment between whites and blacks was narrowed substantially in the 1960s and 1970s. In 1960, about 40 percent of black youngsters finished high school, compared to some 67 percent of whites; by 1980, 70 percent of blacks did so, compared to 82.5 percent of whites. The gap remained, but the progress in reducing it was remarkable.[3]

The democratization of access to higher education did not, as the critics feared, destroy it. Although some public institutions (like the City College of New York) were transformed from elite liberal arts colleges to open-admissions institutions, in response to egalitarian pressures, the occurrence was atypical. American higher education responded to the onrushing tide of students by adopting what one observer has called a "division of labor between and within institutions." Some colleges and universities remained elite in their admissions standards and in their commitment to teaching and research; some other institutions were or became "service institutions," dedicated to preparing young men and women for technical, vocational, and semiprofessional careers. And many big state universities combined both functions within the same institution, providing both high-quality academic departments for those who sought a liberal education and service programs for the career-oriented. This adaptation enabled higher education both to expand to meet the new demand for higher education and to protect the pre-eminence of its research and scholarship functions.[4]

Other seemingly intractable problems were alleviated or dissipated as American society became more educated and more homogeneous. The bitter religious tensions that had long blocked federal aid to education had eased by 1980; Catholics, Protestants, and Jews had become accustomed to working together in an ecumenical spirit on common problems. Although covert anti-Catholicism and anti-Semitism lingered, they had lost their respectability. In the rapid advance of urbanization and modernization, American society had become so secularized that the religious groups most likely to encounter bigotry were Fundamentalists, particularly Protestant and Jewish denominations that clung to biblical commands.

The rising levels of educational attainment resulted from and contributed to a fast-rising standard of living. State and federal governments supported the expansion of educational opportunity because they believed that education was an appropriate way to develop human resources and that it made sense to invest public funds in raising the population's literacy and skills. Broad participation in educational opportunities throughout the nation was both a cause and an effect of the nation's scientific and technological progress.

Yet all was not well. Absolute social progress was accompanied by a rising sense of relative deprivation. In the midst of an affluent society, the persistence of poverty was a reproach to national ideals, even if the actual condition of the poor had improved over time. The shifting demography of the postwar era created new problems. The desire for increased opportunity and the decline of agricultural employment propelled large numbers of poor blacks and Hispanics to the urban centers in the 1950s and 1960s, and the cities developed vast slum areas, where the poor concentrated, dependent on impersonal public institutions, bereft of the sense of family and community that had sustained their counterparts in rural areas. By 1980, most large cities had a black and Hispanic majority in their public schools, reflecting the flight of whites to the suburbs and private schools.

Many of these big-city school systems, having staggered through conflict after conflict, over such issues as desegregation, community control, and fiscal crises, suffered from severe demoralization. For decades they had thought of themselves as the nation's pace-setting school districts, but by the 1960s their middle-class student population was leaving, achievement scores were sinking, disciplinary problems soared, vandalism became common, and the teaching staff became defensive and insulated. More and more children were staying in school longer than ever, but it was not clear to the students, the teachers, or the parents that the quality of education was as good as it had been in less complicated times.

Concern about educational quality was not limited to big-city schools. Once it had become certain that universal access to education at all levels had been largely secured, educators began to turn their attention to the state of learning, which was far from secure. The debate about standards that had been initiated as a result of the decline in SAT scores produced evidence that other standardized test scores had been dropping, beginning in about the fifth grade; that enrollments in advanced courses in mathematics and science in high school had fallen steadily since the mid-1960s; that widely-used textbooks had reduced their reading levels in order to adjust to falling verbal abilities; that homework assignments had been sharply curtailed and that grade inflation was common; that large numbers of easy or nonverbal electives had been added to the schools' curricula as substitutes for demanding courses; that writing skills had declined, at least in part because writing was not systematically emphasized as a part of learning and thinking, and because short-answer quizzes and standardized tests had gained a place alongside of, or in place of, the essay.[5]

The pervasive influence of television, that highly entertaining but passivity-inducing medium of communication, was an important element in the new situation. But also part of the heightened criticism was a question about the fate of humane culture. The issue, which echoed complaints about the permissive aspects of progressive education and open education, was whether a democratic education system best served its students by letting them choose what they wanted to study, if they wanted to study; or whether it served them best by seeing that each and every one of them received a liberal education—including literature and language, science and mathematics, history and the arts. The debate reiterated the old arguments: one side claimed that a democratic school system had to proceed through the willing consent of the governed; the other insisted that a democratic school system had to assure everyone a sound education or suffer the creation of differential elites and of intolerable popular ignorance.

Beyond the obvious gains and losses that had been registered in the course of thirty-five years was a change in climate so basic and yet so elusive that it was difficult to measure or even describe. Although some few big-city high schools were vast educational factories in 1945, most schools, colleges, and even universities were small compared to what was to come. In some communities, teachers "boarded" with families, not because of choice but because of low pay; not a situation they might have chosen, but one that assured intimate familiarity with the community and the children. Even where teachers led independent lives, they were expected to spend after-school hours as supervisors of extracurricular activities and to know their students; they, in turn, could count on parents to support and reinforce the demands made by the school. Colleges and universities never questioned their role *in loco parentis:* they were responsible for the young men and women in their care, as if the institution itself were their parents. Alcohol was seldom permitted on campus, drugs were unheard of, and even the social lives of the students were regulated; infractions of the rules of behavior might be punished by suspension or expulsion.

Much had changed by 1980. The drive to consolidate small schools and small school districts had largely succeeded, helped along by the vast expansion of enrollments in the 1950s and 1960s. Big schools became the rule, not the exception. In a society where bigger was considered better, small districts and small schools were described as backward and inefficient. The number of school districts shrank dramatically, from one hundred thousand at war's end to sixteen thousand in 1980. While total enrollment in elementary and secondary schools nearly doubled during the thirty-five-year span (from 23 million to 40 million), the number of schools dropped from one hundred and eighty-five thousand to eighty-six thousand. More and more students went to larger schools. In higher education, institutions enrolling more than twenty thousand students increased from ten in 1948 to one hundred and fifteen by 1980. Growth had many benefits: efficiency of scale, diversity of curriculum, differentiation of types of students and teachers. Enlargement meant exposure to a more varied setting and interaction with a broader variety of ideas and people than was possible in a small school or college.

The trade-off, of course, was that bigness meant impersonality, bureaucratization, diminished contact between faculty and students, formalization of relationships among colleagues, a weakening of the bonds of community. Colleges and universities withdrew from the *in loco parentis* role that they had previously exercised. No longer part of a community of values shared with students and parents, teachers and administrators found it difficult to administer discipline or even to establish rules that everyone found acceptable. Teachers and professors defended themselves against the new anonymity by joining unions. Students, complaining that no one knew their names, wrote them vividly in the bathrooms and hallways of their schools. The invasion of drugs, first in college in the 1960s, then in high schools and even junior high schools in the 1970s, dulled students' senses and insulated a portion of the student body from adult standards. The lingering influence of the counterculture, that remnant of the 1960s youth rebellion, left many adults wondering whether there were any standards of learning or effort or behavior worth defending.

American education had succeeded in so many ways that were real, tangible, and important—in providing modern buildings, larger enrollment, better materials, better trained teachers, more courses, more departments, and more graduates—that it sometimes seemed difficult for educators to remember what they had accomplished or why they had struggled so hard, or not to wonder whether they had gone wrong somewhere or why so many people criticized the nation's schools, colleges, and universities.

The following vignette, not necessarily representative, is nonetheless true. In 1945, at the beginning of this account, Mrs. Florence Christmas traveled to Washington, D.C., to tell the Senate Committee on Education about the Antioch School, where she was principal. She told them that there were three teachers for 190 children; that she was not only the principal but taught all subjects in four grades. It was a moving story, not just because of the difference between the salaries of the white and black teachers or between the number of months of schooling for white and black students, but because her dedication shone through her testimony. Even more than that, what was apparent was the evident commitment of the parents to the survival of the school and the education of their children, no matter how meager their present chances. Mrs. Christmas died in 1957, not living to see the Antioch School consolidated two years later, along with other small black schools into the Hazlehurst, Mississippi, city school district. The new, all-black, elementary school was much larger; Mrs. Christmas' sister became its principal, and there were six teachers in the first grade alone.[6]

In the late 1960s, under pressure from the federal government, the Hazlehurst district offered its black and white students "free choice" to go to whichever school they wanted. A few black students went to the white school, but most students stayed with their friends. Rowan Torrey, a nephew of Mrs. Christmas, was one of those who chose to stay in the black school; he thought it was better. He liked the school spirit; he liked the way several busloads of kids followed the football team to their matches and cheered them on, and he was proud of the seventy-member band and the school choir. Torrey graduated in 1969 and went to Millsaps College, a small, previously all-white liberal arts college in Jackson. The next year the federal government lowered the boom on Hazlehurst and required the integration of the white and black schools. The town whites promptly opened Copiah Academy, a private school, and abandoned the public schools.

When Rowan Torrey moved back to Hazlehurst in 1980 after serving in the Marines, he went to work for the federal Job Corps, helping young people acquire basic skills and vocational training. Most of his enrollees, including some with high school diplomas, were barely literate. He began to take a close look at the schools. What he saw was a small system that was more than 90 percent black, an integrated staff with white administrators who had suffered "culture shock" after integration and who were "afraid to discipline black kids." Graduation requirements had dropped precipitously during the decade after desegregation, the college preparatory courses had been substantially reduced, students were choosing their own courses, and discipline was lax. But that was not all: the buildings needed repairs, the band instruments had largely disappeared, the choir was a sometime thing, and the football team had a season of 0 and 10.

Born and bred in Mississippi, but college educated and toughened in the Marines, Rowan Torrey decided to fight. As a lay citizen, he took up the family tradition of commitment to public education and agitated for better schools. A new superintendent (a white, third-generation Mississippian who enrolled his daughter in the elementary school) was hired, a strict disciplinarian. Graduation requirements went up, and the district began eliminating options and telling students which academic courses they would have to take. Class size in the district averaged about twenty, though it was smaller in advanced science classes. Even as it tried to right itself, the district weathered a fiscal crisis; only the steady flow of federal funds enabled it to maintain kindergartens, teachers' aides, and special reading and math programs in the early grades.

In Hazlehurst, where there is a black public school system and a white private academy, the schools are not building a new social order but they are making their contribution. In the past decade, new employment opportunities have opened up for educated blacks, as tellers and accountants in local banks, as operators of nationally franchised businesses, as administrators in public agencies. "We had a tremendous opportunity to unite our community, black and white," Rowan Torrey laments, "and we wasted it." It was not the blacks who wasted it, but the whites who fled.

Yet if one had the courage of those who served on the President's Committee on Civil Rights in 1947 and the vision of those who projected the growth of American higher education in the same year, it would be possible to counsel against despair. In the crusade against ignorance, there have been no easy victories, but no lasting defeats. Those who have labored on behalf of American education have seen so many barriers scaled, so much hatred dispelled, so many possibilities remaining to provide the basis for future reconciliation. To believe in education is to believe in the future, to believe in what may be accomplished through the disciplined use of intelligence, allied with cooperation and good will. If it seems naïvely American to put so much stock in schools, colleges, universities, and the endless prospect of self-improvement and social improvement, it is an admirable, and perhaps even a noble, flaw.

NOTES

Introduction

1. Thomas Jefferson, "To George Wythe," *Crusade Against Ignorance: Thomas Jefferson on Education*, ed. Gordon C. Lee (New York: Teachers College Press, 1961), pp. 99–100.

Chapter 1: Postwar Initiatives

1. U.S. Congress, Senate, Committee on Education and Labor, *Federal Aid for Education*, 79th Cong., 1st sess., 1945, pp. 118–21.

2. Ibid., pp. 122–25.

3. Ibid., pp. 187–94.

4. Ibid., pp. 145–46, 147–48, 161.

5. *New York Times*, February 10, 11, 12, 13, 14, 15, 17, 18, 19, 21, 1947. See also Benjamin Fine, *Our Children Are Cheated: The Crisis in American Education* (New York: Henry Holt, 1947).

6. Ben J. Wattenberg, ed., *The Statistical History of the United States: From Colonial Times to the Present* (New York: Basic Books, 1976), pp. 368–89; *General Education in a Free Society: Report of the Harvard Committee* (Cambridge, Mass.: Harvard University Press, 1945), p. 7.

7. *General Education in a Free Society*, pp. 14, 80–81, 96–99.

8. Wattenberg, *Statistical History*, p. 379.

9. Davis R. B. Ross, *Preparing for Ulysses: Politics and Veterans During World War II* (New York: Columbia University Press, 1969).

10. James B. Conant, "Annual Report of the President of the University," *Harvard Alumni Bulletin* 47 (February 3, 1945), cited in Keith W. Olson, "The G.I. Bill and Higher Education: Success and Surprise," *American Quarterly* 25 (December 1973):604; Robert M. Hutchins, "The Threat to American Education," *Collier's*, December 30, 1944, pp. 20–21.

11. "The GI Bill: In 10 Years, 8 million," *Newsweek*, October 4, 1954, pp. 88–91; "Beginning of the End," *Time*, July 30, 1951, p. 58; Olson, "The G.I. Bill and Higher Education," p. 608.

12. "The Class of '49,'" *Fortune*, June 1949, p. 84; Olson, "The G.I. Bill and Higher Education," p. 604; Byron H. Atkinson, "Veteran vs. Non-Veteran Performance at U.C.L.A.," *Journal of Educational Research* 43 (December 1949): 299–302.

13. Keith W. Olson, *The G.I. Bill, the Veterans, and the Colleges* (Lexington: University Press of Kentucky, 1974), pp. 43–48; Sidney A. Burrell, "The G.I. Bill and the Great American Transformation, 1945–1967," *Boston University Graduate Journal* 15 (Spring 1967):3.

14. *Newsweek*, October 4, 1954, p. 91.

15. *Higher Education for American Democracy: A Report of the President's Commission on Higher Education*, 5 vols. (New York: Harper & Bros., 1948), 1:14–23, 27–36, 39–41; 2:25–40.

16. Ibid., 1:36; 2:45–57; 3:30–33; 5:57–58; 65–68.

17. *New York Times*, December 21, 1947; "Revolution on the Campus," *Life*, February 2, 1948, p. 24.

18. For a sampling of the criticism of and support for the report, see Gail Kennedy, ed., *Education for Democracy: The Debate over the Report of the President's Commission on Higher Education* (Lexington, Mass.: D. C. Heath, 1952).

19. " 'Tides of Mediocrity,' " *Time*, February 23, 1948, pp. 52–54; "Federal Aid Without Controls," *Commonweal*, February 13, 1948, p. 435.

20. Robert M. Hutchins, "The Report of the President's Commission on Higher Education," *Educational Record* 29 (April 1948): 107–22.

21. Wendell L. Willkie, "Citizens of Negro Blood," in *Primer for White Folks*, ed. Bucklin Moon (Garden City, N.Y.: Doubleday, 1946), pp. 311–12; "The Negro's War," *Fortune*, June 1942, pp. 78, 164.

22. Willkie, "Citizens of Negro Blood," p. 313.

23. Harry S. Truman, *Memoirs of Harry S. Truman: Years of Trial and Hope*, 2 vols. (Garden City, N.Y.: Doubleday, 1956), 2:180.

24. Transcript, President's Committee on Civil Rights (PCCR), Hanover, New Hampshire, June 30, 1947, p. 490 (Files of Philleo Nash, Papers of Harry S. Truman, Harry S. Truman Library, Independence, Missouri).

25. *To Secure These Rights: The Report of the President's Committee on Civil Rights* (New York: Simon and Schuster, 1947), pp. 20–47, 54–78.

26. Transcript, PCCR, pp. 558–74.

27. Ibid., pp. 584–601; *To Secure These Rights*, p. 168.

28. Margaret Truman, *Harry S. Truman* (New York: William Morrow, 1973), p. 392; *Washington Post*, June 30, 1947; *New York Times*, June 30, 1947; *Washington Star*, June 30, 1947. The reactions of the southern and western press to Truman's NAACP speech are contained in the Files of Philleo Nash, Truman Library. ("Mrs. R." was Eleanor Roosevelt)

29. *New York Times*, January 8, 1948; *New York Times*, February 3, 1948. Reactions to Truman's "10-point civil rights program" are contained in the Files of Philleo Nash, Truman Library.

30. *New York Times*, February 3, 1948; Associated Press dispatch, February 3, 1948, in Files of Philleo Nash, Truman Library.

31. *New York Times*, July 27, 1948.

32. William S. White, *The Taft Story* (New York: Harper & Bros., 1954), p. 50.

33. The best source on the fight for federal aid in the late 1940s is Gilbert Elliott Smith, "The Limits of Reform: Politics and Federal Aid to Education, 1937–1950" (Diss., Teachers College, Columbia University, 1975); it has been published as *The Limits of Reform: Politics and Federal Aid to Education* (New York: Garland Publishing, 1982).

34. *Everson* v. *Board of Education of Ewing Township*, 330 U.S. 1 (1947).

35. "Now Will Protestants Awake?" *Christian Century*, February 26, 1947, p. 262; *New York Times*, February 12, 1947; May 8, 1947.

36. *Cochran* v. *Louisiana State Board of Education*, 281 U.S. 370 (1930); Leo Pfeffer, *Church, State, and Freedom* (Boston: Beacon Press, 1953), pp. 466–69.

37. *New York Times*, January 12, 1948.

38. Paul Blanshard, "The Catholic Church and Education," *Nation*, November 15, 1947, p. 525.

39. Paul Blanshard, *American Freedom and Catholic Power* (Boston: Beacon Press, 2nd ed., 1958, orig. pub., 1949), pp. 303, 322–23.

40. "The Schools and 'The Nation,' " *New York Times*, May 28, 1949; Blanshard, *American Freedom and Catholic Power*, pp. 1–10; see also, T. Robert Ingram, "The Blanshard Book," *Atlantic Monthly*, February 1950, pp. 74–79.

41. *McCollum* v. *Board of Education*, 333 U.S. 203 (1948).

42. *New York Times*, February 18, 1949; see also, Rev. M. J. McKeough, "American Education Week," *Catholic Action*, November 1949, p. 11.

43. U.S. Congress, House, Special Subcommittee of the Committee on Education and Labor, *Public School Assistance Act of 1949*, 81st Cong., 1st sess., 1949, pp. 102, 744.

44. Ibid., p. 532.

45. *New York Times*, June 20, 1949; Smith, *"Limits of Reform,"* p. 317–18; Seymour P. Lachman, "The Cardinal, the Congressmen and the First Lady," *Journal of Church and State* 6 (Winter 1965): 42.

46. Lachman, "The Cardinal, the Congressmen and the First Lady," p. 43; Robert C. Hartnett, "Who's Blocking Federal Aid?" *America*, July 9, 1949, p. 417; *New York Times*, July 7, 1949; Elmer L. Puryear, *Graham A. Barden: Conservative Carolina Congressman* (Buies Creek, N.C.: Campbell University Press, 1979), p. 86.

47. *New York Times,* June 20, 1949; Joseph P. Lash, *Eleanor: The Years Alone* (New York: W. W. Norton, 1972), pp. 156–57.

48. *New York Times,* July 23, 1949.

49. Ibid.

50. Ibid.

51. Lash, *Eleanor,* pp. 155–67.

52. Ibid., pp. 159–60. For Cardinal Spellman's view of the exchange, see Robert I. Gannon, *The Cardinal Spellman Story* (London: Robert Hale, 1962), pp. 311–22.

53. *New York Times,* August 4, 1949; August 6, 1949; Lachman, "The Cardinal, the Congressmen and the First Lady," pp. 49–50; Lash, *Eleanor,* p. 164.

54. *New York Times,* March 2, 3, 7, 1950.

55. Frank J. Munger and Richard F. Fenno, Jr., *National Politics and Federal Aid to Education* (Syracuse, N. Y.: Syracuse University Press, 1962), p. 122.

56. Puryear, *Graham A. Barden,* pp. 92, 227; Munger and Fenno, *National Politics,* pp. 122–24.

Chapter 2: The Rise and Fall of Progressive Education

1. See, for example: State of Indiana, Department of Public Instruction, "Handbook for Evaluating Elementary and Secondary Schools in Indiana," bulletin no. 300, 1950. For a useful review of educational surveying, as well as an example of the activity itself, see Robert Wilson Edgar, "A Survey of the Techniques and Procedures for Curriculum Improvement in the Great Neck Cooperative Study" (Diss., Teachers College, Columbia University, 1949).

2. Hollis L. Caswell, "The Great Reappraisal of Public Education," *Teachers College Record* 54 (October 1952):12–22.

3. Lawrence A. Cremin, *The Transformation of the School: Progressivism in American Education, 1876–1957* (New York: Alfred A. Knopf, 1961), pp. vii–x, 22, 88.

4. Lawrence A. Cremin, "The Revolution in American Secondary Education, 1893–1918," *Teachers College Record* 56 (March 1955):307; U.S. Bureau of Education, *Report of the Committee on Secondary School Studies Appointed at the Meeting of the National Educational Association, July 9, 1892* (Washington, D.C.: Government Printing Office, 1892).

5. U.S. Bureau of Education, *Cardinal Principles of Secondary Education: A Report of the Commission on the Reorganization of Secondary Education Appointed by the National Education Association* (Washington, D.C.: Government Printing Office, 1918), pp. 7, 10–12; Edward A. Krug, *The Shaping of the American High School, 1880–1920* (Madison: University of Wisconsin Press, 1969), p. 385.

6. Eugene Randolph Smith, *Education Moves Ahead: A Survey of Progressive Methods* (Boston: Atlantic Monthly Press, 1924), pp. 30–42; see, William Heard Kilpatrick, *Foundations of Method: Informal Talks on Teaching* (New York: Macmillan, 1926); William C. Bagley, *Education and Emergent Man: A Theory of Education With Particular Application to Public Education in the United States* (New York: Thomas Nelson, 1934), pp. 143–45, 192–94.

7. Walter B. Kolesnik, *Mental Discipline in Modern Education* (Madison: University of Wisconsin Press, 1958), p. 55; Richard Hofstadter, *Anti-Intellectualism in American Life* (New York: Alfred A. Knopf, 1963), p. 349.

8. Franklin Bobbitt, *The Curriculum* (New York: Houghton Mifflin, 1918), p. 42; *How to Make a Curriculum* (New York: Houghton Mifflin, 1924), pp. 8–9; see also, Junius L. Meriam, *Child Life and the Curriculum* (Yonkers-on-Hudson, N.Y.: World Book, 1920); W. W. Charters, *Curriculum Construction* (New York: Macmillan, 1923); Franklin Bobbitt, *Curriculum Investigations* (Chicago: University of Chicago Press, 1926).

9. Harold Rugg and Ann Shumaker, *The Child-Centered School* (Yonkers-on-Hudson, N.Y.: World Book, 1928), pp. vii, 2–5.

10. Samuel Tenenbaum, *William Heard Kilpatrick: Trail Blazer in Education* (New York: Harper & Bros., 1951), p. 141, 185; Kilpatrick, *Foundations of Method,* p. 278.

11. "Curriculum Revision and Development, 1924–1930" (Board of Education, Houston Independent School District, n.d.), foreword, n.p.; Herbert B. Bruner, "Present Status of Curriculum," in *Curriculum Making in Current Practice: A Report of a Conference Held at Northwestern University,* October 30–31, 1931 (Evanston, Ill.: School of Education, Northwestern University, 1932), pp. 12–20; Harold C. Hand and Will French, "Analysis of the Present Status in

Curriculum Thinking," in *The Changing Curriculum* (New York: D. Appleton-Century, 1937), pp. 1–31.

12. See the reading list in Samuel Engle Burr, *A School in Transition: A Study of a Public School Moving from the Use of Traditional Practices to the Acceptance of the Activity Plan of Progressive Education during a Three Year Transitional Period* (Boston: Christopher, 1937), p. 74; Hollis Caswell, *Curriculum Improvement in Public School Systems* (New York: Bureau of Publications, Teachers College, 1950), p. 53.

13. Caswell, *Curriculum Improvement,* pp. 48–49, 68; an invaluable description of the social engineering aspect of curriculum change is Robert William Coleman, "Kurt Lewin's Theory of Social Change Applied to Curriculum Change" (Diss., University of Illinois, 1964).

14. N. C. Turpen, "Cooperative Curricular Improvement: To Formulate a Plan for Securing Community Understanding, Cooperation, and Support in Making Basic Program Changes in the High Schools of Alabama" (Diss., Teachers College, Columbia University, 1941), pp. 129–30; Caswell, *Curriculum Improvement,* pp. 293–94.

15. See Caswell, *Curriculum Improvement,* for accounts of curricular change in Kingsport, Tennessee, and Battle Creek, Michigan. And see Edgar, "A Survey of the Techniques and Procedures," where the point is strongly made that the object of curriculum improvement is not just to change the skills and knowledge of the teacher but to change the teacher's "total personality pattern" (p. 39). For the classic statement of the "social process" involved in curricular change, see Alice Miel, *Changing the Curriculum: A Social Process* (New York: D. Appleton-Century, 1946).

16. William P. Patterson, "Curriculum Improvement in a Junior High School, 1935–1939: A Professional Project to Initiate and Guide the Developing of a Continuous Curriculum Improvement Program in the State Street Junior High School in Hackensack, N.J." (Diss., Teachers College, Columbia University, 1940), p. 48.

17. Patterson, "Curriculum Improvement," p. 159; Caswell, *Curriculum Improvement,* pp. 115, 331; George H. Geyer, "A Secondary School in Transition" (Diss., Teachers College, Columbia University, 1940).

18. Turpen, "Cooperative Curricular Improvement," pp. 22–31, 107–11.

19. Patterson, "Curriculum Improvement in a Junior High School," p. 67; Turpen, "Cooperative Curricular Improvement," pp. 26, 111; Caswell, *Curriculum Improvement,* pp. 236–37; Edgar, "A Survey of the Techniques and Procedures," p. 162; Francis W. Kirkham, "Educating All the Children of All the People," U.S. Office of Education, bulletin no. 11 (Washington, D.C.: Government Printing Office, 1931).

20. Eileen Kathryn Rice, *The Superintendency and the Implementation of Progressive Practices in the Ann Arbor Elementary Schools from 1921–1942* (Ann Arbor, Michigan: Social Foundations of Education Monograph Series, no. 8, 1978), p. 126.

21. Margaret Rouse, "Present Status of the Elementary School Curriculum," *Texas Outlook,* February 1947, pp. 16–17.

22. Mortimer J. Adler, "Shall We Have More Progressive Education? No," *The Rotarian,* September 1941, pp. 30–31. This and other examples of criticism are cited in Sister Mary Ruth Sandifer, *American Lay Opinion of the Progressive School* (Washington, D.C.: Catholic University of America Press, 1943), pp. 10–11.

23. Bagley, *Education and Emergent Man,* pp. 139, 145. When Bagley died, Kilpatrick noted in his diary: "He has long been a hurtful reactionary, the most respectable vocal of all. . . . His going marks the end of an era. No one who professes to know education will henceforth stand forth in opposition as he did" (Tenenbaum, *William Heard Kilpatrick,* pp. 241–42). Carl A. Jessen, "Trends in Secondary Education," U.S. Office of Education, Biennial Survey of Education in the U.S. (Washington, D.C.: Government Printing Office, 1937), p. 39.

24. John Dewey, *Experience and Education* (New York: Collier, 1963, orig. pub., 1938), pp. 21–30, 64–65, 69.

25. *Time,* "Progressives' Progress," October 31, 1938, p. 31; Tenenbaum, *William Heard Kilpatrick,* p. 240; "The Metropolitan School Study Council—A New Pattern in School Cooperation," *Educational Forum* 9 (May 1945):146.

26. Educational Policies Commission, *The Unique Function of Education in American Democracy* (Washington, D.C.: NEA, 1937), pp. 77–78, 82.

27. Harl R. Douglass, *Secondary Education for Youth in Modern America* (Washington, D.C.: American Council on Education, 1937), pp. vii, 1, 6, 8, 20, 29–30, 96.

28. Educational Policies Commission, *The Purposes of Education in American Democracy* (Washington, D.C.: NEA, 1938), pp. 47–48, 147.

29. B. L. Dodds, *That All May Learn*, Bulletin of National Association of Secondary-School Principals, vol. 23, no. 85 (Washington, D.C.: NEA, 1939), pp. 13–14, 21, 33–34, 37–38, 54, 57, 69–70, 122–27, 133.

30. Donald Calvin Doane, *The Needs of Youth: An Evaluation for Curriculum Purposes* (New York: Bureau of Publications, Teachers College, 1942), pp. 113–21.

31. Educational Policies Commission, *Education for All American Youth* (Washington, D.C.: NEA, 1944), p. 142.

32. See, "Democracy in U.S. Schools," *Life*, January 13, 1941, pp. 68–70, for pictures and a description of the Holtville, Alabama, public school; see also, Lavone Hanna, "The Operation of the Core Curriculum in Tulsa," *Curriculum Journal*, February 1940, pp. 66–68; William R. Odell, "Two Approaches to High School Curriculum Revision," *Curriculum Journal*, March 1940, pp. 115–18 (Oakland, California); "Curriculum Revision in the Altoona High School," *Curriculum Journal*, March 1941, pp. 97–98; Roberta LaBrant Green, "Developing a Modern Curriculum in a Small Town," *Progressive Education*, March 1936, pp. 189–97 (Holton, Kansas); A Group of Teachers of the Goldsboro High School, "Active Learning in a High School of North Carolina," *Progressive Education*, December 1938, pp. 629–34 (Goldsboro, North Carolina); Ruth Willard Merritt, "Community Education in Ellerbee, N.C.," *Progressive Education*, February 1938, pp. 121–25; Margaret W. Boutelle, "A School Experiment with Integration," *Curriculum Journal*, May 1937, p. 216 (University of Florida laboratory school); Ethel P. Andrus, "General Procedure at Abraham Lincoln High School, Los Angeles," *Clearing House*, February 1935, pp. 334–39; A. C. Hentschke, "The Basic Course at Eagle Rock High School," *Clearing House*, May 1935, pp. 555–59 (Los Angeles); Glenn Kendall, "The Norris Community Program," *Curriculum Journal*, March 1939, pp. 108–10 (Norris, Tennessee); F. R. Wegner and Harry Langworthy, Jr., "Roslyn, N.Y., Moves Toward Integration," *Clearing House*, October 1936, pp. 84–87; Paul R. Pierce, "The Evolving Pattern of a High School Curriculum," *Curriculum Journal*, February 1941, pp. 70–73 (Chicago); J. C. Moffitt, *The Schools in the Community* (Report to the Board of Education, Provo, Utah, 1941); C. A. Bowes, "The First Junior High to Construct a Golf Course," *Clearing House*, September 1934, pp. 500–501 (Newington, Connecticut); Carlos A. Loop, "Co-ordinating the New Curriculum in Newport News High School," *Virginia Journal of Education*, February 1936, p. 208–10; Parker District High School Faculty, *Parker High School Serves Its People* (Greenville, South Carolina, 1942). For an overview of the "curriculum movement" and examples of progressive practice, see Harold Spears, *The Emerging High-School Curriculum and Its Direction* (New York: American Book, 1940). For a review of experimental high school programs, see Russell Irving Hammond, "A Functional Curriculum for a Small High School" (Diss., Teachers College, Columbia University, 1942).

33. I. L. Kandel, *The Cult of Uncertainty* (New York: Macmillan, 1943), pp. 14–15; Paul R. Mort and William S. Vincent, *A Look at Our Schools: A Book for the Thinking Citizen* (New York: Cattell, 1946), pp. v, 26, 36–37, 41–42.

34. U.S. Office of Education, *Life Adjustment Education for Every Youth* (Washington, D.C.: Government Printing Office, n.d.), p. 15; see also, Harl R. Douglass, *Education for Life Adjustment: Its Meaning and Implication* (New York: Ronald Press, 1950).

35. Dorothy Elizabeth Broder, "Life Adjustment Education: An Historical Study of a Program of the United States Office of Education, 1945–1954" (Diss., Teachers College, Columbia University, 1976), p. 23; Charles Allen Prosser, *Secondary Education and Life* (Cambridge, Mass.: Harvard University Press, 1939), pp. 15–16, 32–36.

36. U.S. Office of Education, *Life Adjustment Education*, pp. 7–10.

37. Franklin R. Zeran, ed., *Life Adjustment Education in Action* (New York: Chartwell House, 1953), p. 45. Other exemplary progressive programs are described in Will French, "Newer Practices in High School Curricula," in *Curriculum Making*, pp. 126–27; and J. Wayne Wrightstone, *Appraisal of Newer Elementary School Practices* (New York: Bureau of Publications, Teachers College, 1938); and in such magazines as *Progressive Education*, *Clearing House*, *Curriculum Journal*, *Nation's Schools*, and *High School Journal*.

38. Grace S. Wright, *Core Curriculum in Public High Schools: An Inquiry into Practices*, U.S. Office of Education, bulletin no. 5 (Washington, D.C.: Government Printing Office, 1949), pp. 17–25.

39. U.S. Department of the Interior, Office of Education, *A Survey of Courses of Study and Other Curriculum Materials Published Since 1934*, bulletin no. 31 (Washington, D.C.: Government

Printing Office, 1937), pp. 60; Ovid Frank Parody, "The Process of Initiating and Developing a New Curriculum at the Drum Hill Junior High School, Peekskill, New York" (Diss., Teachers College, Columbia University, 1948), pp. 17–18; Kenneth Douglass Wann, "Teacher Participation in Action Research Directed Toward Curriculum Change" (Diss., Teachers College, Columbia University, 1950), p. 48; *Materials Prepared by Participants in the Home Economics Group of the Progressive Education Association Summer Workshop, Sarah Lawrence College, Bronxville, New York,* July 2–August 13, 1937 (Columbus, Ohio: Progressive Education Association, 1937), pp. 46–54, 58–63; Donald Roe, "Proposal for the Organization and Administration of a Curriculum Improvement Plan for the New Oak Ridge High School" (Diss., Teachers College, Columbia University, 1950); Joseph McLain, "Plan to Use What Students, Teachers, Parents, and Graduates Think about Secondary Schools to Improve the Educational Program of Mamaroneck Senior High School" (Diss., Teachers College, Columbia University, 1950); Louis V. Nannini, "A Plan for the Improvement of the Curriculum Program of Manhasset High School, Manhasset, New York" (Diss., Teachers College, Columbia University, 1952).

40. Edward A. Krug, *The Secondary School Curriculum* (New York: Harper & Bros., 1960), pp. 258–59.

41. New York State University, *Regents Examinations* (1927, 1937, 1948).

42. Several of these groups and their publications are described in chapter 3. For a list, see Archibald W. Anderson, "The Cloak of Respectability: The Attackers and Their Methods," *Progressive Education,* January 1952, p. 68. For a description of the educational grievances of the antiprogressives, see Mary L. Allen, *Education Or Indoctrination* (Caldwell, Idaho: Caxton Printers, 1955).

43. Caswell, *Curriculum Improvement,* p. 258–62. The superintendent who installed common learnings was Willard Goslin, who left Minneapolis in 1948 to head the Pasadena schools (see chapter 3). Miles E. Cary, "The Fight Over 'Common Learnings' in Minneapolis," *Progressive Education,* May 1951, pp. 205–11.

44. Mortimer Smith, *And Madly Teach: A Layman Looks at Public School Education* (Chicago: Henry Regnery, 1949), pp. 7, 21–24, 42, 59–60, 92–93.

45. "Flapdoodle," *Time,* September 19, 1949, p. 64; Harry J. Fuller, "The Emperor's New Clothes, or Prius Dementat," *Scientific Monthly,* January 1951, pp. 32–41; see also, Louis William Norris, "In Praise of Maladjustment," *School and Society,* February 18, 1956, pp. 55–58.

46. The best collection of articles on the debate is C. Winfield Scott and Clyde M. Hill, *Public Education Under Criticism* (New York: Prentice-Hall, 1954); for a critical collection, see Mortimer Smith, ed. *The Public Schools in Crisis* (Chicago: Henry Regnery, 1956).

47. Anderson, "The Cloak of Respectability," pp. 66–81; see also, Robert A. Skaife, "The Sound and the Fury," *Phi Delta Kappan,* June 1953, pp. 357–62; "N.E.A. Says Modern Schools Teach Three R's Better Than Those of a Generation Ago," *New York Times,* July 8, 1951; Ernest O. Melby, "American Education is in Danger," *ADL Bulletin,* May 1951, pp. 1–7. The June 1953 issue of *Phi Delta Kappan* was devoted to the problem of the attacks on the schools.

48. W. M. Tugman, "Eugene, Oregon," *Saturday Review of Literature,* September 8, 1951, pp. 11–12; *New York Times,* April 13, 1952; Anderson, "The Cloak of Respectability," p. 67–68; Morris Mitchell, "Fever Spots in American Education," *Nation,* October 27, 1951, pp. 344–47.

49. Robert M. Hutchins, *The Conflict in Education in a Democratic Society* (New York: Harper & Bros., 1953), pp. 19–20, 42, 47, 50–51, 54–55.

50. Albert Lynd, *Quackery in the Public Schools* (Boston: Little, Brown, 1953), pp. 14–15, 34–36, 90, 207.

51. Cremin, *Transformation of the School,* p. 344; Arthur Bestor, *Educational Wastelands: The Retreat from Learning in our Public Schools* (Urbana: University of Illinois Press, 1953), pp. 4, 10, 44–47, 57–64, 75.

52. Paul Woodring, *Let's Talk Sense About Our Schools* (New York: McGraw-Hill, 1953), pp. 2, 14–15, 44–47, 63.

53. Caswell, *Curriculum Improvement;* Harold Alberty, *Reorganizing the High-School Curriculum* (New York: Macmillan, rev. ed., 1953, orig. pub., 1947), pp. 8, 15–16, 19, 253–54. Alberty cites Harold Hand, *What the People of Bloomington, Illinois, Think About Their Schools* (Bloomington: Board of Education, 1952), p. 135.

54. Patricia A. Graham, *Progressive Education: From Arcady to Academe: A History of the Progressive Education Association, 1919–1955* (New York: Teachers College Press, 1967), p. 145.

55. Cremin, *Transformation of the School,* p. ix.

Chapter 3: Loyalty Investigations

1. Walter Gellhorn, ed., *The States and Subversion* (Ithaca, N.Y.: Cornell University Press, 1952), p. 375.

2. Irving Howe and Lewis Coser, *The American Communist Party: A Critical History* (Boston: Beacon Press, 1957), pp. 198–201; James A. Wechsler, *The Age of Suspicion* (New York: Random House, 1953), p. 37; Robert W. Iversen, *The Communists and the Schools* (New York: Harcourt, Brace, 1959), pp. 124–47.

3. Daniel Bell, *Marxian Socialism in the United States* (Princeton, N. J.: Princeton University Press, 1967), p. 147. For an account of the schism on the left during and after the 1930s, see William L. O'Neill, *A Better World: The Great Schism: Stalinism and the American Intellectuals* (New York: Simon and Schuster, 1982). For a description of the Popular Front written contemporaneously, see Eugene Lyons, *The Red Decade: The Stalinist Penetration of America* (New York: Bobbs-Merrill, 1941).

4. George S. Counts, *Dare the School Build a New Social Order?* (New York: John Day, 1932), pp. 7, 9–10.

5. Ibid., pp. 28, 40–41.

6. William Heard Kilpatrick, "Launching the Social Frontier," *Social Frontier* 1 (October 1934):2; "Orientation," *Social Frontier* 1 (October 1934):3; "Freedom in a Collectivist Society," *Social Frontier* 1 (April 1935):10. Note: The statement about the close of "the age of individualism" is drawn from the final report of the American Historical Association's Commission on the Social Studies, in which Counts participated (American Historical Association, Commission on the Social Studies in the Schools [New York: Charles Scribner's, 1934], p. 16).

7. Kilpatrick, "Launching the Social Frontier," p. 2; "Teachers and Labor," *Social Frontier* 2 (October 1935):7–8; Theodore Brameld, "Karl Marx and the American Teacher," *Social Frontier* 2 (November 1935):53–56; "Class and Social Purpose," *Social Frontier* 2, (February 1936):135.

8. Harold Rugg, "The American Mind and the 'Class' Problem," *Social Frontier* 2 (February 1936):139; John Dewey, "Class Struggle and the Democratic Way," *Social Frontier* 2 (May 1936): 241–42; William Heard Kilpatrick, "High Marxism Defined and Rejected," *Social Frontier* 2 (June 1936): 272–74.

9. C. A. Bowers, "The *Social Frontier* Journal: A Historical Sketch," *History of Education Quarterly* 4 (September 1964):173; George S. Counts, "Whose Twilight?" *Social Frontier* 5 (February 1939): 135–40. Counts's article was a rejoinder to James A. Wechsler, "Twilight at Teachers College," *Nation,* December 17, 1938, pp. 661–63.

10. "The Changing Scene," *Social Frontier* 5 (May 1939):228.

11. Lawrence A. Cremin, *The Transformation of the School: Progressivism in American Education, 1876–1957* (New York: Alfred A. Knopf, 1961), p. 233.

12. See, Iversen, *Communists and the Schools;* David Caute, *The Great Fear. The Anti-Communist Purge Under Truman and Eisenhower* (New York: Simon and Schuster, 1978), pp. 403–45; Lawrence H. Chamberlain, *Loyalty and Legislative Action: A Survey of Activity by the New York State Legislature, 1919–1949* (Ithaca, N. Y.: Cornell University Press, 1951).

13. Elizabeth Dilling, *The Red Network: A 'Who's Who' and Handbook of Radicalism for Patriots* (Chicago: Elizabeth Dilling, 1934), pp. 258–59.

14. E. Edmund Reutter, Jr., *The School Administrator and Subversive Activities: A Study of the Administration of Restraints on Alleged Subversive Activities of Public School Personnel* (New York: Bureau of Publications, Teachers College, 1951), pp. 8–9, 12.

15. O. K. Armstrong, "Treason in the Textbooks," *American Legion Magazine*, September 1940, pp. 8–9, 51, 70–72; Augustin G. Rudd, "Our 'Reconstructed' Educational System," *Nation's Business*, April 1940, pp. 27–28, 93–94.

16. See, Harold O. Rugg, *The Great Technology: Social Chaos and the Public Mind* (New York: John Day, 1933).

17. Those who followed the affairs of the American Communist party recognized that the Soviet Union had shifted from cooperation to confrontation when Earl Browder, the exponent of peaceful coexistence, was replaced as party leader, on a signal from abroad, by the old Stalinist, William Z. Foster. See Phillip J. Jaffe, *The Rise and Fall of American Communism* (New York: Horizon Press, 1975), pp. 69–85.

18. Gellhorn, "A General View," *States and Subversion*, p. 360.

Notes

19. Reutter, *School Administrator and Subversive Activities*, pp. 15–25.

20. Murray Kempton, *Part of Our Time: Some Ruins and Monuments of the Thirties* (New York: Simon and Schuster, 1955), p. 170.

21. Vern Countryman, *Un-American Activities in the State of Washington: The Work of the Canwell Committee* (Ithaca, N. Y.: Cornell University Press, 1951); Jane Sanders, *Cold War on the Campus: Academic Freedom at the University of Washington, 1946–1964* (Seattle: University of Washington Press, 1979).

22. Iversen, *Communists and the Schools*, pp. 226, 334.

23. Sidney Hook, "Should Communists Be Permitted to Teach?" *New York Times Magazine*, February 27, 1949, pp. 7, 22–29; see also, Sidney Hook, *Heresy Yes, Conspiracy No* (New York: John Day, 1953).

24. Alexander Meiklejohn, "Should Communists be Allowed to Teach?" *New York Times Magazine*, March 27, 1949, pp. 10, 64–66.

25. Alonzo L. Hamby, *Beyond the New Deal: Harry S. Truman and American Liberalism* (New York: Columbia University Press, 1973), pp. 147–68; Norman Thomas, Letter to the Editor, *New York Times Magazine*, March 13, 1949, pp. 2, 4; Walter Goodman, *The Committee: The Extraordinary Career of the House Committee on Un-American Activities* (New York: Farrar, Straus & Giroux, 1968), p. 327; George Counts and John Childs, *America, Russia, and the Communist Party in the Postwar World* (New York: John Day, 1943), p. 62.

26. David P. Gardner, *The California Oath Controversy* (Berkeley and Los Angeles: University of California Press, 1967), p. 45; see also, George R. Stewart, *The Year of the Oath* (Garden City, N.Y.: Doubleday, 1950).

27. Gardner, *California Oath Controversy*, p. 122.

28. Ibid., pp. 250.

29. "The Great Investigation," published by the All-Campus Committee Opposing the Broyles Bills and the Broyles Investigations, University of Chicago, 1949. Part of Hutchins's testimony is cited in E. Houston Harsha, "Illinois: The Broyles Commission," in Gellhorn, *States and Subversion*, pp. 54–139.

30. "The Great Investigation," pp. 2–3; Harsha, "Illinois: The Broyles Commission," pp. 135–39.

31. Eric Bentley, ed., *Thirty Years of Treason* (New York: Viking Press, 1971), pp. 610, 620–21.

32. See, Ellen Schrecker, "Academic Freedom and the Cold War," *Antioch Review* 38 (Summer 1980):313–27.

33. For contemporary expressions of this dilemma, see Irving Kristol, " 'Civil Liberties,' 1952—A Study in Confusion: Do We Defend Our Rights by Protecting Communists?" *Commentary*, March 1952, pp. 228–36; Alan Barth, *The Loyalty of Free Men* (New York: Viking Press, 1952); Arthur M. Schlesinger, Jr., *The Vital Center: The Politics of Freedom* (Boston: Houghton Mifflin, 1949); see also, Mary Sperling McAuliffe, *Crisis on the Left: Cold War Politics and American Liberals* (Amherst: University of Massachusetts Press, 1978); O'Neill, *A Better World*, chap.11.

34. American Association of University Professors, "Academic Freedom and the Quest for National Security" (bulletin 42, 1956), pp. 49–61.

35. *New York Times*, March 31, 1953.

36. *Adler v. Board of Education*, 342 US 485 (1952); Leon Bock, "The Control of Alleged Subversive Activities in the Public School System of New York City, 1949–1956" (Diss., Teachers College, Columbia University, 1971), p. 155–56; U.S. Congress, Senate, Committee on the Judiciary, *Subversive Influence in the Educational Process*, 82nd Cong., 2nd sess., 1952, pp. 2–39. See also, Bella V. Dodd, *School of Darkness* (New York: P. J. Kenedy, 1954).

37. Earl Latham, *The Communist Controversy in Washington: From the New Deal to McCarthy* (Cambridge, Mass.: Harvard University Press, 1966), pp. 378–81.

38. Samuel A. Stouffer, *Communism, Conformity, and Civil Liberties: A Cross-Section of the Nation Speaks Its Mind* (Garden City, N.Y.: Doubleday, 1955), pp. 40–43; Paul F. Lazarsfeld and Wagner Thielens, Jr., *The Academic Mind: Social Scientists in a Time of Crisis* (Glencoe, Ill.: Free Press, 1958), pp. 35–71, 114, 192–236. Schrecker reports that 91 percent of the Rutgers faculty supported the trustees' policy of excluding Communist teachers ("Academic Freedom and the Cold War," p. 326).

39. Kitty Jones and Robert L. Olivier, *Progressive Education Is REDucation* (Boston: Meador, 1956).

40. John Flynn, "Who Owns Your Child's Mind?" *Reader's Digest*, October 1951, pp. 23–28. See footnotes 42 and 47, chapter 2.

41. Houston Independent School District, "Minutes of the School Board Meetings," September 11, 1940; October 24, 1949; March 24, 1952; July 13, 1953; July 15, 1953; April 26, 1954; see also, Don Edward Carleton, "A Crisis in Rapid Change: The Red Scare in Houston, 1945–1955" (Diss., University of Houston, 1978).

42. For the views of the School Development Council, see Mary L. Allen, *Education Or Indoctrination* (Caldwell, Idaho: Caxton, 1955).

43. David Hulburd, *This Happened in Pasadena* (New York: Macmillan, 1951); see also, James B. Conant, "The Superintendent Was the Target," *New York Times Book Review*, April 29, 1951, pp. 1, 27.

44. California Legislature, Senate Investigating Committee on Education, "Education in Pasadena," 8th report, 1951, pp. 25–27, 44.

45. See, for example, Arthur D. Morse, "Who's Trying to Ruin Our Schools?" *McCall's*, September 1951, pp. 26ff.; John Bainbridge, "Danger's Ahead in the Public Schools," *McCall's*, October 1952, pp. 56ff. Articles about school controversies in Scarsdale, New York; Port Washington, New York; Denver, Colorado; Pasadena, California; and Eugene, Oregon are included in C. Winfield Scott and Clyde M. Hill, eds., *Public Education Under Criticism*, (New York: Prentice-Hall, 1954).

46. *Wieman* v. *Updegraff*, 344 U.S. 183 (1952).

47. *Pennsylvania* v. *Nelson*, 350 U.S. 497 (1956); *Slochower* v. *Board of Higher Education of New York City*, 350 U.S. 551 (1956); *Watkins* v. *United States*, 354 U.S. 178 (1956); *Sweezy* v. *State of New Hampshire*, 354 U.S. 234 (1957); *Shelton* v. *Tucker*, 364 U.S. 479 (1960); *Cramp* v. *Board of Public Instruction of Orange County, Florida*, 368 U.S. 278 (1961); *Elfbrandt* v. *Russell*, 384 U.S. 11 (1966); *Keyishian* v. *Board of Regents of the University of the State of New York*, 385 U.S. 589 (1967); *Connell* v. *Higginbotham*, 403 U.S. 207 (1971); *Cole* v. *Richardson*, 405 U.S. 676 (1972).

48. Iversen, *Communists and the Schools*, p. 360; for a different view, see Caute, *The Great Fear*, pp. 403–45; and David L. Marden, "The Cold War and American Education" (Diss., University of Kansas, 1975).

49. Learned Hand, "A Plea for the Open Mind and Free Discussion," in *The Spirit of Liberty*, 3rd ed. (Chicago: University of Chicago Press, 1977), p. 284 (the speech was originally delivered on October 24, 1952).

50. Iversen, *Communists and the Schools*, p. 365.

Chapter 4: Race and Education: The *Brown* Decision

1. John Hope Franklin and Isidore Starr, eds., *The Negro in Twentieth Century America: A Reader on the Struggle for Civil Rights* (New York: Vintage, 1967), pp. 4–5.

2. Howard W. Odum, *Race and Rumors of Race: Challenge to American Crisis* (Chapel Hill: University of North Carolina Press, 1943), pp. 53–141.

3. Gunnar Myrdal, *An American Dilemma: The Negro Problem and Modern Democracy* (New York: Harper & Bros., 1944), pp. 416, 577.

4. Ibid., pp. 426, 518–19, 660–62.

5. *Plessy* v. *Ferguson*, 163 U.S. 537 (1896); see also, Richard Kluger, *Simple Justice: The History of* Brown *v.* Board of Education *and Black America's Struggle for Equality* (New York: Alfred A. Knopf, 1976), chaps. 2–4.

6. "The Availability of Education in the Negro Separate School," *Journal of Negro Education* 16 (Summer 1947): 378, 407; Ambrose Caliver, *Education of Negro Leaders: Influences Affecting Graduate and Professional Studies*, U.S. Office of Education, bulletin no. 3 (Washington, D.C.: Government Printing Office, 1948), p. 27.

7. Martin D. Jenkins, "The Availability of Higher Education for Negroes in the Southern States," *Journal of Negro Education* 16 (Summer 1947): 459–70.

8. *Missouri Ex Rel Gaines* v. *Canada*, 305 U.S. 337 (1938).

9. *Sipuel* v. *Oklahoma Board of Regents*, 332 U.S. 631 (1948).

10. *Sweatt* v. *Painter*, 339 U.S. 629 (1950); *McLaurin* v. *Oklahoma Board of Regents*, 339 U.S. 637 (1950).

11. "Appendix to Petition and Brief in Support of Petition for Writ of Certiorari to the Supreme Court of the State of Texas," 339 U.S. 629 (1950).

12. Leon Friedman, ed., *Argument: The Oral Argument Before the Supreme Court in* Brown

Notes

v. Board of Education of Topeka, *1952–1955* (New York: Chelsea House, 1969), pp. 14, 37.

13. "Brief for Appellants," *Brown* v. *Board of Education,* October 1952, pp. 5–8, 67–68; "Brief for Appellants," *Brown* v. *Board of Education,* October 1953, pp. 16, 22.

14. "The Effects of Segregation and the Consequences of Desegregation: A Social Science Statement," *Minnesota Law Review* 427 (1953); see also, social scientists' testimony in federal district court in *Brown* v. *Board of Education,* 98 F.Supp. 797 (D. Kans. 1951).

15. Friedman, *Argument,* pp. 47–49, 78, 118–21, 187, 202.

16. *Brown* v. *Board of Education,* 347 U.S. 483 (1954).

17. Stephen L. Wasby, Anthony A. D'Amato, and Rosemary Metrailer, *Desegregation from Brown to Alexander: An Exploration of Supreme Court Strategies* (Carbondale: Southern Illinois University Press, 1977), pp. 78–79; "Brief for Appellants," *Brown* v. *Board of Education,* October 1953, pp. 190–97.

18. *Brown* v. *Board of Education,* 349 U.S. 294 (1955).

19. Robert L. Carter and Thurgood Marshall, "The Meaning and Significance of the Supreme Court Decree," *Journal of Negro Education* 24 (Summer 1955):402.

20. Edmond Cahn, "Jurisprudence," *New York University Law Review* 30 (January 1955): 157–58; 163; see also, Alfred H. Kelly, "Clio and the Court: An Illicit Love Affair," in *Supreme Court Review 1965,* ed. Philip Kurland (Chicago: University of Chicago Press, 1965), pp. 119–58; Paul Rosen, *The Supreme Court and Social Science* (Urbana: University of Illinois Press, 1972); Betsy Levin and Philip Moise, "School Desegregation Litigation in the Seventies and the Use of Social Science Evidence: An Annotated Guide," *Law and Contemporary Problems* 39 (Winter 1975): 50–134.

21. Herbert Wechsler, "Toward Neutral Principles of Constitutional Law," *Harvard Law Review* 73 (November 1959): 1–35; see also, Arthur S. Miller and Ronald F. Howell, "The Myth of Neutrality in Constitutional Adjudication," *University of Chicago Law Review* 27 (Spring 1960): 661–95.

22. J. Harvie Wilkinson, III, *From* Brown *to* Bakke: *The Supreme Court and School Integration: 1954–1978* (New York: Oxford University Press, 1979), pp. 29–39, passim.

23. Omer Carmichael and Weldon James, *The Louisville Story* (New York: Simon and Schuster, 1957), pp. 85–86, 100.

24. Jack Greenberg, *Race Relations and American Law* (New York: Columbia University Press, 1959), p. 5.

25. Benjamin Muse, *Ten Years of Prelude: The Story of Integration Since the Supreme Court's 1954 Decision* (New York: Viking Press, 1964), p. 63. For the text of the manifesto, see Hubert H. Humphrey, ed., *Integration vs. Segregation* (New York: Thomas Y. Crowell, 1964), pp. 32–35.

26. "Statistical Summary of School Segregation-Desegregation in the Southern and Border States" (Nashville, Tenn.: Southern Education Reporting Service, 1962); Reed Sarratt, *The Ordeal of Desegregation: The First Decade* (New York: Harper & Row, 1966), pp. 28–46.

27. Muse, *Ten Years of Prelude,* pp. 87–104; see also, George Barrett, "Desegregation: The Clinton Story," *New York Times Magazine,* September 16, 1956, pp. 11ff.

28. President's Press Conference, May 19, 1954; March 14, 1956; September 5, 1956, Papers of President Dwight D. Eisenhower, Eisenhower Library, Abilene, Kansas.

29. Eisenhower Diaries, July 24, 1953, Eisenhower Library.

30. "Statement of Attorney General Herbert Brownell, Jr., on Civil Rights," Cabinet Paper 56–48, March 7, 1956; Maxwell M. Rabb, "Memorandum for the Attorney General. Subject: The President's Views on the Proposed Civil Rights Program," n.d., Ann Whitman Papers, Eisenhower Library.

31. President's Press Conference, July 17, 1957, Eisenhower Library.

32. Muse, *Ten Years of Prelude,* p. 126.

33. Ibid., pp. 127, 135.

34. Ibid., pp. 139–40; "Statement by the President," The White House, U.S. Naval Base, Newport, Rhode Island, September 23, 1957; "Obstruction of Justice in the State of Arkansas: A Proclamation by the President of the United States of America," September 23, 1957; "Text of the Address by the President of the United States, Delivered from His Office at the White House, Tuesday, September 24, 1957," Bryce Harlow Papers, Eisenhower Library; author's conversation with former White House aide Bryce Harlow, July 15, 1981.

35. *Cooper* v. *Aaron,* 358 U.S. 1; see Wasby, D'Amato, and Metrailer, *Desegregation from Brown to Alexander,* pp. 173–80, for the legal summary.

36. "Statistical Summary of School Segregation-Desegregation," p. 3.

37. Eugene Pierce Walker, "A History of the Southern Christian Leadership Conference, 1955–1965: The Evolution of a Southern Strategy for Social Change" (Diss., Duke University, 1978), p. 8; Anthony Lewis, *Portrait of a Decade: The Second American Revolution* (New York: Random House, 1964), p. 97.

38. Alexander Bickel, "After a Civil Rights Act," *New Republic,* May 9, 1964, pp. 11–15.

39. *New York Times,* June 12, 1963.

40. *New York Times,* November 28, 1963; " ' . . . Shall Now Also Be Equal . . . ' " *Newsweek,* July 13, 1964, p. 17.

41. U.S. Congress, House, Committee of the Judiciary, *Hearings on Civil Rights Bill,* 88th Cong., 1st sess., 1963, p. 2144.

42. U.S. Congress, Senate, Committee on the Judiciary, *Hearings on Civil Rights Bill,* 88th Cong., 1st sess., 1963, pp. 298–303.

43. U.S. Congress, House, Committee on the Judiciary, *Hearings on Civil Rights Bill,* 88th Cong., 1st sess., 1963, pp. 1516–17; Section 401 (b), 42 USCA:2000c(b).

Chapter 5: Race and Education: Social Science and Law

1. Michael Harrington, *The Other America: Poverty in the United States* (New York: Macmillan, 1962), p. 159.

2. U.S. Department of Labor and U.S. Department of Commerce, Current Population Reports, *Social and Economic Conditions of Negroes in the United States* (Washington, D.C.: U.S. Government Printing Office, 1967), pp. 6–9.

3. Eric F. Goldman, *The Tragedy of Lyndon Johnson* (New York: Alfred A. Knopf, 1968), p. 363; see also, Eugene Eidenberg and Roy D. Morey, *An Act of Congress: The Legislative Process and the Making of Education Policy* (New York: W. W. Norton, 1969); Frank J. Munger and Richard F. Fenno, Jr., *National Politics and Federal Aid to Education* (Syracuse, N.Y.: Syracuse University Press, 1962), p. 170; Hugh Douglas Price, "Race, Religion and the Rules Committee: The Kennedy Aid-to-Education Bills," in *The Uses of Power,* ed. Alan F. Westin (New York: Harcourt, Brace & World, 1962), p. 67; Philip Meranto, *The Politics of Federal Aid to Education in 1965: A Study in Political Innovation* (Syracuse, N.Y.: Syracuse University Press, 1967).

4. Stephen K. Bailey and Edith K. Mosher, *ESEA: The Office of Education Administers a Law* (Syracuse, N.Y.: Syracuse University Press, 1968), pp. 49–50; National Institute of Education, *Compensatory Education Services* (Washington, D.C.: Government Printing Office, 1977), p. 7.

5. James B. Conant, *Slums and Suburbs* (New York: McGraw-Hill 1961), pp. 24–25.

6. See Diane Ravitch, *The Great School Wars: New York City, 1805–1973* (New York: Basic Books, 1974).

7. David P. Ausubel, "Ego Development Among Segregated Negro Children," *Mental Hygiene* 42 (1956): 362–69.

8. See, for example, Benjamin Bloom, Allison Davis, and Robert Hess, *Compensatory Education for Cultural Deprivation* (New York: Holt, Rinehart & Winston, 1965); Edmund W. Gordon and Doxey A. Wilkerson, *Compensatory Education for the Disadvantaged: Programs and Practices: Preschool Through College* (New York: College Entrance Examination Board, 1966); A. Harry Passow, ed., *Education in Depressed Areas* (New York: Bureau of Publications, Teachers College, 1963).

9. Martin Deutsch, "Minority Group and Class Status as Related to Social and Personality Factors in Scholastic Achievement," (Society for Applied Anthropology, monograph no. 2, 1960), pp. 3–9.

10. Bloom, Davis, and Hess, *Compensatory Education for Cultural Deprivation,* pp. 4, 17, 23, 25–26.

11. Gordon and Wilkerson, *Compensatory Education for the Disadvantaged,* p. 34; Henry T. Hillson, "The Demonstration Guidance Project, 1957–1962: Pilot Program for Higher Horizons," (New York: Board of Education, 1963).

12. Frank Riessman, *The Culturally Deprived Child* (New York: Harper & Row, 1962), pp. x–xi, 1.

13. Ibid., p. 80.

14. Frank Riessman, *Helping the Disadvantaged Child to Learn More Easily* (Englewood Cliffs, N. J.: Prentice-Hall, 1966).

15. Jean Dresden Grambs, "Instructional Materials for the Disadvantaged Child," in *Reaching the Disadvantaged Learner,* ed. A. Harry Passow (New York: Teachers College Press, 1970), p. 172.

16. Sloan Wayland, "Old Problems, New Faces, and New Standards," in Passow, *Education in Depressed Areas,* p. 66; Hylan Lewis, "The Contemporary Urban Poverty Syndrome" (Speech delivered to Howard University Medical School, April 28, 1964), in *Seminar Selections on the Disadvantaged Child,* ed. Elizabeth H. Brady, NDEA Institute for Teachers of Young Disadvantaged Children, Selected Academic Readings (New York: NDEA n.d.), pp. 25–26.

17. Kenneth B. Clark, *Dark Ghetto: Dilemmas of Social Power* (New York: Harper & Row, 1965), p. 131.

18. Edward Zigler and Karen Anderson, "An Idea Whose Time Had Come: The Intellectual and Political Climate for Head Start," in *Project Head Start: A Legacy of the War on Poverty,* ed. Edward Zigler and Jeanette Valentine (New York: Free Press, 1979), p. 12; Lyndon B. Johnson, "Remarks on Project Head Start, May 18, 1965," in *Project Head Start,* p. 69.

19. Louise B. Miller, "Development of Curriculum Models in Head Start," in *Project Head Start,* p. 196; Zigler and Anderson, "An Idea Whose Time Had Come," pp. 12–13.

20. Eveline B. Omwake, "Assessment of the Head Start Preschool Education Effort," in *Project Head Start,* pp. 222–23.

21. Bailey and Mosher, *ESEA,* p. 51; Public Law 89-10, Section 205.

22. Milbrey Wallin McLaughlin, "Implementation of ESEA Title I: A Problem of Compliance," *Teachers College Record* 77 (February 1976): 404; National Institute of Education, *Compensatory Education Services* (Washington, D.C.: Government Printing Office, 1977), p. 5.

23. Lee Rainwater and William L. Yancey, *The Moynihan Report and the Politics of Controversy* (Cambridge, Mass.: MIT Press, 1967), contains the Moynihan report, the president's Howard University speech, and a full account of the controversy.

24. William Manchester, *The Glory and the Dream* (Boston: Little, Brown, 1974), pp. 1062–65; Goldman, *Tragedy of Lyndon Johnson,* p. 509–10.

25. Sarratt, *Ordeal of Desegregation,* p. 350.

26. U.S. Congress, Senate, Committee on the Judiciary, *Hearings on Civil Rights,* 88th Cong., 1st sess., 1963, p. 63; Section 401 (b), 42 USCA: 2000c(b).

27. Gary Orfield, *The Reconstruction of Southern Education* (New York: John Wiley, 1969), pp. 85–101; Bailey and Mosher, *ESEA,* pp. 142–46.

28. Bailey and Mosher, *ESEA,* pp. 153–54.

29. Orfield, *Reconstruction of Southern Education,* p. 146; Bailey and Mosher, *ESEA,* pp. 153–55.

30. Bailey and Mosher, *ESEA,* pp. 155–56; Orfield, *Reconstruction of Southern Education,* pp. 266–304; Gary Orfield, *Must We Bus?: Segregated Schools and National Policy* (Washington, D.C.: Brookings Institution, 1978), pp. 238–39.

31. *Briggs* v. *Elliott,* 132 F. Supp. 776 (E.D.S.C. 1955).

32. Frank T. Read, "Judicial Evolution of the Law of School Integration since *Brown v. Board of Education,*" *Law and Contemporary Problems* 39 (Winter 1975): 20.

33. *Singleton* v. *Jackson Municipal Separate School District,* 348 F. 2d 729 (5th Cir. 1965); 355 F. 2d 865 (5th Cir. 1966); *United States* v. *Jefferson County Board of Education,* 372 F. 2d 836 (5th Cir. 1966); 380 F. 2d 385 (5th Cir. 1967).

34. Alexander Bickel, "Skelly Wright's Sweeping Decision," *New Republic,* July 8, 1967, pp. 11–12.

35. Read, "Judicial Evolution of the Law of School Integration," pp. 20–28; U.S. Commission on Civil Rights, *Twenty Years After* Brown: *Equality of Educational Opportunity* (Washington, D.C.: Government Printing Office, 1975), p. 47.

36. Clayborne Carson, *In Struggle: SNCC and the Black Awakening of the 1960s* (Cambridge, Mass.: Harvard University Press, 1981), pp. 191–211.

37. Jervis Anderson, *A. Philip Randolph: A Biographical Portrait* (New York: Harcourt, Brace, Jovanovich, 1972), pp. 330–44.

38. Section 402, Civil Rights Act of 1964; James S. Coleman et al., *Equality of Educational Opportunity* (Washington, D.C.: Government Printing Office, 1966); James S. Coleman, "Policy Research in the Social Sciences" (Morristown, N. J.: General Learning Press, 1972), p. 9.

39. Gerald Grant, "Essay Review," *Harvard Educational Review* 42 (February 1972): 110.

40. Coleman et al., *Equality of Educational Opportunity,* p. 28.

41. Ibid., pp. 31–32.

42. Alexander Bickel, "Education in a Democracy: The Legal and Practical Problems of School Busing," *Human Rights* 3 (Summer 1973): 54.

43. Ravitch, *Great School Wars*, pp. 252–53; Massachusetts State Board of Education, *Because It Is Right—Educationally* (Report of the Advisory Committee on Racial Imbalance and Education, April 1965); *Fischer* v. *Board of Education, Race Rel. L. Rep.* pp. 730, 733–34; U.S. Commission on Civil Rights, *Racial Isolation in the Public Schools* (Washington, D.C.: Government Printing Office, 1967), p. 230.

44. *Taylor* v. *Board of Education of New Rochelle*, 191 F.Supp. 181 (S.D.N.Y. 1961); *Crisis in the Public Schools: Racial Segregation, Northern Style*, based on reports by Dan W. Dodson (New York: Council for American Unity, 1965); *Bell* v. *School Board of Gary, Indiana*, 213 F. Supp. 819 (N.D. Ind. 1963).

45. U.S. Commission on Civil Rights, *Racial Isolation in the Public Schools*, p. iv–vi.

46. Ibid., pp. viii, 199.

47. Ibid., pp. 203–4.

48. Ibid., p. 205.

49. Ibid., pp. 209–10.

50. Ibid., pp. 106, 117.

51. Preston Wilcox, "Releasing Human Potential: A Study of the East Harlem-Yorkville School Bus Transfers" (New York: New York City Commission on Human Rights, 1961); Stokely Carmichael and Charles V. Hamilton, *Black Power* (New York: Random House, 1967); Ravitch, *Great School Wars*, p. 293.

52. Ravitch, *Great School Wars*, pp. 292–387.

53. *Green* v. *County School Board of New Kent County*, 391 U.S. 430 (1968).

54. Orfield, *Must We Bus?*, pp. 235, 240, 244.

55. *Swann* v. *Charlotte-Mecklenburg*, 402 U.S. 1 (1971).

56. U.S. Commission on Civil Rights, *Twenty Years After* Brown, pp. 49–50.

57. *Keyes* v. *School District No. 1, Denver, Colorado*, 413 U.S. 189 (1973).

58. Orfield, *Must We Bus?*, pp. 20–22.

59. Eleanor P. Wolf, *Trial and Error: The Detroit School Segregation Case* (Detroit: Wayne State University, 1981).

60. *Milliken* v. *Bradley*, 418 U.S. 717 (1974).

61. David J. Armor, "The Evidence on Busing," *Public Interest* 28 (Summer 1972): 90 126; Thomas F. Pettigrew, Elizabeth L. Useem, Clarence Normand, and Marshall S. Smith, "Busing: a Review of 'The Evidence,'" *Public Interest* 30 (Winter 1973): 88–118; David J. Armor, "The Double Double Standard: A Reply," *Public Interest* 30 (Winter 1973): 119–31.

62. "School Expert Calls Integration Vital Aid," *New York Times*, March 9, 1970; "Long-Time Desegregation Proponent Attacks Busing as Harmful," *New York Times*, June 7, 1975; James S. Coleman, "Coleman on 'The Coleman Report,'" *Public Interest* 28 (Summer 1972): 127–28; James S. Coleman, Sara D. Kelley, and John H. Moore, *Trends in School Segregation, 1968–1973* (Washington, D.C.: Urban Institute, 1975); Gregg Jackson, "Reanalysis of Coleman's 'Recent Trends in School Integration,'" *Educational Researcher* 4 (November 1975): 21–25; Christine H. Rossell, "School Desegregation and White Flight," *Political Science Quarterly* 90 (Winter 1975): 675–95.

63. Orfield, *Must We Bus?*, chap. 12.

64. Nancy H. St. John, *School Desegregation: Outcomes for Children* (New York: John Wiley, 1975), p. 85; see also, Harold B. Gerard and Norman Miller, *School Desegregation: A Long-Term Study* (New York: Plenum Press, 1975).

65. Diane Ravitch, "The 'White Flight' Controversy," *Public Interest* 51 (Spring 1978): 135–49.

66. David K. Cohen and Janet A. Weiss, "Social Science and Social Policy: Schools and Race," *Educational Forum*, May 1977, p. 410.

67. Derrick A. Bell, Jr., "Waiting on the Promise of *Brown*," *Law and Contemporary Problems* 39 (Spring 1975): 341–73; Derrick A. Bell, Jr., "A Model Alternative Desegregation Plan," in *Shades of* Brown: *New Perspectives on School Desegregation*, ed. Derrick A. Bell, Jr. (New York: Teachers College Press, 1980), pp. 124–39; *Tasby* v. *Wright*, U.S. District Court, N.D. Texas, 1981, p. 8; Joel L. Fleishman, "The Real Against the Ideal—Making the Solution Fit the Problem: The Atlanta Public School Agreement of 1973," in *Roundtable Justice: Case Studies in Conflict Resolution* (Reports to the Ford Foundation), ed. Robert B. Goldmann (Boulder, Colo.: Westview Press, 1980).

Notes

Chapter 6: From Berkeley to Kent State

1. Ben J. Wattenberg, ed., *The Statistical History of the United States: From Colonial Times to the Present* (New York: Basic Books, 1976), pp. 382–83.

2. Ibid.

3. National Center for Education Statistics, *Digest of Education Statistics, 1980* (Washington, D.C.: Government Printing Office, 1980), p. 89; Wattenberg, *Statistical History*, p. 383.

4. Clark Kerr, *The Uses of the University* (New York: Harper Torchbook, 1973, orig. pub., 1963), pp. 87–88.

5. Ibid., pp. 103–4.

6. Daniel Bell, *The End of Ideology: On the Exhaustion of Political Ideas in the Fifties* (New York: Free Press, rev. ed., 1965, orig. pub., 1960), p. 405.

7. Ronald Berman, *America in the Sixties: An Intellectual History* (New York: Free Press, 1968), p. 2; William L. O'Neill, *Coming Apart: An Informal History of America in the 1960's* (Chicago: Quadrangle Books, 1971), p. 3.

8. See, Morris Dickstein, *Gates of Eden: American Culture in the Sixties* (New York: Basic Books, 1977).

9. C. Wright Mills, *The Power Elite* (New York: Oxford University Press, 1956), p. 361.

10. Paul Goodman, *Growing Up Absurd: Problems of Youth in the Organized Society* (New York: Vintage Books, 1962), pp. xvi, 12–15.

11. Paul Jacobs and Saul Landau, *The New Radicals* (New York: Random House, 1966), pp. 104, 111–12; see, Daniel Bell's reply to Mills, "On C. Wright Mills and the 'Letter to the New Left,'" originally published in *Encounter*, December 1960, reprinted in Daniel Bell, *The Winding Passage: Essays and Sociological Journeys, 1960–1980* (Cambridge, Mass.: Abt Books, 1980).

12. "The Port Huron Statement," in *The New Student Left*, ed. Mitchell Cohen and Dennis Hale (Boston: Beacon Press, 1966), p. 217.

13. Clayborne Carson, *In Struggle: SNCC and the Black Awakening of the 1960s* (Cambridge, Mass.: Harvard University Press, 1981), pp. 99–100, 114; Len Holt, *The Summer That Didn't End* (New York: William Morrow, 1965), pp. 35–51.

14. Oral history interview with Tom Hayden, conducted by Bret Eynon, September 29, 1978, Michigan Historical Collections, Bentley Historical Library, University of Michigan.

15. Bradford Cleaveland, "A Letter to Undergraduates," in *The Berkeley Student Revolt: Facts and Interpretations*, ed. Seymour Martin Lipset and Sheldon S. Wolin (New York: Anchor Books, 1965), pp. 72, 80.

16. Mario Savio, "An End to History," in *Berkeley Student Revolt*, p. 216.

17. Max Heirich, *The Beginning: Berkeley, 1964* (New York: Columbia University Press, 1968), p. 173.

18. Ibid., pp. 155–56. The Academic Senate Ad Hoc Committee studying the suspensions recommended that six students be reinstated as of the date they had been suspended, and that the two demonstration leaders be given six-week suspensions, ending three days after the committee's report was released. The Regents, on recommendation of Kerr and Strong, said that the suspension of all eight students was in force from the date it was imposed (September 30) until the day of the Regents' meeting; in addition, the two demonstration leaders were placed on probation for the few remaining weeks of the current semester.

19. Ibid., p. 195. An FSM leader later said "that if the university had not broken the thing open again . . . by its disciplinary action against four of the FSM leaders," the FSM would have shown a film banned by the university as obscene in order to provoke a clash with the administration. Seymour Martin Lipset and Paul Seabury, "The Lesson of Berkeley," in *Berkeley Student Revolt*, p. 342.

20. Heirich, *The Beginning*, pp. 199–200.

21. Ibid., p. 215.

22. Ibid., pp. 230, 233.

23. Ibid., pp. 247–48.

24. Robert H. Somers, "The Mainsprings of the Rebellion: A Survey of Berkeley Students in November, 1964," in *Berkeley Student Revolt*, p. 536.

25. Mervin D. Field, "The UC Student Protests: California Poll," in *Berkeley Student Revolt*, p. 199.

26. Seymour Martin Lipset and Gerald M. Schaflander, *Passion and Politics: Student Activism in America* (Boston: Little, Brown, 1971), pp. 124–96; Steven J. Novak, *The Rights of Youth:*

American Colleges and Student Revolt, 1798–1815 (Cambridge, Mass.: Harvard University Press, 1977); Seymour Martin Lipset, ed., *Student Politics* (New York: Basic Books, 1967); Kirkpatrick Sale, *SDS* (New York: Random House, 1973), p. 145; Tom Hayden, "The Politics of 'The Movement' " in *The Radical Papers*, ed. Irving Howe (New York: Anchor Books, 1966), pp. 362–77. See also Richard Flacks, "On the New Working Class and Strategies for Social Change," in *The New Pilgrims*, ed. Philip G. Altbach and Robert S. Laufer (New York: David McKay, 1972); Flacks argues that the New Left should stay outside the political system in order to assure that the system continues to fail to change (p. 97).

27. Irving Howe, "New Styles in 'Leftism,' " *Dissent* 12 (Summer 1965): 295–333; Michael Harrington, "Is There a New Radicalism?" *Partisan Review* 33 (Spring 1965):194–202.

28. Everett Carll Ladd, Jr., and Seymour Martin Lipset, *The Divided Academy: Professors and Politics* (New York: McGraw-Hill, 1975), p. 32; Sale, *SDS*, p. 122, 263, 333, 341.

29. Carl Davidson, "Toward a Student Syndicalist Movement, or University Reform Revisited," in *The University Crisis Reader*, 2 vols., ed. Immanuel Wallerstein and Paul Starr, 2:98–99; Sale, *SDS*, pp. 338–39, 391–92.

30. O'Neill, *Coming Apart*, pp. 233–66; *The Free People* (New York: Outerbridge & Dienstfrey, 1969); Theodore Roszak, *The Making of a Counter Culture: Reflections on the Technocratic Society and Its Youthful Opposition* (New York: Doubleday, 1969); Charles A. Reich, *The Greening of America: How the Youth Revolution Is Trying to Make America Livable* (New York: Random House, 1970); Benjamin Zablocki, *Alienation and Charisma: A Study of Contemporary American Communes* (New York: Free Press, 1980).

31. Jerry L. Avorn et al., *Up Against the Ivy Wall: A History of the Columbia Crisis* (New York: Atheneum, 1970), pp. 34–36; see also, the Cox Commission Report, *Crisis at Columbia: Report of the Fact-Finding Commission Appointed to Investigate the Disturbances at Columbia University in April and May 1968* (New York: Vintage, 1968); Roger Kahn, *The Battle for Morningside Heights: Why Students Rebel* (New York: William Morrow, 1970); Dotson Rader, *I Ain't Marchin' Anymore* (New York: David McKay, 1969).

32. Eli Ginzberg, "Black Power and Student Unrest: Reflections on Columbia University and Harlem," *George Washington Review* 37 (May 1969):842.

33. *Columbia Daily Spectator*, April 25, 1968, pp. 1, 6; Mark Rudd, "Columbia," in *University Crisis Reader*, 2:185.

34. *Columbia Daily Spectator*, March 6, 1968, p. 4; April 29, 1968, p. 4.

35. Walter P. Metzger, "The Crisis of Academic Authority," *Daedalus* 99 (Summer 1970): 568–608.

36. Avorn, *Up Against the Ivy Wall*, p. 268; Tom Hayden, "Two, Three, Many Columbias," in *University Crisis Reader*, 2:163–64.

37. Alexander W. Astin et al., *The Power of Protest* (San Francisco: Jossey-Bass, 1975), pp. 37–41.

38. Ladd and Lipset, *Divided Academy*, pp. 26–34; Martin Trow, "Conceptions of the University: The Case of Berkeley," *American Behavioral Scientist* 11 (May-June 1968):15.

39. For coverage of the Chicago sit-in, see *New York Times*, January 30, February 1, 2, 3, 13, 1969.

40. Robert Smith, Richard Axen, and DeVere Pentony, *By Any Means Necessary: The Revolutionary Struggle at San Francisco State* (San Francisco: Jossey-Bass, 1970), p. 56.

41. Lawrence E. Eichel et al., *The Harvard Strike* (Boston: Houghton Mifflin, 1970), pp. 89, 105.

42. Ibid., p. 111.

43. Ibid., p. 186.

44. Ibid., pp. 249–51.

45. "The Report of the Committee to Review the Department of Afro-American Studies," *Harvard University Gazette*, October 30, 1972; see also, Henry Rosovsky, "Black Studies at Harvard: Personal Reflections Concerning Recent Events," *American Scholar* 38 (Autumn 1969): 562–72.

46. Richard B. Freeman, *Black Elite: The New Market for Highly Educated Black Americans* (New York: McGraw-Hill, 1976), p. 47; Current Population Reports, "School Enrollment," 1977.

47. Smith, Axen, and Pentony, *By Any Means Necessary*, p. 30; Astin et al., *Power of Protest*, pp. 71–75.

48. The following books describe the events at San Francisco State College: Smith, Axen, and Pentony, *By Any Means Necessary;* the authors were administrators at the college during

the crisis. Dikran Karagueuzian, *Blow It Up: The Black Student Revolt at San Francisco State College and the Emergence of Dr. Hayakawa* (Boston: Gambit, 1971); the author was editor of the student newspaper. Arlene Kaplan Daniels, Rachel Kahn-Hut, and Associates, *Academics on the Line* (San Francisco: Jossey-Bass, 1970); the authors were professors at the college who went on strike during the crisis. John Summerskill, *President Seven* (New York: World, 1971); the author was president of San Francisco State for two years, until mid-1968.

49. Smith, Axen, and Pentony, *By Any Means Necessary*, p. 155.

50. *New York Times*, March 8, 1969. The article that made Bunzel a target was his "Black Studies at San Francisco State," *Public Interest* 12 (Summer 1968):22–38; see also, John H. Bunzel, " 'War of the Flea' at San Francisco State," *New York Times Magazine*, November 9, 1969, pp. 28 ff.

51. Smith, Axen, and Pentony, *By Any Means Necessary*, pp. 320–24; Karagueuzian, *Blow It Up*, pp. 185, 190–196.

52. Allen P. Sindler, "A Case Study of a University's Pattern of Error" (Paper presented at the annual meeting of the American Political Science Association, New York City, September 1969).

53. Ernest Dunbar, "The Black Studies Thing," *New York Times Magazine*, April 6, 1969, pp. 60, 70.

54. *New York Times*, May 28, 1969.

55. Ibid.

56. *New York Times*, April 30, May 2, 1969.

57. *New York Times*, March 23, May 4, 1969; Louis Harris, *Philadelphia Inquirer*, April 3, 1969.

58. Sale, *SDS*, p. 550.

59. Ibid., chap. 24; but for the PL version of the split, see Alan Adelson, *SDS* (New York: Charles Scribner's, 1972), pp. 225–48.

60. *New York Times*, April 25, 1970; John Taft, *Mayday at Yale: A Case Study in Student Radicalism* (Boulder, Colorado: Westview Press, 1976), pp. 87, 102–3, 105, 116–17, 119–20, 124, 126, 161–162, 167.

61. For descriptions of events leading up to and following the May Day rally, see Taft, *Mayday at Yale;* John Hersey, *Letter to the Alumni* (New York: Alfred A. Knopf, 1970); Robert Brustein, "When the Panther Came to Yale," *New York Times Magazine*, June 21, 1970, pp. 7ff.; an exchange of letters between Brustein and Kenneth Keniston in the same publication on July 12, 1970, pp. 2, 34–35; "And Now Yale . . . " *Time*, May 4, 1970, p. 59; "Panther and Bulldog," *Newsweek*, May 4, 1970, p. 52; "Gentlemen Songsters Off on a Spree," *Newsweek*, May 11, 1970, p. 31; Paul Starr, "Black Panthers and White Radicals," *Commonweal*, June 12, 1970, pp. 294–97. For an article disputing the claim that there was a national campaign to destroy the Panthers, see Edward Jay Epstein, "The Panthers and the Police: A Pattern of Genocide?" *New Yorker*, February 13, 1971, pp. 45–77. For the aftermath of the Panther trials in New Haven, see *New York Times*, September 1, 1970; September 19, 1970; November 18, 1970; May 25, 1971.

62. *New York Times*, May 6, 1970.

63. See generally, *New York Times* for the first two weeks in May; "May Day," *Newsweek*, May 11, 1970, pp. 31–38; Sale, *SDS*' pp. 637–39; Astin et al., *Power of Protest*, p. 39; James Michener, *Kent State: What Happened and Why* (New York: Random House, 1971); *Report of the President's Commission on Campus Unrest* (New York: Arno Press, 1970).

64. *New York Times*, May 9, 1970; see also, Aaron Wildavsky, *The Revolt Against the Masses* (New York: Basic Books, 1971), pp. 29–51.

65. For the firing of Professor H. Bruce Franklin, see Kenneth Lamott, "In the Matter of H. Bruce Franklin," *New York Times Magazine*, January 23, 1972, pp. 12–26; Herbert L. Packer, "Academic Freedom and the Franklin Case," *Commentary*, April 1972, pp. 78–84; Alan Dershowitz, *The Best Defense* (New York: Random House, 1982).

66. Robert Paul Wolff, *The Ideal of the University* (Boston: Beacon Press, 1969), p. 75.

67. Stanley Rothman and S. Robert Lichter, *Roots of Radicalism: Jews, Christians, and the New Left* (New York: Oxford University Press, 1982), p. 388.

68. Zbigniew Brzezinski, "Revolution and Counterrevolution (But Not Necessarily About Columbia!)," *New Republic*, June 1, 1968, pp. 23–25; Bruno Bettelheim, "Obsolete Youth: Towards a Psychograph of Adolescent Rebellion," *Encounter* 33 (September 1969):37; Lewis Feuer, *The Conflict of Generations: The Character and Significance of Student Movements* (New York: Basic Books, 1969); C. Vann Woodward, "What Became of the 1960s?" *New Republic*, November 9, 1974, pp. 18–28.

69. Gerald Rosenfield, "Generational Revolt and the Free Speech Movement (Part 2)," *Liberation,* January 1966, pp. 18–19; reprinted in Jacobs and Landau, *New Radicals,* p. 215.

70. Maryl Levine and John Naisbitt, *Right On* (New York: Bantam, 1970), p. 70; see also, Linda Rennie Forcey, "Personality in Politics: The Commitment of a Suicide" (Diss., State University of New York at Binghamton, 1978), p. 93; Paul Goodman, *The New Reformation: Notes of a Neolithic Conservative* (New York: Random House, 1970), p. 152.

71. Lipset and Schaflander, *Passion and Politics,* pp. 45–61.

72. See, Richard Flacks, "The Liberated Generation: An Exploration of the Roots of Student Protest," *Journal of Social Issues* 23 (July 1967): 52–75; Kenneth Keniston, *Young Radicals: Notes on Committed Youth* (New York: Harcourt Brace Jovanovich, 1968); Kenneth Keniston, *Youth and Dissent* (New York: Harcourt Brace Jovanovich, 1971); Richard G. Braungart, "Youth Movements," in *Handbook of Adolescent Psychology,* ed. Joseph Adelson (New York: John Wiley, 1980), pp. 560–97; James L. Wood, *The Sources of American Student Activism* (Lexington, Mass.: D.C. Heath, 1974). For a comprehensive review and critique of the vast literature on youthful radicalism, see Rothman and Lichter, *Roots of Radicalism.*

73. Astin et al., *Power of Protest,* pp. 45, 180.

74. Ladd and Lipset, *Divided Academy,* pp. 207–9. The magazines *Commentary* and *Public Interest,* which became forums for "neoconservative" opinion, published many articles critical of campus disorders. For a survey of Marxism on campus, see Bertell Ollman and Edward Vernoff, eds., *The Left Academy: Marxist Scholarship on American Campuses* (New York: McGraw-Hill, 1981).

75. Robert Blackburn et al., *Changing Practices in Undergraduate Education* (Berkeley, California: Carnegie Council on Policy Studies in Higher Education, 1976), p. 34; Gerald Grant and David Riesman, *The Perpetual Dream: Reform and Experiment in the American College* (Chicago: University of Chicago Press, 1978), pp. 188–89; James Cass and Max Birnbaum, *Comparative Guide to American Colleges: 1968–1969 Edition* (New York: Harper & Row, 1968); James Cass and Max Birnbaum, *Comparative Guide to American Colleges: Sixth Edition* (New York: Harper & Row, 1973).

76. Lipset and Schaflander, *Passion and Politics,* p. 221.

77. Eugene D. Genovese, "Black Studies: Trouble Ahead," *Atlantic Monthly,* June 1969, p. 38.

Chapter 7: Reformers, Radicals, and Romantics

1. Lawrence A. Cremin, *The Transformation of the School: Progressivism in American Education, 1876–1957* (New York: Alfred A. Knopf, 1961), p. 347; Hyman Rickover, *Education and Freedom* (New York: E. P. Dutton, 1959). See also, for reactions to Sputnik, Kermit Lansner, ed., *Second-Rate Brains* (New York: Doubleday, 1958).

2. Barbara Barksdale Clowse, "Education as an Instrument of National Security: The Cold War Campaign to 'Beat the Russians' from Sputnik to the National Defense Education Act of 1958" (Diss., University of North Carolina at Chapel Hill, 1977), pp. 99–102 (published as *Brainpower for the Cold War: The Sputnik Crisis and the National Defense Education Act of 1958* [Westport, Conn.: Greenwood Press, 1981]).

3. Max Beberman, *An Emerging Program of Secondary School Mathematics* (Cambridge, Mass.: Harvard University Press, 1958). See chapter 2, pp. 72–79.

4. Rockefeller Brothers Fund, *The Pursuit of Excellence* (New York: Doubleday, 1958).

5. James B. Conant, *The American High School Today* (New York: McGraw-Hill, 1959), pp. 15, 37–38; Carnegie Corporation of New York, *Fiftieth Annual Report and Annual Report for the Fiscal Year Ended September 30th, 1961* (New York: Carnegie Corporation, 1961), p. 24; see also, A. Harry Passow, *American Secondary Education: The Conant Influence* (Reston, Va.: National Association of Secondary School Principals, 1977); *New York Times,* February 13, 1978.

6. Paul M. Nachtigal, *A Foundation Goes to School: The Ford Foundation Comprehensive School Improvement Program, 1960–1970* (New York: Ford Foundation, 1972).

7. Edward A. Krug, *The Secondary School Curriculum* (New York: Harper & Bros., 1960), pp. 258–59; President's Commission on Foreign Language and International Studies, *Strength Through Wisdom: A Critique of U.S. Capability* (Washington, D.C.: Government Printing Office, 1979).

8. National Science Foundation, *What Are the Needs in Precollege Science, Mathematics, and Social*

Notes

Science Education? Views from the Field (Washington, D.C.: Government Printing Office, 1980), p. v.

9. Jerome Bruner, *The Process of Education* (Cambridge, Mass.: Harvard University Press, 1960), p. 33.

10. Ronald Gross and Judith Murphy, eds., *The Revolution in the Schools* (New York: Harcourt, Brace & World, 1964), p. 1.

11. Don D. Bushnell, "Computers in Education," in Gross and Murphy, *Revolution in the Schools*, pp. 68–69; Jonathan King, "The New Schoolhouse," in Gross and Murphy, *Revolution in the Schools*, pp. 128–36.

12. Margaret Mead, *American Sociological Review* 26 (June 1961): 504.

13. A. S. Neill, *Summerhill: A Radical Approach to Child Rearing* (New York: Hart, 1960), pp. 4, 25, 29; "Introduction," *Summerhill: For and Against* (New York: Hart, 1970). For a critical assessment of Neill's thought, see Robin Barrow, *Radical Education: A Critique of Freeschooling and Deschooling* (New York: John Wiley, 1978).

14. Paul Goodman, *Compulsory Mis-Education* (New York: Vintage, 1964), pp. 22, 32–33, 55–57, 67, 126, 141.

15. Jonathan Kozol, *Death at an Early Age: The Destruction of the Hearts and Minds of Negro Children in the Boston Public Schools* (New York: Houghton Mifflin, 1967); Herbert Kohl, *36 Children* (New York: New American Library, 1967).

16. Nat Hentoff, *Our Children Are Dying* (New York: Viking Press, 1966); James Herndon, *The Way It Spozed To Be* (New York: Simon and Schuster, 1968); James Herndon, *How To Survive in Your Native Land* (New York: Simon and Schuster, 1971); George Dennison, *The Lives of Children: The Story of the First Street School* (New York: Random House, 1969); Steve Bhaerman and Joel Denker, *No Particular Place To Go: The Making of a Free High School* (Carbondale: Southern Illinois University Press, 1972, rev. ed., 1982); John Holt, *How Children Fail* (New York: Pitman, 1964); George B. Leonard, *Education and Ecstasy* (New York: Delta, 1968); Terry Borton, *Reach, Touch and Teach: Student Concerns and Process Education* (New York: McGraw-Hill, 1970).

17. See Arthur R. Jensen, "How Much Can We Boost IQ and Scholastic Achievement?" *Harvard Educational Review* 39 (1969):1–123. The article and responses to it were printed in *Environment, Heredity, and Intelligence* (Cambridge, Mass.: Harvard Educational Review, 1969). Westinghouse Learning Corporation, *The Impact of Head Start: An Evaluation of the Effects of Head Start on Children's Cognitive and Affective Development* (Washington, D.C.: Clearinghouse for Federal Scientific and Technical Information, June 1969).

18. Joseph Featherstone, "Schools for Children," *New Republic*, August 19, 1967, pp. 17–21; idem, "How Children Learn," *New Republic*, September 2, 1967, pp. 17–21; idem, "Teaching Children to Think," *New Republic*, September 9, 1967, pp. 15–25.

19. Diane-Marie Hargrove Blinn, "Open Education: An Analysis of the Practical Purport, Historical Context, and Parent Doctrine of an Educational Slogan" (Diss., University of Chicago, 1981), p. 3; Ewald B. Nyquist and Gene R. Hawes, eds., *Open Education: A Sourcebook for Parents and Teachers* (New York: Bantam, 1972), p. 82; Beatrice and Ronald Gross, "A Little Bit of Chaos," *Saturday Review*, May 16, 1970, pp. 71–73, 84–85.

20. Blinn, "Open Education," pp. 258–60; also Harold Howe, "Openness—the New Kick in Education" (New York: The Ford Foundation, 1972).

21. Note: In 1972, as federal funds diminished, the New School was absorbed by the University's College of Education and became the Center for Teaching and Learning; its activities were cut back, but its commitment to open education remained undiminished. Blinn, "Open Education," pp. 266–70; Vito Perrone and Warren Strandberg, "The New School," in Nyquist and Hawes, *Open Education: A Sourcebook*, pp. 275–91; Vito Perrone, *Open Education: Promise and Problems* (Bloomington, Ind: Phi Delta Kappa, 1972); Paul M. Nachtigal, *Improving Rural Schools* (Washington, D.C.: Government Printing Office, 1980), pp. 7–8.

22. Blinn, "Open Education," p. 165.

23. See David Hawkins, *The Informed Vision* (New York: Agathon Press, 1974).

24. Blinn, "Open Education," interview with Hawkins, p. 242.

25. Blinn, "Open Education," pp. 333–34.

26. William Hull, "Elementary Science," internal memorandum, ESS, Newton, Massachusetts, September 1968, p. 1 (cited in Blinn, "Open Education," p. 243).

27. Nyquist and Hawes, *Open Education: A Sourcebook*, p. 392; Blinn, "Open Education," pp. 245–49.

28. Beatrice and Ronald Gross, "A Little Bit of Chaos," p. 84.

29. Charles Silberman, *Crisis in the Classroom* (New York: Random House, 1970).

30. Ibid., pp. 13, 21, 28.

31. Ibid., pp. 28–29.

32. Ibid., pp. 10, 11, 122, 152, 173, 207–8.

33. Ibid., pp. 324, 340–48.

34. Ewald B. Nyquist, "Open Education: Its Philosophy, Historical Perspectives, and Implications," in Nyquist and Hawes, *Open Education: A Sourcebook,* p. 83; Howe, "Openness—the New Kick in Education."

35. Bernard Spodek, "Open Education: Romance or Liberation?" in *Studies in Open Education,* ed. Bernard Spodek and Herbert J. Walberg (New York: Agathon Press, 1975), pp. 3–8.

36. Charles H. Rathbone, "The Implicit Rationale of the Open Education Classroom," in *Open Education: The Informal Classroom,* ed. Charles H. Rathbone (New York: Citation Press, 1971), pp. 100, 104.

37. Ibid., pp. 106–7.

38. Roland S. Barth, "Teaching: The Way It Is/The Way It Could Be," *Grade Teacher,* January 1970, p. 101; idem, "When Children Enjoy School," *Childhood Education,* January 1970, pp. 195–200; idem, *Open Education and the American School* (New York: Agathon Press, 1972), pp. 7–48, 50.

39. Ibid., pp. 138, 139, 142, 156.

40. Charles Silberman, ed., *The Open Classroom Reader* (New York: Vintage Books, 1973), p. xvi.

41. The Gallup poll of public attitudes toward education was published each September in *Phi Delta Kappan,* beginning in 1969.

42. Ivan Illich, *Deschooling Society* (New York: Harper & Row, 1970), p. 72; Illich's critique of the free school movement is quoted in Allen Graubard, *Free the Children: Radical Reform and the Free School Movement* (New York: Pantheon Books, 1972), pp. 297–98.

43. Ann Swidler, *Organization Without Authority: Dilemmas of Social Control in Free Schools* (Cambridge, Mass: Harvard University Press, 1979), pp. 2–3; Graubard, *Free the Children,* p. 40.

44. Salli Rasberry and Robert Greenway, *Rasberry Exercises: How To Start Your Own School . . . and Make a Book* (Freestone, California: Freestone, 1970), p. 37; Swidler, *Organization Without Authority,* p. 2–3.

45. William A. Firestone, "Ideology and Conflict In Parent-Run Free Schools," *Sociology of Education* 49 (1976): 169–75.

46. Robert R. Sutcliffe, "Hard Science in a Soft School," *Science Teacher,* September 1973, pp. 30–32; Philip DeTurk and Robert Mackin, "Lions in the Park: An Alternative Meaning and Setting for Learning," *Phi Delta Kappan,* March 1973, pp. 458–60; R. Bruce McPherson, Steven Daniels, and William P. Stewart, "Options for Students in Ann Arbor," *Phi Delta Kappan,* March 1973, pp. 469–70; Richard St. Germain, Roger D. Carten, and James Meland, "Roseville Faces Disaffection with Alternative High Schools," *Phi Delta Kappan,* May 1975, p. 637.

47. Rita M. Hymes and Franklin O. Bullock, "Alternative Schools: Answer to the Gifted Child's Boredom," *The Gifted Child Quarterly* 19 (1974): 340–45; Gene I. Maeroff, "The Traditional School: Keep It Among the Alternatives," *Phi Delta Kappan,* March 1973, pp. 473–75; Frederick S. Bock and Wanda Gomula, "A Conservative Community Forms an Alternative High School," *Phi Delta Kappan,* March 1973, pp. 471–72; Philip G. Jones, "All About Those New 'Fundamental' Public Schools, What They're Promising, and Why They're Catching On," *American School Board Journal,* February 1976, pp. 24–31; Shirley Boes Neill, "Pasadena's Approach to the Classic School Debate," *American Education,* April 1976, pp. 6–10; Community High School, "Course Guide: Community Resource Program" (Ann Arbor, Michigan: Ann Arbor Public Schools, September 1982); Hunter O. Brooks and Paula R. Barker, "Alternative Schools in a Traditional Setting," *Social Education,* November 1973, pp. 650–51; Fred M. Hechinger, "The All-New 'Law and Order' Classroom," *Saturday Review,* May 3, 1975, pp. 40–41; see also, *Phi Delta Kappan* special issue on alternative schools, April 1981.

48. Jerome De Bruin, "A Descriptive Analysis of Experiences of Five First-Year Teachers Attempting Open Education," in Spodek and Walberg, *Studies in Open Education,* p. 214.

49. Joseph Featherstone, "Tempering a Fad," *New Republic,* September 25, 1971, pp. 17–21; Joseph Featherstone, foreword to Roland S. Barth, *Open Education and the American School,* p. x; Roland S. Barth, "Should We Forget about Open Education?" *Saturday Review World,* November 6, 1973. pp. 58–59; idem, "Beyond Open Education,"; *Phi Delta Kappan,* February 1977, pp.

489ff.; Donald A. Myers, "Why Open Education Died," *Journal of Research and Development in Education* 8 (1974):62–63; see also, Donald A. Myers and Daniel L. Duke, "Open Education as an Ideology," *Educational Research* 19 (June 1977): 227–35.

50. Blinn, "Open Education," pp. 444–46; "Back to Basics in the Schools," *Newsweek*, October 21, 1974, pp. 87–95.

51. Neville Bennett, *Teaching Styles and Pupil Progress* (London: Open Books, 1976), pp. 43, 149; British Department of Education and Science, *Primary Education in England: A Survey by HM Inspectors of Schools* (London: Her Majesty's Stationery Office, 1978), pp. 26–27; British Department of Education and Science, *Education 5 to 9: An Illustrative Survey of 80 First Schools in England* (London: Her Majesty's Stationery Office, 1982), pp. 48–49.

52. Brian Simon, "The Primary School Revolution: Myth or Reality?" in *Research and Practice in the Primary Classroom*, ed. Brian Simon and John Willcocks (London: Routledge & Kegan Paul, 1981), pp. 23–24; see also, Maurice Galton and Brian Simon, eds., *Progress and Performance in the Primary Classroom* (London: Routledge & Kegan Paul, 1980), pp. 33–35, and Neville Bennett et al., *Open Plan Schools* (London: NFER Publishing, 1980).

53. Peter W. Greenwood, Dale Mann, and Milbrey Wallin McLaughlin, *Federal Programs Supporting Educational Change, III: "The Process of Change"* (Santa Monica, Calif.: Rand Corporation, 1975), p. 1.

54. Greenwood, Mann, and McLaughlin, *Federal Programs Supporting Educational Change*, pp. 1, 13–14; Malcolm M. Provus, *The Grand Experiment: The Life and Death of the TTT Program as Seen Through the Eyes of Its Evaluators* (Berkeley, Calif.: McCutchan, 1975), p. 146. For a study of the Teacher Corps, see Ronald G. Corwin, *Reform and Organizational Survival: The Teacher Corps as an Instrument of Educational Change* (New York: John Wiley, 1973). For analyses of the Trainers of Teachers Trainers program, see Donald N. Bigelow, ed., *Schoolworlds '76: New Directions for Educational Policy* (Berkeley: McCutchan, 1976), pp. vii–xviii, 287–303.

55. *New York Times*, March 4, 1970; Robert E. Herriott and Neal Gross, eds., *The Dynamics of Planned Educational Change: Case Studies and Analyses* (Berkeley, Calif.: McCutchan, 1979), p. 51.

56. U.S. Office of Education, *Experimental Schools Program, 1971. Experimental Schools Projects: Three Educational Plans* (Washington, D.C.: Government Printing Office, 1972), pp. 149–50.

57. For the plans of these three funded districts, see ibid.; for descriptions of the Berkeley program, see Diane Divoky, "Berkeley's Experimental Schools," *Saturday Review*, September 16, 1972, pp. 44–50; Francisco Hernandez, "Casa de la Raza—An Alternative School for Chicano Students," in *Alternative Schools: Ideologies, Realities, Guidelines*, ed. Terrence E. Deal and Robert R. Nolan (Chicago: Nelson Hall, 1978), pp. 191–8; for the outside evaluation of the Berkeley schools, see Institute for Scientific Analysis, "Educational R&D and the Case of Berkeley's Experimental Schools," a report submitted to the National Institute of Education, November 1976; for an in-depth analysis of the projects in Berkeley, Franklin Pierce, and Minneapolis, see Louise Frankel Stoll, "The Price of a Gift: The Impact of Federal Funds on the Political and Economic Life of School Districts" (Diss., University of California at Berkeley), 1978.

58. Nachtigal, *Improving Rural Schools*, p. 11; see also, Paul M. Nachtigal, ed., *Rural Education: In Search of a Better Way* (Boulder, Colo.: Westview Press, 1982); for an overview of ESP and evaluations of other rural sites, see Herriott and Gross, *Dynamics of Planned Educational Change*.

59. Peter Cowden and David K. Cohen, "Divergent Worlds of Practice: The Federal Reform of Local Schools in the Experimental Schools Program," unpublished study prepared for the National Institute of Education, 1979, pp. 16, 29.

60. Ibid., p. 21.

61. Suzanne Kay Quick, "Secondary Impacts of the Curriculum Reform Movement: A Longitudinal Study of the Incorporation of Innovations of the Curriculum Reform Movement into Commercially Developed Curriculum Programs" (Diss., Stanford University, 1977).

62. Bruce R. Vogeli, "The Rise and Fall of the 'New Math'" (Address delivered at Teachers College, Columbia University, February 5, 1976), pp. 4, 17.

63. Morris Kline, *Why Johnny Can't Add: The Failure of the New Math* (New York: St. Martin's Press, 1973); see also, Seymour B. Sarason, *The Culture of the School and the Problem of Change*, 2nd ed. (Boston: Allyn & Bacon, 1982), chap. 4; Marilyn N. Suydam and Alan Osborne, *The Status of Precollege Science, Mathematics, and Social Science Education: 1955–1975*, vol. 2, *Mathematics Education* (Washington, D.C.: Government Printing Office, 1978), p. 32; Iris Weiss, *Report of the 1977 National Survey of Science, Mathematics, and Social Studies Education* (Research Triangle Park, N. C.: Research Triangle Institute, 1978), p. 79; James T. Fey, "Mathematics Teaching Today: Per-

spectives from Three National Surveys," in *What Are the Needs in Precollege Science, Mathematics, and Social Science Education?* p. 25.

64. *The Status of Precollege Science, Mathematics, and Social Science Education: 1955–1975: An Overview and Summary of Three Studies* (Washington, D.C.: Government Printing Office, 1978), p. 8; Hazel Whitman Hertzberg, *Social Studies Reform, 1880–1980* (Boulder, Colo.: Social Science Education Consortium, 1981), pp. 155–57.

65. James P. Shaver, O. L. Davis, and Suzanne M. Helburn, "An Interpretive Report on the Status of Precollege Social Studies Education Based on Three NSF-Funded Studies," in *What Are the Needs in Precollege Science, Mathematics, and Social Science Education?* pp. 6–12.

66. Peter B. Dow, "Innovation's Perils: An Account of the Origins, Development, Implementation, and Public Reaction to *Man: A Course of Study*" (Diss., Harvard University, 1979), pp. 181, 374, 464; see also, Karen B. Wiley, "The NSF Science Education Controversy: Issues, Events, Decisions" (Boulder, Colo.: Social Science Education Consortium, 1976).

67. See, Karen B. Wiley and Jeanne Race, *The Status of Precollege Science, Mathematics, and Social Science Education: 1955–1975*, vol. 3, *Social Science Education.* (Boulder, Colo.: Social Science Education Consortium, 1977), pp. 299–312; see also, Christopher Dede and Joy Hardin, "Reforms, Revisions, Reexaminations: Secondary Science Education Since World War II," *Science Education* 57 (1973):485–91.

Chapter 8: The New Politics of Education

1. Philip Gleason, "American Identity and Americanization," in *Harvard Encyclopedia of American Ethnic Groups,* ed. Stephan Thernstrom (Cambridge, Mass: Harvard University Press, 1980), p. 55.

2. U.S. Congress, Senate, Committee on Labor and Public Welfare, Special Subcommittee on Bilingual Education, *Bilingual Education,* 90th Cong., 1st sess., 1967, pp. 4–6, 21, 35, 37, 424.

3. Ibid., p. 43.

4. Ibid., pp. 62, 69–70, 74–8.

5. Ibid., pp. 215–17.

6. Ibid., p. 218; Bilingual Education Act of 1968, Title VII of the Elementary and Secondary Education Act of 1965 (P.L. 90–247).

7. J. Stanley Pottinger, "Memorandum to School Districts With More Than Five Percent National Origin-Minority Group Children," Department of Health, Education, and Welfare, Office for Civil Rights, May 25, 1970.

8. *Lau v. Nichols,* 414 U.S. 563 (1974).

9. U.S. Congress, House, Subcommittee on Elementary, Secondary, and Vocational Education of the Committee on Education and Labor, *Bilingual Education,* 95th Cong., 1st sess., 1977, "Statement of Lloyd R. Henderson, Office for Civil Rights," p. 126; U.S. Department of Health, Education, and Welfare, "Task Force Findings Specifying Remedies Available for Eliminating Past Educational Practices Ruled Unlawful Under *Lau v. Nichols,*" Washington, D.C., Summer 1975; Iris Rotberg, "Some Legal and Research Considerations in Establishing Federal Policy in Bilingual Education," *Harvard Educational Review* 52 (May 1982): 148–68.

10. U.S. Congress, House, General Subcommittee on Education of the Committee on Education and Labor, *Bilingual Education Act,* 93rd Cong., 2nd sess., 1974, pp. 38–41, 188.

11. Ibid., pp. 113, 203.

12. Ibid., pp. 314–15.

13. Bilingual Education Act of 1974 (P.L. 93–380).

14. U.S. Congress, House, Subcommittee on Elementary, Secondary, and Vocational Education of the Committee on Education and Labor, *Bilingual Education,* 95th Cong., 1st sess., 1977, pp. 47, 71–81, 99.

15. Ibid., pp. 335–36.

16. Ibid., pp. 141–46; see also, Malcolm N. Danoff, "Evaluation of the Impact of ESEA Title VII Spanish/English Bilingual Education Programs" (Palo Alto, Calif.: American Institutes for Research, 1978).

17. *Bilingual Education,* 1977, pp. 63, 142–43.

18. Danoff, "Evaluation"; *Bilingual Education,* 1977, pp. 143–44.

19. *Bilingual Education,* 1977, p. 69.

20. Abigail M. Thernstrom, "E Pluribus Plura—Congress and Bilingual Education," *Public Interest* 60 (Summer 1980):16.

21. The Bilingual Education Act of 1978 (P.L. 95–561).

22. See Federal Register, August 5, 1980; *Washington Post,* April 24, 1982; *Washington Post,* February 12, 1982.

23. Rotberg, "Some Legal and Research Considerations," pp. 164, 154–56; the international findings cited by Rotberg are drawn from Christina Bratt Paulston, "Bilingual/Bicultural Education," in *Review of Research in Education,* ed. Lee S. Shulman (Itasca, Ill.: Peacock, 1978), p. 187.

24. *Education Week,* June 16, 1982, p. 14; *School Lawyer,* May 11, 1981, p. 1.

25. In the Gallup poll of public education, 82 percent responded that non-English-speaking children should be required to learn English ("Twelfth Annual Gallup Poll of the Public's Attitudes Toward the Public Schools," *Phi Delta Kappan,* September 1980, p. 44); Seymour Martin Lipset and William Schneider, "An Emerging National Consensus," *The New Republic,* October 15, 1977, p. 8–9; see also, Seymour Martin Lipset and William Schneider, "The Bakke Case: How Would It Be Decided at the Bar of Public Opinion?" *Public Opinion,* March/April 1978, pp. 38–44.

26. W. Vance Grant and Leo J. Eiden, *Digest of Education Statistics,* (Washington, D.C.: Government Printing Office 1980), p. 16; U.S. Bureau of the Census, Current Population Reports, 1977 "School Enrollment—Social and Economic Characteristics of Students," p. 8; Richard B. Freeman, *Black Elite: The New Market for Highly Educated Black Americans* (New York: McGraw-Hill, 1976), chaps. 1 and 2.

27. The Civil Rights Act of 1964 (P.L. 33–352), Title IV, Section 401b, Section 407a; Title VI; Title VII, Section 703j.

28. Harold H. Howe, II, "The Time is Now," *Saturday Review,* July 16, 1966, p. 57.

29. Title 41, C.F.R., 60-1.40.

30. J. Stanley Pottinger, "The Drive Toward Equality," *Change,* October 1972, pp. 24, 26–29; Nathan Glazer, *Affirmative Discrimination: Ethnic Inequality and Public Policy* (New York: Basic Books, 1975), pp. 46–49.

31. Richard A. Lester, *Antibias Regulation of Universities: Faculty Problems and Their Solutions* (New York: McGraw-Hill, 1974), pp. 5–6.

32. For criticism of affirmative action policies, see Glazer, *Affirmative Discrimination;* for an extensive bibliography of articles and books about affirmative action, see Kathryn Swanson, *Affirmative Action and Preferential Admissions in Higher Education: An Annotated Bibliography* (Metuchen, N.J.: Scarecrow Press, 1981).

33. Lester, *Antibias Regulation,* pp. 113–14.

34. *Marco Defunis* v. *Charles Odegaard,* 416 U.S. 312.

35. The best single treatment of the *DeFunis* and *Bakke* cases is Allan P. Sindler, *Bakke, DeFunis, and Minority Admissions: The Quest for Equal Opportunity* (New York: Longman, 1978).

36. *Bakke* v. *University of California,* 132 Cal. Rptr. 680, 553 P.2d 1152 (1976); see also, Sindler, *Bakke, DeFunis, and Minority Admissions,* pp. 105, 226–27.

37. Sindler, *Bakke, DeFunis, and Minority Admissions,* pp. 236–37.

38. McGeorge Bundy, "The Issue Before the Court: Who Gets Ahead in America?" *Atlantic Monthly,* November 1977, pp. 41–54.

39. Archibald Cox, *Harvard College Amicus Curiae, DeFunis* v. *Odegaard,* reprinted in *Reverse Discrimination,* ed. Barry R. Gross (Buffalo, N.Y.: Prometheus Books, 1977); the Cox document was also filed as an amicus brief in the Bakke case.

40. *Brown* v. *Board of Education,* Brief for Appellants, October 1952, pp. 5, 67, 79; Brief of the NAACP Legal Defense and Educational Fund, Inc., as Amicus Curiae, October 1976, in *University of California Regents* v. *Bakke,* 438 U.S. 265 (1978).

41. J. Harvie Wilkinson, *From* Brown *to* Bakke: *The Supreme Court and School Integration, 1954–1978* (New York: Oxford University Press, 1979), pp. 298–99; Sindler, *Bakke, DeFunis, and Minority Admissions,* p. 292.

42. *University of California Regents* v. *Bakke,* 438 U.S. 265 (1978).

43. Alexander M. Bickel, *The Morality of Consent* (New Haven, Conn.: Yale University Press, 1975), p. 133.

44. Terry Eastland and William J. Bennett, *Counting by Race: Equality from the Founding Fathers to* Bakke (New York: Basic Books, 1979), pp. 173–76.

45. Eastland and Bennett, *Counting by Race,* pp. 173–74; Federal Register, Vol. 44, No. 14, January 19, 1979, p. 4423; Statement by the United States Commission on Civil Rights on Affirmative Action, July 1, 1978, reprinted in U.S. Commission on Civil Rights, *Toward an Understanding of* Bakke (Washington, D.C.: Government Printing Office, 1979).

46. U.S. Commission on Civil Rights, *Affirmative Action in the 1980s: Dismantling the Process of Discrimination* (Washington, D.C.: Government Printing Office, 1981), p. 40.

47. National Center for Education Statistics, *The Condition of Education, 1979* (Washington, D.C.: Government Printing Office, 1979), pp. 214–15; Richard B. Freeman, *Black Elite: The New Market for Highly Educated Black Americans* (New York: McGraw-Hill, 1976), pp. 53–56; telephone interview, Peter Syverson, National Academy of Sciences, Washington, D.C., February 25, 1983; telephone interview, Loretta Conley, Equal Employment Opportunity Commission, Survey Division (EEO-6 Report), February 28, 1983.

48. George Gallup Organization, poll taken December 5–December 7, 1980.

49. Maren Lockwood Carden, *The New Feminist Movement* (New York: Russell Sage, 1974), pp. 85–99.

50. Ibid., pp. 104, 115.

51. Ibid., pp. 201–17.

52. Ibid., p. 19.

53. Catherine R. Stimpson, ed., *Discrimination Against Women: Congressional Hearings on Equal Rights in Education and Employment* (New York: R.R. Bowker, 1973), p. 61.

54. Ibid., pp. 22, 26, 28, 47–50, 61.

55. Title IX (P.L. 92-318) was part of the Education Amendments of 1972.

56. Pamela Roby, "Institutional Barriers to Women Students in Higher Education," in *Academic Women on the Move,* ed. Alice S. Rossi and Ann Calderwood (New York: Russell Sage, 1973), p. 40; Richard A. Easterlin, *Birth and Fortune: The Impact of Numbers on Personal Welfare* (New York: Basic Books, 1980), pp. 37–70. Estimates of the percentage of faculty members who were women in 1970 vary: Pamela Roby, "Women and Higher Education," *Annals of the American Academy of Political and Social Science* 404 (1972):118–39, includes a bar graph in which women are 22 percent of the faculty in higher education from 1950 to 1970; however, the Carnegie Commission on Higher Education, *Opportunities for Women in Higher Education: Their Current Participation, Prospects for the Future, and Recommendations for Action* (New York: McGraw-Hill, 1973), p. 111, puts the proportion at 19 percent, using data supplied by the National Education Association. See also, Patricia Albjerg Graham, "Women in Academe," *Science,* September 25, 1970, pp. 1284–90.

57. U.S. Bureau of the Census, *Social Indicators III* (Washington, D.C.: Government Printing Office, 1980), chap. 1, pp. 1–7; Easterlin, *Birth and Fortune,* pp. 60–70.

58. U.S. Congress, Senate, Subcommittee on Education of the Committee on Labor and Public Welfare, *Women's Educational Equity Act of 1973,* 93rd Cong., 2nd sess., 1973, pp. 393–96. See Saul D. Feldman, *Escape from the Doll's House: Women in Graduate and Professional School Education* (New York: McGraw Hill, 1974); Jessie Bernard, *Academic Women* (University Park: Pennsylvania State University, 1964); Margaret Gordon and Clark Kerr, "University Behavior and Policies: Where Are the Women and Why?" in *The Higher Education of Women: Essays in Honor of Rosemary Park,* ed. Helen S. Astin and Werner Z. Hirsch (New York: Praeger, 1978), pp. 113–32.

59. *Women's Educational Equity Act,* p. 236.

60. Ibid., pp. 21, 24, 29, 34, 38.

61. Ibid., p. 71.

62. Ibid., pp. 237, 275–84; Federal Register, Vol. 40, No. 108, June 4, 1975, CFR 86.42.

63. *Women's Educational Equity Act,* p. 52.

64. Everett Groseclode, "Sexism and Schools—Feminists and Others Now Attack Sex Bias in Nation's Classrooms," *Wall Street Journal,* October 9, 1973, reprinted in *Women's Educational Equity Act* hearings, pp. 296–98. A sampling from the professional journals: John W. McLure and Gail T. McLure, "Cinderella Grows Up: Sex Stereotyping in the Schools," *Educational Leadership,* October 1972, pp. 31–33; Carole L. Hahn, "Eliminating Sexism from the Schools: An Application of Planned Change," *Social Education,* March 1975, pp. 133–36; Kathryn P. Scott, "Sexist and Nonsexist Materials: What Impact Do They Have?" *Elementary School Journal,* September 1980, pp. 46–52; Women on Words and Images, *Dick and Jane as Victims: Sex Stereotyping in Children's Readers* (Princeton, N.J.: Women on Words and Images, 1972); Linda Oliver, "Women in Aprons: The Female Stereotype in Children's Readers," *Elementary School*

Journal, Febrary 1974, pp. 253–59; Carol Kehr Tittle, "Women and Educational Testing," *Phi Delta Kappan,* October 1973, pp. 118–19; Janice Law Trecker, "Sex Stereotyping in the Secondary School Curriculum," *Phi Delta Kappan,* October 1973, pp. 110–12; Betty Levy and Judith Stacey, "Sexism in the Elementary School: A Backward and Forward Look," *Phi Delta Kappan,* October 1973, pp. 105–9, 123; Richard W. O'Donnell, "Sex Bias in Primary Social Studies Textbooks," *Educational Leadership,* November 1973, pp. 137–141.

65. For measures comparing male and female academic achievement in high school and college, see Carnegie Commission on Higher Education, *Opportunities for Women in Higher Education: Their Current Participation, Prospects for the Future, and Recommendations for Action* (New York: McGraw-Hill, 1973), p. 49–50; Terry N. Saario, Carol Nagy Jacklin, and Carol Kehr Tittle, "Sex Role Stereotyping in the Public Schools," *Harvard Educational Review* 43 (August 1973): 386–416. For an argument against the feminist interpretation of sex-role stereotyping, see Vivian Paley, "Is the Doll Corner a Sexist Institution?" *School Review* 81 (August 1973): 569–76; and Bruno Bettelheim, "Some Further Thoughts on the Doll Corner," *School Review* 83 (February 1975): 363–68. For figures on women as white-collar workers, see Roby, "Women and American Higher Education," table 1.

66. "APA Task Force on Issues of Sexual Bias in Graduate Education: Guidelines for Nonsexist Use of Language," *American Psychologist* 30 (June 1975): 682–84; American Psychological Association, "Guidelines for Nonsexist Language in APA Journals," Publication Manual, Change Sheet 2, June 1977; Harper & Row, "Harper & Row Guidelines on Equal Treatment of the Sexes in Textbooks," 1976; Holt, Rinehart & Winston, "The Treatment of Sex Roles and Minorities," 1976; McGraw-Hill, "Guidelines for Equal Treatment of the Sexes in McGraw-Hill Book Company Publications," n.d.; Prentice-Hall, "Prentice-Hall Author's Guide," 5th ed., 1975; Random House, "Guidelines for Multiethnic/Nonsexist Survey," 1975; Scott, Foresman, "Guidelines for Improving the Image of Women in Textbooks," 1974; John Wiley & Sons, "Wiley Guidelines on Sexism in Language," 1977; National Council of Teachers of English, "Guidelines for Nonsexist Use of Language in NCTE Publications," 1975.

67. Project on the Status and Education of Women (PSEW), "On Campus with Women," November 1974, pp. 3–4; March 1978, p. 1.

68. John H. Bunzel, "The Case of the Jailed Georgia Professor: Let's Cut Through the Intellectual Smog," *Chronicle of Higher Education,* January 12, 1981, p. 96. PSEW, "On Campus with Women," May 1975, p. 2; October 1977, p. 4; Spring 1980, p. 7; Spring 1981, p. 8; Spring 1980, p. 3; Summer 1982, pp. 3–4; Fall 1981, p. 1; May 1975, p. 2; April 1976, p. 2; Spring 1981, pp. 7–8; Winter 1981, p. 5; Spring 1979, p. 8.

69. Lester, *Antibias Regulation,* p. 9. Grove City College in Pennsylvania was one of several that refused to sign the Title IX compliance form; the Federal Appeals Court in the Third Circuit ruled that private educational institutions whose students receive federal loans and grants were subject to Title IX prohibition on sex discrimination, even if the institution itself received no direct funds. On February 22, 1983, the Supreme Court agreed to hear Grove City College's appeal from the Third Circuit ruling (*New York Times,* August 20, 1982; February 23, 1983). In response to the Third Circuit ruling, the economist Milton Friedman observed that the "corner grocer and the A&P are recipient institutions because some of their customers receive social security checks" (Ronald A. Wolk, "The Entangling Web: Federal Regulations of Colleges and Universities" [Washington, D.C.: Editorial Projects for Education, Inc., 1979], p. 3.

70. *Sweezy* v. *New Hampshire,* 354 U.S. 234, 263 (1957).

71. Martha P. Rogers, "The Role of the Equal Employment Opportunity Commission in Higher Education" (Speech to the American Council on Education, Miami Beach, Florida, October 5, 1972); Bernice Sandler, "Affirmative Action on the Campus: Like It or Not, Uncle Sam is Here to Stay" (Speech to the American Council on Education, Miami Beach, Florida, October 5, 1972).

72. Edith Green, "The Road Is Paved with Good Intentions: Title IX and What It Is Not," *Vital Speeches,* February 15, 1977, p. 300.

73. PSEW, "On Campus with Women," Summer/Fall 1979, p. 1; Spring 1979, p. 4; Winter 1980, p. 12; Spring 1980, p. 12; Spring 1981, p. 5; Summer 1982, p. 3; Equal Employment Opportunity Commission, Management Directive EEO-MD 704, September 23, 1980.

74. PSEW, "On Campus with Women," Spring 1980, p. 9; Summer 1982, p. 5; *New York Times,* November 15, 1982; U.S. Department of Labor, *Perspectives on Working Women: A Databook* (Washington, D.C.: Government Printing Office, 1980), pp. 10–11; information about propor-

tion of full professors obtained by telephone interview with W. Vance Grant, information specialist, National Center for Education Statistics, Washington, D.C., February 25, 1983.

75. National Center for Education Statistics, *The Condition of Education* (Washington, D.C.: Government Printing Office, 1979), pp. 232–33; Easterlin, *Birth and Fortune*, pp. 10–13; PSEW, "On Campus with Women," Winter 1980, p. 13.

76. "U.S. Aide's Monitoring of Lectures Stirs Coast Dispute," *New York Times*, January 24, 1980.

77. In the "Statement of Findings and Purpose" in P.L. 94-142, the Education for All Handicapped Children Act of 1975, the Congress "finds that . . . there are more than eight million handicapped children in the United States today."

78. Erwin L. Levine and Elizabeth M. Wexler, *P.L. 94-142: An Act of Congress* (New York: Macmillan, 1981), documents the successful political lobbying of the advocates for the handicapped.

79. Levine and Wexler, *P.L. 94-142*, pp. 38–41; *Pennsylvania Association for Retarded Children v. Commonwealth of Pennsylvania*, 334 F. Supp. 1257 (E.D. Pa. 1971); *Mills v. Board of Education*, 348 F. Supp. 866 (D.D.C. 1972).

80. Levine and Wexler, *P.L. 94-142*, p. 113; Reed Martin, *Educating Handicapped Children: The Legal Mandate* (Champaign, Ill.: Research Press, 1979), p. 19.

81. See Levine and Wexler, *P.L. 94-142*, p. 53, for a description of the "iron triangle" and the lobby for the handicapped.

82. John C. Pittenger and Peter Kuriloff, "Educating the Handicapped: Reforming a Radical Law," *Public Interest* 66 (Winter 1982): 73; P.L. 94-142.

83. Levine and Wexler, *P.L. 94-142*, pp. 188–89; Gene I. Maeroff, *Don't Blame the Kids: The Trouble with America's Public Schools* (New York: McGraw-Hill, 1982), pp. 15–21.

84. H. Rutherford Turnbull and Ann Turnbull, *Free Appropriate Public Education: Law and Implementation* (Denver, Colo.: Love Publishing, 1978), pp. 137–70; Marjorie Wilson, *Mainstreaming* (Washington, D.C.: National Education Association, 1977); Levine and Wexler, *P.L. 94-142*, pp. 139–40, 154–55.

85. *Southeastern Community College v. Davis*, 442 U.S. 397; *New York Times*, June 12, 1979; *Board of Education v. Rowley*, 102, S. Ct. 3034 (1982); *New York Times*, June 29, 1982.

86. National Center for Education Statistics, *The Condition of Education*, 1981 (Washington, D.C.: Government Printing Office 1981), pp. 264–80.

87. Committee on CCCC Language Statement, "Students' Right to Their Own Language," *College English*, February 1975, pp. 709–26. The statement affirmed "the students' right to their own patterns and varieties of language—the dialects of their nurture or whatever dialects in which they find their own identity and style. . . . The claim that any one dialect is unacceptable amounts to an attempt of one social group to exert its dominance over another. . . ."

88. Report of the Advisory Panel on the Scholastic Aptitude Test Score Decline, *On Further Examination* (New York: College Entrance Examination Board, 1977), p. 27.

89. Arthur E. Wise, *Legislated Learning: The Bureaucratization of the American Classroom* (Berkeley and Los Angeles: University of California Press, 1979), p. 2; Family Rights and Privacy Act of 1974.

90. Wise, *Legislated Learning*, p. 2, 151; *Goss v. Lopez*, 419 U.S. 565 (1975); *Martin Luther King Jr. Elementary School Children, Et Al., v. Ann Arbor School District Board* (473 Fed.Supp., 1372–1391); Nathan Glazer, "Black English and Reluctant Judges," *Public Interest* 62 (Winter 1981): 40–54; *Larry P. v. Wilson Riles*, 495 F. Supp. 1926 (N.D. Calif., 1979); Nathan Glazer, "IQ on Trial," *Commentary*, June 1981, pp. 51–59; *Armstrong v. Kline*, 629 F. 2d 269 (1980); *New York Times*, May 17, 1982; *New York Times*, June 10, 1982; *Peter Doe v. San Francisco Unified School District* (California Superior Court, Docket No. 653-312); *New York Times*, February 20, 1977.

91. *San Antonio Independent School District v. Rodriguez* (411 US 1, 1973); *New York Times*, June 24, 1982; Betsy Levin, "State School Finance Reform: Court Mandate or Legislative Action?" (Washington, D.C.: National Conference of State Legislatures, July 1977); Arthur E. Wise, *Rich Schools, Poor Schools: The Promise of Equal Educational Opportunity* (Chicago: University of Chicago Press, 1968); Allan Odden, *School Finance Reform in the States: 1978* (Denver, Colo.: Education Commission of the States, 1978); John E. Coons, William H. Clune, III, and Stephen D. Sugarman, *Private Wealth and Public Schooling* (Cambridge, Mass.: Harvard University Press, 1970).

92. Myron Lieberman, *Public-Sector Bargaining: A Policy Reappraisal* (Lexington, Mass.: D.C.

Notes

Heath, 1980), p. 5; Alan Rosenthal, *Pedagogues and Power: Teacher Groups in School Politics* (Syracuse, N.Y.: Syracuse University Press, 1969), pp. 13–15. Susan Moore Johnson, *Teacher Unions and the Schools* (Cambridge, Mass.: Institute for Educational Policy Studies, Harvard University, 1982), p. 2; Lorraine McDonnell and Anthony Pascal, *Organized Teachers in American Schools* (Santa Monica, Calif.: Rand Corporation, 1979).

93. Lieberman, *Public-Sector Bargaining,* pp. 8–9, 160; Rosenthal, *Pedagogues and Power,* p. 6; see also, Myron Lieberman, "Eggs That I Have Laid," *Phi Delta Kappan,* February 1979, pp. 415–18; Terry Herndon, "The Case for Collective Bargaining Statutes," *Phi Delta Kappan,* May 1979, pp. 651–52; Albert Shanker, "A Reply to Myron Lieberman," *Phi Delta Kappan,* May 1979, pp. 652–54.

94. Johnson, *Teacher Unions and the Schools,* pp. 14–15.

95. At the 1980 Democratic convention, the NEA elected more delegates than any state or any other group; see, Stanley M. Elam, "The National Education Association: Political Powerhouse or Paper Tiger?" *Phi Delta Kappan,* November 1981, p. 169.

96. *New York Times,* February 21, 1980; see also, George W. Angell, ed., *Faculty and Teacher Bargaining: The Impact of Unions on Education* (Lexington, Mass.: D.C. Heath, 1981).

97. Wise, *Legislated Learning,* pp. 18, 24–27, 38–40, 110–11.

98. Gallup polls, published annually from 1974 to 1980 in September issues of *Phi Delta Kappan.*

99. Wise, *Legislated Learning.*

100. J. Myron Atkin, "The Government in the Classroom," *Daedalus* 109 (1980): 85–97.

101. See, James S. Coleman, *The Asymmetric Society* (Syracuse, N.Y.: Syracuse University Press, 1982), pp. 16–19.

102. *New York Times,* October 19, 1980; Wolk, "The Entangling Web," p. 3; Derek C. Bok, "The Federal Government and the University," *Public Interest* 58 (Winter 1980): 96–101.

103. National Center for Education Statistics, *Digest of Education Statistics, 1980* (Washington, D.C.: Government Printing Office, 1980), pp. 187–88.

Epilogue: From 1945 to 1980

1. U.S. Congress, House, Committee on Education and Labor, *Public School Assistance Act of 1949,* 81st Cong., 1st sess., 1949, p. 1.

2. National Center for Education Statistics, *The Condition of Education, 1982* (Washington, D.C.: Government Printing Office, 1982), p. 164; Lawrence E. Gladieux and Thomas R. Wolanin, *Congress and the Colleges: The National Politics of Higher Education* (Lexington, Mass.: D.C. Heath, 1976).

3. National Center for Education Statistics, *Digest of Education Statistics, 1981* (Washington, D.C.: Government Printing Office, 1981), pp. 16–17; U.S. Department of Commerce, Bureau of the Census, *Social and Economic Status of the Black Population in the United States, 1974* (Washington, D.C.: Government Printing Office, 1975), p. 91; National Center for Education Statistics, *The Condition of Education, 1982* (Washington, D.C.: Government Printing Office, 1982), pp. 132–33.

4. Martin Trow, "Reflections on the Transition from Mass to Universal Higher Education," *Daedalus* 99 (Winter 1970): 1–5.

5. Jeanne S. Chall et al., *An Analysis of Textbooks in Relation to Declining SAT Scores* (New York: College Entrance Examination Board, 1977); Report of the Advisory Panel on the Scholastic Aptitude Test Score Decline, *On Further Examination* (New York: College Entrance Examination Board, 1977), pp. 25–31; A. Harnischfeger and D. Wiley, *Achievement Test Score Decline: Do We Need to Worry?* (Chicago: CEMREL, 1975); President's Commission on Foreign Languages and International Studies, *Strength Through Wisdom: A Critique of U.S. Capability* (Washington, D.C.: Government Printing Office, 1979); Diane Ravitch, "Forgetting the Questions: The Problem of Educational Reform," *American Scholar* 50 (Summer 1981): 329–40.

6. Author's telephone conversations in December 1982 with Mrs. Arcola Foster, former teacher, Antioch School, Hazlehurst, Mississippi; Mrs. Carrie N. Wallace, former teacher and principal, Antioch School and Hazlehurst City Elementary School, sister of Mrs. Florence Christmas, now a resident of Lake Providence, Louisiana; Rowan Torrey, Hazlehurst, Mississippi; Jimmy Buchanan, Assistant Superintendent, Copiah County Public Schools; H. T. Overby, Superintendent of Schools, Hazlehurst City Schools.

A NOTE ON SOURCES

The period covered by this book has received a great deal of attention from historians interested in foreign or domestic policy and from biographers of significant political figures, but their works pay little attention to educational issues. To complicate the matter, the best books on the history of American education, if they refer to postwar events at all, do so in a summary fashion. Thus, the reader interested in the educational history of this period must look to general histories for context and, for specific educational issues, to the works of political scientists, sociologists, biographers, and journalists, as well as to a mountain (or, more accurately, a mountain range) of primary source materials.

Postwar Initiatives: Chapter 1

A good general overview of postwar America is Eric F. Goldman, *The Crucial Decade—and After: America, 1945–1960* (New York: Vintage, 1960). Other useful syntheses of an enormously complicated period are William Manchester, *The Glory and the Dream: A Narrative History of America, 1932–1972* (Boston: Little, Brown, 1974); William L. O'Neill, *Coming Apart: An Informal History of America in the 1960's* (Chicago: Quadrangle Books, 1971); Godfrey Hodgson, *America in Our Time* (Garden City, N.Y.: Doubleday, 1976). Cultural histories of particular interest are Ronald Berman, *America in the Sixties: An Intellectual History* (New York: Free Press, 1968); and Morris Dickstein, *Gates of Eden: American Culture in the Sixties* (New York: Basic Books, 1977), both of which cover a longer time span than their titles indicate. Certain political biographies offer a sense of the times and the men who shaped them, such as Alonzo L. Hamby, *Beyond the New Deal: Harry S. Truman and American Liberalism* (New York: Columbia University Press, 1973); and Herbert S. Parmet, *Eisenhower and the American Crusades* (New York: Macmillan, 1972). A useful overview of American educational development is Fred M. Hechinger and Grace Hechinger, *Growing Up in America* (New York: McGraw-Hill, 1975).

The verbatim transcripts of the meetings of the President's Committee on Civil Rights are held by the Harry S. Truman Library in Independence, Missouri. Since these were confidential at the time they were recorded, they provide fascinating insight into what the members of the commission were saying behind closed doors. The document of the commission, *To Secure These Rights* (New York: Simon and Schuster, 1947), is an immensely interesting description of the status of civil rights and civil liberties in 1946/47 and a fine statement of American aspirations. The other major report of the period, *Higher Education for American Democracy: A Report of the President's Commission on Higher Education* (New York: Harper & Bros., 1947), lacks the clarity and interest of the civil rights report but does demonstrate the unbounded (and somewhat unfocused) ambitions of the education profession. Unfortunately, the papers of this commission were "inadvertently destroyed while in storage at the National Archives facility in Suitland, Maryland" (Letter to author from General Reference and Bibliography Division, The Library of Congress, Washington, D.C., March 6, 1978).

The religious issue has its own vast literature. The most comprehensive treatment, favoring absolute separation of church and state, is Leo Pfeffer, *Church, State, and Freedom* (Boston: Beacon Press, 1953). Paul Blanshard, *American Freedom and Catholic Power* (Boston: Beacon Press, 1949, rev. ed., 1958), is an important polemic on the same side of the issue. The Catholic view of the First Amendment is presented in James M. O'Neill, *Religion and Education Under the Constitution* (New York: Harper, 1949); and the same author's response to Blanshard, *Catholicism and American Freedom* (New York: Harper & Bros., 1952). In addition to the presentations by opposing sides, there are also many substantial scholarly works on the legal, philosophical, and political aspects of the issue, including: Richard E. Morgan, *The Politics of Religious Conflict: Church and State in America* (New York: Pegasus, 1968); Philip B. Kurland, *Religion and the Law of Church and State and the Supreme Court* (Chicago: Aldine, 1962); Philip B. Kurland, ed., *Church and State: The Supreme Court and the First Amendment* (Chicago: University of Chicago Press, 1975); Wilber G. Katz, *Religion and American Constitutions* (Evanston, Ill.: Northwestern University Press, 1964). An excellent bibliography is contained in an exhaustively researched dissertation by Ronald James Boggs, "Culture of Liberty: History of Americans United for Separation of Church and State, 1947–1973" (Diss., Ohio State University, 1978).

The history and politics of efforts to pass a federal aid to education bill have been well covered in several excellent studies, such as: Gordon Canfield Lee, *The Struggle for Federal Aid* (New York: Bureau of Publications, Teachers College, 1949); Frank J. Munger and Richard F. Fenno, Jr., *National Politics and Federal Aid to Education* (Syracuse: Syracuse University Press, 1962);

Sidney W. Tiedt, *The Role of the Federal Government in Education* (New York: Oxford University Press, 1966); and Hugh Douglas Price, "Race, Religion, and the Rules Committee: The Kennedy Aid-to-Education Bills," in *The Uses of Power: Seven Cases in American Politics,* ed. Alan F. Westin (New York: Harcourt, Brace & World, 1962). The best single source for this issue is: Gilbert Elliott Smith, *The Limits of Reform: Politics and Federal Aid to Education* (New York: Garland, 1982).

The Rise and Fall of Progressive Education: Chapter 2

The literature about progressive education is voluminous and tends to be either naively celebratory or written in a dense professional jargon. An exception is Lawrence A. Cremin's *The Transformation of the School: Progressivism in American Education, 1876–1957* (New York: Alfred A. Knopf, 1961), which is unsurpassed as a comprehensive history of the progressive education movement. Essential as a starting point in understanding the movement are the seminal works of the founders: John Dewey, Harold Rugg, William Heard Kilpatrick, and George S. Counts. It is then necessary to plow through the extensive literature about progressive pedagogy, curriculum, and practice, much of which is cited in the notes for this chapter. Having gotten that far, I then wondered how all of this theory and exhortation was actually interpreted in the classroom; what were the implications for children? There is something fairly elusive about progressive education; since it is difficult to define, it is also difficult to establish just how widely its influence spread.

But not impossible. First, there are some intriguing documentations of progressive experiments in public schools, such as Samuel Engle Burr, *A School in Transition: A Study of a Public School Moving from the Use of Traditional Practices to the Acceptance of the Activity Plan of Progressive Education During a Three Year Transitional Period* (Boston: Christopher, 1937); and Ellsworth Collings, *An Experiment with a Project Curriculum* (New York: Macmillan, 1923). In addition, I came across a veritable treasure trove of dissertations about school practices, written by superintendents, principals, or teachers who were working toward doctorates in education at Teachers College in the 1930s and 1940s. As a rule, these dissertations were written to demonstrate how a given school or school district had changed from a traditional approach to adopt progressive pedagogy. Three things in these studies are of particular value: first, the detailed description of what the school was like before the change process began; second, how the superintendent or principal persuaded teachers to try new methods; third, what changes were actually tried. The notes for this chapter include references to a large number of these participant-observer studies of schools, and I believe they are a unique resource in trying to get a picture of schools and teachers of another era and in gaining an understanding of how educational ideas are diffused.

A similar resource is the educational survey. The survey movement produced hundreds of school surveys, conducted usually by schools of education. Here, too, is a wonderful, relatively untapped mine of information about what schools were like. Even more interesting, I thought, was the fact that the survey, a seemingly impartial instrument, became a tool of social policy through which the surveyors could translate their assumptions about what constituted good education into a set of expert recommendations for the district. Hollis Caswell, *Curriculum Improvement in Public School Systems* (New York: Bureau of Publications, Teachers College, 1950), offers an excellent review of progressive techniques applied to curriculum change. A good example of an educational survey that also includes a review of the history of surveying is Robert Wilson Edgar, "A Survey of the Techniques and Procedures for Curriculum Improvement in the Great Neck Cooperative Study" (Diss., Teachers College, Columbia University, 1949).

Another place that I looked for evidence of progressive practice was the education journals, where teachers, professors of education, and principals wrote articles about what was happening in their schools. There were many articles about curriculum change and experimentation in places like Tulsa, Atlanta, and Altoona, which suggests that changes were tried in far-flung precincts. On the other hand, the fact that such changes were written up also suggests that they were seen as unusual, as experiments, as deviations from standard practice. So, the possibility remains that progressivism was broadly influential but did not necessarily take root, except in superficial ways. The final judgment must be, at this writing, that the evidence about the true impact of progressive education is not yet in and, given the nature of historical research, may never be conclusive.

Loyalty Investigations: Chapter 3

There is an extraordinarily rich literature devoted to the history of the American left and to the interrelated issues of loyalty, security, subversion, and academic freedom, written during and since the period of state and congressional investigations. From the standpoint of educational issues, the best single secondary source is Robert W. Iversen, *The Communists and the Schools* (New York: Harcourt, Brace, 1959). Other books that deal in a sustained fashion with educational issues are: Robert M. MacIver, *Academic Freedom in Our Time* (New York: Columbia University Press, 1955); Walter Gellhorn, ed., *The States and Subversion* (Ithaca, N.Y.: Cornell University Press, 1952); Lawrence H. Chamberlain, *Loyalty and Legislative Action: A Survey of Activity by the New York State Legislature, 1919–1949* (Ithaca, N.Y.: Cornell University Press, 1951); Edward L. Barrett, Jr., *The Tenney Committee: Legislative Investigation of Subversive Activities in California* (Ithaca, N.Y.: Cornell University Press, 1951); E. Edmund Reutter, *The School Administrator and Subversive Activities: A Study of the Administration of Restraints on Alleged Subversive Activities of Public School Personnel* (New York: Bureau of Publications, Teachers College, 1951); Vern Countryman, *Un-American Activities in the State of Washington: The Work of the Canwell Committee* (Ithaca, N.Y.: Cornell University Press, 1951); Jane Sanders, *Cold War on the Campus: Academic Freedom at the University of Washington, 1946–1964* (Seattle: University of Washington Press, 1979); David P. Gardner, *The California Oath Controversy* (Berkeley and Los Angeles: University of California Press, 1967); George R. Stewart, *The Year of the Oath: The Fight for Freedom at the University of California* (Garden City, N.Y.: Doubleday, 1950); Leon Bock, "The Control of Alleged Subversive Activities in the Public School System of New York City, 1949–1956" (Diss., Teachers College, Columbia University, 1971).

Books about this period written during the 1970s generally share the view that the source of the problem was not Communist activity but hysteria generated by the Cold War, for which anti-Communist liberals were largely responsible. Among such works, those that comment on educational issues include: David Caute, *The Great Fear: The Anti-Communist Purge Under Truman and Eisenhower* (New York: Simon and Schuster, 1978); Mary Sperling McAuliffe, *Crisis on the Left: Cold War Politics and American Liberals, 1947–1954* (Amherst: University of Massachusetts Press, 1978); David L. Marden, "The Cold War and American Education" (Diss., University of Kansas, 1975); and Ellen Schrecker, "Academic Freedom and the Cold War," *Antioch Review*, 38 (Summer 1980): 313–27. A different perspective is provided by William L. O'Neill, *A Better World: The Great Schism: Stalinism and the American Intellectuals* (New York: Simon and Schuster, 1982); O'Neill argues that anti-Stalinist liberals defended democratic values and that the refusal by Communists and fellow travelers to testify in congressional hearings exacerbated public fears of Communist activities.

Though they usually give little or no attention to specifically educational issues, other outstanding secondary works include: Theodore Draper, *The Roots of American Communism* (New York: Viking Press, 1957); David Shannon, *The Decline of American Communism* (New York: Harcourt, Brace,

1959); Irving Howe and Lewis Coser, *The American Communist Party: A Critical History* (Boston: Beacon Press, 1957); Earl Latham, *The Communist Controversy in Washington* (Cambridge, Mass.: Harvard University Press, 1966); Daniel Bell, *Marxian Socialism in the United States* (Princeton, N.J.: Princeton University Press, 1967); Joseph Starobin, *American Communism in Crisis, 1943–1957* (Cambridge, Mass.: Harvard University Press, 1972); Richard M. Fried, *Men Against McCarthy* (New York: Columbia University Press, 1976); Walter Goodman, *The Committee: The Extraordinary Career of the House Committee on Un-American Activities* (New York: Farrar, Straus & Giroux, 1968); Michael Paul Rogin, *The Intellectuals and McCarthy: The Radical Specter* (Cambridge, Mass.: MIT Press, 1967); Robert Griffith, *The Politics of Fear: Joseph R. McCarthy and the Senate* (Lexington: University Press of Kentucky, 1970); Richard H. Pells, *Radical Visions and American Dreams: Culture and Social Thought in the Depression Years* (New York: Harper & Row, 1973).

Many critical accounts of the McCarthy era were written contemporaneously, and some of the best of these are: Alan Barth, *The Loyalty of Free Men* (New York: Viking, 1951); Edward A. Shils, *The Torment of Secrecy: The Background and Consequences of American Security Policies* (Glencoe, Ill.: Free Press, 1956); James A. Wechsler, *The Age of Suspicion* (New York: Random House, 1953); Walter Gellhorn, *Security, Loyalty, and Science* (Ithaca N.Y.: Cornell University Press, 1950); Elmer Davis, *But We Were Born Free* (Garden City, N.Y.: Garden City Books, 1954); Arthur M. Schlesinger, Jr., *The Vital Center: The Politics of Freedom* (Boston: Houghton Mifflin, 1949).

Particularly valuable for the opinion survey materials they contain are Samuel A. Stouffer, *Communism, Conformity, and Civil Liberties: A Cross-Section of the Nation Speaks Its Mind* (Garden City, N.Y.: Doubleday, 1955); and Paul F. Lazarsfeld and Wagner Thielens, Jr., *The Academic Mind: Social Scientists in a Time of Crisis* (Glencoe, Ill.: Free Press, 1958).

There is no secondary source that can adequately substitute for the transcripts of the hearings conducted by the House Committee on Un-American Activities and the Senate Internal Security Subcommittee. They provide in undiluted form as vivid and flavorful a sense of the times and the issues as any interpretive gloss that followed.

Among several excellent collections of articles, largely about the attacks on elementary and secondary schools, are: C. Winfield Scott and Clyde M. Hill, eds., *Public Education Under Criticism* (New York: Prentice-Hall, 1954); Ernest O. Melby and Morton Puner, eds., *Freedom and Public Education,* (New York: Praeger, 1953); Ernest O. Melby, *American Education Under Fire* (New York: Anti-Defamation League, 1951); Theodore Brameld, ed., *The Battle for Free Schools* (Boston: Beacon, 1951); a special issue of *Phi Delta Kappan* 34 (June 1953): 353–432; "Meeting the Attacks on Education," a special issue of *Progressive Education* 29 (January 1952): 65–122. The NEA published several studies of public school controversies, including: National Commission for the Defense of Democracy Through Education, *The Pasadena Story: An Analysis of Some Forces and Factors That Injured a Superior School System* (Washington, D.C.: NEA, 1951); National Commission for the Defense of Democracy Through Education, *Houston, Texas: Report of an Investigation* (Washington, D.C.: NEA, 1954).

Race and Education: Chapters 4 and 5

Again, alas, there is a quantity of primary and secondary source materials which is nearly overwhelming. William L. O'Neill, in *Coming Apart: An Informal History of America in the 1960's* (Chicago: Quadrangle, 1971), notes that "merely reading all the books on racial matters that appeared in the sixties would be a full-time job. They appeared at the rate of eight or ten a week" (p. 433). Necessary background reading includes: C. Vann Woodward, *The Strange Career of Jim Crow* (New York: Oxford University Press, 3rd rev. ed., 1974, orig. pub. 1955); Gunnar Myrdal, *An American Dilemma: The Negro Problem and Modern Democracy* (New York: Harper & Bros., 1944), Henry Allen Bullock, *A History of Negro Education in the South: From 1619 to the Present* (Cambridge, Mass.: Harvard University Press, 1967); David L. Kirp, *Just Schools: The Idea of Racial Equality in American Education* (Berkeley and Los Angeles: University of California Press, 1982); Richard Kluger, *Simple Justice: The History of Brown v. Board of Education and Black America's Struggle for Equality* (New York: Alfred A. Knopf, 1976).

Some early, general accounts that are useful include: Benjamin Muse, *Ten Years of Prelude: The Story of Integration Since the Supreme Court's 1954 Decision* (New York: Viking Press, 1964); Reed Sarratt, *The Ordeal of Desegregation: The First Decade* (New York: Harper & Row, 1966); Anthony Lewis, *Portrait of a Decade: The Second American Revolution* (New York: Random House, 1964).

The changing judicial role is a central element in the story of the civil rights movement, and there are many first-rate studies. Among these are: Stephen L. Wasby, Anthony A. D'Amato, and Rosemary Metrailer, *Desegregation from Brown to Alexander: An Exploration of Supreme Court Strategies* (Carbondale, Ill.: Southern Illinois University Press, 1977); Loren Miller, *The Petitioners: The Story of the Supreme Court of the United States and the Negro* (New York: Pantheon, 1966); Jack Bass, *Unlikely Heroes* (New York: Simon and Schuster, 1981); J. Harvie Wilkinson, III, *From Brown to Bakke: The Supreme Court and School Integration, 1954–1978* (New York: Oxford University Press, 1979); Terry Eastland and William J. Bennett, *Counting by Race: Equality from the*

Founding Fathers to Bakke (New York: Basic Books, 1979). Absolutely invaluable as a source is Leon Friedman, ed., *Argument: The Oral Argument Before the Supreme Court in* Brown *v.* Board of Education of Topeka, *1952–1955* (New York: Chelsea, 1969), which contains the transcripts of the lawyers' presentations and the exchanges between them and the justices of the Supreme Court.

Several dissertations contain material that is not generally available, such as: Byron Richard Skinner, "The Double 'V': The Impact of World War II on Black America" (Diss., University of California, Berkeley, 1978); Eugene Pierce Walker, "A History of the Southern Christian Leadership Conference, 1955–1965: The Evolution of a Southern Strategy for Social Change" (Diss., Duke University, 1978); Stanford Phillips Dyer, "Lyndon B. Johnson and the Politics of Civil Rights, 1935–1960: The Art of 'Moderate Leadership' " (Diss., Texas A&M University, 1978).

The development of federal education policies since 1965 has been well covered in such works as Philip Meranto, *The Politics of Federal Aid to Education in 1965: A Study in Political Innovation* (Syracuse, N.Y.: Syracuse University Press, 1967); Stephen K. Bailey and Edith K. Mosher, *ESEA: The Office of Education Administers a Law* (Syracuse, N.Y.: Syracuse University Press, 1968); Norman C. Thomas, *Education in National Politics* (New York: David McKay, 1975); Gary Orfield, *The Reconstruction of Southern Education* (New York: John Wiley, 1969); Gary Orfield, *Must We Bus?: Segregated Schools and National Policy* (Washington, D. C.: Brookings Institution, 1978); Edward Zigler and Jeanette Valentine, eds., *Project Head Start: A Legacy of the War on Poverty* (New York: Free Press, 1979).

The role of social science in shaping social policy has been the subject of scores of books and hundreds of articles. A seminal social report was James S. Coleman et al., *Equality of Educational Opportunity* (Washington, D.C.: Government Printing Office, 1966), which in turn generated many other studies, including Frederick Mosteller and Daniel P. Moynihan, eds., *On Equality of Educational Opportunity* (New York: Random House, 1972); Christopher Jencks et al., *Inequality: A Reassessment of the Effect of Family and Schooling in America* (New York: Basic Books, 1972); and Donald M. Levine and Mary Jo Bane, eds., *The "Inequality" Controversy: Schooling and Distributive Justice* (New York: Basic Books, 1975). The use of social science data by the courts is discussed in "The Courts, Social Science, and School Desegregation," *Law and Contemporary Problems,* 2 vols., 39 (Winter 1975), 39 (Spring 1975); Paul Rosen, *The Supreme Court and Social Science* (Urbana: University of Illinois, 1972); Nancy St. John, *School Desegregation: Outcomes for Children* (New York: John Wiley, 1975); Charles E. Lindblom and David K. Cohen, *Usable Knowledge: Social Science and Social Problem Solving* (New Haven: Yale University Press,

1979); Eleanor P. Wolf, *Trial and Error: The Detroit School Segregation Case* (Detroit: Wayne State University, 1981). For an unusually perspicacious critique, see Eleanor P. Wolf, "Civil Rights and Social Science Data: Problems in the Use of Research Data to Support Civil Rights Propositions, 1964," *Race, A Journal of Race and Group Relations* (London) 13 (July 1972–April 1973): 155–82.

In addition to social science research that is specifically related to desegregation, there is an imposing body of studies on the education of poor children and black children. Among the most influential were: Kenneth B. Clark, *Dark Ghetto: Dilemmas of Social Power* (New York: Harper & Row, 1965); A. Harry Passow, ed., *Education in Depressed Areas* (New York: Bureau of Publications, Teachers College, 1963); Edmund W. Gordon and Doxey A. Wilkerson, *Compensatory Education for the Disadvantaged: Programs and Practices: Preschool through College* (New York: College Entrance Examination Board, 1966); Frank Riessman, *The Culturally Deprived Child* (New York: Harper & Row., 1962); Martin Deutsch, *The Disadvantaged Child* (New York: Basic Books, 1967); Mario D. Fantini and Gerald Weinstein, *The Disadvantaged: Challenge to Education* (New York: Harper & Row, 1968). Written in the midst of social crisis, these analyses form a specific body of literature, with common assumptions and common terms of reference. Unhappily, there have been few efforts to evaluate this work as a whole, to see whether its assumptions and prescriptions are valid when removed from the context of crisis.

From Berkeley to Kent State: Chapter 6

The best background reading for understanding the campus upheavals includes: Christopher Jencks and David Riesman, *The Academic Revolution* (Garden City, N.Y.: Doubleday, 1968); Martin Trow, "Reflections on the Transition from Mass to Universal Higher Education," *Daedalus* 99 (Winter 1970): 1–42; Martin Trow, "Conceptions of the University: The Case of Berkeley," *American Behavioral Scientist* 11 (May–June 1968): 14–21; Martin Trow, "Bell, Book, and Berkeley," *American Behavioral Scientist* 11 (May–June 1968): 43–48; Stanley Rothman and S. Robert Lichter, *Roots of Radicalism: Jews, Christians, and the New Left* (New York: Oxford University Press, 1982); Morris Dickstein, *Gates of Eden: American Culture in the Sixties* (New York: Basic Books, 1977); Paul Goodman, *Growing Up Absurd: Problems of Youth in the Organized Society* (New York: Random House, 1960); Paul Goodman, *The New Reformation: Notes of a Neolithic Conservative* (New York: Random House, 1970); Clayborne Carson, *In Struggle: SNCC and the Black Awakening of the 1960s*

(Cambridge, Mass: Harvard University Press, 1981); Kirkpatrick Sale, *SDS* (New York: Random House, 1973); Everett Carll Ladd, Jr., and Seymour Martin Lipset, *The Divided Academy: Professors and Politics* (New York: McGraw-Hill, 1975); Seymour Martin Lipset and Gerald M. Schaflander, *Passion and Politics: Student Activism in America* (Boston: Little Brown, 1971); Daniel Bell, *The Cultural Contradictions of Capitalism* (New York: Basic Books, 1976); Nathan Glazer, *Remembering the Answers: Essays on the American Student Revolt* (New York: Basic Books, 1970); Irwin Unger, *The Movement: A History of the American New Left, 1959–1972* (New York: Dodd, Mead, 1974); Philip Altbach, *Student Politics in America: A Historical Analysis* (New York: McGraw-Hill, 1974); John R. Searle, *The Campus War: A Sympathetic Look at the University in Agony* (New York: World, 1971); Adam Ulam, *The Fall of the American University* (New York: Library Press, 1972).

There are several outstanding collections of primary source materials, and among the best of these are: Immanuel Wallerstein and Paul Starr, eds., *The University Crisis Reader*, 2 vols. (New York: Vintage, 1971); Seymour Martin Lipset and Sheldon S. Wolin, eds., *The Berkeley Student Revolt: Facts and Interpretations* (Garden City, N.Y.: Anchor Books, 1965); Mitchell Cohen and Dennis Hale, eds., *The New Student Left* (Boston: Beacon Press, 1967); Philip G. Altbach and Robert S. Laufer, eds., *The New Pilgrims* (New York: David McKay, 1972); Paul Jacobs and Saul Landau, eds., *The New Radicals* (New York: Random House, 1966).

The notes for chapter 6 refer to the best available sources for the events on certain campuses. For reasons known but to Clio, the activities of student rebels on some campuses are very well documented, while on other campuses the record is fragmentary and ephemeral.

Reformers, Radicals, and Romantics: Chapter 7

There are three types of writings that were resources for chapter 7: the crisis literature of the 1960s; the open education literature of the late 1960s and early 1970s; and the evaluation literature of the 1970s.

It is not especially useful merely to list the many books that described the failings of American education; the most influential ones are cited in the notes. The question that cannot be answered with the material presently available is whether the portrait they drew of American schools was anecdotal or representative. One piece of counterevidence is the Gallup poll for 1969 in the *Phi Delta Kappan* 51 (November 1969): 157, 163, which showed high regard for the public schools. Nonetheless, what we have in the crisis literature are snapshots of educational disaster areas, refracted through the eyes of writers with a strong social conscience. There has been, as yet, no systematic effort to test whether this powerful indictment of the schools was accurate.

The crisis literature described the "disease," and for many in education, "the open classroom" was the cure. The difficulties of evaluating whether the original diagnosis was correct and whether the cure was effective are related problems. The events of the 1960s are so recent that the record is still being written. Recent as it is, the story still needs to be assembled in order to understand the connections between ideas and policies. What I have tried to do in this chapter is to create an account of what happened, of the kinds of assumptions that people made, of the kinds of policies they created to act on those assumptions, and of the apparent effects. In looking at a national phenomenon, like open education, there is always the problem of sorting out what people *said* about it (its promoters), from what other people did about it (teachers), and then assessing what difference it made, if any, in the classroom.

The most influential writings on the subject of open education are: Joseph Featherstone's 1967 articles in the *New Republic,* which were collected in *Schools Where Children Learn* (New York: Liveright, 1971); Beatrice Gross and Ronald Gross, "A Little Bit of Chaos," *Saturday Review,* May 16, 1970; in many accounts, teachers and principals mention that they learned about open education by reading one of these articles. Also, articles by Roland S. Barth, including "Teaching: The Way It Is, The Way It Could Be," *Grade Teacher* 87 (January 1970): 98–101; "So You Want to Change to an Open Classroom," *Phi Delta Kappan* 53 (October 1971): 97–99; and *Open Education and the American School* (New York: Agathon Press, 1972). Also notable was Herbert R. Kohl, *The Open Classroom: A Practical Guide to a New Way of Teaching* (New York: Random House, 1969); Lillian Weber, *The English Infant School and Informal Education* (Englewood Cliffs, N.J.: Prentice-Hall, 1971). Open education reached a large national audience with the publication of Charles Silberman, *Crisis in the Classroom* (New York: Random House, 1970). Charles Silberman, ed., *The Open Classroom Reader* (New York: Vintage, 1973) includes many of the significant short writings about open education, as does Ewald B. Nyquist and Gene R. Hawes, eds., *Open Education: A Sourcebook for Parents and Teachers* (New York: Bantam, 1972).

One of the few dissertations on the subject of open education that is written with critical perspective is Diane-Marie Hargrove Blinn, "Open Education: An Analysis of the Practical Purport, Historical Context, and Parent Doctrine of an Educational Slogan" (Diss., University of Chicago, 1981). Unlike progressive education, which was the target of a withering barrage of criticism, the writings directly critical of open education are scarce. An example is: Donald A. Myers and Daniel L. Duke, "Open Education as an Ideology," *Educational Research* 19 (June 1977): 227–35.

In order to find evidence of the practice of open education, I scanned the professional education journals, and these proved to be a rich source of descriptive accounts of innovative activities; from the journals, I was able to find many, many schools that had switched to "openness" or experimented with alternative programs. From such articles, many of which are cited in the notes, it was possible to get a sense of how practitioners interpreted open education and how it was being implemented (though, presumably, only the most successful experiments were written about).

The curious aspect of open education was the rapidity of its ascent and then apparent eclipse as an educational phenomenon. In the early 1970s, there were literally hundreds of articles about open education in the journals. By the mid-1970s, the number began to drop sharply, and an occasional article appeared with a title like "open education is not dead," which implied that someone thought that it was. Word-of-mouth, nothing that could be footnoted, had it that schools were restoring the walls that had been removed to create open classrooms. Yet I found nothing in the literature, nothing from the government agencies and foundations that most vigorously promoted open education, to indicate what had changed. I suspect that open education may turn out to be much like progressive education, which was equally broad in its definition, in that it will be very hard to know whether it was implemented in the right way because there is little agreement on what "the right way" is or even on what "it" (open education) is.

Another angle of vision on the reforms of the late 1960s is provided by federally funded program evaluations and by what is known as "implementation research." Hundreds, probably very many hundreds, of evaluations have been sponsored by the federal government since the passage of federal aid to education in 1965. Some of these evaluations turn out to be rather wonderful documents for the historian of the future, with plenty of detail about curriculum, methods, teachers, students, the community, and efforts to introduce changes. Unhappily, the evaluations for some federally funded projects—especially those that were part of the Experimental Schools Program—are difficult, if not impossible, to obtain. In some cases, the evaluations were rejected by the National Institute of Education for one reason or another (even though they cost hundreds of thousands of dollars); in others, evaluations that were accepted by the federal government were, well, misplaced, lost, not filed in any public repository.

Implementation research is intended to provide understanding of how programs work; to ask, why is it that a program that seems to be well planned and is well funded does not produce the intended results? Why is it that the local school districts do not do what their proposals say they are going to do? Why is it that the money spent has so little effect on educational outcomes? Two opposing answers to these questions are: Eleanor Farrar, John E. DeSanctis, David K. Cohen, "Views from Below: Implementation Research in Education," *Teachers College Record* 82 (Fall 1980): 77–100; and Lois-Ellin Datta, "Changing Times: The Study of Federal Programs Supporting Educational Change and the Case for Local Problem Solving," *Teachers College Record* 82 (Fall 1980): 101–16. There are a number of excellent studies of educational reform programs; in addition to those cited in the chapter notes, Paul M. Nachtigal, ed., *Rural Education: In Search of a Better Way* (Boulder, Colo.: Westview Press, 1982) is highly recommended.

The New Politics of Education: Chapter 8

There are several excellent books on the broad subject of ethnicity, including Stephan Thernstrom, ed., *Harvard Encyclopedia of American Ethnic Groups* (Cambridge, Mass: Harvard University Press, 1980), Andrew M. Greeley, *Ethnicity in the United States: A Preliminary Reconnaissance* (New York: John Wiley, 1974); Nathan Glazer and Daniel P. Moynihan, eds., *Ethnicity: Theory and Experience* (Cambridge, Mass.: Harvard University Press, 1975); Thomas Sowell, *Ethnic America: A History* (New York: Basic Books, 1981); Richard Polenberg, *One Nation Divisible: Class, Race, and Ethnicity in the United States Since 1938* (New York: Viking Press, 1980). Critiques of "the new ethnicity" include: Nathan Glazer, *Affirmative Discrimination* (New York: Basic Books, 1975); Orlando Patterson, *Ethnic Chauvinism: The Reactionary Impulse* (New York: Stein and Day, 1977); Howard F. Stein and Robert F. Hill, "The Limits of Ethnicity," *American Scholar* 46 (Spring 1977): 181–89, a condensation of Howard F. Stein and Robert F. Hill, *The Ethnic Imperative: Examining the New White Ethnic Movement* (University Park: Pennsylvania State University Press, 1977). In addition, the following analyses are valuable: L. Paul Metzger, "American Sociology and Black Assimilation: Conflicting Perspectives," *American Journal of Sociology* 76 (January 1971): 627–47; Lester Singer, "Ethnogenesis and Negro-Americans Today," *Social Research* 29 (Winter 1962): 422–32; Rudolph J. Vecoli, "Ethnicity: A Neglected Dimension of American History," in *The State of American History*, ed. Herbert J. Bass (Chicago: Quadrangle Books, 1970), pp. 70–88.

A Note on Sources

There is a related, but nonetheless distinct, literature on language groups, which provides a context for the issue of bilingual education. Among the most useful works are: Joshua A. Fishman et al., *Language Loyalty in the United States* (The Hague: Mouton, 1966); Theodore Andersson and Mildred Boyer, *Bilingual Schooling in the United States: History, Rationale, Implications, and Planning* (Detroit: B. Ethridge, 1976); Noel Epstein, *Language, Ethnicity, and the Schools: Policy Alternatives for Bilingual-Bicultural Education* (Washington, D.C.: Institute for Educational Leadership, 1977); Heinz Kloss, *The American Bilingual Tradition* (Rowley, Mass.: Newbury House, 1977). There are two excellent summaries of the political evolution of federal bilingual policy: Abigail M. Thernstrom, "E Pluribus Plura—Congress and Bilingual Education," *Public Interest* 60 (Summer 1980): 3–22; and Iris Rotberg, "Some Legal and Research Considerations in Establishing Federal Policy in Bilingual Education," *Harvard Educational Review* 52 (May 1982): 148–68, which also includes a first-rate survey of current research findings.

There has been no accurate assessment of the spread of courses such as black studies and ethnic studies, either in high school or in college and university. An early effort to do so (in higher education) is: Winnie Bengelsdorf, *Ethnic Studies in Higher Education: State of the Art and Bibliography* (Washington, D.C.: American Association of State Colleges and Universities, 1972). For critical discussions of the movement for black studies, see Orlando Patterson, *Ethnic Chauvinism,* pp. 153–58; and Martin Kilson, "Reflections on Structure and Content in Black Studies," *Journal of Black Studies,* 3 (March 1973): 297–314. More than a decade after black studies and ethnic studies were installed in the curriculum, it is not possible to say how many students participated or how many educational institutions established new courses, new departments, or new degree-granting programs, nor is it possible to say whether such courses emphasized the objective study of the subject or particularistic group consciousness.

Many books on the subject of feminism and sexism devote attention to educational institutions because of the importance of "socialization." Books that show how to incorporate feminism into the high school curriculum are: Florence Howe and Jacqueline M. Fralley, eds., *High School Feminist Studies* (Old Westbury, N.Y.: Feminist Press, 1976); Gail Thomas McLure and John W. McLure, *Women's Studies* (Washington, D.C.: NEA, 1977). In addition to the works cited in the notes, I found the newsletters of the Project on the Status and Education of Women (Washington, D.C.) to be an invaluable guide to the developing events of the 1970s. Among the large number of books about sexism in education are: Susan Bereaud, Judith Stacy, and Joan Daniels, eds., *And Jill Came Tumbling After: Sexism in American Education* (New York: Dell, 1974); Nancy Frazier and Myra Sadker, *Sexism in School and Society* (New York: Harper & Row, 1973); Diane Gersoni-Stavn, *Sexism and Youth* (New York: R. R. Bowker, 1974); Casey Miller and Kate Swift, *Words and Women: New Language in New Times* (Garden City, N.Y.: Doubleday Anchor, 1976); Barbara Sprung, *Perspectives on Nonsexist Early Childhood Education* (New York: Teachers College Press, 1978); Phyllis Stock, *Better Than Rubies: A History of Women's Education* (New York: Putnam's, 1978); U.S. Department of Health, Education, and Welfare, *Taking Sexism Out of Education* (Washington, D.C.: Government Printing Office, 1978).

On the issue of unionism in schools and universities, in addition to the works cited, a good reading list would include: Frank R. Kemerer and J. Victor Baldridge, *Unions on Campus* (San Francisco: Jossey-Bass, 1975); Everett Carll Ladd, Jr., and Seymour Martin Lipset, *Professors, Unions, and American Higher Education* (Washington, D.C.: Carnegie Foundation for the Advancement of Teaching, 1973); Charles R. Perry and Wesley A. Wildman, *The Impact of Negotiations in Public Education: The Evidence from the Schools* (Worthington, Ohio: Charles A. Jones, 1970); Marshall O. Donley, Jr., *Power to the Teacher: How America's Educators Became Militant* (Bloomington: Indiana University Press, 1976); Robert J. Braun, *Teachers and Power: The Story of the American Federation of Teachers* (New York: Simon and Schuster, 1972); Thomas Brooks, *Towards Dignity: A Brief History of the United Federation of Teachers* (New York: United Federation of Teachers, 1967); Stephen Cole, *The Unionization of Teachers: A Case Study of the United Federation of Teachers* (New York: Praeger, 1969); Philip Taft, *United They Teach: The Story of the United Federation of Teachers* (Los Angeles: Nash, 1974); and Bruce S. Cooper, *Collective Bargaining, Strikes, and Financial Costs in Public Education: A Comparative Review* (Eugene, Oreg.: ERIC Clearinghouse, 1982).

Despite the very large number of works presently available in most areas mentioned, there remain many unexplored questions, many needs and opportunities for the future scholar. Typically, the surfeit of material consists of books and articles written in the heat of controversy, as advocacy tracts or as rebuttals, which are enormously important in understanding how people viewed educational questions but which are limited as sources by their absence of perspective. Time and emotional distance, one hopes, will produce not only in-depth studies of individual institutions and communities but also balanced interpretations of educational issues in relation to their social, economic, and political context.

INDEX

A. Philip Randolph Institute, 168
Ability grouping, 149, 230
Academic freedom: affirmative action and, 284, 302, 303; loyalty investigations as threat to, 96–100, 102, 110; student radicalism and, 183, 191, 227
Academic standards: and democratization of higher education, 17, 18; debate about, 326; desegregation and, 149; GI Bill and, 13, 14; Sputnik and concern about, 229–31, 235
Accountability laws, 315–16
Addams, Jane, 46
Adelson, Alan, 346n59
Adelson, Joseph, 347n72
Adler, Mortimer J., 58, 334n22
Admissions policies: affirmative action and, 284–91; discriminatory, 16, 24; open, 226, 324
Affirmative action, 271, 280–92; for handicapped, 309; in higher education, 283–92, 302–3, 311
Afro-American Society (AAS) at Cornell University, 213–15
Alabama, University of, 138
Alberty, Harold, 77–78, 336n53
Alexander, Sadie, 23
Allen, Mary L., 336n42, 339n42
Altbach, Philip G., 345n46, 366
Alternative schools, 238, 253–54; federal funding for, 258–59
American Association of School Administrators, 66
American Association of University Professors, 100–101
American Civil Liberties Union (ACLU), 95, 100
American Council on Education, 15, 59; American Youth Commission of, 60
American Education Association, 106
American Farm Bureau Federation, 28
American Federation of Labor (AFL), 89
American Federation of State, County, and Municipal Employees, 314
American Federation of Teachers (AFT), 89, 95, 103, 279, 313, 315
American Historical Association, 105
American Indians: affirmative action and, 283; ethnocentrism and, 270; integration of, 177
American Institutes for Research (AIR), 277–78
American Legion, 90
American Psychological Association, 301
American Vocational Association, 66
Americans for Democratic Action, 97
Anderson, Archibald W., 336n42, n47, n48
Anderson, Jervis, 342n37
Anderson, Karen, 342nn18–19
Andersson, Theodore, 370
Andrus, Ethel P., 335n32
Angell, George W., 356n96

Anti-Communism: among critics of progressive education, 70–71; in denunciations of *Brown* decision, 128; Depression-era, 89–91, 93; *see also* Loyalty investigations
Anti-nepotism rules, 297
Antioch School, 4, 328
Armed forces, discrimination in, 21–22, 25
Armington, David, 242–43
Armor, David J., 179, 343n61
Armstrong, O. K., 337n15
Asians: affirmative action and, 283; innovative education for, 259; integration of, 177
Association of American Universities, 102
Astin, Alexander W., 345n37, 346n63, 347n73
Astin, Helen S., 353n58
Atkin, J. Myron, 317–18, 356n100
Atkinson, Byron H., 331n12
Atlantic Monthly, 73
Ausubel, David P., 341n7
Avorn, Jerry L., 345n31, n36
Axen, Richard, 345n40, n47, n48, 346n49, n51

Baby boom, 6, 41, 70, 182, 226, 229; and decline in female employment, 296–97; higher education enrollments resulting from, 183
"Back to basics" movement, 255, 263, 311–12, 316
Bagley, William C., 49, 55, 58, 69, 333n6, 334n23
Bailey, Stephen K., 341n4, 342n21, nn27–30, 364
Bainbridge, John, 339n45
Bakke, Allan, 285–90
Bakke v. University of California (1978), 286–91
Baldridge, J. Victor, 371
Baldwin, Roger, 101
Bane, Mary Jo, 364
Bank Street College of Education, 242
Barden, Graham A., 33–36, 39–41
Barden bill, 34–36, 39
Barker, Paula R., 349n47
Barrett, Edward L., Jr., 112, 361
Barrett, George, 340n27
Barrow, Robin, 348n13
Barth, Alan, 101, 112, 338n33, 362
Barth, Roland S., 249–50, 255, 349n38, n49, 367
Bass, Herbert J., 369
Beard, Charles, 59–60
"Beats," 186
Beberman, Max, 347n3
Bell, Bernard Iddings, 70
Bell, Daniel, 112, 185, 337n3, 344n6, n11, 362, 366
Bell, Derrick A., Jr., 180–81, 343n67
Bell, Terrell, 274, 279
Bennett, Neville, 350n51, n52
Bennett, William J., 352n44, 353n45, 363

Bentley, Eric, 338*n*31
Bereaud, Susan, 370
Berkeley, University of California at, 190–97; demonstration against HCUA at, 187, 190; Free Speech Movement at, 192–96; national influence of student unrest at, 196–97; "People's Park" issue at, 196
Berman, Ronald, 344*n*7, 357
Bernard, Jessie, 353*n*58
Bestor, Arthur, 70, 75–76, 229, 336*n*51
Bettelheim, Bruno, 222, 346*n*68, 354*n*65
Bhaerman, Steve, 236, 348*n*16
Bickel, Alexander, 166, 170, 290, 341*n*38, 342*n*34, 343*n*42, 352*n*43
Bigelow, Donald N., 350*n*54
Bilingual education, 271–80, 311; civil rights model and, 305; segregation in, 276–77
Bilingual Education Act (1968), 273, 276
Birmingham civil rights demonstrations, 140
Birnbaum, Max, 347*n*75
Black, Hugo, 29, 32
Black Coalition to Maximize Education, 181
Black English, 269, 313
Black Muslims, 147
Black Panther Party, 211, 218–19
Black Student Union (BSU) at San Francisco State College, 211–12
Black studies programs, 209, 211–14, 216, 225, 226, 269
Blackburn, Robert, 347*n*75
Blackmun, Harry, 288–89
Blacks: achievement levels of, 149, 150, 168–73, 179–80; affirmative action and, 280, 281, 283, 291–92; changing social position of, 181, 329; in community control movement, 158, 168, 173–75, 234, 237; emergence of nationalism among, 145–46; ethnocentrism and, 268–70; growing militancy of, 167–68; higher education for, 121, 210, 322; labor force discrimination against, 300; mass support of civil rights movement by, 138–39; Moynihan report and, 160–61; postwar discrimination against, 21–22; poverty among, 146–48, 325; progressive education and, 55; reading books for, 156; restrictions on college admissions of, 16; rioting by, 162, 200; rising level of literacy among, 118–19; segregation of, *see* Segregation; and southern way of life, 115–16; student radicalism and, 189, 190, 201–3, 209–16, 226; in teaching profession, 3–4, 27, 120; urbanization of, 118, 182, 325; violence against, 141; during World War II, 19–20, 116–17
Blanshard, Paul, 31–32, 332*nn*38–40, 358
Blinn, Diane-Marie Hargrove, 348*nn*19–22, *n*24, *n*25, 350*n*50, 367
Bloom, Benjamin, 152, 341*n*8, *n*10
B'nai B'rith, 109
Bobbitt, Franklin, 49, 50, 333*n*8
Bock, Frederick S., 349*n*47
Bock, Leon, 338*n*36, 361
Boggs, Ronald J., 358
Bok, Derek C., 319, 356*n*102
Borton, Terry, 237, 348*n*16
Boutelle, Margaret, 335*n*32
Bowers, C. A., 335*n*32, 337*n*9
Boyer, Mildred, 370
Brady, Elizabeth H., 342*n*16

Brameld, Theodore, 86, 87, 337*n*7, 362
Braun, Robert J., 371
Braungart, Richard G., 347*n*72
Brennan, William, 288
Brewster, Kingman, 218
Briggs dictum, 165–66
Broder, Dorothy E., 335*n*35
Brooks, Hunter O., 349*n*47
Brooks, Thomas, 371
Browder, Earl, 84, 337*n*17
Brown v. Board of Education (1954), 138, 165, 170, 269–70
Brownell, Herbert J., 340
Broyles commission, 99–100
Bruner, Herbert B., 52, 333*n*11
Bruner, Jerome, 232, 348*n*9
Brustein, Robert, 346*n*61
Brzezinski, Zbigniew, 222, 346*n*68
Buchanan, Jimmy, 356*n*6
Budenz, Louis, 93–94
Bullock, Franklin O., 349*n*47
Bullock, Henry Allen, 363
Bundy, McGeorge, 287, 352*n*38
Bunzel, John H., 212, 346*n*50, 354*n*68
Bureau of Education, U.S., 48
Bureau of Education for the Handicapped (BEH), 307
Burger, Warren, 175, 289
Burr, Samuel Engle, 334*n*12, 359
Burrell, Sidney A., 331*n*13
Bushnell, Don D., 348*n*11
Busing, 176, 237, 311; attitudes of blacks toward, 181; legislation prohibiting, 165, 175
Byrnes, James, 135

Cahn, Edmond, 129–30, 340*n*20
Calderwood, Ann, 353*n*56
Califano, Joseph, 308
California, University of: Board of Regents, 98–99, 193; Davis School of Medicine, 285–90; *see also* Berkeley, University of California at
Caliver, Ambrose, 339*n*6
Campbell, Ernest, 168
Campus unrest, *see* Student radicalism
Canwell, Albert F., 94–95
Carden, Maren Lockwood, 353*n*49
Cardinal Principles of Secondary Education (NEA), 47–48, 51, 66
Carey, James, 23
Carleton, Don Edward, 339*n*41
Carlucci, Frank, 275–76
Carmichael, Omer, 340*n*23
Carmichael, Stokely, 167, 343*n*51
Carnegie Corporation, 230, 245–46
Carr, William G., 61
Carson, Clayborne, 342*n*36, 344*n*13, 365
Carten, Roger D., 349*n*46
Carter, Jimmy, 279, 291, 315, 319
Carter, Robert L., 125, 129, 340*n*19
Cary, Miles E., 336*n*43
Cass, James, 347*n*75
Castro, Fidel, 186
Caswell, Hollis L., 45, 54, 333*n*2, 334*nn*12–15, *n*17, *n*19, 336*n*43, *n*53, 360

Index

Catholics: and ecumenical spirit, 325; and federal aid to education, 5, 6, 27–41, 148
Caute, David, 337n12, 339n48, 361
Celebrezze, Anthony J., 143
Chall, Jeanne S., 356n5
Chamber of Commerce, U.S., 27
Chamberlain, Lawrence A., 112, 337n12, 361
Charters, W. W., 333n8
Chicago, University of, 13, 18, 56, 99–100, 152, 206–7
Chicanos: ethnocentrism and, 270; innovative education for, 258, 259
Chief State School Officers, 279
Child-benefit theory, 30, 33, 41
Child-centered schools, 50–51
Childs, John, 86, 98, 338n25
Chinese, bilingual education for, 274
Chisholm, Shirley, 275
Christmas, Florence, 3–5, 328, 356n6
City College of New York (CCNY), 241, 324
City schools, *see* Urban schools
Civil Rights Act (1964), 142–45, 162, 168, 171, 280–81, 294–95; conflicting interpretations of, 165–66; Title VI of, 268, 273
Civil Rights Commission, 135, 164, 171–72
Civil rights movement: anti-Communist attacks on, 90; *Bakke* case and, 286, 288, 290; black violence and, 162; Eisenhower and, 135; emergence of nationalism in, 145–46; ethnocentrism and, 270; higher education and, 210; Johnson and, 142, 144; Kennedy and, 140–41; in legal campaign against segregation, 119–27; "March on Washington" of, 141; mass base of, 138–40; as model for bringing about change, 305–6; Nixon and, 282; pedagogical revolution overshadowed by, 233–34; postwar, 20–26, 118; and racial isolation in North, 177; and urban racial disorders, 148; white students in, 188–92
Clark, Kenneth B., 130, 157–58, 171, 175, 342n17, 365
Cleaveland, Bradford, 344n15
Clowse, Barbara Barksdale, 347n2
Clune, William H., 355n91
Cochran v. Louisiana State Board of Education (1930), 30–31
Cohen, David K., 180, 260, 343n66, 350n59, 364, 369
Cohen, Mitchell, 344n12, 366
Cole, Stephen, 371
Coleman, James S., 168, 171, 179, 342n38, n40, 343n62, 364
Coleman, Robert William, 344n13
Coleman Report, 168–70
Collective bargaining, 314–15
College, *see* Higher education *and specific institutions*
College preparatory courses, declining enrollment in, 56
Collings, Ellsworth, 52, 359
Colorado Education Association, 5
Color-blindness, principle of, 142–46, 165, 268, 270
Columbia University, 83, 130; student unrest at, 200–205; *see also* Teachers College
Colvin, Reynolds, 286
Commager, Henry Steele, 101, 112
Committee of Law Teachers Against Segregation, 123–24

"Common learnings" program, 71
Communist International, 84, 98
Communist party: Depression-era radicalism and, 83–84; New York City public schools and, 102; Popular Front doctrine of, 84–85; public fear of subversion by, 92–93, 104, 107, 108, 112–13; *Social Frontier* group and, 86–89; subversion of liberal organizations by, 97–98; teachers' unions and, 89; university faculty members and, 93–100
Community colleges, 16, 18, 323
Community control movement, 158, 168, 173–75, 234, 237, 325
Compensatory education, 150, 153–54, 231, 234, 238–39; criticism of, 169, 170, 172
Comprehensive high schools, 230
Comprehensive School Improvement Program (CSIP), 231
Compulsory education laws, 10, 153; abolished, to protect segregation, 133; critique of, 236
Conant, James B., 13, 14, 74, 149–50, 230, 331n10, 339n43, 341n5, 347n5
Congress, U.S., 18, 93, 216, 267–68, 317, 321–23; aid to education bills in, 6–9, 28, 29, 33, 34, 229, 306; bilingual education approved by, 273, 276–78; civil rights issues in, 20–23, 25, 119, 134, 140, 141, 146, 148, 164, 165, 167, 172, 288; Department of Education established by, 315; education for handicapped mandated by, 307–10; educational reform programs and, 258; GI Bill in, 13; loyalty investigations in, 90, 92; NSF established by, 231, 244; sex discrimination prohibited by, 294–95, 297; *see also* House of Representatives; Senate
Congress of Industrial Organizations (CIO), 23, 102
Congress of Racial Equality (CORE), 139, 146, 202
Conley, Loretta, 353n47
Connecticut, University of, 242
Consolidated schools, 327, 328
Constitution, U.S.: First Amendment, 29, 196, 299; Fifth Amendment, 101–2; Fourteenth Amendment, 122, 124, 127, 196, 288; Reconstruction-era amendments, 119–20
Coons, John E., 355n91
Cooper, Bruce S., 371
Cooper v. Aaron, 137–38
Copiah Academy, 329
Cordier, Andrew, 204
Core curriculum, 55, 63, 67, 68, 71
Cornell University, 101, 213–16
Corwin, Ronald G., 350n54
Coser, Lewis, 83, 337n2, 362
Council for Exceptional Children, 306
Counterculture, 199–200, 226–27, 328; alternative schools and, 254, 259; free schools and, 252–53
Countryman, Vern, 112, 338n21, 361
Counts, George S., 85–91, 98, 101, 105–6, 337n4, n6, n9, 338n25
Cowden, Peter, 260–61, 350n59
Cox, Archibald, 208, 286, 352n39
Crain, Lucille C., 106, 107
Cranston, Alan, 276
Cremin, Lawrence A., 45–46, 89, 333n3, n4, 336n51, n55, 337n11, 347n1, 359
Cultural deprivation model, 150–58; abandonment of, 160
Curriculum: diversification of, 10–11; impact of

374

student radicalism on, 225, 226; NSF reforms in, 261–65, 318–19; for open education, 243–44; post-Sputnik reforms in, 231–32, 237; in progressive education, 49–50, 52–57, 60, 63, 77–78

Daily Worker, 9
D'Amato, Anthony A., 340*n*17, *n*35, 363
Daniels, Arlene Kaplan, 346*n*48
Daniels, Joan, 370
Daniels, Steven, 349*n*46
Danoff, Malcolm N., 351*n*16, *n*18
Datta, Lois-Ellin, 369
Daughters of the American Revolution (DAR), 27
Davidson, Carl, 345*n*29
Davies, Ronald, 136
Davis, Allison, 152, 341*n*8, *n*10
Davis, Elmer, 112, 362
Davis, Herbert, 98
Davis, O. L., 351*n*65
Deal, Terrence E., 350*n*57
De Bruin, Jerome, 349*n*48
Dede, Christopher, 351*n*67
DeFunis, Marco, 285
Democratic party, 38, 40, 146, 185, 197, 260; Chicago convention of, 206; Congress controlled by, 33, 276, 307, 308; 1944 platform of, 20; in 1948 elections, 25, 29; Popular Front and, 94
Demonstration Guidance Project (New York City), 154
Denker, Joel, 236, 348*n*16
Dennison, George, 236, 348*n*16
Denver School Board, 176–77
Department of Education, U.S., 315, 319–320
Dershowitz, Alan, 346*n*65
DeSanctis, John, 369
Deschooling movement, 238, 251–52
Desegregation, 326; in border states, 131–32; HEW guidelines on, 163–67; of higher education, 210; Kennedy and, 140; massive resistance to, 133–38; Supreme Court ruling on implementation of, 127–30; Title IV definition of, 280–81; Title VI and, 162–64; tracking and, 149; *see also* Integration
DeTurk, Philip, 349*n*46
Deutsch, Martin, 152, 341*n*9, 365
Dewey, John, 46–48, 58–59, 79, 85–86, 105, 334*n*24, 337*n*8
Dewey, Thomas, 29
Dickstein, Morris, 344*n*8, 357, 365
Dilling, Elizabeth, 89–90, 337*n*13
Dilworth Committee, 108–9
Discipline, lack of, 251, 316
Divoky, Diane, 350*n*57
Doane, Donald Calvin, 335*n*30
Dodd, Bella, 89, 93–94, 103, 338*n*36
Dodds, B. L., 61, 335*n*29
Dodson, Dan W., 343*n*44
Donley, Marshall O., 371
Doremus, Richard, 350*n*50
Douglass, Harl R., 60–61, 334*n*27, 335*n*34
Dow, Peter B., 351*n*66
Draper, Theodore, 361
Drug use, 328
Duke, Daniel L., 350*n*49, 368

Dunbar, Ernest, 346*n*53
Dyer, Stanford P., 364

Easterlin, Richard A., 353*n*56, *n*57
Eastland, James O., 25
Eastland, Terry, 352*n*44, 353*n*45, 363
Economic change: blacks and, 116, 118, 119; rise in educational participation and, 9–10
Economic Opportunity Act (1964), 144, 160
Edgar, Robert Wilson, 333*n*1, 334*n*15, *n*19, 360
Education for All Handicapped Children Act (1975), 308–9, 317
Education Development Center (EDC), 242–44
Educational Guardian, 106
Educational Reviewer, 106, 107
Eichel, Lawrence E., 345*n*41
Eiden, Leo J., 352*n*26
Eidenberg, Eugene, 341*n*3
Eisenhower, Dwight David, 41, 109–10, 131, 134–37, 186, 229
Elam, Stanley M., 356*n*95
Elementary Science Study (ESS), 243–44
Elementary and Secondary Education Act (1965), 144, 148–49, 162, 234; Title I, 159–60; Title III, 257
Eliot, Charles, 48
Emerson, Thomas, 123
Employment: discrimination in, 19–20, 22, 147, 281–82; opportunities for blacks during World War II, 116, 117
English language, "de-sexing" of, 298, 300–301
"English as a Second Language" (ESL), 275
Enrollment levels, growth in, 9–10, 15, 19, 327
Epstein, Edward J., 346*n*61
Epstein, Noel, 370
Equal Employment Opportunity Commission (EEOC), 291, 303, 304
Equality of Educational Opportunity (Coleman Report), 168–70
Ernst, Morris, 23
Ervin, Sam, 143, 163
Essentialists, 59
Ethnocentrism, 268–71
Evers, Medger, 141
Everson v. Board of Education of Ewing Township (1947), 29–31, 33, 39, 41
Experimental Schools Program (ESP), 258–61
Eynon, Bret, 344*n*14

"Fair Play for Cuba" committees, 186
Fantini, Mario D., 365
Farrar, Eleanor, 369
Faubus, Orval, 136–37
Featherstone, Joseph, 239–41, 245, 255, 348*n*18, 349*n*49, 367
Federal aid to education, 165, 182, 321–22; as antipoverty measure, 148–49; history of debate over, 5–6; 1945 Senate hearings on, 3–5; opponents of, 27–28; passage of 1965 legislation, 148; postsecondary, 7–8; postwar educational crisis and, 6–8; progressive education and, 70; religious issues in, 27–41, 148, 325; segregation and, 5–7,

Federal aid to education *(continued)*
  22–24, 26–28, 41, 121, 163; Sputnik and, 79, 229
Federal Bureau of Investigation (FBI), 104
Federal Children's Bureau, 39
Federal Housing Administration, 25
Federal programs: for affirmative action, 282–83, 290–92; ban on discrimination in, 163, 281, 282; for bilingual education, 273–79; Catholic school participation in, 27; on civil rights, 25; for compensatory education, 152–53, 158–60, 234, 238–39; for comprehensive change, 258–61; for curriculum development, 261–65, 318–19; and discord about social policy, 161–62; for handicapped, 306–8; higher education and, 15–19; innovation in, 237, 256–58; interest groups and, 316; nonsexist terminology for, 301; open education and, 242, 244; sex discrimination banned in, 294, 301; *see also specific programs*
Feinberg Law, 102–3, 111
Feldman, Saul D., 353n58
Feminism, 292–93, 305; civil rights model and, 305–6; "de-sexing" of English language and, 300–301; political impact of, 294
Fenno, Richard F., Jr., 333n55, 341n3, 358
Feuer, Lewis, 346n68
Fey, James T., 350n63
Field, Mervin D., 344n25
"Filthy Speech Movement," 196
Fine, Benjamin, 6–7, 331n5
Firestone, William A., 349n45
Fishman, Joshua A., 370
Flacks, Richard, 345n26, 347n72
Fleishman, Joel L., 343n67
Flemming, Arthur, 291
Flynn, John T., 106, 338n40
Forcey, Linda Rennie, 347n70
Ford Foundation, 231, 242
Fordham University, 17
Fortune, 14, 19
Foster, Arcola, 356n6
Foster, William Z., 337n17
Fralley, Jacqueline M., 370
Frankfurter, Felix, 126
Franklin, H. Bruce, 346n65
Franklin, John Hope, 339n1
Frazier, Nancy, 370
Free-choice plans, 164, 166, 175, 328
Free school movement, 238, 251–53
Free Speech Movement at University of California at Berkeley (FSM), 192–96
"Free universities," 199, 225
Freeman, Richard B., 292, 345n46, 352n26, 353n47
French, Will, 333n11, 335n37
Fried, Richard M., 362
Friedman, Leon, 339n12, 340n15, 364
Friedman, Milton, 354n69
"Frontier Thinkers," 86, 90, 105–6
Fulbright, William, 4
Fuller, Harry J., 336n45
Fundamentalists, 325

Gaines, Lloyd Lionel, 122
Gallup polls, 251, 292, 316, 349n41, 352n25, 353n48, 356n98

Galton, Maurice, 350n52
Gannon, Robert I., 17, 333n52
Gardner, David P., 338n26, n27, 361
Gardner, John, 230
Gellhorn, Walter, 112, 337n1, n8, 338n29, 361, 362
"General education," 11
Genovese, Eugene D., 347n77
Georgia, University of, 138
Gerard, Harold B., 343n64
Gersoni-Stavn, Diane, 371
Geyer, George H., 334n17
GI Bill of Rights, 12–15
Giamatti, A. Bartlett, 318
Ginzberg, Eli, 345n32
Gitlow, Benjamin, 93–94
Gittelsohn, Roland B., 23
Gladieux, Lawrence E., 356n2
Glazer, Nathan, 112, 352n30, n32, 355n90, 366, 369
Gleason, Philip, 351n1
Goldman, Eric F., 341n3, 342n24, 357
Goldmann, Robert B., 343n67
Gomula, Wanda, 349n47
Goodman, Paul, 187, 223, 236, 344n10, 347n70, 348n14, 365
Goodman, Walter, 338n25, 362
Gordon, Edmund V., 341n8, n11, 365
Gordon, Margaret, 353n58
Goslin, Willard, 107–9, 336n43
Graham, Patricia Albjerg, 78, 336n54, 353n56
Grambs, Jean Dresden, 342n15
Grant, Gerald, 225, 342n39, 347n75
Grant, W. Vance, 352n26, 355n74
Graubard, Allen, 252, 349n42, n43
Great Britain: infant schools in, 239–43, 245–47, 255, 256
Great Cities-Gray Areas Program, 231
Great Depression, 5, 6, 8; blacks during, 20; ideological struggles during, 82–91
Great Society programs, 160, 168, 238; *see also* Elementary and Secondary Education Act and Head Start
Green, Edith, 294–95, 303–4, 354n72
Green, Robert La Brant, 335n32
Green v. New Kent County (1968), 175
Greenberg, Jack, 132, 340n24
Greenway, Robert, 349n44
Greenwood, Peter W., 350n53, n54
Greer, Germaine, 293
Griffith, Robert, 362
Groseclode, Everett, 353n64
Gross, Beatrice, 245, 348n9, n28, 367
Gross, Neal, 350n55
Gross, Ronald, 245, 348n10, n11, n19, n29, 367
Group dynamics, progressive education's use of, 53–54, 79
Guardians of American Education, 106

Hahn, Carole L., 353n64
Hale, Dennis, 344n12, 366
Hamby, Alonzo, 338n25, 357
Hamilton, Charles V., 343n51
Hammond, Russell Irving, 335n32
Hand, Harold C., 333n11, 336n53
Hand, Learned, 111, 339n49

Handicapped children, 306–11; mainstreaming of, 309–11; year-round schooling for, 313
Hanna, Lavone, 335*n*32
Hardin, Joy, 351*n*67
Harlan, John Marshall, 119–20, 124, 142
Harnett, Robert C., 332*n*46
Harnischfeger, A., 356*n*5
Harrington, Michael, 146–47, 197–98, 341*n*1
Harris, Louis, 346*n*57
Harris, William T., 48
Harris Poll, 216–17
Harsha, E. Houston, 338*n*29, *n*30
Harvard University, 13, 17, 48, 100, 101; admissions policy of, 287–88; Department of Afro-American Studies, 209; "Redbook" of, 11; SDS at, 207–9
Hawes, Gene R., 348*n*19, *n*27, 349*n*34, 367
Hawkins, David, 243, 348*n*23
Hayakawa, S. I., 212–13
Hayden, Tom, 188, 205, 344*n*14, 345*n*26, *n*36
Head Start, 158–60, 238–39
Health, Education, and Welfare, U.S. Department of (HEW), 164–67; *see also* Office for Civil Rights; Office of Education
Hechinger, Fred M., 349*n*47, 357
Hechinger, Grace, 357
Heirich, Max, 344*n*17, *n*20
Helburn, Suzanne M., 351*n*65
Hentoff, Nat, 236, 348*n*16
Hentschke, A. C., 335*n*32
Hernandez, Francisco, 350*n*57
Herndon, James, 236, 348*n*16
Herndon, Terry, 356*n*93
Herriott, Robert E., 350*n*55
Hersey, John, 346*n*61
Hertzberg, Hazel Whitman, 351*n*64
Hess, Robert, 152, 341*n*8, *n*10
Hicks, Granville, 100–101
High schools: alternative, 253–54; bilingual education in, 275; comprehensive, 230; growth in enrollment in, 8, 10, open education in, 247, 248; and postwar social change, 10–12; progressive education in, 45, 47–48, 56, 58, 60–69, 76, 78; science and math curriculum in, 231–32
Higher education: access to, 7, 8, 12, 322, 324–25; affirmative action in, 283–92, 302–3, 311; burden of federal regulations on, 318–19; discriminatory admissions policies in, 16, 24; federal courts and, 313; GI Bill and, 12–15; *in loco parentis* role in, 327; "knowledge industry" view of, 184–85; loyalty investigations and, 94–102, 112; postwar growth of, 9, 183–84; recommendations for democratization of, 15–19; segregation in, 121–24; sex discrimination in, 293–97, 301–5; size of institutions, 327; specialization in, 11; student demands for control in, 267; student unrest and, *see* Student radicalism; unionization and, 315
Higher Education for Democracy (Report of the President's Commission on Higher Education), 16–18
Higher Horizons program (New York City), 154
Hill, Clyde M., 336*n*46, 339*n*45, 362
Hill, Robert F., 369
Hillson, Henry T., 341*n*11
Hirsch, Werner Z., 353*n*58
Hispanics: affirmative action and, 283; bilingual education for, 271–72, 277, 279; integration of,

177; labor force discrimination against, 300; urban migration of, 182, 325
Hodgson, Godfrey, 357
Hofstadter, Richard, 49, 112, 333*n*7
Holt, John, 236, 242, 348*n*16
Holt, Len, 344*n*13
Hook, Sidney, 95–97, 101, 338*n*23
House of Representatives, 25, 28–29, 148, 165, 175, 264, 275, 307; Committee on Education and Labor, 33, 35, 38, 40; Committee on Un-American Activities (HCUA), 90, 92–95, 100, 187, 190; Judiciary Committee, 142
Housing, discrimination in, 25, 120, 177
Howard University, 121, 161
Howe, Florence, 370
Howe, Harold, II, 164, 281, 348*n*20, 352*n*28
Howe, Irving, 83, 197, 337*n*2, 345*n*26, *n*27, 362
Howell, Ronald F., 340*n*21
Hulburd, David, 339*n*43
Hull, William, 242–44, 348*n*26
Human potential movement, 236–37
Humphrey, Hubert H., 340*n*25
Hutchins, Robert M., 13, 14, 18, 69, 70, 74–75, 99–101, 112, 331*n*10, 332*n*20, 336*n*49, 338*n*29
Hymes, Rita M., 349*n*47

Illich, Ivan, 238, 252, 349*n*42
Illinois, University of, 75, 229, 242
Institute for Defense Analysis (IDA) at Columbia University, 200–201
Immigrants, 147, 156; assimilation of, 270; educational problems of, 150, 153
Infant schools, British, 239–43, 245–47, 255, 256
Integration: achievement levels and, 169–73, 179–80; dissension, 179–81; educational policy and, 268; social science arguments for, 126, 169–71; southern laws against, 133; suburban schools and, 178; Supreme Court decisions on, 175–78; white flight in response to, 179; *see also* Desegregation
"Interposition," doctrine of, 133
Iversen, Robert, 111, 112, 337*n*2, *n*12, 338*n*22, 339*n*48, *n*50, 360–61

Jacklin, Carol Nagy, 354*n*65
Jackson, Gregg, 343*n*62
Jackson State College, 219
Jacobs, Paul, 344*n*11, 347*n*69, 366
Jaffe, Phillip J., 337*n*17
James, Weldon, 340*n*23
James, William, 46
Jefferson, Thomas, *xi*, 84, 331*n*1
Jencks, Christopher, 364, 365
Jenkins, Martin D., 339*n*7
Jensen, Arthur, 238–39, 348*n*17
Jessen, Carl A., 334*n*23
Jews: affirmative action opposed by, 284, 287; civil rights issues and, 21; ecumenical spirit of, 325; restrictions on college admissions of, 16, 24; among student radicals, 224; in teachers' unions, 174
Johns Hopkins University, 168

Index

Johnson, Susan Moore, 314–15, 356n92, n94
Johnson, Lyndon Baines, 133, 141–44, 148–49, 158–59, 161, 162, 168, 198, 282, 342n18
Jones, Kitty, 338n39
Jones, Philip G., 349n47
Jordan, Vernon, 290
Justice Department, U.S., 25, 123, 165, 175; Civil Rights Division, 135

Kahn, Roger, 345n31
Kahn-Hut, Rachel, 346n48
Kallet, Anthony, 243
Kandel, I. L., 55, 63, 69, 335n33
Kansas City, University of, 101
Karagueuzian, Dikran, 346n48, n51
Katz, Wilber G., 358
Kelley, Sara D., 343n62
Kelly, Alfred H., 340n20
Kemerer, Frank R., 371
Kempton, Murray, 94, 112, 338n20
Kendall, Glenn, 335n32
Keniston, Kenneth, 346n61, 347n72
Kennedy, Edward, 276
Kennedy, Gail, 331n18
Kennedy, John F., 39–40, 140–41, 148
Kennedy, Robert F., 143, 160, 206
Kent State University, 219, 220
Keogh, F. P., 33
Keppel, Francis, 233
Kerr, Clark, 184, 185, 191, 193–95, 344n4, n18, 353n58
Keyes v. School District No. 1, Denver Colorado (1973), 176
Kilpatrick, William Heard, 48–52, 86, 87, 108, 333n6, n10, 334n23, 337nn6–8
Kilson, Martin, 214, 370
King, Jonathan, 348n11
King, Martin Luther, Jr., 139–40, 142, 167, 200, 282
Kingsley, Clarence D., 48
Kirk, Grayson, 201, 203, 204
Kirkham, Francis W., 334n19
Kirp, David L., 363
Kline, Morris, 350n63
Kloss, Heinz, 370
Kluger, Richard, 339n5, 363
Kohl, Herbert, 236, 348n15, 367
Kolesnik, Walter, 49, 333n7
Kozol, Jonathan, 236, 348n15
Kristol, Irving, 338n33
Krug, Edward A., 68, 333n5, 336n40, 347n7
Kuriloff, Peter, 355n82
Kurland, Philip, 340n20, 358

Labor force: women in, 296, 297; see also Employment
Labor movement: civil rights and, 20; see also Unionization
Lachman, Seymour P., 332n45, n46, 333n53
Ladd, Everett Carll, Jr., 224, 345n28, n38, 347n74, 366, 371
Lamott, Kenneth, 346n65
Landau, Saul, 344n11, 347n69, 366
Langer, William, 22

Langworthy, Harry, Jr., 335n32
Lansner, Kermit, 347n1
Lash, Joseph P., 35–36, 38, 333n47, n51, n53
Latham, Earl, 338n37, 362
Lau v. Nichols (1974), 274–75
Laufer, Robert S., 345n26, 366
Lazarsfeld, Paul F., 338n38, 362
Learning-disabled children, 307
Lee, Gordon Canfield, 358
Leonard, George, 237, 348n16
Lesinski, John, 33, 35, 38–40
Lester, Richard A., 352n31, n33, 354n69
Levin, Betsy, 340n20, 355n91
Levin, Maryl, 347n70
Levine, Donald M., 364
Levine, Erwin L., 355nn78–81, n83, n84
Levy, Betty, 354n64
Lewis, Anthony, 341n37, 363
Lewis, Hylan, 157, 342n16
Lichter, Robert S., 346n67, 347n72, 365
Lieberman, Myron, 355n92, 356n93
Life, 17, 73
Life adjustment education, 64–68, 79, 228; critics of, 70, 72
Lincoln, Abraham, 84
Lincoln School, 75
Lincoln University, 122
Lindblom, Charles E., 364
Lippmann, Walter, 83
Lipset, Seymour Martin, 112, 224, 344n15, n19, n26, 345n28, n38, 347n71, n74, n76, 352n25, 366
Little Rock confrontation, 136–38
Local control of schools: desegregation and, 178; federal aid and, 5, 6, 27, 39
Loop, Carlos A., 335n32
Loyalty investigations, 81–113; Depression-era roots of, 82–91; of New York City public schools, 100, 102; progressive education and, 104–9; Supreme Court decisions curbing, 110–11; of university faculty members, 94–102
Loyalty oaths, 82, 90, 93, 98, 110
Lyman, Richard, 220–21
Lynd, Albert, 70, 75, 336n50
Lyons, Eugene, 337n3

McAuliffe, Mary Sperling, 338n33, 361
McCalls, 73, 109
McCarthy, Eugene, 206
McCarthy, Joseph, 45, 82, 92, 103, 109–13
McCollum v. Board of Education (1948), 32
McCormack, John W., 35
McDonald, Milo, 106
McDonnell, Lorraine, 356n92
MacIver, Robert, 112, 361
Mackay, John A., 31
Mackin, Robert, 349n46
McLain, Joseph, 336n39
McLaughlin, Milbrey Wallin, 342n22, 350n53, n54
McLaurin, George W., 123, 124
McLaurin v. Oklahoma Board of Regents (1950), 123–24
McLure, Gail T., 353n64, 370
McLure, John W., 353n64, 370
McPherson, R. Bruce, 349n46
McWilliams, Carey, 112

Maeroff, Gene I., 349*n*47
Magruder, Frank, 107
Mainstreaming, 309–11
Malcolm X, 147–48
"Man: A Course of Study" (MACOS), 264, 316
Manchester, William L., 342*n*24, 357
Mandel, Benjamin, 93
Mann, Dale, 350*n*53, *n*54
Manuel, Hershel T., 272–73
Marden, David L., 339*n*48, 361
Marshall, Thurgood, 125–27, 129, 288, 340*n*19
Martin, Reed, 355
Massachusetts Institute of Technology (MIT), 100, 101; Physical Science Study Committee of, 229
Matthews, J. B., 93–94
Mead, Margaret, 235, 348*n*12
Meharry Medical College, 121
Meiklejohn, Alexander, 95–97, 338*n*24
Meland, James, 349*n*46
Melby, Ernest O., 336*n*47, 362
Mental discipline, theory of, 49
Meranto, Philip, 341*n*3, 364
Meriam, Junius L., 333*n*8
Merritt, Ruth Willard, 335*n*32
Metrailer, Rosemary, 340*n*17, *n*35, 363
Metzger, Walter P., 345*n*35, 369
Mexican Americans, bilingual education for, 272; *see also* Hispanics
Meyers, Agnes, 38
Michener, James, 346*n*63
Michigan, University of, 162
Miel, Alice, 334*n*15
Miller, Arthur S., 340*n*21
Miller, Casey, 371
Miller, Loren, 363
Miller, Louise B., 342*n*19
Miller, Norman, 343*n*64
Millett, Kate, 293
Milliken v. Bradley (1971), 178
Mills, C. Wright, 186–88, 344*n*9, *n*11
Millsaps College, 329
Minton, Sherman, 102–3
Minute Women, 107
Mississippi, University of, 138
Missouri, University of, 122
Mitchell, Morris, 336*n*48
Moffitt, J. C., 335
Moise, Philip, 340*n*20
Molma, John, 278
Mondale, Walter, 298, 299
Montgomery bus boycott, 138–39
Moon, Bucklin, 332*n*21
Moore, John H., 343*n*62
Morey, Roy D., 341*n*3
Morgan, Richard E., 358
Morse, Arthur D., 339*n*45
Morse, Wayne, 24
Mort, Paul R., 59, 64, 335*n*33
Mosher, Edith K., 341*n*4, 342*n*21, *nn*27–30, 364
Moynihan, Daniel P., 160–61, 342*n*23, 364, 369
Munger, Frank J., 333*n*55, 341*n*3, 358
Murphy, Judith, 348*n*10, *n*11
Murray, George, 211
Muse, Benjamin, 340*n*25, *n*27, *n*32, 363
Myers, Donald A., 255, 349*n*49
Myrdal, Gunnar, 20, 117, 118, 144, 339*n*3, 363

Nachtigal, Paul, 347*n*6, 348*n*21, 350*n*58, 369
Naisbitt, John, 347*n*60
Nannini, Louis V., 336*n*39
Nation, The, 31–32, 36
National Association for the Advancement of Colored People (NAACP), 5, 20, 23–26, 28, 118, 120–29, 139, 178, 181, 288
National Association of Elementary School Principals, 279
National Association of Manufacturers, 27
National Association for Retarded Citizens, 306
National Association of School Supervisors and Directors of Secondary Education, 66
National Association of Secondary School Principals, 59, 61, 66, 279
National Catholic Welfare Conference, 33, 34, 66
National Commission on Life Adjustment Education for Youth, 66
National Congress of Parents and Teachers, 5
National Council of State School Officers, 66
National Council of Teachers of English, 301
National Defense Education Act (NDEA), 229
National Education Association (NEA), 5–6, 10–11, 34, 40, 51, 66, 95, 109, 313–15; *Cardinal Principles* pamphlet of, 47–48; Commission on the Reorganization of Secondary Education (CRSE), 48; Committee of Ten, 47; Defense Commission, 74; Educational Policies Commission, 59, 61, 62
National Organization for Women (NOW), 293, 298–300
National School Boards Association, 279
National Science Foundation (NSF), 231, 243, 244, 261–64, 317–18
National Student League, 83
National Urban League, 118
Nation's Business, 90
Neill, A. S., 235–36, 348*n*13
Neill, Shirley Boes, 349*n*47
New Deal, 8, 9, 83, 84
New Left, 187–88; Berkeley and, 196–97; at Harvard, 207; origin of, 185; *see also* Student radicalism
"New math," 232, 262–63
New Republic, 239
New School of Behavioral Studies in Education, 242
New Schools Exchange, 252
New York City Board of Education, 170, 174
New York City Board of Higher Education, 101
New York State Regents' examinations, 69
New York Times, 6–7, 17, 34, 95–97, 132
New York University, 101
New York World Telegraph, 36
Newsweek, 15
Newton, Louie D., 31
Nixon, Richard, 175, 216–17, 219, 257–58, 276, 282
Nolan, Robert R., 350*n*57
Normand, Clarence, 343*n*61
North Dakota, University of, 242
Norris, Louis William, 336*n*45
Norton, E. B., 4
Norton, Eleanor Holmes, 290–91
Novak, Steven J., 344*n*26
Numerus clausus, 16
Nyquist, Ewald B., 248, 348*n*19, *n*27, 349*n*34, 367

Index

Odden, Allan, 355n91
Odell, William R., 335n32
O'Donnell, Richard W., 354n64
Odum, Howard, 116, 339n2
Office for Civil Rights (OCR), 273–74, 282–85, 299, 308, 310
Office of Education, 66–68, 70, 152, 163–64, 276–77; Division of Vocational Education, 64
Ohio State University, 77
Oklahoma, University of, 122–24
Oliver, Linda, 353n64
Olivier, Robert L., 338n39
Ollman, Bertell, 347n74
Olson, Keith W., 331n10, n13
Omwake, Eveline B., 342n20
O'Neill, James B., 358
O'Neill, William, 186, 337n3, 338n33, 344n7, 345n30, 361, 363
Open admissions policies, 226, 324
Open education, 240–50, 326; curriculum development for, 243–44; decline of, 254–56; influence of British infant schools on, 239–43; popularization of, 245–48; problems in defining, 248–49; teacher training for, 241–42
Orfield, Gary, 175, 276–77, 342n27, n29, n30, 343n54, n58, n63, 364
Osborne, Alan, 350n63
Overby, H. T., 356n6
Oxnam, G. Bromley, 31

Packer, Herbert L., 346n65
Paley, Vivian, 354n65
Palmer, A. Mitchell, 93
Parents Council (Minneapolis), 71
Parks, Rosa, 138–39
Parmet, Herbert S., 357
Parochial schools, conflict over aid to, 5, 6, 27–41, 148
Parody, Ovid Frank, 336n39
Pasadena Board of Education, 107–8
Pascal, Anthony, 356n92
Passow, A. Harry, 341n8, 342n15, n16, 365
Patterson, Orlando, 369, 370
Patterson, William P., 334n16, n17, n19
Paulston, Christina Bratt, 352n23
Peace movement: early manifestations of, 186, 187; see also Vietnam war, opposition to
"People's Park," University of California at Berkeley, 196
Pells, Richard H., 362
Pentony, DeVere, 345n40, n47, n48, 346n49, n51
Perkins, James, 213–16
Perrone, Vito, 247, 348n21
Perry, Charles R., 371
Pettigrew, Thomas F., 343n61
Pfeffer, Leo, 332n36, 358
Piaget, Jean, 245
Pierce, Paul R., 335n32
Pittinger, John C., 355n82
Plessy v. Ferguson (1896), 118–20, 122, 125
Plowdern Commission, 239
Polenberg, Richard, 369
Popular Front, 84–85
Pottinger, J. Stanley, 282, 351n7, 352n30

Poverty, 146–48, 325; aid to education as measure against, 148–49; cultural deprivation and, 150–58
Powell, Lewis, 288–90
Power elite, concept of, 186
Prayer in schools, ban on, 316
President's Commission on Higher Education, 15–18
President's Committee on Civil Rights, 20–26
Price, Hugh Douglass, 341n3, 359
Princeton Theological Seminary, 31
Progressive education, 43–80, 326; anti-Communist attacks on, 90, 104–9; basic features of, 44–45; criticism of, 58–59, 69–77; curriculum development in, 49–50, 52–57, 63, 77–78; and decline of academic standards, 229, 230; demise of, 78–80; dissemination of, 51–52; emphasis on social utility in, 59–61; institutionalization of, 46–47; life adjustment education in, 64–68; mental discipline issue in, 49; for poor children, 151, 153; radicalism and, 85–87; reform movement origins of, 45–46; revival of, 235, 241, 242; romantic view of child in, 50–51; scientific claims of, 48–49
Progressive Education Association, 51, 78
Progressive Labor (PL), 198, 207, 217
Progressive party, 25
Project method of education, 50–51
Prosser, Charles Allen, 64–66, 335n35
Protestants: ecumenical spirit of, 325; among student radicals, 224
Protestants and Other Americans United for Separation of Church and State (POAU), 31, 34, 38
Provus, Malcolm M., 350n54
Puerto Ricans: bilingual education for, 272; compensatory education for, 154; cultural deprivation of, 157
Puner, Morton, 362
Purdue University, 61
Pursuit of Excellence (Rockefeller Brothers Fund Report), 229–30
Puryear, Elmer L., 332n46, 333n56
Pusey, Nathan, 207–8

Quick, Suzanne Kay, 350n61
"Quota system" in higher education, 16, 284–91

Rabb, Maxwell M., 340n30
Race, Jeanne, 351n67
Racism: color-blindness and, 114; discredited, 19–20, 119; impact of media on perceptions of, 139; laws supporting, 115–16; violence and, 141; see also Segregation
Rader, Dotson, 345n31
Radicalism, see Student radicalism
Rapp-Coudert Committee (New York), 90
Rasberry, Salli, 349n44
Rathbone, Charles H., 249, 349n36
Read, Frank T., 342n32, n35
Readers Digest, 73, 106
Reagan, Ronald, 196, 211, 219, 320
"Red-baiting," 82, 84
"Redbook," 11

"Red Scare," 8, 104
"Red-ucator Series," 107
Rehabilitation Act (1973), 307–8
Rehnquist, William, 289
Reich, Charles A., 345*n*30
Religion: discrimination on basis of, 24; ecumenical spirit in, 325; and federal aid to education, 5, 6, 27–41, 148; and opposition to progressive education, 74; released-time in public schools for instruction in, 32; student radicalism and, 224
Remedial education, 231, 234
Republican party, 282, 320; and federal aid to education, 6, 26, 29, 33, 40; and loyalty investigations, 94, 110; postwar control of Congress by, 8, 93
Reutter, E. Edmund, Jr., 337*n*14, 338*n*19, 361
"Reverse discrimination," 283–84, 303
Rice, Eileen Kathryn, 334*n*20
Rickover, Hyman, 228, 347*n*1
Riesman, David, 112, 225, 347*n*75, 365
Riessman, Frank, 154–55, 341*n*12, *n*14, 365
Riis, Jacob, 46
Robinson, Spottswood W., III, 127
Roby, Pamela, 353*n*56, 354*n*65
Rockefeller Brothers Fund Report, 229–30
Roe, Donald, 336*n*39
Rogers, Martha P., 354*n*71
Rogin, Michael Paul, 362
Roosevelt, Eleanor, 35–40, 116
Roosevelt, Franklin D., 9, 20, 83, 84, 117, 281
Roosevelt College, 99–100
Rosen, Paul, 340*n*20, 364
Rosenfeld, Gerald, 347*n*69
Rosenthal, Alan, 356*n*92, *n*93
Rosovsky, Henry, 345*n*45
Ross, Davis R. B., 331*n*9
Rossell, Christine H., 343*n*62
Rossi, Alice S., 353*n*56
Roszak, Theodore, 345*n*30
Rotberg, Iris, 279, 351*n*9, 352*n*23
Rothman, Stanley, 346*n*67, 347*n*72, 365
Rouse, Margaret, 334*n*21
Rudd, Augustin, 106, 337*n*15
Rudd, Mark, 200, 204, 217, 223, 345*n*33
Rugg, Harold, 50, 53, 86, 87, 90–91, 105–7, 333*n*9, 337*n*8, *n*16
Rural schools: curriculum revision in, 53, 56; at end of World War II, 4–5, 321; innovation in, 259
Russia, *see* Soviet Union
Rutgers University, 101

Saario, Terry N., 354*n*65
Sadker, Myra, 370
St. Germain, Richard, 349*n*46
St. John, Nancy, 179–80, 343*n*64, 364
Sale, Kirkpatrick, 345*n*26, 366
Sanders, Jane, 338*n*21, 361
Sandifer, Mary Ruth, 334*n*22
Sandler, Bernice, 354*n*71
San Francisco State College, 207, 211–12
Sanford, Terry, 318
Sarason, Seymour B., 350*n*63
Sarratt, Reed, 340*n*26, 342*n*25, 363
Saturday Review of Literature, 73, 74, 109, 245

Savio, Mario, 192, 194–95, 344*n*16
Schaflander, Gerald M., 344*n*26, 347*n*71, *n*76, 366
Schlesinger, Arthur, Jr., 101, 112, 338*n*33, 362
Schneider, William, 352*n*25
Scholastic Aptitude Test (SAT), 69, 255, 311–12, 326
School finance reform movement, 313, 317
School surveys, 52
Schrecker, Ellen, 338*n*32, *n*38, 361
Scientific Monthly, 72–73
Scott, C. Winfield, 336*n*46, 339*n*45, 362
Scott, Kathryn P., 353*n*64
Seabury, Paul, 344*n*19
Seale, Bobby, 218–19
Searle, John R., 366
Segregation, 3, 114–38, 182, 321, 324; abolition of, *see* Desegregation; Integration; academic performance and, 151; as basis of southern way of life, 115, 118, 130–31; in bilingual education, 276–77; black literacy despite, 118–19; de facto, 166, 167, 170–71, 177, 178; de jure, 166, 167, 175–77; and federal aid to education, 5–7, 22–24, 26–28, 41; in higher education, 16–17; in innovative programs, 258; legal campaign against, 119–27; mass protests of 1960's against, 139; progressive education and, 55; Supreme Court decisions upholding, 119–20
Selective Service System, 198
Senate, U.S., 28, 29, 33, 34, 37, 39–41, 110, 148, 175, 307; Committee on Education and Labor, 3–5, 26; Internal Security Subcommittee (SISS), 92, 100, 102–3
"Separate but equal," principle of, 118, 120, 122–25, 127
Serrano v. Priest (1971), 313
Servicemen's Readjustment Act (1944), *see* GI Bill of Rights
Sex discrimination, 271, 292–305; affirmative action against, 282–84, 291, 302–3; in employment, ban on, 280, 282; in higher education, 293–97, 301–5; in progressive education, 18, 56, 62; in textbooks, 298–300
Sexual harassment, 304
Shady Hill School, 242
Shanker, Albert, 315, 356*n*93
Shannon, David, 361
Shaver, James P., 351*n*65
Shils, Edward, 112, 362
Shumaker, Ann, 50, 53, 333*n*9
Silberman, Charles, 245–48, 250, 349*n*29, *n*40, 367
Simon, Brian, 350*n*52
Sindler, Allen P., 346*n*52, 352*n*35
Singer, Lester, 369
Singleton v. Jackson Municipal Separate School District (1965), 166
Sipuel, Ada Lois, 122
Sit-ins: antiwar, 198; at Berkeley, 194; of black students, 215–16; civil rights, 139
Skaife, Robert A., 336*n*47
Skinner, B. F., 233
Skinner, Byron Richard, 364
Smith, Eugene Randolph, 333*n*6
Smith, Gilbert Elliott, 332*n*33, *n*45, 359
Smith, Marshall S., 343*n*61
Smith, Mortimer, 70, 72, 336*n*44, *n*46

Smith, Robert, 211–12, 345*n*40, *n*47, *n*48, 346*n*49, *n*51
Smith Act (1940), 100, 110
Smith College, 98
Social class: cultural differences and, 154–57; impact on learning process of, 150, 151, 153, 158; integration on basis of, 169, 172
Social reform: curriculum revision movement and, 55; progressive education and, 45–46, 75
Socialist party, 84
Somers, Robert H., 344*n*24
Soviet Union: and American Communist party, 98; educational expenditures in, 7; during 1930's, 83–85, 87; nonagression pact with Germany, 85; postwar resumption of tensions with, 92; purges in, 87, 89; Sputnik launched by, 79, 228; totalitarianism of, 112; World War II alliance with, 91
Southern Christian Leadership Conference, 139
Sowell, Thomas, 369
Spears, Harold, 335*n*32
Special education, 306, 308–11
Spellman, Francis, Cardinal, 34–39, 333*n*52
Spodek, Bernard, 349*n*35, *n*48
Sprung, Barbara, 371
Sputnik, 79, 228, 229, 231
Stacey, Judith, 354*n*64, 370
Stanford Research Institute, 220
Stanford University, 220–21
Starobin, Joseph, 362
Starr, Isidore, 339*n*1
Starr, Paul, 345*n*29, 346*n*61, 366
Steffens, Lincoln, 46
Stein, Howard F., 369
Stevens, John Paul, 289
Stewart, George R., 338, 361
Stewart, Potter, 289
Stewart, William P., 349*n*46
Stimpson, Catherine R., 353*n*53
Stock, Phyllis, 371
Stoll, Louise F., 350*n*57
Stouffer, Samuel A., 338*n*38, 362
Strachey, John, 83
Strandberg, Warren, 348*n*21
Strikes: of students, 194–95, 203–4, 208–9, 211–12, 219, 226, 227; of teachers, 7, 174
Strong, Edward M., 191, 194–96, 344*n*18
Studebaker, John W., 66
Student Nonviolent Coordinating Committee (SNCC), 139, 146, 167, 202; Mississippi Summer Project of, 188–89
Student radicalism, 182–83, 186–227, 246; at Berkeley, 190–97; Black Panthers and, 218–19; blacks and, 201–3, 209–16, 226; civil rights movement and, 188–92; at Columbia, 200–205; counterculture and, 199–200; faculty members and, 205–7, 224; during Great Depression, 83; at Harvard, 207–9; institutional change and, 225–26; public response to, 216–17; social origins of, 223–24; Vietnam protests and, 198, 206, 219–23, 226, 246
Students Afro-American Society (SAS) at Columbia University, 201
Students for a Democratic Society (SDS), 187, 197–99, 207, 217; at Columbia, 200–205; at Cornell, 215; at Harvard, 207–9; Port Huron Statement of, 188

Suburban schools: curriculum revision in, 53; integration and, 178
Subversion, fear of, *see* Loyalty investigations
Sugarman, Stephen D., 355*n*91
Summerskill, John, 346*n*48
Supreme Court: affirmative action decisions of, 286–91; on aid to religious schools, 29–32, 39, 41; antisubversive laws and, 102–3, 110–11; on bilingual education, 274–75; desegregation decisions of, 124–25, 137–38, 165, 170, 171, 175–78, 269–70; on handicapped persons' rights, 310; school prayer banned by, 316; "separate but equal" doctrine of, 199–20, 122–25; on teacher unionism, 315; *see also specific decisions*
Sutcliffe, Robert R., 349*n*46
Suydam, Marilyn N., 350*n*63
Swann v. Charlotte-Mecklenburg (1971), 175–76
Swanson, Kathryn, 352*n*32
Sweatt, Heman M., 123, 124
Sweatt v. Painter (1950), 123–24
Swidler, Ann, 252–53, 349*n*43, 44
Swift, Kate, 371
Syverson, Peter, 353*n*47

Taft, John, 346*n*60, *n*61
Taft, Philip, 371
Taft, Robert, 26, 28–29, 33, 322
Taft bill, 28, 33–34
Taylor, Harold, 101
Taylor, Telford, 112
Teacher Corps, 257
Teacher Trainers program, 257
Teachers: in British infant schools, 240; changing relationship with lay public, 323; community involvement of, 327; curriculum revision and, 52–55, 57; and government involvement in educational policy, 317; in Head Start programs, 159; innovative training of, 257; low expectations of, 158; loyalty investigations of, 93–104, 110, 111; loyalty oaths for, 82, 90, 93, 98, 110; NSF curricula and, 263–64; open education and, 241–42, 245, 248–50, 255–56; progressive ideology and, 44–45, 50, 56; qualifications of, 3; radicalism and, 86; salaries of, 3–4, 27, 120; shortage of, 4–7, 26–28, 70; in slum schools, 149, 151–52; special education, 309; unionization of, 89, 313–15
Teachers College, 49, 50, 54, 55, 59, 63, 75, 154, 156; Curriculum Laboratory at, 52; *Social Frontier* group at, 85–88
Teachers Union, 89, 102–3, 174
"Teach-ins," 162, 198
Technological change, 9, 10, 14, 118–19, 325; classroom applications of, 233
Television, influence of, 326
Tenenbaum, Samuel, 333*n*10, 334*n*25
Texas, University of, 123–24
Texas State Department of Education, 57
Textbooks: anti-Communist attacks on, 90–91; censorship of, 107; sexism in, 298–300
Thernstrom, Abigail M., 352*n*20, 370
Thernstrom, Stephan, 351*n*1, 369
Thielens, Wagner, 338*m*38, 362
Thomas, Norman, 97–98, 101, 338*n*25, 364
Thurmond, Strom, 25

Tiedt, Sidney W., 359
Tittle, Carol Kehr, 354*n*64, *n*65
Tobias, Channing, 23
"Token" desegregation, 133, 138
Torrey, Rowan, 328–30, 356*n*6
Tracking, 149; ability grouping vs., 230
Trecker, Janice Law, 354*n*64
Trotsky, Leon, 85, 87
Trow, Martin, 345*n*38, 356*n*4, 365
Truman, Harry S, 9, 15, 20–21, 24–26, 28, 30, 33, 39, 92, 119, 332*n*23, *n*28, *n*29
Truman, Margaret, 332*n*28
Tugman, W. M., 336*n*48
Turnbull, Ann, 355*n*84
Turnbull, H. Rutherford, 355*n*84
Turpen, N. C., 334*n*14, *n*18

Ulam, Adam, 366
Unger, Irwin, 366
Unionization of teachers, 89, 313–15, 325
United Nations, 8, 36, 91
United Public Workers, 102
United States v. Jefferson County Board of Education (1967), 166
Universities, *see* Higher education *and specific institutions*
Upchurch, Wilma, 3, 5
"Urban crisis," 147, 148
Urban schools, 325–26; criticism of, 236; curriculum revision in, 52, 53; desegregation of, 131; at end of World War II, 5; Ford Foundation program for, 231; open education in, 250; poor conditions in, 149–50; proportion of minority students in, 178, 325
Useem, Elizabeth L., 343*n*61
Utilitarianism in progressive education, 51, 59–61, 66, 70, 77, 79

Valentine, Jeanette, 342*n*18, 364
Vanderbilt University, 168
Vecoli, Rudolph J., 369
Vernoff, Edward, 347*n*74
Veterans Administration, 13
Vietnam war, 168; opposition to, 162, 198–208, 223, 270
Vincent, William S., 64, 335*n*33
Vocational education, 10; in alternative schools, 254; and democratization of higher education, 17; GI Bill and, 13; progressive views on, 45, 46, 64–65; sex discrimination in, 297
Vogeli, Bruce R., 262, 350*n*62
Voting rights, 120; restrictions on, 21
Voting Rights Act (1965), 142, 144, 162, 165

Walberg, Herbert J., 349*n*35, *n*48
Walker, Eugene Pierre, 341*n*37, 364
Wallace, Carrie N., 356*n*6
Wallace, George, 138, 140, 162
Wallace, Henry, 25, 100
Wallerstein, Immanuel, 345*n*20, 366

Wann, Kenneth Douglass, 336*n*39
Warren, Earl, 127, 128
Warren, Robert Penn, 71
Wasby, Stephen L., 340*n*17, *n*35, 363
Washington, University of, 94–95
Watergate scandal, 276
Watson, Goodwin, 154–55
Wattenberg, Ben J., 331*n*6, *n*8, 344*n*1, *n*3
Wayland, Sloan, 156–57, 342*n*16
Weatherford, Willis D., 318–19
Weathermen, 204, 217, 220
Weber, Lillian, 241, 245, 247, 367
Wechsler, Herbert, 130, 340*n*21
Wechsler, James A., 83, 112, 337*n*2, *n*9, 362
Wegner, F. R., 335*n*32
Weinberg, Jack, 193–94
Weinstein, Gerald, 365
Weiss, Iris, 350*n*63
Weiss, Janet A., 343*n*66
Wells, H. G., 8
Wendell, Barrett, 17
Westin, Alan F., 341*n*3, 359
Wexler, Elizabeth M., 355*nn*78–81, *n*83, *n*84
White, Byron, 288
White, Walter, 24
White, William S., 332*n*32
"White backlash," 162, 167
White ethnic movement, 270
White flight, 177, 179, 325
White supremacy, 115, 131
Wilcox, Preston, 343*n*51
Wildavsky, Aaron, 346*n*64
Wildman, Wesley A., 371
Wiley, D., 356*n*5
Wiley, Karen B., 351*n*66, *n*67
Wilkerson, Doxey A., 341*n*8, *n*11, 365
Wilkins, Roy, 142
Wilkinson, J. Harvie, III, 340*n*22, 341*n*41, 363
Willcocks, John, 350*n*52
Willkie, Wendell L., 19, 332*n*21, *n*22
Wilson, Marjorie, 355*n*84
Wisconsin, University of, 220
Wisdom, John Minor, 166–67
Wise, Arthur E., 317, 355*nn*89–91, 356*n*97, *n*99
WITCH (Women's International Terrorist Conspiracy from Hell), 292
Wolanin, Thomas R., 356*n*2
Wolf, Eleanor P., 343*n*59, 365
Wolff, Robert Paul, 221, 346*n*66
Wolin, Sheldon S., 344*n*15, 366
Wolk, Ronald A., 354*n*69, 356
Women: discrimination against, *see* Sex discrimination; growth of opportunities for, 323
Women's Educational Equity Act, 298, 299
Women's Equity Action League (WEAL), 293–94, 302
Women's Liberationists, 292, 293
Wood, James L., 347*n*72
Woodring, Paul, 70, 76–77, 336*n*52
Woodward, C. Vann, 346*n*68, 363
World War I, 8
World War II, 19, 91, 116, 117
Wright, Grace S., 335*n*38
Wrightstone, J. Wayne, 335*n*37
Wythe, George, *xi*

Index

Yale University, 218–219
Yancey, William L., 342n23
Yarborough, Ralph, 271
Yeshiva University, 315

Zablocki, Benjamin, 345n30
Zacharias, Jerrold, 229
Zeran, Franklin R., 335n37
Zigler, Edward, 342n18, n19, 364
Zoll, Allen, 106, 108

G. A. C. S. LIBRARY

DATE DUE

SEP 30			
OCT 29 1992			
NOV 17 1993			
APR 13			

DEMCO 38-297